Everything You Want to Know about Chinese Cooking

Pearl Kong Chen   Tien Chi Chen   Rose Y. L. Tseng

Woodbury, New York
Toronto   London   Sydney

© Copyright 1983 by Barron's Educational Series, Inc.

All rights reserved.
No part of this book may be reproduced
in any form, by photostat, microfilm, xerography,
or any other means, or incorporated into any
information retrieval system, electronic or
mechanical, without the written permission
of the copyright owner.

All inquiries should be addressed to:

Barron's Educational Series, Inc.
113 Crossways Park Drive
Woodbury, New York 11797

Credits:

  Color photography:

    Matthew Klein, photographs
    Yoshiko Loomis, food preparation
    Linda Cheverton, stylist

    Porcelain by Ceralene
    Silver by Ercuis
    Crystal by Baccarat
    Linens by Pratesi
    Laboratory glass by Manhattan Ad Hoc
    Flowers by Howe Floral

Black & white photography:

  F D M Photography

Book design by Milton Glaser Inc.
Jacket design by Milton Glaser Inc.

Library of Congress Cataloging in Publication Data

Chen, Pearl Kong.
  Everything you want to know about Chinese cooking.

  Includes index.
  1. Cookery, Chinese. 2. China—Social life and
customs. I. Tseng, Rose Y. L. II. Chen, Tien Chi.
III. Title
TX724.5.C5C5438   1983   641.5951   82-11576
ISBN 0-8120-5361-3

Library of Congress Catalog Card No. 82-11576

Cloth Edition
International Standard Book No. 0-8120-5361-3

PRINTED IN THE UNITED STATES OF AMERICA
  4 5 6   7 9 0   9 8 7 6 5

Introduction

We would like this volume to be a self-learning text on Chinese cookery, a handy reference manual on Chinese cuisine and nutrition, and also a source of entertaining information about the Chinese and their food. We have tried; it is now up to the reader to decide whether our aim has been achieved.

Part 1 is an introduction to Chinese food culture. While the writing style is informal, the contents are the result of years of active research, often through primary sources scattered throughout Chinese literature. Some of the facts uncovered may even surprise most Chinese readers.

This part also contains a discussion of ingredients—from abalone and agar-agar through wawa fish and *shao mai* wrappers—to arm the reader for the needs in the recipe portion of the book, and also possible culinary encounters in China. The part ends with a discussion on tools and techniques. We recommend the use of chopsticks, the Chinese knife, and the wok. They have played a strong role in shaping Chinese cuisine, and their use does make Chinese food preparation easier. Yet we are of course not blind to tools from the Western world, which are reshaping Chinese food practices *now*. Americans may be unprepared to learn that chemicals with Western names are used in Chinese cookery; we have been using them under age-old *Chinese* names. But monosodium glutamate (MSG) can be abused by the careless or the irresponsible; we do not use it ourselves.

Part 2 gives recipes for soups, fish and shellfish, poultry, pork, beef and lamb, soybean products, gluten and seaweed, vegetables, small eats, and sweet dishes. These recipes represent Pearl's efforts to be a creative cook as well as a teacher of cuisine in two continents. They have been tested thoroughly by her and her students in American kitchens, and cover the range from simple family fare to banquet offerings. She is most attached to Emerald Shrimp, an East China dish which mystified Hong Kong gourmets until Pearl found the key to greening in a Chinese book. But she is also partial to Sauce-blasted Chicken Ding from Peking, tangy, robust and hearty; Chrysanthemum Fish Chowder from Fujian, with three unlike ingredients blending together their aroma, texture, and taste in utter harmony; dry-fried Beef Shreds from Sichuan, nutlike yet chewy and as scorching as can be; Stuffed Crab Legs, a showy variation of a Chaozhou dish designed for the dungeness crab; Braised Orange Duck, a roasted-then-braised Chinese duck in a Westernized sauce; and Steamed Almond Custard, an exquisite dessert from a lone outpost of the dairy-product cuisine in South China.

Part 3 describes how the Chinese people handle their food. Menu planning is not easy until one has acquired a feel for the principal techniques and their sequencing; we show explicit menus with detailed timing to aid the readers, who will later plan and execute menus of their own choice.

The serving of beverages during Chinese meals is a matter of some controversy; we offer our views here. We also provide glimpses of Chinese food tradition in festivities, folk medicine, and folk beliefs.

INTRODUCTION

The book also features a discussion of the nutritional aspects of Chinese cuisine. The reader will find Chinese cuisine to be based on modern scientific knowledge, and therefore is provided with both the art and science of good cooking.

The Chinese culture has been in existence for over ten thousand years. Chinese cookery has always been a special enjoyment to the Chinese people and serves to bind them together, keep them healthy, and help them overcome calamities, natural or man-made. It is thus understandable that some Chinese may become so proud of their food as to think that Chinese cookery has long reached perfection in total isolation, and is both unchanging and unchangeable. Serious scholarship disputes this extremist view.

For Chinese cuisine has evolved throughout history, and is still changing every-day. One of the prime movers in this evolution has been external contact. It is hard to imagine a northern Chinese cooking without sesame oil, yet twenty-two centuries ago sesame was totally unknown to the Chinese; it was brought back from Central Asia by the great traveller Zhang Xian. It would even be more unthinkable for a Sichuanese chef to do without red-hot chili peppers, imported indirectly from the New World only about four centuries ago. We can think of no higher praise for Chinese cuisine than that it is vibrantly alive, ever seeking to become even better than it already is.

Outside influence is most evident in Cantonese cookery, owing to geography and the receptive temperament of the Cantonese. Two of us (T.C. and Pearl) are Cantonese, and half of the recipes convey a Cantonese flavor. However, a gen-uine effort has also been made to include representative culinary practices of North China, East China, Sichuan-Hunan, and Fujian-Taiwan. We intend to show that authenticity in cooking transcends the mere choice of ingredients and utensils; it lies in the way ingredients are skillfully blended to achieve taste har-mony.

While Chinese cuisine has helped the survival of the Chinese people, it itself is not immune to attacks. It came through the Cultural Revolution, which almost buried the entire culture of Continental China. It is battered and shaken, but has fully recovered its prestige at home while steadily winning friends abroad. Yet a nagging question remains about it and sister cuisines all over the world: Should taste be supplanted by flashy showmanship, instant chemistry, and make-believe? This book is dedicated to those who think otherwise.

We have been working on this book for at least five years. Ten years ago, Pearl was invited by Dr. Tseng to share the teaching of menu planning at San Jose State University, California. The questions from our students could not be answered by any book in print, and we began to think of writing a book. Later as Pearl volunteered to cater and teach for the American Cancer Society, she was pep-pered with questions about Chinese *haute cuisine,* and T.C. started to trace the development of Chinese cooking through twenty-five official histories of China. The three of us had a draft of the book accepted by Barron's in 1979, when T.C. took a sabbatical appointment in Hong Kong, and lectured in Shanghai, Sian, Peking, and Canton. We used these occasions also for exchanges in food culture, and collected material for improving the book. During 1981–1982, the entire collection of recipes was revised and the accompanying portions rewritten. Pearl worked on the menus and recipes; T.C. covered the background information, beverages, folklore and beliefs; and Rose included her information on nutrition, after in-depth analyses of the healthful aspects of Chinese cooking.

The authors of *Everything You Want To Know About Chinese Cooking* take plea-sure in sharing the history, culture, and food of China. We take pride in having the privilege of sharing another way of learning about people.

Acknowledgments

Pearl would like to dedicate her work to the memory of Kong Hungyun, her grandfather and reigning gourmet in Canton for half a century, for teaching her how good "good food" could be. For abetting her to offer *haute cuisine* banquets using the American kitchen for the American Cancer Society in her mother's memory, she is grateful to Chan Mongyan, her mentor and for the past three decades the leading food critic in Hong Kong, and also to Mrs. Chan.

Pearl thanks her students in America and in Hong Kong, for their inquisitive questions and for testing her recipes. She owes a particular debt to those students who selflessly served in her volunteer catering group: Frank Mauer, Edna Hansen, Grace Okazaki, Joyce Shen, Anne Liu, Marlene Louie, Diane Stephens, Jackie Torres, Andy Anderson, Pat Concklin, Belinda Chan, Yee Wong, Jeannie Hsu. Sharon Lee, her own daughter, plunged into the volunteer effort unflinchingly. Melissa Yau assisted in her teaching and tested most of the advanced recipes. In preparing the manuscript Pearl is indebted to Coleen Carr and Betty Clamp, both of Ohlone College, Mary Little Mueller of Metropolitan Adult Education Program, San Jose, and also her numerous friends on both sides of the Pacific for their criticism, support, and encouragement.

T.C. acquired his interest in Chinese cuisine and folk traditions from Suenming Tu Chen, his late mother. He thanks his father, Dr. Ping-Chuan Chen, for filling gaps of half-forgotten Chinese history and for encouragement in general. He is indebted to Professor S. S. Chern, mathematician and gourmet, for reading and criticizing a draft, and also to Dr. George Fan for discussions on beverage use.

Rose Tseng would like to thank her many colleagues and students at San Jose State University who had urged her to offer her first Chinese cooking class in 1972, and provided her with continuous stimuli to pursue this project. Special appreciation must go to Mary Ann Sullivan who gave the most valuable original input and numerous helpful suggestions. She would also like to thank her understanding husband Raymond and loving children Jennifer and Frank for their daily encouragement and support throughout the years.

All three of us thank Adele Horwitz for encouragement and promotion, Cathy Chang for an expert job in scrutinizing the draft, and Carole Berglie for an outstanding job in fitting the latter into the present format.

And last, but certainly not least, we would like to acknowledge with immeasurable gratitude the assistance and counseling provided us by the noted food consultant and admirer of Chinese cuisine, George Lang. He put our thoughts into perspective and helped us make evident to the reader the unique qualities of Chinese cooking.

Conversion Tables

The following are conversion tables and other informational items applicable to those converting the recipes in this book for use in other English-speaking countries. The cup and spoon measures given in this book are U.S. Customary; use these tables when working with British Imperial or Metric kitchen utensils.

Liquid Measures

The old Imperial pint is larger than the U.S. pint; therefore note the following when measuring liquid ingredients:

U.S.

1 cup = 8 fluid ounces
½ cup = 4 fluid ounces
1 tablespoon = ¾ fluid ounce

Imperial

1 cup = 10 fluid ounces
½ cup = 5 fluid ounces
1 tablespoon = 1 fluid ounce

U.S. Measure	Metric	Imperial*
1 quart	946 ml	1½ + pints
1 pint	473 ml	¾ + pint
1 cup	236 ml	− ½ pint
1 tablespoon	15 ml	− 1 tablespoon
1 teaspoon	5 ml	− 1 teaspoon

Weight and Volume Measures

U.S. cooking procedures usually measure certain items by volume, although in the Metric or Imperial systems they are measured by weight. Here are some approximate equivalents for basic items appearing in this book.[†]

	U.S. Customary	Metric	Imperial
Apples (peeled and sliced)	3 cups	500 g	1 pound
Beans, dried (raw)	2½ cups	450 g	1 pound
Butter	1 cup	250 g	8 ounces
	½ cup	125 g	4 ounces
	¼ cup	62 g	2 ounces
	1 tablespoon	15 g	½ ounce
Cheese (grated)	½ cup	60 g	2 ounces
Cornstarch	1 teaspoon	10 g	⅓ ounce
Cream of Tartar	1 teaspoon	3-4 g	⅛ ounce
Flour, all-purpose (sifted)	1 cup	128 g	4¼ ounces
	½ cup	60 g	2⅛ ounces
	¼ cup	32 g	1 ounce
Herbs, fresh	¼ cup whole	15 g	½ ounce
	2 tablespoons chopped	7 g	¼ ounce
Mushrooms, fresh (chopped)	4 cups	300 g	10 ounces
	1 cup	112 g	4 ounces
Nut meats	1 cup	450 g	1 pound
Peas, fresh (shelled)	2 cups	450 g	1 pound
Potatoes (mashed)	¾ cup	125 g	4 ounces
Raisins (or Sultanas)	1 cup (raw)	225 g	8 ounces
Rice	3 cups (cooked)	225 g	8 ounces
	½ cup	285 g	10 ounces
Spinach, fresh (cooked)	1 cup	240 g	8 ounces
Sugar:	½ cup	120 g	4 ounces
granulated	¼ cup	60 g	2 ounces
	1 tablespoon	15 g	½ ounce
	1 cup	140 g	5 ounces
Confectioners'	½ cup	70 g	3 ounces
	¼ cup	35 g	1 + ounce
	1 tablespoon	10 g	¼ ounce
	1 cup	160 g	5⅓ ounces
Brown	½ cup	80 g	2⅔ ounces
	¼ cup	40 g	1⅓ ounces
	1 tablespoon	10 g	⅓ ounce
	1½ cups	450 g	1 pound
Tomatoes, fresh (peeled, seeded, juiced)	3½ cups (sliced)	450 g	1 pound
Zucchini	2 cups (grated)	450 g	1 pound

Oven Temperatures

Gas Mark	¼	2	4	6	8
Fahrenheit	225	300	350	400	450
Centigrade	107	150	178	205	233

---

*Note that exact quantities cannot always be given. Differences are more crucial when dealing with larger quantities. For teaspoon and tablespoon measures, simply use scant quantities, or for more accurate conversions rely upon metric measures. Since the Australian cup measures 250 ml, add 1 tablespoon liquid measure for each cup.

[†]So as to avoid awkward measurements, some conversions are not exact.

Contents

Part 1

Background Information

Food in Chinese Culture

China is a vast subcontinent embracing a great diversity in geographic features, nationalities, and cultures. With an area of 3.7 million square miles, China is twice the size of Europe (excluding the Soviet Union).

Chinese culture can be traced through twenty-six centuries of written history, ten thousand years of farming communities, eventually to Peking Man half a million years ago, and perhaps even to stone-wielding Yuanmou Man in Southwest China 1.7 million years ago. With such a cultural continuity, it is no wonder that China is now the most populous country on earth, with a billion people comprising no fewer than thirteen major nationalities.

By far the largest ethnic group in China is the Han people, living in the eastern half of China and constituting fully 94 percent of the population. In addition, 3.5 million Tibetans spread over the Southwest Highlands, almost a quarter of the total area of China. Northwest China is inhabited by 6.3 million Turkic people, most Uygurs, and twenty-two thousand Indo-European Tajiks. Some 2.7 million Mongols live along a three-hundred-mile-wide strip bordering Mongolia, while 1.7 million Koreans are in Southeast Manchuria, just north of the Yalu River. The 12 million Zhuang are descendents of the ancient Yue people. They and a million relations live in Southwest China, as do the Yi (4.8 million), the Miao (3.9 million), and the Yiao (1.2 million). The mountains on Hainan Island are inhabited by 680 thousand Li, and those on Taiwan are home to the 400 thousand Polynesian Gaoshan ("High Mountain") people.

The ancestors of the 2.6 million Manchus started in Manchuria; but after ruling China for nearly three hundred years before being overthrown in 1911, the Manchus have largely become indistinguishable from the Han majority. On the other hand, 6.5 million Chinese Moslems have a cultural, if not racial, identity. They live in hundreds of communities all over China, particularly along the Gansu Corridor, the starting point of the fabled Silk Road to Central Asia and eventually Western Europe.

This book is concerned mainly with the five principal cuisines of the Han people. The Han Chinese represent much more than a racial group. Ethnic purity might have existed at one time in the ancient past, four thousand years ago when the Han controlled only a small part of North China, but subsequent territorial expansion engulfed natives with differing backgrounds, and the influx of outsiders, peaceable or otherwise, has added vitality. "Han" was the name of a great dynasty, noted for its triumph over the Huns; yet half of the Hun population has been absorbed into the Han nation, as have virtually all other nomad invaders.

The Han people have also contributed to the current minority stock. Intermarriage in border areas has been common, and many Chinese princesses have married foreign rulers, as tokens of good will.

In this book the word *Chinese* is used to mean "Han Chinese," with due apologies to the minority groups whose cuisines are largely unknown to the Han majority. There are, however, two significant exceptions. Elements of Mongolian cookery have become a basic part of Peking cuisine, and restaurants run by Chinese Moslems are well liked throughout the country.

SOME GEOGRAPHIC FACTORS

While China and the United States are roughly the same size (China is 1.5 percent larger) and occupy the same latitudes, their climates are very different. Because there are fewer ocean currents affecting the weather, a point in China tends to be cooler in the winter, warmer in the summer, and drier all year round than a corresponding point at the same latitude in the States. Only Southeast China has abundant moisture, like the Southeast in the United States. West China on the whole is dry, with less than ten inches of rain per year. The high elevation (10,000 feet) and stupendous size (Tibet alone has more than half a million square miles) of the Southwest Highlands really defy comparison.

Only 10 percent of China is under routine cultivation. While food supply is adequate in normal times, the large population has known starvation and want. Almost everything edible has been consumed at one time or another.

Corn, potatoes, and peas are grown throughout China. North China, being relatively cold and dry, produces soybeans, kaoliang (a relative of the sorghum), wheat, oats, millet, but little rice. It is also where Chinese cabbage *(bok choy)*, napa cabbage, garlic, root vegetables, eggplants, persimmons, pomegranates, peaches, pears, apples, grapes, jujube dates, chestnuts, walnuts, and peanuts are grown.

The temperate climate along the Yangtze River is well suited for rice and tea, but is also known for green vegetables, bamboo shoots, lotus roots, lotus seeds, water chestnuts, melons, squash, pumpkins, gourds, and beans.

South China boasts of exotic fruits such as lychee, longan, loquats, citrus fruits, olives, guava, bananas, papayas, pineapples, and coconuts. This area also produces snow peas, Chinese broccoli, taros, tiger lily, bitter melons, and fuzzy melons. In subtropical areas along the coast, abundant sunshine and rain bring two rice harvests per year.

Xinjiang in the Northwest is famed for a sweet melon shaped like an oversized American football and for grapes made into salted raisins. It is little known that rhubarb is native to Mongolia and Tibet, and that it was first shipped to Western Europe in the days of Marco Polo, not as a vegetable, but as a laxative.

A great variety of mushrooms and fungi are cultivated or collected in China. Black and straw mushrooms come from South China, while the moogoo (as in Moogoo Gai Pan) is from Inner Mongolia. Snow mushrooms (silver fungi) grow in Sichuan, Fujian, and Taiwan, as do wood, stone, elm, cloud, and yellow fungi.

Chickens, ducks, pigs, and cattle are raised throughout the eastern half of China. Geese being fattened serve also as watchdogs in many Yangtze households. Beef comes, not from the southern water buffalo, but from the northern "yellow cattle." Lamb and kid are common only in North and West China. Game includes deer, roebucks, rabbits, raccoons, wild ducks, wild geese, squab, and quail. Bear's paw is a treasured delicacy, and so is camel's hump, of which every Chinese camel is endowed with two.

The China Sea teems with yellow fish, eels, turtles, cuttlefish, and conch. Cod is plentiful along the North China coast, while oysters, mussels, and clams are found along the southeastern coast. Jellyfish is commonly harvested in East China, while huge meaty shrimp are collected in the North. Yangtze Valley freshwater shrimp, on the other hand, are much smaller and more delicate in taste. Brackish waters near Canton and Xiamen (Amoy) are noted for crab, but the most respected crustacean is the freshwater hairy crab from East China, with a bunch of hair on each claw. The most famous freshwater fish in all China is perhaps the Yellow River golden carp, but other favorites include sturgeon, perch, and shad from the Yangtze River and its tributaries. Dace raised in ponds is the second major industry in Sundak district near Canton (the first is silkworm culture).

CHINESE FOOD
THROUGH THE AGES

The Chinese are among the most history-conscious people in the world, with twenty-six centuries of written history. However, until recently, food in China has been deemed either unfit or too familiar to merit the written word. Nevertheless, when archaeological discoveries are matched with occasional literary references, it is possible to discover a cultural continuity, from the unseasoned roast deer of Peking Man half a million years ago, to the magnificent multicourse banquets of today.

The Beginnings of Food in the North
Peking Man lived in North China half a million years ago, using only stone implements for hunting. Yet he already knew the enjoyment of good food—he was the earliest man to cook his meat. His diet consisted mainly of large-horned deer and wild plants, but also included saber-toothed tiger, rhinoceros, elephant, camel, and water buffalo.

During neolithic times the Yellow River Valley inhabitants domesticated animals while growing millet, then rice, and later wheat. Recent excavations at Banpo, a suburb of the city of Xian in North China, uncovered a village occupied from about 5000 BC to about 3000 BC. Within the village was found the earliest known vessel for steaming food. It is believed that such vessels were used for unhusked millet, which would burst upon steaming. The eater would then chew to extract the soft, starchy part and spit out the husks. Besides millet, Banpo residents also consumed chickens, carp, and wild animals, including elephants and vultures.

Yu, founder of the Hsia Dynasty, was said to be the first Chinese king to sample wine, probably fermented from millet. He was also the first to issue a decree restricting its consumption.

In 1650 BC, the Shang Dynasty burst upon the scene like a comet and brought the Chinese Bronze Age to full flower. It was mere coincidence that the first Shang king was named Tang ("soup"). This name probably also inspired the fiction that his prime minister came to his attention by posing as a roadside chef, extolling the harmonious blending of food ingredients in soup as the perfect analogue of sound government.

Shang artistry produced magnificent bronze vessels with intricate animal motifs, mostly ceremonial containers for wine and grains. However, meat was commonly presented in tall, wooden containers. (Among the speculations as to why may be that bronze imparts a disagreeable taste upon contact with meat.) But Shang food certainly included cattle and turtle. The cracking patterns of charred cattle thigh bones and turtle shells had been interpreted by priests for divination, and thousands of these oracle devices have been unearthed in Henan province. The last Shang king was pictured by his enemies as a cruel despot who ignored his kingly duties while indulging in food and drink. An example of his excesses was the presumed invention of ivory chopsticks.

Shang was overthrown by Chou, an agricultural kingdom from the west. The Chou kings were descendents of Hou Ji ("Lord Millet"), an agriculture hero, and it is intriguing that their capital was not far from Banpo, where millet was steamed and eaten fully two thousand years earlier.

The Book of Poetry was compiled during this time, and it contains traditional folk songs, official odes, and ritualistic hymns. The busy life of early Chou peasants was captured in the song "The Seventh Month." The farmers grew millet, rice, wheat, hemp, melons, gourds, and Chinese chives; boiled celery and soybeans; foraged for wild edible plants; picked jujube dates; and gathered mulberry leaves for the silkworms. They made rice wine "to help longevity." They hunted boars, offering the larger catch to the feudal lords while keeping the younger ones for themselves. In the fall they enjoyed a lamb feast in the lord's hall and drank from rhinoceros' horns to the health of all.

Official Chou banquets were somber affairs. "When the Guests Commence to Dine," another ode, showed how the sedate ceremonies and ritualistic games of skill during a banquet could be spoiled by inebriated guests who failed to remove themselves.

Li Ji (*The Book of Rites*) was devoted to prescriptions for proper gentlemanly conduct. It contains, among other things, very explicit recommendations for the preparation, presentation and consumption of food. For instance,

> *For seasoning, mostly sourness in the spring, mostly bitterness in the summer, mostly spiciness in the autumn, mostly saltiness in the winter, moderated always with smooth and sweet seasonings. . . .*
>
> *Spring is suited for lamb and pork, pan-fried in cattle fat; summer is suited for dried pheasant and dried fish, pan-fried in dog fat; autumn is suited for veal and venison, pan-fried in chicken fat; winter is suited for fresh fish and winged birds, pan-fried in mutton fat.*

There was sophistication in the choice of animal fat to blend with the ingredients, but the reader gets the uncanny feeling that barriers have been erected against further blending. The prescription on seasoning throughout the year is especially restrictive.

Elsewhere in *Li Ji* and two companion texts are found the proper pairing of vegetables with meat, ingredients for stews, and meat sauces fermented by mixing wine and grain products with chopped beef, pork, venison, rabbit, fish, snails, wasps, or ants' eggs. Vinegar, probably made from changed wine, was all-important, serving as seasoning, pickling agent, and meat tenderizer. Today cooks in Shanxi Province, just north of the old eastern Chou capital of Loyang, are known for their fondness for vinegar, possibly a direct cultural link with the ancient Chou cookery.

Eight primary methods for cooking were described in *Li Ji*. One involved baking an entire animal encased in mud, and this is the forerunner of the present-day Beggar's Chicken. This method was recommended for pig and lamb, in both cases with a smartweed stuffing.

About 600 BC, the dukedom of Chi became powerful. Master chef Yi Ya became a confidante to Duke Huan of Chi, and was said to have butchered his own infant son for the duke's table. When the duke died, Yi Ya tried to seize power for himself, and nearly succeeded. Though thwarted in life, he became the patron saint of Chinese restaurants.

Confucius (about 500 BC) opined on table manners and dietary rules, but was regarded as a gourmet only in a negative sense. He became oblivious to the taste of meat for three months after attending a recital of great music. Mencius, bearer of his spiritual mantle two hundred years later, at least showed a preference for good food by saying: "Fish I desire, and bear's paw I desire; if both cannot be had together, leave fish and take bear's paw."

Just before Confucius' time, the despotic Duke of Jin executed his chef for serving Braised Bear's Paw underdone. This dish, which takes hours of patient preparation, was already the height of *haute cuisine* then, and it remained a North China favorite for twenty-five centuries.

Early Food in the South

Areas to the south, along the Yangtze River, contributed significantly to early Chinese culinary culture. Its antiquity, just unfolding before the archaeologists, appeared even to surpass that in North China. For instance, cord-marked pottery made 10,000 years ago was found south of the Yangtze in a district appropriately called Myriad Years (Wannian). Fragments of neolithic pottery dating to 4000 BC have been found on Hangzhou Bay, just south of the Yangtze Delta. Inhabitants there consumed peaches, melons, peanuts, and water chestnuts. They cultivated rice, using animal shoulder blades as plows.

During the Spring-Autumn Era (722–418 BC), Hangzhou Bay and areas to the south belonged to the militant kingdom of Yue. The Yangtze River Delta and areas to the north belonged to the kingdom of Wu, and the great expanse of the Middle Yangtze was the dominion of the kingdom of Chu. These three kingdoms together controlled the entire South China. They were considered semibarbaric by historians, yet there was nothing barbaric about the keenness of Wu swords, the fragile beauty of Yue maidens, and the flights of fancy in Chu poetry.

In "Beckoning the Souls," a Chu ode summoning departing souls to return, the vagrant spirits were promised the enticements of "sour and bitter soup of Wu"— also rice and noodles mixed with honey, roast lamb in sugarcane sauce, and braised tendons from fat cattle. Ancient Yangtze cuisine deviated from that of the North in the use of local ingredients but, more importantly, also in the blending of tastes (sourness and bitterness) attributed to the kingdom of Wu. To this day tendons of beef and pork are still gourmet favorites in East China. Pungent

and Hot Soup is common in North China; it could be related to the soup of Wu.

While Yangtze cuisine may have altered the eating habits in North China, the court of Chu also developed a fondness for Braised Bear's Paw, the elaborate dish from the North. After a palace coup in 625 BC, the deposed Chu king asked for one last taste of this delicacy before committing suicide. His own son, the coup leader, saw through this delaying tactic and denied the request.

The First Unification and the Introduction of Foreign Ingredients

In 221 BC the Qin king conquered the other warring states and unified China, crowning himself First Emperor. He annexed two outlying regions, Sichuan in Central China and Guangdong in South China; both achieved renown eventually as centers of cuisine. Fujian along the southeast coast remained semiautonomous for yet another century under descendents of the ancient Yue kings.

The First Emperor died while touring the empire. His death was kept a secret, and the tour continued with an extra load of salted fish to mask the smell of his decomposing body. The first line of defense for his tomb has only recently been excavated near Xian. It consists of an army of 7,500 terra-cotta warriors, life sized and lifelike, with real weapons of bronze.

Soon after his death the Qin Empire crumbled in a conflagration of popular uprisings. A commoner, Liu Bang, defeated all opposition in 206 BC and founded the Han Dynasty. In an expedition against the Huns, he had to bribe his way out of a siege. The defeat of the Huns became the preoccupation of Wu-di (a posthumous name meaning Militant Emperor), his great-grandson. To outflank them, Wu-di sent Zhang Xian on two remarkable expeditions to "the Western Lands," the first of which was even through Hun lines. The path traced by Zhang Xian became the Silk Road, the main thoroughfare to Central Asia and beyond.

He went as far as Bactria, north of the present Afghanistan. He and his successors brought back grapes, pomegranates, walnuts ("foreign peach"), squash, peas, coriander, garlic, and, most important, sesame ("foreign hemp") which few North China chefs today can do without.

The tomb of the Marquess of Tai, who lived about this time, was recently excavated. A complete menu written on bamboo strips was found inside; most of the dishes were meat stews. Spices and seasonings found in the tomb included Sichuan peppercorns, cinnamon bark, mustard, ginger, galangal, soy sauce, and fermented salted black beans. All these seasonings are still in use today. The body of the Marquess was so well preserved that muskmelon seeds were found inside her stomach.

Another glimpse of Han cuisine is seen in a canto written about 100 BC. There was the expected Braised Bear's Paw. Also mentioned was Unborn Leopard and stew of fat dog with venison. Carp and meat were served (raw?), finely sliced. Bamboo shoots from Sichuan were prized then, as was lychee, the exotic perfumed fruit. The latter was sent later (in 100 AD) by pony express from Canton to the Royal Palace in Loyang, a thousand miles to the north.

An important development during the Han Dynasty was the invention of noodles, shortly after the technique of flour-milling was apparently imported from India. Much less certain was the invention of bean curd (tofu).

The Han court encouraged the theory of the cosmological dualism of *yin* and *yang,* which later became the basis of Chinese medicine. The same theory, combined with the nihilistic philosophy of Lao Tze, led to the Taoist religion, noted for the experimental pursuit of the elixir of life. Bean curd, formed by combining vegetable matter (soybean milk) with a mineral (calcium sulfate, or plaster of paris), was just the thing a Taoist-alchemist would concoct, and its invention was attributed to Prince Liu An, a great expounder of Taoism.

The House of Han fell after a series of *coups d'état* caused by palace intrigues. China split into three kingdoms: Wei, Shu, and Wu. Wei owned the entire Northeast China, Shu developed Sichuan, while Wu cultivated areas south of the Yangtze.

The center of fine cookery was undoubtedly in Wei, which took over the Han government. The greatest poet of the era was Cao Zhi, a Wei prince. He wrote about the skill of chefs in cutting the white meat of black bears into cicadawinglike slivers: "Piled, they are as folded gauze; released, like scattered snow."

Cao Zhi's most famous poem, however, was one on boiled beans, composed under threat by his brother, the Emperor:

> *The beans were boiled by burning stalks;*
> *The beans wept softly in the pot:*
> *"But we were born from roots the same,*
> *Why, then, are you so scalding hot?"*

He was released by his shame-faced brother.

The other two kingdoms were noted less for food than for culinary substitutions. The last emperor of Wu substituted tea for wine, out of respect for an old, teetotaling official. This fact was recorded in the *History of Wu,* marking the first known reference to the word *tea* in official history. Prior to that time, tea was mentioned under several alternative names.

In an expedition to the Southwest, the Shu Prime Minister replaced human heads in tribal sacrifices by a look-alike bun. The steamed bun is still called Manto (Savage's Head) to this day.

The three kingdoms were united briefly, but the country was soon torn apart by internecine warfare. The Huns and four other nomadic tribes asserted themselves, and had a free run of North China for three centuries (304–577). A Sinicized Hun Emperor executed a prince for "failing to supply fish and crabs." Food served in Northern courts, however, consisted mainly of mutton and milk products.

The southern half of China remained Chinese. Chinese *haute cuisine* there, according to a canto dated about 300 AD, included new delicacies from the south such as gorilla's lips, cooked autumn oranges, coconuts, lotus seeds, and longan (dragon-eye fruit). One of the two kinds of alcoholic drinks mentioned was bamboo leaf green from the North; a distilled spirit by this name is still in great demand today, though it could not possibly be the same thing, as the art of distillation was yet to be invented in China.

The Sui Dynasty (581–618) reunited China long enough to build a canal to ship Yangtze grains into the Yellow River Valley. The city of Yangzhou, where the canal meets the Yangtze, became Sui's southern capital. It remained a bustling metropolis for fifteen centuries and was the birthplace of Fried Rice, Wo Noodles (a large noodle soup), Dim Sum, and Lion's Head, an oversize meatball.

Further Sophistication and Refinement

The "Chinese-ness" of the entire subcontinent remained in doubt until consolidation under the Tang Dynasty (618–907). Even then, the crown prince of the great Tang Emperor Tai-zong (Supreme Forebear) had a tent installed inside his own palace, preferring to live and eat (!) like a Turk.

Perhaps fortunate for Chinese culture, a different prince succeeded Tai-zong. Nevertheless, many nomad customs and products became firmly established. The Tang populace consumed "foreign cookies" with a sesame-seed coating. Already in use during Tang was the wok and the art of stir-frying. Two dumplings have recently been excavated in the Turfan area along the Silk Road. Tang poets sang praises for grape wine, made and served by Turkic people. Later (about 840 AD) they adored "burnt wine" from Sichuan, showing that Chinese distilled spirit was first invented there.

Tang traded with Central and West Asia, not only by land, but also by sea via Canton and Quanzhou (in Fujian). Foreign trade brought the eggplant, spinach (Persian vegetable), pumpkin (the Chinese type tastes like the American butternut squash), dill, nutmeg, saffron, and peppercorns. The most significant import during Tang, however, was Mahayana Buddhism.

Buddhism had already reached China during Han, and it became widespread throughout the nomad kingdoms in the North during the Age of Chaos. But in Tai-zong's reign Monk Xuan-zhuang trekked to India and returned after sixteen years with the classics of Mahayana Buddhism written in Sanskrit. The news of his triumphal return had the same electrifying effect on Chinese Buddhism as Charles Lindbergh's transatlantic flight had on American aviation. Buddhist practices led to a vegetarian cuisine incredible in variety, complexity, and taste. Many Chinese vegetarians shun garlic and scallions because of their strong flavor, yet they may accept mussels as a vegetable. There was the legend that once the starving Xuan-zhuang prayed for a vegetarian meal on a barren lakeshore, and found mussels adhering to his scepter.

Tang power dissipated into the hands of warlords. The Song Dynasty (960–1297) allied with the emergent Nuzhens to defeat the nomadic Khitans in the North, but were soon defeated by the conquering Nuzhens also. A century and a half later, Song gave up North China and settled in scenic Hangzhou. To seal a treaty with the Nuzhens, Song Prime Minister Qin Hui killed the ablest Chinese general on trumped-up charges. This infamous character is deep-fried in near effigy, torn to shreds by the teeth, and swallowed for breakfast with congee or bean milk in millions of Chinese households every morning. The product of hate is Oil (Fried) Strips, still called Oil-fried Ghost in Peking and Canton; the word *ghost* is pronounced "gui."

Though a military and diplomatic failure, Song was an outstanding success in economic and cultural matters. The development of the southern half of China, accelerated by the introduction of an early harvesting rice from Vietnam, led to a height of prosperity never before known. Great works of philosophy and literature were printed by presses with movable types, and these works were debated under the benign influence of excellent wine and tea, held in porcelain vessels unparalleled in artistic subtlety. Banknotes were invented, freely exchangeable with salt and tea. Chinese junks, equipped with the first marine compasses, sailed to all major ports in Asia, trading silk, porcelain, rhubarb, and (later) tea for precious stones, ivory, incense, and spices.

Three culinary regions generally were recognized then: North China for lamb and noodles, Lower Yangtze for fish and rice, and Sichuan for hot food based on

Sichuan peppercorn. Cantonese lychee was praised by poets, but the Cantonese were known mainly for their fondness for snake.

On the scenic Westlake in the southern capital of Hangzhou, Song Wusao (fifth sister-in-law of the Song family), a refugee from the old Song capital of Kaifeng, peddled lake Fish Soup into fame and received an audience with the emperor. She was also thought to have invented the current Hangzhou specialty dish Vinegar-Slipped Fish. Southern Song cuisine was surely a blend of the old Kaifeng tradition with the abundant local ingredients. A book written during the last days of Hangzhou as capital named more than four hundred dishes; many were the same as those mentioned in another book written more than a century earlier about the heyday of Kaifeng. But many dishes of this time were new. An example is Soup-Filled Dumplings, probably from nearby Yangzhou. Many Kaifeng dishes continue to be appreciated, even today; an example is Stir-fried Crabs. It is strange that lamb, kid, and mutton, prominent in both texts, are now uncommon south of the Yangtze. A plausible explanation is the reaction against the century of Mongol rule (1297–1369).

The Mongols lived on mutton and fermented mare's milk. Alone of all nomad invaders, they successfully resisted assimilation. Folklore credited the bulky mooncakes for the popular uprising against the Mongols. Their size was certainly right for hiding the secret message: "Kill the Tartars at the mid-autumn fullmoon." The exchange of mooncakes by the Chinese was never intercepted by the Mongols, who were not at all curious about Chinese food. When finally chased back into the Gobi Desert by Chinese calvary, the Mongols largely took their cooking with them; Steak Tartare is no Chinese fare. Mongol dishes in present-day Peking probably came from Inner Mongolia much later. The Mongols were more adaptable when it came to liquid refreshments. They became avid drinkers of Chinese tea.

The Development of Modern Chinese Cuisine

The Chinese cuisines as we know them today evolved during the past six centuries under the Ming (1368–1644) and the Qing (1644–1911), when the country was largely at peace. *Haute cuisine* during these periods was patronized by the rich and the powerful: court officials in Peking (which again became the capital after a brief interlude), flood control constructors in Henan and Jiangsu provinces, salt merchants in Yangzhou, and later foreign traders in Shanghai, Ningpo, Fuzhou, Xiamen, and Canton. Foreign trade led to the importation of snow peas ("Holland peas" in Canton), watercress ("West Ocean vegetable"; Portugal was known as "the Great West Ocean Nation"), and tomatoes ("foreign eggplant"). Vegetable foods from the New World created an agricultural, hence culinary, revolution. Previously barren soil was now planted with corn and sweet and white potatoes. Green and red chili peppers now supply most of the fire and much of the vitamins in dishes from Central China.

The Early Ming navy made seven expeditions to impress countries in the South seas and on the shores of the Indian Ocean, three quarters of a century before Vasco da Gama sailed around the Cape of Good Hope. These expeditions, led by a Moslem eunuch called Zheng He, certainly promoted the exchange of food products and populations. The later popularity of shark's fin and bird's nest, both from tropical South Asia, quite conceivably resulted from international trade since that time. Bird's nest has also been used as tribute from Malaya to the Ming court.

The Japanese during the Ming era were the Vikings of the Far East, plundering all along the Southeast China Coast. To match their considerable mobility, Ming general Chi Ji-guang invented a tasty donut-shaped hard cookie to be threaded by the bundle and worn by his soldiers. This popular invention is now called Guang Cookie, with or without the center hole.

At the invitation of a Ming general, the Manchu military machine entered the Great Wall to quell a rebellion. It elected to stay. All resistance was crushed mercilessly; Yangzhou saw massacre for ten full days, and Canton for three. However, initial Manchu cruelty was later redeemed by several long, prosperous reigns, and the fierce Manchus ended up as Chinese as anybody else.

Not noted for their own cuisine, the Manchus became patronizers of good food establishments. They surely had the leisure to do so, as all Manchus were pensioned for life. The most elaborate banquet in Hong Kong today is still called the Man-Han (i.e., Manchu-Chinese) Complete Feast. In 1977, a Japanese group flew to Hong Kong for a two-day Man-Han Complete Feast, and enjoyed such delicacies as elephant's trunk, bear's paw, and sparrow's tongue. The bill came to $1,750 per person.

But the palate could become tired of exotica and long for plain, country food. It was said that Emperor Qian-long, during one of his famous visits south of the Yangtze, was greatly impressed by a plain dish of Boiled Bean Curd with Spinach and wanted to know its name. A quick-witted official invented the high-sounding name Red-Beaked Green Parrots on Slabs of White Jade. This story was probably apochryphal. The learned Qian-long surely knew that bean curd had been called "boards of jade" in a famous Sung poem. Besides, his own grandfather, Emperor Kang-xi (1662–1722), even offered a bean curd recipe to an elderly court official.

Writings about food became respectable during Ching. Li Yu (alias Li Li-weng) wrote a chapter on food, emphasizing crisp textures and delicate flavors. He was particularly fond of bamboo shoots, crabs, and the pungent mustard. He was considered to be a fake by Yuan Mei, whose *Menu of Easygoing Garden* gave practical recipes in the East China idiom.

Both authors traveled widely. Li described his joy upon discovering the hair vegetable in its native Shaanxi; it has now become a common, if expensive, ingredient for New Year celebrations in China (see p 479). In East Guangdong, Yuan was delighted with Bird's Nest and Wintermelon Soup which "matches softness with softness, and clarity with clarity"; a fresh eel soup; and a meat dumpling named (would you believe?) Dienbuling. Yuan also mentioned blackfish roe, now a Taiwan delicacy, and many South Seas products such as bird's nest, shark's fin, sea cucumbers, and abalone. The only New World plant mentioned by either was tobacco. Yuan cautioned against dropping tobacco ashes on food.

These two authors preserved for us a glimpse of the culinary state of China two centuries ago. North China and East China cuisines were well-established, and Cantonese cuisine, light and elegant, was beginning to be known by gourmets like Yuan. Fujian was mentioned by Li as a place for exotic seafood. But it probably took many more years for Central China to evolve a new cuisine based on New World chili rather than the native Sichuan peppercorns. The importation of South Seas delicacies was probably negligible until Yuan's time, as the earlier Li text mentioned them not at all, and Yuan noted that they were only a recent rage.

At the beginning of Ming, China still led the world in science and technology. But China slept while Western Europe experienced first the cultural Renaissance, then the Industrial Revolution. The Manchus handled internal affairs accept-

ably, but were unprepared for confrontation with Western fire power. After the humiliation of several disastrous wars, China became a republic in 1911, and Westernization became a watchword. Few advocated dropping Chinese cuisine, yet Western cookery practices have left their mark. Custard tarts, French style, appeared in Cantonese teahouses in the 1920s. Ceylon Tea, served with milk and sugar, became fashionable in big-city cafés despite purist disapproval. Dairy products, largely absent since the Mongols left six hundred years ago, made a frontal assault on Chinese children in the form of ice cream. In the 1930s monosodium glutamate, a Japanese invention, reached the remotest village in China proper. Western utensils and appliances began to appear in the late 1920s—first enamelled platters and aluminum pots, then gas stoves and refrigerators.

The late 1930s began a generation of the greatest upheaval in Chinese history. When the Japanese attacked Pearl Harbor on December 7, 1941, they had already occupied Manchuria for a decade and most of the China coastal areas for up to four years. While more than half the Chinese population had to suffer Japanese subjugation, many millions, motivated by anger, fear, or want, migrated westward to Central China, seeing for the first time the true expanse of the country and incidentally experiencing the variety of its cuisine.

After returning home during the euphoria of the Japanese surrender, the Chinese soon faced the stark realities of a full-scale civil war between the Nationalists and the Communists. Another great migration ensued, this time from the North toward the Southeast. In 1949, the People's Liberation Army swept over the entire Chinese mainland, and the Nationalist Government moved to Taiwan. Even when hostilities subsided, many still found themselves stranded, far from home. And many who have since come home acquired a taste of the food from the places they have been. Nostalgia joined enterprise to spread Chinese regional cuisines far from their origin, all over the world. Significantly, in America all five major cuisines are now represented, and large cities usually have at least three of them.

Continental China woke up in the late 1970s after more than a decade of devastation in the name of the Great Cultural Revolution, and determined to regain her culinary splendor. A series of visiting demonstrations in America by Chinese regional chefs showed that their special cuisines are alive and rapidly recovering. Old master chefs are encouraged to teach and write, and young cooks are once more taking them seriously. The loss of contact with special ingredients during the intervening years is being made up through exchange with prosperous, international Hong Kong, where support for *haute cuisine* has never wavered.

With improved transportation, specialty foods are now reaching palates thousands of miles away, and tourists travel just as far for a taste of Chinese morsels in their original setting. But communication also accelerates the blurring of identity. Already today several regional cuisines sport the same dishes in slightly altered forms, their true origins having been largely forgotten. It is possible that Chinese regional cuisines as we know them may not exist in thirty years. Yet the blending may lead to something more glorious than the parents, and variety— truly the spice of life in food enjoyment—may reassert itself in unexpected ways.

More disturbing is a trend toward oversimplification, stressing visual impact at the expense of substance and taste and equating extravagance with excellence. In the long run, a cuisine can be no better than its clientele, and the global popularity of Chinese cuisine calls for a steady supply of discerning tasters to match it.

MAJOR CHINESE
CUISINE TODAY

The great diversity of climate and tradition and the previous lack of communications led to separate developments in cookery. Within China proper, there are at least five major culinary regions; each region also contains many identifiable areas with distinct styles of food preparation.

North China is roughly represented by the food native to Peking; East Central China by the cities of Shanghai, Hangzhou and Yangzhou; Central China by Sichuan and Hunan. In Southeast China, Fujian and Taiwan have an individual style, and the spokesman of Guangdong Province is Canton, its capital city.

North China Cuisine

What is commonly called Peking cuisine covers the entire northeast plain of China, the cradle of Chinese civilization, bounded on the south by a line roughly midway between the Yellow River and the Yangtze, and on the northwest by Inner Mongolia. It includes the classical cuisines from the provinces of Hebei, Henan, and Shandong, ancient traditions of Shanxi and Shaanxi. Manchurian cookery is basically Shandong in outlook.

North China, being cold in the winter, has a short growing season. It produces little rice; the chief staples are wheat, millet, and soybeans. A large variety of food made from wheat flour is prepared with great skill, particularly in Shandong. Tangy sauces made from soybeans are specialties. A wine mash is used in cooking and preserving goose eggs. Nuts, jujube dates, persimmons, apples, peaches, pears, and grapes are famous, as are napa cabbage, bok choy, and vegetables of the onion family. A prized Henan mushroom, shaped like a monkey's head, is so named. The sea yields a giant shrimp known all over China.

Peking is not far from the site where Peking Man (400,000 BC) was found and has been a capital for the past one thousand years, with brief interruptions. It is justly famous for Peking duck. The duck is first force-fed for weeks. After slaughter, the cavity is sewn up, then the carcass is blown up to separate the skin before roasting. The duck is roasted, and the crispy skin is then cut up and served with a tangy sauce and scallion threads. Thin crêpes are provided so the diner can make his or her own rolled crêpe. *Guo-tiehs* (pansticker) are dumplings with a meat-and-vegetable filling, pan-fried on one side and served upside down to reveal the neatly charred bottom. A favorite of children is the hot, candied apple chunks that are quenched in icy water; these are called *basi* (pull-thread) apples.

Peking also sports a number of Mongol dishes; these came not from Kublai Khan's court but Inner Mongolia, whose princes allied with the Manchus. Trade with Inner Mongolia required camel caravans, and Camel's Hump is a great delicacy.

Shandong has long been prosperous because of a hard-working people, a silk culture, and the bountiful sea. It was also the birthplace of Confucius, whose influence on food, however, was far less than that of Yi Ya, master chef and another native son. One railway town in Shandong Province called Dezhou (Virtue City) is nationally famous for its tender braised chicken. Shandong is known for apples, peaches, and grapes; Qingdao (Tsingtao), once leased to the Germans (1879–1914), has excellent beer and a thriving grape-wine industry, following the German tradition.

Most of Manchuria is now populated by the industrious Shandongese. The orig-

inal inhabitants were the Manchus, who left in 1644 for literally the greener pastures of Peking, thus Manchurian cuisine may be more visible in Peking than in Manchuria. There is reason to believe, however, that the conquering Manchus were better gourmets than chefs. An official Manchurian feast featured tray-upon-tray of boiled pork, without seasoning of any kind. A Manchurian contribution to Chinese cuisine is *hasma*, the dried ovaries from a frog, used in soups in the winter, partly as a tonic. It was said that Manchu Emperor Qian-long was so fond of Fragrant Concubine, a Moslem, that he created a Moslem town within the forbidden city. Anyway, Peking has a large Moslem population, and throughout North China there are many Moslem restaurants featuring lamb, kid, beef, and horse and donkey meat.

The Chinese culinary orthodoxy had its start in Henan, which housed the ancient capitals of four dynasties. For centuries Henan was the site for great engineering projects to dam the Yellow River: "China's Sorrow," which has overflowed and changed its course several times in the past thousand years. Henan's greatest claim to fame is Braised Bear Paw. Oil-dipped Kidney is done with tender care to ensure crispiness. Sweet and sour dishes are favorites. Yellow River golden carp, which have jumped upstream to reach the town of Dragon Gate, are said to have qualified to change into dragons; they also qualify for the wok of the discriminating.

The ancient provinces of Shanxi and Shaanxi also belong to the North China culinary region. Both are known for their strong liquors distilled from grains. *Fen* liquor from Shanxi is the main ingredient in Spicy Cold Beef. Western Phenix liquor from Shaanxi tastes initially like *moutai* and finally like *fen* liquor. Shaanxi also produces a deliciously mild rice wine, milky-white in color. Also, Shaanxi is famous for its lamb stew with dunked buns and the use of half-grown bean sprouts for stir-frying. Shanxi is known for its partiality for vinegar, which is applied to virtually all dishes.

East China Cuisine

The East China culinary region includes the entire lower Yangtze River Valley, covering the provinces of Jiangsu, Zhejiang, Anhui, and Jiangxi. It is the traditional home of "fish and rice," also of scholars and merchants. It includes the metropolis of Shanghai, the business city of Ningbo, the scenic city of Hangzhou, the canal city of Yangzhou, and Suzhou, the center of embroidery. Each of the above cities is famed for its individual cuisine.

Shanghai is known for its Red-cooked Pork Shoulders with Rock Candy, the tastiest part being the dark reddish brown skin—soft, rich, and distinctly sweet. Red-cooked Water Paddles uses the fin portions of fish. A meat aspic is served cold. Whole Family Prosperity is braised meatballs, chicken, shrimp, sea cucumbers, black mushrooms, and bamboo shoots in a thick gravy. The green turtle is cherished for its taste and medicinal value.

Ningbo makes extensive use of locally abundant seafood. The cookery tends to be salty and sometimes overly odorous by outside standards. Notable among the more curious dishes is Salt-preserved Stems of Amaranth.

Scenic Hangzhou sports a number of famous local dishes, such as Vinegar-slipped Fish, using the local red vinegar and grass carp from the West Lake. *Hua diao* (Flower Engraved), probably the best Chinese wine, tastes vaguely like a dry Spanish sherry. The green Dragon Well tea, picked in the spring before the Grain Rain Festival (about April 20), is a chief ingredient in the local stir-fry called Dragon Well Shrimplets. Ham from Jinhua (Golden Flower) is often considered the best in China.

West of Shanghai, Yangzhou was the South Capital of the Sui Dynasty and the center of the salt trade until it was eclipsed by Shanghai in the nineteenth Century. Yangzhou is the birthplace of many dishes, including Lion's Head (a tender, fist-sized meatball), Stir-fried Shrimplets, Cabbage Mash, Fried Rice (using a Supreme Stock), Noodle Soup, and Soup-filled Buns in small bamboo "cages." Nanjing, capital of seven dynasties and the Republic of China, is known for a salted preserved duck. The freshwater hairy crab out of Yangcheng Lake, midway between Shanghai and Nanjing, is the best crab in all of China. Suzhou is known for its unmatched embroidery industry, its beautiful women, and its delicate dim sum. A dish there known as the "Number one dish under Heaven" is Shrimplets with Sizzling Rice.

Also belonging to the East China sphere of cookery are Jiangxi and Anhui. Jiangxi is most well known for a dried salted duck made at its southern border with Guangdong. Anhui is the source of Keemun (Qimen) tea, the most well-known Chinese red tea. An Anhui oddity is hairy bean curd, covered with inch-long white mould.

Central China Cuisine

Sichuan in Central China is the gateway to the mountain provinces of Guizhou and Yunnan; Hunan and Hubei are east of Sichuan down the Yangtze River. Sichuan, Hunan and Guizhou share a love for hot peppers. Hubei and Yunnan have personalities all their own.

Sichuan ingredients includes the delicate, crystalline snow mushroom, the delayed-action Sichuan peppercorn (*fagara*) and of course red hot peppers. Hunan produces and consumes even more red peppers than Sichuan. Yunnan ham rivals Qinhua ham in East China. From Guizhou, *moutai* wine—actually a whisky made from wheat and kaoliang—is aged in urns for decades and can be lit with a match; its potency is masked by its smoothness and its unique aroma of new-mown hay. Yunnan and Sichuan both boast of preserved vegetables.

The Sichuan Basin is ringed by steep mountains. Its relative isolation, coupled with abundant varieties of food, naturally leads to a unique cuisine. Self-sufficient in food, it even has large deposits of rock salt. The only thing in short supply is fish, because of the rapidly flowing rivers. Dishes called "fish-flavored" are flavored not with fish, but with a combination of seasonings (vinegar, hot bean paste, ginger, garlic, and scallions). Examples are Fish-flavored Pork Shreds, Fish-flavored Beef Shreds, and Fish-flavored Eggplants. These are red-hot and oily dishes; Sichuan cuisine thrives on red-hot peppers and searing vegetable oil. Curiously, Sichuan banquet food tends to be mild in flavor.

Other Sichuan specialties include Twice-cooked Pork: boiled first, then stir-fried with peppers and oil; Camphor and Tea Leaf Duck: smoked with camphor wood and tea leaves; Sand-pot Simmered Fish Head; Ma Po (Pock-marked Grandma's) Bean Curd, which goes well with white rice; Bang Bang Chicken; Strange-Flavor Chicken, combining five flavors; Peppery Beef Tripe. The name Ants (Crawling) Up the Tree may raise goose bumps in the uninitiated; it is actually ground meat with transparent bean noodles.

A Guizhou specialty is Gung Bao Chicken Ding, which is a sauce-blasted diced chicken with scorching peppers, often also with corn or peanuts added. It was invented by an official whose rank in the Manchu Court was Gung Bao (Guardian of the Palace), the Junior Guardian of the Royal Heir. This particular Gung Bao happened to have the surname Ding also.

Hunan food is on the whole even richer in seasoning than Sichuan. Hunan dishes include Dongan Chicken, Ham in Honey Sauce, Rice-flour Steamed Pork, and Squab Soup Steamed in Bamboo Section. Dried preserved meat features in many Hunan dishes.

In Hubei and Yunnan, red-hot dishes are present yet do not overpower. Hubei cookery practices share characteristics with North China and East China cuisine. Pepper-hot dishes do not predominate there, and special attention is paid to cutting skill and color and appearance. Interesting dishes include Vinegar-slipped Thousand-Year-Old Eggs and Coiled Dragon Roll-cut, which is a neatly coiled, sliced meat roll with skin made of eggs. Wuchang fish, a fresh-water bream, has been famous for three thousand years.

Yunnan cookery is heavily influenced by local ingredients and the minority population there. A curious but useful Yunnan cooking device is the air pot, a steaming vessel in the form of a pot. When this pot is immersed in boiling water, a jet of steam shoots up the center, bounces off the bottom part of the cover, to spread throughout the interior of the vessel. Air Pot Chicken is occasionally served in Sichuan restaurants in America.

Fujian–Taiwan Cuisine

Subtropical Fujian is bounded by mountains on three sides and the sea on the fourth. Taiwan is a large island about a hundred miles offshore. Both were relatively unaffected by Imperial Chinese rule in ancient times. With the development of sea travel, the Fujianese took to the sea (and seafood) as a fish takes to water. Descendents of the seafaring Fujianese populated Taiwan and spread all over Southeast Asia.

Fujian and Taiwan are best known as producers of tea. Fujian-Taiwan cuisine is known for soups; in a banquet there usually are several. A unique practice is the addition of cracked raw chicken bones to the soup to provide a fresh zing. Atop the soup may float what appear to be wontons but their skin, translucent and tasty, is made of pounded lean pork.

The most well-known North Fujianese dish is probably Southern Pan-fried Pork Livers. The thin slices are first dipped in egg white, then coated with starch before pan-frying to just-doneness. Many Northern Fujianese dishes feature the use of a sweet red wine mash for cooking.

A specialty of Southern Fujian and Taiwan is *poopia* (thin cakes) which is a do-it-yourself crêpe. The eater takes a thin pancake eight inches in diameter, and wraps up, spring-roll style, a selection of from twenty or more finely shredded meat and vegetable ingredients. The skill in *poopia* preparation is not only in the pancake itself, but most certainly in the artistry of fine shredding.

A Fujianese dish very popular in Hong Kong is Fu Tieo Qiang (Buddha Jumping Over the Wall). It consists of shark's fin, sea cucumber, fish lips, dried abalone, dried scallops, dried cuttlefish, dried tendon of pork, the tip of pork maw, pork, chicken meat, duck meat, ham, and black mushrooms—all simmered in a large earthenware jar. When the jar is eventually opened, the aroma is so irresistible that even Buddha, the confirmed vegetarian, would presumably jump over the wall for a morsel.

The most popular places for inexpensive quick meals in Singapore are the food stalls, run under government supervision. About ten of them are spread all over the city. Many offerings there are Fujian-Taiwan in origin, such as Sparerib Tea,

a soup made with spareribs and Chinese medicinal herbs. Oysterette Pan-fry is the Fujian-Taiwan version of the American Hangtown Fry, with oysters in an egg pancake.

Cooking in Southeast Asia is affected by the hard-working Chinese residents, most of whom are Fujianese by origin though with significant Chaozhou and Hakka contributions. Bami, an Indonesian noodle dish loved by the Dutch, is believed to be Fujianese. Indonesian *nasi goreng* is an adaptation of Chinese fried rice. In Singapore and Malaysia, the use of Chinese techniques with local ingredients (coconut milk, curry mixtures) has led to a distinctive style of cookery called Nonya cuisine. One of its foremost proponents is the mother of Prime Minister Lee Kwong Yew of Singapore. *Nonya* is the Malay word for a girl with a Chinese father and a Malay mother. Fujian-Taiwan cuisine also contains features of Southeast Asian cookery, notably *saté* sauce from Indonesia, and fish sauce from Vietnam and Thailand.

THE CANTONESE PEOPLE AND THEIR FOOD CULTURE*

"Eat in Canton" is an old Chinese saying. The South China province, now known as Guangdong, is a relative newcomer to Chinese history. Established in 220 BC as part of China proper with Canton as capital, Guangdong was known at first as a haven for adventurers and exiles, distinguished in a culinary sense only for exotic fruits such as the lychee with its firm, crystalline flesh filled with perfumed sweetness. With waves of great southward migrations, Guangdong inherited Northern traditions, adapting them for the local environment.

Guangdong is blessed with a mild climate and is abundant in rice, fruits, vegetables, poultry, pork, fish, and crustaceans. The city of Canton, situated at the Pearl River Delta a short distance from the sea, grew prosperous with twenty centuries of trade, first with Arabs, Persians (probably including Jews), and Hindus, then with the Dutch, the Portuguese, the Spaniards, the British, and the French. Cantonese sailors and merchants ranged throughout Southeast Asia. Canton accordingly developed a distinctive cuisine with a greater variety than any other region in China.

The Cantonese people have a reputation of being clever, innovative, adventurous, and energetic; they are said to be temperamental, impatient, opinionated, and not too consistent. How is the Cantonese character reflected in the cuisine?

An Obsession for Capturing Peak Flavor   The Cantonese demand the freshest food and try their best not to overcook it. They are particularly squeamish about leafy vegetables, most of which should look appetizingly green and crisp to the bite. Chicken and fish, purchased live, are usually served with a tinge of pink in the bones.

---

*In Canton we have one of the many examples of linguistic transmigration common during the early days of East-West contact. *Canton* is a corruption of Guangdong, the name of a province. The word *Canton* now means Guangzhou, the capital of Guangdong. However *Cantonese* now means "pertaining to Guangdong" or at least "pertaining to a wide area centered at Canton." Cantonese cuisine is the cuisine of the entire Guangdong Province, plus the eastern portion of neighboring Guangxi.

Natural Appearance   Cantonese dishes tend to be colorful, less through meticulous cutting and patient decoration than through the choice of ingredients, the treatment they receive, and the tasteful yet simple arrangements on the platter after cooking.

A Long List of Ingredients   Practically anything edible is grist for the Cantonese gourmet. Guangdong is richly endowed with excellent ingredients, and what the province lacks can arrive by sea.

The Cantonese is fond of "light soy sauce," pale in color and fresh in taste. Other typical ingredients include black beans, oyster sauce, shrimp paste, salted fish, crabmeat, Cantonese sausages, and roast pork. Bean cheese—pungent and salty—goes well in a stir-fry with watercress or green beans. Fresh coriander, Chinese broccoli, and water chestnuts are used more often in Cantonese food than elsewhere. Examples of unusual ingredients are lychees, cashew nuts, coconuts, pineapples, papayas, tiny young watermelons, tender pea leaves, chrysanthemum petals, skins of pomelo (a Chinese cousin of the grapefruit). Seafood such as White-dipped Conch Slices and Stir-fried Cuttlefish are specialties. Oysters and large crabs thrive in brackish water near Canton, giving forth dishes as Minced Oyster Fluff and Crab Foo Yung. A whole array of animals and animal parts are eaten, including poisonous snakes and the pupae of the silkworm.

A Huge, Ever-Improving Repertoire   Every medium-sized Cantonese restaurant displays hundreds of items on its menu, and new dishes are being invented every day. Some of the dishes have metaphoric riddle names: an easy example is Dragon Piercing the Wings of Phoenix, with slivers of Chinese ham displacing the bones in the mid-sections of chicken wings.

An Open-Mindedness About Other Cuisines   From India came Curry Chicken, and from Indonesia, Saté, a miniature shish-kebab. While other regional Chinese cuisines may strain to be traditional, the Cantonese adopt foreign methods with relish but seldom, if ever, copy blindly. Western foods served in Hong Kong restaurants often taste vaguely Chinese; the temptation to innovate and modify must be hard to resist.

Even within the broad Cantonese classification, there are at least two distinct subcuisines. The residents near Chaozhou, near Fujian, are known not only for their taste for tea, but also for Marinated Goose, Red-roasted Conch, Fried Crab Balls, and Braised Shark's Fin in a Small Pot. The latter is sold in many small shops in Chinatown, Bangkok, with a large Chaozhou population.

The Hakka people spread all along the coast in Guangdong and Fujian. They are famous for Salt-baked Chicken, Fish-stuffed Bean Curd, and crispy meatballs made of beef, fish, or shrimp.

The arts of stir-frying, white-cooking, steaming, and oil-dipping are developed to the highest degree, as these techniques tend to bring out the natural food flavors. Very rich foods and prolonged cooking, on the other hand, tend to be identified more with East China and Central China cooking. The Cantonese are particularly respected for their multifarious ways for preparing chicken. A common order in a Cantonese restaurant is One Chicken in Three Flavors.

The hungry Cantonese can eat snacks at least twenty hours a day, though major restaurants have limited hours. Congee shops serve congee (rice porridge) plain, with raw fish slices to be scalded to doneness, with roast duck, with meatballs, and with pork or beef organs. Also served are deep-fried pastries and thin steamed rice crepes called Pig's Intestines. Wonton shops serve wonton noodles (the Cantonese prefer a chewy type), plain wontons, or water crescents (soup dumplings) (which resemble wontons in taste but contain different ingredients). Cool tea shops sell piping-hot herb teas with a "cooling" humor. Cafés sell coffee, tea, various sweet teas, egg custard, iced tea, iced red bean soup, ice cream, and cookies and cakes. In the summer, flower of bean curd is served chilled with syrup of brown sugar.

Tiny shops abound in Canton, specializing in ready-to-eat roasts, such as whole roast suckling pigs, whole roast ducks, whole roast geese, roast pig's liver, and roast duck's webbed feet. They also offer pre-cooked food, simmered in a spicy sauce, such as chicken, squab, pig's feet, and pig's maw. The aroma of the food alone is a treat, and the sight of a well-roasted goose is irresistibly tempting.

A tea house serves about two hundred kinds of steamed and fried *dim sums*. Some of the popular ones are shrimp dumplings, *shao mai*, buns stuffed with sweet lotus-seed paste or roast pork, and fried rice wrapped in lotus leaves; all are to be washed down with tea, which comes in scores of varieties. The hungry folk may order, in addition, fried chicken noodles or rice sticks stir-fried with beef, bell peppers, and black beans. Many businessmen conduct their transactions in the tea house at six in the morning and finish the day's work by ten.

The great restaurants in Canton vie not only for excellence, but they also claim uniqueness in having special recipes, special chefs, or proprietary techniques. The Supreme Stock, a master flavoring agent made of chicken, Chinese ham, lean pork, and sometimes duck and squab, is maintained for years, differing from one great restaurant to the next. It is expensive because of the ingredients and the upkeep, but to the Cantonese gourmet it is the very soul of the restaurant.

Guangxi also belongs to the Cantonese culinary region, but it is mostly known as a supplier of ingredients and games. It produces the best starchy taro, the best water chestnut, and the best pomelo. Forbidding Ten-myriad Big Mountains is combed for poisonous snakes for the tables in Canton and Hong Kong in the fall.

Paper-wrapped Chicken is a specialty of Wuzhou, at the Guangdong border. Tiny Moslem restaurants in scenic Guilin offer Horse-meat Rice Noodles in tiny bowls; a dozen per person is considered normal. The meat is cut paper thin and is cooked by scalding in the soup. Guilin's special chili-pepper sauce goes well with the noodles, or also everything.

CHINESE FOOD IN AMERICA

The Cantonese first came to the Continental United States more than a hundred years ago, seeking gold. Later, when the Transcontinental Railroad was being built, young Chinese males were recruited to do the manual labor, digging and dynamiting their way from San Francisco to Utah. After the mining and the railroad building, many workers remained and took the only jobs available to them. They became laundrymen and cooks. Descendents from these hardy folk now account for the bulk of the Chinese Americans, and they own perhaps 80 percent of the Chinese restaurants in the United States, advertising Cantonese food.

Most of the original Chinese gold-miners and railroad builders came from the neighborhood of Taishan, a hilly district on the sea one hundred miles southwest

of Canton. Taishan is now known as Little Canton; but this nickname came after the overseas Chinese returned with their hard-earned money, not before their departure. Taishan cooking is not representative of Cantonese city cuisine, and the miners and railroaders were not particularly trained as chefs. What they brought with them was a tradition of good country cookery and a genius for adaptation. The Chinese Americans in Hawaii trace their origins to the Zhongshan district, the birthplace of Dr. Sun Yat-sen, the founder of the Chinese Republic. Zhongshan is closer to Canton in tradition than Taishan is, and the Chinese food in Hawaii in general is closer to Cantonese city cooking.

Chinese American food has a patron saint: Ambassador Li Hongzhang from the Imperial Manchu court to the United States in the late 1800s. A scholar-general turned diplomat, he was credited with the invention of Chop Suey. As the story goes, one late afternoon he suddenly remembered having invited a number of guests for supper. With no time for shopping and only leftovers in his hands, his chef whipped up a tasty hodge-podge, which became an instant success. Ambassador Li was immortalized in culinary history when he had to tell approving guests the name of the dish. Chop Suey means the conglomeration of oddments.

As Ambassador Li had a frugal mother who (so it was said) insisted on eating only leftovers, his household had no lack of this magic ingredient. In fact, the filial son often would order a full complement of banquet dishes to be left untouched overnight in order to be warmed over the next day, leftover style, to please his mother. In Chop Suey, it seems, mother is the necessity of invention.

Does Chinese American food define a cuisine? Probably not. It is sound cooking, adopted to the needs of an impatient, uncritical society. Chop Suey is a commercialized stir-fry with similar ingredients, often simmered like stew in a huge pot, then ladled to order. It can be very tasty, reminding one of the Mash Paste Cabbage of East China, where Ambassador Li came from.

Chow Mein (stir-fried noodles) in the least expensive version is just Chop Suey poured over crunchy deep-fried noodles. It aimed to be the Cantonese pan-fried noodles, not quite reaching that state owing to the demand for quick service. Subgum (roughly, "many-splendored") Chow Mein has a made-to-order Cantonese topping; Chow Mein Cantonese Style is genuinely Cantonese.

Chinese-American fried rice, dark with soy sauce, is a departure from the original Yangzhou tradition, which called for flavoring by a nearly colorless Supreme Stock to display the natural rainbow colors of the ingredients. Likewise, the brown, tasty Egg Foo Yung is a far cry in appearance from the Cantonese original, which is colorful, soft, and moist, like the big foo yung (hibiscus) flower for which the dish was named. Chinese American Egg Foo Yung actually resembles a Cantonese Egg Pancake (a silver dollar-sized omelet), enlarged to facilitate handling.

Lobster Cantonese Style (sometimes called Lobster Boston Style) and Jumbo Shrimp in Lobster Sauce are welcome additions to Cantonese cuisine. Sea-going Taishan is well familiar with seafood, and neighboring Yangjiang is famed for salted black beans. Ground pork and eggs make the black bean sauce hearty and delicious, blending marvelously with white rice.

Other old-time Chinese American restaurant favorites include Egg Rolls, Wontons, Sweet and Sour Pork, and Moogoo Gai Pan (chicken slices with button mushrooms). In general, the egg rolls have thicker skin for easier handling. The wontons, often prepared long in advance, may omit shrimps to avoid spoilage, and a dried fish ingredient ("great earth fish") is also omitted, partly to accommodate the American lack of enthusiasm for fish. The sweet and sour dishes exaggerate the color; their gravy, derived from canned pineapples and catsup, might be extra-sweet. The more expensive, made-to-order Chinese-American dishes do approximate the true Cantonese counterparts. Moogoo Gai Pan is a true-to-life Cantonese stir-fry, tending to be more gravy-laden for blending with white rice. Since it looks to true Cantonese cuisine as an ideal, Chinese American cookery is not a cuisine, but an off-shoot of one.

In big American cities, the Cantonese restaurants catering to the Chinese have been conscientiously practicing Cantonese cuisine. A trend toward sophistication became quite noticeable after the Second World War, when relaxed immigration rules enabled big-city relatives of Chinese American restaurateurs to practice their art in the United States. During the period from 1950 to 1960, a substitution of quality for quantity was seen in a shrimp dumpling in New York tea houses. Its size shrank by at least one-half, the skin became conspicuously more translucent and less lumpy, and the taste was greatly improved. The expanded supply of Chinese ingredients, plus the proliferation of restaurants featuring Shanghai, Peking, Sichuan, and Hunan cuisines have contributed to raise the overall level of Chinese cookery in America. Some of the best-known Chinese chefs have established themselves in this country, and outstanding examples of their regional cuisines can now be found in major cities, especially New York, Washington, D.C., San Francisco, and Los Angeles.

The Ingredients

Chinese cuisine commands a much larger repertoire of ingredients than probably any other cuisine on earth. There is heavy use of both fresh ingredients and preserved specialties. Also interesting is that the Chinese make no strong distinction between foods and seasonings. Foods can be used in either way, as in the use of dried shrimp as a flavoring for soup, or young gingerroot as a vegetable in stir-fries. Lastly, oil and lard but not butter are used for frying. Indeed, there is nearly a total absence of dairy products. On the other hand, the Chinese have multiple uses for the ancient soybean, from cooked plain beans through bean sprouts, bean sheets, and bean curd, to soy sauce.

THE IMPORTANCE OF FRESH INGREDIENTS

The Chinese often demand utmost freshness in their food, particularly their poultry, fish, and vegetables. The Chinese homemaker shops daily in the market and develops a fastidiousness for fresh food, matched in America only by the mania for young corn. (It is ironic that many Chinese favor well-ripened corn for its chewiness.) There is no substitute for fresh green vegetables just picked and shipped from the farm, or fish just caught from nearby waters.

You should develop the same fastidiousness for fresh ingredients. When possible, use fresh-killed chicken. The chicken should also be well drained of blood, lest a gamey flavor defeat the more delicate preparations, especially in White-chopped Chicken. Freshness in meats and in duck is of less importance, and these days quick-frozen shrimp can taste as fresh as can be, even though live ones are firmer in texture. Improperly frozen shrimp, however, have an unpleasant taste.

In America, the variety of vegetables available in average supermarkets is not large, although freshness is often adequate. If possible, visit a grocery in the Chinatown in your section of the country, and you will be impressed by the much greater choice of Chinese vegetables. There you will often see Chinese cabbage (*bok choy*), Chinese broccoli, napa cabbage (celery cabbage), eggplants that are thinner than the usual American variety, bitter melons, mustard greens (*gai choy*), Chinese parsley (coriander), white radishes, and snow peas.

Fresh ingredients should be kept in the vegetable drawer or bin of your refrigerator. Those not readily available in supermarkets, and that require extra effort to obtain, can be given some added protection. Wrap them first with a clean towel or paper towel, then put them in a plastic bag for refrigeration. The aim is to avoid spoilage induced by close contact with moisture. Scallions and leeks should be put in a special plastic container to localize odor.

PRESERVED SPECIALTIES FOR ADDED INTEREST

A huge variety of preserved foods, spices, and seasoning agents are used daily by the Chinese cook. Many consider their food naked without the presence of soy sauce, small dried shrimps, slivers of pickled turnips, star anise, red dates, or black mushrooms.

Dried rice sticks, upon deep-frying, give Wooly Lamb its fluffy coat. Chinese wizardry turns ordinary duck eggs into thousand-year-old eggs in three short weeks. Salted duck eggs are prized for the yolks; they are the little moons inside Mooncakes.

Chinese ham is dark red in color, aromatic and salty, and although hard to find here, is well approximated by the Smithfield ham. Chinese sausages, preserved duck, and preserved meats—formerly only available in the winter—are now found in grocery stores all year round with the blessings of modern refrigeration.

The tangy smell of salted fish and purple shrimp paste might not appeal to the uninitiated, but oyster sauce, a Cantonese product, is loved by almost all. Its Fujianese counterpart is fish sauce, often imported to the United States from Thailand and Malaysia. Sichuan cookery calls for red-chili pepper oil, hot bean paste, and *ma-la* sauce made by powdered fagara and sesame oil. (Don't be too trigger happy with sesame oil! It has a mild laxative effect.)

Tiny dried mung beans taste exactly like lentils; they grow into bean sprouts in water. Red bean paste makes a sweet red or black stuffing for steamed buns and pastries. Sesame paste is chewier, and winter melon paste is crisp and transparent. Most elegant, perhaps, is the paste made with dried lotus seeds. Fermented black beans, tangy and salty, are a favorite household seasoning. The versatile dried soybean is responsible for soy sauce, bean curd (tofu), and soybean sticks (fuzhu). Fuzhu is a major ingredient in meatless cooking, appearing as vegetarian chicken or vegetarian roast duck; the imitation often surpasses the original in flavor, texture, and nutrition.

Walnuts are used for stir-frying with diced chicken, so are almonds and cashews. Chestnuts are for braised chicken chunks; the Chinese chestnut is among the best in the world, and, besides, its tree is impervious to the American chestnut blight. Dried red dates (jujube) are solid honey, each with a tiny spindle for a seed. Olives come in a huge number of preserved forms and are eaten like candy together with preserved plums. The seed inside the stone of large black olives is prized for its flavor (like pine nuts) and unique texture.

A store in China (or a Chinatown in the United States) where preserved foods are sold reminds one of a museum. Exotic dried shark's fins and fish maws hang from the ceiling of the store, looking like delta wings or fantastic shaped coils. On the shelves in glass jars are found dried treasures such as bird's nest, jade pillars, abalone, octopi, sea cucumbers, squid, and jellyfish. Dozens of teas are displayed:

black Pu Erh, pressed into pancakes; green Dragon Well, whose leaves open in hot water like flowers; dried tiny white chrysanthemums, for the only tea to be served with sugar; bitter herb teas, to drive off colds. Thousand-year-old eggs and salted duck eggs are stacked in huge earthen jars. Black mushrooms, cloud ears, snow mushrooms, noodles, and beans are sold in dried form; but the best bamboo shoots, straw mushrooms, and boiled abalone in the United States are found only in tins. A bottled bean cheese made in San Francisco has won critics' approval in Hong Kong.

Dried foods weigh much less, and often fetch much higher prices than their fresh counterparts. For example, a good grade of dried abalone sells for twenty times the fresh; jade pillars (dried "scallops") fetch about five times the price of filet mignon. But dried vegetables are consumed regularly, sometimes together with fresh ones, to improve the flavor of the dishes. Similarly, dried and fresh meats are often found in the same soup (Ham Hock and Pork's Feet Soup or Watercress Soup with Fresh and Dried Gizzards).

Dried ingredients usually keep indefinitely at room temperature. These include rice, flour, noodles, dried seafood, dried vegetables, and dried beans. We often put the more valuable dried ingredients in sealed jars, and place them in the refrigerator for additional protection against insects, especially tiny beetles.

Dried meat products may "sweat" and turn rancid; we put them in plastic bags in the freezer. Wet-preserved ingredients should be kept in glass or porcelain containers, as the liquid often interacts with metal or plastic. Bean pastes and similar products should be transferred to plastic or glass containers. Add some fresh oil on the surface to keep the contents moist.

Canned bamboo shoots and canned water chestnuts should be drained, rinsed, then put into fresh water before refrigeration. The water should be changed at least every 2 days to best retain the flavor.

Oyster sauce, soy sauce, and fish sauce keep indefinitely in bottles. Vegetable oil, however, may turn rancid, and you should not keep more than a month's supply.

A GLOSSARY OF CHINESE INGREDIENTS

The following listing includes discussion of the major ingredients for most Chinese dishes.

Abalone

Canned abalone from Mexico, Australia, and Japan is readily available in Oriental markets and specialty food stores. It comes already shelled and cooked in salted water, and is very versatile. It can be served directly, sliced and arranged neatly in a cold platter; it also makes an excellent stir-fry with vegetables and oyster sauce. Shredded abalone is used much like Chinese ham in Northern cuisine. Avoid overcooking, or its texture turns rubbery.

Dried abalone from Japan commands extraordinarily high prices in specialty stores, and besides is difficult to prepare properly. Dried abalone from North China are smaller.

Fresh abalone is found along the West Coast of North America. Tasty but often tough, it is pounded to tenderness and sold in seafood stores there. It is quite different from canned abalone.

Agar-Agar

A Japanese seaweed product sold in the form of 8-inch-long bars with 1-square-inch cross-section or thin sticks ⅛ inch in diameter. Basically colorless but sometimes dyed a deep red, it is used much like clear gelatin, but has an altogether different texture; while gelatin gels are resilient, gels made of agar-agar break cleanly on the bite. For best results, pass the boiled agar-agar liquid through a sieve to remove the undissolved particles before gelling.

Agar-agar sticks, cut into 2-inch lengths, are often mixed with fresh cucumber shreds and soy sauce in a Northern salad. A favorite agar-agar dessert is Almond Bean Curd, which is agar-agar gel flavored with milk, sugar, and almond essence, but no bean curd.

Almonds

Chinese almonds ("apricot seeds" in Chinese) are seeds of the apricot, and come in two varieties: southern almonds are mild, interchangeable in taste with American almonds; northern almonds are more bitter. A soup recipe may call for both types. American almonds are known to the herbist as flatpeach seed.

Amaranth

Young leaves and stems of this decorative plant are a common vegetable *(xiancai)* in East and South China. Salt-preserved Amaranth Stems, thick as a thumb, is an East China specialty.

Aniseeds

Seeds from the anise plant, similar to fennel in both taste and appearance.

Bacon, Chinese

Meat from the belly of the pig, with lean and fat layers interlaced and skin attached, is called five-flower meat in China, and is used extensively, especially in braised dishes in which ¼-inch-thick slices are separated by slices of starchy vegetables such as taro. Winter-preserved meat *(laro)*, often called Chinese bacon, also employs this cut, and is marinated first, then dried in the winter sun.

Bamboo Fungi (zhusun, *"bamboo plant"*)

Often mistaken to be the lining of the hollow bamboo stem, these are actually a relative of the American stinkhorn. The scientific name is *Dictyophora duplicata*. With a unique crisp texture reminding one of bamboo shoots, they are among the most expensive edible fungi in China, fetching three or more times the price of French truffles. There is hope, however, that the price may soon come down with artificial cultivation.

Bamboo-leaf Green

A potent (about 95 proof) medicated Fen liquor from Shanxi Province. Its pale green coloration is from young bamboo leaves, one of its twelve ingredients.

Bamboo-leaf Green made a thousand years ago was almost certainly not a distilled liquor, and may be close to a wine now made under the same name in Zhejiang Province.

Bamboo Shoots
Bamboo plants propagate by issuing shoots from below the ground. The texture of the shoots changes with the seasons. Winter shoots, stubby and firm, have a meatlike chewiness; spring shoots are slender and tender; most commonly available are summer shoots, looser in texture, succulent though inclined to be bitter. In America fresh shoots are a rarity, and the quality of canned shoots varies greatly with the brand. Winter and spring shoots are so specified on cans; unspecified ones are summer shoots, which should be ivory-white rather than yellow, and firm rather than mushy.

After the can is opened, the shoots should be rinsed, then transferred to an airtight glass container where they can be kept refrigerated for up to ten days. For utmost freshness, change the water daily. Blanch before cooking to eliminate the metallic taste common in most canned shoots.

Bean Cheese
Also called fermented bean cake, or *furu* (*fuyu* in Cantonese). A fermented soybean product in the form of tiny yellow bricks, it is soft, salty, and pungent. Americans seem to avoid it as much as the average Chinese abhor cheese. An excellent fresh kind is made in Chinatown, San Francisco. It is used to accompany congee and oil-strips for breakfast, or in Chinese country-style dishes such as Fuyu Stir-fried Empty-hearted Vegetables. Red and subtle-tasting red bean cheese (*nanru; namyu* in Cantonese) is used extensively to flavor pork dishes and Cantonese snacks.

Bean Curd
See pages 322–323.

Bean Products
See pages 322–323 and CELLOPHANE NOODLES.

Bean Sprouts
Sprouts from both soybeans and mung beans are used extensively in Chinese cooking. Mung-bean sprouts, found in many American supermarkets, have a fresh taste and a crisp, almost crystalline texture. This is true also of the stems of soybean sprouts. The large, yellow head of the latter, however, is chewy and meatlike.

Both sprouts are used mainly in country cooking; but the crisp stems of mung-bean sprouts are invariably served with Braised Shark's Fin in Cantonese cooking and just-sprouted mung beans are a specialty dish in Shaanxi and Gansu Provinces. Soybean sprouts are the main ingredient in the Supreme Stock of South China vegetarians.

Bean sprouts should be fresh; canned versions are not really adequate on this score. Sprouting kits are available from health food stores for those who prefer to grow their own.

Bean Threads
See CELLOPHANE NOODLES.

Bear's Paw
Front paws of the bear, esteemed for thirty centuries in North China. Paws collected in the spring, called cinnabar paws because of their reddish color, are considered the best.

Bicarbonate of Soda (baking soda)
Used extensively in South China as a meat tenderizer (do not forget to neutralize afterwards!) and as a latter-day replacement of lye solution for controlled leavening of pastries.

Big-head Vegetable
See VEGETABLES, PRESERVED.

Bird's Nest
Nests of swallows in Malaysia, Thailand, and Indonesia, made of dried saliva and formed on sheer cliffs. The best ones are crystalline white, sometimes tinged with pink. Lower grades may be gray with adhered swallow down. Very expensive and getting rarer every year.

Black Beans, Fermented
These beans come already cooked, fermented, and seasoned with salt and ginger. This inexpensive ingredient is widely used in stir-frying and steaming in country cooking all over South China. Americans might not take to the down-to-earth flavor and strong smell upon first encounter, but it is the main seasoning in Steamed Spareribs in Black Bean Sauce or Shrimp in Lobster Sauce. They can be kept indefinitely in a closed jar at room temperature.

Blackfish Roe
Dried roe of the blackfish (*wu* fish), thin slices are roasted and consumed as a snack in Fujian and Taiwan.

Broad Beans (fava beans)
A very common bean, especially in North China. The pods are poisonous, and some unlucky people may be allergic to the beans as well. Served as a vegetable in stir-fries, in soups, as a paste, or as a snack. Fresh broad beans are delicious, in our opinion better than lima beans. Sprouting broad beans are an East China favorite. Broad beans found in markets are from an Italian species of equal quality.

Brown Sugar
Chinese brown sugar comes in slabs like an elongated domino, and can be nibbled like candy. Each slab looks like a sandwich, brown and solid top and bottom, and lightly yellow and powdery in between. Common brown sugar serves essentially the same purpose except for the appearance.

Camel's Hump
Widely praised in the classics, this delicacy is now found in frozen form in specialty markets in Hong Kong. It is very fatty and appears to have been overrated.

Camphor Wood Chips
Used for smoking duck for Camphor and Tea Leaf Duck. These can be approximated by American hickory chips.

Cashew Nuts
Crunchy and naturally sweet, this is a newcomer to Chinese cuisine. I stir-fry whole ones with vegetables and meat, and grind the chipped ones for pastry fillings.

Cassia Blossoms, Preserved (guihua)
Tiny yellow flowers of the osmanthus (not cassia) preserved either in sugar or in salt, are used extensively in East and North China for their sweet fragrance in dumplings, pastries, and sauces.

Caul or Lace Fat (wangyou, "net-fat")
This is a net of stringy fat which forms a casing for the stomach of pigs, used for wrapping food before cooking for a self-braising effect, to improve external appearance and to add special chewiness.

Cellophane Noodles (fensi, "flour threads," also called bean threads)
Dried white threads made of the flour of the mung bean, they turn transparent and resilient when cooked, and are important in country cooking. A related product is *fenpi* ("flour skin"), which is a platter-size sheet of the same material. Do not confuse with rice sticks, which turn white and soft on cooking.

Chestnuts
One of the best companions to chicken, available fresh or dried. The Chinese chestnut is easy to peel and has a smooth surface. Dried chestnuts should be soaked for hours before use. Chestnut paste is used commonly in North China for cakes and fillings of pastries or puddings.

Chili Pepper Products
Chili pepper oil is red as a rose, and carries a mighty sting. Use sparingly. *Chili pepper sauce* is a common table condiment, and comes in two types: those made of ground chilis are orange red, somewhat like Tabasco sauce, but are thicker in consistency and are not vinegary; those made of crushed chilis often contain added ingredients such as ginger, fermented black beans, and shallots. *Dried chili peppers* are used liberally in Sichuan and Hunan cooking. *Chili pepper powder* is not too common in Cantonese kitchens.

Chives, Chinese
Chinese chives, often called Chinese leeks, have the shape of chives and an odor

like leeks. They are used for stir-frying, for making egg pancakes, and for stuffing dumplings in North China cuisine. Yellow chives are Chinese chives grown in the dark; they are pale yellow and tender. Both Chinese chives and yellow chives are available in large Chinatowns. In Hong Kong the flowering stalks of Chinese chives are a crunchy vegetable.

Chrysanthemums

Fresh white chrysanthemum petals are edible, and are used as a garnish for a number of banquet dishes. They also play prominent roles in Chrysanthemum Hot Pot in North China, and Snake Soup in Canton and Hong Kong. Be sure that the plant has not been sprayed with insecticide recently. Tiny Hangzhou white chrysanthemums are used as tea, often mixed with Dragon Well tea leaves.

Cloves

Commonly available. Used with other spices to make a spicy mixture for lo, the Southern simmering sauce.

Coconut Milk

Fresh coconut milk is a refreshing summer drink. Canned concentrated coconut milk from Hawaii or the Philippines is excellent for making curry, sweet teas, or puddings.

Conches

Called "loud shell" *(xiangluo)* because the shells are used as a blowing horn. Good for stir-frying when very fresh, for soup whether fresh, frozen, or dried. East Coast conches are smaller than Chinese ones, but are just as good.

Congee

Boiled rice porridge. Plain congee with oil-strips, bean cheese, and pickles is a standard breakfast for many Chinese. Common in South China is congee with meat, chicken, roast duck, animal organs, and/or peanuts. A Cantonese specialty congee scalds thinly sliced raw fish right in the bowl. *Congee* is a Hindu word; the Chinese name is *zhou* (*juk* in Cantonese).

Coriander

Also known as Chinese parsley, Mexican parsley, and cilantro, this is the most common herb in Chinese cuisine. Its graceful, tender leaves have a unique spicy flavor, and are used extensively but sparingly in South and East China as a garnish and as an accessory in soups, congees, salads, and scrambled egg dishes. In North China it is used as a vegetable.

Corn, Miniature

Two-inch-long miniature ears of corn, sold in cans, are crisp and sweet. They are a recent addition to Chinese cuisine.

Cucumbers

Cucumbers are used extensively in clear soups, in stir-fries, and in Steamed

Stuffed Cucumbers. They are the most common ingredient for salads in Chinese cooking, rather than any leaf vegetable. Pickled cucumbers are used as a condiment, a side dish, as an ingredient for cooking, or as companion to breakfast congee. Preserved sweet cucumbers, made from white-skinned tiny cucumbers, are used in steamed minced pork, steamed fish, and soups.

Curry

We prefer the curry powder or curry sauce from Madras, India. However, the success of a Chinese curry dish depends less on the brand of curry than on the use of good coconut milk.

Cuttlefish

See OCTOPI, SQUID, AND CUTTLEFISH.

Dace

A freshwater fish grown in ponds in South China. Canned fried dace, with or without fermented black beans, is a common sight in Oriental markets.

Dates, Chinese Red

Also called jujube dates, these are sold in dried form. They are used in soups, steamed chicken as garnish, and also as a filling for pastries.

Dragon Well Tea

This is the most well-known green tea, grown in Hangzhou near Dragon Well Spring, the water from which is almost as famous for tea-making.

Duck, Preserved (laya, *"winter-preserved duck"*)

A salted whole duck, flattened into a roughly circular disc and dried. The best ones come from Nanan in Jiangxi Province, just north of the border with Guangdong. Preserved duck from Nanking is called *banya* ("board duck").

Eggplants

The Chinese prefer the long, narrow type (called Japanese eggplant in the United States) as much more suitable for stuffing. They also have more skin, pound for pound; skin is needed in many dishes. We recommend Braised Eggplant with Bean Paste and Steamed Eggplant in Mustard and Sesame Sauce.

Eggs, Salted Duck

Salted duck eggs are pretty, with their snow-white egg white and bright red yolk. They are used often for steamed minced meat and for soups. The yolks are the major ingredient for the mooncake and many pastries.

Eggs, Thousand-Year-Old

These are duck eggs that have been preserved in potash. They acquire a blue-black yolk and a transparent, brown egg white.

Fen
See NOODLES, RICE STICKS, AND FEN.

Fen Liquor
Very potent (130 proof) kaoliang liquor from Fenyang in Shanxi Province. Excellent for marinating beef.

Fennel
An important ingredient in five-spice powder and in lo, the South China simmering sauce. Often replaced by aniseed.

Fish, Dried
See GREAT EARTH FISH.

Fish, Freshwater
Steamed East Coast shad is delicious (the Chinese steam shad with the scales on), though its season is short. Midwest walleyed pike is outstanding, and so is West Coast big-head carp grown by the Chinese and called *sung* fish in Chinatown. Fresh trout, carp, and catfish are established favorites, but freshwater salmon is a new Northwest delicacy.

In China, look for dace in the South, shad (*shi* fish), perch (*lu* fish), and Mandarin perch (*gui* fish) in the East; Wuchang fish (a freshwater bream) in Central China; and golden carp in the North. The *grass carp* in Hangzhou is unusually tender and delicious.

Fish Lips and Fish Maws
Fish lips are meaty parts of the shark near the mouth and fins. Fish maws are dried, deep-fried floats of large fish, usually cod; unfried floats are known as white flower gel. All three are banquet delicacies.

Fish, Salted
Not necessarily to the taste of Americans, this oldtime Chinese favorite comes in many varieties and is often as salty as salt itself, with a penetrating odor. Formerly food for the peasants, it is now expensive enough to grace banquet tables in Hong Kong in the form of Salted Fish Fried Rice with Diced Chicken.

Fish Sauce
Fermented from fish, this is a seasoning originally from Southeast Asia; Thailand is now the main supplier. It is used in Fujianese and Chaozhou cooking.

Fish, Sea
The Chinese Americans enjoy scrod and sea bass in the East, rock cod in the West, and salmon in either. Sole and sand dab are fine for steaming, and cod and halibut are well-suited for stir-fried fish chunks. The flaky texture of Chinese yellow fish (also called yellow croaker) is unique; it is available frozen in the United States. Fujian and Taiwan are noted for eels; some canned eels are found in American markets too. The Cantonese in Hong Kong value their rock cod

(called *garupa* there) above its American cousin; one kind, called *mouse garupa*, can cost a hundred American dollars each in a restaurant. But if price is really no object, Hong Kong live seafood is among the best in the world, with huge varieties (try the live green parrotfish, called green dress) (Cantonese: *chingye*), excellent preparation (the best should be steamed), and romantic ambiance, in huge restaurant boats offshore.

Five-spice Powder
A mixture of five ground spices: star anise, cinnamon bark, fennel, Sichuan peppercorn, and clove. Commonly used in South China to marinate pork and poultry. Available now in most supermarkets. Five-spice salt is another mixture, a recipe for which is on page 193.

Flours and Starches
All-purpose flour contains 5 to 10 percent gluten, *high-gluten flour* contains 11 to 20 percent. *Gluten flour,* available in health food stores, contains almost 80 percent gluten and is best for making gluten without going through the rinsing process. The starch rinsed from wheat flour after fermentation becomes *wheat starch,* an important ingredient for making dim sum wrappers. *Glutinous rice flour* is ground from glutinous rice, widely used for Chinese sweet puddings and dumplings. *Rice flour* is ground from long-grain rice, used the same way as glutinous flour; it also is the chief ingredient for rice sticks *(fen)*. *Tapioca powder* is made from cassava, a plant grown in the tropics; it is used often in South China cooking for sealing the cut-up ingredients when seasoning. It is interchangeable with *arrowroot powder,* and can often be substituted by *cornstarch.* The latter cannot give the clear glossy appearance desired in thickening soups and sauces, but being less sticky, excels in coating pieces of ingredients for deep-frying. For thickening clear banquet soups, the starch from water chestnuts, called *Water chestnut powder,* should be used.

Fowl
America makes chicken the best bargain in the market. Many years ago, the Chinese in America complained of the gamey taste in chicken; this was due more to the methods of dressing and refrigeration than to the species used. Look for freshly killed, well-drained chicken. Chinatown chicken often costs much more, but the Chinese gladly pay the difference.

Long Island ducks, said to be Chinese in origin, are excellent, though Chinese ducks may be less fatty. American (and Canadian) geese seem to vary widely in tenderness, perhaps owing to differences in species and raising. It is best to stick to one supplier to ensure consistency.

To many Chinese, the height of cuisine is not the American Thanksgiving turkey. It is too big, and the meat is too uniform and hard to season. But the cornish game hen, just the opposite of the ponderous turkey, in time should win acceptance by the Chinese.

Peking duck is deservingly famous; it is beginning to be available frozen in large Oriental markets. When in Hong Kong or Canton, look at the restaurant menus for the huge variations for preparing chicken. Also try Marinated Goose in a Chaozhou restaurant. As the Chaozhou folk had mastered goose-raising, most of the roast ducks sold in Hong Kong today are really roast geese. The webbed feet of the goose have climbed the social ladder to reach Cantonese banquets, braised together with abalone.

Fungi
See MUSHROOMS AND FUNGI.

Game
Game can be handled like conventional meat or poultry, the problem is how to dispel the gamey odor. A few slices of gingerroot will suffice in a stir-fry or in a braised dish; garlic, leek, and fermented black beans are also effective. In Supreme Scholar's Snake Soup, named after my grandfather, century-old tangerine peel and very finely cut lemon leaves serve the purpose. One of my students applied to moose meat my recipe for Beef in Oyster Sauce with great success.

In China game includes roebucks, deer, "fruit" raccoons, hare, quail, partridges, wild ducks, cranes, armadillos, tortoises, and snakes. The rarer game are valued as tonic during fall and winter, and are slow-cooked with Chinese herbs.

Ginger
Used mainly for flavoring, it is sold in knobs in most supermarkets. Fairly common in the United States now, pieces of about 2 ounces will suffice for ten or more dishes spread over more than a week. After each use, wrap tightly with plastic wrap and store in the refrigerator without rinsing. It will keep for up to two weeks. If used only sparingly, scrape the skin off the root and put the whole knob in a glass jar. Add sherry to cover and keep jar tightly capped. The jar can be stored in the refrigerator for over a month.

Ginger juice often is used as a seasoning, along with wine. To achieve maximum output, do not slice the gingerroot first. Instead grate as much ginger as needed into a small bowl, then add the wine, blending the ginger and wine together. Pour the mixture through a small strainer into another bowl and squeeze the gratings against the wall of the strainer to extract all the juice. Another method is to prepare a larger quantity, and keep it stored in the refrigerator in a small glass jar. It will last up to two weeks. A normal slice of gingerroot is about the size and thickness of an American quarter.

Ginger, Sand
This is a South China root used for seasoning chicken and also as a component of curry. It is used most commonly as one of the spices to make lo, the simmering sauce in Cantonese cooking.

Ginkgo
Dried meat inside the stone of the ginkgo fruit, looking like tiny yellow eggs. Chewy and aromatic, it is used extensively in vegetarian cookery and as a snack.

Glutinous Rice
See RICE.

Golden Needles
See TIGER LILIES.

Great Earth Fish

The Cantonese name *(daiday)* for dried flounder, used as a soup base, also for seasoning dim sums and wontons. Roast to remove skin and bones, then deep-fry the meat and pound into bits before use.

Green Beans and Yard-long Beans

Green beans in America are plentiful and excellent in quality. They correspond to four-seasons beans *(siji dou)* in China; Dry-braised Green Beans is a Sichuan specialty. Yard-long beans come in two types; the Cantonese prefer the green, crunchy type in a stir-fry with roast pork to the whitish, softer type which is actually more versatile.

Hair Vegetable (facai)

A freshwater algae from creeks in North China, with the appearance of coarse, dull, black human hair. Valued in vegetarian cuisine, also during New Year's celebrations, as *facai* sounds like "get rich" in Chinese.

Hairy Crab

A freshwater crab. The best is found in Yangcheng Lake, not far from Shanghai. Male crabs are more treasured for their orange coral.

Ham, Chinese

The most prized Chinese hams come from Jinhua ("Gold Flower") in Zhejiang Province. Almost as famous are those from Yunnan Province. Smithfield Ham in the United States is by far the closest substitute, and it is available in Chinese markets, specialty meat markets, and delicatessens. It is usually sold both whole or cut up. If a whole ham is purchased, ask the butcher to cut it into 2-inch-wide slabs. Trim off all fat, wrap well, and put in the freezer; Smithfield ham does not turn rancid easily and can be kept frozen for up to two years. Though seldom served as a main dish, it is important for decoration and seasoning. The most common way to prepare Chinese-style ham is to steam the trimmed ham with a little honey.

Hasma

These are dried ovaries of the Manchurian tree frog, used for soup as a winter tonic. Very expensive, but an ounce will feed a party of eight.

Hua Diao ("flower-engraved")

The best yellow wine from Xiaoxing, so-called because of the colorful designs put on the earthen jars. See WINES AND SPIRITS FOR COOKING.

Jade Pillars (yiuchue *in Cantonese; Mandarin:* yaozhu) *("Dried Scallops")*

These are dried, cylindrical muscles (pillars) of river jade, a sea clam shaped like a narrow triangle. Invariably sold as "dried scallops," though not from a scallop; true dried scallops, much smaller and less tasty, should be called *ganbei* in Chinese.

Good jade pillars are cylinders about 1 inch in diameter and ½ inch in height, looking somewhat like a piece of brownish yellow jade. They are expensive but

indispensible in many famed soups and banquet dishes. Sold in small bags in Oriental stores, a little will go a long way for soups.

Jasmine Tea

A jasmine flower-flavored tea. It has been around for 700 years, and is now common throughout China, especially in Peking and Tianjin, its sister city. The best jasmine tea may have no jasmine petals; the scent of fresh flowers has been baked into the tea leaves.

Jellyfish

A special ingredient for North China salads, the edible, semi-transparent jellyfish comes salted, either preshredded or in large sheets, in Oriental markets. Store in a cool place; refrigeration is not needed.

Kaoliang

A cousin of the sorghum, grown as a staple to 10 feet high in fields in North China. Also a grain liquor made of kaoliang.

Keemun Tea

Bright red, excellent tea from Qimun, in Anhui Province.

Lace Fat

See CAUL.

Lo (Cantonese; lu in Mandarin)

A South China simmering sauce made from a spicy mixture, soy sauce, wine, and sugar. Now available in bottles in Oriental markets. If salt is used instead of soy sauce, the sauce is called *white lo*.

Longan (Cantonese: "dragon-eye")

A relative of the lychee, longan also has a tough shell and juicy meat inside. It is sweeter and less fragrant. Candy made with dried longan, such as Walnut and Longan Cake, is found in Oriental markets. Dried longan is used in meat soups and sweet teas.

Lotus Root, Lotus Leaves, and Lotus Seeds

Lotus roots (actually rhizomes) grow underwater to 3 feet long in several segments, each resembling the chubby arms of a baby. They are starchy when cooked, but crisp and refreshing when raw. Lotus leaves are not edible, but lend a fresh fragrance to food cooked in them; Lotus Leaf (wrapped) Rice is an example. Lotus seeds can be eaten raw, but are found in the U.S. either dried or canned. They are used in vegetarian cooking, in soups, in sweet teas, and for mashing into a paste for sweet pastries, especially Mooncakes. At the center of each seed is a green bud, which is very bitter and should be removed before cooking.

Lychee (lizi in Mandarin)

This is a highly perfumed, sweet fruit with a tough but easily peelable skin.

Canned lychees are good, but even better are fresh ones, now grown in Hawaii and Florida and sold in the Chinatowns of large cities in the summer. Used as dessert or in sweet-sour dishes. Dried lychees are enjoyable as a snack.

Malt Sugar or Maltose

Also called Chinese malt sugar, this is a chewy sweetener made from germinating barley, commonly used as a coating for roasts. When twirled into a bulb on a chopstick, it is the Chinese version of a lollipop. Can be replaced by honey if not available.

Mandarin Orange

A sweet Chinese citrus fruit looking like an oversized tangerine. Available in supermarkets in canned form, sometimes even fresh if in season. Dried peels *(chenpi)* are valued as both a drug for coughs and as a seasoning. Also made from tangerines, chenpi are known here as *tangerine peels.*

Melon, Bitter

Wrinkled green squash up to 8 inches in length, with a refreshing, bitter taste. Often blanched before preparation to lessen the bitterness.

Melon, Fuzzy

A South China melon with tender flesh but stubby hair which must be scraped off together with the skin before cooking. Tender and faintly sweet, it is excellent for stuffing with pork and jade pillars.

Melon, Winter

Grown in the summer rather than the winter, despite the name. Whole melons, weighing up to 20 pounds, can last for several months after harvesting; unprotected cut-up pieces, however, will spoil in several days in a refrigerator. A winter melon has a thick, dark green, waxy skin and white flesh which turns transparent during cooking. One of the most elegant soups in Cantonese cuisine is Winter Melon Pond, in which the melon itself, with skin intricately carved with designs, serves as the soup tureen.

Monkey's Head Mushrooms

These are fist-sized fungi grown on trees in the rough shape of a monkey's head, with brown hair but no face. A delicacy in North China cuisine.

Monosodium Glutamate

Also called MSG, this flavor-enhancer should be used sparingly or not at all. We consider the indiscriminate use of large amounts of this chemical a bad habit, and people are known to develop allergic reactions to it, varying from excessive thirst to spasms.

Moutai

This is probably the most renowned Chinese grain liquor (110 proof). Produced in Guizhou Province from kaoliang and wheat.

Mushrooms and Fungi
See also BAMBOO FUNGI, MONKEY'S HEAD MUSHROOMS, SNOW MUSHROOMS.

Button mushrooms, common in Europe and America, were virtually unknown until recently; they are now grown in China for export and internal consumption. Moogoo Gai Pan, the well-known Chinese-American dish, means Button Mushrooms with Chicken Slices. But before the button mushroom became widely grown, the word *moogoo* was reserved for its firm-fleshed tasty cousin from Inner Mongolia, which is known today as *koumo* (abbreviation for Zhangjia *moogoo*). The most common mushrooms are *black mushrooms,* called *donggu* (winter mushroom) by the Chinese, and often found in Oriental markets under the Japanese name *shiitake.* They are sold in dried form in several grades; the best ones are thick, with cracks on the crown. Fresh black mushrooms are found in New York and the West Coast; they are delicious if grown properly. The tastiest fresh mushrooms might be straw mushrooms, available only in canned or dried form in the United States.

To the Chinese, a mushroom (Mandarin: *gu*) is usually a spongy umbrella, while an ear (Mandarin: *er*) refers to a fungus which is thin, crunchy, and shaped like an ear. The most common ear is the *cloud ear,* which is grayish brown, translucent and pliant. The *wood ear* is thicker, opaque, and darker, with a gray underside, and is much crunchier in texture. The velvety *stone ear* is jet black with a lighter underside. *Elm ears* are brown, transparent, and meaty yet gelatinous, and so are *yellow ears,* which are yellow and fragrant like chanterelles. Aromatic *Cassia ears* are found on stems of the osmanthus. *Snow ears* (snow mushrooms, silver ears) are pale yellow, transparent, and shaped like a delicate flower.

Noodles, Rice Sticks, and Fen
Chinese egg noodles are available fresh in some markets, and dried in others. They come in several widths, and the fresh variety have a lower egg content.

Noodles made of rice flour are called *fen* ("flour"). The best fen, often called *saho* (*shahe* in Mandarin), after its place of birth, a suburb of Canton. Freshly made saho fen are found in noodle shops in large Chinatowns, and sheets of saho fen are rolled into *"pig-intestine fen"* an inch in diameter. *Rice sticks* in the United States are narrowly cut fen, dried and hardened into sticks or folded sticks. Saho fen, for example, can be bought in folded rice stick form, to be boiled at home. (Note that cellophane noodles are from the mung bean, and not strictly speaking a fen.)

Nutmeg
One of the spices used in making the simmering sauce for meat and poultry. Use the whole nutmeg rather than the ground variety common in Western cooking.

Octopi, Squid, and Cuttlefish
Dried ones are found in Chinatown, and are excellent for soups. Dried cuttlefish is soaked to life size and stir-fried, sometimes together with fresh ones in the same Cantonese dish, called Gold and Silver Cuttlefish. Fresh squid is found all along the shores in the United States, and is very tasty.

Oils and Fats
The Chinese usually cook with vegetable oil or pork lard, but not butter. Peanut

oil is considered the best cooking oil by the Cantonese. Places in North China may use lard (called "big oil"). Sesame oil is a seasoning but not meant for frying except by North China Moslems.

Oil Strips

Two strips of leavened dough attached along the long side, and deep-fried to a golden yellow color, soft yet crunchy at places. A standard breakfast item in China, and focus of nostalgia by the Chinese in the United States. This peasant food is now found in American cities with large Chinese populations.

Olives and Olive Nuts

Olives are enjoyed raw for their pucker taste and chewiness. Preserved olives are an important snack. Olive oil is seldom used as a cooking oil.

Jumbo purple-black olives from South China are boiled with sugar as a snack, and are preserved in salt for use in country cooking. There are three long seeds inside each stone; these are extracted, skinned, and sold as olive nuts. Their rich taste and crumbly texture make them excellently suited for pastries (e.g., inside mooncakes) and in banquets. Available in Oriental markets.

Oolong Tea

Excellent tea from Fujian and Taiwan, commonly served in Chinese restaurants in the United States. It is intermediate in flavor between the fragrant green tea and the robust red (black) tea. Ti Kuan Yin (iron Buddhisattva) and shuixian (waternymph or waterlily) are both oolong in type. Jasmine tea is after flower-flavored oolong.

Organ Meats

Practically all internal organs of the pig are consumed by the Chinese, including the lung (for soup with two kinds of almonds) and the kidney (in a quick stir-fry with Chinese celery). Street-corner shops roast pig's livers, and marinate by the lo process the stomach, the nose, the ears, the tongue, and a washboardlike piece in the upper mouth cavity of the pig. Brains, bone marrow, and blood are found in country dishes and sometimes banquets. Organs of cattle, lamb, and fowl are similarly enjoyed. In East China there is an artistic dish with circles within circles; these are cross-sections of intestines within intestines. An East China dish with cross-sections of the large intestines of pigs is called Fried Elephant's Eyes. In Anhui Province, there is a dish with pig bronchial tubes braised with pig bone marrow.

Oyster Sauce

A rich brown sauce made from thickened, concentrated oyster broth. Strangely, this product is not fishy, and actually goes well with beef and green vegetables. As a table sauce, it is used like soy sauce. It comes in bottles or in 5-pound cans, sometimes labeled as "oyster-flavored sauce."

Parsley, Chinese
See CORIANDER.

Pepper, Chili
See CHILI PEPPER PRODUCTS.

Pepper, White
The Cantonese prefer white pepper to the black. Do not substitute with the latter because it is not the same—not only in color, but also in taste.

Peppercorns, Sichuan
Also called fagara peppercorns, these are an important spice in Sichuan cooking, but also are used throughout the rest of China. They are one of the spices for making the simmering sauce (lo). Sichuan peppercorn oil is also used in Sichuan cooking.

Plaster of Paris
Something with such a Western-sounding name need not be foreign to the Chinese. Calcined calcium sulfate, called stone-paste *(shigau)*, has been used by the Chinese as a coagulant for bean curd (tofu) for a thousand years.

Plums, Preserved
Used by the Cantonese as a condiment in seasoning meat and poultry, these come in jars and are found in most Oriental markets.

Pomelos
A pomelo looks like an oversized grapefruit with a tapered top. Its flesh is sweet though inclined to be dry. Pomelo skin makes an unusual Cantonese dish when braised with dried shrimp roe.

Potatoes and Sweet Potatoes
Both are New World importations. Sweet potatoes are found everywhere in China, and few Chinese would suspect their foreign origin. They are used as staples, in snacks, and in country cooking. The leaves are also stir-fried with meat. Potatoes are treated as a minor vegetable in Canton, used mainly in curries and soups. In North China, they are often called ground beans *(tudou)*.

Pu Erh Tea
This is a mellow, dark red tea from Yunnan Province, valued for its power to dissolve grease and aid digestion. The best are a hundred years old, to be enjoyed like a claret.

Radishes, Chinese White
Also called *daikon* in Japanese, these are a white, long, spicy root vegetable. They can be used raw in salads or pickled, braised, or stir-fried. Sold in most Oriental markets.

Red Beans
Tiny in size and red in color, red beans are used in making sweet teas, congee, and, most commonly, mashed into a paste for stuffing dim sums and pastries.

Red Rice and Red Wine Mash
The red color comes from an edible mold, *monascus purpureus*, which functions as

a yeast. Red rice is dried cooked rice coated with this benign mold, which acts on boiled glutinous rice to produce red wine mash used extensively in Fujian cuisine. *Red bean cheese* is bean cheese fermented by the same mold.

Rice

America is now the world's leading producer of rice. The quality of American rice is excellent. The Chinese are bewildered by the occasional presence of talc as an additive, but they always wash and rinse their rice before cooking, and talc would be discarded naturally.

The Cantonese use long-grain rice; short-grain rice is favored in East China, also in Fujian-Taiwan. Glutinous rice is used for desserts and for stuffings, as well as in wine making. See also RED RICE AND RED WINE MASH.

Rice Sticks

See NOODLES, RICE STICKS, AND FEN.

Rock Sugar

Crystallized from raw syrup, this is the same as the American rock candy. Used widely by the Cantonese in sweet teas, it also is used to add a special glaze to red-cooked dishes. Though replaceable by granulated sugar or brown sugar, it has a better taste. Comes in lumps and should be crushed into smaller pieces before use.

Saltpeter

The common name for sodium nitrate, this has been used by the Chinese for generations to preserve meat, in the same way as by the West.

Sausage, Chinese

Excellent pork sausages in the Cantonese tradition are found in Chinatowns all over America, all year round, with or without duck livers. These can be steamed over rice for a delicious side dish.

Scallions

Also called green onions, these are sold in most markets and supermarkets in bunches. They can be kept for about one week in a plastic bag in the refrigerator.

Scallops, Dried

See JADE PILLARS.

Sea Cucumbers

Also called *bêche-de-mer* (sea slug). Sold in Oriental markets in dried form in sizes up to 8 inches. They require prolonged soaking, during which they swell to several times the dried size. Commonly served in banquets, they have little taste of their own, but can pick up seasoning quite readily. It is a pity that most Americans find their slippery, gelatinous texture objectionable.

Seasonings and Condiments

See pages 317–318; also CHILI PEPPER PRODUCTS, FISH SAUCE, OYSTER SAUCE, SESAME PASTE, SHRIMP PRODUCTS, VINEGAR.

The Cantonese use *light soy sauce* to preserve the flavor of delicate food. Elsewhere *dark soy sauce* is more common. Usually only a tiny dish of soy sauce is found on the Chinese family dining table. In banquets one would find, in addition, *chili pepper sauce* and *hot mustard;* also special sauces and condiments with particular dishes. *Red vinegar,* for example, accompanies Shark's Fin Soup.

A number of flavorful thick sauces, or pastes *(jiang),* are fermented from soybeans and/or flour. *Hoisin* means "seafood" in Cantonese, but *hoisin sauce* contains no seafood and is not even served with seafood. Fermented from flour, spices, and sugar, this sauce is dark red in color, with a sweet-sour tangy taste well suited for Roast Duck, Spareribs and Char Siu. *Sweet flour paste* goes well with Peking Duck and Moshu Pork. *Brown bean paste* (also called yellow paste or ground bean paste) is the ground version of *whole bean paste,* both common in Chinese cooking. *Sichuan hot bean paste* is fermented from fava beans and crushed chili peppers. All these pastes are found in Oriental markets in cans and bottles. They keep indefinitely, but should be removed from the can and put in jars for best flavor. Put a tablespoonful of fresh oil on top to keep it moist.

Cantonese cuisine in Hong Kong and the United States often involves imported table seasonings, such as Worchestershire sauce for Roast Squab (together with Chinese spiced salt), A-1 sauce for spareribs, and sometimes Maggi sauce for poultry. The Chinese like American catsup and British mustard powder. Inside the kitchen, bouillon cubes and bouillon powder are handy for instant broth, and the Chinese in America and Hong Kong often use bottled curry and curry powder from India and fish sauce from Thailand. Saté is a Malayan shish kebab with a spiced peanut sauce, but the Fujianese make their own saté sauce for spiced stir-fries.

Seaweeds

A number of dried seaweeds are consumed in Chinese cooking. Purple vegetable *(zicai;* known in the United States under the Japanese name *nori)* is a purple-colored seaweed that comes in thin dried sheets. All over China it is used to add a taste of the sea to clear soups. *Kelp* is a broad-leaved seaweed, dark green in color and much thicker than nori. It is often packaged in large envelopes and sometimes it is preseasoned, cut, and tied into small bundles. Available in Oriental markets.

Sesame Oil

Pressed from roasted sesame, and used for flavoring in salads, congees, and pastries, particularly in North China. Better buy small bottles as it turns rancid easily when exposed to air. Use sparingly. Cold-pressed sesame oil is not a substitute.

Sesame Paste

Roasted sesame seeds are ground into a thick aromatic paste, used in dressing for salads or in marinades for meat and poultry. Available in Oriental stores, or can be approximated by peanut butter.

Sesame Seeds

These tiny, flat nutty-tasting seeds are used often in pastry as stuffings and coatings or in salads. Common and available in most supermarkets. Black sesame seeds have an earthier taste, and are used in sweet teas.

Shallots

A mild member of the onion family, these small bulbs are available in markets, though at high prices. They are actually easy to grow. When green leaves begin to sprout, plant the bulbs in loose soil; for one bulb planted, about eight to ten new bulbs will be harvested. Shallots add a subtle but pleasant flavor to soups and braised dishes.

Shark's Fin

The pale yellow, transparent ligaments within the fins of the shark. Whole fins are very difficult to handle, but prepared, dried shark's fin can be bought in Oriental markets. Shark's Fin Soup or Braised Shark's Fin are considered the height of a Cantonese banquet. In these dishes the gristles furnish the texture, while the taste is mostly from the supreme stock and accompanying ingredients.

Shrimp, Lobsters, and Crabs

These are in excellent quality and (except possibly for lobsters) quantity in the United States. The two most notable Chinese-American dishes are Lobster Cantonese Style and Shrimp in Lobster Sauce. Large prawns, caught in North China waters, are available frozen in Oriental markets. They are delicious pan-fried; the Chinese value the taste of their head above their meat. West Coast dungeness crabs are large, meaty, and flavorful; Eastern blue crabs are smaller, lighter in taste, and more delicate in texture. See also HAIRY CRAB.

Shrimp Products

Dried shrimps, each less than an inch in length, are found in Oriental markets in cellophane bags, already shelled. They are used to season almost everything, especially soups and boiled country dishes. Dried shrimp powder is also available, serving essentially the same purpose without being noticed. *Shrimp roe* looks like a million tiny red pearls, and is an elegant seasoning for braised dishes. At the other extreme, *shrimp paste* is pungent in odor, purple in color, and earthy in its salty taste; it is important in Cantonese country cooking. *Shrimp chips,* a crispy snack, are deep-fried shrimp-flavored starch chips.

Snow Mushrooms
See MUSHROOMS AND FUNGI.

Snow Peas

These green, flat pods are used widely as a crunchy vegetable. Sold only in winter in China, but they can be found in American supermarkets fresh or frozen all year round. The frozen variety tend to lose some of the crispness. A favorite vegetable in Hong Kong is the young leaves of snow peas, called *pea shoots.*

Soybean Products
See pages 317–336 for explanations of the many products derived from soybeans, including bean curd (tofu), bean milk, fupi, fuzhu, soy-tin, and soy sauce. See also BEAN CHEESE, BEAN SPROUTS, SEASONINGS AND CONDIMENTS.

Squash, Butternut
American butternut squash is the closest thing to the *Chinese pumpkin* (*nangua,* "south melon"). Excellent in braising with spareribs and black beans. The American pumpkin would be too soft.

Squash, Luffa (in Chinese: sigua, *"silk melon")*
Ribbed green squashes used in stir-fries, also in clear soups in the summer, and valued for their cooling humor and refreshing taste. Dried fibrous skeletons from old luffa squash are used as sponges.

Squid
See OCTOPI, SQUID, AND CUTTLEFISH.

Star Anise
Also called "eight corners" by the Chinese, this is an important spice for red-cooking. It is also a component of five-spice powder and lo.

Supreme Stock
An almost clear, concentrated stock made of meat, fowl, and Chinese ham, used for seasoning quality food in good Cantonese restaurants. Not for sale anywhere. A poor substitute by many miles is chicken stock.

*Tangerine Peel (*chenpi, *"old skin")*
See MANDARIN ORANGE.

Taro
A relative of *poi* in Hawaii, this root vegetable comes in many varieties. The Cantonese like the large, starchy type with internal purple veins. The Shanghai people like a different type, the size of a Ping Pong ball, flavored with cassia flowers, as a snack.

Tea
See pages 465–469 for a detailed discussion. See also DRAGON WELL TEA, JASMINE TEA, KEEMUN TEA, OOLONG TEA, and PU ERH TEA.

Tendons
Tendons of pig and cattle have been enjoyed by the Chinese for more than two thousand years. A more recent delicacy is tendons of deer. All are now available in Oriental markets in dried form.

Tiger Lilies (golden needles)
These are 2-inch-long edible dried flower buds of the tiger lily. Used in vegetar-

ian cooking, also braised with meat. They have a sweetish taste and a special chewiness. Remove the knob at one end before cooking.

Tomatoes

Not a native of China, tomatoes are enjoyed by the Cantonese when cooked with beef. Eating raw tomatoes is a habit not yet acquired by the average Chinese.

Turtles and Tortoises

The most common edible turtle in China is armored fish (*jia* fish), a green fresh-water turtle valued in East China. The gelatinous edge of its shell is especially prized. Tortoises are said to strengthen the body and rid it of poison and diseases; the best one for the purpose is the gold coin tortoise, available in large Chinatowns.

Vegetables, Leaf

See also pages 347 and 348.

Napa cabbage (celery cabbage) is one of the oldest Chinese vegetables. In North China the crop is either pickled to become *paocai,* or buried underground to last through the winter, using Mother Nature as an icebox. *Bok choy* (Cantonese for "white vegetable," *beicai* in Mandarin), with white, sturdy stalks, is also very versatile. *Vegetable heart* may mean either the flowering stem of fully grown bok choy, or an altogether different vegetable (*yau choy* in Cantonese, "oil vegetable"). What is sometimes called chop suey vegetable should be more properly called *chrysanthemum greens;* it is featured in hotpots in the winter. In Chinatown you can find green, crunchy *Chinese broccoli;* it is a Cantonese vegetable, excellent in a stir-fry with beef strips and yellow wine (the Chinese in America use whiskey); *empty-hearted vegetable,* a relative of the sweet potato, excellent with either bean cheese or purple shrimp paste. In Hangzhou look for *chuncai* or water-shield, an aquatic vegetable with tiny, slippery leaves; apparently California Indians enjoy its tuberous root.

Mustard greens in Chinatown have large, fleshy stalks which remain firm after cooking. It originated from Chaozhou, near Canton. Believed to have a cool humor, this vegetable makes an excellent summer soup or stir-fry; it is also boiled and covered with crabmeat sauce as a banquet dish. *Watercress* is common in Cantonese soups. But Spinach Velvet Soup is a favorite of Pearl's grandfather. The Chinese cook their lettuce, including the East China *celtuce* with an overdeveloped root. *Chinese celery* is thinner, greener, and more aromatic than the American variety. *Rhubarb* is not used as a vegetable despite its Chinese ancestry. See also AMARANTH.

Vegetables, Preserved

Many preserved vegetables belong to the mustard or the turnip families. A significant exception is *paocai* ("soaked vegetable"), often made with napa cabbage in North China, just as *kim chee,* its Korean counterpart.

In salt-preserved vegetables, it is hard to tell where the mustard ends and turnip begins. Surely most preserved root vegetables are turnips, but crisp, pleasant *big-head vegetable* from Yunnan uses the bulbous root (the size of a human's head) of a variety of mustard green. When finely chopped, it adds a pleasant crunchy texture to soft minced meat patties. They also can be sliced to steam with fish or meat. Steamed alone, they go well with breakfast congee. *Sichuan jar* (i.e., pressed) *preserved vegetables* use the irregularly swollen stems of a different variety of mustard greens. *Red-in-snow*, a favorite in Northland East China, uses the leaves of yet another species with a bulbous root. It is slightly salty yet crunchy; we recommend rinsing for a lighter taste.

Vinegar is used to pickle ginger and shallots. Cantonese country food includes pickled tiny watermelons and pickled taro stalks. The best way to prepare sweet and sour fish is to start from a bottle or can of Chinese *assorted pickled vegetables*, which contains cucumbers, red and green peppers, green papayas, and tiny onions. The large-stalked mustard green from Chaozhou is the basis for *sour vegetable*. Another variety produces *Mei vegetable*, salty-sweet and lightly vinegared; Mei Vegetables Steamed with Pork is a famous Hakka country dish.

Sugar is used to preserve lotus roots, lotus seeds, kumquats, melons, and coconuts. These are snacks important in New Year's entertaining.

Vinegar, Chinese
Chinese red (rice) vinegar from Zhejiang is transparent and tangy. It is often mixed with finely cut fresh gingerroot or used at the table to go with seafood (even shark's fin), noodles, and dumplings. White rice vinegar has a hint of glutinous rice, its main ingredient. Both are uniformly low in acid and can easily be substituted with American wine vinegars. A kind of dark, rich vinegar is used to marinate pigs feet, hard-boiled eggs, and ginger to strengthen women after childbirth.

Water Chestnuts
These are a sweet Chinese root vegetable with a unique crunchiness, even after cooking. They can be found fresh in Chinese markets around the Chinese New Year. The canned product is nearly as good, and can be kept using the same method as for canned bamboo shoots.

Wawa Fish
A tree-climbing spotted salamander which cries like a baby (*wawa* is Chinese for "baby," not its cry), this is an amphibian, not a fish. Found in Guangxi and Guizhou Provinces, now served in restaurants in major cities in China as a tonic and delicacy.

Wild Rice
Common a thousand years ago, wild rice is now seldom consumed as a staple in China. A great pity. The stem of the wild rice plant, stimulated by the edible mold *ustilago esculenta*, swells to the diameter of a banana, and becomes *jiaosun* ("jiao shoots"), one of the most succulent vegetables in existence, very common in East and South China in the summer, but unfortunately not found in the United States.

Wines and Spirits for Cooking
See also BAMBOO-LEAF GREEN, FEN LIQUOR, HUA DIAO, MOU TAI, RED RICE AND RED WINE MASH.

Wine mash, fermented from glutinous rice, is fragrant and sweet; it is used as a seasoning, for preserving eggs, and as an East China snack with added sweet dumplings. The unique flavor in Fujian-Taiwan and Chaozhou cuisine is often due to *red wine mash;* the latter also figures indirectly in Cantonese cuisine through red bean cheese, in seasoning braised dishes.

Yellow wine, used extensively for cooking throughout China, has an alcohol content of about 18 proof, similar to a sherry, but with a personality all its own. The best is *hua diao* from Shaoxing, in Zhejiang Province. It could be substituted by a sherry with a good aroma.

Fen liquor is important for marinating beef, and for preparing Drunken Chicken. If not available, use vodka, white rum, or brandy.

Wrappers and Skins
Spring roll wrappers, or Cantonese spring roll skins, are made of wheat flour dough, about seven inches square in size. The Shanghai spring roll wrapper is round in shape, white in color, much thinner, more prone to breakage, but is very much crispier upon deep-frying. Wonton wrappers vary from the round-shaped soup dumpling skin to the much thinner shao mai wrappers.

All these wrappers are found in Oriental markets. They can be kept frozen indefinitely, but should be wrapped properly to avoid drying out in the freezer. Thaw in the refrigerator until soft.

Tools and Equipment

Chinese cuisine has evolved around the fact that the cleaver is used for cutting, the wok is used for cooking, and chopsticks are used to put food into the mouth. Nevertheless, Chinese food can be prepared using American equipment with almost equal effectiveness.

Food is pre-cut in the kitchen, or made tender enough to be pried apart later with chopsticks. In general, more effort is spent in the initial preparation than in the actual cooking. This is especially true with stir-fried dishes.

The traditional Chinese kitchen is totally Spartan. There are only two brick stoves fueled by firewood or coal; one of them supports an eighteen-inch wok, in which most of the dishes are prepared. The other stove is used for cooking rice and soups or for boiling water. In a corner nearby is a special counter-sink with a four-inch-high, round chopping board cut from a pine tree. The Chinese cleaver is never out of sight, nor is the spatula for stir-frying. A container cut from a large bamboo section holds a bundle of chopsticks. Spoons, ladles, bowls, and plates are kept on a little shelf; on top of the shelf, under a wire-screen cover, might rest leftover food from the previous meal, waiting to be warmed over.

The above was a common sight in the late 1940s for a family of five of above-average income in a typical South China city. Would you believe that such a kitchen could turn out—for every lunch and supper—four tasty dishes, one soup, plus white rice? In the past three decades, those who could afford them began to acquire some appliances, such as a refrigerator and an electric rice cooker. Yet the first sight of a gadget-packed American kitchen fills the Chinese homemaker with disbelief.

We do not advocate a return to simplicity. Nevertheless, it is good to know that excellent Chinese food can be prepared with a minimum of equipment and with inexpensive, fresh ingredients.

SECRET WEAPONS OF THE CHINESE CHEF

Despite the simple appearance of the Chinese kitchen, there are implements that the Chinese chef will not do without and the American cook can adopt with profit. Foremost among them are the wok and the Chinese cleaver.

The Chinese cleaver is a four-by-seven-inch steel rectangle with a handle. With one hand chopping at the pace of several strokes per second and the free hand pressing ingredients under the blade, the chef seldom pays attention to the clea-ver but often engages in small talk all the while. There is never danger in losing a finger; the broad center of the blade, guided by pressing against the knuckles above the fingertips, prevents the user from any mishap. With the same cleaver, the chopped food is scooped up from the chopping board and the chopping board is scraped clean. The cleaver is also excellent for cutting fowl because it chops through the bones crisply.

When the going gets tough, the free palm pounds on the dull edge of the cleaver squarely, directing extra force to the stroke. The same dull edge is used to daze live fish, tenderize meat, and crush scallions and spices. The broad side is for pounding ginger, and the end of the handle is used to mash garlic and salted black beans. Only the four-inch edges serve no specific purpose, though they are used sometimes to pry open glass jars and even to substitute for a screw-driver.

The cleaver comes in three weights: the heavyweight version is for chopping bones; the lightweight is for slicing and cutting soft foods; and the medium weight serves both purposes, except it cannot chop through hard bones such as those for beef and pork. For the one-cleaver kitchen, the medium weight is recommended. Carbon steel is stronger than stainless-steel, and the cleaver will not rust if properly taken care of. After each use, clean it with hot soapy water (or just very hot water). Dry it thoroughly, then apply a thin layer of vegetable oil on both sides of the blade. Keep the cleaver sharp at all times to cut faster and cleaner.

Another instrument of the Chinese chef is the wok, that now-familiar hemispher-ical shell made of iron, steel, stainless steel, aluminum, or nonstick metal. The center can be heated to a dull red, yet the edge remains barely warm to the touch. This temperature gradient is exploited to the fullest: for stir-frying, the pieces which are done sooner can be kept warm away from the center, while the rest are seared to perfection. Several ingredients, each calling for different degrees of cooking, can be stir-fried in the same wok and be ready at the same time.

The wok is also used for steaming, traditionally done by resting the bowl of food on two bamboo chopsticks placed parallel three inches apart on the bottom of the wok. For dim sum (tea dumplings) or bao-zi (steamed buns), the bowl is replaced by a many-layered bamboo steamer.

Just a little oil in the center of the round-bottomed wok is enough to ensure good deep-frying; much more oil would be needed for flat-bottomed woks and pans. In Chinese pan-frying, the proper degree of golden crispness is obtained by pressing the food with the curved spatula against the curved side of the wok.

Many Chinese-American housewives have difficulty with electric stoves. The flat heating surface offers little contact with the wok, and the wok center receives the least heat. Even with the support of a metallic wok ring, the hemispherical wok tends to be under-heated. If higher temperature is required, use a flat-bottomed wok, which is almost as convenient as the rounded variety. (You could also use a regular cast-iron skillet or Dutch oven.) The same size wok can be used for large or small quantities of food. We like iron or spun steel woks 14 to 16 inches in diameter for the American family, with a large, tall aluminum cover to fit on top. A smaller wok, equipped with a handle, is handy for tilting.

Often a new iron wok comes with a tough coat of plasticlike film to prevent it from rusting. Scrub the inside surface thoroughly with a Nylon scrubber and use very hot soapy water to remove the coating, then wipe dry. Grease the inside

surface by rubbing evenly with a piece of unseasoned pork fat (or a small paper towel soaked with peanut oil) several times. Set the wok in a 200-degree oven and bake for two hours, then take it out and cool it to room temperature. Some woks have screwed-on wooden handles; they should be removed before baking.

Wipe the wok clean with a paper towel and rub the inside again with pork fat (or peanut oil), then bake for an additional hour. After it is wiped a second time, the wok is ready for cooking.

After each use, clean the wok with hot soapy water. Should anything stick to the surface, rub with a Nylon scrubber. Do not scour or scrub with metal pads such as steel wool. Be sure the wok is completely dry before putting it away. The best method is to wipe it dry, then set it over low heat to drive off the remaining moisture.

Under proper care, the wok will not rust. Upon detection of rust, scour the rust off and repeat the greasing procedure.

Still another important cooking implement is the chopsticks. With special bamboo chopsticks ten inches long, it is easy to pull chestnuts out of the fire; indeed this is a favorite pastime of Chinese children, as is picking up deep-fried dumplings from boiling oil for the Chinese New Year. Use bamboo chopsticks in the kitchen, as plastic ones may deform or even melt in the presence of heat. Chopsticks are used to select food slivers for tasting, to arrange food on a platter for attractive appearance, to toss salads and noodles, to move ingredients around during a stir-fry, to mix seasonings with ingredients, to guide the flow of liquids into a bottle, to beat eggs and then guide the eggs into a clear broth to make Egg-flower Soup.

Try to obtain these tools and learn to use them well. It will take some practice to master the use of chopsticks and the cleaver, but the effort will be amply rewarded. Is it absolutely necessary to use these implements before becoming a proficient Chinese cook? No. In most cases, these tools merely add to the efficiency of preparation, not the quality of the product.

LABOR-SAVING DEVICES

We do not embrace the traditionist view that everything should be done the old way. A blender with a stainless-steel blade is useful for making purées, fresh shrimp paste, and chicken velvet, also for grinding tender meat. Some Chinese families use it to make their own soybean milk and bean curd as well.

We found the modern food processor, however, a curious mixed blessing for Chinese cookery. It is powerful and fast, excellent for grinding small quantities of meat often needed in some dishes. It slices frozen meat beautifully. For slicing vegetables, however, the cutting is often uneven. The cross sections are rough rather than smooth, especially in the case of fibrous vegetables. Fine-chopping must be done with care, for the powerful motor reduces the food to a paste all too quickly. In the making of pastes of shrimp or fish, though, air bubbles are beaten in; the pastes when cooked have an interesting fluffiness which could be very desirable indeed, but the recipe may require firm texture instead. It appears that the food processor is a definite labor-saver, but experimentation is needed for each new ingredient. Also, the fastidious cook may want to rinse the bowl after each use.

The American oven adds a new dimension to Chinese home cooking. The roast duck and roast pork heretofore available only from specialty shops and restaurants are now within easy reach. For small amounts of food, the convection oven is fast and economical. No substitute for the regular oven, the microwave oven is in a class by itself, excellent for steaming fish, reheating food before serving, and warming leftovers.

The electric rice cooker takes the guesswork out of rice cooking. Most electric woks have limited heating power, and can do only a small amount of stir-frying, but are great for Chinese fondue (Mongolian Fire Pot) and fried rice.

In South China, slow cooking is often done in an elaborate pagodalike charcoal burner called daybreak chicken (*ng gang gai* in Cantonese), which is about two feet tall and eight inches in diameter. It is a pleasure to report that some electric slow cookers (with removable crock casserole) perform the same job much more conveniently and cleanly. Gourmet Chinese cookery requires a clear Supreme Stock made by simmering meats, fowl, and bones; the slow cooker is ideal for this purpose.

A pressure cooker can reduce hours of stewing to minutes, and is excellent for a North China red-cooked dish or a Cantonese Spicy Beef Tongue.

I use a heavy duty mixer to mix dough, to beat minced meat, fish paste and shrimp paste to yield firm texture.

OTHER TOOLS

You should have a large, tall wok cover which covers the wok snugly. The flat cook top in American stoves is not designed to hold the round bottom wok; the wok ring holds the wok securely, but also separates the wok from the heat source. I use the largest cooktop available, and use the wok ring upside down, with the larger opening on top, to reduce the separation. For most gas stoves, the iron grill work often can be turned up to hold the wok acceptably, without the wok ring.

The professional Cantonese chef uses, with great skill and flourish, a large ladle in one hand and a handled strainer in another for all stir-frying. Their practice is not recommended for the average American kitchen. However, a set of handled wire-mesh strainers is very useful. I use four-, six-, and eight-inch ones. The smallest one, made of fine wire mesh, is for skimming scum from soups and scraping sediments from oil during deep-frying. The six-inch one, with coarser mesh, is to remove food from liquids. The largest one is for collecting wontons, dumplings, and noodles from the pot. For deep-frying I use an eight-inch handled strainer which is made of a sheet of metal with punched holes ¼-inch in diameter. Wire-mesh there would stick and break the surface of the fried pieces. For draining food after oil dipping I use a strainer-lined bowl; the strainer here must be several inches in height and diameter.

The oddly shaped Chinese spatula is designed for use with the wok. It is most efficient with the Chinese stir-frying. Use it to toss many pieces together, using its rigid spade with full curved edge (which fits the wok), or individually using one of the pointed tips. It can scoop up the finished product including the juices, as its back edges are turned up to hold liquids. American kitchen spatulas can be used, but at some loss in efficiency; some are too pliant, and none can hold liquids. I use a stainless-steel Chinese spatula; it is easier to clean.

Some American implements are handy. I use a boning knife to remove meat from bones, a pair of kitchen shears to cut off ligaments, and Nylon pot scrubbers to scrub the yellow film off chicken skins. I also use a food mill for purées in preparing sweet stuffings, and a mechanical noodle maker for rolling out the dough for flat bread and noodles, though noodle-making without it is more fun. A nonstick pan is excellent for low-temperature cooking. A meat thermometer can be helpful in deep-frying, though I use the traditional testing method by throwing a piece of scallion green into the oil. I also use the two-inch diameter American rolling pin, though I have another one, a rod one inch in diameter, for pastry making.

Techniques of Food Preparation

We divide this part of the book into two sections: the first deals with techniques of cutting the food and readying it for cooking; the second describes the actual cooking techniques used by Chinese cooks. See also pages 61–104 with photographs of some techniques.

CUTTING TECHNIQUES

The knife is not found at the Chinese dining table. Large pieces of food can be cooked so tender that they are easily pried apart with chopsticks or spoons, but more commonly they are precut in the kitchen either before or after cooking. Furthermore, in order to stir-fry effectively and quickly, all the ingredients must be of uniform size and definite shape.

Cutting has many facets. According to the position with which the knife is held, the basic techniques include vertical cutting, sloped cutting, and horizontal cutting. The desired shape may be slices, dice, bits, shreds, or wedges. Particular ingredients may call for special techniques such as roll-cutting, scoring, and mincing.

All techniques, except horizontal cutting with thin pieces, can be done with any Western-style knife. But in all cases, the Chinese cleaver is more efficient and is highly recommended.

Basic Cutting Techniques

Vertical Cutting   It is the most common form of cutting. The knife is held vertically, perpendicular to the cutting board, giving excellent control over the thickness of each piece. The knife can also be held perpendicular to the piece being cut (straight vertical cut), or it can form an angle with the latter (diagonal vertical cut) to yield a larger cross section.

Slope Cutting   The knife is held at an angle of roughly 45 degrees to the cutting board, usually away from the user. This produces pieces with a larger cross section than with the vertical cutting, although the effect can also be achieved with the vertical diagonal cutting.

Horizontal Cutting The knife is held parallel to the cutting board, sawing through the food which is placed flat on the board. The technique is not easy to master, particularly if a Chinese cleaver is *not* used. There often is no alternative to this method if a thin slice is to be made even thinner.

Special Cutting Techniques

Roll Cutting With vegetable pieces which are narrow and conical in shape, an irregular wedge shape is called for. This is actually a diagonal vertical cut with the piece under the knife rotated around the long axis of the cylinder between cuts. Generally the amount of rotation is a quarter turn; turn up the previously diagonally cut surface each time before a new cut is made.

Scoring With this, the cook makes incisions on the surface of the food, either to improve the appearance or to allow faster penetration by heat and/or seasoning. A typical example is the scoring of squid: one side of each piece is lightly scored with a criss-cross pattern. Upon heating, the scored side expands at the expense of the unscored side, and the cooked piece is curled into a cylinder. With kidneys and gizzards, the scored parts also expand but to a lesser degree. For cooking a whole fish, it is customary to make several incisions on each side about one inch apart for faster cooking.

Mincing This is to chop the food into fine bits. The food is scraped up and turned over from time to time to form a new heap. Chopping is continued until the desired texture is achieved. The efficiency doubles if two Chinese cleavers, held parallel, are used at the same time.

Shapes and Sizes of Cut Pieces

Domino Slices A standard shape of meat is a rectangular slab about 1¾ by ¾ inches with a thickness of about ⅛ inch. This size is best for chopstick handling, although the thickness may vary from one ingredient to the next.

Shreds and Strips The standard length is about 1¾ inches, and the width and thickness are roughly ⅛ inch. An easy way to cut shreds is to start with domino slices first. The larger version of the shreds are strips.

Dice and Bits Usually *dice* means "cubes" (the Chinese word is *ding*), ⅜ inch on each side. Bits are much finer dice, often needed in gourmet cooking. One good way to obtain dice is to start with shreds with proper cross-sections.

Wedges Wedges are usually cut from bulk vegetables such as melons, eggplants, tomatoes, peppers, and onions or from lemons and oranges for garnishing. With narrow and conical-shaped vegetables such as turnips and carrots, irregular wedges are made by roll-cutting.

COOKING TECHNIQUES

Although cooking with fire has long been known to both East and West, the Chinese have evolved over thirty unique cooking methods. Some may appear superficially similar to Western ones, but are very different in practice. Also, a recipe often involves several techniques in succession. This may seem unduly

complex to the beginner, but usually becomes very easy. The most important skill to acquire is a sense of timing and getting to know, through looking at the food as it cooks, when foods are finished.

We give you the basic cooking techniques here, so you can try the recipes in this book.

Major Cooking Techniques

Stir-Frying   Stir-frying is a unique Chinese technique that has been used regularly by the Chinese for at least a thousand years. Although it resembles French sautéing, it is very different. It is the fastest way to cook food, often taking less than five minutes, but to benefit from this technique, the ingredients must be cut properly to ensure even heating.

Stir-frying actually consists of several steps, and there are minor variations. The entire process is easy to learn, and readily becomes second nature. A typical sequence is as follows:

1 Preheat wok on high heat until very hot (dull red), then pour in a small amount of oil. Swish the oil around to coat the surface of the wok. This prevents the ingredients from sticking to the wok and helps to heat the food evenly.

2 Put in flavoring agents such as garlic, ginger, or scallions.

3 Drop in the pre-cut ingredients. Stir, spade, and turn over with the spatula to coat all surfaces with the hot oil. Bring the underdone pieces closer to the hot center of the wok and put the pieces which are nearly done closer to the cooler rim. Add seasoning, unless the food has been preseasoned.

4 Add water if necessary (for example, when stir-frying fibrous vegetables), then cover the wok. Leafy vegetables, meat, and seafood usually do not need this step.

5 Stream in a small amount of wine along the edge of the wok, for added flavor and aroma.

6 If cooking meat with vegetables, each are cooked separately, then combined at this step for the remainder of the cooking time.

7 If a sauce is desired, thicken the juices with a starch-and-water mixture before serving.

If you don't have a wok, you can substitute a cast-iron skillet, but you lose a certain amount of control over the cooking process.

Steaming   Steaming is an ancient technique as well. Special pottery steamers were used five thousand years ago in China, but the most common steamer today is a bamboo stack with several close-fitting layers, topped with a domed cover. Each layer can hold a quantity of food to be steamed, and the dome lid ensures that most of the condensed steam drips down the sides rather than on the food itself. The steamer is usually set into a wok, which has some boiling water in it. The steam from the water circulates freely within the steamer, heating the food on contact.

There is a modern steamer made of aluminum or steel that is similar in construction to the bamboo version, and it usually includes a base for the water, thus allowing you to place the whole container on the stove directly. Unfortunately, the top is often flat, causing the condensed steam to drip onto the food. If you are using such a steamer, you can protect the food by wrapping the cover snugly with a kitchen towel to absorb the moisture.

If you have neither the bamboo nor another type of steamer, just cut off both ends of a small, short (2 inches) can and place it in the center of any tall pot. Use the can to support the dish containing the food to be steamed. The bottom of the pot should be lined with a small kitchen towel to spread the action of the boiling water, otherwise the stand would topple into the water.

When steaming food in a dish, be sure the dish is heatproof and that it has turned-up edges to hold the liquid. Avoid using soft plastic; enamel or porcelain are best. The water level in the pot or wok should be about one inch below the steamer rack or dish, and the water should be boiling vigorously before you put the dish into the steamer. If using a pot to steam your food, be sure the diameter of the pot is at least two inches larger than that of the dish, to permit free circulation of steam. Do not peek at the food as it steams, as heat escapes with each little peek. Make sure that there is enough water in the base and keep a kettle of boiling water ready to replenish if necessary.

Deep-Frying This is a technique of cooking ingredients using a large quantity of heated oil. It was featured in ceremonial feasts in the Chou Dynasty, more than twenty-five centuries ago. Chinese deep-frying differs from the Western version in that the Chinese season the ingredients first, then add an unseasoned coating or batter. (The Western approach is just the opposite; the ingredients are usually not seasoned but the batter is.)

The most common oil for deep-frying is a vegetable oil such as peanut oil. Lard is sometimes used with Northern cooking, but never butter. The amount of oil required depends on the size of the pieces to be deep-fried and the diameter and depth of the wok or pot. Normally four to six cups of oil will reach a depth of two to three inches in a round-bottom wok; this depth is usually sufficient to cover the ingredients and heat all pieces uniformly. More oil is needed with a flat-bottomed wok or a regular frying pan. Also, deep-frying a whole fowl or fish requires more oil. The oil should be at the proper temperature, not too hot nor too cold, or the pieces will be ruined. Rather than use a thermometer to test the oil, the Chinese evolved a much simpler method: just throw a small piece of scallion green or any tiny piece from a vegetable leaf into the oil. Watch for the following results to determine if the oil is how you want it:

1 If the green remains undisturbed, the oil has not been heated sufficiently for any deep-frying.

2 If small bubbles appear around the green slowly, the oil is about 200 to 250 degrees.

3 If small bubbles appear around the green immediately with sizzling, the oil is about 275 to 300 degrees.

4 If the green sizzles and moves about quickly, the oil is about 325 to 350 degrees.

5 If the green sizzles noisily and soon turns brown, the oil is about 375 degrees.

6 If the green turns brown quickly and a haze appears above the surface, the oil is about 400 degrees.

In Chinese deep-frying, the medium (325 to 350 degrees) and high (375 degrees) temperatures are mainly used. Low (250 to 275 degrees) temperature is used in

CHRYSANTHEMUM FISH CHOWDER
PAGE 127

STEAMED WHOLE FISH, WITH GINGER AND SCALLION SAUCE
PAGE 135

deep-frying wontons and puff pastries, however, and only when deep-frying rice crusts and rice sticks is the smoking-hot (400 degrees) oil needed.

If the oil is too cold, heat it further. If it is too hot, add a small amount of cold oil to bring the temperature down. Do not put all the ingredients into the oil at once; this would lower the temperature too suddenly. It is best to introduce them a few pieces at a time. This way the oil temperature is easier to maintain, and the pieces will not stick together.

Large chunks of food require two deep-frying stages: first fry in small batches to a pale yellow color, and drain. Later put all the pieces together back into the heated oil until deep golden. The food is cooked in the first stage to about 75 percent doneness and the second frying crisps the outside without overheating the interior. This two-stage frying process works particularly well because you can do the first frying hours ahead and just finish up prior to serving.

Frying oil can be reused four or five times as long as you have not cooked fish. (Keep the oil for frying fish separate.) Add some fresh oil after each time you use the oil and reheat the oil to evaporate the moisture. Let it cool at room temperature for several hours and allow the scraps and particles to settle to the bottom. Then pour the cold oil through a large funnel lined with a paper towel into a bottle. Keep the oil covered or stored in the refrigerator for further use. When the oil turns brown, do not use any further.

Pan-Frying Pan-frying—very common in Chinese home-cooking—makes full use of the round-bottomed wok. Cut-up or whole pieces are arranged in a layer in the preheated wok to which a small amount of oil has been added. The food is fried on one side until brown, then turned and fried on the other side. More oil is later whirled in along the edge and runs eventually into the center. The wok is tilted and turned every now and then so that each piece receives even temperature and the oil coats the wok all the way around. Very often a sauce is introduced at the last stage to give the ingredients a glossy coating.

You can use a cast-iron skillet or nonstick frying pan equally well for pan-frying.

Red-Cooking Red-cooking is similar to Western braising. It is the simmering of large pieces of food in a soy sauce-based liquid. The food can be prepared one or two days ahead and merely warmed before serving.

To red-cook, often you would first marinate the meat or fowl, then brown it in a pot or a wok to seal in the natural juices. After browning, remove the excess fat and place the meat in a bowl. Rinse the pot and wipe it dry, then place the meat back in. Add a spicy sauce liquid to reach half the height of the meat and cover the pot. Cook slowly and evenly until tender. When the meat or fowl is done, remove it from the pot and degrease the braising liquid. At this point, if you desire a thicker liquid, add a mixture of starch and water. If you want to heighten the flavor, add a bit of wine. Cut up the food and serve with the sauce. The soy sauce in the braising liquid imparts a reddish color, hence the name.

The Chinese prefer to use an earthen pot (with only the inside surface glazed), but a heavy Dutch oven, a cast-iron pot, or an enameled pot works equally well. When red-cooking a whole fish, the cooking time is much reduced since fish cooks faster. Also, sometimes the meat or fowl is cut up, browned, and then braised; this process is also called red-cooking, but it is more akin to stewing.

White-Cooking   White-cooking is a typical Cantonese technique to cook a whole fowl or fish by immersing it in a pot of boiling water. The heat is then turned off, and the pot is covered for exactly the right duration.

White in Chinese means "plain." The liquid in which the food is cooked is usually plain water: colorless and unseasoned except for the addition of a few slices of gingerroot as a freshener. In white cooking a chicken, usually the neck, back, bones, and giblets are put back into the plain liquid, which is then simmered into a clear flavorful stock for soups or for use in white-cooking yet another chicken. Very often white-cooking is done in clear broth for added flavor.

White-cooking differs from poaching in that the hot water is not heated continuously during the immersion. The Cantonese may also poach a fowl but seldom a fish. White-cooked fish tastes tender and fresh, just like steamed fish, and is easier to do. Often "steamed fish" in restaurants are in reality white-cooked.

Roasting   Though Peking Man was perhaps the first ever to roast food regularly, in China today most roasting is done in commercial ready-to-eat food shops; the household oven is a rarity.

A Chinese oven is very different in design. It is usually built with bricks in the shape of an oblong box with an iron door in front. Racks are provided inside the upper portion of the oven for hanging food. There is a water-filled tray to catch the drippings and to prevent smoking. Marinated ingredients, cut-up or whole, are hung vertically in the oven to produce a self-basting effect.

In the United States the oven is a commonplace; roasting is thus possible in any kitchen. The cubical shape of the oven cavity, however, allows only limited vertical roasting. For hanging cut-up strips of meat, use steel skewers about 8 inches long with the last 1½ inches of the blunt ends bent into hooks. A piece of carrot or celery is threaded onto the skewer first to prevent charring the top part of the meat strip. Another piece of carrot (or cork from a wine bottle) is then skewered at the bottom to keep the meat from sliding off.

S-shaped hooks made of stainless steel serve the same purpose. Simply hook a piece of meat at one end and use the other curved end for hanging in the oven. However, the meat browns very easily unless there is a protective covering on top. The limited height of the American oven does not allow hanging a whole fowl, but you can follow the Western practice of laying the fowl on a roasting rack.

Sauce-Simmering   Simmering in a spicy sauce is a very strong Cantonese culinary tradition. The food is then cut up and served cold as an appetizer, as a main dish with rice, or even alone as a snack. It is aromatic and flavorful, and yet very easy to prepare. Ready-to-eat poultry and meat made this way—from beef tripe to squabs—are sold almost everywhere in small eateries in Canton. Customers can easily order any particular piece by pointing.

The Catonese name of the spicy sauce is called *lo,* and the sauce-simmered goodies are called *lo mei* (*mei* means roughly "goodies"). A variety of Chinese spices is simmered into a concentrated mixture, which is later combined with strong wine (or even liquor), rock candy, and soy sauce. The spices used vary from shop to shop or from chef to chef, each claiming a specialty of his own "secrets." Generally, the combination of spices would consist of star anise, sand ginger, licorice stem, nutmeg, cinnamon bark, clove, fennel, Sichuan peppercorns (*fagara*), ani-

seed, white peppercorns, aged tangerine peel, gingerroot, and garlic, plus some "secret" items. The aged tangerine peel can be the most crucial ingredient: it mellows with age and is very expensive. Some shops even boast of the use of "hundred-year-old" tangerine peels. The spices are premixed in a traditional proportion, sold in small packages in almost all Chinese herb stores, and many Oriental markets in the U.S. A dried "frog's head" was often added in the old days as a preservative! In this book, only the common spices easily accessible to the reader are used.

The master sauce is used again and again, over a long period of time. Proper care should be exercised to maintain the freshness of the aged sauce as follows:

1 After the spices are cooked, wrap and keep them in the freezer.

2 The best container for the sauce is a covered ovenproof porcelain casserole or pot. It can be heated directly on the stove and stored away in the refrigerator.

3 Raw ingredients should first be blanched in boiling water and rinsed to remove any scum. Large pieces of meat should be cooked separately to 70 percent doneness before simmering.

4 After each use, bring the sauce back to a boil over low heat before refrigerating. Before each use remove the solidified fat on top. There will be a thick deposit in the bottom of the container. Scoop out and discard as much as possible.

5 After the sauce is used two or three times, it will be reduced in volume and lose part of its spicy flavor. Make more spicy mixture with the spices which have been used once before, then add to the master sauce with more wine, rock candy, and soy sauce. The spices should not be used more than twice. Remove the used ginger and garlic; add some fresh pieces each time.

The *lo* prepared in the above-mentioned manner is called *brown lo* because of the soy sauce used. *White lo* is prepared the same way only concentrated saltwater is used instead of soy sauce.

Oil-Dipping

Oil-dipping—an important cooking technique commonly used in banquet dishes—resembles deep-frying, but the quantity of oil used is smaller and the temperature and timing vary according to the sizes and types of ingredients to be cooked. In oil-dipping, ingredients such as meat, poultry, or seafood are given a quick bath in heated oil to seal in the natural juices. The partially cooked pieces separate easily. Then they are removed to drain in a bowl lined with a strainer or a sieve. Afterwards the food joins other ingredients in the last stage of stir-frying.

With elegant banquet dishes, oil-dipping is always the preferred technique as a pre-treatment to the ingredients before stir-frying. But if the food is not properly drained, the dishes may become greasy. There are three major kinds of oil-dipping techniques:

Cool Oil-dipping This technique should be used with fine shreds, thin slices of meat, and minced meat. First set the wok over high heat until very hot. Pour in the oil and add the ingredients immediately, stirring gently until separated; then remove together with the oil to drain in a strainer-lined bowl.

Warm Oil-dipping This technique should be used with slices of meat, small to medium-sized shrimp, poultry dice, meat dice, or small scallops. Set the wok over high heat until very hot, then add oil. Wait two to three minutes for the oil to warm up before adding the ingredients.

Hot Oil-dipping This technique is used with chunks or thick slices of meat (¼ inch or thicker) and seafood such as jumbo shrimp, large scallops, fresh oysters, and fish chunks. Unlike the previous two kinds of oil-dipping, it uses more oil and the waiting time is longer (about four to five minutes to heat the oil).

Since different ingredients call for different timing, the reader should follow the recipes closely. A round strainer or a colander about eight inches in diameter inside a large stainless-steel mixing bowl is ideal for straining the food. The drained oil can be directly heated in the bowl over low heat to evaporate the moisture. After it is cooled, pour the oil through a funnel lined with a paper towel into a bottle for storing. The oil can be reused for cooking or for further oil-dipping.

Secondary Techniques

Blanching Blanching means dipping food into boiling water for a short while until partially cooked, then removing it and immediately running it under cold water to stop the cooking process. Usually this technique is a pre-treatment:

1 To pre-cook vegetables for stir-frying.
2 To seal in natural juices of coated pre-cut meats.
3 To remove scum and strong taste from meat and bones for soup stock and sauce simmering, film from oysters, or blood from liver.
4 To remove the metallic taste of canned vegetables such as bamboo shoots, straw mushrooms, and miniature corn.
5 To remove the skin of nuts and tomatoes.

Smoking Food is often smoked after simmering in master sauce or after deep-frying for additional flavor. It is placed on a rack in a wok filled with burning smoking agents. The wok is then covered and the smoke circulates to impart its special zing to the food. Tea leaves and camphor chips are the most commonly used smoking agents. One special Cantonese recipe even calls for the addition of a scented flower. Curiously, smoked fish in East China cuisine is usually deep-fried without the smoking step.

Illustrated Techniques

The following is a photographic guide to various Chinese cooking techniques mentioned in the book. For additional information, also see Techniques of Food Preparation, pages 53–60.

CUTTING TECHNIQUES

Since the flank steak is most commonly used in a Chinese beef stir-fry, it is used here to exemplify the cutting technique with a Chinese cleaver.

A piece of flank steak weighs from 1½ to 2½ pounds. Choose one just under 2 pounds and trim away visible fat. Cut it in half along the grain. Each half will weigh about 12 ounces, which is the optimum load for an average wok. The other half can be kept frozen for another meal. Some people prefer to freeze their flank steak and cut it in a semithawed state.

1

Domino Slices
Lay the half flank piece flat on the cutting board. Press it firmly with fingers of the left hand and, while the right hand holds the cleaver roughly at a 45° angle with the beef, slope-cut across the grain into the desired thickness—normally from ⅛ to ¼ inch, depending on the recipe (**1**). The broad side of the cleaver should rest on the knuckles of the left-hand fingers, which are kept at the same angle. The finger tips should be turned in slightly away from the blade. After each cut, the left-hand fingers are moved backwards, to govern the thickness of the next slice. The slope-cut tends to enlarge the narrow side of

2

the cross-section. Vertical-cutting can be employed also, only the slices would appear to have come from a thinner piece of beef **(2).**

1

Shreds

First vertically cut the half flank steak across the grain into slices about 1¾ inches long and ³⁄₁₆ inch thick. Overlap several pieces at a time to form a stepped pile, so that the beef slices can be held firmly together when shredding. Then cut the pile vertically, starting from the long side, into strips the same width (about ³⁄₁₆ inch) as they are thick **(1).** Owing to its coarse fiber and a tendency to break, beef shreds should be larger and have a larger cross-section than that of pork or chicken.

Beef shreds sometimes are cut along the grain to withstand the constant stirring called for in some recipes such as Sichuan Spicy Fried Beef Shreds. Start with a strip of half a flank steak. Cut into several large pieces about 1¾ inches wide, and use a horizontal cut to obtain slices ³⁄₁₆ inch thick as follows:

Lay one piece flat on the cutting board and press it firmly downward with the palm of the left hand, while the fingers are pointed slightly upward to clear the way. Hold the cleaver horizontally with the right hand parallel to the cutting board. Make a shallow cut ³⁄₁₆ inch from the bottom. Saw the cleaver into the piece, from right to left, slowly and gently until a slice is cut off. Remove the slice and continue to cut horizontally in the same manner, each time slicing off a thin piece nearest the cutting board, until the whole piece is used up. Arrange all the slices in an overlapping manner to form a stepped pile. Vertical-cut the pile along the grain into strips ³⁄₁₆ inch thick. Follow the same method to finish slicing the remaining pieces.

1

Other Cutting Techniques
The illustrations **(1–5)** show the techniques described on pages 53–54.

Straight vertical cutting

2

Diagonal vertical cutting

3

Horizontal cutting

4

Roll-cutting

5

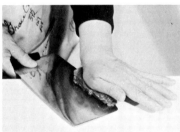

Scoring

1

Mincing
Many recipes call for minced foods. In addition to the illustrations **(1–3),** see the information on mincing, page 54.

2

3

WORKING WITH CHICKEN

Chicken is used in many different forms. Given here are techniques first for boning, then slicing and dicing chicken breasts. Also shown are techniques for boning wings and thighs and for cutting up a whole chicken

1

Boning a Chicken Breast
Remove the skin.

2  Using a sharp boning knife, cut around the wishbone to partially free the meat. Tuck the index finger into the incision on one side of the wishbone and tear briskly to free the meat for about 2 inches.

3  Do the same with the other side of the chicken, so that a flap of meat hangs down.

4  Press the gristle with the flat side of a cleaver to hold the meat firmly on the board. Scrape and pull to detach the meat.

5  A fillet, embedded on each side of the breastbone, will be revealed. Use your fingers to break the membrane of the embedded fillet.

6  Pry the membrane away from the breastbone gently to remove the fillet.

Removing Membranes from a Chicken Breast

Elegant chicken breast dishes should be free from tough membranes, which separate layers of meat. For dicing, slicing, and shredding, removing the membranes is not as critical as for mincing, which calls for only tender chicken breast meat, free of gristle and membranes. You may find the task quite difficult at first, usually ending up with too much waste and too little meat, but this takes some practice. Once the technique is mastered, you will not want to use any chicken breast without removing the membranes.

1

Remove the skin. Cut the whole breast meat lengthwise into symmetrical halves. Trim white gristle in the center.

2

On a cutting board, lay one piece of breast meat flat, membrane-side down. Cut gently along the main gristle, as far down as the membrane (do not cut through), to free the meat of the smaller side from the gristle. Press the larger side of the breast meat firmly with the flat side of a cleaver (see #4), and scrape and pull very carefully with your fingers to detach the meat from the gristle.

3

Turn the remaining breast meat with the main gristle on the far side. Cut along the gristle at an angle, almost as far down as the membrane, but do not cut through.

4  Hold the chicken breast by the top with one hand while the other hand grasps the flap of meat firmly, tearing the meat quickly away from the bone, all the way down.

5  Now the breast meat is free from the membranes and gristle.

6  For the fillet, hold the white gristle in the middle with one hand, and scrape the meat away with a cleaver.

1

Dicing, Slicing, Shredding, and Mincing a Chicken Breast

To dice, cut chicken meat vertically along the grain into strips the same width desired for the dice. Rearrange all strips to line up in a straight line on the right-hand side, one parallel to the other, leaving the left ends uneven **(1).** Cut vertically from the right end across the grain the same width as the strips to form unform dice **(2).**

2

3

4

To slice, cut chicken meat along the grain into pieces about 1½ by 1 inch in size **(3).** Lay 1 piece of breast meat flat on the cutting board as close to the edge as possible to ease slicing. Hold the cleaver at a very small angle or almost parallel to the cutting board, then from the bottom up make a shallow cut the same thickness as desired for the slice. Press the breast meat firmly with the palm of the other hand, with the fingers slightly pointed upward to clear the way, and at the same time slowly and gently move the cleaver horizontally from right to left in a sawing motion until a slice is cut off **(4).** Remove the slice and continue to slice the remainder of the piece in the same manner **(5).**

5

6

To shred, start with breast meat sliced about ⅛ inch thick. Place one slice on top of the other, several pieces at a time to form a pile. Press the pile firmly with fingers of one hand and, with the cleaver held by the other hand, shred the piled-up slices *along the grain* into fine strips about ⅛ inch thick **(6).**

7

To mince, cut breast meat into coarse shreds first, then chop into bits, adding a little cold chicken broth (or water) at a time until the amount called for is used up and blended with the minced meat. Fold one-half of the breast meat over, making a right turn. Continue to mince until a paste is formed **(7).**

ILLUSTRATED TECHNIQUES

Boning a Whole Chicken

Boneless chicken parts are used most frequently in Cantonese cooking. It is always easier to clean and more economical to start with a whole chicken.

If a conventionally dressed (not Chinese-style) chicken is used, rub it with a Nylon scrubber to remove any yellow film. Rinse and pat dry with paper towels.

1 On a cutting board, place the chicken, breast-side down, preferably on a kitchen towel to prevent slipping. Cut along the spine with a boning knife from neck to tail without cutting through the bones.

2 Probe with your fingers to locate the joint between the wing and the shoulder. Sever. Do both sides.

3 Cut breast meat around the wishbone. Hold chicken by the neck with one hand. With the other hand, hold the upper portion of one wing and pull briskly to loosen breast meat. Do the same with the other side.

4 Pull the entire piece of meat all the way down to the oysters.

---

5  Separate the oysters from the carcass.

6 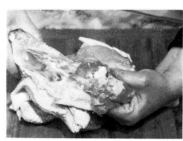 Snap the joints between the thighs and the carcass.

7 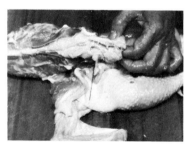 Continue to pull the chicken meat all the way down to the tail bone. Detach.

8  At this point, the remaining chicken bones can be removed.

9  Or cut the chicken up into five major pieces for later use.

1

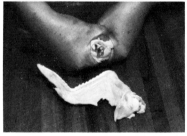

2

3

4

5

Boning a Chicken Wing

By boning in this manner, you have the makings for a mock drumstick, used in several recipes.

Use the near tip of a Chinese cleaver to cut a slash along the skin between the first portion and the other portion (mid-portion and wing tip together).

Hold the wing with both hands, making sure that force is stressed by the right hand (or left hand, if left-handed) that holds the mid-portion and the wing tip.

Bend upward to break the joint.

The cap of the main bone of the first portion will come out easily with this bending.

Pull the first portion downward to free the meat from the main bone. Cut to detach at the first joint.

6  Turn the skin inside out to form a mock drumstick. Reserve the remaining portion for another use.

1
Boning a Chicken Leg and Thigh
Turn inside part of thigh out. Lay flat on a cutting board. Slit along the bone.

2  Spread meat to the sides.

3  Insert a carving knife under the bone. Cut to free meat from the smaller end first.

4  Then hold the bone by the smaller end. Scrape to push meat toward the larger end.

5

Place the piece close to the edge of the cutting board. Hold the main bone in an upright position. Cut at an angle to detach the meat, leaving as much of the thick membranes with the bone as possible.

6

For boning the leg, break the smaller end of the drumstick with the blunt edge of a cleaver, then detach by cutting. Use the same method as boning the thigh to free the meat.

Cutting Up a Cooked Fowl for Serving

When serving a whole fowl, the traditional Chinese method would include the head, neck, liver, gizzard, heart, and even feet. The bones stay in and are chopped through by using a cleaver. Since the bones can be a problem for some people, here is a simple method for boning the fowl before chopping which retains the Chinese way of serving.

1

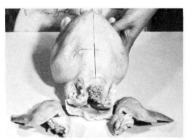

Make two incisions in the form of a cross on the back of chicken as shown. Detach wings at the joints.

2

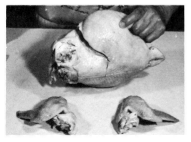

Lay chicken flat on one thigh, and cut through the skin around the other thigh until the knife reaches the arm of the cross.

BACKGROUND INFORMATION

3

Hold chicken by the leg, and pull to loosen. Do the same with the other side.

4

Cut each wing into two pieces at the first joint. Keep the wing tip attached to the mid-portion. Bone the upper portion and arrange the meat in the center of an oval serving platter (see #8).

5

Separate the breast from the backbone section by cutting down from the tail to the neck.

6

Carve away skin and meat from the backbone section. Cut into 1¼ by 2½-inch pieces, arranging them in a straight row together with the upper wing meat.

7

Lay the chicken breast on its skin. Remove the wishbone as well as the main bone by hand.

8

With the skin-side up, cut breast meat length-wise in half, then chop crosswise into pieces about ¾ inch wide.

9

Transfer breast meat, one-half at a time, with the blade of a cleaver and arrange breasts on top of the carved pieces on the platter.

10

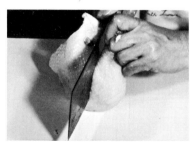

Separate the leg and the thigh through the joint, one piece at a time.

11

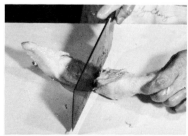

12

Slit the inside of the thigh and remove the bones.

13  Repeat for the chicken legs.

14  Chop the legs and the thighs crosswise, the same width as the breast meat. Arrange them on each side of the breast halves (see #15).

15  Arrange the two wings, one on each side, near the upper part of the breast meat. Put the head (if any) between the wings and the tail between the legs. Now the original shape of the chicken is approximated.

SHAPING TECHNIQUES

Many recipes in the book require specialized rolling, folding, or shaping techniques. You'll find them explained in the text on the appropriate pages, but the following step-by-step photos are offered as an additional aid.

1

Shrimp Bunnies, recipe page 160
Shell shrimp, leaving tails on.

ILLUSTRATED TECHNIQUES

2 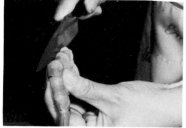 Cut deeply down the back, along the vein, but do not cut through.

3  De-vein. Proceed with cleaning.

4  Place shrimp with split-side down on a cutting board. Flatten with the blunt edge of a cleaver.

5  Put a piece of sausage on the near edge. Roll shimp toward the tail.

6  Keep the tail open like the ears of a bunny. Secure with two red toothpicks for the eyes.

1 *Pearly Balls, recipe page 276*
Scoop up a handful of the meat mixture.

2 Squeeze the meat mixture through your fist until it reaches the size of a walnut. Scrape it off with a wet spoon onto the sweet rice.

3 Roll the pork ball in rice until the surface is evenly coated.

1 *Spring Rolls, recipe page 398*
Place a wrapper with the smooth side down. Put about 2 tablespoons of filling on the lower center, directly below the diagonal.

2 Lift the near corner and turn to cover the filling.

3    Bring the two side corners to the center so they overlap each other. Tuck securely.

4    Roll toward the tip, to form a 4 by 1½-inch envelope. Keep it as firm as possible. Press to eliminate any excess air inside.

5    Seal by moistening the far edges with a tapioca-and-egg mixture.

6    The finished spring rolls.

1    To make miniature spring rolls, make the following modifications:

Cut the spring-roll skin on a diagonal into two triangles. From each triangle trim off two corners. Use the cut-out portions to form a small rectangle as a reinforcement in the center.

2

Put 1 rounded tablespoon of filling onto the reinforced area.

3

Bring up the bottom edge to fold over filling, matching the top edge of the reinforcement.

4

Fold both sides to the center so they overlap one another.

5

Roll toward the tip of the triangle.

6

Seal with a dab of egg wash to form a mini spring roll.

1 *Steamed Shrimp Rolls, recipe page 164*
Prepare an egg sheet.

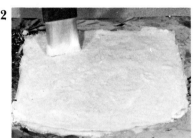

2 Arrange the egg sheet flat on a piece of aluminum foil. Dust tapioca powder evenly on the egg sheet with a pastry brush.

3 Spread one layer of shrimp paste on the egg sheet, with the upper and lower edges much thinner than the center for easy rolling. Arrange about 20 parsley leaves on the shrimp paste.

4 Roll up, in a jelly-roll fashion.

5 Dust the rolled-up surface with tapioca powder for adherence.

6 Dust more tapioca powder on the top edge to seal.

7 Roll the foil in the same direction to wrap the shrimp roll securely.

8 The finished shrimp roll.

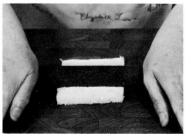

1 *Crispy Shrimp Rolls, recipe page 166*
Cut all the edges off a slice of sandwich bread.

2 Roll the bread hard with a rolling pin to yield a very thin slice.

3 Spread shrimp paste on the pressed bread, covering ¾ of the surface. Leave the far edge uncovered. Place a few parsley leaves on the shrimp paste. Lay a strip of ham crosswise, close to the near edge.

4 Roll securely into a cylinder.

5 Seal the roll with egg yolk wash.

6 Lightly coat with cornstarch and shake off the excess.

1 *Cantonese Soup Dumplings, recipe page 404*
Place about 1½ tablespoons of the filling in the center of the upper half of a dumpling skin.

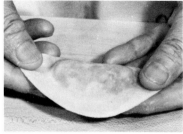

2 Fold the lower half over. Press lightly so the skin adheres to the filling and excess air is expelled. A half-moon shape is formed.

3 Gather the edges toward the center.

4 A finished dumpling.

1 *Wontons in Soup, recipe page 400*
Place 1 full teaspoon of filling into the center of the second quarter of a wonton skin.

2 Fold the corner of the first quarter over to cover the filling.

3

Fold the first and second quarters over to cover the third, leaving the top corner as a flap.

4

Bend the two ends at the base inward, pressing with the thumbs to expel the air inside.

5

Moisten one end with egg yolk to paste it to the other angle. A wonton is formed.

1

Wonton Ears with Lychee Sauce, recipe page 403

Place ½ teaspoon of the filling in the center, half way between the diameter and the edge.

2

Bring the small edge up to cover the filling.

3

Pull the two corners down. Moisten one corner with water and adhere to the other corner.

4

A shell-shaped wonton is formed.

1

Char Siu Buns, recipe page 413

Divide dough into 4 equal parts. Roll one part by hand to form a rod. Hold the dough rod in the left hand, with one section sticking out from the opening formed by the thumb and index finger, and tear briskly with the right thumb and index finger to break off small dough rods.

2

Flatten the small dough rods with the palm.

3

With a rolling pin, roll each dough rod out into a round, making a quarter turn after each rolling.

4 Roll to leave the center thicker while the edge is thinner.

5 Place about 1½ tablespoons of the filling at the center of each dough round, with the flat side up.

6 Gather the edges by pleating counterclockwise.

7

8

BACKGROUND INFORMATION

9

10

11

12

Twist to seal securely.

13

Place the bun, with the pinched side up, on a piece of wax paper about 2 inches square.

Pan-Stickers, recipe page 409

Divide the dough into 4 equal parts and roll each part by hand into a rod, then cut each rod into 10 small pieces. Roll each small piece into a round wrapper about 3 inches in diameter. Sprinkle flour lightly on the kneading board if necessary. Then fill and shape as follows:

1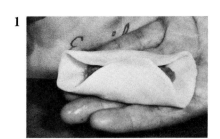

Place about 1 to 1½ tablespoons of the filling in the center of a wrapper. Fold the wrapper in half and pinch the edges together at the center of the round, leaving the two ends open.

2

With your fingers, make about 3 to 4 pleats on one side of the opening.

3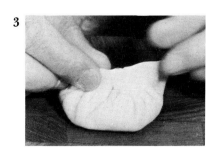

Make pleats the same way with the other opening.

4

Pinch all along the edges to seal.

5 Place pan stickers in a floured tray, arranging them closely together.

1 *Curried Crescents, recipe page 417*
Flatten the spiral dough roll and bring both ends up.

2 Press to taper both ends and make them overlap at the center.

3 Roll the pastry dough out making a round about 3 inches in diameter, with a thin edge for easy sealing and ridging.

4 Place the pastry round on one palm. Brush half the edge with beaten egg yolk.

5

Put about 1 tablespoon of the filling in the center.

6

Fold the pastry round together and press the edge firmly to make a half moon.

7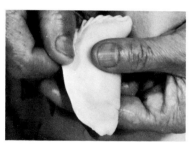

Make ridges along the edge.

8

The finished crescent.

1

Shao Mai, recipe page 406
Place a shao mai wrapper on a slightly cupped left palm. Using the right hand, scoop up with a butter knife about 1 tablespoon of the filling and place it on the center of wrapper.

2

Insert the butter knife downward into the bulk of the filling; both the filling and the wrapper will stick to the blade of the butter knife.

3

Withdraw the left palm. Form a ring with the left thumb and left index finger; gently push the wrapper and filling together toward the butter knife. The filling now roughly assumes the shape of a cylinder slice (shao mai) loosely encased in the wrapper.

4

Withdraw the butter knife. Use the flat side of the blade to pack the filling, to increase the contact between filling and wrapper, and to smooth the top of the shao mai.

5

Place a small dot of orange shrimp paste on the smooth top of shao mai for decoration.

6

Arrange shao mai closely together on a well-greased plate. Set the plate in the steamer.

1

BATTERS AND DOUGHS

Cantonese Flat Bread, recipe page 412
Divide the dough in half. Roll one-half out into a very thin, long strip (thinner than ⅛ inch and about 4 inches wide).

2

Roll each end of the strip onto a rolling pin for easy handling.

3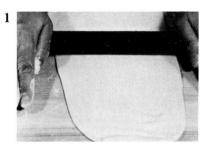

Roll and stretch to maintain thinness.

4

Generously grease a sheet of wax paper for lining the steamer. Start by laying one end of the dough strip in the center of the wax paper.

5

Brush oil on the dough to separate layers.

6  Fold the dough back and forth until the whole strip is used. Roll the second half of the dough into a strip to join the end of the first strip. Brush and fold in the same manner.

7 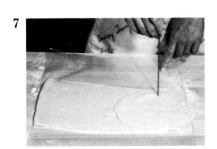 Pierce holes through the dough pile with a trussing needle so that the bread will rise evenly.

8  The dough pile is ready for steaming.

1

Mandarin Pancakes, recipe page 411
Divide dough into four equal parts. Roll each part into a rod. Divide each rod into ten equal pieces.

2  Flatten each piece into a 2-inch round.

3 Brush sesame oil evenly on the surface of one round.

4 Place another round on top, forming a two-layered round.

5 Roll into a thin pancake about 6 inches in diameter and ⅛ inch thick.

6

7 To cook, set a griddle over medium heat. Pan-fry the pancake for 1 minute or until the surface bubbles.

8

Turn the pancake over and fry for another 30 seconds.

9

Use a spatula to separate the two layers while hot.

10

Stack the pancakes on a platter and cover with a lightly dampened cloth.

1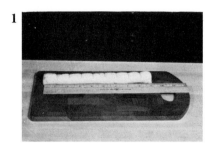

***Classic Chinese Flaky Pastry Dough,
recipe page 416***

Divide the water dough into four equal parts. Roll each part by hand into a solid rod, 9 inches by ¾ inch. Cut each rod into nine equal pieces (36 pieces altogether).

2

Flatten the oil dough into a 9-inch square. Cut the large square into 36 1½-inch squares.

3

Press a piece of water dough flat with your palm to form a round. Roll a square of oil dough between two palms to make a small ball.

4

Place the oil-dough ball above the water-dough round.

5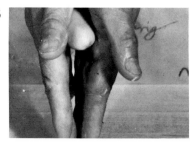

Bring the edges up, pleating and clipping to seal into a nugget.

6

Holding your two palms vertically, roll the nugget into a cylinder 3 inches long, ½ inch in diameter.

7

Lay the cylinder flat on a kneading board.

8

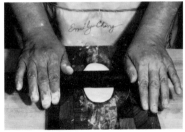

Flatten with a rolling pin to make a very thin dough strip about 12 by 1½ inches.

9

10

Starting from the narrow end, roll up the dough with your fingers.

11

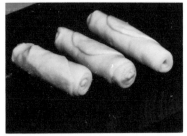

This multi-layered dough roll can now be shaped into flaky crescents, buns, discs, or spiral crescents.

1

Flaky Spiral Disc, recipe page 440
Cut the multi-layered dough roll in half cross-wise.

2  Flatten each half into a round.

3  Roll out each to a round about 2 inches in diameter.

4  Place one round on your palm. Brush the edge with beaten egg in a band about ¼ inch wide. Put one piece of filling in the center. Cover with the other round of dough.

5  Press the edge firmly to make it thinner and to seal opening. Flute the edge.

6  *Left:* Deep-fried flaky disc.
Right: Uncooked flaky disc.

OTHER TECHNIQUES

Rinsing of Gluten, recipe page 337
Place the dough in a bowl or saucepan and put in the kitchen sink.

Hold the dough under gently running cold water, rubbing and squeezing all the while.

Starch will be washed out, making the water cloudy.

Keep on washing and squeezing until the water in the bowl runs clear.

Now gluten is left. Place it in a colander set over a bowl to drain.

6

Clockwise from the top:
Gluten puffs.
Raw gluten.
Cut-up gluten pieces.
Cooked gluten piece.

1

Home-made Bean Curd, recipe page 326
Pour bean paste into a sack and squeeze to extract as much bean milk as possible. Drain milk into a saucepan placed beneath.

2

Heat bean milk to boiling. Mix coagulant with water in a deep pan. Stir well to mix. Pour boiling bean milk all at once into the pan. Do not stir.

3

In about 15 minutes, the bean milk will coagulate into flower of bean curd.

4

Spoon off the foamy layer on top and discard.

5  Scoop flower of bean curd into a mold lined with cheesecloth.

6  Fold the extra cheesecloth over to wrap bean curd securely.

7  Place lid on mold.

8  Weight the lid with a heavy cutting board, then a pile of books or other heavy object.

9  Remove the lid and mold from bean curd.

10  Unwrap the bean curd.

11  Cut into pieces.

Part 2

Major Chinese Cuisine

Difficulty Symbols

The following symbols have been used to show the approximate levels of difficulty for each of the major recipes in the book. Actual times of preparation and levels of difficulty may vary, depending upon personal experience and familiarity with the recipe and/or ingredients.

EASY TO PREPARE

MODERATE

REQUIRES SOME EXPERIENCE

DIFFICULT

Soups

The Chinese always have soup with their meals; they seldom serve another liquid food on the dining table. With everyday meals, a clear vegetable soup is often served with very little meat in it, and this kind of soup is cooked so quickly that it deserves the name "minute soup." "Thickened soups" prepared with more effort are often served in North China. At an elegant banquet, however, only "gourmet soups" with exotic ingredients are served.

The soup stock is the essence of good Chinese cooking. It is the liquid obtained by simmering meat and poultry together with additional bones and scraps. Ham and other choice ingredients are added in gourmet cooking for the Supreme Stock, for which the ham imparts such a distinct flavor and taste that very little additional salt is needed.

For everyday family cooking a clear, flavorful, and concentrated stock is good as the basis for almost everything: soups can be used to braise meat, poultry, and vegetables; to white-cook a fowl or a whole fish; or to make sauces (with a little thickener) to bind the food together during the last stage of cooking.

It is extremely easy to prepare a stock. For everyday cooking, save all the scraps when boning pork chops and spareribs, the membranes and gristle when boning chicken breasts, and the poultry giblets and neck bones that come with fresh chickens. Keep these ingredients frozen until enough are on hand, then make soup stock to last you a couple of weeks. The amount not used immediately can be frozen too.

The Chinese seldom mix beef and pork together for a stock. They claim that the strong beefy taste would overpower the delicate pork. Instead, beef bones and scraps are made into a special stock used in cooking beef only, or mainly for making a soup itself. Fish is also seldom used in stock. And since they treasure the simple taste of the meat, Chinese almost never use any flavoring vegetables such as onion, garlic, leek, or celery. They do use a few slices of gingerroot, however, to chase away the gamey taste of some ingredients.

Although homemade stock is preferable, you may not always have it available when you want it. Clear canned chicken broth is a reasonable substitute, but read the labels carefully and select only those brands that have no added seasoning vegetables. The chicken fat contained in the broth does not agree with the Chinese palate, and the liquid should be degreased first. (Chill in the refrigerator until the fat congeals on top.) When canned broth is used as a soup base, dilute each can with half a can or more of water. For sauces, use the broth straight.

Chicken bouillon powder or bouillon cubes can also be used occasionally for convenience. Again, be careful in selecting the best brands; some contain mostly chicken fat, artificial flavoring, and MSG.

⊛Basic Soup Stock

Yields 3 quarts
Time 30 minutes preparation
5 to 6 hours cooking

上湯

This stock is the foundation for a number of soups. In addition, it can be the basis for a secondary stock, useful for braising meat and vegetables.

Ingredients

1 stewing hen, about 5 pounds
3 to 4 pounds lean pork, preferably from the leg

6 slices gingerroot, about ½ ounce

PREPARATION

1 Cut hen into 8 or 10 pieces. Discard the fat.

2 Keep the pork in 1 piece, but trim off some of the fat.

3 Combine the hen and pork in an 8-quart stockpot. Add water to cover and set over high heat. Bring to a boil with pot uncovered and boil for 10 minutes or until the scum rises to the surface. If the water starts to boil over, bring it down by pouring in 1 cup of cold water, then return to a boil.

4 Pour the contents of the pot into a colander and rinse hen and pork with cold water.

COOKING

1 Rinse stockpot. Put hen and pork back into the pot and add ginger. Add water to cover until the pot is 80 percent full. Set over high heat and bring to a boil. Immediately turn heat to low.

2 Simmer stock, with pot uncovered, for 5 or 6 hours or until liquid is reduced to about 3 quarts.

3 To strain, pour the stock through a very fine sieve or a colander lined with cheesecloth. Reserve the hen and pork to make the secondary stock. Cool the primary stock at room temperature, then refrigerate overnight. The next day, remove the solidified fat from the surface. Stock is ready to use.

Note: To make the Supreme Stock, add 1 pound of Chinese ham hock to the stock. Blanch it in boiling water for 10 minutes, and rinse with cold water to remove scum and any spices, then add to the stockpot before the long simmering begins. (The ham hock is blanched separately to prevent its spices from mixing with the other ingredients.)

Substitute a Smithfield ham hock for the Chinese ham hock if the latter is not available. Also, a roasting hen is a fair substitute for a stewing hen.

VARIATION: Secondary Stock

If you have on hand some additional chicken bones, pork bones, or meat scraps, blanch them in boiling water then rinse with cold water. Add these to the cooked chicken and pork in the stockpot and pour in enough water to cover. Set over high heat and bring to a boil. Immediately turn the heat to low and simmer stock for 3 to 4 hours or until it has been reduced to 5 to 6 cups. Strain and degrease as described above. This recycled stock is less concentrated and not as flavorful, but is useful for cooking with vegetables or braising meat.

MINUTE SOUPS

These soups can be prepared very quickly. First we give you a general recipe, then three versions.

⊛ Basic Minute Soup

Serves 4
Time   10 minutes preparation
            10 to 15 minutes cooking

一般滾湯

Ingredients

¾ pound desired
  vegetables
4 ounces fish or meat
  (beef or pork)
1 tablespoon oil
2 slices gingerroot

1 teaspoon salt
3 cups thin stock

Seasonings

1 teaspoon oil
2 teaspoons light soy
  sauce mixed with 1
  teaspoon tapioca
  powder (for meat
  only)

PREPARATION

1 Cut the vegetables either in lengths, slabs, or shreds. Generally leafy vegetables should be cut in 2-inch lengths; fibrous vegetables should be cut in lengths, but stalks and leaves should be kept separate. Melons, squash, or cucumbers should be cut into slabs about 1 by 1½ inches. Preserved vegetables and bamboo shoots can sometimes be cut into shreds.

2 Slice the fish no thicker than ³⁄₁₆ inch thick. Season with oil.

3 Slice the meat as thin as possible (about ¹⁄₁₆ inch). Season with mixture of soy sauce and tapioca powder, then stir in oil.

COOKING

1 Place saucepan over high heat and, when hot, add the oil. Flavor oil with ginger, then add salt. Pour in stock and bring to a boil.

2 To cook the vegetables, add them to the hot stock depending upon their texture; most leafy vegetables are added late and cooked only until soft and their color turns bright green. Stalks of fibrous vegetables should be cooked first, for about 5 minutes, then leafy parts added and cooked only until soft. Melons take a few more minutes to cook than fibrous vegetables.

3 To cook the meat, add beef slices to the soup, cooking until the soup returns to a boil; stir to separate slices. For pork, continue to cook for 2 more minutes after soup returns to a boil.

4 To cook the fish, immerse slices in the boiling soup, push them to the bottom of the pot, and remove the pot from the heat. After 1 minute, the fish will be done.

Note: The minute soup made with vegetables plus a small amount of meat is a good supplement to an all-meat dish. Preparation time is minimal and the cooking is just as fast. While the minute soup is on the stove, the cook can usually prepare another dish.

Pork and Winter Melon Soup with Salted Duck Eggs

Serves 4
Time 10 minutes preparation
15 minutes cooking 鹹旦 冬瓜肉片湯

A Cantonese clear soup in the home style, with salted duck eggs added. The whites add snowflakes and a surrealistic landscape with a cheeselike flavor. The yolks are usually shared but could be awarded to the guests of honor at the table.

Ingredients

1 pound winter melon
2 salted duck eggs
4 ounces lean boneless pork, cut from loin
3 teaspoons oil

2 slices gingerroot
3 cups Basic Soup Stock (page 108)
Salt

Seasonings

2 teaspoons light soy sauce
1 teaspoon tapioca powder
2 teaspoons oil

PREPARATION

1 Cut green skin off the melon. Remove seeds and pulp. Cut melon into slabs about 1 by 1½ by ¼ inch.

2 Separate yolks and whites of eggs. Lightly beat whites until smooth. Set yolks aside.

3 Slice pork across the grain into thin slices about 1 by 1½ by 1/16 inch. Add seasonings and mix well.

COOKING

1 Set a 4-quart saucepan over high heat. When hot, add oil. Flavor oil with ginger slices for 10 seconds. Add the stock, bring to a boil, then add melon slices and egg yolks, cooking over medium heat with pan covered. Cook for 10 minutes or until melon is soft.

2 Add pork slices to soup, stirring to separate pieces. After the soup returns to a boil, continue to cook for 1 minute more. Stream in the egg whites, then remove pan from heat. Stir to mix egg whites with the other ingredients.

3 Correct seasoning, being careful that soup is not too salty (eggs are salted). Serve hot.

Note: Winter melon can be substituted with mustard greens. Cook only 5 minutes instead of 10.

⊚Tomato and Beef Soup

Serves 4
Time 10 minutes preparation
10 minutes cooking

番茄牛肉湯

The Cantonese are now beginning to appreciate raw tomatoes, but cooked tomato dishes like this clear soup have been part of their culinary tradition for a century.

Ingredients

1 pound medium
  tomatoes
4 ounces boneless beef
  flank
4 teaspoons oil
1 egg
1 slice gingerroot
3 cups Basic Soup
  Stock (page 108)

Salt
1 tablespoon chopped
  scallion (both white
  and green parts)

Seasonings

2 teaspoons light soy
  sauce
1 teaspoon pale dry
  sherry
1 teaspoon tapioca
  powder
½ teaspoon sesame oil
Dash of white pepper

PREPARATION

1 Pour boiling water over tomatoes and soak for 5 minutes. Peel. Cut each tomato crosswise in half and squeeze out the seeds. Cut each half into 3 or 4 segments.

2 Slice the beef as thinly as possible (1/16 inch) into 1 by 1½-inch pieces.

3 Mix seasonings, then blend with meat. Add 2 teaspoons oil, mixing well.

4 Beat egg lightly.

COOKING

1 Set a 2-quart saucepan over high heat. When hot, add the remaining oil. Flavor oil with ginger until brown, then remove ginger.

2 Stir-fry tomatoes for 1 minute. Add the stock, bring to a boil, and cook for 2 minutes.

3 Add beef slices and bring soup back to a boil. Turn off heat and stir to separate pieces of meat.

4 Stream in egg and wait for 20 seconds, then stir to mix well. Correct the seasoning and garnish with chopped scallion. Serve hot.

●Watercress Soup with Fish Slices

Serves 2
Time 10 minutes preparation
10 minutes resting
5 to 7 minutes cooking

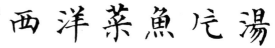

The Cantonese claim that the combination of ginger, preserved sweet cucumber, watercress, and Chinese parsley in this soup can soothe a sore throat. Fish adds extra flavor without affecting its lightness.

Ingredients

1 bunch watercress	Chinese sung fish;
2 tablespoons	sole, sand dab could
preserved sweet	also be used)
white cucumber	1 tablespoon oil
6 sprigs Chinese	4 slices gingerroot,
parsley	shredded
6 ounces freshwater	2 cups water
fish fillets (such as	1¼ teaspoons salt
pike, catfish or	

PREPARATION

1 Remove the tough stems from the watercress, using only the tender parts (about 3 inches from the tops). Rinse and drain. You should have 2 cups of greens.

2 Rinse cucumber and shred finely.

3 Trim roots of parsley and break sprigs into 2-inch lengths. Rinse and dry.

4 Cut fish across the grain into ³⁄₁₆-inch slices. If sole or sand dab is used, cut into slabs about 1 by 1½ inches. Mix with oil and ginger. Set for 10 minutes.

COOKING

1 In a saucepan, combine the water, salt, and cucumber. Bring to a boil over high heat and cook for 1 minute.

2 Add the watercress and parsley, cooking until the color of the vegetables turns bright green and they are soft, about 3 to 4 minutes.

3 Add the fish slices to the soup, pushing them to the bottom of the pan. Turn heat off and wait for 1 minute.

4 Correct seasonings. Pour soup into a serving bowl.

CLEAR SOUPS

The simple elegance in these clear soups is created by adding the ingredients to soup stock without thickening the soup.

Fish Ball Soup with Preserved Vegetables

Serves 6
Time 10 minutes preparation
30 minutes chilling
15 minutes cooking

榨菜魚丸湯

A refreshingly hot soup from Hunan, this country-style dish uses the Sichuan jar vegetable (mustard greens preserved in salt and red-pepper powder).

Ingredients

½ pound cod fillets
6 medium black mushrooms
1 cup warm water
½ cup Sichuan preserved vegetables
½ cup bamboo shoots
1 ounce cellophane noodles

4 cups Basic Soup Stock (page 108)
2 tablespoons oil
2 slices gingerroot
Salt
1 whole scallion, shredded
2 teaspoons sesame oil

PREPARATION

1 Prepare fish paste following the general recipe on page 145, but using half the fish and seasonings. Chill for 30 minutes.

2 Soak mushrooms in water until soft. Trim stems and squeeze to extract moisture. Shred mushrooms finely. Reserve soaking liquid.

3 Rinse preserved vegetables and shred finely.

4 Shred bamboo shoots finely, then blanch in some boiling water for 1 minute. Run cold water over to rinse, then drain.

5 Soak cellophane noodles in cold water until soft. Cut into 3-inch lengths, then cook a few minutes until transparent. Drain and rinse.

COOKING

1 Put stock in a 4-quart saucepan and heat.

2 While stock is heating, grasp fish paste by one hand, squeezing out a small ball about 1 inch in diameter, and drop it into the stock. Continue to make fish balls until all the paste is used up.

3 Cook soup slowly over medium-low heat until the fish balls all float to the surface. Remove balls to a bowl, using a slotted spoon. Use immediately to assemble soup or keep refrigerated until later. Reserve fish stock.

4 Set a saucepan over high heat. When hot, add the oil. Flavor oil with ginger and discard ginger when brown. Add the bamboo shoots, mushrooms, and preserved vegetables, stirring for 1 minute.

5 Add the mushroom liquid and the fish stock. Bring to a boil, turn heat to medium, and then add cellophane noodles.

6 Cook soup 5 minutes, then add fish balls. Bring soup back to a boil and test for seasoning, adding salt if necessary.

7 Add scallion to soup and stir in sesame oil. Mix and serve.

⊛⊛Eight-Treasure Winter Melon Soup

Serves 8 to 10
Time 30 minutes preparation
20 to 25 minutes cooking

八寶冬瓜粒

The Cantonese have an ingenious way of putting many cut ingredients together to achieve a dazzling color combination and a curious harmony of taste and texture. Here is one more example, similar in taste to the famed Winter Melon Pond, but much easier and much more foolproof because the melon this time is used in the soup rather than used as the container.

Ingredients

2 pounds winter melon
6 medium black
  mushrooms
1 cup warm water
12 straw mushrooms
  (canned)
¼ cup shelled green
  peas
2 chicken fillets
2 teaspoons tapioca
  powder
4 ounces lean boneless
  pork, cut from loin

8 shrimp in the shell
2 ounces crabmeat
1 ounce Smithfield
  ham
1 cup water
4 cups Basic Soup
  Stock (page 108)
1½ teaspoons salt
Dash of white pepper
Few drops of sesame
  oil

PREPARATION

1 Remove green skin from melon. Discard fibers and seeds and dice pulp. Melon and all other ingredients should be cut into ⅜-inch cubes.

2 Soak black mushrooms in warm water until soft, then trim stems. Squeeze to extract moisture and dice. Reserve soaking liquid.

3 Blanch straw mushrooms in some boiling water for 1 minute. Run cold water over to rinse, then drain and dice.

4 Blanch peas in boiling water for 30 seconds. Rinse with cold water to stop the cooking process, then set aside.

5 Dice chicken and coat with 1 teaspoon tapioca powder. Blanch with boiling water over high heat for 30 seconds. Remove and rinse with cold water. Drain and reserve.

6 Dice pork and coat with remaining tapioca. Blanch with boiling water over high heat for 1 minute. Remove and rinse with cold water. Drain and reserve.

7 Cook shrimp in boiling water over high heat until the shells turn red. Remove and rinse with cold water. Shell and devein. Dice.

8 Flake crabmeat lightly and set aside.

9 Dice ham and set aside.

COOKING

1 In a 4-quart saucepan, place the melon and water. Cook over high heat for 10 minutes with the pan covered, until the melon turns transparent and soft, but not mushy.

2 Combine the stock, reserved mushroom liquid, black mushrooms, ham, and straw mushrooms in another saucepan. Cook over high heat until boiling, then turn the heat to medium and cook for 3 minutes more. Add melon cubes and water in which melon was cooked.

3 Bring soup to a boil and add chicken and pork. Cook for 2 minutes, then add shrimp, crabmeat, and peas. Season with salt and stir soup to mix ingredients. Correct seasoning; add more salt if needed.

4 Bring soup back to a boil and remove from the heat. Flavor with white pepper and sesame oil and serve hot.

⊛⊛⊛Sizzling Rice Soup

Serves 4 to 6
Time 30 minutes preparation
20 minutes cooking

鍋 巴 湯

This is an East China favorite, to enjoy first with your ears, then with your nose, finally with your palate.

Ingredients

6 medium black mushrooms
1 cup warm water
12 medium shrimp in the shell
Salt
4 ounces boneless pork, cut from loin
½ cup bamboo shoots
¼ cup shelled green peas
1 tablespoon granulated sugar
2 cups water

2 scallions (white part only)
2 tablespoons oil
6 cups Basic Soup Stock (page 108)
12 pieces Rice Crust, 1 by 2 inches (page 384)
3 cups oil for deep-frying

Seasonings

¼ teaspoon salt
½ egg white
2 teaspoons tapioca powder
2 teaspoons light soy sauce
1 teaspoon tapioca powder
1 teaspoon sesame oil
Dash of granulated sugar
Pinch of white pepper

PREPARATION

1 Soak mushrooms in warm water until soft. Squeeze to extract moisture, then trim stems. Shred into very thin strips about ¹/₁₆ inch wide. Reserve the soaking liquid.

2 Shell and devein shrimp. Clean with salt (see page 151), then rinse and drain. Pat dry with paper towels, then cut into ½-inch cubes. Season with salt, egg white, and tapioca powder, then chill while you complete remaining preparations.

3 Shred pork finely into strips ⅛ by 1 by 2 inches. Mix with remaining seasonings and chill.

4 Shred bamboo shoots the same size as pork. Set aside.

5 Blanch peas in boiling water with sugar for 30 seconds. Remove and rinse with cold water to stop the cooking process. Drain thoroughly and set aside.

6 Shred scallions finely and set aside.

COOKING

1 Set a 4-quart saucepan over high heat. When the pan is very hot, add 2 tablespoons oil. Stir-fry the pork shreds for 30 seconds, then add the shrimp, stirring constantly. Add the mushrooms and bamboo shoots. Stir again.

2 Pour in the stock and the reserved mushroom liquid. Bring to a boil and turn the heat to low. Simmer soup until ready to use. Correct the seasonings.

3 While soup is simmering, set a wok over high heat. When the wok is hot, add remaining oil. Wait for about 5 to 7 minutes, or until the oil has reached the

boiling point. Test temperature by dropping a small piece of rice crust in. If it puffs up immediately, the oil is hot enough (about 400 degrees).

4 Deep-fry the rice crust in very hot oil until puffy and light gold. Remove immediately to line a serving bowl.

5 Add peas to soup and pour into another serving bowl. Bring soup and rice crusts immediately to the table. Pour soup onto the rice crusts. A sizzling noise should be heard when the soup comes in contact with the rice crusts. (No waiting time should be allowed.) Add scallion shreds, stir, and serve!

◎◎Clear Chicken Soup with Ham and Black Mushrooms

Serves 4 to 6
Time 25 minutes preparation
1 hour simmering stock
10 minutes cooking

雞 火 清 湯

A light and flavorful soup. There is no substitute for the Smithfield ham, except Chinese ham, so omit it altogether if neither is available.

Ingredients

1 whole chicken breast, about 12 to 14 ounces
1 slice gingerroot
4 cups water
6 medium black mushrooms
1 cup warm water
2 ounces Smithfield ham
½ cup bamboo shoots
1 bunch spinach, about 1 pound
2 cups Basic Soup Stock (page 108)
Salt

Seasonings

1 egg white
2 tablespoons water
1 tablespoon tapioca powder
½ teaspoon salt
1 tablespoon pale dry sherry
½ teaspoon granulated sugar
Dash of white pepper

PREPARATION

1 Skin and bone the chicken breast. Remove all visible gristle and membranes. Slice horizontally into thin pieces about 1 by 1½ by ¹⁄₁₆ inch.

2 Combine the egg white, water, and tapioca powder in a bowl, then add chicken. Mix with your fingers until well blended, then add remaining seasoning ingredients and mix again. Chill until ready to use.

3 Simmer the chicken bones and scraps with the ginger and water for 1 hour to make about 2 cups of thin secondary stock.

4 Soak mushrooms in warm water until soft. Trim and reserve stems. Squeeze to extract moisture, then slice each mushroom cap diagonally into ¼-inch pieces. Add stems and soaking liquid to simmer with the chicken bones.

5 Slice ham across the grain into ¹⁄₁₆-inch-thick pieces, about 1 by 1½ inches. Set aside.

6 Blanch bamboo shoots in boiling water for 1 minute. Rinse with cold water and cut shoots into pieces the same size as ham.

7 Choose the tenderest leaves from the center of the spinach. Rinse and drain; there should be about 1 cup of leaves.

COOKING

1 Combine basic stock with secondary stock to make 4 cups stock. Put stock in a 4-quart saucepan over medium heat. While waiting for it to boil, blanch chicken in boiling water in a smaller saucepan for 30 seconds, stirring until slices separate. Remove chicken to a colander and run cold water over to stop cooking process. Drain.

2 When stock boils, add ham and mushrooms. Turn heat to medium, cooking for 5 minutes. Add bamboo shoots and spinach leaves, cooking until the soup boils again. Add chicken slices, cooking enough to just heat through. Test for salt.

3 Pour soup into a tureen, then serve.

⊚⊚Red-in-Snow and Fava Bean Soup

Serves 4 in a family meal
Time 20 minutes preparation
30 minutes soaking
20 minutes cooking

雪菜豆瓣湯

A simple family soup popular in the summer. This soup originated in East China, but is now enjoyed even in Hong Kong. The sprouting fava beans acquire a special taste, and provide extra vitamin C.

Ingredients

1 cup sprouted fava beans (page 359)
¼ cup dried shrimp
½ cup hot water
¼ cup Sichuan preserved vegetable

¼ cup red-in-snow
1 tablespoon oil
5 cups thin Basic Soup Stock (page 108)
2 teaspoons sesame oil

PREPARATION

1 Remove skin from fava beans.

2 Soak shrimp in hot water for 30 minutes. Reserve soaking liquid.

3 Rinse Sichuan preserved vegetables and cut into ⅛-inch slices about 1 by 1¼ inches in size. Also rinse red-in-snow and cut into 1-inch lengths.

COOKING

1 Set a 2-quart saucepan over high heat. When hot, add oil, then the shrimp, stirring for about 1 minute or until the shrimp flavor becomes noticeable.

2 Add the thin stock, reserved shrimp liquid, and fava beans and bring to a boil. Cover saucepan, turn heat to medium, and cook 10 minutes.

3 Add the Sichuan preserved vegetables and red-in-snow to the pot. Cook for 5 more minutes. Add sesame oil to soup and serve.

THICK SOUPS

These soups are based on thickened soup stock. They are more filling than clear soups but are not necessarily harder to prepare.

⊛Mock Bird's Nest Soup

Serves 6
Time 40 minutes preparation
10 minutes cooking

冬茸燕窩湯

The delicate texture of grated winter melons closely resembles that of bird's nest. The latter is expensive and tedious to clean, and some diners may not cherish the fact that bird's nest is actually the dried saliva of South Seas swallows. This soup comes very close to offering a taste of that wonderful original, with much less effort.

Ingredients

3 pounds winter melon
2 ounces Smithfield
    ham
4 cups Basic Soup
    Stock (page 108) or
    strong canned broth
3 tablespoons water
    chestnut powder

⅓ cup chicken stock
3 egg whites, lightly
    beaten with 1
    tablespoon water
Salt
1 teaspoon sesame oil

PREPARATION

1 Remove the fiber and seeds from the melon and peel off the green skin. Cut the meat into 1-inch chunks and put in a blender. Blend at high speed until the melon is reduced to a purée (timing depends on the efficiency of the blender; make sure that purée is not reduced too fine). Pour purée into a bowl lined with a strainer to drain excess moisture. You'll find the melon more controllable if puréed in small batches. Reserve the juice that drains off.

2 Cut ham into thin slices. Chop about 1 tablespoon's worth for a garnish. Cook the remaining ham with the melon juice over medium-low heat for 30 minutes. Discard the ham slices but reserve the liquid.

COOKING

1 In a heavy saucepan, cook the melon purée over medium heat until soft and transparent. Add the soup stock and ham-flavored juice. Bring to a boil.

2 Meanwhile, mix the water chestnut powder with the chicken stock, then stream gradually into the soup, stirring all the while to prevent lumping. When the soup returns to a boil, whirl in the egg whites.

3 Remove saucepan from the heat and wait 30 seconds. Stir to mix well. Correct seasoning, then glaze soup with sesame oil. Pour soup into a tureen and garnish with chopped ham. Serve hot.

Note: In preparing this soup, you may find it helpful to purée the melon in advance—as much as a night ahead. Then cook the soup the day of serving and at the last minute just warm it, thicken it, and pour the egg white in.

⊛⊛⊛Spinach Velvet Soup

菠 菜 茸

Serves 6 to 8
Time 30 minutes preparation
10 minutes cooking

This is the favorite of my grandfather, the ruling gourmet in old Canton for half a century.

Ingredients

3 bunches spinach, about 6 cups of leaves loosely packed
1 tablespoon granulated sugar
3 egg whites
1 tablespoon water
4 tablespoons tapioca powder

5⅓ cups Basic Soup Stock (page 108)
2 tablespoons chopped Smithfield ham
Salt
1 teaspoon sesame oil
2 tablespoons oil

PREPARATION

1 Remove stems from spinach and reserve for another use. Rinse leaves thoroughly and drain.

2 Half fill a 4-quart saucepan with water. Set over high heat and bring water to a boil. Sprinkle in the sugar (to keep the spinach green) and add spinach, stirring until water boils again. Pour immediately into a colander, running cold water over the spinach to stop the cooking process.

SHRIMP IN THE YIN/YANG STYLE: EMERALD SHRIMP (PAGE 155)
AND CLEAR-FRIED SHRIMP IN YELLOW WINE (PAGE 153)

ASPARAGUS IN CRAB SAUCE
PAGE 168

3 Squeeze the spinach leaves to extract as much moisture as possible. Press between the hands to form a lump. Mince finely with a Chinese cleaver (do not use a blender).

4 Beat the egg whites with water until smooth but not foamy.

5 Mix tapioca powder and ⅓ cup stock together in a bowl.

COOKING

1 Heat the remaining stock in a 4-quart saucepan over high heat. Bring to a boil, then turn heat to medium. Add half the ham and cook for 5 minutes. Turn heat to high and add the spinach, stirring until it boils.

2 Season soup with salt. Restir the tapioca mixture and stream it into the soup, stirring until soup thickens.

3 Remove saucepan immediately from the heat and whirl in the egg whites. Wait 30 seconds, then stir to mix, adding sesame oil and other oil for glazing.

4 Pour soup into a tureen and garnish with remaining ham. Serve immediately.

Note: Do not prepare this soup in advance. The spinach cannot take reheating without losing its beautiful, bright green color.

◉◉◉Chinese Corn Chowder with Chicken Velvet

Serves 8 to 12
Time 30 minutes preparation
1 hour chilling
15 minutes cooking

鷄茸粟米羹

This chowder combines the freshness of New World corn with the Old World elegance of chicken velvet. While canned or frozen corn are possible substitutes, it would be vastly better to use the freshest, sweetest corn possible, preferably that picked the same day.

Ingredients

6 ears fresh corn or 3 cups frozen or canned corn
1½ cups water
1 whole chicken breast, approximately 12 to 14 ounces
2 eggs, separated, + 2 whole eggs
5¼ cups Basic Soup Stock (page 108)

2 tablespoons minced Smithfield ham
1½ tablespoons cornstarch
Salt
1 tablespoon oil
1 teaspoon sesame oil

Seasonings

1 tablespoon tapioca powder
1 teaspoon pale dry sherry
½ teaspoon salt
¼ teaspoon granulated sugar
1 teaspoon sesame oil
Dash of white pepper

PREPARATION

1 If using fresh corn, cut kernels off cobs. Put corn into blender and whirl 1 minute at high speed, adding 1 cup of water while beating. Pour corn mixture into a bowl lined with a fine sieve to drain the juice. Press mixture against the wall of sieve to extract as much juice as possible. Reserve the corn juice and discard the husks.

2 Skin and bone the chicken breast. Remove all visible membranes and gristle. Cut flesh coarsely into small cubes, then mince as fine as possible, adding some water (about 4 teaspoons) at a time, until chicken is reduced to a paste.

3 Remove chicken to a mixing bowl and add egg whites, 1 at a time, stirring with a wire whisk until well blended. Add seasonings.

4 Add ¼ cup chicken stock to chicken paste gradually, stirring until a velvety thin paste is formed. Chill at least 1 hour.

5 Beat the reserved egg yolks with the 2 additional eggs.

COOKING

1 In a saucepan, combine the remaining stock with half the ham. Set over high heat and bring to a boil. Immediately add the corn mixture and turn heat to medium-low. Return to a boil, then reduce heat to low.

2 Transfer about 2 cups of corn mixture from saucepan to smaller pan (for easy stirring), setting it over very low heat. Add the chicken velvet, stirring rapidly with a wire whisk to break up the lumps. When the color of the chicken turns white, remove the pan from the heat.

3 Mix cornstarch with 3 tablespoons water and stream mixture into corn soup in the large saucepan, stirring constantly until thickened. Add the chicken velvet in the smaller saucepan to combine with the corn soup, stirring all the while until the soup boils again. (This takes a while because the pan is on low heat.) Add salt, but do not over-salt.

4 Whirl in the egg mixture and wait for 10 seconds, then stir to mix well. Glaze the soup with the oil and the sesame oil. Pour into a tureen and garnish with the remaining ham. Serve hot.

Note: The chicken velvet can be prepared easily with a blender fitted with a baby food jar. Add all the seasonings, chicken, egg whites, and chicken stock into the jar. Beat at high speed just for 20 seconds, and the mixture will turn to a very fine paste, more delicate than that which is minced manually.

◉◉Pungent and Hot Soup

Serves 6 to 8
Time 30 minutes preparation
15 minutes cooking

酸辣湯

Different versions of this soup are found in North, East, and Central China, even in South China. This North China version has the lightest color.

Ingredients

6 medium black
  mushrooms
1 cup warm water
4 ounces lean boneless
  pork, cut from loin
½ ounce wood ears
¾ cup bamboo shoots
1 piece (12 ounces) soft
  bean curd
1 whole scallion,
  trimmed
1 sprig Chinese parsley
4 cups Basic Soup
  Stock (page 108)
3 tablespoons tapioca
  powder
2 tablespoons water
2 eggs, lightly beaten

Seasonings

2 teaspoons tapioca
  powder
1 tablespoon light soy
  sauce
½ teaspoon granulated
  sugar

Pungent and hot mixture

1 tablespoon sesame oil
2 tablespoons light soy
  sauce
1 teaspoon white
  pepper
2 tablespoons red rice
  vinegar
1 teaspoon granulated
  sugar

PREPARATION

1 Soak the black mushrooms in warm water until soft. Squeeze to extract moisture and trim and discard stems. Shred mushrooms into pieces ⅛ by ⅛ by 2 inches. Reserve soaking liquid.

2 Shred pork the same size as mushrooms.

3 Soak wood ears in plenty of hot water until soft and expanded. Trim the tough ends and rinse thoroughly. Shred to match black mushrooms.

4 Mix seasonings in a bowl and add to pork shreds. Mix well.

5 Shred bamboo shoots into pieces ⅛ by ⅛ by 2 inches. Blanch in boiling water for 1 minute, then rinse with cold water. Drain.

6 Shred bean curd into pieces the same size as bamboo shoots. Drain excess moisture.

7 Shred scallion and cut Chinese parsley into 2-inch pieces.

8 Mix together the pungent and hot mixture.

COOKING

1 Combine the stock and mushroom soaking liquid in a 3-quart saucepan set over high heat. Bring to a boil and add mushrooms, bean curd, bamboo shoots, wood ears, and pork shreds. Bring back to a boil, then turn heat to medium. Stir to separate pork shreds and cook for 5 minutes. Turn heat to low.

2 Mix tapioca powder with water and add gradually to soup, stirring constantly until thickened. Stream the egg mixture, in a whirling manner, into the soup. Allow soup to set for 10 seconds, then add scallion and parsley. Turn off heat.

3 Restir pungent and hot mixture and add to soup. Mix. Serve immediately.

Note: For a darker soup, use dark soy sauce in the pungent and hot mixture.

⊛Seaweed Soup

Serves 6
Time 15 minutes preparation
10 minutes cooking

紫 菜 湯

This nutritious East China soup is easy to prepare, pleasant to look at, tasty to eat, yet very inexpensive.

Ingredients
6 sheets dried seaweed
  (*nori*)
¼ cup dried shrimp
½ cup hot water
4 ounces lean boneless
  pork, cut from loin
2 whole eggs
3 tablespoons tapioca
  powder
⅓ cup water
2 tablespoons oil
5 cups Basic Soup
  Stock (page 108)
Salt
1 teaspoon sesame oil
1 whole scallion,
  chopped finely

Seasonings
1 teaspoon light soy
  sauce
1 teaspoon pale dry
  sherry
1 teaspoon tapioca
  powder
Dash of white pepper

PREPARATION

1 Cut *nori* with scissors into ½-inch squares. Loosen pieces.

2 Soak shrimp in hot water until soft. Chop into soybean-sized pieces. Reserve soaking liquid.

3 Cut pork into fine shreds about ⅛ by ⅛ by 1½ inches. Mix with seasonings.

4 Beat eggs lightly.

5 Mix tapioca powder with water and set aside.

COOKING

1 Set a 4-quart saucepan over high heat. When hot, add oil. Stir-fry shrimp pieces for 1 minute, then add pork shreds, stirring 1 more minute until the pink color disappears. Add stock and water in which shrimp was soaked. Bring to a boil, then turn heat to low.

2 Restir thickener and stream into soup, stirring constantly until thickened. Scatter seaweed squares on soup, stirring to mix well. Add salt to taste.

3 Whirl in the eggs, using the prongs of a fork to guide the pouring so as to form egg flowers.

4 Wait for 10 seconds, then glaze soup with sesame oil. Mix well, and pour soup into a tureen. Garnish with scallion and serve hot.

⊛Egg Flower and Minced Beef Soup

Serves 6
Time 15 minutes preparation
15 minutes resting
10 minutes cooking

蛋花牛肉湯

The Chinese name of this Cantonese soup—West Lake Beef Soup—has bewildered Northern Chinese gourmets, as the most well-known West Lake is in East China, a thousand miles from Canton. The West Lake in question here is only about 100 miles east of Canton. The original West Lake Beef Soup uses only egg whites; we use whole eggs here for added taste.

Ingredients	Seasonings
¼ pound extra-lean ground beef	1 tablespoon light soy sauce
2 tablespoons oil	2 teaspoons pale dry sherry
2 eggs + 1 egg yolk	½ teaspoon granulated sugar
1 whole scallion, trimmed	1 teaspoon sesame oil
5 cups Basic Soup Stock (page 108)	2 teaspoons tapioca powder
3 tablespoons tapioca powder	1 egg white
2 tablespoons water	⅛ teaspoon white pepper
Salt	

PREPARATION

1 Mix seasonings in a bowl, adding beef as well. Stir with chopsticks in one direction until the beef holds together.

2 Add oil and stir. Set at room temperature for 15 minutes.

3 Beat eggs and yolk together lightly. Chop scallion finely.

COOKING

1 In a 4-quart saucepan, add stock. Set over medium-high heat with the pan uncovered. While waiting, mix tapioca powder and water, and stream into the soup when it boils, stirring constantly to prevent lumps. Turn heat to low.

2 Transfer about 2 cups of boiling soup to a smaller saucepan (for ease in stirring). Add the ground beef and beat with a wire whisk to separate the meat.

3 Add the beef mixture to the larger saucepan. Turn heat to medium and return to a boil. Turn off the heat and, using a fork, guide the egg mixture into the soup, pouring through the prongs and whirling around while pouring. Wait for 10 seconds, then stir gently to blend.

4 Test for seasoning and correct if necessary. Pour soup into a tureen and decorate with scallion. Serve hot.

⊛Crabmeat and Bean Curd Soup

Serves 6
Time 10 minutes preparation
15 minutes cooking

蟹 肉 豆 腐 羹

Crabmeat, bean curd, and soup stock make this soup the easiest to prepare, with the possible exception of Egg Flower Soup, and yet this dish is smooth and delicate enough to surprise your guests.

Ingredients	Seasonings
1 piece (12 ounces) soft bean curd	1 teaspoon sesame oil
4 ounces cooked crabmeat	¼ teaspoon salt
2 tablespoons Smithfield ham	1 teaspoon pale dry sherry
2 whole eggs	Dash of white pepper
4 cups Basic Soup Stock (page 108)	
3 tablespoons tapioca powder	
¼ cup chicken stock	
Salt	
1 teaspoon sesame oil	
Dash of white pepper	

PREPARATION

1 Cut bean curd into strips ¼ by ¼ by 1 inch. Drain excess moisture.

2 Flake crabmeat and mix with seasonings.

3 Chop ham finely.

4 Beat eggs until smooth but not foamy.

COOKING

1 Set a 3-quart saucepan over medium-high heat. Add the stock and bring to a boil. Turn heat to medium and add 1 tablespoon of the ham. Cook 5 minutes, then add the bean curd. Return to a boil.

2 Mix tapioca powder with chicken stock and gradually add to soup, stirring gently until thickened. Add the crabmeat and season with salt if needed.

3 Whirl in the eggs and remove saucepan from heat. Allow to set 30 seconds, then stir gently to mix well.

4 Glaze soup with sesame oil and sprinkle pepper on top. Stir and pour soup into a tureen. Decorate with the remaining ham and serve soup hot.

⊛⊛⊛Chrysanthemum Fish Chowder

Serves 6 to 8
Time 30 minutes preparation
10 minutes cooking

菊 花 魚 羹

Chrysanthemum petals add a refreshing chewiness to the fish chowder in this Fujianese recipe. This is a fine example of the blending of different textures in one soup.

Ingredients

12 ounces gray sole (weight after cleaning & removing head and tail)
2 tablespoons oil
3 slices gingerroot
1 tablespoon pale dry sherry
3 cups water
6 medium black mushrooms
1 cup hot water
½ cup bamboo shoots
1 piece (12 ounces) soft bean curd
2 tablespoons Smithfield ham

2 egg whites
2 large white chrysanthemums
1 tablespoon salt dissolved in 4 cups water
6 sprigs Chinese parsley
5 cups Basic Soup Stock (page 108)
Salt
3 tablespoons tapioca powder
¼ cup chicken stock

Seasonings

1 tablespoon light soy sauce
⅛ teaspoon white pepper
2 teaspoons sesame oil
½ teaspoon granulated sugar
¼ teaspoon salt

PREPARATION

1 Rinse fish and pat dry. Set a 3-quart saucepan over high heat, and, when hot, add the oil. Flavor oil with ginger until lightly brown. Sizzle in the sherry and immediately add 3 cups of water. Bring to a boil and add the fish, then return to a boil.

2 Turn the heat to low and cook fish for 10 minutes, or until it flakes easily. Remove saucepan from the heat and remove fish; reserve fish and stock.

3 Soak mushrooms in hot water until soft. Trim stems and shred caps finely. Reserve soaking liquid.

4 Blanch bamboo shoots in boiling water for 30 seconds. Rinse with cold water and drain. Shred finely.

5 Cut bean curd into strips about ¼ by ¼ by 2 inches. Drain off excess water.

6 Shred ham finely.

7 Beat egg whites lightly.

8 Shake mums in salted water to rinse. Break off the petals and wrap them loosely in a kitchen towel. Chill.

9 Break off the leafy parts of the parsley and cut into 2-inch lengths. Rinse.

10 Take 1 piece of fish at a time and place it on a platter. Use a spatula to scrape the meat from the main bone and put it in a bowl. Bone remaining fish, then add seasonings to fish and mix well. Strain fish stock and discard the ginger.

COOKING

1 In a saucepan, combine the stock, mushroom liquid, ham, and fish stock. Bring to a boil over high heat and then add mushrooms and bamboo shoots. Turn heat to medium and cook for 2 minutes.

2 Add bean curd to the soup, cooking until soup returns to a boil. Add the fish and return to a boil, then season with salt.

3 Meanwhile, mix the tapioca powder with the chicken stock and stream into the soup, stirring gently until thickened. Whirl in the egg whites, stirring to mix with all the ingredients.

4 Pour the soup into a tureen and place chrysanthemum petals and parsley leaves in separate saucers for the diners to sprinkle on top of their individual bowls of soup.

Note: Any flat white fish can be used.

BANQUET SOUPS

A large bowl of delicious soup, made with exotic ingredients, is often the high point of a Chinese banquet. Note that in banquet soups, a Supreme Stock (page 108) is used; also, water chestnut powder is often used as a transparent thickener. The ingredients include dried foods like shark's fin, bird's nest, fish maw, hasma (ovaries of a Manchurian tree frog), dried abalone, dried scallops, and the meat of unusual game animals and fowl such as raccoons, cranes, owls, tortoises, giant Wawa fish. In Southern China in the fall, restaurants feature Supreme Scholar's Snake Soup, immortalizing my grandfather. The Snake Soup uses five kinds of poisonous snakes, and is mixed with fresh lemon leaves cut fine as human hair and fresh chrysanthemum petals.

◉◉Chicken Velvet and Jade Pillars Chowder

Serves 10 to 12
Time 30 minutes preparation
2 hours chilling
2 hours soaking
30 minutes cooking

鷄茸瑤柱

Jade pillars are dried clam muscles highly regarded by the Chinese, as can be seen in the name. Here is a refined banquet soup that justifies this respect. The scattered muscle fibers add to the texture and taste in a way no other ingredient can match.

Ingredients

1 whole chicken breast, about 14 ounces
2 ounces jade pillars
¾ cup warm water
1 tablespoon pale dry sherry
2 slices gingerroot
2 eggs + 2 egg yolks
½ cup + 1 tablespoon chicken stock
¼ cup water chestnut powder

2 tablespoons Smithfield ham
8 cups Supreme Stock (page 108)
Salt
1 teaspoon sesame oil

Seasonings

½ cup cold chicken stock
½ teaspoon salt
1 teaspoon sesame oil
2 teaspoons pale dry sherry
Dash of white pepper
Pinch of granulated sugar
2 egg whites
1 tablespoon tapioca powder

PREPARATION

1 Skin and bone the chicken breast. Remove all gristle and membranes. Cut into ½-inch cubes and put cubes in a blender (preferably one with a baby food attachment).

2 Add the first 6 seasoning ingredients to the chicken. Blend at high speed until chicken turns into a purée (about 1 minute). Add egg whites and tapioca powder and blend again to mix well. Chill in refrigerator for at least 2 hours or until firm. (Note: chicken velvet can be prepared a day ahead.)

3 In a heatproof bowl, soak the pillars in warm water for at least 2 hours. Add the sherry and ginger and steam over high heat for 30 minutes. Discard the ginger and let cool, then break pillars into fine shreds, combining pillars with juice. Reserve.

4 Beat the eggs with the yolks and blend with 1 tablespoon of chicken stock until smooth.

5 Mix the water chestnut powder with the remaining chicken stock and blend with a wire whisk until smooth.

6 Chop ham finely.

COOKING

1 Combine the soup stock, pillar shreds and juice, and half the ham in a 4-quart saucepan. Set pan over medium heat until the soup boils. Turn heat to low and continue to simmer for 20 minutes.

2 Scoop out about 2 cups of hot soup (soup only) and place in a 2-quart saucepan. Add the chicken velvet and beat with a wire whisk to break up any lumps until the mixture is smooth and velvety.

3 Turn the heat to medium and restir the thickener and then stream it into the soup, stirring constantly until it thickens. Add the chicken velvet mixture to the soup, stir, and bring to a boil. Correct the seasoning, then turn heat off.

4 Whirl in the egg mixture quickly and stir gently to mix well. Flavor soup with a little sesame oil, then pour into a serving bowl. Decorate soup with the remaining ham and serve hot.

Note: Jade pillars are available in Chinese markets. Ask for "dried scallops."

⊛Steamed Chicken with Black Mushroom Soup

Serves 8 to 10
Time 25 minutes preparation
2½ hours cooking

北菇燉雞

This is a clear soup that requires very little attention while it steams.

Ingredients

2 ounces black
  mushrooms
2 cups hot water
1 small frying chicken,
  about 2½ pounds
3 slices gingerroot

2 ounces Smithfield
  ham, in 1 piece
5 to 6 cups boiling
  water
2 teaspoons salt

PREPARATION

1 Rinse the mushrooms and soak them in hot water until soft. Trim the stems and squeeze caps to extract moisture. Reserve soaking liquid.

2 Rub chicken with a Nylon scrubber to remove any yellow film on the skin. Remove excessive fat. Rinse and then blanch in boiling water for 3 minutes. Transfer chicken from water and place in a colander. Run cold water over to rinse again.

3 Cut chicken in half lengthwise. Place it in a heatproof casserole, adding ginger slices, ham, mushroom soaking liquid, and boiling water. Cover casserole.

COOKING

1 In an 8-quart saucepan, place a towel to line the bottom. Put in a cake rack on top of the towel and place the casserole on the rack. Pour water into the saucepan to come halfway up the sides of the casserole. Turn the heat to high and when the water boils vigorously, cover the saucepan. Reduce the heat to medium-low and steam soup for 2 hours. Replenish pot with boiling water if necessary.

2 The above steps can be done well ahead of time. Half an hour before serving, bring water in saucepan back to a boil over high heat. Add the mushrooms and liquid to the casserole and continue to steam for 30 minutes. Season with salt.

3 Remove casserole from the saucepan and wipe dry. To serve, break chicken with chopsticks or a fork at the table. Scoop chicken, mushrooms, and soup into individual bowls and serve hot.

⊛⊛⊛Snow Mushroom Soup with Chicken Shreds

Serves 12
Time 30 minutes preparation
15 minutes cooking
1 hour chilling

雪 耳 雞 絲 湯

Rivaling bird's nest and shark's fin in texture and greatly exceeding them in visual beauty, the relatively inexpensive snow mushrooms represent the best buy for Chinese *haute cuisine*.

Snow mushrooms from Taiwan are usually bleached, ranging from yellowish white (partly bleached) to almost pure white (fully bleached). In water they expand into beautiful flowers with large, intricately linked petals. They are never meant to be overcooked, especially the fully bleached white ones. The bleaching has taken away their firmness, and the slightest overheating turns the beautiful clusters into a gluey mash, tasting like hot Jello. Fujianese snow mushrooms, grown around the city of Zhangzhou, are yellowish in color, crunchy in texture, with much smaller petals than their Taiwan counterparts. They call for special treatment. The most expensive snow mushrooms come from Sichuan. After they are expanded, they are almost as white as the Taiwan variety and as crunchy as the Fujianese variety. Unfortunately in the United States, the access to Sichuan snow mushrooms is limited.

Ingredients

1½ ounces snow mushrooms (see note)
1 whole chicken breast, about 12 to 14 ounces
1 ounce Smithfield ham

3 tablespoons water chestnut powder
6¼ cups Supreme Stock (page 108)
1 cup oil
Salt

Seasonings

1 egg white
2 tablespoons water
½ teaspoon salt
2 teaspoons tapioca powder
1 teaspoon pale dry sherry
1 teaspoon sesame oil
Dash of white pepper

PREPARATION

1 Soak mushrooms in cold water in a large mixing bowl until they are expanded. Trim and discard tough ends, then drain mushrooms in a colander. Pour a kettle of boiling water over them and rinse with cold running water immediately. Drain thoroughly.

2 Skin, bone, and remove membranes and gristle from chicken breast. Shred as fine as possible.

3 In a small bowl, combine the egg white and water for seasonings. Beat lightly to mix, adding chicken shreds and mix by hand until water is absorbed. Add the next 5 seasonings, mixing again until well blended. Chill at least 1 hour.

4 Shred ham finely.

5 Mix water chestnut powder with ¼ cup stock in a small bowl.

COOKING

1 In a 4-quart saucepan, place stock and all but 1 tablespoon of the ham. Set stock over medium heat (high heat will turn the stock milky) until it boils. Cook 5 minutes, then add the snow mushrooms. Lower heat and simmer soup.

2 Set a small saucepan over high heat. When very hot, add the oil. Remove saucepan immediately from the heat and add the chicken shreds, stirring to separate for 30 seconds. Pour the oil and chicken together through a sieve into a bowl.

3 Raise the heat from simmer to medium to bring the soup to a boil. Restir thickener and stream into soup, stirring constantly until it thickens. Return chicken shreds to soup, stirring again to mix well. Correct seasoning.

4 Pour soup into a tureen and garnish with the remaining ham. Serve hot.

Note: If Fujianese snow mushrooms are used, instead of pouring boiling water over, cook them in a saucepan over medium heat for 5 minutes, then cover pan. Let stand 20 minutes and then rinse with cold water. Add mushrooms to the Supreme Stock at the same time as the ham.

VARIATION: Shark's Fin Soup with Chicken Shreds

Double the quantity of the shark's fin called for in Cassia Flower Shark's Fin (page 185). Then follow the preparation steps 1 and 2 for soaking, cleaning, and braising to substitute for the snow mushrooms in the master recipe and proceed to finish the soup the same way. Two optional teaspoons of dark soy sauce can be added to give a light brown color to the soup.

Fish and Shellfish

Fish holds a respected place in Chinese cookery, and a choice fish—steamed, deep-fried, or braised—is often the high point of a banquet. Or a small platter of seasoned fish fillets, steamed atop a pot of boiling rice, can be found in even the most humble Chinese household. Fish is plentiful in the United States, so you can experiment with many of these specialties.

A large whole fish, weighing over 2½ pounds, should be white-cooked; smaller whole fish can be steamed quite successfully. Whole fish can also be pan-fried, usually sprinkled with salt first to firm up the flesh. (The salt is then rinsed off prior to cooking.) Pan-frying at an even temperature gives the fish a crisp and tasty brown skin, and can be served with a little soy sauce or a thin ginger-and-scallion sauce.

Fillets are often minced and mixed with chopped scallions to form a paste, out of which come chewy and firm fish balls, fish cakes, and fish sticks, as well as the stuffing for bean curd, eggs, eggplant, or green peppers. Chinese fish balls are in sharp contrast to the softer Swedish fish ball, Jewish gefilte fish, or French fish quenelle.

One requirement common to all fish recipes is freshness. The following are important points to note:

1 The fish should have a fresh, neutral aroma; it should not smell "fishy."

2 The fish meat should not be a dull gray, or slimy. The flesh should be firm, and elastic, leaving no impression when pressed with a finger.

3 The fish should have bright red gills and clear eyes. The skin should glisten.

When serving fish, remember that the Chinese prefer to serve whole fish with the head and fins still on. Many Chinese love the fish cheeks, and relish the fins and tails.

Depending upon where you live in the United States, fresh shellfish can be either a staple or a luxury. Foods like dungeness crabs, Maryland blue crabs, or Maine lobsters are best enjoyed in their area of origin or elsewhere as the budget allows. However, the Chinese use shellfish regularly in their cookery, and you will find many of these recipes use quantities small enough to make preparing the dishes possible.

The Chinese enjoy crab, and in the United States, you'll find that dungeness crab from northern California is full of tasty meat, well suited for their crab dishes. The Maryland blue crab has excellent crystalline flesh, but it is smaller and takes more shelling labor. Alaskan king crab is easiest to shell, but the meat is a bit too sweet to duplicate the Chinese dishes; use it as a substitute only when you can't get dungeness. The most celebrated crab in China is a freshwater crab with hairy claws from Yangcheng Lake, near Shanghai.

Fresh shrimp meat is minced like fish fillets into a paste called Hundred Flower Paste, used in elegant Cantonese banquets. Many exquisite dishes are prepared with shrimp, either stir-fried or deep-fried. Although fresh shrimp are best, frozen shrimp from Texas or Louisiana are firm and crisp, and are a suitable substitute. The small shrimp from California are great for fried rice dishes and spring roll fillings.

Though some Cantonese are brave enough to eat raw fish, they usually shudder at the thought of eating raw oysters or clams. On the other hand, squid is well-liked by the Chinese, and the American version is small and tender, excellent for stir-frying. Fresh bay and sea scallops are used, and jade pillars enjoy a particularly esteemed place in gourmet cooking. But the queen of a luxury banquet is still the shark's fin with dried abalone, fish maw, fish lips, and sea cucumbers in her retinue.

FISH

⊛Steamed Whole Fish

Serves 2 to 4 as a main dish
depending on the size of fish,
served with rice, vegetable,
and/or thick soup
Time 5 minutes preparation
10 minutes cooking

Steaming brings out the natural flavor of fish. It is considered by the Cantonese as the best way to cook fresh fish; this view is also shared by masters of the French *Nouvelle Cuisine*. In seafood restaurants in Hong Kong, where swimming fish are sold by the ounce, perhaps two-thirds of the fresh fish served are steamed.

Any firm, white-meat fish such as rock cod, striped bass, snapper, perch, sole, or pike or any freshwater fish is suitable for steaming. The proper size should be about 1 to 1½ pounds for this recipe.

Ingredients

1 whole firm fish, with
head and tail on,
about 1½ pounds
2 whole scallions,
trimmed

PREPARATION

1 Clean and scale the fish or have the fish market do it for you. Rinse the inside and out of the fish, then pat dry with paper towels.

2 Arrange scallions lengthwise on a heatproof oval fish platter; the platter should be large enough to hold the fish and yet small enough to be accommodated by the steamer. Place the fish on top of the scallions so that the steam will pass underneath.

COOKING

1 Bring enough water in the base of the steamer to a boil over high heat. If a pot and rack are used (see page 56), the water level should come to 1 inch below the rack on which the platter is set. When water boils vigorously, set the fish in the steamer (or on the rack inside the pot). Cover and steam for 10 minutes or until a chopstick can go easily into the thickest part.

2 Remove platter from steamer and drain excess liquid. Discard the scallions. Prepare one of the sauces given on pages 136–137 and pour over fish. Serve hot.

Note: Using a microwave oven, you can steam the fish even more quickly. Arrange the scallions on the platter, then place fish on top. Cover with plastic wrap and poke a few holes in the wrap to relieve pressure. Cook for 7 minutes,

being sure to turn the platter twice while cooking so that fish is cooked evenly. Remove fish from oven, discard scallions, and pour out liquid. Serve with sauce poured over.

To steam the fish in the oven, preheat the oven to 450 degrees. Set a roasting rack inside a baking pan and add boiling water to the pan to a depth of about ¼ inch. Place the fish on the rack; it should not touch the water. Wrap the whole pan securely with aluminum foil, piercing holes in the wrap to allow steam to escape. Bake for 15 minutes for each pound of fish, then remove from oven. Take out rack, and set fish gently on a pre-warmed serving platter.

Ginger and scallion sauce

¼ cup oil
2 teaspoons sesame oil
⅛ teaspoon white
  pepper
¼ teaspoon salt
3 slices gingerroot,
  shredded finely
2 whole scallions,
  shredded finely
3 tablespoons light soy
  sauce
2 sprigs Chinese
  parsley, cut into
  2-inch lengths

1 Combine oil and sesame oil in a small saucepan and set over low heat. When fish is done, sprinkle pepper and salt over fish and spread ginger and scallion shreds on top.

2 Change heat to high and cook oil until very hot. Pour oil evenly over fish, then add soy sauce. Garnish with parsley.

Ginger and vinegar sauce

2 teaspoons sesame oil
2 tablespoons red rice
  vinegar
2 tablespoons dark soy
  sauce
1 tablespoon brown
  sugar
½ teaspoon salt
¼ cup oil
2 cloves garlic, minced
2 slices gingerroot,
  grated
2 sprigs Chinese
  parsley, cut into
  2-inch lengths

1 After fish is in steamer, combine sesame oil, vinegar, soy sauce, brown sugar, and salt in a small saucepan and heat over low heat.

2 Set another small saucepan over low heat and add the oil. When fish is done, raise heat under oil to high and cook until very hot. Add garlic and ginger, stir just once, and pour over fish. Follow by pouring over soy sauce mixture, then garnish with parsley.

White sauce with chopped ham

4 tablespoons oil
2 slices gingerroot
1 tablespoon pale dry
  sherry
¾ cup chicken stock
2 tablespoons
  Smithfield ham,
  finely chopped
½ teaspoon salt
⅛ teaspoon white
  pepper
1 teaspoon granulated
  sugar
2 teaspoons tapioca
  powder mixed with 2
  tablespoons chicken
  stock
2 egg whites, beaten
  with 1 tablespoon
  water
1 teaspoon sesame oil
2 sprigs Chinese
  parsley, cut into
  2-inch lengths

1 After fish is in steamer, prepare sauce. Set a heavy 2-quart saucepan over high heat. When hot, add 2 tablespoons of oil. Flavor oil with ginger for 20 seconds, then discard. Sizzle in the wine and immediately add the stock, ham, salt and pepper, and sugar. Turn heat to low and bring gradually to a boil.

2 When fish is done, remove from steamer and place on a warmed serving platter. Stream tapioca mixture into sauce and stir until thickened. Add egg whites, stirring until sauce turns white, then glaze with remaining oil and the sesame oil. Pour sauce over fish and garnish with parsley.

VARIATION: White-Cooked Whole Fish

If the fish weighs over 2 pounds, it is better to white-cook it than to steam it. The ideal utensil is a French fish poacher. It is oblong in shape and has a rack with handles for easy lifting (see diagram). To white-cook, add enough water to cover the fish. Bring water to a boil over high heat, then drop in 3 to 4 slices of gingerroot. Meanwhile, grease the rack and place the fish on it. Lower rack into the water, cover poacher, and turn off heat. In about 15 minutes (allow 7 to 8 minutes for each pound of fish), when a chopstick can go through the thickest part easily, the fish is done. Lift rack from the water and gently slip the fish onto an oval serving platter. Prepare one of the sauces, and pour it over the fish and serve.

Other utensils such as an oval roasting pan or a wok will suit the same purpose but manipulating a cooked fish is extremely troublesome. The Chinese often use a bamboo liner (see diagram) and place the fish on it, which is then lowered into the boiling water in a wok or a roasting pan. When the fish is done, it is removed by lifting the bamboo liner and then transferring the fish carefully to the serving platter. Or you may use a piece of cheesecloth to wrap the fish and lift the cheesecloth and fish together from wok when done.

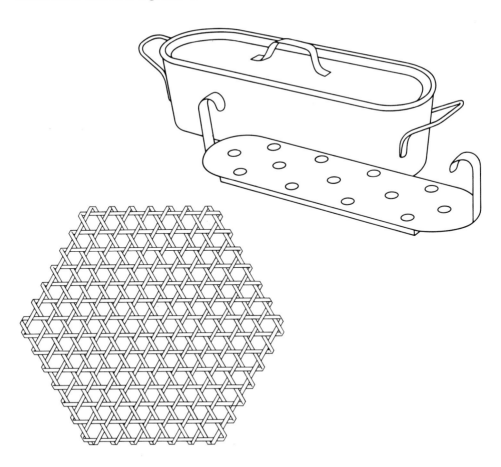

❀❀Fillet of Sole Roulade in White Sauce

Serves 4 as a main dish with rice, vegetables, and a minute soup, or 12 in a banquet

Time 30 minutes preparation
30 minutes chilling
15 minutes cooking

白 汁 魚 卷

This is a light dish made even lighter with an egg-white sauce.

Ingredients	Marinade	Sauce mixture
12 fillets of sole, about 1½ pounds	2 tablespoons oil	¼ teaspoon granulated sugar
2 scallions (white part only)	1 tablespoon tapioca powder	½ cup chicken stock
3 medium black mushrooms	1 teaspoon salt	2 teaspoons tapioca powder
4 slices bamboo shoots, each ⅛ inch thick and 2 by 3 inches	½ teaspoon granulated sugar	Salt
4 slices Smithfield ham, cut ⅛ inch thick, 2 by 1 inch	1 teaspoon ginger juice	
1 sprig Chinese parsley	1 teaspoon sesame oil	
2 egg whites	Dash of white pepper	
2 teaspoons water		
Tapioca powder		
2 tablespoons oil		
1 clove garlic, flattened		
1 tablespoon pale dry sherry		
1 teaspoon sesame oil		

PREPARATION

1 Pat fillets dry. Mix marinade ingredients in a bowl and add the fish. Mix well with your fingers.

2 Lightly pound the scallions with the back of a cleaver. Put scallions between fillets and chill for 30 minutes.

3 Soak mushrooms in warm water until soft. Trim the stems and squeeze caps to extract moisture. Cut each cap into ¼-inch strips.

4 Cut bamboo shoots into ⅜ by 2 by ⅛ inch strips.

5 Cut ham into same size strips as bamboo shoots.

6 Rinse parsley and break leaves off from stems.

7 Mix ingredients for sauce in a bowl and set aside.

8 Lightly beat the egg whites with the water. Set aside.

9 Put 1 strip each of bamboo shoots, ham, and mushrooms on the near end of each fish fillet. Roll it up and seal edge with tapioca powder. Arrange fish roulades, sealed edge down, in rows on a heatproof oblong serving platter.

COOKING

1 Steam the fish over high heat for 10 minutes. Remove from steamer and pour juices into a bowl.

2 Set a heavy 2-quart saucepan over high heat. When very hot, add the oil. Flavor oil with garlic for 10 seconds, then remove and discard garlic. Sizzle in the wine.

3 Restir sauce mixture and add to the pan, stirring constantly until bubbly. Turn heat to low and add fish juices to the sauce. Bring back to a boil. Whirl in the egg whites, then remove from the heat.

4 Glaze sauce with sesame oil, stirring to mix well, then pour sauce over fish. Garnish with parsley and serve immediately.

VARIATION: Deep-Fried Fillet of Sole Roulade

Assemble the fish roulades as in the master recipe but do not steam. Omit the sauce. Instead, wilt a bunch of scallion greens in boiling water and then run cold water over to stop the cooking process. Use 1 wilted green to tie each roulade around the center. Dip the roulade in egg white, then coat with cornstarch. Deep-fry in moderately hot oil (about 350 degrees) until golden. Serve with lemon wedges and five-spice salt (see page 193) in separate saucers.

◉◉Fillet of Fish in Tomato Sauce

Serves 2 with vegetable and rice as a
main dish, or 4 to 6 in a
multi-dish family meal

Time 10 to 15 minutes preparation
10 minutes cooking

茄 汁 魚 塊

This is a Westernized Cantonese dish, just as popular in Hong Kong as Sweet
and Sour Pork, yet much lighter and simpler.

Ingredients	Seasonings	Tomato sauce
1 pound fillets of fish (cod, red snapper, sole, etc.)	1 tablespoon pale dry sherry	½ cup chicken stock
2 whole scallions, green and white parts separated	Juice of 2 slices gingerroot	1 tablespoon red wine vinegar
1 egg white	¾ teaspoon salt	3 tablespoons catsup
Cornstarch for coating	Dash of white pepper	2 tablespoons brown sugar
4 cups + 1 tablespoon oil		2 teaspoons dark soy sauce
1 clove garlic, minced		1 tablespoon tapioca powder
1 tablespoon pale dry sherry		
2 teaspoons sesame oil		

PREPARATION

1 Pat fillets dry with paper towels. Lay flat on a cutting board and, with your
fingers, locate any bones and remove with a knife. Cut across the grain diagonally
into slices ¼ inch thick.

2 Combine the seasonings in a bowl and add the fish. Mix with your fingers.

3 With the flat side of a cleaver, lightly pound the scallion whites. Put them in
between the fish slices. Chop and reserve the greens.

4 Mix ingredients for tomato sauce in a bowl and set aside.

5 Remove the scallion whites from the fish, chop them fine and add to the greens.
Add the egg white to the fish and mix well. Coat each piece evenly with cornstarch and shake off the excess.

COOKING

1 Set a wok over high heat. When very hot, add 4 cups of oil. Wait for 5 minutes,
then test temperature by dropping a small piece of scallion green into the oil. If
bubbles appear around the green and the green sizzles and moves about quickly
in the oil, the oil is hot enough (about 350 degrees). Drop in the fish slices 1 at a
time and deep-fry until lightly golden. Remove and drain. Keep warm in the
oven.

2 Wipe wok clean and set again over high heat. When very hot add remaining tablespoon of oil. Flavor oil with garlic for 10 seconds, then sizzle in the sherry along the edge of the wok. Restir the tomato sauce and immediately add to the wok, stirring constantly. Turn heat to low.

3 When sauce thickens, glaze with sesame oil and add the fish and scallions. Mix together. Serve hot.

◉ Pan-Fried Fish Fillets

Serves 2 to 3 as a main dish with rice, vegetable, and a clear soup

Time 10 minutes preparation
1 hour chilling
20 minutes cooking

This is one of the best ways to handle frozen fish the Chinese way.

Ingredients	Seasoning	Sauce mixture
1 pound fresh or frozen fish fillets (cod or turbot)	1 egg white	⅓ cup chicken stock
	1 tablespoon light soy sauce	2 teaspoons light soy sauce
2 scallions (white part only)	1 tablespoon pale dry sherry	¼ teaspoon salt
Flour for coating	Juice of 2 slices gingerroot	1 teaspoon granulated sugar
1 whole egg + 1 egg yolk	⅛ teaspoon white pepper	
¼ cup oil	2 teaspoons sesame oil	
1 tablespoon pale dry sherry	½ teaspoon granulated sugar	

PREPARATION

1 If using frozen fillets, thaw them first, then pat dry with paper towels. Cut fish into pieces about 2½ by 1½ inches.

2 Combine the seasonings in a bowl. Add the fish pieces and mix well with your fingers.

3 Flatten the scallions with the back of a cleaver. Put slices between the fish pieces and keep fish refrigerated for at least 1 hour.

4 Mix ingredients for sauce and set aside.

5 Remove scallions from the fish and then lightly coat each piece with flour. Arrange pieces on a platter in 1 layer.

6 Beat whole egg and egg yolk together in a bowl.

COOKING

1 Set a heavy skillet over high heat. When very hot, add the oil. Dip fish pieces 1 at a time into the egg mixture, then into the oil in quick succession. When the fish has browned on 1 side, turn to brown on other side.

2 Sizzle in the wine and immediately add the sauce mixture. Turn the heat to medium and cover the skillet. Cook about 1 minute, or until the sauce has evaporated. Serve hot.

⊛Oil-Poured Fish Chunks

Serves   2 as a main dish with rice,
vegetables, and a thick soup
Time   5 to 10 minutes preparation
7 minutes cooking

油 泡 魚 球

Fish fillets tend to break easily after heating, thus are not suitable for regular stir-frying. The hot oil dip in this recipe seals the natural juices rapidly, giving the fish chunk a tender texture.

Ingredients
12 ounces fillet of cod,
  snapper, or ocean
  perch (with skin on)
2 whole scallions,
  trimmed
½ teaspoon salt
2 cups oil
1 clove garlic, sliced
2 slices gingerroot
1 tablespoon pale dry
  sherry
1 teaspoon sesame oil

Sauce mixture
3 tablespoons chicken
  stock
1 teaspoon oyster sauce
1 teaspoon light soy
  sauce
½ teaspoon granulated
  sugar
⅛ teaspoon white
  pepper
2 teaspoons tapioca
  powder

PREPARATION

1 Wipe the fillets with a dampened towel. Cut them lengthwise into 1-inch strips, then into 1½-inch chunks. Chill until ready to use.

2 Mix ingredients for sauce in a small bowl. Set aside.

3 Cut scallions into 1-inch lengths.

4 Remove fish from refrigerator and sprinkle salt evenly over. Mix well.

COOKING

1 Set a wok over high heat. When very hot, add the oil. Wait for about 4 to 5 minutes, then test temperature by dropping in a piece of scallion green. If bubbles appear and the green moves about and soon turns brown in the oil, oil is ready (about 375 degrees).

---

2 Add the fish chunks to the hot oil, stirring rapidly just a few times around the wok. Pour oil and fish together into a strainer-lined bowl to drain, leaving about 1 tablespoon of oil in the wok.

3 Reset the wok over high heat. When hot, add the garlic, ginger, and scallions to flavor the oil. Immediately sizzle in the wine, add the sauce mixture, and stir until bubbly.

4 Return fish to wok and stir once. Remove wok from heat and glaze fish with sesame oil. Serve very hot.

◉Vinegar-Slipped Fish Chunks

Serves 3 as a main dish with rice and vegetables
Time   7 to 10 minutes preparation
1 hour chilling
5 minutes cooking

This is a North China dish. The fish is "slipped" through the vinegar sauce, to be glazed by it, with the fresh taste still intact.

Ingredients	**Marinade**	**Vinegar sauce**
1 pound fillet of cod, red snapper, or sole	2 egg whites	¾ cup chicken stock
2 scallions, white and green parts separated	2 tablespoons tapioca powder	2 tablespoons red rice vinegar
3 cups oil	1 tablespoon pale dry sherry	2 tablespoons granulated sugar
1 clove garlic, crushed	¾ teaspoon salt	2 teaspoons tapioca powder
1 tablespoon pale dry sherry	Juice from 2 slices ginger	¼ teaspoon salt
2 teaspoons sesame oil		

PREPARATION

1 Rinse the fish and pat dry with paper towels. Remove any bones, then cut fillets lengthwise into strips about 1 inch wide. Cut each strip into chunks about 1 by 1½ inches. Put fish in a large bowl.

2 Mix ingredients for marinade and add to fish. Use your fingers to mix well.

3 Cut scallion whites into 4-inch lengths, then flatten with a cleaver. Put them between the fish chunks and chill for at least 1 hour.

4 Chop the scallion greens very fine and set aside.

5 Mix ingredients for sauce in a small bowl and set aside.

6 Before cooking, remove scallion whites from fish and chop fine. Combine whites with scallion greens.

COOKING

1 Set a wok over high heat. When very hot, add the oil. Wait about 4 to 5 minutes, then test the temperature by dropping a piece of scallion green into the oil. If the green sizzles and soon turns brown, the oil is ready, about 375 degrees.

2 Add the fish chunks to the oil, lightly stirring in a spading manner to separate (about 30 seconds). Pour fish and oil together into a bowl lined with a strainer to drain, leaving about 1 tablespoon of oil in the wok.

3 Replace wok over high heat. When very hot, add the garlic, stirring 10 seconds. Sizzle in the wine along the edge of the wok, then add the sauce mixture. Turn heat to low and stir sauce until thickened.

4 Glaze sauce with sesame oil, then slip in the fish chunks. Add the chopped scallions and mix together. Correct seasoning, then serve.

⊚⊚Fish Paste

Yields	2 cups	
Time	20 minutes preparation	
	1 hour chilling	

Just as versatile as Hundred-Flower Paste (page 161), fish paste is much easier to prepare and yet is only about a quarter of the cost. In Cantonese home cooking, the paste is made of freshwater fish. In America, saltwater fish is commonly used.

Ingredients

1 pound firm fish
  fillets (cod, sea bass,
  red snapper, or
  perch)

1 teaspoon salt
⅛ cup water

PREPARATION

1 Rinse fish fillets. Pat dry with paper towels. Lay 1 piece of fish flat on a cutting board with the inside up. Press the smaller end with the fingers of your hand, while the other hand holds a cleaver to scrape flesh out. The fish will be a mash and you will have a thin red layer at the bottom of the fillet.

2 Put the fish mash into a large mixing bowl and discard the red layer. Finish scraping the remaining fillets.

3 Dissolve the salt in the water and add to the fish in a gradual stream, stirring with chopsticks or a wooden spoon in 1 direction until the mash holds together as a paste.

3 Scoop up the paste with your hand and beat it back to the bowl several times until it is elastic. Chill for at least 1 hour to firm. Use as specified in recipes.

Note: A heavy-duty electric mixer with a paddle can help in the beating process. The paste turns out more elastic and firmer.

◉◉Chrysanthemum Fish Balls

Yields	2 dozen balls for an appetizer in a multi-dish family meal or as an hors d'oeuvre in a cocktail party
Time	30 minutes preparation 1 hour chilling 10 minutes cooking

炸菊花魚球

This is a specialty from Phoenix City. When chrysanthemums are in full bloom during autumn, the petals are often used to mix with the fish paste.

Ingredients

2 tablespoons dried shrimp
½ cup hot water
¼ cup pine nuts
1 large white football mum (optional)
1 tablespoon salt dissolved in 4 cups water
2 scallions (white part only)
2 sprigs Chinese parsley

2 Chinese pork sausages
Fish paste made from 1 pound of fillets (page 145), not chilled
4 cups oil
½ head iceberg lettuce, shredded

Seasonings

⅛ teaspoon white pepper
1 teaspoon sesame oil
½ teaspoon granulated sugar
1 tablespoon tapioca powder

PREPARATION

1 Soak dried shrimp in hot water for 30 minutes. Chop finely.

2 Put pine nuts in a heavy 1-quart saucepan, and set it over medium heat. Stir nuts constantly until light golden. Chop finely.

3 Shake mum in salted water to rinse. Break off the petals. Pat dry with kitchen towel.

4 Chop the scallions, parsley, and sausages finely.

5 Fold seasonings, nuts, chrysanthemum petals, scallions, sausages, and parsley into fish paste. Mix together with fish paste and chill at least 1 hour to firm.

COOKING

1 Set a wok over high heat. When very hot, add the oil. Wait for about 5 minutes, then test the temperature by dropping in a piece of scallion green. If bubbles appear around the green and it sizzles, the oil is moderately hot (about 325 degrees). Turn heat to medium.

2 Scoop up a handful of the fish paste and squeeze it up through your fist until it reaches the size of a walnut. Dip a spoon into some fresh oil to grease it and use it

to scrape off the fish ball, then drop fish ball into the hot oil. Make half of the fish balls and deep-fry in 1 batch until golden. Remove and drain on paper towels.

3 Finish forming the remaining balls and deep-fry. Drain as before.

4 Serve fish balls on shredded lettuce.

⊛⊛Braised Fish-Stuffed Eggplants

Serves	4 to 6 in a multi-dish family meal
Time	30 minutes preparation
	1 hour chilling
	15 minutes cooking

魚 肉 釀 茄 子

The following is another homecooking favorite, easy to make and quite presentable. The long Chinese eggplants are often called Japanese eggplants here in the United States. They are better because, pound for pound, they have fewer seeds and more skin than the bulb-shaped Italian ones, and they maintain their shape better after braising.

Ingredients
¼ cup dried shrimp
⅔ cup hot water
2 scallions, green and white parts separated
1 pound firm fish fillets (cod, sea bass, snapper, perch or pike)
1 medium Italian eggplant or 4 Chinese eggplants, about 1½ pounds
Cornstarch
5 tablespoons oil
1½ teaspoons tapioca powder mixed with 1 tablespoon chicken stock

Seasonings
⅛ teaspoon white pepper
1 teaspoon sesame oil
½ teaspoon granulated sugar
1 tablespoon tapioca powder

Braising sauce
1 cup chicken stock
1 tablespoon oyster sauce
1 tablespoon dark soy sauce
2 teaspoons granulated sugar
1 tablespoon pale dry sherry
1 teaspoon sesame oil

PREPARATION

1 Soak dried shrimp in hot water until soft. Chop finely; reserve soaking liquid.

2 Chop the white and green parts of the scallions separately.

3 Prepare the fish paste, following the instructions on page 145. Before chilling, mix in the shrimp, scallion whites, and seasonings and beat the paste back to the bowl a few more times. Chill for at least 1 hour to firm.

4 Trim stem from Italian eggplant and cut in half. Lay half flat on a cutting board with the skin side up, and cut and discard about 1 inch off both ends. Vertically cut the piece into ¾-inch slices. (If using Chinese eggplants, vertical slope-cut to obtain larger pieces.) Make a slit in the middle of each slice and cut two-thirds of the way down, forming a double layered slice with the skin side not cut through all the way. Gently open up the double layer and brush the inside surface lightly with cornstarch. Slice and brush the remaining half the same way, noting that they are not uniform in size but in thickness only.

5 For each piece of eggplant, stuff about 1 tablespoon or more of the fish paste between 2 layers, pressing with your fingers to help the fish paste adhere to the eggplant. Smooth the stuffing along the opening with a moistened knife.

COOKING

1 Set a skillet over high heat. When very hot, add 3 tablespoons of oil, spreading it evenly over the bottom. Place the stuffed eggplant pieces skin side up in the skillet and pan-fry over medium heat until brown. Turn and brown on the other sides (only the skin side is not pan-fried), adding a tablespoon of oil to the skillet each time the pieces are turned.

2 Mix ingredients for braising sauce and add the reserved shrimp soaking liquid. Pour the sauce into the skillet and cover. Cook for 4 to 5 minutes or until most of the liquid is absorbed and the eggplant is soft.

3 Restir the tapioca mixture and add it to the skillet, stirring until thickened. Sprinkle the chopped scallion greens on top and serve hot.

VARIATION: Stuffed Eggplant with Minced Pork
Prepare half the recipe for Pearly Balls (page 276) as a substitute for the fish paste. Stuff and pan-fry the eggplant pieces in the same manner, but allow 3 or 4 more minutes for braising.

VARIATION: Sichuan Stuffed Eggplant
This version uses a fish-flavored braising sauce.

Ingredients
½ pound lean ground pork
3 Chinese long eggplants, or 1 medium Italian eggplant, about 1 pound
2 scallions (white part only)
4 slices gingerroot
2 cloves garlic
2 whole eggs
⅛ teaspoon salt
Cornstarch for coating
4 cups + 1 tablespoon oil
1 teaspoon sesame oil

Seasonings
¼ teaspoon salt
1 tablespoon light soy sauce
1 teaspoon pale dry sherry
½ teaspoon granulated sugar
1 teaspoon grated gingerroot
2 teaspoons tapioca powder
1 tablespoon chopped scallion
1 teaspoon sesame oil

Braising sauce
½ cup chicken stock
1 tablespoon Sichuan hot bean paste
1 tablespoon dark soy sauce
1 tablespoon red rice vinegar
1 tablespoon brown sugar

PREPARATION

1 In a large mixing bowl, combine the pork with the salt and soy sauce for the seasonings. Mix with your fingers and scoop up the pork mixture with your hand, beating it back into the bowl several times until firm. Add the remaining seasonings and mix well, beating several more times.

2 Follow the instructions for the master recipe regarding the cutting and stuffing of the eggplant pieces.

3 Chop the scallions, ginger, and garlic and put together in a small bowl. Set aside.

4 Mix the ingredients for the braising sauce in a bowl and set aside.

5 About 10 minutes before cooking, beat the eggs with the salt until smooth. Dip each piece of stuffed eggplant into the egg mixture, then coat with cornstarch. Shake off excess cornstarch.

6 Set a wok over high heat. When hot, add the 4 cups of oil. Wait 5 minutes, then test the temperature by dropping in a small piece of scallion green; if bubbles appear around the green, and the piece moves in the oil and begins to turn brown, the oil is ready (about 375 degrees).

7 Add the eggplant pieces in succession to the oil and deep-fry until the coating is set, then remove. Reheat oil to very hot and return all the eggplant pieces to the oil. Deep-fry until golden, then remove and drain on paper towels.

8 Pour out the oil and wipe the wok clean. Set it again over high heat. When hot, add remaining tablespoon of oil. Stir in the scallions, ginger, and garlic, stirring for 1 minute. Restir the braising sauce and add to the wok. Bring to a boil, then put all the eggplant pieces into the wok and cook until the sauce is almost absorbed (about 3 minutes).

9 Glaze eggplant with sesame oil and serve hot.

SHELLFISH

Stir-Fried Shrimp

Serves 2 as a main dish with rice and
vegetables
Time 20 minutes preparation
2 hours chilling
5 minutes cooking

炒蝦

The secret of good stir-fried shrimp is making the shrimp crispy. Restaurants often do this by soaking them in baking soda, but it often leaves a strong, caustic taste and sometimes changes the texture. In this recipe, we offer a more effective way using salt and water alone.

Ingredients	Seasonings
1 pound shrimp in the shell	1 egg white
Salt	¾ teaspoon salt
2 scallions (white part only)	1 teaspoon sesame oil
	Dash of white pepper
3 tablespoons oil	1 tablespoon tapioca powder
1 clove garlic, crushed	¼ teaspoon granulated sugar
1 tablespoon pale dry sherry	

PREPARATION

1 Shell and devein the shrimp. Put shrimp in a colander and rub generously with table salt, then run cold water over to rinse.

2 Repeat the salting and rinsing process 1 more time. When the shrimp meat turns translucent, stop the rinsing. Drain.

3 Arrange shrimp meat, in 1 layer, on several layers of paper toweling. Pat dry, then roll the towels up into a jelly roll with the shrimp meat inside. Chill in refrigerator for at least 1 hour but don't keep more than 24 hours.

4 One hour before using the shrimp, mix the seasonings in a bowl. Add the shrimp and mix with your fingers to blend well. Chill again until it is used.

5 Cut scallions into 1-inch lengths.

COOKING

1 Set a wok over high heat and, when very hot, add the oil. Flavor oil with garlic and remove when brown. Add the shrimp, stirring and turning constantly until separated. The color will have turned pink.

2 Sizzle in the wine along the edge of the wok and then add the scallions, stirring to mix well. Remove to serve immediately or reserve for combining with stir-fried vegetables.

Stir-Fried Shrimp with Miniature Corn and Straw Mushrooms

Serves 4 with an all-meat dish and rice
Time 20 minutes preparation
2 hours chilling
5 minutes cooking

小玉米草菇炒蝦

This is just the ideal recipe to practice stir-frying with special Chinese vegetables.

Ingredients

1 pound shrimp in the shell
Salt
1 cup straw mushrooms
1 cup miniature corn
5 tablespoons oil
2 cloves garlic, 1 whole and 1 shredded
1 teaspoon chicken bouillon powder
2 slices gingerroot, shredded

1 tablespoon Chinese yellow wine
1 whole scallion, trimmed

Seasonings

1 egg white
1 tablespoon tapioca powder
½ teaspoon granulated sugar
1 teaspoon sesame oil
Dash of white pepper
¾ teaspon salt

PREPARATION

1 Shell and devein the shrimp. Put them in a colander and use about 2 tablespoons of salt to rub the meat against the sides of the colander. Run cold water over to rinse and repeat the salting, rubbing, and rinsing once more or until the color of the shrimp meat turns translucent (about 5 minutes). Drain thoroughly, then arrange the shrimp on paper towels to dry. Wrap and chill for at least 1 hour or until ready to use.

2 Blanch the mushrooms and the corn in boiling water for 1 minute. Drain and run under cold water to rinse.

3 About 1 hour before cooking, take shrimp out of refrigerator and put into a bowl. Add the seasonings. Mix with your fingers, then chill.

4 Cut scallion into 1-inch lengths.

COOKING

1 Set a wok over high heat. When very hot, add 2 tablespoons of oil. Flavor the oil with the whole garlic, then remove the garlic when it has browned. Add the

mushrooms and corn, and season with bouillon powder, stirring constantly for 2 minutes. Remove and reserve.

2 Rinse wok and set again over high heat. When very hot, add remaining 3 tablespoons of oil. Flavor oil with shredded garlic and ginger for 10 seconds, then add the shrimp, stirring constantly to separate. Whirl in the wine along the edge of the wok, then add the scallions and stir.

3 Return the corn and mushrooms to the wok and stir to mix well. Serve hot.

◉◉ Shrimp in Lobster Sauce

Serves 4 as a main dish with rice and
vegetables
Time 30 minutes preparation
1 hour chilling
5 minutes cooking

蝦龍糊

Τhis is very much a Chinese-American invention. The sauce, normally used for Lobster Cantonese Style, is served here with shrimp.

Ingredients
1 pound shrimp in the
shell
3 tablespoons
fermented black
beans
1 tablespoon pale dry
sherry
1 teaspoon granulated
sugar
2 slices gingerroot
4 ounces lean ground
pork
¼ cup oil
1 clove garlic, sliced, +
2 cloves, minced
1 tablespoon pale dry
sherry
2 eggs, lightly beaten
with 1 egg yolk
2 whole scallions,
chopped finely

Meat seasonings
1 teaspoon tapioca
powder
½ teaspoon sesame oil
1 tablespoon light soy
sauce
1 teaspoon pale dry
sherry
½ teaspoon granulated
sugar

Shrimp seasonings
1 egg white, lightly
beaten
1 tablespoon tapioca
powder
½ teaspoon salt

Sauce mixture
1 cup chicken stock
2 teaspoons tapioca
powder
1 teaspoon sesame oil

PREPARATION

1 Shell, devein, and clean shrimp (see page 151). Pat dry with paper towels. Chill until ready to use.

2 Rinse the black beans and put in a heatproof bowl with the wine, sugar, and ginger. Steam over medium heat for 20 minutes, then discard the ginger.

STUFFED CLAMS
PAGE 184

SPICY SOY SAUCE CHICKEN
PAGE 196

3 Combine the pork with the seasonings and mix well. Chill.

4 About 1 hour before cooking, remove the shrimp from the refrigerator and put into a bowl. Add egg white, mixing with your fingers, then add tapioca powder and salt. Mix again, and chill until ready to use.

5 Mix ingredients for sauce in a small bowl and set aside.

COOKING

1 Set a wok over high heat. When very hot, add the oil. Flavor the oil with garlic slices for 10 seconds, then add the shrimp, stirring constantly until separated and pink. Sizzle in the wine along the edge of the wok, stirring several times. Remove shrimp, leaving as much oil as possible in the wok.

2 Add minced garlic and black beans to the wok, stirring for 30 seconds. Add ground pork and stir until the pink color disappears.

3 Restir the sauce mixture and pour it gradually into the wok, stirring constantly to prevent lumps. When the sauce thickens, turn heat to low and whirl in the beaten eggs. Add the shrimp to the sauce and mix well. Add the scallions, mix, and serve.

◉ Clear-Fried Shrimp in Yellow Wine

Serves 4 with a meat and vegetable dish, a minute soup, and rice; or serves 8 in an informal banquet

Time 10 minutes preparation
1 hour, 30 minutes chilling
5 to 7 minutes cooking

黄酒蝦仁

This is a specialty from Zhejiang Province, the producer of the best yellow wine in East China.

Ingredients	Seasonings
1½ pounds shrimp in the shell	1 egg white
4 whole scallions	1 teaspoon salt
3 cups oil	1½ tablespoons tapioca powder
2 tablespoons yellow rice wine	1 teaspoon sesame oil
	Dash of white pepper

PREPARATION

1 Shell and devein the shrimp. Clean as described on page 151. Pat dry with paper towels and chill until ready to use.

2 About 30 minutes before cooking, combine the shrimp and seasonings in a bowl. Mix well with your fingers and chill.

3 Cut off about 4 inches of the green ends of the scallions and cut the remaining white portions into ½-inch lengths.

COOKING

1 Place a strainer over a bowl and set it within easy reach for oil-dipping.

2 Set a wok over high heat. When very hot, add the oil. Wait for about 4 minutes, then add the shrimp, stirring constantly until separated. Pour shrimp and oil into the strainer to drain, leaving about 1 tablespoon of oil in the wok.

3 Set wok again over high heat. When hot, add the scallions and stir for about 5 seconds. Return shrimp to wok, sizzle in the wine along the edge, and stir until liquid is evaporated. Remove and serve.

VARIATION: Hot and Spicy Shrimp

The added tang suggests that this dish be served with white rice. Follow the above recipe to prepare the shrimp to the point of draining the oil into a strainer-lined bowl. Prepare sauce, then stream in mixture after the shrimp is returned to the wok, stirring until the sauce thickens. Glaze with sesame oil and serve hot.

Sauce mixture

1 tablespoon Sichuan
  hot bean paste
2 teaspoons red rice
  vinegar
1 tablespoon brown
  sugar

2 tablespoons chicken
  stock
1 teaspoon tapioca
  powder
2 teaspoons sesame oil

VARIATION: Stir-Fried Yin-Yang Shrimp

Two styles of stir-fried shrimp served together for contrast of color and taste.

Hot and spicy sauce

1 tablespoon tomato
  catsup
1½ teaspoons Sichuan
  hot bean paste
1 teaspoon brown
  sugar

1 teaspoon red rice
  vinegar
1 teaspoon dark soy
  sauce
½ teaspoon tapioca
  powder

1 Mix together the catsup, bean paste, sugar, vinegar, soy sauce, and tapioca powder before oil-dipping the shrimp.

2 Follow the method given above for Clear-fried Shrimp and prepare and stir-fry the shrimp up to the point of sizzling in the wine.

3 Dish out only half the shrimp in the wok and arrange on 1 side of an oval platter. Push the remaining shrimp to the side, streaming the hot and spicy mixture into the center of the wok. Stir constantly until the sauce thickens.

4 Mix shrimp and sauce together and remove to other side of serving platter, forming a 2-colored dish. Serve hot.

◎◎◎ Emerald Shrimp

Serves	4 with a meat and vegetable dish, a minute soup, and rice; or serves 10 in a formal banquet
Time	15 minutes preparing shrimp 4 hours chilling 30 minutes preparing spinach paste 5 minutes cooking

翡 翠 蝦 仁

Usually one can tell whether something is animal, vegetable, or mineral, but not so readily with this conversation starter from East China, which is shrimp coated a bright emerald green after a spinach bubble bath.

Ingredients
1½ pounds medium shrimp in the shell
2 scallions (white part only)
1 ounce Smithfield ham
1 pound flat-leaf fresh spinach
2 cups water
3 cups oil
1 clove garlic
1 tablespoon light dry Puerto Rican rum

Seasonings
2 egg whites (small)
¾ teaspoon salt
1½ tablespoons tapioca powder
½ teaspoon sesame oil
½ teaspoon granulated sugar
Dash of white pepper

PREPARATION

1 Shell and devein the shrimp by cutting a slit about ⅓ inch deep along the back but not cut through. Clean as described on page 151. Pat thoroughly dry with paper towels. Arrange the shrimp in 1 layer on double paper towels. Roll shrimp up like a jelly roll and chill for at least 2 hours.

2 Roll-cut the scallions in ½-inch lengths. Slice the ham thinly, then cut to ½-inch cubes.

3 Rinse spinach thoroughly and break leaves off stems. You will need 4 cups altogether. (Use *only* fresh spinach. The stems can be reserved for stir-frying.)

4 Chop spinach leaves coarsely. Put them in a blender, adding 1 cup of water and beat at high speed until reduced to a purée. Pour the purée into a very fine mesh strainer which has been placed over a bowl. Press the puréed spinach against the wall of the strainer to extract liquid.

5 Transfer the spinach purée from the strainer to a bowl and thin it with remaining cup of water. Pour it through the strainer to combine liquid with the previously extracted spinach juice.

6 Add spinach juice to a 2-quart saucepan and set it over high heat. Attend watchfully. In about 2 minutes the juice will almost reach the boiling point. At this moment you will see small bubbles start to appear gradually along the sides of the pan until the liquid foams. Remove saucepan *immediately* from heat.

7 Set a coffee filter into a cone, then skim the spinach foam from the saucepan into the filter. Let it drain thoroughly, then gather the filter and squeeze to extract all liquid; you will have about 1 tablespoon of very fine spinach paste. Put paste in a small bowl, cover, and chill until ready to use. Discard the juice in pan.

8 Unroll the shrimp. Blot again with paper towel to ensure dryness, or else the green spinach coloring will not adhere. Put shrimp in a bowl and dredge in 1 teaspoon of the spinach paste, mixing it well by hand. Dredge shrimp in more spinach paste, ½ teaspoon at a time, mixing well after each addition until each shrimp is tinted evenly with green coloring. You will need at least 2 teaspoons of spinach paste but no more than 3 teaspoons. (Over-coloring should be avoided.)

9 In a small bowl, mix seasonings with a wire whisk until smooth. Add to the green shrimp, mixing well by hand until evenly coated. Wrap and chill for at least 2 hours.

COOKING

1 Have ready a strainer put over a bowl for oil-dipping.

2 Set a wok over high heat. When very hot, add about ¼ cup of the oil for dipping. Swish the oil around the wok to grease the surface, then pour oil out into the bowl. Add the remaining oil to wok and heat until hot (drop in a piece of scallion green; if it bubbles, sizzles, and moves around, oil is about 325 degrees and ready). Give the shrimp mixture a quick stir, then add the whole batch to the oil at once. Stir to separate shrimp quickly, about 20 seconds. Pour shrimp and oil into the strainer to drain oil, leaving about 1 tablespoon oil in wok.

3 Set wok back on high heat. Add garlic. Remove wok quickly from heat and let garlic cook in hot oil for 10 seconds, then discard. (This ensures the oil in wok is clear.)

4 Reset wok on high heat. Return the shrimp to wok, stirring 3 to 4 times around. Sizzle in the rum, stirring some more. Add scallion and ham pieces. Stir and serve immediately. Total stirring time should not exceed 30 seconds.

⊛ Pan-Fried Jumbo Shrimp

Serves 3 as a main dish with rice,
vegetables, and a clear soup
Time 10 minutes preparation
30 minutes chilling
5 minutes cooking

This is the most famous shrimp dish in Canton, made using a technique called dry pan-frying. The shrimp is deveined but not shelled, the better to pick up the pungent sauce.

Ingredients	Tomato sauce mixture	Hot sauce mixture
1 pound jumbo shrimp in the shell	½ cup chicken stock	½ cup chicken stock
1 teaspoon salt	3 tablespoons tomato catsup	1 tablespoon Sichuan hot bean paste
3 tablespoons oil	2 teaspoons granulated sugar	2 teaspoons dark soy sauce
1 tablespoon pale dry sherry	1 teaspoon tapioca powder	1 tablespoon brown sugar
4 scallions (white part only), shredded	1 teaspoon sesame oil	1 tablespoon red rice vinegar
4 slices gingerroot, shredded	Salt and pepper	1 teaspoon tapioca powder
1 clove garlic, minced		2 teaspoons sesame oil
1 teaspoon sesame oil		

PREPARATION

1 With a pair of sharp kitchen scissors, trim the tails and feet from the shrimp, if still on. Slit along the back to reveal the vein and remove it from each. Put shrimp in a colander and add salt, mixing together gently. Place a platter under the colander to catch drippings and keep refrigerated for 30 minutes.

2 Pat shrimp thoroughly dry.

3 Mix ingredients for either sauce.

COOKING

1 Set a heavy skillet over high heat. When hot, arrange the shrimp in 1 layer in the skillet, roasting 1 side until the shells turn red. Turn to the other side and roast until the moisture is evaporated.

2 Whirl in 2 tablespoons of oil and tilt skillet so that oil can run evenly in between the shrimp. Pan-fry both sides of the shrimp until brown.

3 Sizzle in the wine, stirring constantly, for 30 seconds. Push shrimp to the side and add remaining tablespoon of oil. Add scallions, ginger, and garlic, and stir for 10 seconds.

4 Add the sauce mixture of your choice, stirring until it boils. Cook the shrimp quickly until the sauce is reduced enough to just coat the shrimp. Glaze with sesame oil and serve hot.

Pepper and Salt Shrimp

Serves 5 to 6 as part of a multi-dish
family meal
Time 20 minutes preparation
30 minutes chilling
10 minutes cooking

椒盐蝦

The best-tasting part of this famous Hong Kong dish is the shell, and we recommend that you taste it.

Ingredients

1 pound shrimp in the
  shell
1 tablespoon salt
3 cups water
1½ tablespoons
  all-purpose flour
4 cups oil
2 cloves garlic, minced
¾ teaspoon salt
¼ teaspoon white
  pepper

PREPARATION

1 Trim the feet from the shrimp. Make a shallow cut about ⅛ inch deep into the meat near the tail to break the vein. Arrange the shrimp flat with its back up and locate the vein showing on the other end. Pull it out carefully. Repeat for others.

2 After all the shrimp have been deveined, soak them in salt water for 30 minutes in the refrigerator.

3 Rinse and drain shrimp, and arrange on paper towels; pat dry for immediate use, otherwise chill until ready to use but no longer than 8 hours.

4 Mix flour with shrimp to coat, then shake off excess.

COOKING

1 Have a bowl lined with a strainer ready for deep-frying the shrimp.

2 Set a wok over high heat. When hot, add the oil. Wait for about 6 or 7 minutes, or until a haze appears above the surface (about 400 degrees), and add all the shrimp, stirring constantly until most of the moisture is evaporated and the color of the shells turns red.

3 Pour the oil and shrimp together into the strainer, leaving about 1 tablespoon of oil in the wok.

4 Reheat the wok to very hot and add the garlic, stirring for 20 seconds. Return shrimp to wok and sprinkle with salt and pepper. Toss quickly until well mixed and serve immediately.

◉Oil-Blasted Shrimp

Serves 6 to 8 as part of a multi-dish
family meal, or on a cold
platter for a party
Time 30 minutes preparation
1 hour chilling
10 minutes cooking

This is a very popular appetizer of East China. The original recipe calls for freshwater shrimp, but Gulf shrimp serve just as well.

Ingredients

1 pound medium Gulf
 shrimp in the shell
2 tablespoons salt
3 tablespoons pale dry
 sherry
2 scallions (white part
 only)
4 slices gingerroot
4 cups oil
1 tablespoon
 granulated sugar
2 tablespoons dark soy
 sauce
1 teaspoon sesame oil

PREPARATION

1 Trim the feet from the shrimp. Devein and clean the shrimp as described on page 158, using 2 tablespoons salt. Be careful not to break the shells.

2 Drain and dry shrimp, then mix with 2 tablespoons of the sherry. Chill for 1 hour.

3 Mince the scallions and grate the ginger.

COOKING

1 Set wok over high heat. When very hot, add the oil. Wait for about 5 to 7 minutes or until a small piece of scallion green dropped in sizzles noisily and soon turns brown (about 375 degrees).

2 Add the shrimp, stirring constantly until the shells turn red. Continue to stir for 1 minute, then pour oil and shrimp together into a strainer-lined bowl to drain, leaving about 2 tablespoons of oil in the wok.

3 Reset wok over high heat. When hot, add the scallions and ginger, stirring for 30 seconds. Return shrimp to wok and sizzle in the remaining sherry.

4 Add the sugar, then the soy sauce, stirring again. Glaze with sesame oil and serve, either hot or cold.

◉◉Shrimp Bunnies

Makes 16
Time 40 minutes preparation
30 minutes soaking
30 minutes chilling
10 minutes cooking

玉 兔 蝦

The delicate taste and firm texture of fried shrimp is enhanced by the embedded pieces of Chinese sausage. The tails of the shrimp become bunny ears, to be held by finger-happy nibblers. Techniques for shaping are shown on pages 76–77.

Ingredients	Seasonings
16 large shrimp in the shell	2 egg whites
4 cups water	1 teaspoon sesame oil
2 tablespoons salt	2 tablespoons cornstarch
2 Chinese sausages	Dash of white pepper
16 red toothpicks, broken in half	1 teaspoon brandy
4 cups oil	½ teaspoon salt
	½ teaspoon granulated sugar

PREPARATION

1 Shell the shrimp but leave the tails on. Cut deeply down the back along the vein of each and devein. Soak in salt water for 30 minutes in the refrigerator. Drain and rinse with cold running water, then lay flat on paper towels to dry.

2 Steam the sausages for 20 minutes, then cut each into 2-inch lengths. Divide each length into 4 equal strips for a total of 16 strips.

3 Combine the seasonings in a mixing bowl and beat with a wire whisk until smooth. Add the shrimp and chill for 30 minutes.

ASSEMBLING

1 Place a shrimp with the split side down on a cutting board. Flatten it with the blunt edge of a cleaver, then put a piece of sausage on the near edge.

2 Roll the shrimp toward the tail, but keep the tail open like the ears of a bunny. Secure with 2 toothpick halves as eyes.

COOKING

Set a wok over high heat. When hot, add the oil. Wait for about 6 or 7 minutes, then test the temperature of the oil by dropping a small piece of scallion green into the oil. If the green sizzles noisily and turns brown soon, it is hot enough (about 375 degrees). Drop in the shrimp bunnies in succession. Deep-fry until golden brown, then drain on paper towels. Serve hot.

Note: The bunnies can be assembled ahead of time. Wrap and chill until ready to cook.

Shrimp Paste (Hundred Flower Paste)

Makes 1½ cups shrimp paste
Time 30 minutes preparation
5 hours chilling

百 花 膠

Fifty years ago, one of the four greatest dishes in Canton was South China Hundred Flower Chicken, which was shrimp paste stuffed under chicken skin. At least since then, the crisp, firm shrimp paste has been called the Hundred Flower Paste, and it is found as a stuffing for all kinds of dishes.

Relatively uncomplicated, this shrimp paste is used frequently in homecooking also. The old Chinese mincing technique is contrasted here with the labor-saving appliances. I get best results with a mixer.

Ingredients

1¼ pounds shrimp in
  the shell
¾ teaspoon salt
2 egg whites (small)
1 tablespoon tapioca
  powder

1 teaspoon sesame oil
1 teaspoon pale dry
  sherry
Dash of white pepper

PREPARATION

Shell and devein the shrimp. Clean with salt (see page 151), then pat dry with paper towels. Chill for 2 hours, or up to 8 hours.

BY HAND

1 Cut shrimp meat coarsely into ½-inch pieces. Take about ¼ cup at a time and spread it on a chopping board (place shrimp close to the near edge of the board for ease in mashing). Hold the cleaver flat with 1 hand while the other palm presses down on the cleaver and moves horizontally from one side to the other. Mash the shrimp meat underneath while moving along, then finish mashing the remaining shrimp meat in the same manner. Put shrimp in a large mixing bowl.

2 Add salt to shrimp, stirring with a wooden spoon or chopsticks in 1 direction until the mixture is elastic. Then add egg whites, 1 at a time, stirring again in 1 direction until blended in. Add the tapioca powder, sesame oil, sherry, and pepper, stirring again. Scoop up the shrimp mixture by the hand and beat it back to the bowl. Repeat this scooping and beating process until the paste becomes elastic (about 5 minutes). Chill until firm, about 3 hours.

BY BLENDER

Cut the shrimp meat coarsely and put it into a blender. Add the salt and egg whites first, and beat at high speed for 30 seconds, then add the remaining seasonings. Beat another 30 seconds, then scrape mixture into a bowl. Chill in refrigerator until firm, about 3 hours.

BY MIXER

Mash the shrimp meat by hand with a cleaver, then put it into the mixing bowl of a heavy-duty electric mixer with a paddle. Add the salt, egg whites, then seasonings in succession. Beat at high speed until elastic, then chill for 3 hours to firm.

⊚⊚ Deep-Fried Shrimp Balls

Yields about 20 shrimp balls
Time approximately 30 minutes
preparation
2 hours chilling
10 minutes cooking

炸蝦丸

This is originally a dish from Chaozhou, east of Canton. It makes a fine main dish, also a wonderful appetizer or party snack.

Ingredients

2 ounces pork fatback
2 tablespoons
  Smithfield ham
8 water chestnuts
2 scallions (white part
  only)

1 sprig Chinese parsley
Shrimp Paste (page.
  161), made from 1¼
  pounds shrimp
1 egg yolk
4 cups oil

PREPARATION

1 Blanch fatback in boiling water until transparent. Soak it in ice water until firm, then chop as fine as mung beans.

2 Chop the ham finely.

3 Rinse water chestnuts well with hot water. Pat dry with paper towels, then chop finely.

4 Follow instructions on page 161 to prepare the shrimp paste. Add the pork fat, water chestnuts, and ham, stirring with a wooden spoon in 1 direction* until the ingredients hold together. Scoop up the shrimp mixture with your hand and beat it back to the bowl until elastic. Chill for about 2 hours.

COOKING

1 Set a wok over high heat. When hot, add the oil. Wait for about 5 to 7 minutes, then test the temperature by dropping in a piece of scallion green. If the green sizzles noisily and it soon turns brown, the oil is ready (about 375 degrees).

---

* **Note:** Stirring the shrimp paste in 1 direction creates an evenness of texture and eliminates the air spaces in the mixture. The result is a nearly homogeneous elastic mixture. Do not change directions in stirring, for that would create rough spots with pockets of air, undoing earlier work.

2 Scoop up a handful of the shrimp paste and squeeze it up through your fist until it reaches the size of a walnut. Scrape it off with a spoon greased with oil and drop it into the hot oil.

3 Finish shaping the shrimp balls, then turn heat under wok to medium. Deep-fry the balls until all rise to the surface. Drain on paper towels.

VARIATION: Deep-Fried Crispy Shrimp Balls

Essentially this is the previous recipe with the diameter of the shrimp balls expanded to fully 2 inches through the use of bread cubes. It never fails to attract favorable comments.

Ingredients
1 loaf (1 pound) white
  sandwich bread, 2 or
  3 days old
1 batch shrimp ball
  paste
6 cups oil

1 Trim edges from the bread and cut into ⅜-inch cubes. Spread cubes on a platter.

2 Follow instructions for making shrimp balls and roll them in the bread cubes, making sure to pat cubes evenly on the surface of the balls.

3 Deep-fry the balls as instructed and serve as an appetizer.

VARIATION: Poached Shrimp Balls in Clear Soup

Much lighter and more delicate in taste than the deep-fried version, this dish must be served directly from kitchen to table.

Ingredients
1 batch shrimp ball
  paste
3 cups diluted chicken
  stock (½ stock and
  ½ water)

1 When making shrimp balls, omit the water chestnuts, pork fat, and ham. Do not chop parsley, but rather cut it into 1-inch lengths.

2 Bring diluted stock to a simmer and keep over low heat. Scoop up a handful of the shrimp paste and squeeze it up through your fist, until it reaches the size of a walnut. Scrape it off with a wet spoon and drop the shrimp balls, 1 by 1, into the stock and cook slowly until the balls float to the surface.

3 If served as a soup, correct the seasonings and garnish with parsley. If used to cook with other ingredients, remove balls with a strainer and reserve the cooking liquid as a stock.

VARIATION: Stir-Fried Shrimp Balls with Mixed Vegetables

Ingredients
1 batch shrimp ball
  paste
4 ounces snow peas
1 cup straw
  mushrooms
3 tablespoons oil
1 clove garlic, sliced
½ teaspoon chicken
  bouillon powder
2 teaspoons sesame oil
Salt

Sauce mixture
¼ cup shrimp stock,
  from Poached
  Shrimp Balls in
  Clear Soup
2 teaspoons light soy
  sauce
1 teaspoon oyster sauce
2 teaspoons tapioca
  powder
½ teaspoon granulated
  sugar

1 teaspoon sesame oil
Dash of white pepper

1 Follow instructions to prepare the poached shrimp balls. Cut each ball in half and set aside.

2 String the peas. Rinse and drain.

3 Blanch the mushrooms in boiling water for 1 minute. Rinse with cold water and drain.

4 Mix ingredients for sauce in a bowl.

5 Set a wok over high heat. When very hot, add 2 tablespoons of oil. Flavor oil with garlic for 15 seconds, then add pea pods, stirring for 1 minute. Remove peas from wok.

6 Add remaining tablespoon of oil to wok. Stir-fry the mushrooms for 1 minute; season with bouillon powder.

7 Restir the sauce mixture and stream it into the center of the wok, stirring constantly until thickened. Add the shrimp ball halves, pea pods, and stir. Test for salt. Glaze with sesame oil and serve hot.

⊚⊚⊚ Steamed Shrimp Roll

Serves 10 to 12 as part of a cold
        platter for a banquet
Time   approximately 45 minutes
        preparation
        1 hour chilling
        20 minutes cooking

蒸蝦卷

This is an eye-appealing dish with the pink of the shrimp balanced by the yellow of the egg spiral and the green of the Chinese parsley. It has a clean, fresh taste, with just the right amount of chewiness. Techniques for shaping are shown on pages 71–82.

Ingredients

1¼ pounds shrimp in
  the shell
Tapioca powder
2 teaspoons water
2 whole eggs
⅛ teaspoon salt
2 sprigs Chinese
  parsley

PREPARATION

1 Follow the instructions on page 161 for preparing the Hundred Flower Paste. Chill until ready to use.

2 Mix 1 teaspoon of tapioca powder with the water and add the eggs and salt. Beat with chopsticks or a wire whisk until light but not foamy.

3 Brush the bottom surface of a 9-inch nonstick skillet evenly with oil. Set over medium heat for 1 minute, then pour in the egg mixture, spreading with a spatula to cover the entire surface. When egg sets and the sides detach from the skillet, remove carefully to lay browned side down on a piece of aluminum foil, 12 by 8 inches.

4 Rinse the parsley and remove the stems.

ASSEMBLING

1 With a pastry brush, dust tapioca powder lightly on the egg sheet. Spread the shrimp paste on in 1 layer, with the upper and lower edges much thinner than the center.

2 Smooth the surface with a moistened spatula, then arrange about 20 parsley leaves over the paste.

3 Roll the egg sheet in jelly roll fashion and dust the rolled-up surface with tapioca powder. Roll the foil in the same direction to wrap the shrimp roll securely. Chill for at least 1 hour.

COOKING

1 Set a steamer over high heat and bring the water in the base to a boil. Add the shrimp rolls and steam for 20 minutes. Remove the foil and chill in the refrigerator until cool.

2 Just before serving, slice the shrimp roll vertically into ⅜-inch pieces and serve cold.

◉◉◉Crispy Shrimp Roll

Yields about 16 rolls
Time 1 hour preparation
2 hours chilling
20 minutes cooking

脆皮蝦卷

This is a delightful appetizer or main dish: eye-pleasing, delicious, and easy to make. The shrimp paste and the Chinese parsley flavor are especially Cantonese; the sandwich bread is a compromise for the original Cantonese Flat Bread (see also page 412). The techniques for shaping are shown on pages 82–83.

Ingredients

1¼ pounds shrimp in
 the shell
1 loaf (1 pound) white
 sandwich bread
2 slices cooked ham,
 about 4 ounces

2 sprigs Chinese
 parsley
Cornstarch for coating
1 egg yolk
5 cups oil

PREPARATION

1 Follow the recipe on page 161 to prepare the shrimp paste. Chill for 2 hours.

2 Cut all the edges off each piece of bread. Roll the slices hard with a rolling pin to yield very thin slices.

3 Cut the ham into strips about ¼ by ¼ by 3 inches.

4 Rinse the parsley and remove the stems.

ASSEMBLING

1 Spread the shrimp paste on the pressed bread slices, covering three-fourths of the surface of each. Leave the far end uncovered. Place a few parsley leaves on the shrimp paste, then put a strip of ham crosswise, close to the near edge.

2 Roll each slice securely into a cylinder and seal the edge with egg yolk. Lightly coat each roll with cornstarch and shake off the excess.

COOKING

1 Heat oil in a wok over medium heat for 10 minutes. Test the temperature by dropping a piece of parsley leaf into the oil. If it sizzles and soon moves about, the oil is ready, about 350 degrees.

2 Add the shrimp rolls in succession and deep-fry until light golden. Remove to drain on paper towels.

3 Cut each roll into three 1-inch cylinders. Arrange pieces, cut side up, on a serving platter and serve hot.

VARIATION: Shrimp Toast or Sesame Shrimp Toast

After trimming the edges, cut the bread on the diagonal into 4 equal triangles. Spread the shrimp paste on top of each triangle and decorate with parsley leaf (or coat with sesame seeds). Deep-fry as you would for the rolls until golden. Makes about 32 shrimp toast.

◉◉Crab Foo Yung

Serves 3 as a luncheon dish with
vegetables or salad
Time 10 minutes preparation
30 minutes soaking
15 minutes cooking

This dish clearly differs from the Cantonese version, but it is not necessarily inferior. A major advantage of this recipe is that the foo yung can be pan-fried in advance, then warmed in the oven. A pouring of hot sauce on top and it is ready for the table.

Many Chinese-American restaurants use bean sprouts. This adds to the texture, but it introduces excess water, requiring then the use of starchy absorbents. We suggest bamboo shoots instead.

Ingredients	Seasonings	Sauce mixture
6 ounces cooked crabmeat	1 tablespoon pale dry sherry	½ cup chicken stock
6 medium black mushrooms	⅛ teaspoon white pepper	1 tablespoon oyster sauce
¾ cup warm water	¼ teaspoon salt	1 tablespoon tapioca powder
1 cup bamboo shoots	½ teaspoon granulated sugar	2 teaspoons light soy sauce
2 whole scallions	1 teaspoon sesame oil	1 teaspoon granulated sugar
2 sprigs Chinese parsley	**Egg mixture**	Dash of white pepper
6 tablespoons oil	6 whole eggs	
1 clove garlic, flattened	1 tablespoon cornstarch	
¼ teaspoon salt	1 tablespoon water	
1 teaspoon granulated sugar	2 tablespoons oil	
1 teaspoon sesame oil	½ teaspoon salt	

PREPARATION

1 Lightly flake the crabmeat and mix with the seasonings. Keep refrigerated until ready to use.

2 Soak mushrooms in warm water for 30 minutes or until soft. Trim the stems and squeeze moisture from caps. Shred as fine as possible. Reserve soaking liquid.

3 Shred bamboo shoots into strips about ⅛ by ⅛ by 1½ inches. Blanch in boiling water for 1 minute. Rinse with cold water and drain. Pat dry with paper towels.

4 Rinse and cut scallions into 2-inch lengths. Shred finely.

5 Rinse and break parsley into 2-inch lengths.

6 Combine ingredients for egg mixture in a mixing bowl and beat until light, but not foamy, using a wire whisk. Add scallion shreds and parsley.

COOKING

1 Set a square-shaped nonstick skillet over high heat. When hot, add 2 tablespoons oil. Flavor oil with garlic and remove garlic when brown. Add mushrooms, stir, then add bamboo shoots. Season with salt and sugar, then keep stirring for 1 minute. Remove to mix with crabmeat, then combine with the egg mixture.

2 Rinse skillet and wipe dry. Set again over high heat. When hot, add 2 more tablespoons of oil. Turn heat to medium high and spread oil to coat the surface evenly. Use a regular ladle and drop the foo yung mixture into the corners of the skillet, 1 ladleful at a time. Pan-fry 3 foo yungs in 1 batch. When the bottom sides are brown, turn to brown on other side. Remove to serving platter.

3 Add 2 more tablespoons of oil and pan-fry the remaining 3 foo yungs. Add the last batch to the first.

4 Mix ingredients for the sauce and add reserved mushroom soaking liquid. Add sauce to the skillet, stirring constantly until bubbly and thickened.

5 Glaze sauce with sesame oil, pour over foo yungs, and serve.

⊛ Asparagus in Crab Sauce

Serves 4 with an all-meat dish and
rice, or 10 to 12 in a banquet
Time 15 minutes preparation
15 minutes cooking

蟹 扒 黎 筍

This sauce can also be used on Chinese mustard greens, celery cabbage, straw mushrooms, broccoli, and many other vegetables.

Ingredients

2 pounds asparagus
2 tablespoons
Smithfield ham
2 egg whites
1 tablespoon water
6 tablespoons oil
2 cloves garlic, 1
crushed and 1 whole
1 teaspoon salt
1 teaspoon sugar

¼ cup chicken stock
2 teaspoons pale dry
sherry
6 ounces crabmeat
1½ tablespoons tapioca
powder mixed with 2
tablespoons water
1 teaspoon sesame oil

Sauce mixture

1 cup chicken stock
½ teaspoon granulated
sugar
Dash of white pepper
Salt

PREPARATION

1 Break asparagus and discard white parts. Peel the skin; rinse and drain.

2 Chop ham finely.

3 Mix ingredients for sauce in a small bowl and set aside.

4 Lightly beat the egg whites with water until smooth but not foamy.

COOKING

1 Set a wok over high heat. When very hot, add 3 tablespoons of oil. Flavor oil with crushed garlic, then discard garlic when brown. Add asparagus, stirring constantly until every piece is well coated with oil. Season with salt and sugar.

2 Pour in the chicken stock around the edge of the wok and stir for 1 minute. Cover wok, cook 1 minute, and let stand for 1 minute. Remove asparagus and arrange on a round serving platter in a sundial position, or on an oval platter in 2 bundles with spearheads pointing outwards.

3 Clean wok and wipe dry. Put over high heat and, when hot, add 2 tablespoons oil. Flavor oil with whole garlic for 10 seconds, then discard the garlic. Immediately sizzle in the wine, then also add the sauce mixture.

4 Add the crabmeat and half the ham, bring back to a boil, and turn heat to low. Restir tapioca mixture and stream into sauce, stirring to prevent lumps. Test for salt.

5 Stir egg whites into crab mixture and glaze sauce with sesame oil and remaining tablespoon of oil. Pour over the asparagus and decorate with the remaining ham. Serve hot.

◉◉◉◉ Crispy Stuffed Mushrooms with Crabmeat

Serves 12 as a hot platter in banquet
or as hors d'oeuvre
Time 1 hour preparation
30 minutes chilling
10 minutes cooking

脆皮蟹釀蘑菇

The secret ingredient in this delightful dish, which I often serve as an appetizer in banquets, is caul or lace fat (*crépine* in French), which encases the paunches of pigs. This is a large, thin, transparent membrane with lacy fatty veins. Though not a standard meat market item, fresh or frozen caul, gathered into a ball weighing about 1½ pounds, is available in Chinese meat markets and can be ordered through specialty butchers. In Chinese gourmet cooking caul is used for wrapping food to be deep-fried. It seals in moisture, imparts an unusual crispiness to the coating, yet retains its own chewy texture.

Before using the caul, thaw it completely. Loosen the mass gently in a sink filled

with warm water (about 90 degrees). Shake to remove trapped hair or dirt if any. Drain water and repeat until it is thoroughly clean. Clip off areas with heavy veins, which are difficult to cook. Turn a plastic dish rack upside down, and spread the caul on it to drain and air-dry thoroughly (about 30 minutes). Peel gently and scissor into pieces roughly 5 inches square. Other wares besides the dish rack can be used, but they should have ample amounts of air space to avoid sticking and consequent tearing; otherwise water may have to be sprayed through the bottom side to free the delicate caul.

Ingredients

1 ball caul, about 1½ pounds
12 fresh mushrooms, about 1¾ inches in diameter
½ teaspoon salt
1 whole scallion
1 sprig Chinese parsley
2 eggs
3 tablespoons oil
2 tablespoons minced shallots
2 tablespoons all-purpose flour

½ cup chicken stock
1 tablespoon minced Smithfield ham
3 ounces crabmeat
Cornstarch for coating
4 cups oil for deep-frying

Seasonings

2 teaspoons pale dry sherry
¼ teaspoon salt
⅛ teaspoon white pepper
½ teaspoon granulated sugar
1 teaspoon sesame oil

PREPARATION

1 Clean and dry lace fat as instructed above. Cut 12 square pieces about 5 inches in size.

2 Wipe mushrooms with a dampened towel to clean. Remove the stems and chop them into fine bits.

3 Arrange mushroom caps, hollow side down, and sprinkle lightly with salt. Set aside.

4 Chop scallion and parsley finely.

5 Separate eggs into whites and yolks.

6 To prepare stuffing: Set a heavy small saucepan over high heat. When hot, add the oil, then the shallots. Stir constantly until shallots turn limp, about 1 minute. Add mushroom stems and stir 30 seconds. Turn heat to medium and mix in the flour. Gradually add chicken stock in a stream, stirring vigorously to break up lumps until sauce is smooth.

7 Remove saucepan from heat and mix in egg yolks 1 at a time. Season mixture. Fold in ham, scallion, parsley, and crabmeat. Test for salt. Chill for 30 minutes.

8 Spoon stuffing evenly to fill each cap so that the stuffing is round in shape.

9 Lay 1 piece of lace fat flat on a platter with 1 corner facing you. Place mushroom, cap side down, below the diagonal at the center. Bring the corner up to cover the mushroom, then roll it over twice and fold up the corners. Put mushroom in palm and squeeze to increase contact.

10 Dip wrapped mushrooms in egg white. Coat with cornstarch evenly, then shake off the excess starch.

11 Finish the remaining mushrooms in the same manner. Use immediately or wrap and chill until ready to use.

COOKING

1 Set a wok over high heat. When hot, add 4 cups oil. Heat about 4 or 5 minutes, then test the temperature by dropping a piece of scallion green into the oil. If bubbles appear immediately around the green, which also moves around in the oil, the temperature is moderately hot, about 325 degrees.

2 Dip a Chinese deep-frying strainer into the hot oil just to grease it once, then remove. Arrange all 12 mushrooms in 1 layer in the strainer. Lower the strainer and its contents into the oil. Turn heat to medium high. Deep-fry mushrooms for 1 minute, or until the coating is set.

3 Remove strainer with mushrooms from oil to rest over a large mixing bowl.

4 Use a very fine-mesh, small strainer to remove sediments in oil.

5 Turn heat to high. Place all mushrooms back into the oil and deep-fry until golden, about 2 minutes. Remove mushrooms to drain on paper towels.

6 Serve immediately with five-spice salt (page 193) on the side.

◉◉◉ Stuffed Crab Legs

Serves 12 in a banquet or as an
             appetizer
Time   1 hour or more preparation
          2 hours chilling
          10 to 12 minutes cooking

釀 蟹 脚

Rather than stuffing the ingredients into the crab legs, the latter are inserted into balls of stuffing to become handles. The stuffed crab legs are assembled under a cooked shell, looking roughly like a complete crab. This is an impressive dish, but it tastes even better than it looks.

Ingredients

1 dungeness crab,
   about 2 pounds, live
   or fresh-cooked
Paste for Deep-fried
   Shrimp Balls (page
   162)

¼ cup cornstarch
¼ cup bread crumbs
6 cups oil

PREPARATION

1 Steam the crab over very high heat for 12 to 15 minutes. (Omit the steaming if using fresh-cooked crab.)

2 Remove the shell and separate the meat. Chill until ready to use.

3 Rinse the shell thoroughly. Break each claw by hand into 2 prongs, also 2-inch tips from each leg. These are the handles for the stuffed crab legs. Wipe dry and reserve.

4 Add crabmeat to the shrimp paste and stir with a wooden spoon in 1 direction until mixture holds together and feels resilient. Chill until firm, at least 2 hours.

5 Divide the crab and shrimp mixture into 12 equal portions. Shape each into an oval ball and insert a handle into 1 end with the leg tip or claw end.

6 Mix together the cornstarch and bread crumbs, then roll each ball in the coating mixture.

COOKING

1 Heat the oil in a wok until very hot, about 10 minutes. Test temperature of the oil by dropping a small piece of scallion green into the oil. If it sizzles noisily and quickly turns brown, the oil is ready (about 375 degrees).

2 Drop in all the crab balls rapidly in succession. Turn the heat to medium and deep-fry until the balls rise to the surface and become golden. Remove to drain excess oil on paper towels.

3 Quickly dip the shell in the hot oil to make it shiny. Drain.

4 Arrange crab balls in an oval on a serving platter. Place the shell on top and serve.

◉◉◉ Crab Imperial

Serves 2 as a main dish with
vegetable and rice
Time 30 minutes preparation
30 minutes cooking

This is a popular Cantonese variation on a Western theme. Note that the sauce base is very similar in principle to the French velouté.

Ingredients
2 ounces pork fatback
6 medium black
mushrooms
2 sprigs Chinese
parsley
1 fresh-cooked
dungeness crab,
about 1¾ pounds
2 tablespoons oil
2 tablespoons minced
shallots or scallions
(white part only)
2 tablespoons chopped
Smithfield ham
3 eggs + 2 egg yolks
Bread crumbs for
coating
oil for deep frying

Sauce base
2 tablespoons oil
2 tablespoons
all-purpose flour
⅔ cup chicken stock

Seasonings
2 teaspoons sesame oil
1 tablespoon brandy
½ teaspoon granulated
sugar
½ teaspoon salt (use
less if crabmeat is
preseasoned)
⅛ teaspoon white
pepper

PREPARATION

1 Cook the fatback of pork in some boiling water until translucent, about 10 minutes, then soak it in ice water to firm. Chop finely.

2 Soak mushrooms in warm water until soft. Trim the stems, then squeeze caps to extract moisture. Shred finely, then cut into ⅜-inch lengths.

3 Rinse and chop parsley finely.

4 Shell the crab and lightly flake the meat. Mix with the seasonings.

5 In a small, heavy saucepan, heat the oil for the sauce base over medium-low heat. Add the flour, cooking slowly about 2 minutes. Gradually stream in the stock, stirring with a wire whisk or chopsticks to blend until boiling. Set aside.

COOKING

1 Set a heavy 2-quart saucepan over medium heat. When hot, add the oil. Flavor oil with shallots until limp but not brown, then add the mushrooms and stir for 1 minute.

2 Remove the saucepan from heat. Mix in the pork fat and the ham, crabmeat, and the sauce, stirring to blend well.

3 Beat the eggs and yolks together until smooth. Add the eggs to the crabmeat mixture, then fold in the parsley and mix. Correct seasonings.

4 Clean, dry, and grease the interior of the crab shell, if you are using the dungeness crab. Put all the crab mixture into the shell, making sure the stuffing reaches the corners. Lightly pack stuffing and smooth the surface with a moistened spoon. Coat with bread crumbs and brush off excess.

5 Put stuffed crab in steamer and steam over high heat for 15 minutes. Pat the crab shell dry.

6 Heat 4 cups of oil until very hot, about 375 degrees. Place the crab, shell side down, in a deep-frying strainer and put it in the oil. Use a ladle to scoop hot oil over the crabmeat, ladle by ladle, until the surface turns golden. Remove to drain on paper towels.

7 Cut crab shell in half with kitchen shears. Serve as a main dish or as a luncheon treat.

Note: This recipe can be made with 6 Eastern blue crabs. Reserve the shells as containers and prepare in the same manner.

VARIATION: Miniature Crab Casserole

You can use 12 ounces of cooked crabmeat for this version. Prepare the crab mixture in the same manner. Grease 6 individual souffle dishes, about 2¾ inches in diameter and 1 inch tall, and coat them with bread crumbs, then brush with oil.

1 Preheat oven to 375 degrees.

2 Add about ¼ inch of boiling water to a roasting pan. Put the souffle dishes into the pan.

3 Bake crabmeat for 20 minutes or until a toothpick inserted comes out clean. Broil to brown the surface. Serve as an appetizer.

◉◉◉◉ Jade Pillars with Garlic Cloves

Serves 10 to 12 in a Chinese banquet
Time 4 hours soaking
30 minutes preparing garlic cloves
2½ hours steaming
5 to 7 minutes cooking sauce

瑶柱蒜脯

This is a banquet dish from Canton. A gourmet friend of ours searched for it for ten years in the United States before he found it in our house. While the jade pillars are impressively packed and delicious, the best part is actually the garlic which has absorbed the juice of the pillars. Leftover garlic and sauce can be ground into a pastelike sauce, great for topping a beef medallion steak or a deep-fried quail.

Ingredients

19 medium jade pillars, about ½ pound
8 whole heads of garlic, about 1¼ pounds
Oil for deep-frying garlic
1 cup boiling water
1 tablespoon granulated sugar mixed with 1 teaspoon salt for blanching

1½ teaspoons tapioca powder
1 tablespoons water
2 tablespoons oil
2 teaspoons brandy
1 teaspoon sesame oil

Seasonings

1 tablespoon pale dry sherry
1 teaspoon granulated sugar
2 slices gingerroot

PREPARATION

1 Break off the tough new-moon shaped muscle that is attached on the side of each jade pillar. (This small piece, though tough, is flavorful for soup stock.) Rinse gently.

2 Select the largest pillar to place in the center of a heatproof bowl which is no more than 6 inches in diameter and 2½ inches in depth. Surround the center piece with 6 pillars to form a tight circle and surround the circle with 12 more.

3 Add just enough water to cover all pillars, and set aside; the water will be absorbed in about 1 hour. Add water again, to the same level to replenish the amount absorbed and repeat until the water level does not lower significantly after 1 hour. By this time the pillars are fully reconstituted and saturated. This soaking process should take about 3 to 4 hours. (Because the pillars vary widely, their ability to absorb water cannot be predetermined.)

4 Meanwhile, separate the garlic cloves. Use only the uniform ones, leaving the remaining cloves for some other use. Soak selected garlic cloves in boiling water for 5 minutes for easy peeling. Peel garlic skin and pat dry with paper towel. You will have about 1½ cups of peeled garlic cloves.

5 Set a wok over high heat. When hot, add oil. When the oil is hot (about 375 degrees), add the garlic cloves to the oil. Turn heat to low and deep-fry garlic until the cloves float to the surface and the skins turn crinkly and golden, about 2 to 3 minutes. Remove.

6 Blanch the fried garlic cloves in boiling water with sugar and salt for 1 minute; this will mellow the sharp taste. Remove to drain in a colander. Run cold water over to rinse away any grease. Drain well and reserve.

COOKING

1 Add enough water to the pillars in the bowl to make sure the water level again comes up to the edge of the pillars. Add seasoning.

2 Support the bowl with a deep dish to catch any overflowing juices from steaming. (The juice is flavorful for later use as a sauce base.) Steam over medium heat for 1½ hours.

3 Add garlic to the bowl of jade pillars, spreading out evenly. Spoon out some juice if needed. Continue to steam for 1 more hour or until pillars are soft to the bite.

4 Remove the bowl from steamer and put a platter about ¼ inch smaller than the bowl over pillars and garlic (I use the cover of a 1-quart saucepan). Press the platter firm to hold contents in shape, then tip the bowl to drain as much juice as possible into a mixing bowl; you will have about less than 1 cup. Keep contents in the bowl, and keep warm in the steamer.

5 Mix tapioca powder with water.

6 Set a small saucepan over high heat. When hot, add 1 tablespoon of the oil. When the oil is hot, sizzle in brandy. Immediately add the reserved juice to pan and bring to a boil. Reduce heat to low, then stream in tapioca mixture, stirring constantly until sauce thickens. Test for seasoning, and glaze sauce with remaining oil and sesame oil. Turn heat off and cover pan.

7 To serve, remove the smaller platter from pillars. Cover the bowl with a round serving platter about 10 to 11 inches in diameter, then hold the platter and bowl together firmly and flip them over quickly. Remove the bowl. The jade pillars now form a dome, resting on the serving platter.

8 Reheat sauce and spoon it evenly on surface of pillars. Serve hot, best with plain steamed rice.

◉◉ Oil-Dipped Fresh Scallops

Serves 4 as a main dish with a beef and vegetable dish plus rice, or 6 to 8 in a multi-dish family meal

Time 10 minutes preparation
2½ hours chilling
7 minutes cooking

油泡帶子

Fresh scallops are one of the great wonders of the culinary world. Oil-dipping at high temperatures seals in the natural juices without affecting the sweet taste and delicate texture.

Ingredients	Seasonings	Sauce mixture
1 pound fresh scallops	1 egg white	¼ cup chicken stock
4 medium black mushrooms	1 tablespoon tapioca powder	1 teaspoon oyster sauce
4 scallions (white part only)	Juice of 2 slices gingerroot	1 teaspoon sesame oil
4 cups oil	1 teaspoon pale dry sherry	½ teaspoon granulated sugar
1 clove garlic, thinly sliced	⅔ teaspoon salt	1 teaspoon tapioca powder
1 tablespoon pale dry sherry	Dash of white pepper	
1 teaspoon sesame oil		

PREPARATION

1 Remove the small tough muscle attached along the side of each scallop. Rinse clean of sand and drain in a colander. Arrange scallops in 1 layer on paper towels to dry, then wrap and chill for at least 2 hours.

2 Soak mushrooms in warm water until soft. Squeeze to extract moisture and trim stems. Cut caps into quarters.

3 About 30 minutes before cooking, mix seasonings in a bowl. Add the scallops and mix well with your fingers. Chill.

4 Cut scallions into 1-inch pieces.

5 Mix ingredients for sauce in a small bowl and set aside.

COOKING

1 Have ready a bowl lined with a strainer for oil-dipping. Set it within easy reach.

2 Set wok over high heat. When very hot, add the oil. Wait for about 5 minutes, or until a piece of scallion green dropped in sizzles noisily and soon turns brown (about 375 degrees).

3 Add the scallops to the oil, stirring to separate pieces with a spatula. Then pour together with oil into the bowl, leaving about 1 tablespoon of oil in the wok.

4 Reheat the wok over high heat until very hot. Flavor oil with garlic for 10 seconds, then add the mushrooms, stirring for 10 seconds.

5 Return scallops to the wok and sizzle in the wine along the edge, stirring gently until the wine is evaporated.

6 Push scallops to the side of the wok and restir the sauce mixture. Stream sauce into the center of the wok, stirring until thickened. Add the scallions, glaze with sesame oil, and mix well. Remove and serve immediately.

VARIATION: Leaf-Veined Scallops

By tinting the scallops with spinach paste (see Emerald Shrimp, page 155), the color enters the tiny crevices but leaves the smooth part of the surface untinted. The scallops look like pieces of white jade with bright green lotus-leaf veins. Choose large, unbroken scallops for best visual effect.

To prepare, follow step 1 of the master recipe to prepare the scallops. Use 2 teaspoons of spinach paste to mix with the scallops after the first chilling, then add seasonings and chill for another hour. Omit the mushrooms and the oyster sauce in the sauce mixture. Oil-dip the scallops as in the master recipe.

⊛ Deep-Fried Oysters

Serves	4 with a beef or pork stir-fried main dish and rice, or serves 6 in a multi-dish Chinese family meal
Time	15 minutes preparation 30 minutes chilling 10 minutes cooking

酥 炸 生 蠔

Oysters are almost never eaten raw by the average Chinese, but deep-fried oysters are a Cantonese favorite. The complexity of texture and taste defies description.

Ingredients	Seasonings	Batter
24 medium shucked oysters	1 teaspoon salt	½ cup all-purpose flour
2 tablespoons salt	1 tablespoon pale dry sherry	⅔ cup ice water
4 cups oil	Juice of 2 slices gingerroot	1 tablespoon oil
Flour for coating	Dash of white pepper	¾ teaspoon baking powder
¼ head iceberg lettuce		
1 lemon, cut into wedges		
1 tablespoon Five-Spice Salt (page 193)		

PREPARATION

1 Mix salt with oysters. Let stand for 10 minutes, then rinse with cold water to remove film. Drain.

2 Set a 4-quart saucepan half-filled with water over high heat. Bring water to a boil, then add the oysters. Cover the saucepan and remove from the heat. After 1 minute, drain in a colander. Arrange oysters on paper towels to dry.

3 Put oysters in a mixing bowl and add seasonings. Mix gently, then chill 30 minutes.

4 Mix ingredients for batter and chill for 20 minutes.

COOKING

1 Set a wok over high heat. When very hot, add the oil. While waiting for the oil to get hot, coat each oyster with the flour, shaking off excess.

2 Test temperature of oil by dropping in a piece of scallion green. When bubbles appear around the green and it begins to move in the oil, and soon turns brown, temperature is hot enough (about 375 degrees).

3 Dip the oysters, 1 by 1, into the batter and then into the oil. Deep-fry until golden, then remove to drain on paper towels.

4 Shred the lettuce finely to line a serving platter. Arrange the fried oysters on top of the lettuce and garnish with lemon wedges. Serve five-spice salt separately in a little dish.

◉ Quick-Braised Oysters with Ginger and Scallions

Serves 4 with a meat-vegetable dish and rice

Time 10 minutes preparation
4 to 5 minutes cooking

羗 葱 生 蠔

The unusual aspect of this Cantonese dish is the oyster sauce, commonly a seasoning for meat. The texture of this dish is tender, the taste is zesty, and there is a tangy flavor with the browned ginger and scallion mixture. Many claim that the best-tasting part is the scallions.

Ingredients

1½ pounds shucked
  oysters
3 tablespoons salt
8 slices gingerroot
2 tablespoons distilled
  white vinegar

6 whole scallions,
  trimmed
3 tablespoons oil
1 tablespoon pale dry
  sherry

Sauce mixture

2 tablespoons chicken stock

1 teaspoon tapioca powder

1 teaspoon sesame oil

2 tablespoons oyster sauce

2 teaspoons light soy sauce

1 teaspoon granulated sugar

Dash of white pepper

PREPARATION

1 Place oysters in a colander. Add 2 tablespoons of salt, mixing gently. Let set for 5 minutes, then rinse with cold water to remove any film.

2 Half-fill a 3-quart saucepan with water. Set over high heat and when the water boils, add 4 slices of ginger, remaining tablespoon of salt, and vinegar. Boil for 1 minute, then add the oysters.

3 Remove saucepan from the heat. Cover and let sit for 1 minute, then pour oysters into a colander to drain. Arrange on paper towels to dry.

4 Trim off 3 inches from the scallion greens and discard. Cut the remaining portions into 1½-inch lengths.

5 Shred the remaining ginger finely.

6 Mix the ingredients for the sauce in a small bowl and set aside.

COOKING

1 Set a wok over high heat. When very hot, add the oil. When oil is hot, place in the ginger, stirring until brown. Then add the scallions, stirring constantly until limp and brown—about 2 minutes.

2 Sizzle in the wine and immediately add the oysters, stirring and turning gently until oysters are heated through, about 1 minute.

3 Push the oysters to the side of the wok and restir the sauce mixture. Add sauce to the wok, stirring until thickened. Mix all ingredients together and serve hot.

Braised Abalone with Black Mushrooms in Oyster Sauce

Serves 10 to 12 in a formal Chinese banquet
Time 25 minutes preparation
25 minutes cooking

蠔油鮑片會冬菇

The exquisite taste of black mushrooms from Japan and the tender abalones from Mexico blend well with the oyster sauce. This is a favorite holiday dish for the Cantonese.

Ingredients

1 can (16 ounces) abalone
24 medium black mushrooms
1 cup warm water
1 piece chicken fat, about 2 to 3 ounces
4 slices gingerroot
3 tablespoons oil
1 clove garlic, flattened

1 tablespoon pale dry sherry
2 teaspoons water chestnut powder mixed with 1 tablespoon abalone juice
1 teaspoon sesame oil
2 sprigs Chinese parsley

Seasonings

1 teaspoon granulated sugar
1 tablespoon pale dry sherry

Sauce mixture

1½ tablespoons oyster sauce
1 teaspoon dark soy sauce

PREPARATION

1 Drain juice from abalone and reserve. Slice abalone horizontally (so that slices will be larger than if sliced vertically) into ⅛-inch thick pieces.

2 Rinse mushrooms and soak in warm water until soft. Trim stems and reserve soaking liquid.

3 In a heatproof bowl, combine the mushrooms, soaking liquid, and seasonings. Place a piece of chicken fat and the ginger slices on top of the mushrooms. Steam over high heat for 20 minutes or until chicken fat has melted. Discard the ginger and any residue of chicken fat.

4 Drain the juice into a small bowl, adding abalone juice to make ¾ cup of liquid. Mix this with the sauce ingredients and set aside.

COOKING

1 Set a heavy 2-quart saucepan over high heat. When hot, add 2 tablespoons of oil. Flavor oil with garlic and discard when brown. Sizzle in the wine, adding the sauce mixture immediately after. Add the mushrooms and bring to a boil. Turn heat to low.

2 Stream water chestnut mixture into the pan, stirring until thickened. Add abalone slices and cook just to heat through (it cannot withstand prolonged, high-heat cooking).

3 Transfer abalone slices to a serving platter, with slices overlapping each other. Put mushrooms, caps up, in the center. Glaze sauce with remaining oil and sesame oil and pour over mushrooms. Garnish with parsley leaves and serve hot.

◉◉ Stir-Fried Squid in Garlic and Wine

Serves 2 as a main dish with Chinese mixed vegetables and rice
Time 45 minutes preparation
3 minutes cooking

酒蒜爆鮮魷

Squid is delicious, especially in a Cantonese stir-fry such as this.

Ingredients

2 pounds squid
2 tablespoons salt
6 to 8 cups water
4 tablespoons oil
1 tablespoon minced garlic
2 tablespoons pale dry sherry
2 teaspoons sesame oil
2 sprigs Chinese parsley, chopped finely

Sauce mixture

Juice of 2 slices gingerroot
1 tablespoon chicken stock
1½ teaspoons tapioca powder
1 teaspoon granulated sugar
1 tablespoon light soy sauce
Dash of white pepper
¼ teaspoon salt

PREPARATION

1 Hold the head and tentacles of the squid very firmly, pulling them away from the body. The ink sac will come out at the same time. Pull out the yellow jelly pouch and the transparent center bone inside the body.

2 Reserve only the body for this recipe and discard the rest or keep the tentacles for some other use. Open up the body cavity with scissors and rub the purplish outer skin with the fingers, peeling it off. Detach and discard the fins, leaving only the triangular piece of white meat. Process all remaining squid as described.

3 Rub and squeeze squid with salt in a colander. Rinse and drain.

4 Turn the inner side of a piece of squid up, scoring gently and diagonally at ¼-inch intervals, forming diamond-shaped criss-crosses so that the pieces will curl up when cooked.

5 Bring water to a boil in a saucepan. Remove from the heat and add the squid immediately. Stir once and pour into a colander to drain. Arrange in 1 layer on a kitchen towel and pat dry thoroughly with another towel.

6 Prepare ingredients for sauce in a small bowl. Set aside.

COOKING

1 Set a wok over high heat. When very hot, add the oil. Flavor the oil with the garlic for 10 seconds, then add squid, stirring for 1 minute.

2 Push squid to the side and restir the sauce mixture, then add it to the center of the wok, stirring until thickened. Sizzle in the wine along the edge of the wok, stir to mix all ingredients, and glaze with sesame oil. Sprinkle with chopped parsley and mix well. Serve hot.

◉◉◉ Stir-Fried Lobster Meat with Chicken

Serves 2 as a main dish with rice and vegetables
Time 30 minutes preparation
15 minutes resting
30 minutes chilling
10 minutes cooking

龍蝦雞片

Sliced chicken and lobster meat, featuring oil-dipping to preserve the natural flavor and tender texture, typifies the Cantonese approach to ingredients.

Ingredients	Seasonings for chicken	Seasonings for lobster
1 chicken breast, about 12 ounces	½ egg white	½ egg white
2 cups + 1 tablespoon oil	1 tablespoon water	2 teaspoons tapioca powder
1 large frozen lobster tail, about 12 ounces	2 teaspoons tapioca powder	⅓ teaspoon salt
½ sweet red pepper	¼ teaspoon salt	
4 medium black mushrooms	¼ teaspoon granulated sugar	
Salt	½ teaspoon pale dry sherry	
2 whole scallions, trimmed	Dash of white pepper	
4 thin slices gingerroot		
1 tablespoon pale dry sherry		
1 teaspoon sesame oil		

PREPARATION

1 Skin and bone the chicken breast. Remove as much visible membrane and gristle as possible. Cut horizontally into slices about ⅛ inch thick and 1 by 1½ inches in size.

2 To season, beat the egg white with water in a small bowl, then add the chicken. Mix well and let sit for 15 minutes. Then add the remaining seasoning ingredients and mix again.

3 Stir 1 tablespoon of oil into the chicken mixture to separate the slices. Chill for at least 30 minutes.

4 Thaw the lobster tail completely, then slit along the underside. Remove the shell (yields about 7 ounces of meat). Cut meat lengthwise in half, then into ¾-inch chunks. Pat dry with paper towels.

5 Mix seasonings for the lobster and add lobster meat. Stir well and chill for 30 minutes.

6 Remove seeds and pulp from the pepper. Cut into ⅝-inch strips, then into diamond-shaped pieces.

7 Soak mushrooms in warm water until soft. Squeeze out excess moisture, then quarter each mushroom.

8 Trim scallions 4 inches from the green tops. Roll-cut the remaining stalks into ½-inch wedges.

COOKING

1 Set a wok over high heat. When very hot, add the 2 cups of oil. Immediately add the chicken, stirring constantly about 15 seconds or until the slices separate. Remove from the oil quickly with a spatula to a strainer, resting it over a large bowl.

2 Continue to heat the oil in the wok for about 3 minutes. While waiting, remove chicken to a platter.

3 Add the lobster to the oil, stirring until the color turns pink and opaque. Pour the oil and lobster together into the strainer-lined bowl to drain, leaving about 1 tablespoon of oil in the wok.

4 Reset the wok over high heat. When hot, flavor oil with ginger. Add mushrooms and pepper, and stir until every piece is coated with oil.

5 Season ingredients in wok with salt and return chicken and lobster, adding also the scallions. Sizzle in the wine along the edge of the wok, and stir until wine is evaporated. Glaze with sesame oil and mix all ingredients. Serve hot.

VARIATION: Cantonese Surf and Turf
Replace the chicken slices with slices of filet mignon. Follow the recipe for Stir-Fried Beef Shreds with Peppers (page 290) to prepare and cook the beef. Combine with lobster at the last stage of stir-frying.

◉◉◉ Stuffed Clams

Yields 24 stuffed clams, for an hors
d'oeuvre or as part of a hot
platter in a banquet

Time 1 hour preparation
2 hours chilling
30 minutes cooking

This is an excellent hors d'oeuvre. The deep-fried version is a common dish for the Cantonese New Year, partly because the Chinese word for "clam" rhymes with *renown* (that is, prosperity).

Ingredients

12 littleneck clams
Tapioca powder
6 black mushrooms
2 Chinese sausages
8 water chestnuts
4 scallions (white part only)
2 sprigs Chinese parsley
½ pound lean ground pork
12 shrimp in the shell
2 tablespoons oil
1 teaspoon minced gingerroot

1 clove garlic, minced
1 tablespoon pale dry sherry
Bread crumbs for coating
4 cups oil

Seasonings

1 tablespoon light soy sauce
2 teaspoons pale dry sherry
1 tablespoon tapioca powder
1 whole egg
2 teaspoons sesame oil
¼ teaspoon salt
Dash of white pepper
1 teaspoon granulated sugar

PREPARATION

1 Brush sand off the shells of the clams and rinse. Steam over medium-high heat for 20 minutes, or until opened.

2 Remove clam meat and wipe shells dry. Dust each half shell with tapioca and set aside. Chop the clam meat into fine bits.

3 Soak the mushrooms in warm water until soft. Squeeze out moisture and trim stems. Chop into fine bits.

4 Chop the sausages, chestnuts, scallions, and parsley separately into fine bits.

5 Combine seasonings and pork in a large bowl. Mix with your fingers.

6 Shell and devein shrimp. Rinse. Cut into fine bits.

COOKING

1 Set a wok over high heat. When very hot, add the oil. Flavor oil with ginger and garlic for 10 seconds, then add the clam meat, stirring constantly until moisture has evaporated.

GOLD FLOWER AND JADE TREE CHICKEN
PAGE 200

BLACK BEAN CHICKEN
PAGE 211

2 Add the sausages to the wok, stirring until the fat turns transparent. Add the mushrooms, water chestnuts, and scallions and stir a few more times.

3 Sizzle in the wine along the edge of the wok and stir. Remove to cool for 30 minutes, then combine with the pork mixture in the bowl. Add the shrimp meat and the parsley and mix well, then chill for 2 hours.

4 Fill the clam shells with the filling and coat with bread crumbs. Shake off the excess.

5 Arrange the clams in a steamer. Steam over high heat for 10 minutes. Remove the clams to dry on paper towels (so as to eliminate splashing when deep-frying).

6 Set a wok over high heat. When very hot, add oil. Wait for about 5 to 7 minutes or until a piece of scallion green dropped in moves about in the oil and soon turns brown (about 375 degrees). Add half of the clams in succession and deep-fry until golden. Remove to drain on paper towels.

7 Deep-fry the remaining clams in the same manner. Serve.

Note: Stuffed clams can also be baked. After bread crumbs are put on the clams, brush the surface with oil. Arrange clams in a baking pan. Bake in a preheated 375-degree oven for 30 minutes or until small grease bubbles appear around the stuffing.

Cassia Flower Shark's Fin

Serves 10 in a banquet as appetizer
Time Overnight soaking
2 hours resting
30 minutes cleaning
2 hours simmering
10 minutes preparation
10 minutes cooking

炒桂花翅

Shark's Fin Soup, though well known as a Chinese delicacy, is not necessarily to the taste of the non-Chinese. In many expensive banquets in Hong Kong, when this is served, foreign guests often would consume the soup and leave behind the transparent "needles" which are actually the most expensive part of the soup. On the other hand, shark's fin is virtually a tasteless texture food, and one of the best ways to appreciate its texture is to serve it in solid food such as this one.

A gourmet's Egg Foo Yung if you like, this Cantonese specialty is beautiful to look at (like a cluster of cassia flower), and its texture is loved even by all who encounter shark's fin the first time.

The preparation of all shark's fin dishes requires patience, especially when one starts from the whole fin. We suggest the use of pre-processed shark's fin cakes which eliminate the labor to quite an extent.

Ingredients

4 ounces dried shark's fin cake
4 to 5 cups water
1 knob gingerroot, about 1 ounce, sliced
4 scallions (white part only)
2 tablespoons yellow wine or sherry
3 ounces Smithfield ham, in 1 piece
1 cup + 3 tablespoons oil
1 cup Supreme Stock (page 108)
Dash of white pepper
1 teaspoon salt
2 teaspoons sesame oil
¾ pound bean sprouts

1 sprig Chinese parsley
2 teaspoons tapioca powder mixed with 1 tablespoon chicken stock
6 whole eggs
2 ounces cooked crabmeat

PREPARATION OF SHARK'S FIN

1 Soak shark's fin cake in a large bowl with cold water overnight.

2 Pick over fins and discard meatlike brown bits and foreign particles if any.

3 Bring about 4 to 5 cups of water to a boil in a 2-quart saucepan. Add the shark's fin and bring water back to boil. Cover pan and set off the heat until water becomes cool.

4 Pour shark's fin into a large, fine-mesh strainer, at least 6 inches in diameter. Rinse with cold water and swish and rub the fin against the wall of the strainer, running cold water over to rinse. Repeat the rubbing and rinsing 3 to 4 times until most of the jellylike particles have been rinsed off, leaving only "fin needles" in the strainer.

5 Put the shark's fin in a saucepan. Add water, ginger slices, 3 scallions, and 1 tablespoon of the yellow wine or sherry. Simmer for 2 hours or until both ends of a thick needle droop down when picked up by a pair of chopsticks.

6 Discard ginger and scallions. Put fin needles in the strainer and repeat the rubbing and rinsing one more time. Now the fin needles are free of fishy smell. You should have about 1 cup packed.

BRAISING OF THE SHARK'S FIN

1 Shred about 2 tablespoons of the ham and keep the remainder intact.

2 Set a saucepan over high heat. When hot, add 1 tablespoon of oil. Sizzle in the remaining wine and immediately add the stock, the shark's fin, and the whole piece of ham. Cover pan and simmer over low heat until most of the liquid has evaporated, about 40 minutes to 1 hour.

3 Remove fin needles to drain in a colander. Discard ham. Add a dash of pepper, half the salt, and half the sesame oil. Toss well. Test for seasoning. The fin needles are now ready for use in stir-frying (or in soup).

RECIPE PREPARATION

1 Remove heads and tails from bean sprouts (a must for this dish), and soak them in cold water. Chill in refrigerator until 1 hour before using, then drain well. You will have about 1½ cups.

2 Shred the remaining scallion finely. Break off parsley leaves and set aside.

3 Mix tapioca powder with stock.

4 Beat eggs in a bowl until smooth. Add salt, 1 tablespoon of oil, crabmeat, shredded ham, and braised shark's fin needles. (If shark's fin has been chilled in the refrigerator, reheat over low heat to soften.) Mix all ingredients well.

COOKING

1 Have ready a large bowl lined with a strainer for oil-dipping.

2 Set a wok over high heat. When hot, add the remaining tablespoon of oil and the ½ teaspoon of salt. Add bean sprouts, stirring a few times around the wok until bean sprouts start to wilt, about 20 seconds. Remove immediately to drain excess moisture in a colander. Reserve.

3 Rinse wok and wipe it dry. Set the wok over high heat. When very hot add the cup of oil, swishing the oil around 3 to 4 times to coat the surface of wok evenly. Put in half of the egg mixture, stirring rapidly until almost set, about 40 seconds. Pour egg mixture and oil together into the strainer, leaving about 3 tablespoons of the oil in the wok. Turn heat off.

4 Shake the strainer to drain off as much oil as possible into the bowl. Combine the cooked egg mixture with the uncooked egg mixture and mix well.

5 Reset wok on high heat. When the oil is very hot, add all the egg mixture, stirring quickly until almost set. Push egg mixture to the side, add tapioca mixture to the center of the wok, and stir until it thickens. Add bean sprouts and scallion shreds, mixing with all the ingredients in wok. Glaze with remaining sesame oil, then remove to a serving platter. Sprinkle parsley leaves on top and serve.

Note: Stir-frying the egg mixture in 2 batches is the classical technique to ensure the lightness of the egg. The perfect Cassia Flower Shark's Fin should be smooth but not runny.

Poultry

It is interesting to note that the Chinese respect chicken above pork and beef. Live chicken, from a good breed and properly raised, commands several times the price of frozen ones. The Cantonese in particular go out of their way to preserve the tenderness and flavor of chicken. Toward this end, hundreds of recipes are created, utilizing all the parts and employing many different cooking techniques. Accordingly, recipes for chicken receive the major emphasis in this chapter, while the special techniques for boning, cutting, chopping, and serving are discussed on pages 64–76.

The Chinese are not fussy about duck, but most feel that the American duck generally has too much fat, tougher meat, and harder bones. A duck is usually braised whole until it is very tender, so that the diner can then pry the meat apart with chopsticks. In Peking the famous Peking duck is fattened by force-feeding, just as the French force-feed their geese half a world away. But while the French aim for the goose liver, the Chinese value the skin of the duck.

Squab is used more often for banquets than family meals. Although it is not readily available in average U.S. supermarkets, in Chinatowns fresh and cooked squab are nearly as common as chicken and duck.

Recipes for ducks are generally applicable to geese after allowances for the latter's increased size and tougher skin. Roast goose hung in front of restaurants, together with roast duck and roast pork, is a familiar sight in Canton. In Quangdong province geese are raised so successfully that what is called "roast duck" in neighboring Hong Kong often turns out to be roast goose.

The Chinese seldom use Cornish game hens or turkey. Turkey especially is too large to be handled like chicken, and the meat is too uniform in texture. The game hen, however, has size and meat texture straddling the chicken and the squab, but it comes across with a gamey taste unwelcome to the Chinese palate. We include two recipes using the game hen, in which gaminess is neutralized by the cooking technique.

Soups made of wild fowl are valued more for their medicinal properties than their taste. The livers and gizzards of all poultry are esteemed in China everywhere, and we include a recipe here for Deep-fried Spicy Liver.

CHICKEN

The Chinese always prefer to cook with a freshly killed chicken, and their choice bird should be plump, with a pale skin and no blemishes. If possible, use a Chinese-dressed chicken, which has had the thin layer of yellow film on the skin removed. When this film is removed the skin takes on a smooth, yellowish white color when white-cooked or a reddish brown hue when simmered in a spicy soy sauce. If you must use a conventionally dressed chicken, try to remove the yellow film by rubbing it with a Nylon pot scrubber, holding the bird under a steady stream of warm water.

A broiling chicken of about 2 pounds (dressed weight) is suitable for deep-frying or quick braising whole. The frying chicken, between 2½ and 3½ pounds, is perfect for cutting up in chunks for steaming and braising. The heavier roaster is usually used for white-cooking, simmering in sauce, or roasting because of its firm but tender texture. A larger fryer of about 4 pounds can be used for the same purpose. Only the big stewing hens are suitable for making either Supreme Stock or a regular chicken stock.

The chicken breast is best for stir-fries, and is excellent for mincing into Chicken Velvet; use whole ones for easier boning. Legs and thighs are fine for red-cooking, and the wings are multi-purposeful.

Frozen chicken is a poor substitute for a fresh-killed bird. If you must use one, thaw it completely before cooking and do not use it for white-chopped dishes.

◉◉ Lemon Chicken

Serves 4 as a main dish with rice,
vegetable, and a thick soup
Time 15 minutes preparation
1 hour marinating
15 minutes cooking + 40
minutes simmering

檸檬雞

The emphasis in this dish is not on tartness, but rather the aromatic tang from the lemon rind when subtly modified by the shallot, ginger, and garlic. Braising ensures that the flavor permeates the chicken. This is a Cantonese specialty.

Ingredients	**Marinade**	**Sauce**
1 frying chicken, about 4 pounds	1 tablespoon brandy or vodka	2 fresh lemons
3 tablespoons oil	2 tablespoons dark soy sauce	3 tablespoons brown sugar
1 tablespoon sesame oil	2 teaspoons salt	1½ cups chicken stock (or water)
2 teaspoons tapioca powder		
1 tablespoon water	**Seasonings**	
	2 ounces shallots (about 8 heads)	
	2 cloves garlic	
	4 slices gingerroot	

PREPARATION

1 Rub chicken with a Nylon pot scrubber to remove any yellow film on the skin. Rinse chicken inside and out, then pat dry with paper towels.

2 Mix marinade in a large bowl, then add chicken. Rub the marinade evenly on the skin and in the cavity. Let stand at room temperature for at least 1 hour, turning the chicken occasionally in the marinade. Drain chicken and reserve marinade.

3 For the sauce, grate the rind from the lemons, then squeeze the juice from 1½ of the lemons, leaving the remaining half for a garnish. Mix lemon juice and rind with remaining ingredients for the sauce.

4 Peel the shallots and pound lightly to flatten each. Crush the garlic lightly. Have ginger ready.

COOKING

1 Set a wok over high heat and heat until very hot. Add 2 tablespoons of the oil and swish it around to coat the wok evenly. Place in the chicken and turn heat to medium. Move the chicken around in the wok so as to brown on all sides. Remove the chicken from the wok when it is browned.

2 Flavor the oil in the wok with shallots, garlic, and ginger, stirring for 20 seconds.

3 Add reserved marinade to the sauce mixture, then stir and add to wok. Bring liquid to a boil and return the chicken to the wok. Cover wok and cook the chicken over low heat for about 40 minutes. Turn the chicken occasionally as it cooks.

4 Test for doneness by inserting a toothpick through the thigh. If the juice comes out clear, the chicken is done; if it comes out pink, cook several minutes longer and test again.

5 When done, remove chicken from wok and rest on a rack. Brush sesame oil evenly over the skin. Transfer cooking liquid to a bowl.

6 When chicken is completely cooled, chop into bite-sized pieces and arrange on a serving platter so that the original shape of the chicken is approximated (see page 76). Cover with plastic wrap and keep warm until ready to serve.

7 Place cooking liquid in a saucepan over medium heat and bring back to a boil. Mix the tapioca powder with the water and gradually add the mixture to the boiling sauce, stirring constantly until thickened. Test for seasoning, especially for tartness. Add more brown sugar if desired.

8 Glaze the sauce with the remaining oil and pour over the chicken. Garnish with lemon slices cut from the remaining half lemon and serve.

⊛⊛Shredded Chicken in Oyster and Ginger Sauce

Serves 3 as a main dish with rice and
a minute soup
Time 15 minutes preparation
2 hours marinating
20 minutes cooking + 30
minutes simmering

蠔油手撕雞

The sauce, rich and flavorful, is based on the natural juices resulting from steaming the chicken. Since most of the steps can be done in advance, this dish is a true favorite of the busy Cantonese homemaker.

Ingredients	Marinade	Sauce mixture
1 frying chicken, about 3½ pounds	1 tablespoon pale dry sherry	Chicken juices from steaming, combined with enough chicken stock to make 1 cup liquid
4 teaspoons sesame oil	2 teaspoons ginger juice	
3 tablespoons peanut oil	2 teaspoons salt	
4 cloves garlic, crushed		1 tablespoon tapioca powder
1 tablespoon pale dry sherry		2 teaspoons granulated sugar
2 whole scallions, shredded		2 tablespoons oyster sauce
Leaves from 2 sprigs Chinese parsley		

PREPARATION

Rub chicken with a Nylon scrubber to remove any yellow film on the skin. Mix together marinade and rub evenly on the skin and in the cavity. Place chicken in a heatproof bowl (large enough to hold it snugly), and leave it at room temperature for at least 2 hours, or keep refrigerated overnight. Turn the chicken occasionally as it marinates.

COOKING

1 Steam the chicken in the bowl with the marinade over high heat for 30 minutes. Test for doneness by inserting a toothpick into the thickest part of the thigh; if juices run clear, chicken is done. If chicken needs to cook longer, cover steamer and let chicken stand for 10 minutes longer. When done, rest chicken on a rack and brush the skin with 2 teaspoons of sesame oil to keep it moist. When cool, cover with aluminum foil.

2 Strain the steaming juices through a very fine mesh strainer and skim the fat. Add the juices to the remaining sauce ingredients and mix well.

3 When ready to serve, bone the chicken by tearing meat into *irregular* bite-sized pieces. Resteam chicken over high heat just to heat through, about 2 minutes.

4 Meanwhile, prepare the sauce. Set a heavy, small saucepan over high heat. When hot, add the peanut oil and flavor oil with garlic for 10 seconds; do not brown garlic. Sizzle in the sherry. Mix ingredients for sauce mixture, then add half to the oil-sherry mixture. Turn heat to low, restir the remaining sauce mixture and then stream it into the saucepan, stirring until it thickens. Test for seasoning, and then glaze the sauce with remaining sesame oil.

5 When chicken is hot, scatter scallion shreds and parsley leaves on top. Pour on sauce, toss, and serve.

Note: The chicken can be steamed and boned ahead of time, then reheated quickly just prior to serving. A microwave oven serves admirably here, though steaming is the traditional reheating technique.

◉◉Chinese Roast Chicken

Serves	4 as a main dish with rice, vegetables, and a clear soup
Time	20 minutes preparation
	6 to 8 hours hanging time
	70 minutes roasting

燒雞

The Chinese roasted chicken differs from Western versions in that a spicy seasoning is sprinkled into the cavity and a sugar-based mixture is brushed on the outside to make the skin appetizingly crisp.

Ingredients	Five-spice salt	Brushing mixture
1 roasting chicken, about 4 to 5 pounds	3 teaspoons salt	3 tablespoons vinegar
1 teaspoon tapioca powder	1 teaspoon five-spice powder	2 tablespoons Fen liquor, vodka or brandy
2 teaspoons water		1 tablespoon Chinese malt sugar or honey
1 lemon, cut into wedges		

PREPARATION

1 Rub the chicken with a Nylon scrubber to remove any yellow film on the skin. In a large pot of boiling water placed over high heat, plunge the chicken breast side down for 1 minute, then back side down for an additional minute. Remove and drain, patting the cavity and skin dry.

2 Roast the salt and five-spice powder in a small frying pan over medium heat until brown. Sprinkle the spice mixture into the chicken cavity and spread it around. Skewer the opening near the tail.

3 Combine the brushing mixture ingredients in a small saucepan. Cook over low heat until well mixed.

4 Mix the tapioca and water and add to the brushing mixture. Stir well, then brush the mixture evenly on the chicken skin 2 or 3 times. Tie the wings with string and

hang the chicken in an airy place to dry until the skin is no longer sticky and the excess moisture has drained—about 6 hours.

COOKING

1 Preheat the oven to 375 degrees.

2 Place the chicken on a rack, breast side up. Roast for 40 minutes, then turn and roast another 30 minutes on other side, or until skin is evenly brown. Test for doneness by inserting a toothpick into the thickest part of the thigh. If juices run clear, it is done; otherwise roast 10 more minutes.

3 Remove chicken from oven when done and cool on rack at least 10 minutes. Chop into bite-sized pieces and arrange on a serving platter in approximately the shape of a whole chicken (see page 76). Garnish with lemon wedges.

◉◉ Cold-Tossed Roast Chicken

Serves 6 as a luncheon dish
Time 40 minutes preparation
6 to 8 hours hanging
50 minutes cooking

涼拌燒鷄絲

Here is a Chinese-American dish popular on the West Coast. This version uses the roast chicken to add subtlety to the blending of textures and a mustard-lemon dressing for piquancy without heaviness. Excellent for an informal party, but prepare enough as guests invariably have appetite for more.

Ingredients

1 frying chicken, about 4 pounds
4 tablespoons sesame seeds
8 to 10 sprigs Chinese parsley
3 whole scallions
3 cups oil
2 ounces Chinese rice sticks
1 small head iceberg lettuce
Freshly ground black pepper

Dressing

3 tablespoons lemon juice
1½ tablespoons dry mustard
1 tablespoon water
¼ cup peanut oil
1 tablespoon sesame oil
1 tablespoon granulated sugar
1 teaspoon chicken bouillon powder
2 tablespoons light soy sauce
½ teaspoon salt
1 clove garlic, minced

PREPARATION

1 Follow the recipe for Chinese Roast Chicken (page 193) to prepare the chicken until it is ready for roasting.

2 Toast the sesame seeds in a small pan over medium heat until they are light brown, about 1 minute; do not allow to burn. Set aside.

3 Mix the ingredients for the dressing in a bottle and chill in refrigerator.

4 Clean the parsley and break the leaves from the stems. Discard stems; you should have about 1 cup of leaves.

5 Trim and shred the scallions finely. Set aside.

COOKING

1 Preheat oven to 375 degrees. Place the chicken on a rack with the breast side down. Roast for 30 minutes, then turn and roast on other side for 20 minutes or until the skin is golden brown and crispy. Remove chicken from oven and allow to cool.

2 Remove skin from the chicken and drain juice and reserve. Bone the chicken, then tear the meat into julienne shreds. Cut the skin also in julienne strips.

3 Set a wok over high heat. When the wok is very hot, add the oil. Wait for about 10 minutes, then test the temperature by throwing a few inches of rice sticks into the oil. The temperature is hot enough if the rice sticks puff up immediately (about 400 degrees). Otherwise, wait a little longer and test again.

4 When the oil is hot and smoke starts to appear on the surface, add about ¼ of the rice sticks. They should puff up and cover the surface of the oil instantly. Turn them quickly and deep-fry the other side until puffy. Remove from oil quickly; you want the sticks creamy white, not brown. Finish frying the remaining rice sticks and keep all warm in a warm oven.

5 Shred the lettuce just before serving; you should have about 3 cups of greens.

6 Combine the shredded lettuce and scallions, parsley leaves, shredded chicken, chicken juice, and sesame seeds in a large bowl. Add dressing and black pepper to taste and toss well.

7 Spread rice sticks on top of salad and serve warm.

◉◉Spicy Soy Sauce Chicken

Serves 4 with rice, vegetable, and a
thick soup
Time 20 minutes preparation
30 minutes cooking

豉 油 雞

This is an aromatic, flavorful offering from Canton. In Chinatowns in the United States, the chicken may be found hanging in windows of food shops. The homemade version is better, since this dish does not withstand reheating.

Ingredients
1 large frying chicken
  or small roaster,
  about 4 pounds
3 cups light soy sauce
1 cup dark soy sauce
1 cup pale dry sherry
4 ounces rock candy or
  brown sugar
4 slices gingerroot
4 whole scallions
2 cloves garlic
1 tablespoon sesame oil

Spice mixture
2 whole star anise
2 whole nutmeg,
  lightly cracked
2 sticks cinnamon,
  about 2 inches each
2 teaspoons Sichuan
  peppercorns, or ½
  teaspoon crushed
  black peppercorns
2 teaspoons aniseed
½ teaspoon cloves
1 teaspoon fennel
  seeds
4 cups water

PREPARATION

1 Rub chicken with a Nylon scrubber to remove any yellow film on the skin, then rinse inside and out with warm water. Pat dry with paper towels and rest on a rack to drain.

2 Combine spices for spice mixture with water in a saucepan. Cook over high heat until reduced to 1 cup of liquid. Strain through a fine sieve and reserve liquid for recipe; wrap spices in plastic wrap and store in freezer for use in another recipe.

COOKING

1 Combine the spice mixture liquid with the soy sauce, sherry, rock candy, ginger, scallions, and garlic in a 4-quart saucepan. Set over medium heat (too high a heat will cause the soy sauce mixture to boil over) and bring to a boil. Add the chicken and bring liquid back to a boil. Turn chicken over.

2 Put a wooden spoon into the rear opening of the chicken, hold the handle with 1 hand, and scoop the hot soy sauce mixture into the opening, allowing the soy sauce to drain through the neck opening. Repeat this 6 or 8 times, then turn the heat low, cover pot, and simmer for 15 minutes.

3 Turn chicken over and continue to simmer, covered, for 15 minutes more. Test for doneness by inserting a toothpick into the thickest part of the thigh; if the

liquid runs clear, the chicken is done. If the chicken is not done, simmer for 10 minutes more and test again.

4 Remove chicken and rest on a rack. Brush sesame oil evenly on the skin of the chicken, then allow to cool to room temperature. Use aluminum foil to make a tent to cover the chicken loosely and set aside; do not refrigerate.

5 When ready to serve, chop chicken into bite-sized pieces and arrange them on a serving platter into roughly the original shape of a whole chicken. Boil spicy soy sauce in the pan over medium heat. Scoop about 1 cup of the sauce to cover the chicken pieces, then drain the sauce back to the pan. Do this 3 or 4 times. Serve the chicken warm.

Note: Setting an aluminum foil tent over a sauce-simmered fowl can avoid the discoloring of the reddish-brown color of the skin, which would normally happen if the fowl is covered by plastic wrap.

VARIATION: Soy Sauce Squab

Serves 2 with green vegetables and
rice as a main meal, or 10 to
12 in a formal banquet
Time 5 minutes preparation (with
ready-made simmering sauce)
45 minutes cooking

1 Substitute the chicken with 2 plump young squab, about 1 pound each. Trim the feet (if any) and wing tips. Rinse, then wipe skin and cavity dry with paper towels. In a Dutch oven, add Brown Simmering Sauce (see pages 59 and 196) and bring to a boil over medium heat. Add the squab, breast side down, and spoon hot sauce into the cavities several times until the sauce comes to a boil. Turn heat off and cover pot. Allow to sit in hot sauce for 20 minutes, then turn the squab, cover pot again, and let sit for another 20 minutes. Test for doneness by inserting a toothpick into the thickest part of 1 thigh; if juices run clear, they are done.

2 Remove squab to a rack to rest, brush each with sesame oil, and allow to cool for at least 1 hour. When cool, chop squab into bite-sized pieces, and arrange on a serving platter so as to reconstruct roughly the original shape of a squab (see page 76). If not served immediately, wrap loosely in aluminum foil until it is used, up to 3 hours.

3 When ready to serve, heat about ¼ cup of the Simmering Sauce, then pour it over the squab. If the squab is served cold, use the same sauce at room temperature.

⊛⊛⊛My Lord's Smoked Chicken

Serves 4 as a main dish with vegetables, soup, and rice; or 6 to 8 persons with several other dishes; or 10 to 12 as a cold platter as part of a banquet

Time 10 minutes preparation
20 minutes smoking time

This was a very popular Cantonese dish during the early 1890s. In the original recipe, green tea and dried cassia blossoms were used as the smoking agent. In the United States, jasmine tea is an excellent pre-mixed substitute.

Ingredients	**Smoking agent**
1 frying chicken, about 3 to 4 pounds	¼ cup jasmine tea leaves
½ cup brown sugar	2 tablespoons all-purpose flour
Oil for brushing	

PREPARATION

1 Follow the instructions given for preparing Spicy Soy Sauce Chicken (page 196), using the spicy braising liquid or the ready-made Brown Simmering Sauce (page 59). There is no need to brush the bird with sesame oil, however.

2 Roast the smoking agent in a wok over medium heat until the flour turns light brown. Remove and mix with brown sugar, then set aside.

COOKING

1 Line a wok and its cover with heavy aluminum foil (to prevent staining). Spread the smoking agent evenly over the bottom of the wok. In the wok, place a stand about 2 inches tall and on top of it rest a round cake rack. Place chicken on rack and cover wok tightly. Turn the heat to medium-high and smoke chicken for about 15 to 20 minutes.

2 Remove chicken from wok and brush with oil. Cool.

3 Chop chicken into bite-sized pieces and arrange on a serving platter to reconstruct the shape of a chicken (see page 76). Serve.

VARIATION: Smoked Cornish Game Hen

Use 3 Cornish game hens instead of a chicken; the texture proves to be much firmer. After simmering the hens in the sauce for 15 minutes, turn them over, cover, and simmer 10 additional minutes. Drain chicken, then proceed with smoking as for chicken.

⊛White-Chopped Chicken

Serves 4 with vegetables and rice
Time 15 minutes preparation
5 to 7 minutes cooking + 35
minutes resting

白切雞

This is the quintessence of Cantonese white-cooking, simple to make yet with the full, delicate flavor of fresh chicken. Normally the chicken is served with any of several sauces; the best loved by the Cantonese is the one with grated ginger and scallions. Save the bones and cooking liquid to make a clear chicken stock.

Ingredients

1 large frying chicken
or 1 small roasting
chicken, about 4
pounds
4 slices gingerroot
2 teaspoons sesame oil

Garlic and hot chili sauce

2 dried chili peppers
2 cloves garlic, crushed
1 teaspoon granulated
sugar
¼ cup peanut oil
¼ cup light soy sauce
1 tablespoon red rice
vinegar
1 tablespoon sesame oil

Oyster sauce

1 tablespoon light soy
sauce
2 tablespoons oyster
sauce
2 tablespoons peanut
oil
1 tablespoon chicken
stock

Ginger and scallion sauce

2 teaspoons grated
gingerroot
2 whole scallions,
shredded
2 teaspoons salt
¼ cup peanut oil,
heated to boiling

PREPARATION

1 Rub chicken with a Nylon scrubber to remove any yellow film on the skin. Rinse and pat dry with paper towels.

2 Mix all ingredients for oyster sauce in small bowl and set aside.

3 Combine ginger and scallions for ginger and scallion sauce with salt in a heat-proof bowl. Pour in oil and stir to mix. Set aside.

4 Chop chili peppers fine, then combine with the garlic and sugar in a heatproof bowl. Heat the oil until very hot, then pour it over the chili mixture. Add soy sauce, vinegar, and sesame oil. Mix well and set aside.

COOKING

1 Fill a 4-quart saucepan with enough water to cover the chicken and set over high heat. Bring water to a boil and add the ginger slices. Put in chicken and bring

water back to a boil, then turn chicken over, cover pan, and turn off heat. Allow to sit in hot water for 20 minutes.

2 Turn the chicken over in the water and bring water back to a boil over medium heat. Cover pan, turn off heat, and allow to rest for 15 minutes.

3 Test to determine if chicken is cooked by inserting a toothpick into the thickest part of the thigh. If juice runs clear, chicken is done. If not, cover pan and allow to sit for 10 more minutes.

4 Remove chicken to a colander and run cold water into the cavity and over the skin to stop the cooking process, for about 5 minutes. This drastic change of temperature will help tighten the skin and firm up the meat. Allow to cool.

5 When chicken is cool, place it on a rack. Brush with sesame oil and cover well with plastic wrap. Leave at room temperature until ready to serve, if a few hours.

6 To serve, chop chicken into bite-sized pieces and arrange them on a platter to reconstruct the original shape of the chicken. Serve cold with any of the 3 sauces, or all of them.

◉◉◉◉◉ Gold Flower and Jade Tree Chicken

Serves 12 in a banquet, 4 for a main dish in a family meal
Time 15 minutes preparation
1 hour resting
1 hour cooking

金華玉樹雞

Jinhua, the town where the best Chinese ham is produced, literally means "gold flower." The "jade tree" here is the broccoli flowerettes placed around the boneless chicken pieces interlaced by slices of ham. This is a very popular banquet dish, and easy to prepare, too.

Ingredients

1 small roasting chicken, about 4 pounds, or a fresh Chinese-dressed chicken the same size
4 ounces center-cut Smithfield ham, or Chinese Jinhua ham
3 teaspoons granulated sugar
4 slices gingerroot
3 teaspoons sesame oil
1 bunch broccoli, about 1½ pounds
4 tablespoons oil

1 clove garlic, crushed
2 teaspoons pale dry sherry
1 tablespoon peanut oil

Sauce thickener

¼ cup chicken stock
1 tablespoon water chestnut powder

Sauce mixture

¾ cup chicken stock
½ teaspoon granulated sugar
½ teaspoon salt
Dash of white pepper

Seasonings

½ teaspoon salt
1 tablespoon brandy
1 teaspoon ginger juice
¼ cup chicken stock

PREPARATION

1 Rub the chicken with a Nylon scrubber to remove any yellow film that adheres to the skin. Rinse, then drain.

2 Rub the ham with 1 teaspoon of the sugar. Steam the ham over medium heat for 15 minutes, then chill to firm for easy slicing. When completely cool, cut the ham across the grain into slices ⅛ inch thick, 1 × 1¾ inches in size. Reserve the ham juice.

COOKING

1 To white-cook the chicken, fill a 4-quart saucepan with enough water to cover the chicken well. Set over high heat and bring to a boil. Add the ginger, put in the chicken, and bring water back to a boil. Turn the chicken over, cover pot, and turn heat off.

2 After 20 minutes, turn the chicken and bring the water back to a boil over medium heat. Cover pot again, turn off heat, and wait for 20 minutes. Test for doneness by inserting a toothpick into the thickest part of the thigh. If the juices run clear, the chicken is done. If they are pink, cover pan for 10 minutes more.

3 Remove chicken to a colander. Run cold water into the cavity and over the skin to stop the cooking process, about 5 minutes. When chicken is cool, place on a rack and brush with 2 teaspoons of sesame oil. Reserve the cooking liquid. Cover chicken well with plastic wrap and leave at room temperature for at least 1 hour.

4 Rinse the broccoli and trim the stems. Break flowerettes off, keeping each about 2 inches in length.

5 **One hour before serving, remove the bones from the chicken and chop meat into bite-sized pieces. Arrange chicken on an oval platter to reconstruct roughly the original shape of the bird (page 76). Interlace the chicken with ham slices and cover lightly with plastic wrap.**

6 Just before serving, mix the sauce ingredients with juice from steaming ham. Also blend together the chicken stock and water chestnut powder. Set aside.

7 Bring the liquid for cooking the chicken to a boil and warm over low heat.

8 Set a wok over high heat. When very hot, add 3 tablespoons of oil. Sprinkle the ½ teaspoon salt on the oil, then add broccoli, stirring constantly until each piece is well coated with oil. Sizzle in the brandy and ginger juice, adding the remaining sugar. Stir and add the chicken stock. Cover wok for 1 minute, then remove broccoli to drain in a colander.

9 Set a small, heavy saucepan over high heat. When very hot, add remaining tablespoon of oil. Flavor oil with garlic for 15 seconds, then discard garlic. Sizzle in the wine and immediately add the sauce mixture. Bring to a boil, stream in the water chestnut mixture, and stir until sauce thickens. Turn heat to a simmer.

10 Scoop about 1 cup of the cooking liquid to cover the chicken in the platter, then drain the stock back to the pan. Repeat this 3 or 4 times to keep the chicken warm, or set the platter of chicken in a microwave oven to warm for 1 minute.

11 Arrange the broccoli around the chicken on the platter. Glaze the sauce with peanut oil and remaining teaspoon of sesame oil, then pour evenly over the chicken. Poke the chicken with a fork so that sauce can slip in between the slices. Serve warm.

◉ Salt-Water Chicken

Serves 10 to 12 as part of a cold
platter
Time 10 minutes preparation
30 minutes simmering
10 minutes cooking
40 minutes setting
overnight chilling

盐 水 雞

A Cantonese country cold dish using a white simmering sauce, this recipe can be prepared days ahead.

Ingredients	Spice mixture	Salt-water mixture
1 plump frying chicken, about 4 pounds, or a small roasting chicken	2 whole star anise	2 tablespoons oil
	2 whole nutmegs, flattened	4 slices gingerroot
	2 tablespoons aniseed	2 cloves garlic, flattened
4 slices gingerroot	1 teaspoon Sichuan peppercorns or coarsely ground black peppercorns	4 whole scallions
2 teaspoons sesame oil		4 sprigs Chinese parsley
2 sprigs Chinese parsley		1¼ cups pale dry sherry
	4 cups water	¼ cup salt
	2 cups diluted chicken stock (½ stock, ½ water)	½ cup granulated sugar

PREPARATION

1 Cook ingredients for spice mixture with water in a small saucepan over high heat until reduced to 1 cup. Strain liquid and discard solids. Mix the spice mixture with diluted chicken stock and keep it frozen.

2 Rub the skin of the chicken with a Nylon scrubber to remove any yellow film. Rinse cavity, then drain.

COOKING

1 Add water to about a half depth in a 6-quart saucepan. Bring the water to a boil over high heat, then add the ginger slices. Immerse the chicken in the boiling water, turning it once. Bring water back to a boil and turn the heat off. Cover pan for 20 minutes.

2 Uncover saucepan and turn heat back to high. Turn chicken over and bring the water back to a boil. Turn heat off again and cover pan for another 20 minutes.

3 Test for doneness of chicken by inserting a toothpick into the thickest part of the thigh. If liquid runs clear, chicken is done. Otherwise, cover pan for 10 minutes more.

4 Remove chicken to a colander and run cold water over the skin and into the cavity to tighten the skin and firm up the meat. Reserve the liquid in which the chicken is white-cooked.

5 Place a saucepan over high heat until very hot, then add oil for salt-water mixture. Flavor oil with ginger, garlic, scallions, and parsley until greens are limp. Sizzle in wine, then add 4 cups of the reserved chicken stock. Bring to a boil and add the salt and sugar, cooking over medium heat for 2 minutes. Remove greens and pour liquid into a deep stockpot. Add the frozen spice mixture to bring down the temperature of the salt water.

6 Immerse the chicken in the salt water, scooping up enough salt water to fill the cavity. Cover and set in refrigerator overnight.

7 The next morning, turn the chicken. About an hour before serving, remove chicken from salt water and leave at room temperature until the jellied salt water liquifies.

8 Brush sesame oil over the skin of the chicken, then chop chicken into bite-sized pieces. Pour about ⅓ cup of the salt-water mixture over the meat and serve cold. Garnish with remaining Chinese parsley.

◉Drunken Chicken

Serves	10 to 12 as a part of a cold platter	
Time	5 minutes preparation	
	10 minutes cooking	
	30 minutes setting	
	4 hours + overnight chilling	

This is an East China specialty originally made with yellow wine. We recommend the use of light Puerto Rican rum for its potency, light color, and added aroma.

Ingredients	**Marinade**
1 small frying chicken, about 3 pounds	1 cup chicken stock
4 slices gingerroot	1 cup light Puerto Rican rum or Chinese yellow wine
	1 tablespoon salt
	1 tablespoon granulated sugar

PREPARATION
Remove yellow film from skin of the chicken, using a Nylon scrubber. This will ensure the white look of the chicken after it is cooked.

COOKING
1 Half-fill a 3-quart saucepan with water and set it over high heat. Bring water to a boil, then add the ginger and cook for 1 minute. Put in chicken, back side down, and let it sit in the boiling water for 1 minute, then turn the chicken breast side up. Bring back to a boil, cover pot, and turn off heat. Set timer for 15 minutes and allow to rest.

2 Uncover pot, bring water back to a boil, then cover again and turn off the heat. Let chicken sit for another 15 minutes.

3 Remove chicken from the pot and wrap it in plastic wrap and chill in the refrigerator until bird is cool, about 1 hour.

4 When chicken has cooled, cut off wings (use the middle portions and tips only), legs, thighs, and breasts from chicken; reserve. Put the carcass, first portion of wings, neck, and giblets (not the liver) in the cooking liquid. Cook over low heat with the pot uncovered for at least 1 hour to make a clear, concentrated broth. Remove fat and drain liquid through a fine sieve. Reserve stock.

5 Slightly slash the soft bone on the underside of the chicken breast. Flip up both sides to flatten. Chop off about 1 inch of skin and bone from the small end of the legs.

6 Arrange the chicken pieces closely together in a deep pan. Mix together the marinade and pour over to cover, then chill in the refrigerator overnight.

7 Turn the chicken pieces the next day and chill again for several hours.

8 Remove the bones from the chicken pieces and cut them up in bite-sized pieces. Leave the wings intact. Arrange the chicken in such a manner that the original shape of the chicken is reconstructed. Serve.

Note: Drunken Chicken can be kept for up to a week in the refrigerator. Do not cut up the chicken until 30 minutes before serving.

⚫⚫⚫Strange-Flavored Chicken

Serves	4 for a main dish in a family meal
Time	30 minutes preparation
	5 to 7 minutes cooking
	35 minutes resting

怪味鷄

This is a famous dish from Sichuan, so named because it is salty, sweet, sour, and pepper-hot and fragrant all at once.

Ingredients
1 small roasting
   chicken, about 4
   pounds
2 teaspoons Sichuan
   peppercorns
2 tablespoons sesame
   seeds
2 whole scallions
2 cloves garlic

**Strange-flavored
sauce**
½ teaspoon ground
   roasted Sichuan
   peppercorns
2 teaspoons chili oil
1 tablespoon sesame oil
1 tablespoon peanut oil
2 tablespoons Chinese
   red rice vinegar
2 tablespoons sesame
   paste

1 tablespoon sugar
1 tablespoon dark soy
   sauce
1 tablespoon light soy
   sauce

PREPARATION

1 Follow the recipe for White-chopped Chicken (pages 199–200): white-cook the chicken and chop into bite-sized pieces, then arrange on a platter to reconstruct the original shape of the chicken.

2 Roast Sichuan peppercorns in a small saucepan over medium heat until a spicy fragrance escapes, about 3 minutes. Remove peppercorns to a small stainless-steel mixing bowl and smash with the end of the handle of the Chinese cleaver until very fine. Put ground peppercorns through a very fine mesh sieve to separate the tiny husks. Reserve the fine pepper powder (about 1 teaspoon).

3 Roast sesame seeds until light golden. Put them in between 2 pieces of wax paper and roll with a rolling pin or grind with a mortar and pestle until sesame seeds are broken. Reserve. (Do not use a food processor or a blender. This recipe calls for rolled sesame seeds, light and fluffy in texture.)

4 Chop scallions and garlic finely and put them together.

5 Combine ingredients for sauce in a mixing bowl. Use a wire whisk to blend them until smooth.

6 When ready to serve, restir sauce to mix well. Pour evenly over chicken and sprinkle with chopped scallion and garlic, then sesame seeds. Serve cold.

◉◉Foil-Wrapped Chicken

Serves 10 to 12 as an hors d'oeuvre
Time approximately 30 minutes
preparation
30 minutes chilling
15 minutes baking

This is a modified version for Parchment Chicken, famous in Wuzhou in Guangsi province, just over the border of Guangdong. The original recipe involves deep-frying the chicken pieces wrapped in an absorbent Chinese paper. Foil-wrapping and baking makes the chicken juicier and less greasy, besides being more convenient in the American kitchen.

Ingredients	Seasonings	
2 pounds chicken thighs	Juice of 2 slices gingerroot	⅛ teaspoon white pepper
8 ounces bacon strips	2 teaspoons brandy	1½ tablespoons tapioca powder
6 whole scallions	1 tablespoon peanut oil	
	2 teaspoons sesame oil	
	1 teaspoon granulated sugar	
	1 tablespoon oyster sauce	
	2 teaspoons dark soy sauce	

PREPARATION

1 Remove skin from the chicken thighs. Slit thighs along the center lengthwise and spread the meat to the sides. Insert a carving knife from one long side through the meat underneath the main bone, sliding and cutting to free meat at both ends. Trim off excess fat and any visible gristle.

2 Cut thighs into pieces about 1 by 1½ inches. Put meat in a bowl and add the seasonings. Mix well with your fingers, then chill at least 30 minutes or until ready to use.

3 Cut bacon into 1-inch pieces.

4 Using the lower 3 inches of each scallion, cut each into 1-inch lengths. Split each length in half, then separate the layers.

5 Cut aluminum foil into 3-inch squares. You will need about 24 to 30 pieces.

ASSEMBLING

1 Place a piece of chicken and a strip of scallion in between 2 pieces of bacon. Position above the center of a piece of aluminum foil.

2 Bring the other half of the foil over to form a fold, with ends meeting.

3 Seal all around the sides (except on the fold-over side) by turning the edges over about ¼ inch. Repeat for remaining chicken.

COOKING

1 Preheat oven to 450 degrees.

2 Arrange foil bags in 1 layer on a baking sheet. Place in the center of the hot oven and bake for 15 minutes or until brownish bubbles appear breaking through the folds. Serve hot.

◉◉Fried Chicken Thighs, Hong Kong Style

Serves   3 to 4 as a main dish with rice and vegetables
Time   10 minutes preparation
30 minutes marinating
25 minutes cooking

炸雞腿

Cosmopolitan Hong Kong is always ready to experiment with ingredients from the West. This dish, using tomato catsup, Worcestershire sauce, and citrus juices, is a good example.

Ingredients

2 pounds chicken
  thighs, about 8 to 9
  pieces
1 medium yellow onion
6 cups + 2 tablespoons
  oil
2 egg whites, lightly
  beaten
Cornstarch for dusting
1 clove garlic, minced

Marinade

2 tablespoons light soy
  sauce
1 tablespoon brandy
1 teaspoon ginger juice
2 teaspoons granulated
  sugar

Sauce

½ cup chicken stock
2 tablespoons tomato
  catsup
2 tablespoons
  Worcestershire
  sauce
Juice and rind of ½
  lemon
1 tablespoon tapioca
  powder
¼ teaspoon salt
2 tablespoons brown
  sugar

PREPARATION

1 Rub the skin of the chicken thighs with a Nylon scrubber to remove any yellow film. Rinse and pat dry. Follow the instructions on page 72 for boning the thighs, being sure to trim as much gristle and fat as possible. Prick the skin and inside part of each thigh with a fork so marinade can penetrate.

2 Mix marinade ingredients in a bowl, then put in chicken. Allow to rest at room temperature for at least 30 minutes, or keep refrigerated for several hours. Turn the thighs twice while marinating. Drain and reserve marinade.

3 Combine marinade with ingredients for sauce in a bowl. Mix well and set aside.

4 Peel the onion, then cut it in half lengthwise. Slice each half crosswise into ¼-inch strips. Separate strips.

COOKING

1 Set a wok over high heat until very hot, then add 6 cups oil. While waiting for oil to heat, dip the thighs in egg white, then dredge in cornstarch. Shake off excess cornstarch.

2 Test the oil temperature by dropping a piece of scallion green into the oil. If it sizzles and turns brown quickly, the oil is ready (about 375 degrees). Add thighs, piece by piece, and deep-fry until the coating sets and is lightly brown. Remove the chicken to a strainer. Turn heat off.

3 Use a fine-mesh strainer to remove sediment from the oil, then reheat oil over high heat to very hot and return thighs to wok. Deep-fry until golden brown, then drain again.

4 Put onion strips in a small basket and lower basket into hot oil. Shake basket gently until onion is soft and transparent, about 1 minute. Remove basket and pour out oil. Wipe wok clean.

5 Set wok again over high heat and add 1 tablespoon of oil. Put in garlic and stir, about 10 seconds. Restir sauce mixture and add to wok, stirring constantly until it thickens. Turn the heat to low, then glaze the sauce with remaining oil. Turn heat off.

6 Arrange thighs in 1 layer on a deep serving dish and decorate with fried onion strips. Pour sauce over thighs and serve immediately.

VARIATION: Braised Chicken Thighs in Pineapple Sauce
This is another example of fruit used in the cooking of Hong Kong.

Ingredients
1 small can (12 ounces)
  pineapple chunks
2 pounds chicken
  thighs, about 8 to 9
  pieces

Sauce
1 teaspoon chicken
  bouillon powder
2 tablespoons tomato
  catsup
1 tablespoon red rice
  vinegar
1 tablespoon light soy
  sauce
2 teaspoons granulated
  sugar
¼ teaspoon salt
1 tablespoon tapioca powder

1 Drain pineapple and reserve all the canning juice (about ¾ cup) for the sauce.

2 Mix ingredients for sauce in a small bowl, add pineapple juice, and set aside.

3 Follow the master recipe to bone, marinate, and deep-fry the chicken.

4 Cook the sauce in the same manner as in master recipe. Add pineapple chunks to the sauce before glazing. Serve.

◉◉ Curry Chicken

Serves 4 with rice and stir-fried
  green vegetables
Time 15 minutes preparation
  20 minutes resting
  25 minutes cooking

咖喱鷄

This recipe, using coconut milk, is Chinese-Malaysian. It also excludes the traditional potato, keeping the sauce light.

Ingredients
1 frying chicken (about
  3 pounds), cut up
1 large yellow onion
½ pound carrots
¼ cup oil
1 clove garlic, flattened
2 tablespoons curry
  powder
⅛ teaspoon cayenne
  pepper (optional)

1 tablespoon pale dry
  sherry
1½ cups coconut milk
1½ cups water
½ teaspoon salt
1 tablespoon tapioca
  powder mixed with 2
  tablespoons water

Seasonings
2 tablespoons light soy
  sauce
Juice from 2 slices
  gingerroot
1 teaspoon granulated
  sugar
½ teaspoon salt
Dash of white pepper

PREPARATION

1 Trim any excess skin and fat off chicken parts. Cut the breast in half lengthwise, then cut each half into pieces about 1 by 2 inches. Cut to disjoint legs and thighs, then cut them into pieces the same size as chicken breast. Cut wings at the joints to yield 6 pieces.

2 Combine seasonings and chicken in a large bowl and mix with your fingers to blend well. Set at room temperature for at least 20 minutes.

3 Quarter the onion lengthwise, then cut each quarter crosswise in half. Separate the layers.

4 Peel carrots. Roll-cut (see page 63) into wedges. Cook with some water for 5 minutes, then drain and set aside.

COOKING

1 Set a wok over high heat. When very hot, add oil. Put in onion, stirring until each piece is well coated with oil, then remove and leave as much oil in the wok as possible. Set onion aside.

2 Add garlic to flavor the oil in wok for 20 seconds. Add chicken and stir constantly until pink color disappears, about 5 minutes.

3 Sprinkle curry powder (and cayenne pepper if used) on chicken, immediately sizzle in wine, stirring again, then add the coconut milk and water to cover the chicken pieces. Bring to a boil, turn heat to medium, cover, and cook 15 minutes.

4 Add the carrots, onion, and salt to chicken. Cover, and cook 5 minutes more.

5 Stream the tapioca mixture into the sauce, stirring to prevent lumps. When sauce thickens, test for salt. Mix sauce with chicken, then remove to a casserole and serve.

Note: Frozen coconut milk in a 12-ounce can from Hawaii is the best. Canned coconut milk from Malaysia or the Philippines is slightly less flavorful, but still serves excellently in this recipe.

◉◉◉Gung Bao Chicken Ding

Serves 3 to 4 as a main dish with
rice, vegetables, and a minute
soup
Time 15 minutes preparation
30 minutes resting
1 hour chilling
10 to 15 minutes cooking

Developed by Ding Bao-zhen, erstwhile governor of Yunnan and Guizhou with the rank of Gung Bao ("Guardian of the Royal Heir's Palace"), this fiery dish features maize corn in its native Guizhou, but peanuts almost everywhere else in China. Ding, incidentally, means "dice."

Ingredients	Seasonings	Sauce
2 pounds chicken thighs	1 egg white, from medium egg	1 tablespoon red rice vinegar
2 tablespoons water	1 tablespoon dark soy sauce	1 tablespoon brown sugar
2 cups oil	1 tablespoon tapioca powder	1 teaspoon tapioca powder
¾ cup blanched unsalted peanuts	½ teaspoon salt	1 teaspoon dark soy sauce
4 dried chili peppers, broken in half		
2 cloves garlic, crushed		
2 slices gingerroot, minced		
1 tablespoon pale dry sherry		
4 scallions (white part only), cut into ¼-inch pieces		
2 teaspoons sesame oil		

PREPARATION

1 Remove skin from chicken and bone the thighs (see page 72). Trim as much fat and gristle as possible, then cut meat into cubes about ½ by ½ by ¾ inch in size.

2 Combine chicken with water in a bowl and allow to rest for 30 minutes, or until water is well absorbed.

3 Mix the ingredients for the seasonings and add to the chicken. Chill at least 1 hour or until ready to use.

4 Mix sauce ingredients in a small bowl and set aside.

COOKING

1 Set a wok over high heat. When the wok is very hot, add the oil. Deep-fry the peanuts until just lightly golden, then remove with a strainer to drain.

2 Turn off heat and immediately add the chicken to the oil, stirring for about 30 seconds, then pour chicken and oil together into a strainer-lined bowl to drain. Leave about 2 tablespoons of oil in the wok.

3 Again set wok over high heat. When the oil is hot, add the chili peppers, stirring just once, then add the garlic and ginger. Immediately return the chicken to the wok, sizzle in the wine, and stir for 20 seconds.

4 Push the chicken to the side of the wok and restir sauce mixture. Stream sauce mixture into the center of the wok, stirring constantly until thickened.

5 Add the scallions and mix all ingredients together. Add the sesame oil to glaze the sauce and serve with peanuts on top.

◉◉◉Black Bean Chicken

Serves	4 as a main dish, with rice and vegetables
Time	35 minutes preparation
	15 minutes resting
	10 minutes cooking

豆 豉 雞

The versatile black bean goes with everything, but ordinarily is the mark of country food. This dish, however, is elegant enough to be popular in large-city restaurants. Steaming the black beans in wine and sugar mellows their sharp taste, and makes the dish more subtle.

Ingredients

1 small frying chicken, about 3 pounds
3 tablespoons fermented black beans
2 slices gingerroot
3 tablespoons yellow wine or pale dry sherry
1 tablespoon granulated sugar

3 cups oil
8 small shallots, lightly crushed
2 dried chili peppers (optional)
2 cloves garlic, minced
2 teaspoons sesame oil

Seasonings

2 tablespoons light soy sauce
1 tablespoon tapioca powder
¼ teaspoon salt

Sauce

1 teaspoon tapioca powder
1 tablespoon chicken stock

PREPARATION

1 Rub the chicken with a Nylon scrubber to remove any yellow film, then pat with paper towels to dry inside and out. Bone chicken, following instructions on page 69. Trim all fat and excess skin, then cut into 2- by 1-inch chunks.

2 Combine seasoning ingredients, then mix with chicken. Allow to rest at room temperature for at least 15 minutes.

3 Rinse the black beans and place them in a small heatproof bowl. Add ginger, 1 tablespoon sherry, and sugar, and steam over medium heat for 20 minutes.

4 Mix the ingredients for the sauce with juice from steaming the beans, then set aside.

COOKING

1 Set a wok over high heat. When very hot, add the oil and wait 6 to 7 minutes until oil is very hot, about 375 degrees. Add the chicken, stirring to separate, for about 30 seconds. When the pink color disappears, pour oil and chicken together into a strainer placed in a bowl, leaving about 2 tablespoons of oil in the wok.

2 Reset the wok over high heat and add the shallots, stirring until transparent. Add the chili peppers, garlic, and black beans, stirring 15 seconds.

3 Return chicken to wok, then sizzle in the remaining wine. Stir and turn until the moisture is evaporated. Cover wok for 1 minute, then uncover and push ingredients to the side. Restir the sauce mixture and stream it into the center, stirring until thickened. Glaze sauce with sesame oil, mix with chicken, and serve.

◉◉Red-Cooked Chicken with Chestnuts

Serves 4 as a main dish with vegetables and a clear soup
Time 40 minutes preparation
30 minutes cooking

紅炆栗子雞

Chestnuts and chicken are a delightful combination as seen in this dish from North China, where the best chestnuts are grown.

Ingredients

1 pound chestnuts in the shell
1 small frying chicken, about 3 pounds
2 tablespoons oil
4 whole scallions, cut into 2-inch lengths
2 slices gingerroot
2 tablespoons pale dry sherry
1½ cups chicken stock
¼ cup dark soy sauce
2 teaspoons granulated sugar

2 teaspoons tapioca powder
2 tablespoons water
2 teaspoons sesame oil

PREPARATION

1 Using a sharp paring knife, peel a small strip of shell from each chestnut. Put chestnuts in a 3-quart saucepan and add cold water to cover. Bring to a boil over high heat, boil 1 minute, then remove from heat. Take out 3 or 4 chestnuts at a time and peel off the shells and inner skins, leaving the unshelled chestnuts in the saucepan. Continue to shell and skin until all are done, then set them aside.

2 Rub chicken with a Nylon scrubber to remove any yellow film on skin. Rinse with water occasionally while rubbing, then pat dry with paper towels. Chop chicken into bite-sized pieces about 2 inches by 1 inch, but do not include the back bone and neck bone (reserve these for soup stock).

COOKING

1 Set a heavy Dutch oven over high heat until very hot. Add the oil and flavor oil with scallions and ginger. Stir for 20 seconds, then add the chicken and stir constantly until pink color disappears, about 5 to 7 minutes.

2 Sizzle in the wine, stirring again, then add the chicken stock, soy sauce, and sugar. Bring to a boil, turn heat to medium, cover, and cook for 15 minutes.

3 Add the chestnuts to the pot and cook 10 minutes more.

4 While chicken is cooking, mix together the tapioca and water.

5 When chicken and chestnuts are done, gradually add the tapioca mixture, stirring gently to prevent lumps. When sauce thickens, correct seasoning and then glaze with sesame oil.

6 Mix sauce with the chicken and chestnuts. Serve hot.

Note: When fresh chestnuts are not in season, you can substitute dried ones. Soak ½ pound of dried chestnuts in hot water for 5 to 6 hours or overnight. Drain, then put in a 3-quart saucepan, adding enough cold water to cover, about 4 cups. Bring to a boil over high heat, then turn heat to low. Cover pot and cook 30 minutes, or until chestnuts are soft but not mushy.

◉◉Steamed Chicken with Chinese Sausages and Black Mushrooms

Serves	4 as a main dish with vegetables and rice
Time	20 minutes preparation 30 minutes resting 20 minutes cooking

冬 菇 腊 腸 蒸 雞

Popular in old Canton in the winter, the season for dried marinated meats, this dish is now served year-round. A Cantonese family dish, it is commonly one of three dishes from a single chicken. Omit the sausage and jujube if not available.

Ingredients	Seasonings
1 whole chicken breast, about 12 ounces	1 tablespoon light soy sauce
1 pair of chicken legs and thighs	1 tablespoon oyster sauce
6 medium black mushrooms	1 tablespoon brandy
4 Chinese red dates (jujube)	2 tablespoons peanut oil
2 slices gingerroot	1 teaspoon sesame oil
2 scallions (white part only), cut into 1-inch lengths	1 teaspoon granulated sugar
2 Chinese sausages	1 tablespoon tapioca powder
	Dash of salt

PREPARATION

1 Rub chicken with a Nylon scrubber to remove any yellow film. Rinse and pat dry with paper towels, then chop into bite-sized pieces about 2 inches by ¾ inch, bones and all.

2 Combine seasonings in a mixing bowl. Add the chicken pieces and mix well, then set aside for at least 30 minutes.

3 Soak mushrooms in hot water until soft. Trim stems, and squeeze mushrooms to extract moisture. Cut diagonally into slices about ⅜ inch wide.

4 Soak dates in hot water until soft. Remove the pits and cut each date into 6 to 8 pieces.

5 Shred the ginger finely, then combine with scallion and add to the resting chicken meat.

6 Slice sausages diagonally into ⅛-inch pieces.

COOKING

1 Place chicken, along with seasonings, scallions, ginger, mushrooms, and dates, into a heatproof dish. Arrange the sausages in 1 layer on top.

2 If you are using a steamer, bring the water in the base to a boil over high heat. When the water boils vigorously, set the dish in the top layer, then cover the steamer. Steam for 15 to 20 minutes, or until the pink color of the meat disappears, and the fat part of the sausages turns transparent. If the "dish-in-the-pot" steaming method is used (see page 56), line the bottom of the pot with a small kitchen towel, then put in a stand. Add water to come up 1 inch below the dish. When the water boils vigorously, set the dish on the stand and keep the pot covered. Steam as for above method.

3 Remove chicken and other ingredients from the steamer and serve.

◉◉◉Deep-Fried Chicken Breast in Shrimp Roe Sauce

Serves	3 to 4 as a main dish with vegetable and a clear soup in which chicken is not the major ingredient
Time	10 minutes preparation 15 minutes steaming 10 minutes cooking

蝦子雞脯

Dried shrimp roe is one of the ideal seasoning agents. It can be sprinkled like salt to impart both color and taste to all foods. Shrimp roe sauce is simple to prepare and invariably pleasing. It goes excellently with chicken (as shown here), duck, mushrooms, green beans, bamboo shoots, and even asparagus.

Ingredients

2 whole chicken breasts, about 14 to 16 ounces each
1½ teaspoons salt
1 tablespoon dried shrimp roe
2 tablespoons yellow wine
2 slices gingerroot

1 whole egg
⅓ cup cornstarch
4 cups + 1 tablespoon oil
1 clove garlic, crushed
1 tablespoon tapioca powder mixed with 2 tablespoons water
2 teaspoons sesame oil

Sauce mixture

1 cup chicken stock
2 tablespoons oyster sauce
1 teaspoon sugar
Dash of white pepper
Salt

PREPARATION

1 Remove bones and the 2 fillets from each breast, leaving the meat with skin intact. Reserve fillets for other use.

2 Lay each piece of chicken breast on a cutting board with the skin side down. Score diagonally about ¼ inch deep, in 1 direction first at ½-inch intervals, then cross-wise also at ½-inch intervals to form diamond-shaped incisions. Sprinkle salt evenly on the chicken, and rub it into the incisions. Set aside.

3 Combine shrimp roe, 1 tablespoon of the yellow wine, and gingerroot in a small heatproof bowl. Steam over medium high heat for 15 minutes. Discard ginger.

4 Shortly before cooking, pat chicken breasts with a kitchen towel to absorb excess moisture. Beat the egg and pour it onto the chicken breasts to coat both sides evenly, then dredge each piece in cornstarch and dust off the excess.

COOKING

1 Set a wok over high heat. When the wok is very hot, add 4 cups of oil. Wait for 5 minutes, then test the temperature by dropping a piece of scallion green into the oil. If the green sizzles noisily and soon turns brown, the oil is about 375 degrees. Put chicken in rapid succession into the oil, and deep-fry until the coating sets and turns light golden, about 2 minutes. Remove chicken from oil.

2 Use a fine-mesh strainer to remove sediments in oil. Reheat oil to 375 degrees again, then return the chicken breasts to the oil and deep-fry until golden. Remove to drain on paper towels.

3 Pour oil out, leaving about 1 tablespoon oil in the wok. Flavor oil with garlic for 10 seconds, then discard garlic. Sizzle in the remaining wine along the edge of the wok and immediately pour in the sauce mixture and the shrimp roe. Turn heat to medium and cook sauce for 1 minute.

4 Restir the tapioca mixture and stream it gradually into the boiling sauce, stirring until thickened. Glaze sauce with remaining oil and sesame oil. Test seasoning.

5 To serve, chop each breast into half lengthwise, then chop each half into ¾-inch-wide pieces. Arrange in 2 rolls on a serving platter. Pour shrimp roe sauce over and serve.

VARIATION: Deep-Fried Chicken Breast in Lemon Sauce

This is a famous dish from Hong Kong, where East meets West. Follow the master recipe to prepare, deep-fry, and cut up the chicken breast but substitute the shrimp roe sauce with a lemon sauce.

Ingredients

1½ fresh lemons
¾ cup water
2 teaspoons chicken
   bouillon powder
1 tablespoon light soy
   sauce
2 tablespoons brown
   sugar

1 tablespoon tapioca
   powder
2 tablespoons oil
2 small heads of
   shallot, flattened
1 clove garlic, crushed
Salt
1 teaspoon sesame oil

1 Juice the lemons and combine with the next 5 seasoning ingredients for the sauce. Set it aside.

2 Follow cooking steps 1 and 2 above. After the chicken breasts are removed to cut up and the oil poured out from the wok, set the wok back on high heat. When

BRAISED ORANGE DUCK
PAGE 234

**TEA LEAF EGGS
PAGE 242**

very hot, add 1 tablespoon of the oil. Flavor oil with shallots and garlic until they are slightly brown, then give the lemon sauce a quick stir and stream it gradually into the wok, stirring until it thickens. Test for seasoning, especially for tartness; add more brown sugar if needed. Add the remaining oil and the sesame oil to glaze, then pour sauce over chopped chicken breast and serve.

◉◉◉Almond Chicken

Serves 4 as a main dish with a thick
soup
Time 10 minutes preparation
35 minutes resting
7 minutes cooking

杏 仁 雞 丁

A fine meal in itself. With a combination of chicken, vegetables, and nuts, the dish is nutritious, delicious, and eye-pleasing—deservedly popular.

Ingredients

2 whole chicken
  breasts, about 12
  ounces each
2 tablespoons water
1 cup + 6 tablespoons
  oil
8 medium black
  mushrooms
1 cup hot water
½ medium green bell
  pepper
½ medium red sweet
  pepper or ½ cup
  diced carrot
½ cup bamboo shoots
¾ cup shelled almonds

1 clove garlic, sliced
2 whole scallions, cut
  into ½-inch lengths
½ teaspoon salt
1 teaspoon granulated
  sugar
1 tablespoon pale dry
  sherry

Seasonings

½ teaspoon salt
1 tablespoon light soy
  sauce
1 tablespoon pale dry
  sherry
1 egg white
1 teaspoon sesame oil
½ teaspoon granulated
  sugar
Dash of white pepper
2 tablespoons tapioca
  powder

PREPARATION

1 Skin and bone breasts, removing as much fat, membranes, and gristle as possible. Cut chicken into ⅜-inch cubes and place in a mixing bowl, adding the water. Mix well and set aside for 5 minutes.

2 In a small bowl, combine all the seasonings and add to the chicken. Mix with your fingers (or a wooden spoon) to blend well. Add 2 tablespoons of oil and mix again, then refrigerate for at least 30 minutes.

3 Soak mushrooms in hot water to cover until soft. Trim the stems and squeeze to extract moisture. Dice caps.

4 Remove seeds and pulp from peppers, then dice. If substituting carrot, dice, blanch in boiling water for 1 minute, then rinse in cold water and set aside.

5 Dice the bamboo shoots, then blanch in boiling water for 1 minute. Rinse in cold water and drain.

6 Blanch almonds in boiling water for 2 minutes, then remove skins. Open each into halves and place on paper towel to dry.

COOKING

1 Set a wok over high heat. When very hot, add 1 cup of oil and wait for 2 to 3 minutes, then test temperature by dropping a small piece of scallion green into the oil. If bubbles appear around the green immediately, then the oil is ready (about 300 degrees). Otherwise wait a minute and test again.

2 When oil is ready, add almonds. Stir 2 or 3 times, then remove wok completely from heat, leaving almonds in the oil until lightly brown, then remove. Pour oil out.

3 Again set wok over high heat. When very hot, add 4 tablespoons of oil, then flavor oil with garlic for 10 seconds. Add chicken, stirring rapidly until the dice separate and the pink color changes to white. Push the chicken to the side and tilt the wok slightly to keep oil away. Remove chicken; there will be about 2 tablespoons of oil left in the wok.

4 With the remaining oil in the wok very hot, add the mushrooms, bamboo shoots, peppers, and scallions in succession, stirring for a total of 2 minutes. Season with salt and sugar.

5 Return the chicken to the wok and immediately sizzle in the wine along the edge, stirring constantly until wine is evaporated and all ingredients are mixed well. Remove to a serving platter and sprinkle almonds on top. Serve immediately.

VARIATION: Walnut Chicken or Cashew Chicken

If walnuts are used to replace almonds, blanch them in boiling water for 1 minute, then remove the skins. Spread the walnut meats on paper towels to dry, then deep-fry as with the almonds.

If cashews are used, deep-fry the cashews the same as for almonds.

◉◉Sauce-Blasted Chicken Ding

Serves	4 as a main dish with vegetables and rice or plain noodles
Time	10 minutes preparation
	1 hour chilling
	5 minutes cooking

醬 爆 雞 丁

A dish from North China, where the sweet bean paste has been used for two thousand years.

Ingredients
2 whole chicken breasts, about 1 pound each
2 cups oil
1 tablespoon pale dry sherry
4 scallions (white part only), cut into ¼-inch slices
2 teaspoons sesame oil

Seasonings
2 tablespoons water
1 tablespoon tapioca powder
1 egg white, from medium egg
¼ teaspoon salt
Juice of 2 slices gingerroot

Sauce
3 tablespoons sweet bean paste
2 tablespoons granulated sugar

PREPARATION

1 Skin and bone the breasts. Remove all possible gristle and any membranes, then cut into ⅜-inch cubes.

2 Combine water and tapioca for seasonings and add chicken cubes; mix well with your fingers. Then blend in the remaining seasonings, mixing well. Chill at least 1 hour or until ready to use.

3 Combine sauce ingredients in a small bowl and set aside.

COOKING

1 Set a wok over high heat. When very hot, add the oil. Wait for about 3 minutes, then add chicken, stirring quickly to separate cubes. When pink color of the meat disappears—in about 40 seconds—pour chicken and oil into a strainer-lined bowl to drain, leaving about 2 tablespoons of oil in the wok.

2 Reset wok over high heat. When oil is hot, add sauce ingredients, stirring until the sugar dissolves and the bean paste becomes thin. Sizzle in the wine, adding also the chicken. Put in scallions, stirring to mix all ingredients, then add sesame oil. Mix and serve.

Stir-Fried Chicken Slices with Fresh Mushrooms

Serves 2 as a main dish with rice and
a thick soup
Time 30 minutes preparation
30 minutes resting
1 hour chilling
5 minutes cooking

蘑 菇 雞 片

Restaurants differ somewhat in how they prepare this dish (also called Moogoo Gai Pan), perhaps the most well known in the United States next to wonton soup. This version stresses the natural flavor and beauty of the ingredients without the veil of a heavy, dark sauce.

Ingredients
1 whole chicken breast, about 1 pound
5 tablespoons oil
1 teaspoon sesame oil
¼ pound button mushrooms
¼ cup sliced carrots
4 ounces snow peas
1 clove garlic, crushed
½ teaspoon salt
1 tablespoon pale dry sherry

Seasonings
2 tablespoons water
½ egg white
1 tablespoon tapioca powder
½ teaspoon salt
1 teaspoon light soy sauce
1 tablespoon pale dry sherry
Dash of white pepper
¼ teaspoon granulated sugar

Sauce
1½ teaspoons tapioca powder
2 tablespoons chicken stock

PREPARATION

1 Skin and bone the chicken. Remove all visible gristle and membranes, then cut the meat into 1- by 2-inch pieces, then horizontally into slices about ¹⁄₁₆ inch thick (for cutting method, see page **68**).

2 Combine water and egg white for seasonings in a bowl, then add chicken slices. Mix with your fingers until each piece is well coated, then set for 30 minutes.

3 Add the remaining seasonings to the chicken, mixing well. Blend in 2 tablespoons of oil and the sesame oil to separate the slices, then chill at least 1 hour or until ready to use.

4 Trim the tough ends of the stems of mushrooms and wipe the caps clean with a dampened cloth. Cut the mushrooms vertically into ¼-inch slices.

5 Blanch carrots in boiling water for 30 seconds, then run cold water over to stop cooking. Drain well and set aside.

6 String the snow peas, rinse, and drain. Set aside.

7 Mix sauce ingredients in a bowl and set aside.

COOKING

1 Set a wok over high heat. When very hot, add the remaining oil, then flavor oil with garlic for about 10 seconds. Remove garlic and add chicken slices, then immediately remove the wok from the heat and stir quickly to separate the slices. Push the chicken to the side and tilt the wok to allow excess oil to run to the center. With a spatula, scrape the chicken into a strainer to drain, leaving as much oil in the wok as possible.

2 Reset wok over high heat. When very hot, add the mushrooms, stirring about 20 seconds. Add snow peas, stirring until natural mushroom juices are released and pea pods turn bright green. Season with salt and sprinkle with a little water if necessary.

3 Return chicken to wok and add carrots. Sizzle in wine, stirring all ingredients together.

4 Restir sauce mixture and stream it into the center of the wok, stirring until it thickens. Remove and serve immediately.

◉◉◉Chicken Velvet with Green Peas

Serves 3 as a main dish with rice and
a thick soup
Time 30 minutes preparation
2 hours chilling
20 minutes cooking

青豆芙蓉雞

This dish shows that North China food can be as delicate as the lightest of Cantonese food.

Ingredients	Seasonings	Clear sauce
1 whole chicken breast, about 14 ounces	1 tablespoon tapioca powder	1 cup chicken stock
½ cup chilled chicken stock	1 teaspoon pale dry sherry	1 tablespoon water chestnut powder or tapioca powder
6 egg whites	¾ teaspoon salt	Dash of white pepper
1 cup shelled green peas	Dash of white pepper	Pinch of granulated sugar
2 cups water	½ teaspoon granulated sugar	Salt
1 tablespoon granulated sugar		
3 cups oil		
1 clove garlic, crushed		
1 tablespoon pale dry sherry		
1 teaspoon sesame oil		
2 tablespoons chopped Smithfield ham		

PREPARATION

1 Skin and bone the chicken breast. Remove all membranes and gristle (see page 64). Cut the meat coarsely into ½-inch cubes.

2 Mince the chicken cubes as finely as possible with a cleaver, adding a few teaspoons of stock at a time while mincing, until meat is reduced to a paste. Remove to a large mixing bowl and add egg whites 1 at a time, stirring with a wire whisk to blend until all whites are incorporated.

3 Add seasonings to chicken paste and stir well to mix. Chill chicken to firm the paste, at least 2 hours.

4 Blanch peas in boiling water with the sugar for 1 minute. Drain in a colander and immediately run cold water over to stop the cooking process. Drain well.

5 Mix the sauce ingredients in a bowl and set aside.

COOKING

1 Set a wok over high heat. When hot, add the oil. Turn heat to medium-low and wait for about 2 minutes, then test temperature by dropping a small piece of scallion green into the oil. If bubbles appear around the scallion very slowly, then the oil is ready (about 200 degrees); oil should be low in temperature, or the chicken velvet will lose its smoothness and tenderness.

2 Turn heat to low. Dip a tablespoon in cold oil, then fill it with the chicken paste and flatten it into an oval shape. Drop spoonful by spoonful into the hot oil until one-third of the paste is used. The chicken is cooked when it sets and rises to the surface; pieces should be creamy white in color. If the oil gets too hot, add ½ cup of cold oil to the wok. Also, to prevent the paste from sticking to the spoon, dip the spoon in cold oil frequently between batches. Drain the chicken velvet pieces in a strainer and continue to cook the 2 remaining batches of paste as for first.

3 Pour oil out of wok, leaving about 1 tablespoon of oil. Turn heat to medium and, when hot, flavor remaining oil with garlic for 10 seconds, then remove garlic. Sizzle in the wine. Quickly restir the sauce mixture and add it to the wok, stirring constantly until bubbly.

4 Add the peas and 1 tablespoon of the ham to the wok and bring sauce back to a boil. Glaze the sauce with sesame oil, then return chicken pieces to the wok, stirring to mix. Correct seasoning.

5 Remove chicken and sauce to a deep serving platter and decorate with the remaining ham. Serve immediately.

Note: The mincing of the chicken and the beating with egg whites can be done in a blender with excellent results. Add chicken, chicken stock, and the seasonings in the blender. Beat at high speed for 1 minute. Then add the egg whites, beating at low speed until they are well blended with the chicken into a thin paste. Be sure not to overbeat the egg whites. Chill at least 2 hours.

For a low-fat version of this dish, instead of cooking chicken in oil, fill a Dutch oven half-full with cold water and set it over medium-low heat. Spoon the chicken paste into the water, piece by piece, until all pieces float to the surface. Wet the spoon frequently to prevent sticking.

⊛⊛⊛Chicken Shreds and Red-in-Snow

Serves 4 to 6 in a multi-dish meal
Time 20 minutes preparation
30 minutes resting
1 hour chilling
7 minutes cooking

雪 菜 鷄 絲

Red-in-snow is a preserved green popular in East China. Its unique salty flavor recommends this dish as an accompaniment to other dishes and with rice.

Ingredients	Seasonings	Sauce
1 whole chicken breast, about 1 pound	2 tablespoons water	1½ teaspoons tapioca powder
1 small can (7 ounces) red-in-snow	1 egg white	2 tablespoons chicken stock
6 medium black mushrooms	2 teaspoons tapioca powder	
1 cup bamboo shoots	½ teaspoon salt	
1 cup + 2 tablespoons oil	1 teaspoon granulated sugar	
1 teaspoon granulated sugar	1 teaspoon sesame oil	
1 clove garlic, shredded	Dash of white pepper	
1 tablespoon pale dry sherry		
1 teaspoon sesame oil		

PREPARATION

1 Skin and bone the chicken. Remove all visible gristle and membranes, then shred finely (for cutting method, see page 68).

2 Combine chicken shreds in a bowl with water for seasonings. Mix together with your fingers, then add egg white, stirring and mixing until well blended. Allow to rest for 30 minutes.

3 Add remaining seasonings to the chicken and mix well. Chill at least 1 hour or until ready to use.

4 Soak red-in-snow in cold water for 5 minutes to remove excess salt. Squeeze to extract any moisture, then cut into ¼-inch pieces.

5 Soak black mushrooms in warm water until soft. Trim stems and squeeze to extract moisture. Shred finely.

6 Cut bamboo shoots into shreds ⅛ by ⅛ by 1½ inches. Blanch in boiling water for 1 minute, then rinse with cold water and drain.

7 Mix sauce ingredients in a small bowl and set aside.

COOKING

1 Set a wok over high heat. When very hot, put in bamboo shoots and red-in-snow, stirring constantly until most moisture has evaporated. Whirl in 2 tablespoons of oil and season with sugar. Remove vegetables from wok and set aside.

2 Rinse the wok and wipe it dry. Set it again over high heat and, when very hot, add the remaining 1 cup of oil. Immediately add the chicken and remove the wok from the heat. Stir quickly to separate the shreds, about 10 seconds. Pour the oil and the chicken into a strainer-lined bowl to drain, leaving about 1 tablespoon of oil in the wok.

3 Reset the wok over high heat. Add the garlic, stirring once, then add the mushrooms, stirring for 10 seconds. Return chicken to the wok, sizzle in the wine along the edge, and then add the bamboo shoots and red-in-snow. Stir and mix all ingredients together.

4 Restir sauce mixture and add to the center of the wok, stirring constantly until it thickens. Glaze with sesame oil and mix well. Remove and serve.

Note: After cooking salty ingredients, rinsing the wok is a must, or else the wok will turn sticky and the beautiful color of the chicken shreds will also be greatly affected.

VARIATION: Chicken Shreds with Sichuan Preserved Vegetables
Red-in-snow can be replaced by Sichuan preserved vegetables. Cut into shreds ⅛ by ⅛ by 1½ inches. Rinse, soak, and cook in the same manner.

Braised Chicken Wings

Serves   3 with rice and a thick soup
Time   5 minutes preparation
20 minutes marinating
30 minutes cooking

炆雞翼

Chicken wings, very inexpensive in America, are esteemed in China for the firm skin in the mid-portion and the tender meat beneath the skin. They are said to have been a favorite of Empress Dowager Ci-xi of the Qing Dynasty.

This recipe came from the one for Royal Consort Chicken, a famous northern dish. However, we use only the mid-portion of the wing, which is, conveniently, the byproduct of boning the chicken wings for Deep-Fried Mock Drumsticks.

Ingredients

16 chicken wings,
mid-portions only
2 tablespoons oyster
sauce
1 cup chicken stock
4 cups spinach leaves
5 tablespoons oil
4 teaspoons granulated
sugar

2 tablespoons pale dry
sherry
1 clove garlic, crushed
Salt
1 teaspoon tapioca
powder
1 tablespoon water
1 teaspoon sesame oil

Marinade

1 tablespoon dark soy
sauce
1 tablespoon pale dry
sherry
2 teaspoons ginger
juice

PREPARATION

1 Rub chicken wings with a Nylon scrubber to remove any yellow film on the skin. Rinse and pat dry with paper towels. Add wings to marinade in a bowl, mixing well. Set at room temperature for 20 minutes. Drain chicken and reserve marinade.

2 Combine marinade with oyster sauce and chicken stock. Set aside.

3 Rinse and drain spinach leaves thoroughly.

COOKING

1 Set a heavy Dutch oven over high heat until hot. Add 3 tablespoons of the oil. Arrange wings in the pot in 1 layer and pan-fry until both sides are brown. Add 2 teaspoons of the sugar, stirring until dissolved (the melted sugar helps the skin to take on the reddish brown color of the sauce), then sizzle in the wine. Add the marinade mixture and turn heat to medium low. Cover pot and cook for 20 minutes.

2 Five minutes before the wings are done, you can start to cook the spinach. Set a wok over high heat and, when hot, add the remaining oil. Flavor oil with garlic for 10 seconds, then add salt. Put in spinach, stirring and turning until wilted. Sprinkle the remaining sugar on top and keep on stirring until the spinach turns to a bright green and becomes soft. Remove and drain, then arrange spinach on both ends of an oval serving platter.

3 Mix the tapioca with the water and add to the center of the pot, stirring until the sauce thickens. Correct seasonings. Glaze sauce with sesame oil.

4 Arrange wings in 2 rows on the center part of the serving platter and pour the hot sauce over. Serve immediately.

Deep-Fried Mock Drumsticks

Serves 8 as an appetizer
Time about 20 minutes preparation
30 minutes marinating
15 minutes cooking

炸假雞腿

One of the most inexpensive, yet most impressive Chinese hors d'oeuvre to be served for any occasion, this dish is easiest using our method. The upper portion of a chicken wing turns handily into a mock drumstick, ready for deep-frying.

Ingredients	Marinade	Batter
16 whole chicken wings	2 tablespoons light soy sauce	¾ cup all-purpose flour
6 cups oil	1 tablespoon pale dry sherry	1 cup ice water
	1 teaspoon ginger juice	1 tablespoon oil
	½ teaspoon salt	1¼ teaspoons baking powder
	2 teaspoons granulated sugar	
	2 teaspoons sesame oil	
	¼ teaspoon five-spice powder	

PREPARATION

1 Bone the upper portion of each wing to form a mock drumstick (see page 71). Reserve the middle portion and tip intact for another use.

2 Mix the marinade in a bowl, then add drumsticks. Mix well with fingers, then set at room temperature for 30 minutes. Drain and discard marinade. Mix ingredients for batter, then chill.

COOKING

1 Set a wok over high heat. When hot, add oil. Wait for about 8 to 10 minutes, then test temperature by dropping a small piece of scallion green into the oil. If the green quickly turns brown, the oil is ready (about 400 degrees).

2 Twirl the chicken wings, 1 at a time, into the batter, then drop them into the hot oil. Deep-fry half the wings until the batter sets and the color is light golden. Drain in a strainer while you reheat the oil to very hot and continue to deep-fry the remaining half of the chicken in the same manner. Turn heat off.

3 Skim the oil and remove any particles. Reheat to very hot over high heat, then return all pre-fried wings to the oil. Deep-fry until rich golden brown. Remove and drain on paper towels, then serve.

Note: The crispy batter is a little thin, thus the oil must be very hot so as to set it immediately, otherwise the batter will fall into the oil.

⦿Deep-Fried Spicy Liver

Serves 4 as part of a family meal, or
makes about 24 appetizers
Time 15 minutes preparation
20 minutes marinating
15 minutes cooking

A very delightful Cantonese appetizer, this inexpensive dish is also easy to prepare. It can be served also with other dishes in a Chinese-style meal.

Ingredients	Marinade
1 pound chicken livers	1 tablespoon brandy
1 large egg, lightly beaten	Juice of 2 slices of gingerroot
Cornstarch for coating	¼ teaspoon five-spice powder
4 cups oil	
1 cup shredded iceberg lettuce	1 teaspoon granulated sugar
1 lemon, cut into wedges	1 tablespoon light soy sauce
1 tablespoon Five-Spice Salt (page 193)	¾ teaspoon salt

PREPARATION

1 Remove all fat and gristle from livers. Cut each in half. Fill a 4-quart saucepan half full with water, set it over high heat, and bring water to a boil. Add livers, then remove pan from the heat. Cover and let rest about 30 seconds, then pour the contents into a colander to drain. Pat livers with paper towels to dry.

2 Combine seasonings for marinade in a bowl and add livers. Mix well, then set at room temperature for 20 minutes.

3 Drain livers and discard marinade. Add the egg to the livers and mix.

COOKING

1 Coat each piece of chicken liver with cornstarch.

2 Set a wok over high heat. When very hot, add the oil, then wait about 5 minutes. Test temperature by dropping a piece of scallion green into the oil. If the green sizzles noisily and soon turns brown, the oil is ready (375 degrees).

3 Add half the livers, piece by piece. Turn the heat to medium and deep-fry the livers until golden. Remove to drain. Reheat the oil to very hot and finish deep-frying the remaining livers.

4 Line a serving platter with the shredded lettuce, and arrange livers on top. Serve garnished with lemon wedges and five-spice salt on the side as appetizer.

 Gold Coin Chicken

Serves 12 in a banquet
Time 1 hour preparation
marinate overnight
35 minutes roasting

金錢鷄

This dish usually contains neither chicken nor gold coin. It is so called because the pieces are gold coin in size, and tender as chicken. I substitute chicken liver for the traditional pork liver to make it even more tender. And at least, there is now something of the chicken in this multi-layer banquet "sandwich."

Ingredients
1 pound pork fatback
4 ounces Smithfield ham
12 ounces pork tenderloin
1 pound chicken livers
1 medium turnip
3 skewers (see cooking techniques, page 58)
3 corks from wine bottles
48 flat bread rounds (see Cantonese Flat Bread, page 412)
⅓ cup honey
2 tablespoons sesame oil

Marinade for pork fat
2 tablespoons brandy
2 tablespoons granulated sugar
½ teaspoon salt

Marinade for pork tenderloin
1 tablespoon light soy sauce
2 tablespoons oyster sauce
1 teaspoon granulated sugar
1 tablespoon brandy
Dish of white pepper

Marinade for chicken liver
1 knob gingerroot
1 teaspoon brandy
1 tablespoon light soy sauce
1 teaspoon granulated sugar
½ teaspoon salt
⅛ teaspoon white pepper

PREPARATION

1 Slice pork fat into 24 slices about ⅛ inch thick and 1½ inch square in size (reject the part with nonuniform texture). Cut off the corners to make them round in shape. Discard the rejected parts.

2 For pork fat marinade, mix brandy, sugar, and salt in a small bowl. Add pork fat slices and mix well. Wrap and chill in refrigerator overnight, turning twice.

3 Cut ham across the grain into 24 slices, the same size and shape as pork fat.

4 Also cut pork tenderloin across the grain into 24 thin slices of same size and about ³⁄₁₆ inch thick.

5 For pork marinade, mix soy sauce, oyster sauce, sugar, brandy, and pepper in a bowl. Arrange half the slices in 1 layer in a deep dish. Pour seasonings over. Put the remaining slices on top. Set at room temperature for 15 minutes, then turn pork. Wrap and chill overnight.

6 On the day of serving, prepare chicken livers. Remove visible gristle and slice the larger pieces in half horizontally. For the smaller pieces, make a horizontal cut half way through the center, and spread open to make them close to the size of the larger pieces.

7 Grate about 2 slices of ginger from the knob. Strain it through a fine-mesh strainer into a mixing bowl; press the ginger pulp against the wall of strainer to extract juice. Add brandy, soy sauce, sugar, salt, and pepper. Mix well and put in liver to mix with the seasonings. Chill for 30 minutes.

8 To skewer, cut the turnip crosswise into ⅓-inch slices. Thread 1 piece of turnip first to protect the meat from burning. Then thread, in sequence, 8 sets of meat ingredients, each consisting of 1 piece of pork fat, 1 piece of ham, 1 piece of pork loin, and 1 piece of chicken liver. Push the sharp end of the skewer into a cork to secure the meat. Thread the remaining skewers likewise.

COOKING

1 Preheat oven to 375 degrees.

2 Place a roasting pan on the lowest level of the oven. Add about 1 cup of water; this keeps the meat moist during roasting.

3 Hang the skewers vertically at the highest level of the oven rack. Roast for 25 minutes.

4 During this time, arrange flat breads on a platter. Cover them with a paper towel to trap the moisture and steam for 5 minutes. Keep steamer cover on until ready to serve.

5 Remove skewers from oven. Brush first with honey all around, then with sesame oil.

6 Raise oven temperature to 450 degrees.

7 Empty the water from the roasting pan, then rehang skewers on rack and reset pan in oven. Roast for 10 minutes.

8 Remove skewers and discard corks. Use a fork to scrape meat from skewers onto a serving platter. Discard turnip pieces. Surround the "gold coins" with steamed flat bread rounds in an overlapping style. Serve hot. The diners prepare their own sandwiches with 1 set of meat slices, starting with a piece of pork fat, between 2 pieces of flat bread rounds.

DUCK

 Braised Onion-Stuffed Duck

Serves 4 as a main dish with rice and
a clear soup
Time 20 minutes preparation
1 hour marinating
2 hours simmering
30 minutes cooking

The duck meat is chopstick-soft and the onion melts in your mouth. The sauce adds just the right flavor to plain rice. This East China dish is great for special family occasions.

Ingredients
1 young duckling,
about 5 pounds
4 tablespoons oil
1 pound small boiling
onions
1 clove garlic, crushed
1 cup + 2 tablespoons
water
2 teaspoons tapioca
powder
1 teaspoon sesame oil

Marinade
1 tablespoon brandy or
vodka
2 tablespoons dark soy
sauce
1 teaspoon salt
Juice of 2 slices
gingerroot

Braising sauce
1½ cups chicken stock
1 tablespoon oyster
sauce
1 tablespoon
granulated sugar

Green vegetables
4 cups spinach leaves
2 tablespoons oil
1 clove garlic, crushed
½ teaspoon salt
2 teaspoons granulated
sugar

PREPARATION
1 Rinse duck and pull out all loose fat from the tail and neck. Cut off the mid-portion and tip of the wings (reserve for stock), and press the duck on the back with both palms to flatten. Pat dry with paper towels.

2 Mix marinade ingredients and rub over the skin and cavity. Set at room temperature for at least 1 hour, turning the duck several times.

3 Drain duck and reserve marinade.

COOKING
1 Set a wok over high heat. When very hot, add 2 tablespoons of oil. Lightly brown the onions on all sides and then remove. Turn heat to medium high and place in the duck, turning it frequently to brown on all sides, about 20 minutes.

2 Remove duck from wok and discard fat. Stuff the onions into the cavity.

3 Set a heavy Dutch oven over high heat. When very hot, add 1 tablespoon oil. Flavor oil with garlic until brown, then add braising sauce ingredients and 1 cup water. Bring to a boil and add the duck. Return to a boil, cover, and simmer over low heat for about 2 hours, turning the duck occasionally. Add more water if necessary to keep up level of liquid.

4 Test for doneness of duck meat by inserting a chopstick through the thickest part of the thigh. It should go through very easily; otherwise, cook another 30 minutes (the timing depends on the quality of the duck).

5 If the duck is to be used immediately, remove from the pot. Take onions out of cavity and lay duck flat on an oval serving platter, breast side up, to warm in the oven until served. If duck is to be used several hours later, refrigerate the duck in the pot, then remove solidified fat on top when ready to reheat.

6 Skim fat from sauce, add onions, and cook over medium heat until it comes to a boil. Mix the tapioca powder with 2 tablespoons of water, and then stream it into the sauce, stirring constantly until the sauce thickens. Glaze sauce with sesame oil and remaining tablespoon of oil.

7 If a green vegetable is desired, follow the instructions for Braised Chicken Wings (page 224) to stir-fry the spinach. Drain.

8 Arrange spinach (if used) around the duck first, then place the onions on top of the spinach. Pour the sauce over the duck and onions and serve whole, to be pried apart at the table.

⊚⊚Red-Cooked Duck in Yellow Wine

Serves	4 as a main dish with vegetables and rice or as a cold platter	酒炆鴨
Time	5 minutes preparation 1 hour, 35 minutes cooking	

Fragrant, delightful, and very easy to make, this dish can be served hot or cold and is always welcome at parties.

Ingredients

1 young duckling, about 5 pounds
½ cup yellow wine
1 can (12 ounces) light beer
¾ cup light soy sauce
¼ cup sesame oil
2 tablespoons granulated sugar
4 slices gingerroot

2 whole scallions, trimmed
3 cloves garlic, crushed
1 whole star anise
1 tablespoon Sichuan peppercorns

PREPARATION

1 Thaw duck if frozen. Pull off excess fat along the neck and around the tail.

2 Rinse and pat dry.

COOKING

1 In an oval Dutch oven (or another pot large enough to hold the duck snugly), place the wine, beer, soy sauce, sesame oil, sugar, ginger, scallions, and garlic. Bring to a boil over medium-high heat.

2 Tie the star anise and peppercorns in a piece of cheesecloth and add the spice bag to the braising liquid.

3 Put duck into Dutch oven, breast side up. Cover pot and cook over medium-low heat for 30 minutes. Turn duck and cook another 30 minutes. Then turn duck to rest on its side, first 15 minutes on one side and then 15 minutes on the other. The duck should be evenly colored. Remove to a rack to cool.

4 To serve, chop duck into bite-sized pieces, Chinese style, or remove bones and cut up in pieces (see page 73).

5 Reheat braising liquid, skim fat, and pour about ¾ cup over duck. Serve warm.

Note: The duck can also be served cold. Chill in refrigerator until the fat solidifies on top, then remove the fat before cutting up the duck.

Camphor and Tea Leaf Duck

Serves	4 as a main dish with Pungent and Hot Soup, rice and vegetables
Time	30 minutes preparation
	2 days marinating
	2 hours steaming
	30 minutes smoking
	20 minutes deep-frying (optional)

樟茶鴨

The authentic Sichuan method of preparing duck is to marinate it with spices, smoke it with tea and camphor wood, steam it, then deep-fry it. The complicated processing put tremendous pressure on the family cook and, as a consequence, this dish is seldom served in homes.

This recipe, designed for home-cooking, steams the duck before smoking, thus eliminating the unpleasant splashing of duck fat on the cinders. The last deep-frying step is necessary if one desires the crispy skin. Otherwise, the duck is just as aromatic, indeed somewhat juicier.

It is traditional to use a tiny amount of saltpeter, a chemical used by the Chinese for over a thousand years to make the duck meat hamlike in color, taste, and texture. It could be omitted if desired.

Ingredients

1 young duckling,
about 5 pounds
2 tablespoons Sichuan
peppercorns
2 tablespoons salt

1 teaspoon saltpeter
(optional)
6 cups oil for
deep-frying

Smoking agents

½ cup black tea leaves
½ cup fine chips of
camphor wood
½ cup brown sugar

PREPARATION

1 Thaw the duck if frozen. Pull out all loose fat from the tail and neck. Cut off the tips and midportions of the wings. Rinse and drain.

2 Roast the peppercorns and salt in a small skillet over medium heat until brown. Cool, then mix the spicy salt with the saltpeter (if used) and rub it over the skin and cavity of the duck.

3 Put the duck in a bowl, cover, and chill in the refrigerator overnight. Turn the duck over several times during the next day. Allow to sit overnight again and into the next day; the total curing time is about 48 hours.

4 Rinse the duck to remove the peppercorns and salt. Transfer it to a shallow bowl large enough to hold the duck snugly.

COOKING

1 Set the bowl with the duck into a steamer and bring water in the base to a boil. Cover and steam the duck over medium heat for 2 hours or until soft. Set duck on a rack to cool completely.

(Note: Duck can be prepared ahead of time up to this stage.)

2 Fully line the inside surface of a wok with heavy-duty aluminum foil. Also line the inside surface of the cover. Mix the tea leaves, sugar, and camphor wood chips together and add the mixture to the center of the wok, spreading them in a thin layer.

3 Place a rack in the wok, its height being at least 1 inch above the surface of the smoking agents. Put the duck on the rack, then set the wok over high heat. When smoke arises, cover the wok tightly and smoke will circulate inside the cover. Turn heat to medium. Smoke the duck for 20 minutes.

4 Turn off heat under wok and keep duck covered for 10 more minutes.

(Note: If you are not deep-frying the duck, then serve the duck at this stage. Allow to cool 15 minutes, then chop into bite-sized pieces.)

5 If deep-frying, set wok over high heat. When very hot, add the oil. Wait for about 7 minutes, or test the oil with a piece of scallion green; if green sizzles and moves about quickly when dropped in, then oil is ready (about 350 degrees). Place duck in a deep-frying strainer, then put into the oil. Pour oil over the duck, ladle by ladle, until one side is brown, then turn duck to the other side and deep-fry in the same manner. It should take about 7 minutes to brown each side.

6 Remove duck from the oil and rest on a rack for at least 10 minutes. Chop duck into bite-sized pieces and arrange pieces on a serving platter so that the original shape of the duck is reconstructed.

Note: The natural juice from steaming the duck can be used as part of the stock for Pungent and Hot Soup (pages 122–123). You can substitute hickory chips for the camphor wood.

⊛⊛⊛Braised Orange Duck

Serves	4 as a main dish with rice or Rice Crusts (page 384) and vegetables, or serves 10 to 12 as part of a banquet
Time	40 minutes preparation 4 hours hanging 30 minutes roasting 1½ hours braising

橙子鴨

This duck is first roasted, then braised in an orange sauce to become moist and tender. The best way to use the tangy sauce is to pour it over sizzling rice crusts, making it a meal in itself.

Ingredients
1 Long Island duckling, about 5½ pounds
2 teaspoons salt
½ teaspoon white pepper
3 tablespoons oil
4 shallots, peeled and flattened
2 tablespoons brandy
1 navel orange
1 teaspoon sesame oil
2 sprigs Chinese parsley

Brushing mixture
1 tablespoon honey
2 tablespoons vodka
3 tablespoons distilled vinegar

Braising mixture
3 navel oranges (or 1½ cups orange juice)
1 tablespoon lemon juice
2 cups duck stock
1 tablespoon light soy sauce
2 teaspoons dark soy sauce
3 tablespoons brown sugar

Sauce thickener
2 tablespoons orange liqueur
1 tablespoon chicken stock
1 tablespoon tapioca powder

PREPARATION

1 Thaw duck. Pull out all loose fat from the tail and neck, and cut off the middle and tip portions of wings (reserve for soup stock). Press duck on the back with both palms to flatten, then immerse in a large pot of boiling water. Bring water back to a boil, then turn the duck. When water boils, remove duck to a colander and run hot water over it to rinse the film on the skin. Drain and gently pat dry inside and out with paper towels. Season cavity with salt and pepper.

2 Prepare brushing mixture by combining ingredients in a small saucepan. Set pan over low heat, stirring until well blended. Brush mixture on duck skin, then repeat. Be sure that all areas are evenly coated with the mixture.

3 Tie the neck with a kitchen string and hang duck in an airy place to dry for at least 4 hours.

4 Boil the neck, giblets, and wings with 4 cups of water until reduced to 2 cups of thin stock for braising the duck.

COOKING

1 Preheat oven to 450 degrees, then roast duck for 30 minutes, or until skin is lightly brown.

2 While duck is roasting, juice the oranges for the braising mixture, then grate the rind from half of 1 orange. Combine the juice and grated rind with the remaining braising mixture ingredients. Mix well and set aside. When duck is ready, remove from oven and set aside.

3 Set a heavy oval Dutch oven (just large enough to hold the duck snugly) over high heat. When hot, add 2 tablespoons of oil and stir-fry the shallots until light brown. Sizzle in the brandy and immediately add the braising mixture. Add the duck, bring liquid to a boil, then turn heat to low. Scoop several ladlefuls of liquid into the cavity of the duck. Cover pan and braise duck for 1½ hours or until a chopstick goes through the thigh easily. Turn duck twice during the cooking.

4 While duck is braising, remove rind from the orange and cut it in half vertically, then slice into ¼-inch thick half-rounds. Set aside.

5 (If duck is being prepared several hours ahead, simply refrigerate duck in braising liquid, then later remove solidified fat.) Transfer duck carefully to a deep bowl, about 8 inches in diameter, with the breast side down. Slit duck along the backbone and remove all bones, making sure to keep the meat intact. Cover bowl with aluminum foil or chill until ready. Reserve braising liquid.

6 About 1 hour before serving, add about 2 tablespoons of braising liquid to the duck.

7 Preheat oven to 300 degrees, then heat the duck in the bowl (with foil still on) for 20 minutes (30 minutes if the duck has been chilled), then keep warm until needed.

8 Reheat the braising liquid and drain it through a strainer into a small saucepan. Discard any solids. When sauce comes to a boil, turn heat to a simmer. Mix sauce ingredients and stream into the liquid, stirring until clear and thick. Correct the seasoning and glaze sauce with sesame oil and remaining tablespoon of oil, stirring to blend.

9 Remove duck in bowl from oven and discard foil. Cover bowl with a round platter (deep enough to hold sauce and large enough to cover bowl). Flip and turn the bowl and platter over and remove the bowl. A dome-shaped piece of duck meat is now set on the platter. Arrange orange slices around and pour sauce over. Garnish with parsley and serve. Diners are to pry duck meat from dome with chopsticks.

Note: If you prefer to serve with sizzling rice crusts, deep-fry 12 pieces of rice crusts (see page 116). Arrange them immediately in the platter to surround the orange slices and pour sauce over at the table.

Cantonese Oven-Hung Duck

Serves 8 in a formal dinner, 12 in a banquet
Time 30 to 40 minutes preparation
10 hours hanging
1 hour, 10 minutes roasting

掛爐鴨

This is the Cantonese counterpart of Peking Duck. The skin is crisp, the meat juicy and tasty, and the bones can also make a flavorful soup stock.

Ingredients	Brushing mixture	Duck sauce
1 young duckling, about 5 pounds	3 tablespoons red rice vinegar	1 tablespoon oil
1 tablespoon Five-Spice Salt (page 193)	2 tablespoons vodka	2 cloves garlic, minced
4 whole scallions (white and green parts), trimmed	1 tablespoon Chinese maltose or honey	3 tablespoons hoisin sauce
1 bamboo chopstick		1 tablespoon sesame oil
6 3-inch pieces of scallion (white part only)		2 tablespoons chicken stock
24 pieces Cantonese Flat Bread (page 412)		

PREPARATION

1 If using a frozen duck, thaw completely before beginning recipe. Pull loose fat off duck from the tail and neck. Cut off the tips and mid-portions of the wings (save for stock), then immerse duck in a large pot of boiling water. Turn heat off and turn duck over carefully, using 2 spatulas. Bring water back to a boil, then remove pot from heat and let duck stand in hot water for 5 minutes.

2 With spatulas, remove duck from water to rest in a colander. Run warm water over duck to remove excess grease on skin, then pat inside and out until thoroughly dry.

3 Sprinkle and rub five-spice salt into duck cavity. Put in whole scallions, truss tail and neck openings securely. Cut off 2 2-inch lengths from a bamboo chopstick and use 1 for each side to prop wings against duck back.

4 Mix brushing ingredients in a small saucepan over low heat, stirring until well blended. Brush mixture evenly on the duck skin, then repeat. Tie duck around the neck with a kitchen string and hang in an airy place for about 10 hours, or until skin is no longer sticky.

COOKING

1 Preheat oven to 450 degrees. Set duck on the rack of a roasting pan, back side down. Roast about 15 minutes, then turn to roast on other side for an additional 15 minutes.

2 Turn oven heat to 375 degrees, and continue to roast duck on each side for 20 minutes, or until skin is golden brown, ending with breast side up. When turning duck, be sure not to break the skin; use a mitten or towel.

3 While duck is roasting, prepare the sauce. Set a small saucepan over high heat and add oil. Flavor oil with garlic for 15 seconds, then add the hoisin sauce, sesame oil, and chicken stock, stirring well until blended and bubbly. Remove sauce from heat and pour into 2 separate shallow dishes to be served on the side later.

4 Cut each 3-inch piece of scallion in half crosswise, then split each half in half lengthwise (24 strips). Set aside.

5 When duck is turned the last time, prepare flat bread by placing them on an 8-inch platter in several layers. Bring water in the base of a steamer to a boil and reduce heat to keep just steadily boiling. Set flat bread in the steamer, covering with a piece of paper towel to absorb steam. Steam over low heat until needed.

6 When duck is done, remove from oven. Discard chopsticks and trussing strings. Hold duck by the neck with a towel and let juice drain out of cavity. Rest duck in a colander in an upright position.

7 Have several layers of paper toweling ready. Use a sharp knife to carve out pieces of skin, mostly from the breast and thighs, making a total of 24 pieces, each about 1½ inches by 2¼ inches. Lay each piece on a paper towel immediately after carving so that the excess grease and moisture underneath the skin can be absorbed and the crispness is maintained.

8 Arrange pieces of skin on a serving platter. Serve with duck sauce, scallion strips, and piping-hot flat bread just fresh from the steamer. The diner takes a piece of flat bread, places a piece of skin on 1 end, dots it with duck sauce, and puts a scallion strip on top. Then the diner folds the flat bread over, forming a little sandwich, and eats the sandwich with his or her fingers.

Note: The rest of the duck—the duck meat and bones—is also to be used. The duck meat can be used to substitute for roast chicken in a cold-tossed roast chicken or for pork shreds in Mo Shu Pork (page 260), or in Stir-fried Pork Shreds with Bean Sprouts (page 270). The bones, wings, and giblets make a delicious soup with napa cabbage.

◉◉ Red-Cooked Duck with Napa Cabbage

Serves 4 as a main dish with rice, or
10 to 12 in a banquet
Time 30 minutes preparation
1 hour marinating
2 hours cooking

西 湖 鴨

T his is a well-known banquet dish. Everything can be prepared in advance and kept warm in an oven until the final moment of serving when the sauce is poured over. This dish fits nicely into the busy schedule of any cook and is a proven crowd-pleaser besides.

Ingredients

1 young duckling,
about 4½ pounds
3 tablespoons oil
2 cloves garlic,
flattened
2 whole scallions,
trimmed
1 whole star anise
1 head napa cabbage,
about 3 pounds
½ cup chicken stock
Salt
2 teaspoons tapioca
powder
1 tablespoon water
1 teaspoon sesame oil

Marinade

2 teaspoons ginger
juice
2 tablespoons brandy
2 tablespoons dark soy
sauce
½ teaspoon salt

Braising mixture

2 cups chicken stock
1 tablespoon oyster
sauce
1 tablespoon
granulated sugar

PREPARATION

1 If using a frozen duck, thaw completely before beginning recipe. Pull out all the loose fat from the tail and neck, then press the duck with both palms until flat. Rinse and pat dry thoroughly with paper towels. Prick the skin with a fine stainless-steel trussing skewer around the thighs and breast, then place the duck in a large bowl.

2 Prepare marinade and then rub it evenly on the skin and into the cavity. Set the duck at room temperature for at least 1 hour, turning the duck occasionally.

COOKING

1 Drain the duck, reserving excess marinade. Set a wok over high heat and, when hot, add 2 tablespoons of oil. Swish oil around the bottom, then place in duck. Turn heat to medium, and brown the duck slowly and evenly on all sides.

2 Mix together the braising mixture in an oval Dutch oven, then set the pot over high heat. Bring to a boil and add the duck, then return liquid to a boil.

3 Add reserved marinade, garlic, scallions, and star anise. Cover pan and turn heat to low. Simmer for 1½ hours to 2 hours, or until a chopstick goes through the thigh easily.

(Note: The duck may be prepared ahead of time up to this point. If used immediately, remove the duck and degrease the sauce with a separating spoon. Otherwise cool the duck and the sauce in the pan and keep refrigerated. Discard solidified fat.)

4 Rinse and separate the cabbage leaves. Cut into 4-inch lengths, then boil in the chicken stock until soft. Season with salt, remove, and drain.

5 When ready to serve, place Dutch oven over medium heat and bring liquid to a boil. Heat until duck is hot, then remove the duck carefully and place on an oval serving platter. Discard any solids in the cooking liquid. Keep the duck warm in the oven.

6 Add the cabbage to the sauce and bring it back to a boil. When hot, remove cabbage with chopsticks (or a slotted spoon) and arrange on both sides of the duck. Keep sauce at a simmer.

7 Mix the tapioca powder with the water and add to the sauce in a gradual stream, stirring constantly until thickened. Correct seasoning, then glaze sauce with sesame oil and remaining tablespoon of oil. Pour the sauce over the duck and cabbage and serve hot.

SQUAB

⊛⊛ Roast Squab

Serves 2 as a main dish with rice and vegetables
Time 15 minutes preparation
3 hours hanging
25 minutes roasting

燒乳鴿

American ovens brown the skin of a squab crisply while keeping the meat juicy and tender. This recipe is a short-cut to the typical Cantonese Oil-poured Squab.

Ingredients	Spice mixture	Brushing mixture
2 young squab, about 1 pound each	2 cups water	1 tablespoon honey
½ cup light soy sauce	1 whole star anise	2 tablespoons vodka
½ cup dark soy sauce	¼ teaspoon crushed black peppercorns	3 tablespoons apple cider vinegar
½ cup pale dry sherry	2 teaspoons aniseed	1 teaspoon tapioca powder
¼ cup brown sugar	1 2-inch piece cinnamon stick	1 teaspoon water
2 slices gingerroot		
2 cloves garlic		
½ teaspoon salt		

PREPARATION

1 Combine water and spices for spice mixture in a small saucepan. Cook over medium heat until liquid is reduced to 1 cup. Drain through a fine strainer into a 3-quart saucepan. Reserve the spices for another use.

2 Blanch squab in boiling water for 1 minute to tighten the skin. Rinse immediately with cold running water to remove scum, then pat with paper towels to dry each squab inside and out.

3 Add soy sauces, sherry, brown sugar, ginger, garlic, and salt to the spice liquid. Bring to a boil, then add 1 squab to the sauce mixture. Put a wooden spoon into the rear of the cavity, and pour the hot sauce along the handle of the spoon so that the liquid will drain from the neck. Repeat the pouring 5 or 6 times, then remove squab to a colander. Repeat for other squab.

4 Combine the honey, vodka, and vinegar in a small saucepan, warming over low heat until well blended. Then mix in the tapioca and water and add to pan. Brush the skin of the squab evenly, twice.

5 Tie the wings of the squab with kitchen string and hang the squab in an airy place to drain excess moisture for about 3 hours.

COOKING

1 Place an oven rack on the highest level of the oven and another on the lowest. Preheat oven to 400 degrees.

2 Fill a roasting pan with ½ inch of boiling water and set on the lowest level of the oven to catch the drippings.

3 Hook 1 curved end of an S-shaped curtain hook through the neck bone of each squab; make sure each is secure. Hook the other curved end to the rack, keeping each squab about 5 inches apart. Roast squab 15 minutes, or until the upper portion of the birds turns lightly brown.

4 Remove squab from oven and pour water out of pan. Reset the pan in the oven. Hook the tail part securely in the same manner and hang the squab back in the oven, upside down this time. Roast another 10 minutes or until squab are evenly brown.

5 To serve, offer squab whole, which would be American style, or cut each into 8 pieces. Serve with five-spice salt (page 193) in a small saucer.

VARIATION: Roast Cornish Game Hen

Cornish game hen is not native to China, but it can be treated like squab for the above recipe. It has a skin just as crisp as squab, and the meat is juicier. What is different about the game hen is a slight gamey flavor not present in squab.

◉◉◉ Oil-Poured Squab

Serves 10 to 12 in a banquet
Time 1 hour preparation
5 hours hanging
1 hour, 15 minutes cooking

油淋乳鴿

With crispy skin and tasty dark meat, the oil-poured squab features one of the most popular dishes in Cantonese restaurants, where the ready set-up for deep-frying makes the procedure easy.

Ingredients	Spice mixture	Brushing mixture
2 squab, about 1 pound each	3 cups water	3 tablespoons red rice vinegar
2½ cups light soy sauce	2 whole star anise	2 tablespoons vodka
2 cups pale dry sherry	1 stick cinnamon, about 2 inches	1 tablespoon Chinese malt sugar
1 cup rock candy	2 whole nutmeg	1 teaspoon tapioca powder
6 slices gingerroot	½ teaspoon crushed black peppercorns	2 teaspoons water
2 cloves garlic	1 teaspoon Sichuan peppercorns	
2 whole scallions, trimmed	2 teaspoons aniseed	
6 cups oil	2 quarters dried mandarin orange peel	
1 ounce shrimp chips		
1 lemon, cut into wedges		
1 tablespoon Five-Spice Salt (page 193)		

PREPARATION

1 Combine spices for spice mixture with water in a 2-quart saucepan. Cook over low heat until the water is reduced to 1 cup. Drain and reserve the liquid; use spices for another recipe.

2 In a 4-quart Dutch oven, add 1 cup of spice mixture, soy sauce, sherry, rock candy, ginger, garlic, and scallions. Set over medium-low heat and bring to a boil. Turn the heat to a simmer.

3 Rinse the squab and pat dry thoroughly with paper towels, drying both inside and out.

4 Bring mixture in Dutch oven back to a boil and add the squab, turning once. Put a wooden spoon into the rear opening of the cavity of 1 squab. Holding the spoon with the left hand, use a ladle to pour the hot sauce down the spoon handle into the cavity, allowing the sauce to drain from the neck opening. Repeat this 6 to 8 times and then do same for other squab.

5 Turn heat to a simmer, cover pot, and cook squab 10 minutes. At this point the squab are almost done; remove and drain on a rack.

6 Combine the vinegar, vodka, and malt sugar in a small saucepan. Cook over low heat until the ingredients blend together.

7 Mix tapioca powder and water together and add to the brushing mixture, stirring to mix well.

8 Tie each squab with a piece of kitchen cord around the neck (for neckless squab, tie around the wings). Hang in an airy place. Brush mixture evenly on skin of squab and allow to hang for 4 to 5 hours.

COOKING

1 Set a wok over high heat. When very hot, add the oil. It will take about 8 to 10 minutes for the oil to get very hot. Test the temperature by dropping in a piece of scallion green; if haze appears above the surface of the oil and the green turns brown, the oil is very hot (about 400 degrees).

2 Add shrimp chips to the oil, deep-frying until puffed. Remove and drain on paper towels.

3 Put the squab, 1 at a time, into a Chinese deep-frying strainer. Scoop boiling oil over the skin of the squab, a ladle at a time for 1 minute, then turn the heat to medium high. Continue to pour oil over the skin of the squab until the bird is golden brown. Remove and cool for 10 minutes while you repeat for other squab.

4 Chop each squab into 8 pieces. Serve with shrimp chips, lemon wedges, and five-spice salt.

EGGS

⊛Tea Leaf Eggs

Yields 8 servings
Time 10 minutes preparation
45 minutes cooking

茶 葉 蛋

The brown marinade enters through deliberately created cracks in the shell to deposit a cracked porcelain pattern. Each egg looks like a rare thousand-year-old porcelain masterpiece, and this is food to feast the eyes as well as the palate.

Ingredients
8 large eggs

Tea-leaf mixture
3 cups water
1 tablespoon dark soy sauce
1 whole star anise
2 teaspoons salt
2 tablespoons green tea leaves

PREPARATION

1 Place eggs in a 3-quart saucepan. Add cold water to cover and bring to a boil over high heat. Cook for 10 minutes.

2 Remove and immerse eggs in a large bowl of cold water until they are cool. Tap the shells gently to make fine cracks, using a tablespoon.

3 Combine ingredients for tea-leaf mixture in a small saucepan. Set pan over high heat and bring to a boil. Add the cracked eggs and bring back to a boil. Turn heat to simmer and cook eggs for 30 minutes.

4 Remove saucepan from the heat and cool eggs to room temperature.

5 Shell the eggs and cut in half or in quarters. Serve cold.

●Assorted Egg Pâté

Yields   60 slices
Time   15 minutes preparation
40 minutes baking
20 minutes steaming
3 hours chilling

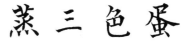

T hree kinds of eggs are blended loosely in aspic. Cutting the aspic reveals cross sections of smoked quartz, marble, and coral.

Ingredients

5 thousand-year-old
  eggs
4 salted duck eggs
6 whole eggs

1 cup chicken stock
¼ cup water
1 teaspoon sesame oil

PREPARATION

1 Cut thousand-year-old eggs into ⅜-inch cubes.

2 Separate yolks and whites of salted duck eggs. Cut 2 yolks also into ⅜-inch cubes and cut remaining yolks in half. Flatten each half with the blade of a cleaver, pressing it on a cutting board; make 2 egg-yolk sheets about ⅛-inch thick.

3 Beat the regular eggs and salted egg whites together with chopsticks until light but not foamy. Add the chicken stock, water, and sesame oil. Blend well.

4 Fold in the thousand-year-old egg cubes and the salted duck egg yolk cubes. Mix with egg mixture.

5 Grease an 8 by 4 by 3-inch loaf pan and add the egg mixture. Arrange the salted egg yolk sheets on top as a garnish. Either bake or steam the egg mixture.

BAKING

1 Preheat the oven to 275 degrees.

2 Set a loaf pan in a baking pan and pour boiling water around to come half way up the sides of the loaf pan.

3 Cover loaf pan with foil and place in bottom third of oven. Bake for about 40 minutes, or until a bamboo skewer inserted in the center comes out clean.

4 Remove pan from oven and cool to room temperature, then chill for at least 3 hours. Cut into ¼-inch slices and serve cold.

STEAMING

1 Bring the water in the base of a steamer to a boil over medium heat. Turn heat to low and set in loaf pan.

2 Wrap the cover of the steamer with a kitchen towel to absorb condensed steam.

3 Steam over medium-low heat for 20 minutes or until a bamboo skewer inserted in the center comes out clean. Remove from steamer immediately.

4 Blot surface of pâté dry with paper towels and chill for 3 hours. Cut into ¼-inch slices and serve cold.

⊛Scrambled Egg with Crabmeat

Serves	4 as a luncheon, or as a main dish with a thick soup, rice, and vegetable
Time	10 minutes preparation 7 minutes cooking

This Cantonese recipe aims to capture its radiant colors while preserving the natural flavors of the ingredients. The nonstick skillet makes the cooking really easy.

Ingredients

6 ounces cooked fresh crabmeat (do not use frozen)
2 whole scallions, trimmed
2 sprigs Chinese parsley
6 whole eggs
4 to 5 tablespoons oil
¼ teaspoon salt

Seasonings

2 teaspoons pale dry sherry
½ teaspoon salt
2 teaspoons sesame oil
⅛ teaspoon white pepper

PREPARATION

1 Flake the crabmeat lightly and mix with the seasonings. (If crabmeat is preseasoned, reduce the amount of salt in the seasoning mixture.)

2 Cut the scallions into 2-inch shreds.

3 Clean and chop parsley into 2-inch lengths.

4 In a mixing bowl, beat the eggs with 2 tablespoons of oil and the salt until smooth but not foamy. Add the crabmeat, scallion shreds, and parsley. Mix well.

COOKING

1 Set a nonstick skillet (or wok) over medium heat. Wait 3 minutes and add the remaining 2 tablespoons of oil (3 if using a wok). Pour in the egg–crabmeat mixture and spread it over the bottom.

2 When the egg starts to set, push the cooked egg to the side, letting the uncooked mixture run back to the heated surface of the pan. Continue to push back with the spatula until no more egg mixture runs out. Serve immediately.

⊚Steamed Egg with Fresh Scallops

Serves 4 to 6 as part of a Chinese family meal
Time 10 minutes preparation
15 minutes cooking

帶 子 蒸 旦

This is a great family dish. The texture of the egg is velvety and delicate.

Ingredients
4 ounces fresh scallops
4 whole eggs
1½ cups chicken stock
4 or 5 Chinese parsley leaves

Seasonings
Dash of white pepper
½ teaspoon salt
1 teaspoon pale dry sherry
1 teaspoon sesame oil

PREPARATION

1 Remove the small tough muscle attached to the side of each scallop. Rinse clean of sand and drain thoroughly. Cut each scallop in half crosswise and arrange on paper towels. Pat to dry, then chill until ready to use.

2 Beat eggs lightly with a wire whisk until smooth but not foamy. Add the chicken stock and the seasonings and mix well. Remove any foam from the surface.

3 Arrange the scallop pieces in 1 layer in a deep heatproof dish. Pour the egg mixture through a fine strainer into the dish.

COOKING

1 Bring enough water in the base of your steamer to a vigorous boil over high heat. Reduce the heat to medium-low and place in the dish of the egg mixture. Cover steamer and steam for 12 to 15 minutes, or until a chopstick inserted comes out clean.

2 Arrange a few parsley leaves on top of the egg mixture for decoration. Serve hot.

Note: Fresh scallops can be replaced with fish fillets or shrimp. Dried shrimp are most often used by the Cantonese.

◉◉Pan-Fried Egg Crescents

Serves	4 in a multi-dish family meal, or 16 small crescents for an appetizer
Time	20 minutes preparation 1 hour chilling 15 minutes cooking

煎蛋角

This is a typical example of Cantonese homecooking. The crescents are stuffed with fish.

Ingredients

½ pound firm fish fillets (cod, sea bass, snapper, perch, or pike)
2 tablespoons dried shrimp

½ cup warm water
2 whole scallions, trimmed
4 whole eggs
¼ teaspoon salt
4 to 5 tablespoons oil

Seasonings

1 teaspoon sesame oil
2 teaspoons tapioca powder
Dash of white pepper
¼ teaspoon granulated sugar

PREPARATION

1 Prepare a fish paste, following the instructions on page 145, using half the salt, water, and seasonings called for in that recipe.

2 Soak dried shrimp in warm water until soft. Chop finely.

3 Chop the scallions finely and set aside.

4 Before chilling the fish paste, add dried shrimp, scallions, and seasonings. Stir in 1 direction with a wooden spoon until fish paste is elastic. Chill for at least 1 hour to firm.

5 Beat the eggs with the salt until they are smooth.

COOKING

1 Set a wok over high heat. When hot, add 2 teaspoons of oil and swish it around to coat the surface. Turn the heat to medium and add about 1 tablespoon of the egg mixture to the center of the wok. Immediately it will spread and puff up into a pancake about 3 inches in diameter.

2 Place 1 heaping teaspoon of the fish filling in the center of the pancake, turning 1 side over to cover filling, forming a crescent. Press the crescent lightly with a spatula to seal the edges.

3 Turn the crescent over and push it to the side of the wok. Pan-fry both sides until golden, leaving the center space empty.

4 Add another teaspoon of oil to wok and repeat for next pancake. Each time you make a crescent, push it to the side, leaving the center open for the next one. Add 1 teaspoon of oil for pan-frying each pancake.

5 Remove the crescents 1 by 1 as they turn brown. It takes about 2 minutes for a crescent to cook but several can be cooked simultaneously.

⊚⊚⊚⊚⊚Deep-Fried Custard (Guozha)

Serves	10 to 12 in a banquet as appetizer	鍋 炸
Time	30 minutes preparation Overnight chilling 15 minutes cooking	

Deep-fried soup, if you please. The outside is fried a golden yellow, while the interior is a thickened, tasty soup. Be careful when taking this banquet dish, as fresh fried Guozha can be scorching to the tongue.

Ingredients

3 cups Supreme Stock (page 108)	2 teaspoons lard
Scant ½ cup cornstarch (about 3 ounces)	Cornstarch for coating
	6 cups oil
3 whole eggs + 2 egg yolks	2 tablespoons extrafine sugar
Salt	

PREPARATION

1 Combine stock, cornstarch, eggs, and egg yolks in a blender. Beat on the lowest speed until the ingredients are well mixed but not foamy. Pour the mixture through a fine-mesh strainer into a nonstick 2-quart saucepan.

2 Set the saucepan over medium heat and stir the mixture constantly to prevent lumping. In about 10 minutes, the mixture will become thick and bubbly. Continue to cook 5 to 7 more minutes to assure doneness.

3 Season custard with a little salt and add the lard, stirring some more (the amount of salt depends on the quality of the stock; it may not be necessary to add salt at all).

4 Grease a 9 by 9-inch shallow pan with oil. Pour in custard mixture and shake the pan to level the surface. Cool at room temperature, then wrap in plastic and chill overnight or at least 6 hours. The custard should be firm enough for handling.

COOKING

1 Have ready a strainer-lined bowl and a deep-frying strainer.

2 Shortly before deep-frying, cut custard into ¾-inch-wide strips, then cut the strips diagonally into diamond-shaped pieces about 2 inches long. Coat each piece evenly with cornstarch; be sure to shake off the excess starch.

3 Set a wok over high heat. When the wok is hot, add oil. Wait for about 8 to 10 minutes, then test the temperature by dropping a piece of scallion green into the oil. If the green turns brown quickly and a haze appears above the surface, the oil is ready (about 400 degrees). Dip the deep-frying strainer in the hot oil to grease, then arrange half of the custard pieces in 1 layer in the strainer and lower it gently into the oil. Deep-fry custards until golden.

4 Remove custard pieces to drain in the strainer-lined bowl. Keep the oil temperature very hot throughout and deep-fry the remaining pieces in the same fashion.

5 Serve custards immediately with sugar on the side.

Note: If Supreme Stock is not available, dilute 2½ cups canned chicken broth with 1½ cups water. Cook over medium heat with 2 ounces of Smithfield ham slices until stock is reduced to 3 cups. Discard ham and strain stock. Chill to solidify the fat on top, then skim it off. After practicing 2 to 3 times successfully, the reader can try a thinner consistency by reducing ½ ounce of cornstarch so that the center of each piece is more soup-like.

◉◉◉Stir-Fried Milk with Egg White

Serves 8 to 10 in a banquet
Time 10 minutes preparation
10 to 12 minutes cooking

鳳城炒牛奶

A unique main dish from Phoenix City, this is milk that is stir-fried with egg whites, crabmeat, and slivers of ham. Then it is surrounded by deep-fried rice sticks, intricately intertwined and crispy. Deep-fried olive nuts are sprinkled on top to complete the texture harmony.

Ingredients

6 eggs whites
½ cup half and half
¼ cup heavy cream
2 tablespoons cornstarch
½ teaspoon salt
3 ounces cooked crabmeat

2 tablespoons coarsely chopped Smithfield ham
2 cups oil
1 ounce rice sticks
½ cup olive nuts (or pine nuts)
1 sprig Chinese parsley, leaves only

Seasonings

1 teaspoon sesame oil
¼ teaspoon granulated sugar
1 teaspoon light rum or brandy
Dash of white pepper

STIR-FRIED MILK WITH EGG WHITE
PAGE 248

HAM IN CANDY SAUCE
PAGE 255

PREPARATION

1 In a large mixing bowl, add the egg whites (with embryonic chards removed) and beat with a wire whisk until smooth but not frothy. Add half and half and cream gradually, beating gently until well blended with egg whites. Stir in cornstarch and salt.

2 Mix crabmeat with seasonings and add to the milk mixture. Fold in chopped ham.

COOKING

1 Line a large mixing bowl with a strainer and have a deep-frying strainer ready within easy reach.

2 Set a wok over high heat. When very hot, add the oil. Wait for about 3 to 4 minutes, then test temperature by dropping a piece of scallion green into the hot oil. If the green sizzles and moves about quickly, the oil is about 350 degrees. Give the milk mixture a quick stir and add about ⅓ to the oil. Pull the wok completely from heat, stirring gently around 3 to 4 times or until set. Remove with the deep-frying strainer to the strainer-lined bowl to drain.

3 Reheat the oil to 350 degrees. Pour in another ⅓ of the mixture and stir in the same fashion as step 2. Remove set milk to combine with the first batch. Be sure to pull the wok away from heat while stirring.

4 Do the same with the remaining ⅓ of the milk mixture. All 3 batches are now in the strainer.

5 Reheat the oil in the wok to very hot. Remove with a fine strainer any residue milk mixture which rises to the surface of the oil upon heating. Test temperature by dropping a length of rice stick. If it puffs up immediately, the oil is ready. Add the rice sticks and deep-fry until puffed up. Remove to drain on paper towels.

6 Turn heat off. Put the olive nuts in a fine strainer and dip it in the oil, then take it out. Repeat this dip-in and take-out procedure 3 to 4 times or until the olive nuts are lightly brown. Drain on paper towels.

7 Shake the stir-fried milk in the strainer to drain off as much excess oil as possible. Remove to a serving platter. Arrange rice sticks to surround the milk, then sprinkle olive nuts on top. Decorate with parsley leaves. Serve immediately.

Pork

Pork is the favorite meat in China. Its fine texture and flavor have been enjoyed for thousands of years. Only the Chinese Moslems and vegetarians avoid pork completely. Almost all parts of the pig are eaten, and it is hard to ruin a good piece of pork by improper cooking.

Foot-long pieces of red roast pork, slightly charred on the edges, are hung in windows of ready-to-eat shops in Canton, usually next to a medium-sized, bottom-up whole roast pig, which has been done to a crispy golden brown. The rump pieces of the roast pig are the best and often command higher prices.

Chinese sausages, always served hot, are chewy and tasty, their fatty parts transparent and crisp. Chinese bacon, dried in the winter sun, is a specialty of Hunan, while the hams from Zhejiang and Yunnan are famous. The sausages are found in Oriental markets in large U.S. cities, but the hams are best substituted with Smithfield ham, which comes close in texture and flavor.

Five-Flower Meat, actually a fresh bacon slab with five alternate layers of fat and lean meat with skin on, is a wintertime favorite. It is the main ingredient for Twice-Cooked Pork.

Pig's snout, ears, feet, tongue, tail, kidneys, liver, lungs, heart, stomach, and intestines are simmered in a soy-sauce mixture to produce delightful Cantonese snacks. The Shanghaiese braise pork shoulders with rock candy; they also cure fresh hams with saltpeter. Pork fluff from Fujian is light as cotton candy. The Chinese uses of pork are almost limitless.

Buying the Pork

If you need pork for slicing and shredding, you could use the butt, lean meat cut from the loin, or loin chops. The loin chops, though expensive, are best for this purpose because the uniformity of the grain saves trouble when cutting.

For dicing and chunking, the butt is better because of its marbling. Use shoulder or loin for cooking whole pieces of meat from three to five pounds.

◉◉ Cantonese Roast Pork (Char Siu)

Serves 6 to 8 as a main dish with vegetables and rice
Time 20 minutes preparation
3 hours marinating
1 hour cooking

The Cantonese roast pork is moist and tasty. Even more versatile than our Western cooked ham, it can be served independently as a snack, main dish, or as the chief ingredient in stir-fries, fried rice, noodles, and dim sums. Half a pound per person may seem to be a lot, but do not underestimate the appetite of your diners.

Ingredients

3 pounds lean pork butt (trimmed weight)
2 carrots
½ cup honey
2 tablespoons sesame oil

Marinade

¼ cup pale dry sherry
2 cloves garlic, crushed
3 tablespoons light soy sauce
1 tablespoon sesame paste
2 tablespoons brown bean paste
2 tablespoons hoisin sauce
1 teaspoon salt
½ teaspoon five-spice powder
¼ cup granulated sugar

PREPARATION

1 Trim fat from meat and cut into 1- by 1- by 8-inch strips.

2 Combine all ingredients for marinade in a bowl. Use a wire whisk to mix well. Add pork strips, mixing with fingers. Cover and set at room temperature for at least 3 hours or keep refrigerated overnight. Turn pork occasionally.

3 Cut carrots into 2-inch lengths, then cut each vertically in half.

4 Put a skewer through the center of a piece of carrot; push it toward the hook. Thread a piece of pork on the skewer lengthwise. Secure the other end with another piece of carrot (or a cork) to prevent the pork from sliding off. Thread remaining pork on skewers in the same manner.

COOKING

1 Preheat oven to 375 degrees. Fill a shallow roasting pan with boiling water to a 1-inch depth to catch drippings and to prevent smoking. Place pan on the lowest rack of the oven and hook the skewers to the highest rack, each 2 inches apart. Roast meat for 40 minutes. Turn oven to 450 degrees.

2 Remove skewers from oven and brush meat with honey, then with sesame oil. Reserve any juices that are given off.

3 Empty the water from the roasting pan, then put pan back into oven to catch more drips. Hang the skewers the same way as before and roast 10 minutes more.

4 Cut pork strips diagonally into slices about ¼ inch thick. Serve with meat juices that collected in the pan.

VARIATION: Barbecued Spareribs

Not as versatile as Char Siu, but they are more fun to eat with your fingers for informal occasions or as an appetizer. They can be kept frozen for months without losing their nutlike flavor.

Substitute 1 whole piece of pork spareribs, about 3 to 4 pounds. Cut the ribs into smaller pieces, in between the ribs, at an interval of every 3 ribs. Marinate as for roast pork and hang rib sections by skewers or S-shaped hooks. Roast in the same manner.

◉◉Red-Cooked Pork Shoulder with Rock Candy

Serves	6 to 8 in a multi-dish family meal
Time	10 minutes preparation
	2 hours marinating
	1 hour soaking
	2 hours cooking

氷糖肘子

The best part of this Shanghai specialty is actually the skin; it must be tasted to be appreciated.

Ingredients

1 whole pork shoulder, about 3½ pounds
4 cups oil
6 cups black tea, made from 3 tea bags (optional)
Chicken stock to cover
1 large head iceberg lettuce or 2 pounds fresh spinach

⅛ cup granulated sugar
2 teaspoons tapioca powder mixed with 2 tablespoons water
1 teaspoon sesame oil

Marinade

2 tablespoons dark soy sauce
1 tablespoon salt

Seasonings

½ cup dark soy sauce
3 ounces rock candy
¼ cup yellow wine or pale dry sherry
2 teaspoons salt

PREPARATION

1 Blanch pork in a large pot of boiling water over medium heat for 10 minutes until the skin tightens. Rinse with cold running water, then pat dry with paper towels. Place pork in a bowl and rub marinade evenly over. Set at room temperature for at least 2 hours (so the color of the soy sauce can adhere to the skin). Turn the meat and rub with marinade occasionally. Drain well before deep-frying.

2 Set a cast-iron casserole over high heat. When very hot, add oil. When the oil is hot, add the meat. Deep-fry all sides until brown, then remove. Rinse with cold water to stop the cooking process. If desired, soak in black tea for 1 hour to remove grease.

COOKING

1 Put meat in a heatproof casserole. Mix seasonings and add to pot, then pour in enough chicken stock to cover. Steam over medium heat for 3 hours (or cover and bake in the lower part of a 350-degree oven for 2½ hours). Turn meat several times while it cooks. The meat should be soft enough for a chopstick to go through easily.

(Note: The pork can be prepared ahead of time up to this stage. If it has been chilled after cooking, then warm it in a 350-degree oven before preparing sauce.)

2 Rinse the lettuce and break it into 2-inch pieces. Bring water to a boil and add the sugar, then blanch lettuce for 1 minute, or until limp but not soggy. Rinse with cold water to stop the cooking process, then drain.

3 Turn hot or reheated pork out onto a deep serving dish. Use about ½ cup of the cooking liquid to just reheat the lettuce in a saucepan, then arrange it around the meat.

4 Heat the cooking liquid over medium-low heat until it boils. Stream in the tapioca mixture, stirring until the sauce is thick and bubbly. Glaze with sesame oil and pour over meat. Serve hot.

White-Cooked Pork in Garlic Sauce

Serves 8 as a cold dish
Time 30 minutes cooking
1 hour resting
2 hours chilling
10 minutes slicing

蒜茸白切肉

Popular in North China, this dish is possibly related to the Manchurian boiled pork. However, the latter is served without seasoning of any kind. In this recipe, the garlic sauce makes the dish.

Ingredients

1 pound lean pork, cut from the leg
4 slices gingerroot
1 white scallion, trimmed
2 tablespoons yellow wine or pale dry sherry

Garlic sauce

1 tablespoon minced garlic
2 teaspoons red rice vinegar
2 tablespoons dark soy sauce
2 tablespoons cooking liquid from the meat

4 teaspoons sesame oil
2 teaspoons granulated sugar
Salt

COOKING

1 Place the meat in a 3-quart saucepan and add enough water to cover. Set pan over high heat and bring water to a boil. Skim off any foam, then add the ginger, scallion, and wine. Cover the pan and cook for 20 minutes over medium heat.

2 Turn the meat in the pan and bring the liquid back to a boil, then turn off heat. Keep pan covered until the meat cools, about 1 hour, then remove meat from pot and chill in the refrigerator for 2 hours or until the meat is firm to ease slicing. Reserve the cooking liquid.

3 Mix ingredients for garlic sauce. Test for salt.

4 Slice the meat across the grain into pieces 2 inches by 1½ inches by ⅛ inch. Arrange in layers on a serving platter and pour sauce over. Serve cold.

Note: The pork can be prepared 1 day in advance. Do not slice it until ready to serve, so as to keep the meat moist.

Ham in Candy Sauce

Serves 10 to 12 in a Chinese banquet
Time Overnight pre-soaking of ham
2 hours soaking of lotus seeds
40 minutes for preparing
lotus seeds
2 hours for chilling ham
approximately 2 hours
cutting, steaming, and saucing

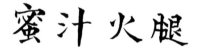

This sweet dish, served as the last main course (before the noodles and sweets), is characteristic of banquets in East China, especially on the shores of the West Lake in Hangzhou. The lake furnishes unrivaled scenery and lotus seeds as perfect companions to unskinned ham from Jinhua nearby. Jinhua ham does not travel well and is hard to find in the United States; we suggest a center cut of Smithfield ham as an excellent alternative.

Ingredients

2 teaspoons baking
soda
1 2-inch center-cut slab
of Smithfield ham,
about 2 pounds
1 cup dried skinless
lotus seeds
3 cups boiling water
4 ounces Chinese rock
candy
1 tablespoon pale dry
sherry

1 tablespoon preserved
cassia blossoms
(optional)
1 tablespoon
granulated sugar
1 tablespoon water
chestnut powder
1 tablespoon water
1 tablespoon oil
1 recipe Cantonese Flat
Bread (page 412)

PREPARATION

1 Half-fill a soup kettle with boiling water. Add baking soda (to help loosen spices) and the ham. Cover and set at room temperature until water becomes cool, about 1½ hours.

2 Use a Nylon brush to scrub off the spices found adhering to the ham. Remove the bone marrow with a chopstick and trim off and discard the spicy dark brown layer on the skinless side until the red color of the ham shows.

3 Place the ham in a large bowl and add about 2 quarts of cold water to soak overnight. Then discard the soaking water.

4 Soak lotus seeds in boiling water in a covered pan for 2 hours. Split each seed in half and remove the green parts in the center, if any. Rinse. Simmer lotus seeds in water for about ½ hour or until tender but not too soft. Drain well.

5 Put ham flat into a 2-quart saucepan. Add water to come up about ½ inch over the ham and set pan over high heat. Bring to a boil, turn heat to low, cover pan, and simmer for about 1½ hours or until the main bone sticks out; turn once during cooking.

6 Remove the main bone. Wrap the ham and chill in refrigerator for 2 hours or until firm for easy slicing. Reserve the ham juice and chill to degrease.

COOKING

1 Have ready a heatproof bowl about 6 inches in diameter and at least 2 inches deep. Place ham on the flat side and slice carefully from the smaller end, into pieces about ³⁄₁₆ inch thick. Arrange ham slices, skin side up, in overlapping fashion along the inside surface of the bowl, forming a spiral pattern. Fill up the space in the center with remaining ham slices.

2 Crush the rock candy lumps into small pieces about the size of a soybean. Add half the rock candy to cover the ham slices in the bowl, then add the degreased ham juices to come up to about ½ inch below the rim of the bowl. (The remaining ham juice can be frozen for other purpose.)

3 Steam ham over high heat for 15 minutes or until the rock candy is dissolved. Drain the ham juice into a small saucepan.

4 Add sherry and ¼ of the lotus seeds to cover the ham in the bowl. Top the ham slices with the remaining rock candy and steam over low heat for 45 minutes.

5 Meanwhile, combine the remaining lotus seeds with the ham juice in the small saucepan. Cook over low heat for 15 minutes. Then strain juice into another small saucepan, and add the cassia blossoms and sugar, cooking over low heat until the sugar dissolves.

6 Drain the cassia blossom juice into a bowl. Rinse saucepan and put juice back. Discard cassia blossoms. (Now you have the ham in the steaming process, the lotus seeds in 1 small saucepan, and the cassia-flavored ham sauce in another saucepan.)

7 When the ham is ready, remove from the steamer and strain excessive juice to combine with the cassia-flavored ham sauce. Bring sauce back to boil over medium heat. Put ham back in steamer to keep warm.

8 To thicken the cassia-flavored ham sauce, mix water chestnut powder with water. Stream mixture into sauce, stirring until thickened and clear. Turn heat to very low and cover pan.

9 To serve, place a deep dish about 12 inches in diameter over the ham in the bowl. Turn the bowl and dish together quickly upside down, then remove the bowl. The ham slices should form a pleasant-looking dome. Reheat the lotus seeds and arrange them to surround the dome evenly. Add oil to glaze the sauce and pour sauce over the ham and lotus seeds. Serve hot, with steamed flat bread.

◉◉ Twice-Cooked Pork

Serves 4 to 6 as part of a multi-dish family meal
Time 10 minutes preparation
1 hour chilling
45 minutes cooking

回鍋肉

This is one of the three most popular dishes from Sichuan, the other two being Fish-flavored Pork Shreds and Camphor and Tea Leaf Duck.

Ingredients

1 pound fresh bacon (with skin, also known as five-flower pork)
2 cups water
4 slices gingerroot
2 whole scallions, trimmed
1 sweet red or green pepper

1 leek (white part only)
3 tablespoons + 2 teaspoons oil
1 clove garlic, minced
1 tablespoon pale dry sherry

Sauce mixture

3 tablespoons sweet bean paste
1 tablespoon Sichuan hot bean paste
1 tablespoon dark soy sauce
2 teaspoons granulated sugar
1 teaspoon sesame oil

PREPARATION

1 Simmer meat in a small saucepan with the water, ginger, and scallions for about 40 minutes. Remove and run cold water over to stop the cooking process, then chill meat in the refrigerator for at least 1 hour.

(Note: This first cooking step can be done ahead of time.)

2 Slice the meat thinly into 1 by 2-inch pieces, about 1/16 inch thick.

3 Seed the pepper and remove pulp. Cut into 1-inch pieces.

4 Roll-cut the leek into 1-inch wedges, then separate the layers.

5 Mix ingredients for sauce in a bowl and set aside.

COOKING

1 Set wok over high heat and when very hot, add 3 tablespoons of oil. Flavor oil with garlic for 20 seconds, then add the pork, stirring for 1 minute. Add the sauce mixture, stirring to mix with the meat. Sizzle in the wine along the edge of the wok, stirring again.

2 Push the ingredients to the side of the wok and add remaining 2 teaspoons of oil to the center. Stir-fry the pepper and leek for 30 seconds, then mix all ingredients together and serve hot.

❋❋❋ Home-Cured Pork

Serves Up to 12 in a party as part of
a cold platter
Time 4 to 5 days curing
2 hours steaming
6 hours pressing

醃肉

Zhenjiang City on the Yangtze River is known for this home-cured ham, aromatic with Sichuan peppercorns. It is common in cold platters at the beginning of a banquet.

Ingredients
3 tablespoons salt
1 tablespoon Sichuan
peppercorns
2 teaspoons saltpeter
1 boneless pork
shoulder, about 3 to
4 pounds

Ginger and vinegar sauce
1 knob gingerroot,
about 1 ounce,
shredded finely
3 tablespoons red rice
vinegar
1 teaspoon sesame oil

PREPARATION

1 Roast the salt and Sichuan peppercorns in a small saucepan over medium heat, stirring constantly until brown. Cool, then mix with the saltpeter.

2 Rub the meat evenly with the salt mixture. Put in a plastic bag and tie opening. Keep refrigerated for 4 to 5 days and turn the meat in the bag every day.

3 Remove meat from bag and discard marinade. Wash away the peppercorns with cold running water. Tie meat securely with heavy string to form a block and put into a deep bowl.

COOKING

1 Steam the meat over medium heat for 2 hours or until the skin of the pork becomes soft. Reserve the natural juices that form in the bowl.

2 Wrap the meat in muslin while hot and put a piece of board on top. Place heavy weights to press the meat for 5 to 6 hours.

3 Remove muslin wrapper and untie meat. Soak meat in the reserved juices. It can be kept refrigerated up to a week.

4 When ready to use, cut meat into slices about ⅛ inch thick. Serve cold with ginger and vinegar sauce.

Note: The whole ham can be kept for months in the freezer after curing, to be steamed when needed.

For those concerned about the use of saltpeter in this recipe, it would be best not to attempt the dish by simply omitting it. Whereas sometimes the saltpeter is used only as a preservative, in this recipe the saltpeter is vital for authenticity. The Chinese name for this dish is "Saltpeter Pork."

⊛⊛⊛ Sweet and Sour Pork

Serves	3 or 4 as a main dish with rice and a minute soup
Time	20 minutes preparation
	30 minutes marinating
	30 minutes cooking

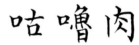

The authentic Cantonese sweet and sour sauce uses the traditional dried crab-apple wafers to provide color and tartness, but American pickled crabapples are fresher and more tangy, although a little bit spicy. This dish is fairly time-consuming to prepare, but worth the trouble.

Ingredients	Marinade	Sweet and sour sauce
1½ pounds lean pork butt (trimmed)	1 tablespoon light soy sauce	2 pickled crabapples
1 can (8 ounces) pineapple chunks in heavy syrup	1 tablespoon pale dry sherry	2 tablespoons wine vinegar
½ green pepper	1 whole egg	2 teaspoons dark soy sauce
½ sweet red pepper	½ teaspoon salt	1 tablespoon tapioca powder
1 medium onion		1 teaspoon chicken bouillon powder
½ cup bamboo shoots		2 tablespoons granulated sugar
Cornstarch for coating		¼ cup water
4 cups + 3 tablespoons oil		Salt
1 clove garlic, crushed		
½ teaspoon salt		
1 tablespoon pale dry sherry		
2 teaspoons sesame oil		

PREPARATION

1 Cut meat into ¾-inch cubes. Put meat in a mixing bowl and add ingredients for marinade. Mix with a wooden spoon or your fingers, then set at room temperature for at least 30 minutes (or keep refrigerated until you are ready to use it).

2 Drain the pineapple chunks and set aside; reserve syrup.

3 Cut peppers, onion, and bamboo shoots into pieces about 1 by ¾ inch. Set aside.

4 In a mixing bowl, mash the crabapples with a spoon. Add the vinegar and reserved pineapple syrup, stirring to blend. Press the mash against the sides of the bowl to extract all the remaining juice, then discard the mash. Drain mixture through a fine sieve into another bowl. Add the other ingredients for the sauce and blend well.

COOKING

1 Coat each piece of meat with cornstarch. Shake off excess, then arrange the pieces separately on a platter.

2 Heat 4 cups of oil in wok over high heat for about 5 minutes, then test the temperature of the oil by dropping a piece of scallion green into the oil. If the green
   sizzles noisily and soon turns brown, the oil is ready, about 375 degrees. Drop in
   half the pork, 1 piece at a time, until the meat loses its softness and the coating is
   lightly browned. Remove the meat, piece by piece, into a strainer-lined bowl to
   drain. Deep-fry the remaining half.

3 With a fine strainer, remove as much deposit or sediment as possible from the oil.
   Keep the oil still very hot. When the moisture in the oil is fully evaporated, test
   the temperature again. If very hot, return the pork pieces to wok and deep-fry
   for about 5 minutes, or until golden brown. Remove pork to drain. Pour out
   oil.

4 Wipe the wok clean with paper towels (no need to rinse) and set it over high heat.
   When very hot, add 2 tablespoons of oil. Flavor oil with garlic for 10 seconds,
   then add onion, stirring for 30 seconds. Add the bamboo shoots, peppers, and
   stir again. Season with salt and remove from wok.

5 Rinse wok, then set over high heat. When very hot, add the remaining tablespoon
   of oil. Whirl in the sherry along the edge of the wok, then add the pineapple
   chunks immediately. Cook for 30 seconds, then restir the sauce mixture and add
   it also to the wok. Stir to prevent lumps from forming.

6 When the sauce has thickened, add the vegetables and pork to the wok and mix
   well. Test for salt. Glaze with the sesame oil and stir, then serve hot.

Note: If sweet red peppers are not available, substitute carrot pieces. Also, 3
tablespoons of tomato catsup could be substituted for the crabapples.

◉◉◉ Mo Shu Pork

Serves 4 as a meal with a thick soup
Time   approximately 30 minutes
            preparation, depending on
            shredding ability
            15 minutes resting   木 須 肉
            10 minutes cooking

In this dish, scrambled eggs are used to symbolize the *muxu,* a fragrant yellow
flower of northern China. This specialty has become a favorite of Americans in
northern restaurants. In a sense, it is many dishes in one, as within the Mandarin
pancake each ingredient retains its own unique texture, and the taste combination varies with each bite. The wrapping gives the diner a welcome chance to
exercise fingers on both hands while eating.

Some people use half a Syrian bread with its built-in pocket to hold the stuffing.
This certainly saves time, but the bread has a coarse and absorbent texture. We
prefer to use the Mandarin pancakes, which are easy to make or can be purchased from Chinese markets. A Mexican wheat tortilla is a reasonable substitute.

Ingredients

2 ounces tiger lily buds
½ ounce wood ears
8 medium black mushrooms
1 cup bamboo shoots
12 ounces lean pork, cut from the loin
9 tablespoons oil
4 whole scallions, trimmed
4 whole eggs
Dash of salt
2 teaspoons tapioca powder

¼ teaspoon chicken bouillon powder
16 to 20 Mandarin Pancakes (page 411)
2 cloves garlic, 1 crushed and 1 minced
1 teaspoon granulated sugar
1 tablespoon pale dry sherry

Seasonings

1 tablespoon dark soy sauce
1 tablespoon tapioca powder
1 teaspoon granulated sugar
¼ teaspoon salt
1 teaspoon sesame oil
1 tablespoon pale dry sherry

PREPARATION

1 The ingredients in this recipe are to be shredded finely into strips about ⅛ by ⅛ by 1½ inches.

2 Soak tiger lilies in warm water until soft. Rinse well, then trim tough ends. Cut each in half.

3 Soak wood ears in plenty of hot water to cover. Allow to soak until soft and expanded, then rinse and trim tough ends. Shred finely.

4 Soak black mushrooms in warm water until soft, then squeeze to extract moisture. Reserve the soaking liquid and shred mushrooms finely.

5 Shred the bamboo shoots, then blanch in boiling water for 1 minute. Remove to a colander and run cold water over the shoots to stop the cooking.

6 Shred the pork and put it in a bowl, then add the seasonings. Mix well.

7 Add 2 tablespoons of oil to the pork mixture, stir to separate the shreds, and let sit at least 15 minutes (or chill until needed).

8 Shred the scallions and set aside.

9 Beat the eggs with salt until smooth.

10 Mix the tapioca powder and instant chicken bouillon powder with ½ cup of the reserved mushroom liquid.

11 Prepare the Mandarin pancakes according to the directions on page 411. If using frozen pancakes, thaw in the refrigerator.

COOKING

1 Set a steamer over high heat and bring water in base to a boil. Arrange the pancakes on a heatproof platter, then place in steamer. Cover pancakes with a clean kitchen towel to prevent condensed steam from dropping onto the surface. Steam pancakes for 10 minutes, then keep covered until ready to serve.

2 While steaming the pancakes, set a wok over high heat. When very hot, add 2 tablespoons of oil. Flavor the oil with crushed garlic and discard the garlic when

browned. Add the tiger lilies, wood ears, and black mushrooms, stirring for 1 minute. Add the bamboo shoots and season with salt and sugar. Remove from wok.

3 Rinse wok and reset over high heat. When very hot, add 2 more tablespoons of oil. Flavor with minced garlic for 10 seconds, then add the meat, stirring constantly until the shreds separate. Sizzle in the wine along the edge of the wok.

4 Push ingredients to the side of wok and restir the tapioca mixture. Add mixture to the center of the wok, stirring sauce until it thickens. Return the tiger lilies, wood ears, black mushrooms, and bamboo shoots to wok; mix and remove.

5 Rinse wok again and set over high heat. When hot, add remaining 3 tablespoons of oil. Scramble the eggs until almost set, then return all ingredients to the wok, adding also the scallion shreds. Mix well and remove.

6 Serve with steamed Mandarin pancakes as wrappers.

◉◉◉ Lychee Pork

Serves 4 with vegetable, rice, and a
minute soup
Time 10 minutes preparation
30 minutes marinating
25 minutes cooking

荔 枝 肉

The lychees perfume and sweeten the meat in this Fujianese sweet-and-sour specialty.

Ingredients
1½ pounds lean pork butt
1 can (16 ounces) lychees
1 egg, lightly beaten
4 cups + 2 tablespoons oil
Cornstarch for coating
1 clove garlic, flattened
2 teaspoons pale dry sherry
2 teaspoons sesame oil

Marinade
2 tablespoons light soy sauce
1 tablespoon pale dry sherry
⅛ teaspoon five-spice powder
½ teaspoon salt

Lychee sauce
¾ cup lychee canning juice
1 teaspoon chicken bouillon powder
2 tablespoons tomato catsup
3 tablespoons white wine vinegar
1 tablespoon tapioca powder
1 tablespoon granulated sugar
¼ teaspoon salt

PREPARATION

1 Trim excess fat from the pork. Cut into pieces about 1 by 1½ inches. Score each piece on one side about halfway down in a checkerboard pattern with incisions about ¼ inch apart.

2 Combine ingredients for marinade in a bowl and add pork. Mix well with your fingers and then set at room temperature for 30 minutes.

3 Drain lychees and reserve juice for sauce. Cut each lychee in half.

4 Mix ingredients for lychee sauce and set aside.

5 Remove meat from marinade and drain excess liquid. Add the egg to the pork and mix together.

COOKING

1 Set wok over medium heat. When hot, add 4 cups of oil. While waiting for the oil to heat, coat each piece of pork lightly with cornstarch, shaking off excess.

2 Raise heat under wok to high. Test temperature by dropping a piece of scallion green into oil. If the green sizzles noisily and soon turns brown, the oil is ready (about 375 degrees).

3 Add half the pork in succession to the oil and deep-fry until the coating sets and the color turns light golden. Remove to drain in a strainer. Continue to deep-fry the remaining pork in the same manner.

4 Skim off as much sediment from the oil as possible, then heat the oil until very hot. Return all the meat to the oil at once and deep-fry until golden brown. Pour oil and pork together into a strainer-lined bowl to drain.

5 Wipe wok clean with paper towels, then set over high heat. Add 1 tablespoon of oil. Flavor oil with garlic, then remove the garlic when it is brown. Sizzle in the wine and immediately restir the sauce mixture and add it to the wok. Stir constantly until the sauce thickens, then add lychees. Bring sauce to a boil again and taste for salt and tartness. Add sesame oil and remaining tablespoon of oil to glaze. Return meat to the wok, mix, and serve.

⊛ Cantonese Pork Chops

Serves 2 as a main dish with
stir-fried vegetables and a
clear soup
Time 20 minutes preparation
25 minutes marinating
10 minutes cooking

煎 猪 扒

The Western pork chop gets a Cantonese treatment in this dish, one of my family's favorites from as early as half a century ago. It is proper to take bites from the chop on your plate, alternating it with intakes of other foods for variety. Sometimes the chops are cut to domino size, to be handled by chopsticks. This cutting is done after the cooking, however, to retain the natural juices.

Ingredients	Marinade	
6 center-cut pork chops, cut ³⁄₈ inch	1 tablespoon light soy sauce	1 teaspoon granulated sugar
1 medium onion	1 tablespoon dark soy sauce	⅛ teaspoon white pepper
5 tablespoons oil	1 tablespoon pale dry sherry	2 tablespoons cornstarch
3 tablespoons chicken stock or water	2 teaspoons sesame oil	
Salt		

PREPARATION

1 Remove bones so that the pork chops can lay flat in the wok or skillet to receive even temperature. Tenderize each piece by pounding both sides lightly with the blunt edge of the cleaver, crosswise and lengthwise.

2 With a wire whisk, mix marinade in a bowl. Arrange the chops in 1 layer in a deep dish and pour marinade over. Set at room temperature for 15 minutes, then turn chops and set for another 10 minutes. Use immediately or chill until ready to use.

3 Cut onion lengthwise in half. Slice each half crosswise into ¼-inch slices. Separate layers.

COOKING

1 Set a wok over high heat. When very hot, whirl in 3 tablespoons of oil along the edge of the wok. When oil runs to the center, swish the oil around the inside surface using a spatula.

2 Add the chops, arranging them in 1 layer, then turn heat to medium-high. Tilt the wok in different positions so that each piece will receive equal amounts of heat. Pan-fry the chops until one side is brown, then turn to brown on other side, adding more oil if necessary. When golden brown, remove chops to a platter.

3 Add onion strips to wok, stirring constantly until limp. Turn heat to high and add broth and season with salt. Cook until the moisture is evaporated, then place onion strips around the chops on the platter. Serve whole or cut up.

VARIATION: Deep-Fried Pork Chops
Instead of pan-frying, deep-fry the chops.

◎◎ Deep-Fried Pork Cubes in Vinegar Sauce

Serves 2 as a main dish with
vegetables and rice
Time 10 minutes preparation
30 minutes marinating
20 minutes cooking

糖醋肉

This is a popular sweet and sour pork dish in the East China manner.

Ingredients

1 pound lean pork butt
(trimmed weight)
4 cups + 1 tablespoon
oil
3 tablespoons
all-purpose flour

1 clove garlic, crushed
2 teaspoons sesame oil

Marinade

1 tablespoon pale dry
sherry
1 tablespoon light soy
sauce
½ teaspoon salt
1 whole egg

Vinegar sauce

3 tablespoons red rice vinegar

3 tablespoons brown sugar

1 tablespoon dark soy sauce

2 tablespoons chicken stock

2 teaspoons tapioca powder

PREPARATION

1 Cut meat into 1-inch cubes.

2 Mix marinade in a bowl. Add the pork cubes and mix well with your fingers. Set aside for 30 minutes.

3 Combine ingredients for vinegar sauce in a small bowl. Set aside.

COOKING

1 Set a wok over high heat. When wok is hot, add 4 cups of oil. While waiting for oil to heat, add flour to the pork. Mix with the fingers until each piece is well coated with flour.

2 Test the temperature of the oil by dropping a piece of scallion green into the hot oil. If the green sizzles and soon turns brown, the oil is ready (about 375 degrees). Otherwise wait for 2 more minutes and test again. Drop in half the cubes in quick succession into the oil. Deep-fry until the coating sets and the color turns light golden. Remove pork piece by piece to a strainer to drain. Continue with remaining meat.

3 Reheat the oil in the wok for about 3 minutes. Return all the pork to the oil and deep-fry until golden brown. Remove to drain on paper towels.

4 Pour out oil and wipe wok clean with paper towels. Add about 1 tablespoon of fresh oil to wok and set it over high heat. Flavor oil with garlic for 15 seconds, then discard the garlic. Restir the sauce mixture and add to the wok, stirring constantly to prevent lumps from forming. Cook until thickened and bubbly.

5 Glaze sauce with sesame oil and return pork cubes to wok, stirring and turning until pieces are coated with sauce. Serve hot.

◉◉◉ Fish-Flavored Pork Shreds

Serves 4 to 6 as part of a Chinese family meal
Time 20 minutes preparation
30 minutes soaking
8 to 10 minutes cooking

魚 香 肉 絲

Do not be misled by the name of this dish. There is no fish in this oily, pepper-hot, and chewy offering from fish-starved Sichuan. The flavor is adapted from the sauce used in braising fish.

Ingredients	Seasonings	Sauce mixture
8 medium wood ears	2 tablespoons dark soy sauce	1 tablespoon Sichuan hot bean paste
12 ounces lean boneless pork, cut from loin	1 tablespoon tapioca powder	1 tablespoon red rice vinegar
8 water chestnuts		1 tablespoon dark soy sauce
2 cups + 2 tablespoons oil		1 tablespoon granulated sugar
¼ teaspoon salt		1 teaspoon tapioca powder
2 scallions (white part only), chopped fine		
4 slices gingerroot, grated		
2 cloves garlic, minced		
1 tablespoon pale dry sherry		
2 teaspoons sesame oil		

PREPARATION

1 Soak wood ears in warm water for 30 minutes until soft. Trim the tough ends, then cut remainder into strips about ⅛ inch wide.

2 Trim meat of excess fat. Shred into thin strips about ⅛ by ⅛ by 2 inches. Put meat in a bowl with the seasonings and mix well.

3 Cut water chestnuts into ⅛-inch strips.

4 Mix ingredients for sauce mixture in a bowl and set aside.

COOKING

1 Set a wok over high heat. When the wok is very hot, add 2 cups of oil. Wait for about 1 minute, then add the pork shreds, stirring to separate. Pour both meat and oil into a strainer-lined bowl to drain, leaving about 1 tablespoon of oil in the wok.

2 Place wok again over high heat and add the wood ears and water chestnuts, stirring for 1 minute. Season with salt, stir, and remove.

3 Add remaining 2 tablespoons of oil to the wok. When oil is hot, add the scallions, ginger, and garlic. Stir for 15 seconds, then return pork to wok. Sizzle in the wine along the edge of the wok, stirring constantly. Add the wood ears and water chestnuts.

4 Restir the sauce mixture and add to the center of the wok, stirring until thickened. Glaze sauce with sesame oil, mix well, and serve.

Stir-Fried Pork Slices with Vegetables

Serves 2 as an accompaniment to a main dish

Time 10 to 15 minutes preparation
15 minutes resting
5 minutes cooking

肉片炒菜

This is a general recipe which, in the United States, is called Chow Yok, meaning "stir-fried pork." You could use almost any vegetable.

Ingredients	Seasoning	Optional sauce
½ pound lean boneless pork, cut from loin	1 tablespoon light soy sauce	1 teaspoon tapioca powder mixed with 1 tablespoon water or stock
3 tablespoons oil	2 teaspoons dark soy sauce	
3 cups vegetables for stir-frying (see page 349)	2 teaspoons tapioca powder	
1 clove garlic, sliced	1 teaspoon sesame oil	
1 tablespoon pale dry sherry	2 teaspoons pale dry sherry	
	½ teaspoon granulated sugar	
	Dash of white pepper	

PREPARATION

1 Slice the pork across the grain into pieces about 1 inch by 1½ inches and ⅛ inch thick.

2 Mix ingredients for seasoning and blend with pork. Use your fingers to mix well.

3 Stir in 1 tablespoon of oil to separate the pork slices. Set meat at room temperature for 15 minutes.

4 Meanwhile, rinse, cut, and drain the vegetables.

COOKING

1 Stir-fry the vegetables by following the general recipe. Discard excess oil and juice, if any.

2 Rinse wok and wipe dry. Set it over high heat. When very hot, add 2 tablespoons of oil. Flavor oil with garlic for 20 seconds, or until lightly browned. Add the meat, spreading slices evenly on the bottom of the wok. Cook in a pan-frying manner for 1 minute, then turn to cook the other side for another 1 minute. Stir quickly until slices separate and pink color disappears.

3 Sizzle in the wine along the edge of the wok, add the vegetables, and stir constantly to mix all ingredients well. The wine will evaporate.

4 If desired, mix tapioca powder with water and add to the center of the wok, stirring until sauce is thickened.

5 Serve pork and vegetables, either with or without sauce, while hot.

◉◉◉ Two-Tone Pork

Serves	2 as a main dish or 4 in a Chinese meal
Time	15 minutes preparation
	15 minutes soaking
	2 hours chilling
	7 minutes cooking

雙 色 肉

From the same cut of pork, two distinct ways of preparation lead to two dishes with different colors, texture, and taste. The two are served on the same platter, encircled by jade-green Chinese parsley to heighten the contrast. This two-in-one dish asserts the chef's mastery of the art of both the palate and the palette.

Ingredients	Seasonings for white-colored pork	Seasonings for brown-colored pork
2 pieces center-cut pork chop, each about 1½ inches thick	1 egg white	1 egg yolk
2 cups water	2 teaspoons tapioca powder	1½ tablespoons cornstarch
2 ounces Chinese parsley	1 teaspoon Fen liquor or light rum	1 tablespoon dark soy sauce
2 cups oil	1 teaspoon sesame oil	1 teaspoon granulated sugar
	½ teaspoon sugar	½ teaspoon ginger juice
	¼ teaspoon salt	¼ teaspoon finely minced garlic
	Dash of white pepper	1 teaspoon yellow wine or sherry
		1 teaspoon sesame oil
		⅛ teaspoon salt

PREPARATION

1 Remove the bone from the pork chops. Trim excess fat and remove membranes; each piece of meat should yield about 5 ounces. Reserve the bones for soup stock.

2 Slice 1 piece of pork across the grain into very thin slices about $\frac{1}{16}$ inch thick and 1 by 2 inches in size. Put pork slices in a bowl and soak with water for 15 minutes, then drain. Squeeze meat gently to extract excess moisture. Arrange slices in 1 layer on double paper towels. Place another paper towel on top to blot dry. Mix white seasonings in a small bowl and add the pork slices. Blend well and chill in refrigerator for 2 hours. This is the white-colored pork.

3 For the brown-colored pork, slice the remaining piece of pork across the grain the same size as the white-colored ones, but double the thickness, to about $\frac{1}{8}$ inch. Mix brown seasonings with pork in another small bowl and chill also for 2 hours.

4 Cut and remove roots from Chinese parsley. Rinse and separate stems. Drain.

COOKING

1 Have a bowl lined with a strainer ready for oil-dipping.

2 Set a wok over high heat until very hot. Add about 2 tablespoons of the oil and swish it around the wok to coat the surface evenly, then pour oil out.

3 Reheat the wok to very hot and add the remaining oil. Give the white-colored pork a quick stir, then add to the oil, stirring rapidly until slices separate, about 40 seconds. Use a deep-frying strainer to remove the pork slices to drain oil over a bowl.

4 Remove sediments in the oil if any. Reheat the oil to about 375 degrees or until a piece of scallion green dropped in the oil sizzles noisily and soon turns brown. Add the brown-colored pork slices in quick succession, and deep-fry until slices start to float at top of the oil. Remove pork slice by slice to drain in the strainer. Turn heat off.

5 Arrange the white-colored pork on one side of the serving platter, then the brown-colored pork on the other side, forming a yin-yang pattern if you like.

6 Drop the parsley into the hot oil and give it just a stir to half-cook. Remove parsley immediately to drain on paper towels, then arrange around the pork. Serve at once.

⊛ Stir-Fried Pork Shreds with Bean Sprouts

Serves 2 as part of a multi-dish
family meal
Time   30 minutes preparation
10 minutes resting
5 minutes cooking

銀 芽 炒 肉 絲

Bean sprouts are served in a banquet only after the heads and tails have been removed, whereas in the home, the whole sprouts are eaten. The happy medium is to retain the head and stem and remove only the stringy root. The Chinese almost never eat bean sprouts raw; they compare the taste to that of raw grass.

Ingredients

1 pound fresh bean
  sprouts
4 black mushrooms
1 center-cut pork chop,
  cut 1 inch thick and
  with bone removed
2 whole scallions,
  trimmed
1 cup + 2 tablespoons
  oil
2 slices gingerroot
½ teaspoon salt
2 teaspoons pale dry
  sherry

Seasonings

1 tablespoon light soy
  sauce
1 teaspoon pale dry
  sherry
1 teaspoon sesame oil
1 teaspoon granulated
  sugar
Dash of white pepper
2 teaspoons tapioca
  powder

PREPARATION

1 Fill the kitchen sink with cold water, then put in bean sprouts. The green husks will sink to the bottom and the roots will rise to the surface. Stir gently with your hand to loosen the ends, then take a handful of sprouts at a time and put in a colander to drain. There will be about 3 cups after cleaning. (For a more elaborate version, remove the heads and tails from the sprouts. Soak in a bowl of water and chill; drain before using.)

2 Soak mushrooms in warm water until soft. Squeeze to extract moisture, then trim stems. Shred finely, about ⅛ inch thick.

3 Trim fat from pork and then cut vertically into slices ⅛ inch thick. Cut the slices from the small sides vertically into shreds also ⅛ inch thick.

4 Mix seasonings in a bowl and add the meat. Stir well, then set aside for 10 minutes.

5 Cut and discard about 3 inches of the green part of scallions. Shred the rest finely into 2-inch lengths.

COOKING

1 Set a wok over high heat. When very hot, add 2 tablespoons of oil. Flavor oil with ginger until lightly brown, then remove and discard the ginger. Add salt, then immediately add the sprouts, stirring and turning quickly until their color turns from solid to translucent. Remove to drain.

2 Rinse wok and wipe dry. Set over high heat and when very hot add remaining cup of oil. Immediately add the pork shreds, stirring for 15 seconds or until separated. Remove pork shreds together with the oil and pour into a strainer-lined bowl, leaving about 1 tablespoon of oil in wok.

3 Set wok back on high heat and, when oil is hot, add mushrooms, stirring them around the wok a few times. Return pork to wok and sizzle in the wine along the edge. Add the scallion shreds and sprouts, stirring just once again.

4 Remove meat and vegetables from wok and serve immediately to retain crunchiness.

◉◉ Metropolis Spareribs

Serves 4 as a main dish with rice, vegetables, and a clear soup
Time 10 minutes preparation
1½ hours resting and marinating
30 minutes cooking

京都排骨

Like the recipes from many large cosmopolitan cities, this one uses seasonings from all over.

Ingredients	Marinade	Sauce mixture
2 pounds extra-lean pork spareribs	2 tablespoons light soy sauce	3 tablespoons red rice vinegar
1 teaspoon unseasoned meat tenderizer (optional)	1 tablespoon pale dry sherry	3 tablespoons brown sugar
¼ cup all-purpose flour	¼ teaspoon five-spice powder	2 tablespoons A-1 sauce
1 egg, lightly beaten	¼ teaspoon salt	1 teaspoon tapioca powder
6 cups + 1 tablespoon oil		
2 cloves garlic, minced		
3 small shallots, minced		

PREPARATION

1 Cut spareribs into pieces about 1 by 1½ inches (or have butcher do this for you). Remove the fat and rinse off any bone dust. Put ribs in a large bowl and, if desired, add tenderizer; mix well. Set for 30 minutes.

2 Mix ingredients for marinade and add to meat. Keep meat at room temperature for at least 1 hour or refrigerate for several hours until ready to use.

3 Mix ingredients for sauce together in a small bowl and set aside.

4 Shortly before cooking, drain ribs. Discard marinade and then put ribs back into bowl. Add the flour first, mixing and turning with your fingers, then the egg and mix again, making sure every piece is evenly coated.

COOKING

1 Set a wok over high heat. When very hot, add the 6 cups of oil. Wait for about 8 minutes, then test temperature by dropping in a piece of scallion green. If bubbles appear around the green immediately and the green also sizzles and turns brown, the temperature is hot enough (about 375 degrees). Otherwise, wait a little longer and test again.

2 Drop spareribs, piece by piece, into the oil until you have about 15 pieces in the wok. Deep-fry until lightly brown, then remove to drain. Heat the oil to very hot again and repeat for more ribs; continue until all ribs are cooked.

3 Reheat the oil to very hot again and return all the ribs to the oil; deep-fry until golden brown, then remove and drain. Pour out oil.

4 Set wok over high heat again. When very hot, add the 1 tablespoon of oil. Flavor oil with garlic and shallots until brown, then add sauce mixture, stirring constantly until it bubbles. Return ribs to wok and stir and turn until each piece is well coated with the sauce. Remove and serve hot.

VARIATION: Tangy Spareribs

Follow the previous recipe to cut, marinate, and deep-fry the ribs, but use the following fruit sauce to replace the sweet and sour sauce for a more delicate flavor.

Fruit sauce mixture

Juice of ½ lemon	1 tablespoon tapioca
Juice of 1 orange	powder
Juice of 2 tangerines	¼ teaspoon salt
1 teaspoon chicken	2 tablespoons oil
bouillon powder	1 clove garlic, minced
1 tablespoon brown	1 teaspoon sesame oil
sugar	

1 Mix fruit juices with chicken bouillon powder, brown sugar, tapioca powder, and salt in a bowl. Set aside.

2 After deep-frying the ribs, remove oil from wok. Wipe clean with paper towels, then set wok over high heat again. When hot, add 1 tablespoon of oil. Flavor oil with garlic, stirring just once around the wok.

3 Add half the reserved sauce mixture, then gradually stream in the remainder, stirring constantly until the sauce thickens. Correct the seasonings, adding more sugar if desired.

4 Glaze sauce with sesame oil and remaining tablespoon of oil. Add the spareribs, stir, and serve hot.

Steamed Spareribs in Black Bean Sauce

Serves 3 with rice, vegetable, and a thick soup
Time 15 minutes preparation
10 minutes resting
20 minutes cooking

豉 汁 排 骨

This is a Cantonese country dish.

Ingredients

1 pound small extra-lean spareribs
2 tablespoons fermented black beans
2 cloves garlic, crushed
2 tablespoons oil

Seasonings

1 tablespoon light soy sauce
1 tablespoon tapioca powder
1 teaspoon sesame oil
2 teaspoons pale dry sherry
2 teaspoons fresh lemon juice
1 tablespoon granulated sugar
1/4 teaspoon salt

PREPARATION

1 Have butcher cut the spareribs crosswise into 1-inch pieces. Rinse and drain, then pat dry with paper towels. Put ribs in a bowl and add the seasonings. Mix, then let sit at room temperature for at least 10 minutes.

2 Rinse the black beans, and combine with garlic in a small bowl. Crush beans with the handle of a cleaver into a paste, then stir in the oil. Add bean mixture to spareribs and blend well.

3 Transfer ribs to an 8-inch dish with a 1-inch-high rim. Steam spareribs over high heat for 20 minutes, then serve hot.

VARIATION: Steamed Spareribs in Plum Sauce

Plum sauce goes well with two Cantonese steamed dishes: spareribs and goose. For this version, omit the lemon juice and use 2 tablespoons of brown bean paste (whole bean) instead of the black beans. Mash the brown bean paste with the garlic and add 4 pitted preserved plums. Add a red chili pepper also if desired. Steam as for above and serve hot.

◉◉ Pigs' Feet in Aspic

Yields about 60 slices
Time 20 minutes preparation
2 hours simmering
Overnight chilling

猪 脚 凍

This is a Chaozhou counterpart to head cheese. The Chinese are fond of putting their (pig's) foot in their mouth.

Ingredients
2 pigs' feet, about 2
  pounds total
2 fresh ham hocks,
  about 1 pound total
4 cups water
1 package unflavored
  gelatin

Seasonings
½ cup fish sauce
2 ounces rock candy

COOKING

1 Blanch the pigs' feet and ham hocks for 10 minutes, then run under cold water.

2 In a 4-quart saucepan, bring water to a boil and add seasonings. Add pigs' feet and ham hocks and return to a boil. Reduce heat to low, cover pot, and cook about 2 hours. Test for doneness by inserting a chopstick into the ham hock. If it goes through easily, the pork is soft enough. Otherwise, cook about 20 to 30 minutes. Remove, leaving the cooking liquid in the pan.

3 Remove all bones from the pigs' feet and ham hocks. Set meat aside.

4 Strain the cooking liquid through a fine sieve and replace in saucepan. Skim as much fat as possible.

5 Dissolve the gelatin in ¼ cup water, then bring the cooking liquid to a boil and add the gelatin mixture. Cook until completely dissolved and clear.

6 Arrange the pieces of meat in a small loaf pan (4 by 3 by 8 inches) and pour in the gelatin mixture. Poke it with a fork to allow the liquid to penetrate to the bottom, then chill loaf in the refrigerator overnight or until firm.

7 To serve, scrape off any solidified fat on top of the loaf and slice into ¼-inch pieces. Serve cold.

Note: You can only use part of the loaf and freeze the remainder. To later use the frozen part, thaw and reheat, then chill again until needed.

◉ Quick-Fried Pork Liver

Serves 2 as a main dish with rice and
vegetables
Time 30 minutes preparation
10 minutes marinating
15 minutes soaking
5 minutes cooking

閩 式 豬 肝

This is a Fujianese specialty. The natural juice of the liver is well sealed in by the coating and the warm oil-dipping preserves the tender texture. This should be served immediately over a bed of stir-fried crunchy vegetables.

Ingredients

1 pound fresh pork
liver (trimmed
weight about 12
ounces)
2 cups oil
3 tablespoons tapioca
powder
4 whole scallions, cut
into 1-inch lengths

1½ teaspoons
granulated sugar
1 tablespoon pale dry
sherry
2 teaspoons sesame oil

Marinade

1 egg white
2 tablespoons dark soy
sauce
2 teaspoons pale dry
sherry
Pinch of salt

PREPARATION

1 Soak the liver in cold water for 15 minutes. Wipe dry with a paper towel, then trim away the tough membranes. Slope-cut into thin slabs about 1 by 1½ by ⅛ inch.

2 Put liver in a bowl and add the marinade. Set at room temperature for no longer than 10 minutes.

COOKING

1 Set a wok over high heat. When hot, add the oil. While waiting for oil to heat, coat each piece of liver with the tapioca powder, shaking off the excess.

2 Test temperature of the oil by dropping a piece of scallion green into the oil. If it sizzles and moves around quickly, the oil is ready (about 325 degrees). Add all the liver pieces to the oil, stirring to separate, and deep-fry for about 15 seconds. Pour the oil and liver together into a strainer-lined bowl to drain, leaving about 1 tablespoon of oil in the wok.

3 Set wok back on high heat. When very hot, add the scallions, stirring until each piece is coated with oil. Add the sugar and liver, then sizzle in the wine. Stir quickly to mix well.

4 Glaze ingredients with sesame oil, then stir and serve immediately.

◉◉ Pearly Balls

Serves 3 as a main dish with
vegetables, or about 8 as an
appetizer
Time 20 minutes preparation
3 hours soaking and chilling
30 minutes cooking

珍 珠 丸 子

Walnut-sized meatballs are given a coating here of glutinous rice. This dish from East China is also known as Porcupine Meatballs. Techniques for shaping are shown on page 78.

Ingredients	Seasonings	Vinegar and ginger sauce
1 cup glutinous rice	½ teaspoon salt	¼ cup red rice vinegar
1 pound lean ground pork	2 tablespoons light soy sauce	4 slices gingerroot, finely shredded
1 cup bamboo shoots	1 whole egg	
2 scallions (white part only), chopped	1 tablespoon pale dry sherry	
	1 teaspoon granulated sugar	
	2 teaspoons grated gingerroot	
	1 tablespoon sesame oil	
	1 tablespoon tapioca powder	
	Dash of white pepper	

PREPARATION

1 Rinse the rice, then soak in cold water for at least 1 hour. Drain thoroughly and spread in 1 layer on a cookie sheet lined with paper towels.

2 In a large mixing bowl, add the pork to the soy sauce and salt for the seasonings. Mix with your fingers and scoop up the pork mixture by the hand, beating it back into the bowl several times until firm. Add the remaining seasonings to the meat, scooping and beating several more times.

3 Blanch the bamboo shoots in boiling water for 2 minutes. Run cold water over to stop the cooking process, then shred and cut into bits about the size of a bean. Put in the center of a kitchen towel and wrap; squeeze to extract as much moisture as possible.

4 Add the scallions to the pork, together with the bamboo shoot bits. Mix well, then chill for at least 2 hours or until ready to use.

SHAPING THE BALLS

1 Scoop up a handful of the meat mixture and squeeze it up through the fist until it reaches the size of a walnut. Scrape off with a wet spoon.

---

2 Drop the pork ball onto the rice, rolling it around until the surface is evenly covered with rice. Place the balls on a greased heatproof platter, allowing about ½ inch space between balls.

3 Continue to shape the balls until all the meat is used.

COOKING

1 Place the platter with the meatballs into a steamer.

2 Bring water in base of steamer to a boil and steam meatballs over high heat for 30 minutes, or until the rice turns shiny and transparent. Serve hot or warm with vinegar and ginger sauce.

VARIATION: Sweet and Sour Pork Balls
Ingredients

	Sweet and sour sauce
1 pound lean ground pork	1 cup chicken stock
Cornstarch for coating	2 tablespoons tapioca powder
4 cups + 2 tablespoons oil	3 tablespoons red rice vinegar
1 clove garlic, minced	3 tablespoons brown sugar
2 teaspoons pale dry sherry	½ teaspoon salt
2 teaspoons sesame oil	1 tablespoon dark soy sauce

1 Follow the above recipe to prepare and shape the balls but do not roll them in the glutinous rice.

2 Drop each pork ball onto a small platter of cornstarch and roll it around until the surface is evenly and lightly coated. Arrange the balls on a tray; if not used immediately, chill.

3 Set a wok over high heat. When very hot, add 4 cups of oil. Wait about 5 to 7 minutes, then test the temperature by dropping in a piece of scallion green. If it sizzles and moves about quickly, the oil is ready, about 350 degrees. Drop in half the balls in succession, and deep-fry until just light brown. Remove and drain. Continue to deep-fry the remaining half, then remove and drain.

4 Skim off as much sediment from the oil as possible with a fine strainer. Reheat the oil until very hot, then return all the pork balls to the oil. Deep-fry until golden, then pour both balls and oil into a strainer-lined bowl to drain. Wipe the wok clean with paper towels.

5 Set the wok over high heat. When very hot, add 1 tablespoon of oil. Flavor the oil with the garlic for 10 seconds, then sizzle in the wine along the edge of the wok. Add the sauce mixture immediately and stir constantly until sauce thickens. Glaze with sesame oil and remaining tablespoon of oil.

6 Remove balls to a serving bowl and pour the sauce over.

⊛ Steamed Minced Pork with Salted Eggs

Serves 4 to 6 as part of a family meal
Time 10 minutes preparation
20 minutes cooking

Very often the Chinese steam a dish of food atop boiling rice. A dish with a 1-inch rim is ideal for holding the natural juices and then later for removing from the pot. However, remember that the pot should be large enough to hold a dish at least 6 inches in diameter; there should be at least 3 cups of rice to generate sufficient steam; the dish and its rack should not be in position until small craters appear on the surface of the cooking rice. Then the heat is turned to a simmer and the pan is covered. When the rice is done, so is the dish on top.

Minced pork can be steamed with different ingredients, such as minced jade pillars, dried squid, Sichuan preserved vegetables, Cantonese preserved vegetables, or well-salted fish. They are all great with plain rice and, for the Chinese, are just as common as American meatloaf.

Ingredients	**Seasonings**	
2 salted duck eggs	1 tablespoon light soy sauce	2 teaspoons chicken stock or water
½ pound lean ground pork	2 teaspoons tapioca powder	1 tablespoon oil
1 whole egg	½ teaspoon granulated sugar	1 teaspoon sesame oil
1 tablespoon oil		Dash of white pepper

PREPARATION

1 Separate the whites and yolks of the duck eggs. Beat the salted egg whites with the whole egg and the oil until smooth. Remove any foam and set aside. Reserve the salted egg yolks.

2 Combine the seasonings in a bowl, then add the pork. Blend ingredients well with your fingers. Scoop the meat mixture by the hand and beat it back into the bowl. Repeat the scooping and beating several times until the mixture holds together and is firm. This beating process helps keep the pork mixture smooth and elastic.

3 Arrange the meat in a heatproof dish with a 1-inch rim and a 6- to 7-inch diameter. Fold in the beaten egg mixture.

4 Grease one side of the blade of a cleaver and use it to flatten the egg yolks into 4 thin rounds about 1½ inches in diameter. Place the yolks on top of the pork mixture, pressing them lightly into the meat.

COOKING

1 Steam the pork over a pot of boiling rice (see comments above) or steam it in a steamer over medium heat for 20 minutes. (Do not set the dish in before the water in the base boils.)

2 Steam meat until done; do not overcook it or the egg will be grainy. Remove dish from steamer or rice pot and serve immediately.

VARIATION: Minced Pork with Dried Shrimps and Black Mushrooms
Ingredients

½ pound lean ground
   pork
¼ cup dried shrimp
1 scallion (white part
   only)
4 black mushrooms

1 Follow the instructions in previous recipe to season and beat the pork until it is firm. To the seasonings, add 1 more teaspoon tapioca powder and ¼ teaspoon salt.

2 Soak the dried shrimp in ½ cup hot water until soft, then chop finely. Reserve the soaking liquid.

3 Chop the scallion finely and set aside.

4 Add the dried shrimp, black mushrooms, and scallion to the pork mixture and mix well. Scoop and beat the mixture in the same manner until all ingredients hold together.

5 Spread the pork on a 6-inch-deep dish with a 1-inch rim. Moisten the surface with 1 tablespoon of the shrimp juice.

6 Steam the meat over boiling rice or in a steamer, setting the steamer over high heat for 15 minutes. Cook until the pink color of the pork disappears and the natural juices run out. Serve hot.

◉◉ Pork Brains

Yields about 12 ounces cooked
           brains
Time   15 minutes preparation
           3 hours soaking
           15 minutes steaming

豬腦

The Chinese believe that animal brains will impart extra brain power to the eater. While European cuisine favors brains from calves or lamb, pork brains find special favor in the Chinese cuisine. They are stir-fried, deep-fried, braised, or made into omelettes or added to soups. They are also served in banquets.

Ingredients	**Seasonings**	
1 pound pork brains (veal or lamb brains)	½ teaspoon salt	1 tablespoon yellow wine
2 tablespoons distilled vinegar mixed with 4 cups water	1 teaspoon ginger juice	Dash of white pepper
	1 teaspoon chicken bouillon powder	

PREPARATION

1 Soak the brains in cold water, changing the water every 30 minutes for a total of 2 hours. Then soak brains in vinegar water for another hour.

2 Take a piece of brain and, using a toothpick to roll on some of the thickest part of the membrane, gently pull off the membrane by rolling the toothpick over the brain. Trim off the white opaque bit at the base and slip the brain into a large bowl of cold water. Rinse the brain carefully to avoid breakage, then remove to a heatproof deep dish.

3 Finish the remainder of the brains the same way, arranging the brains in a deep dish in 1 layer; drain off as much water as possible.

4 Mix seasonings in a small bowl and spoon over the brains.

5 Steam the brains over high heat for 15 minutes, then set the brains at room temperature in their natural juices until cool. If the brains are used immediately, spread each piece on paper towels to dry; otherwise, keep refrigerated until ready to use, then drain and dry.

❀❀❀ Stir-Fried Pork Brains

Serves 6 as part of a Chinese meal
Time 10 minutes preparation
  1 hour chilling
  5 to 7 minutes cooking

炒豬朥

It was said that a live-in tutor to the young son of a rich merchant wearied of the taste of rich food, and begged for plain bean curd. It came and was much tastier than his memory indicated. A trip to the kitchen showed him why. In the corner were thrown a dozen dead pigs with their brains carved out. This dish shows that pork brains do not have to be disguised to be delicious.

Ingredients

6 ounces cooked Pork Brains (see page 279)
6 ounces shrimp in the shell
1 ounce Smithfield ham

1 whole scallion, trimmed
6 whole eggs
1 cup + 5 tablespoons oil
¼ teaspoon salt

Seasonings

½ egg white
1½ teaspoons tapioca powder
½ teaspoon oil
¼ teaspoon salt

PREPARATION

1 Cut brains into ⅜-inch dice.

2 Shell and devein shrimp. Clean and rinse (see page 151). Pat shrimp thoroughly dry with paper towels, then dice to the same size as the brains.

3 Mix seasonings in a small bowl, add the shrimp, and mix well. Chill for at least 1 hour.

4 Slice the ham thinly and cut into ⅜-inch squares.

5 Cut scallion into ¼-inch lengths.

TWO-TONE PORK
PAGE 268

PEARLY BALLS
PAGE 276

6 In a large bowl, beat eggs with 2 tablespoons of the oil and the salt until smooth. Add the brains, ham, and scallion. Set aside.

COOKING

1 Set a wok over high heat until very hot. Add the cup of oil and heat 1 minute. Give the shrimp a quick stir, then add to the oil, stirring until dice separate. Pour oil and shrimp together into a strainer put over a bowl to drain. Turn the heat off.

2 Add the cooked shrimp to the egg mixture and mix well.

3 Reheat the wok to very hot over high heat. Add 2 tablespoons of the oil, then pour in the egg mixture, stirring constantly until half the mixture is set, then whirl in the remaining tablespoon of oil along the edge of the wok, stirring until the egg mixture is set and not runny. Serve immediately.

◉◉◉ Braised Pork Brains in Brown Sauce

Serves 6 as part of a Chinese meal
Time 10 minutes preparation
30 minutes soaking
15 minutes cooking

黃燜豬腦

Though very similar in taste to its French counterpart, this northern dish is truly Chinese.

Ingredients	Seasonings	Sauce mixture
6 medium black mushrooms	2 teaspoons light soy sauce	½ cup chicken stock
½ cup hot water	1 teaspoon tapioca powder	1 tablespoon oyster sauce
3 ounces lean pork (cut from the loin)	¼ teaspoon granulated sugar	1 teaspoon dark soy sauce
1 whole scallion, trimmed	½ teaspoon sesame oil	1 teaspoon granulated sugar
12 ounces cooked Pork Brains (see page 279)	Dash of white pepper	
1 egg, lightly beaten		
Cornstarch for coating		
¼ cup + 2 tablespoons oil		
1 clove garlic, shredded		
1 tablespoon yellow wine		
1 teaspoon tapioca powder mixed with 1 tablespoon water		
1 teaspoon sesame oil		

PREPARATION

1 Soak mushrooms in hot water until soft; trim stems. Squeeze caps to extract moisture, then cut into ⅛-inch strips. Reserve the soaking liquid.

2 Shred the pork into ⅛-inch strips and mix with the seasonings. Chill for 30 minutes.

3 Chop scallion finely. Mix sauce with the mushroom liquid in a bowl and set aside.

4 Shortly before cooking, drain juice from the cooked brains, arranging them on paper towels to dry.

5 Dip the brains, piece by piece, into the egg first, then coat lightly with cornstarch.

COOKING

1 Set a wok over high heat. When very hot, add ¼ cup of the oil and swish it around to coat the wok evenly. Turn heat to medium, then arrange the brains in 1 layer in the wok, tilting to change position for even heating.

2 Pan-fry the brains until one side is brown, then turn to brown the other side, adding 1 more tablespoon of oil if needed. Remove brains to a platter.

3 Raise heat to high and add the remaining oil. Flavor oil with garlic for 5 seconds, then add the pork, spreading it out in 1 layer. Fry the pork for 30 seconds, then turn it over, stirring constantly until shreds separate. Sizzle in the wine and add the mushrooms. Stir 1 minute.

4 Add the sauce mixture and bring it to a boil. Return brain pieces to the wok and cook until half the sauce is absorbed. Push the brains to the side and stream the tapioca mixture into the center of the wok. Stir sauce constantly to prevent lumps. Add sesame oil to sauce, then mix sauce with the brains. Remove to a serving platter and decorate with scallion and serve.

◉◉◉ Pork Fluff

Makes	about 3 cups
Time	5 minutes preparation
	3 hours cooking

豬肉鬆

Pork fluff is one of the many small eats served with plain rice congee in China at breakfast and even makes a delicious sandwich. Though Fujianese in origin, this recipe requires no Fujianese wine mash, hard to find in the United States.

Ingredients

1½ pounds lean pork,
   cut from the loin
3 tablespoons oil

Braising sauce

¼ cup light soy sauce
2 tablespoons pale dry
   sherry
1½ tablespoons
   granulated sugar

2 slices gingerroot
4 cups water
¼ teaspoon salt

PREPARATION AND COOKING

1 Trim fat from the pork and cut into 1-inch chunks, then put the meat in a 3-quart saucepan. Add the braising sauce and set over high heat. Bring to a boil, turn heat to medium-low, and cover pan. Cook for 2 hours or longer, until the pork is very tender and the sauce is reduced to 1 cup.

2 Remove the pork to a cutting board while it is still hot. Pound it with a rolling pin, a little at a time, to break up the meat into fine shreds. Make sure the pork is finely and evenly shredded.

3 Strain the remaining sauce through a fine sieve into a nonstick skillet. Add the pork shreds and set over high heat. Cook, stirring all the while, until the sauce is dried up.

4 Reduce heat to medium, tossing and turning the pork constantly, for about 30 minutes.

5 Whirl in the oil and continue to toss and turn until the shreds become fluffy and crispy. When the color changes to golden, remove from the heat.

6 Store in a glass jar when completely cool. The pork fluff can be kept for several weeks.

⊚⊚⊚ Lettuce Wraps

Serves 6 as an appetizer, or 12 in a banquet

Time approximately 30 minutes preparation, depending on cutting skill
5 to 7 minutes cooking

生 菜 包

This colorful dish, originally from Phoenix City in Shunde District near Canton, usually uses minced squab or quail as the major ingredient instead of the ground pork here. It is perhaps one of the most exquisite Cantonese offerings to be eaten with both hands.

Ingredients

½ pound lean ground pork
6 black mushrooms
6 ounces bamboo shoots
12 water chestnuts
½ medium sweet red pepper
3 Chinese pork sausages
9 medium shrimp
3 scallions (white part only)

3 sprigs Chinese parsley
12 iceberg lettuce leaves
1 cup + 1 tablespoon oil
½ teaspoon salt
1 teaspoon granulated sugar
1 clove garlic, minced
1 tablespoon pale dry sherry

Seasonings

1 tablespoon light soy sauce
2 teaspoons oyster sauce
1 teaspoon sesame oil
1 teaspoon granulated sugar
2 teaspoons tapioca powder
Dash of white pepper

PREPARATION

1 All ingredients are to be cut into bits approximately the same size as a mung bean, or even smaller.

2 Mix pork with seasonings and set aside.

3 Soak mushrooms in warm water to cover until soft, then trim the stems. Squeeze to extract moisture, then cut into small bits.

4 Blanch bamboo shoots in boiling water for 1 minute. Rinse with cold water, then drain and cut into small bits.

5 Rinse water chestnuts with very hot water. Cut into small bits.

6 Remove seeds and pulp from pepper and cut finely.

7 Cut sausages into small bits.

8 Cook shrimp in boiling water until the shells turn red. Shell and devein, then cut into small bits.

9 Chop scallion whites and parsley finely.

10 Trim lettuce with scissors into 4-inch rounds to be used as wrappers. Rinse, then arrange on a serving tray. Wrap and chill until used (no more than 2 hours, or the cut edges of lettuce will turn rusty).

COOKING

1 Set a wok over high heat. When very hot, add 1 cup of oil. Immediately add the ground pork, stirring quickly to separate the bits. Remove meat and oil together and pour into a strainer-lined bowl, leaving about 2 tablespoons of oil in the wok.

2 Reheat wok to very hot, and add the bamboo shoots and water chestnuts, stirring until most of the moisture evaporates. Add pepper and season with salt and sugar, stirring a few times. Remove to a bowl.

3 Add sausage to wok, stirring until the fatty parts turn transparent. Add mushrooms, shrimp, and scallion whites, stirring to mix. Add to vegetables in a bowl.

4 Rinse wok and wipe dry. Set it over high heat. When very hot, add remaining tablespoon of oil. Flavor oil with garlic for 10 seconds, then return pork to wok. Sizzle in wine along the edge and mix well.

5 Return all cooked ingredients to wok, stirring constantly. Correct seasoning and add chopped parsley. Mix well, then remove to a serving platter.

6 To serve, place lettuce leaves in one platter, and the minced pork in another. Each diner takes a piece of lettuce by hand and on it places a heaping tablespoon of the minced pork. The diner then picks up the 2 opposite ends of the lettuce leaf with the fingers, taco-style, and enjoys.

Beef and Lamb

Beef, lamb, and kid are very much northern ingredients. In the old days, beef from South China was tough in texture, and deemed unworthy of the banquet.

Nowadays many farms in southern China raise cattle for meat alone, no longer toughening their flesh by toil, and dishes made with high-quality beef are appearing more and more at formal occasions.

The supply of lamb and kid, however, remains limited in the south. American beef and lamb are high in quality; the best Steak Cantonese Style in Hong Kong often uses American beef.

The Chinese cook is not sensitive to the cuts and grades of beef, but is most careful about the grain. With few exceptions, each piece of beef is to be cut across the grain because heat travels along the muscle fibers much easier than across, and uniform heating is essential to stir-frying. The most popular cut is flank steak because of its uniform grain and relative absence of gristle and fat. Cutting a flank steak across the grain gives domino-sized slices just right for stir-frying.

When Chinese-style steaks demand larger pieces of meat with a crosswise grain, the more tender top sirloin is preferred. For the same purpose, one could also use the cross rib or round steak (less expensive) or the flatiron steak (chuck blade). Lean top round is very often used for minced meat.

Beef shank is the favorite cut for Five-spiced Beef Shank served as a cold appetizer; the gristle forms a delightful geometric pattern after slicing. If a whole shank is not available, use standard 2-inch slabs, although it will be a bit more difficult to slice them into eye-pleasing pieces.

Chinese people like neither the taste nor the look of beef fat, and in red-cooking, the meats are degreased (done easily by refrigeration). Oftentimes the Cantonese tenderize their beef by soaking it first in a solution of baking soda. If you like to use this method, we advocate the extra neutralizing step with lemon juice following to cancel out the metallic taste.

The Chinese tend to use the same word for lamb, sheep, kid, and goat with no further qualifications. Once common throughout China, their use has almost disappeared south of the Yangtze River except when slow-cooked with herbs as tonic in the winter.

In the Chinese Northwest, lamb and kid are the staple of the Turkic peoples, the Chinese Moslems, and the Mongols. They are also popular in the North, especially in Moslem restaurants. The whole-lamb feast, popular as a tourist attrac-

tion in the western parts of China, had been a standard feature in the Imperial Chinese Court for the entertainment of Moslem dignitaries. This royal feast included forty-four to seventy-two courses, each featuring a different part of the lamb, but none using the word *lamb* explicitly in the name. For example, "the fan which greets the wind" featured the tips of the lamb ears. The most popular mutton dish in Peking today is Mutton Fire-Pot, the best of which uses the castrated small-tail sheep from Inner Mongolia.

Veal is very uncommon in China, probably because a calf is too valuable to be slaughtered (in contrast to suckling pigs, which are served in every Cantonese restaurant in Hong Kong, and eaten with gusto).

BEEF

Stir-Fried Beef Slices with Vegetables

Serves 2 as a main dish with rice
Time 10 minutes preparation
30 minutes chilling
5 to 6 minutes cooking

牛肉片炒菜

Perhaps this is the most basic recipe for stir-frying meat and vegetables together. Any kind of vegetable goes well with beef.

Ingredients
½ flank steak, 2 inches wide (about 12 ounces)
3 cups vegetables for stir-frying (see page 349)
2 tablespoons chicken stock
1 teaspoon tapioca powder
5 tablespoons oil
Salt
1 clove garlic, sliced
1 tablespoon pale dry sherry
2 teaspoons sesame oil

Seasoning
½ egg white
1 tablespoon dark soy sauce
1 tablespoon light soy sauce
2 teaspoons pale dry sherry
½ teaspoon granulated sugar
3 teaspoons tapioca powder
Dash of white pepper
2 tablespoons oil
1 teaspoon sesame oil

PREPARATION

1 Trim all visible fat from the steak. Slope-cut across the grain into slices as thin as possible (⅛ inch or thinner), about 1 by 2 inches in size.

2 In a mixing bowl, mix egg white and beef slices. Add the soy sauce, sherry, sugar, tapioca powder, and white pepper to season. Stir in the oil to separate the slices. Chill meat at least 30 minutes.

3 Rinse and drain the vegetables. Prepare for cooking (see pages 347–349).

4 Mix together the chicken stock and tapioca powder in a small bowl and set aside.

COOKING

1 Use 3 tablespoons of oil to stir-fry the vegetables according to the directions on page 349. Remove when almost done and set aside.

2 Rinse the wok and wipe dry. Set over high heat and when very hot, add remaining 2 tablespoons of oil. Flavor the oil with the garlic, stirring for 10 seconds, then remove and discard.

3 Add the beef to the wok, spreading the slices in 1 layer in the center. Cook in a pan-frying manner for 1 minute, then turn to cook on the other side for 30 seconds. Stir and turn beef until the slices separate.

4 Sizzle in the wine along the edge of the wok, stirring several times around. Push the beef to the side, leaving a space in the center. Restir the tapioca mixture and gradually add to the center space, stirring constantly until the sauce thickens.

5 Return the vegetables to the wok, mixing them with the beef. Whirl in the sesame oil to glaze, and remove and serve immediately.

◉ Scallion-Blasted Beef Slices

Serves 2 as a main dish with rice
Time 10 minutes preparation
30 minutes marinating
5 minutes cooking

葱爆牛肉

This is a favorite dish in northern China. Scallions are bright green and crunchy, and their pungent aroma is modified by the searing oil. Try the same recipe with lamb instead of beef and/or leeks instead of scallions.

Ingredients	Marinade
½ flank steak (about 12 ounces)	1 egg white
8 whole scallions, trimmed	1 tablespoon oil
2 cups oil	Juice of 2 slices gingerroot
2 cloves garlic, thinly sliced	2 teaspoons pale dry sherry
1 tablespoon pale dry sherry	1 teaspoon granulated sugar
2 teaspoons sesame oil	3 teaspoons tapioca powder
	2 tablespoons dark soy sauce
	Salt

PREPARATION

1 Trim meat of all visible fat, then slice across the grain diagonally into very thin pieces, ⅛ inch thin or thinner.

2 Combine the oil and egg white for the marinade in a bowl. Beat with a wire whisk until smooth, then add the remaining ingredients and stir. Add the meat and mix well. Keep refrigerated for at least 30 minutes, then restir just before using.

3 Trim off about 3 inches from the scallions (green ends) and discard. Cut the remaining portions into 2-inch lengths.

COOKING

1 Set a wok over high heat. When very hot, add the oil. Wait for about 2 or 3 minutes, then add beef slices to the oil, and stir beef quickly until the slices are separate. Pour the oil and beef together into a strainer-lined bowl to drain, leaving about 2 tablespoons of oil in the wok.

2 Reset the wok over high heat and when smoke starts to rise, add the garlic to flavor the oil for 10 seconds. Add the scallions, stirring a few times.

3 Return the beef to the wok and immediately sizzle in the wine, stirring until it evaporates. Glaze the meat with sesame oil and serve hot.

⊛⊛ Sichuan Spicy Fried Beef Shreds

Serves 4 to 6 as part of a multi-dish
family meal
Time 15 minutes preparation
30 minutes marinating
20 minutes cooking

乾燒牛肉絲

Deliberately dry, chewy, and scorching, this dish exemplifies the Sichuan genius for doing the unexpected.

Ingredients

1 small flank steak
(about 20 ounces)
2 stalks celery
½ medium carrot
4 fresh hot chilis
½ cup + 1 tablespoon
oil
2 cloves garlic,
flattened

4 dried hot chilis, seeds
removed
½ teaspoon salt
1 tablespoon sesame oil

Marinade

4 tablespoons dark soy
sauce
Juice of 3 slices
gingerroot
1 tablespoon pale dry
sherry
2 teaspoons sesame oil
1 tablespoon
granulated sugar

PREPARATION

1 Trim meat of excess fat. Split the steak lengthwise in half, then cut each half into pieces about 2 inches in length. Lay 1 piece of steak flat on the cutting board. Press with the palm of one hand while the other holds a cleaver horizontally. Slice the meat in a sawing motion into thin pieces about ⅛ inch thick. Stack several pieces of meat together into a stepped pile and cut vertically from the smaller side along the grain into strips ⅛ inch wide. Repeat for the remaining half.

2 Mix the ingredients for the marinade in a bowl, then add the beef strips. Mix well and set at room temperature for at least 30 minutes. Turn the meat occasionally as it marinates.

3 Shred the vegetables into the same size strips as the meat.

COOKING

1 Set a wok over high heat. When very hot, add ½ cup oil. Flavor the oil with the garlic, then remove garlic when it is brown. Add the meat, stirring and turning constantly for about 5 to 7 minutes, or until strips separate. Turn heat to medium-low and continue to stir until the strips turn brown. This takes about 15 minutes; the texture of the meat is now dry and chewy. Remove.

2 Rinse wok and wipe dry. Set over high heat and, when hot, add remaining 1 tablespoon of oil. Flavor oil with dried chili until brown, then remove. Add carrot, celery, and chili, stirring for 1 minute. Season with salt.

3 Return meat to the wok and mix with the vegetables. Glaze the meat with sesame oil and serve with rice.

Stir-Fried Beef Shreds with Peppers

Serves 2 as a main dish with rice
Time 10 to 15 minutes preparation
30 minutes chilling
5 minutes cooking

青椒牛肉絲

This dish is made lighter with the filet mignon; flank steak could be used with nearly the same effect. Note that the shreds are cut with the grain to avoid breaking up. Even heating is maintained because of the small diameter of the shreds.

Ingredients

1 piece filet mignon, about 1½ inches thick (trimmed weight 6 to 8 ounces)
5 tablespoons oil
1 medium green pepper
½ medium sweet red pepper or ½ cup shredded carrot
4 scallions (white part only)

¼ teaspoon salt
½ teaspoon granulated sugar
1 clove garlic, shredded
1 tablespoon pale dry sherry
1 teaspoon sesame oil

Marinade

½ egg white
2 teaspoons tapioca powder
1 tablespoon oyster sauce
1 teaspoon light soy sauce
½ teaspoon granulated sugar
1 teaspoon sesame oil
Dash of white pepper

PREPARATION

1 Trim all visible fat and gristle from meat. Cut vertically into ⅛-inch slices, then arrange the slices in a pile. Cut slices along the grain into shreds about ⅛ inch wide.

2 Mix ingredients for marinade in a bowl, then add the meat. Stir gently to mix well.

3 Add 2 tablespoons of oil to the meat, stirring to separate the shreds. Chill for at least 30 minutes.

4 Cut the peppers in half and remove seeds and core. Shred into ⅛-inch strips. If substituting carrot for the red pepper, be sure the carrot shreds are also ⅛ inch wide.

5 Shred the scallions finely.

COOKING

1 Set a wok over high heat. When hot, add 1 tablespoon of oil. When the oil is hot, add the peppers (or carrots), stirring constantly until every strip is coated with oil. Season with salt and sugar, then remove.

2 Add 2 remaining tablespoons oil to the wok. When hot, flavor oil with garlic for 10 seconds. Add the beef, spreading it in 1 layer to cover the center of the wok.

Cook in a pan-frying manner for 30 seconds, then turn to cook on the other side for 20 seconds. Sizzle in the wine along the edge of the wok, stirring constantly until the wine is evaporated. Test for salt.

3 Glaze the beef with the sesame oil. Add the scallions and peppers, stirring to mix well. Serve immediately.

◉ Saté

Makes 12 skewers of beef
Time 15 minutes preparation
1 hour marinating
5 minutes cooking

沙爹

Saté is a small-scale shish-kebab flavored with a spicy peanut sauce, originally from Indonesia. This version is Fujian-Taiwanese in style. It is excellent as a main course with rice, also ideal as an appetizer, or as a party snack.

Ingredients	Seasonings	
½ flank steak (about 12 ounces)	2 teaspoons ground coriander	¼ teaspoon salt
Oil for brushing	1 teaspoon cumin powder	2 cloves garlic, minced
12 bamboo skewers (6 inches long)	½ teaspoon turmeric	1 tablespoon sesame paste
	¼ teaspoon black pepper	Juice of ½ fresh lemon
	Pinch of red chili powder	1 tablespoon dark soy sauce
	1 tablespoon minced shallot	1 tablespoon light soy sauce
		1 teaspoon granulated sugar

PREPARATION

1 Slope-cut the steak across the grain into slices about ⅛ inch thick.

2 Combine the seasoning ingredients in a bowl and mix well. Add the meat, mixing with a wooden spoon until well blended. Marinate at room temperature for at least 1 hour or keep refrigerated for several hours.

3 Thread about 3 slices of meat on each bamboo skewer.

COOKING

1 Preheat broiler.

2 Brush meat with oil on both sides. Arrange skewers on a broiling pan and set pan on the highest level of the oven. Broil 2 minutes, then turn skewers and broil other side until brown, about 1 minute.

3 Serve hot.

Note: There will be juice in the broiling pan. Do not discard it because it is great over plain rice. Also, in this recipe, the beef can be replaced with pork, chicken, or lamb.

◉◉ Beef Steak, Cantonese Style

Serves 3 as a main dish with vegetables and rice or 12 in a banquet

Time 20 minutes preparation
1 hour, 15 minutes marinating
15 minutes cooking

中式牛柳

This could be the best of two worlds: Cantonese technique applied to a favorite Western meat. It is very popular in Hong Kong.

Ingredients

1¼ pounds filet mignon
1 medium onion
4 tomatoes
1 sprig Chinese parsley
4 cups oil
1 tablespoon water
½ teaspoon salt

Marinade

1 knob gingerroot
2 tablespoons cornstarch
1 tablespoon brandy
1½ tablespoons oyster sauce
1 tablespoon dark soy sauce
1 clove garlic, minced

1 teaspoon granulated sugar
1 egg white
Dash of white pepper
1 teaspoon sesame oil
1 tablespoon oil

PREPARATION

1 Trim as much visible fat and thick membranes from beef as possible. Slice beef across the grain into pieces about ½ inch thick.

2 Using the blunt edge of a cleaver, tenderize the beef by making criss-crosses on both sides. Be sure not to cut into the meat.

3 Grate about ¼ inch from the ginger knob into a small bowl. Strain it through a fine-mesh strainer into a mixing bowl. Press the ginger pulp against the wall of the strainer to extract juice.

4 Combine cornstarch with brandy, ginger juice, oyster sauce, and soy sauce in a mixing bowl. Whisk to blend well. Add garlic, sugar, egg white, pepper, sesame oil, and oil. Mix until smooth.

5 Arrange half the beef slices in 1 layer on a large platter. Pour on half the marinade to cover evenly. Put the remaining slices on top and cover with remaining marinade. Set for 15 minutes. Turn the beef slices over. Cover and chill for at least 1 hour or until ready to use.

6 Cut onion in half lengthwise. Cut each half across into ¼-inch slices. Loosen slices to have strips.

7 Shortly before cooking, slice tomatoes the same thickness as onion and arrange in overlapping style to surround the edge of a round serving platter.

8 Rinse parsley. Break off stems and reserve leafy parts.

COOKING

1 Set a wok over high heat. When hot, add oil. Wait for about 5 minutes, then test temperature by dropping a piece of scallion green into the oil. If bubbles appear around the green which soon turns around in the oil, the temperature is about 325 to 350 degrees. Drop half the beef slices, one after another, into the oil. Deep-fry one minute or until brown. Remove to drain on paper towels. Finish deep-frying the remaining pieces in the same manner.

2 Pour oil into a heatproof bowl, leaving about 1 tablespoon of oil in wok.

3 Heat wok to very hot and add onion. Stir constantly until onion is soft, then add water and salt. Cook until water evaporates.

4 Remove onion strips to line the center space of the serving platter. Arrange beef slices on top. Put a small bunch of parsley leaves on beef as decoration. Serve.

Beef in Oyster Sauce

Serves 2 as a main dish with
vegetables and rice
Time 5 minutes preparation
1 hour tenderizing (optional)
30 minutes marinating
3 to 4 minutes cooking

蠔油牛肉

This is the classical Cantonese dish. Beef and oyster sauce belong together as do ham and eggs in America.

Ingredients	Marinade	Oyster sauce mixture
½ flank steak (about 12 ounces)	1 tablespoon dark soy sauce	2 tablespoons oyster sauce
½ teaspoon baking soda (optional)	2 tablespoons tapioca powder	1 tablespoon chicken stock
2 tablespoons water (optional)	2 teaspoons pale dry sherry	1 teaspoon tapioca powder
2 teaspoons lemon juice (optional)	2 tablespoons oil (omit if cooked oil-dipping style)	1 teaspoon granulated sugar
4 scallions (white part only)		
2 slices gingerroot		
1 clove garlic		
3 tablespoons oil		
1 tablespoon pale dry sherry		
2 teaspoons sesame oil		

PREPARATION

1 Trim meat of all visible fat. Slope-cut across the grain into slices about ⅛ inch thick.

2 If tenderizing the meat, mix the baking soda with the water in a mixing bowl. Add the meat and stir; set at room temperature for 30 minutes. Stir in the lemon juice and allow to set for another 30 minutes.

. 3 Drain meat, then combine with ingredients for marinade and marinate for 30 minutes. Drain and discard marinade.

4 Mix the ingredients for the oyster sauce mixture and set aside. Roll-cut the scallions into 1-inch wedges. Shred the ginger and slice the garlic.

COOKING

1 Set a wok over high heat. When very hot, add the oil. Flavor the oil with the garlic and ginger for 10 seconds, then add beef slices, spreading them out in 1 layer. Pan-fry the beef for 1 minute, then turn to other side and pan-fry for 30 seconds. Stir quickly to separate the slices, then add scallions.

2 Sizzle in the wine along the edge of the wok, stirring while it evaporates. Push the beef to the side of the wok.

3 Restir the oyster sauce mixture and stream it into the center of the wok, stirring until it thickens. Mix well with the beef, then glaze with sesame oil, remove, and serve.

Note: To prepare this dish oil-dipped style, set the wok over high heat. When very hot, add 2 cups of oil and wait for about 3 minutes. Add the beef, stirring quickly to separate the slices. Pour the beef and oil together into a strainer-lined bowl to drain, leaving about 2 tablespoons of oil in the wok. Reheat wok to very hot. Flavor oil with garlic and ginger for 10 seconds. Return beef to wok. Sizzle in the wine, then mix and push beef slices to the side. Restir sauce mixture and stream into the center of wok, stirring constantly until sauce thickens. Add scallions and sesame oil. Stir to mix and serve.

◉◉◉ Leek-Stuffed Short Ribs of Beef

Serves 4 as a main dish with vegetable and rice
Time 35 minutes preparation 2 hours braising

蒜 塞 牛 排 骨

The giant scallion in North China is two feet long, much of it dazzling white and gentle in flavor. It keeps for months in the frigid winter, supplying vitamin C to the North Chinese, who view it as a cure-all and universal tonic. It is the best accompaniment to Peking duck slices and is the main ingredient in the Sichuan dish Scallion-stuffed Pork Spareribs.

In America, scallions are too green and too small for that dish. Leeks have the right texture and color, but the taste overpowers the pork. This latter problem calls for another substitution, meeting the strong flavor of leek with the robust beef short-ribs. The result is a Chinese one-pot dish in the red-cooking tradition. Make a lot to last for several days; it actually tastes better on reheating.

Ingredients

4 pounds extra lean short ribs of beef	1 tablespoon granulated sugar
2 knobs gingerroot, each about the size of a walnut	½ cup dark soy sauce Salt
4 whole scallions, trimmed	2 tablespoons light soy sauce
½ cup + 1 tablespoon yellow wine or sherry	4 dried red chili peppers (optional)
6 to 8 whole leeks, trimmed	1 tablespoon tapioca powder mixed with 2 tablespoons water
2 tablespoons oil	2 teaspoons sesame oil

PREPARATION

1 Trim as much visible fat from short ribs as possible. Rinse off bone dust.

2 Peel skin from gingerroots. Smash with the flat side of the cleaver. Rinse scallions and tie them in a bunch.

3 Half-fill a 4-quart saucepan with water. Set it over high heat to bring water to a boil. Add short ribs and bring water back to boil. Use a fine strainer to remove the scum on the surface of the water. Turn heat to medium. Cook 10 minutes.

4 Set a colander over a very large bowl (or a pot). Into the colander pour together the beef ribs and the cooking water. Place the colander in the sink, running cold water over to rinse off scum.

5 Clean the saucepan. Add beef ribs, ginger, scallions, and ½ cup wine. Pour the cooking water for beef through a fine strainer into the saucepan.

6 Set the saucepan over high heat. When water boils, cover the pan. Turn heat to low, simmer beef ribs for 1 hour or until the bones stick out. Remove beef ribs to cool.

7 Meanwhile, wash the leeks thoroughly to remove fine dirt. For smaller leeks (about ½ inch in diameter), use them whole. For larger ones (from 1 inch to 1¼ inches in diameter), cut them in half or in quarters lengthwise. Trim the round ends to form a uniform stick. Discard any withered greens.

8 Take out the bone from each rib carefully and replace it with a piece of leek white of the same size and length. Do the same with the remaining ribs. Reserve all greens of leek, and cut them into 2-inch lengths.

9 Spoon off grease from the beef broth. Scoop out 1 cup and set it within easy reach.

COOKING

1 Set a wok over high heat. When very hot, add oil. Arrange beef ribs in wok and tilt the wok around for even heating. Brown the ribs on one side, then turn to brown on the other side, changing position of the beef while turning.

2 Sizzle in the remaining 1 tablespoon of the wine. Immediately sprinkle in sugar, stirring to mix with beef. Add dark soy sauce and stir some more. Add the cup of reserved beef broth, bring it to a boil.

3 Lay the greens of leeks in 1 layer in the saucepan with the beef broth and pour all the contents in the wok back into the saucepan. Season beef lightly with salt and light soy sauce. (If hot taste is preferred, add dried chili at this stage.) Cover pan. Simmer for 45 minutes to 1 hour or until a chopstick can go through the beef easily.

4 Remove ribs and leeks with a slotted spoon. There should be about 2 cups of sauce left in the pan; thin the sauce with boiling water, or reduce it with high heat as necessary. Stream in tapioca mixture, stirring until sauce thickens. Test for seasoning, then glaze sauce with sesame oil.

5 Return beef and leeks to pan to mix with the sauce. Serve hot.

Beef Roll Stuffed with Shrimp and Pine Nuts

Serves 3 as a main dish or 12 in a banquet

Time   30 minutes preparation
1 hour chilling
15 minutes cooking

松 子 牛 肉 卷

This is an East China banquet dish with a delicious blend of shrimp meat, chopped pine nuts, and tender beef.

Ingredients

8 ounces tenderloin of beef (trimmed weight), about 2 inches thick
12 medium shrimp in the shell
¼ cup pine nuts
1 red chili pepper
½ teaspoon salt
⅛ teaspoon white pepper
2 egg whites

⅓ cup cornstarch
3 cups oil
1 clove garlic, minced
2 whole scallions, trimmed
1 teaspoon sesame oil

Sauce mixture

1 cup chicken stock
1 tablespoon red rice vinegar
1 tablespoon dark soy sauce
1 tablespoon brown sugar
2 teaspoons tapioca powder
1 tablespoon pale dry sherry

PREPARATION

1 Trim excess fat and membrane from beef. Cut across the grain into 12 slices about ³⁄₁₆ inch thick. (You could freeze the meat for 1 hour for easy slicing.)

2 Put 1 slice of beef on a cutting board. Hold a Chinese cleaver in one hand. Use the other palm to press the flat side of the cleaver on the beef, moving crosswise from one end to the other to make the slice thinner and larger, about 2½ by 3½ inches in size.

3 Continue to thin the remaining beef slices the same manner, and set them aside.

4 Shell and devein the shrimp (see page 151). Rub with some salt to clean and rinse thoroughly with cold running water. Drain, then wrap with a kitchen towel. Chill for at least 30 minutes.

5 Roast pine nuts over medium heat in a wok, stirring constantly for 2 minutes or until nuts are light brown. Remove to cool. Chop nuts finely and put in a small bowl. Use the end of the handle of the cleaver to mash the nuts into a paste. Set aside.

6 Remove seeds of chili. Shred finely. Mix ingredients for sauce.

7 To assemble rolls, lay 1 piece of beef on a platter with the smaller end near you. Sprinkle on salt sparingly, then the pepper. Split a shrimp along the back lengthwise in half and place half a shrimp on the near end. Put a strip about ¼ inch wide of the pine nut paste on the shrimp, then put the other half of the shrimp on top with the tail on the larger end so to produce a uniform strip of stuffing. Roll the beef up tightly and seal with a little egg white. Finish the remaining rolls the same manner. If not to be used immediately, chill in the refrigerator.

COOKING

1 Shortly before cooking, dip each beef roll in remaining egg white first, then dredge it in cornstarch to coat evenly; shake off the excess cornstarch.

2 Set a wok over high heat. Add oil, then wait for about 5 minutes, and test the temperature of oil by dropping in a small piece of scallion green. If the green sizzles noisily and soon turns brown, the oil is ready (about 375 degrees). Drop half the beef rolls in succession into the oil until the coating sets and the color turns light brown. Remove to drain in a strainer-lined bowl and continue to deep-fry the remaining beef rolls in the same manner and drain.

3 Reheat the oil to very hot, then return all the beef rolls to the wok. Deep-fry for about 2 minutes or until the rolls turn golden brown. Remove to drain. Pour oil out, leaving about 1 tablespoon of oil in the wok.

4 Set wok back on high heat. Flavor oil with garlic, scallion, and chili pepper. Restir the sauce mixture and add to wok, stirring to prevent lumps. Add beef rolls and turn heat to medium. Cook until sauce is reduced just enough to cover all the rolls. Glaze with sesame oil and serve.

⊛⊛ Red-Cooked Spicy Beef with Onions

Serves 4 to 6 as a main dish with a minute soup and rice
Time 15 minutes preparation
2 hours cooking

红烧洋葱牛

This is an excellent way to use inexpensive chuck roast. There is no need to finish it in one meal, either; it can be refrigerated and reheated without losing its delightful flavor. If more vegetables (for example, potatoes, celery) are added, this dish becomes a Chinese-style beef stew.

Ingredients

3 pounds boneless chuck roast
1 pound small white onions
2 carrots, scraped
1 whole star anise
½ teaspoon crushed black peppercorns
4 tablespoons oil
2 cloves garlic, crushed
4 slices gingerroot
2 whole scallions, trimmed
¼ cup dark soy sauce

4 cups thin Basic Soup Stock (page 108)
2 tablespoons granulated sugar
¼ cup pale dry sherry
1 tablespoon tapioca powder mixed with 2 tablespoons water
2 teaspoons sesame oil

PREPARATION

1 Trim as much fat and gristle from the meat as possible.

2 Peel the onions. Roll-cut the carrots, then cook them in boiling water for 10 minutes; drain and reserve.

3 Wrap the anise and peppercorns in a piece of cheesecloth and tie loosely.

COOKING

1 Set a heavy Dutch oven over high heat. When very hot, add 2 tablespoons of oil and stir-fry the onions until lightly brown. Remove and set aside.

2 Add the meat in 1 piece and brown on both sides. Remove and set into a colander. Run hot water over the meat to rinse off any grease.

3 Rinse the pot, then set over high heat again. When very hot, add the remaining 2 tablespoons of oil. Flavor oil with garlic, ginger, and scallions, stirring for 1 minute.

4 Add the soy sauce, stock, sugar, and wine to the pan, and bring to a boil. Add the meat and the spice bag and bring back to a boil. Turn heat to low, cover pot, and simmer for about 1½ hours, or until the beef is tender.

5 When meat is done, remove from the pot and skim the fat off the cooking liquid. Add carrots and onions to the pot and cook over medium heat for 15 minutes. There should be about 1 cup of liquid left; replenish with hot water or reduce over high heat if necessary.

6 Cut the meat into 1-inch cubes and add to the vegetables in the pot. Stir in the tapioca powder mixture and bring liquid back to a boil. Glaze sauce with sesame oil and serve hot.

◎◎ Quick-Braised Beef Shank with Cloud Ears and Tiger Lilies

Serves 4 as a main dish, or 6 to 8 in a multi-dish meal
Time 30 minutes preparation
30 minutes seasoning
40 minutes cooking

金針雲耳焗牛腒

A winter specialty of small Cantonese restaurants, this is often served in earthen pots called *sa bo* (sand pots).

Ingredients
1 pound boneless beef shank
½ ounce cloud ears
1 ounce tiger lily buds
4 tablespoons oil
2 slices gingerroot
2 cloves garlic, crushed
1 tablespoon pale dry sherry
1 tablespoon chicken stock mixed with 1 teaspoon tapioca powder
2 teaspoons sesame oil

Seasoning mixture
Juice of 2 slices gingerroot
1 tablespoon pale dry sherry
1 tablespoon light soy sauce
2 teaspoons tapioca powder

Braising sauce
1 cup chicken stock
1 tablespoon oyster sauce
1 teaspoon granulated sugar
2 teaspoons dark soy sauce

PREPARATION

1 Remove any tough membranes around the beef shank. Straight-cut across the grain into slices about ⅛ inch thick.

2 Mix seasoning mixture in a bowl, then add the meat. Keep at room temperature for at least 30 minutes, or refrigerate for several hours. Turn the meat occasionally.

3 Soak the cloud ears and tiger lilies separately in warm water until soft. Trim tough ends. Rinse and drain.

4 Prepare the braising sauce and set aside.

COOKING

1 Set a wok (or Dutch oven) over high heat. When hot, add 1 tablespoon of oil. Stir-fry the cloud ears and tiger lilies until the moisture is evaporated. Remove.

2. Add 3 remaining tablespoons of oil to the wok. When the oil is hot, flavor with ginger and garlic for 20 seconds. Add the beef shank, spreading the slices in 1 layer. Pan-fry the beef for 1 minute, then turn to the other side and pan-fry for another minute.

3 Sizzle in the wine along the edge of the wok, stirring quickly to separate the meat slices. Add the braising sauce, cloud ears, and tiger lilies. Bring to a boil, then turn heat to low. Cover wok and cook slowly for 30 minutes, or until a chopstick goes through the beef slices easily.

4 Restir tapioca powder mixture. Push ingredients in the wok to the side and add the mixture, stirring constantly until the sauce is transparent. Correct the seasoning, then glaze with sesame oil. Serve.

◉◉ Five-Spiced Beef Shank

Serves 10 to 12 as a part of the cold
platters
Time overnight marinating
15 minutes preparation
2 hours cooking

五香牛肉

This is one of the mainstays of an East China cold platter. The transparent pattern of meat grains form a natural decoration on the red slices.

Ingredients
2 small whole beef
shanks, about 1 to
1¼ pounds each
2 tablespoons salt
¼ cup strong liquor,
such as Chinese Fen,
vodka, or whiskey
1 tablespoon sesame oil

Braising mixture
½ cup dark soy sauce
½ cup light soy sauce
¼ cup Chinese rock
candy
1 cup pale dry sherry
2 pieces (quarters)
dried tangerine peel
4 slices gingerroot
1 whole scallion,
trimmed

2 cloves garlic
2 whole star anise
1 teaspoon black
peppercorns
1 stick cinnamon, 2
inches long

PREPARATION

1 Trim excess fat from meat. Use a sharp metal skewer to pierce meat all over so that marinade can penetrate.

2 Mix salt and liquor in a bowl large enough to hold the meat snugly. Add meat, turning several times, then wrap and chill for at least 24 hours (or up to 2 days) in the refrigerator. Turn the meat occasionally in the marinade.

3 Rinse meat and tie it with kitchen strings at 1-inch intervals.

COOKING

1 Blanch the meat in boiling water for 5 minutes. Remove to a colander and rinse with cold water.

2 Into a 3-quart saucepan add the braising mixture. Bring to a boil over high heat, then add the meat and just enough water to cover. Cover and simmer for 1½ hours. Replenish with water to maintain the same level.

3 Test the meat to determine if it is done by inserting a chopstick into the thickest part of the shank. If it goes in easily all the way, it is done. Otherwise, cover pot and cook longer; test again. (The timing depends greatly upon the diameter of the shank, as well as the quality of the meat.)

4 When the meat is done, place pot with meat and cooking liquid in the refrigerator to chill. It can be refrigerated up to 4 or 5 days.

5 When ready to serve, remove strings from meat. Cut meat vertically across the grain into very thin slices (about ⅛ inch). Arrange slices around the edge of a round serving platter, overlapping them slightly. Decorate the center of the platter with pickled cabbage (see page 377) and brush braising liquid first, then sesame oil over the slices. Serve cold.

Note: For best color, slice the meat as close to serving time as possible.

⊛⊛ Red-Cooked Beef in Aspic

Serves 12 to 15 as a part of a buffet
Time 20 minutes preparation
2 hours, 10 minutes cooking
overnight chilling

牛 肉 凍

This cold platter is common to all culinary regions in China except Canton. Moslems in North China often use mutton or lamb instead of beef.

Ingredients

1½ pounds boneless
 chuck roast
2 tablespoons oil
2 cloves garlic, crushed
4 slices gingerroot
2 whole scallions,
 trimmed
1 whole star anise
1 teaspoon Sichuan
 peppercorns

1 envelope (1 tablespoon)
 unflavored gelatin
¼ cup cold water
1 tablespoon Fen
 liquor or brandy
1 teaspoon sesame oil

Braising sauce

¼ cup dark soy sauce
2 cups thin stock
2 tablespoons
 granulated sugar
¼ cup pale dry sherry

PREPARATION

1 Trim as much fat and gristle from meat as possible. Set a heavy Dutch oven over high heat and, when very hot, add 1 tablespoon of oil. Place beef in pot and brown on both sides.

2 Discard any fat and rinse the pot. Blanch the meat in boiling water for 2 minutes.

COOKING

1 Set Dutch oven over high heat again. When hot, add remaining tablespoon of oil. Flavor oil with garlic, ginger, and scallions, stirring for 1 minute.

2 Add braising sauce to pot and bring to a boil. Place in the meat, adding more water if necessary, to cover meat well.

3 Wrap star anise and peppercorns in a piece of cheesecloth and tie loosely. Add to the braising liquid. Cover and simmer beef over medium-low heat for at least 2 hours, or until the meat can be flaked easily with a fork.

4 Remove meat to cool. Flake finely along the grain, then cut into ½-inch lengths. Arrange meat in a greased loaf pan, about 8 by 4 by 2 inches.

5 Discard the spice bag and any solids in the pot. Skim off as much fat as possible, then reduce or add water to measure 1½ cups of liquid.

6 Bring braising liquid to a boil. While waiting for the boil, sprinkle the gelatin over the cold water and mix well. As braising liquid boils, add gelatin mixture and stir until well blended. Add liquor and sesame oil, again mixing well.

7 Pour liquid into loaf pan and use a fork to poke meat so that the sauce can slip through and fill pan. Wrap and chill overnight.

8 To serve, turn beef aspic out from the mold and cut with a sharp knife into slices about ½ inch thick. Serve cold.

VARIATION: Jellied Lamb

Substitute 2 pounds leg of lamb (weight including skin, bones and fat). Blanch the lamb in boiling water for 5 minutes instead of browning. Follow the same procedure as above to red-cook the lamb. When done, take off skin carefully in 1 piece to line the mold, then remove bones and fat. Proceed with the molding in the same manner.

◉ Stir-Fried Minced Beef with Green Peas

Serves 2 as a main dish with rice
Time 15 minutes preparation
1 hour chilling
5 minutes cooking

青豆牛肉末

It is easy to practice Cantonese cuisine using typically American ingredients, as seen in this recipe which takes so little time to prepare.

BEEF AND LAMB

Ingredients

½ pound lean ground
  beef
4 black mushrooms
½ cup hot water
1 cup shelled green
  peas
¼ cup finely diced
  carrots
1 medium onion
1 teaspoon tapioca
  powder
1 teaspoon chicken
  bouillon powder
4 tablespoons oil
½ teaspoon salt
1 clove garlic, minced
1 tablespoon pale dry
  sherry

Seasonings

1 egg white
2 teaspoons tapioca
  powder
1 tablespoon oyster
  sauce
1 tablespoon light soy
  sauce
1 teaspoon granulated
  sugar
1 teaspoon sesame oil
Dash of white pepper
2 tablespoons oil

PREPARATION

1 Mix seasonings together and add to the meat. Blend with chopsticks in one direction until the meat holds together. Chill for at least 1 hour or until used.

2 Soak mushrooms in hot water until soft. Trim the stems and squeeze caps to extract moisture. Dice and set aside. Reserve soaking liquid.

3 Blanch peas and carrots in boiling water for 30 seconds. Remove and run cold water over to stop the cooking process. Drain.

4 Dice the onion.

5 Mix the tapioca powder with the reserved mushroom liquid and add the bouillon powder. Set aside.

COOKING

1 Set a wok over high heat. When very hot, add 2 tablespoons of oil. Flavor oil with onion, stirring until onion is limp. Add mushrooms, carrots, and peas, stirring until heated through. Season with salt and chicken bouillion powder. Mix well and remove.

2 Add remaining 2 tablespoons of oil to the wok and heat until hot. Flavor oil with garlic, then add the beef. Stir quickly to separate bits of meat, then sizzle in the wine along the edge of the wok. Stir meat, then add vegetables and mix well.

3 Push the ingredients to the side of the wok, and restir the sauce mixture. Stream the sauce into the center of the wok, stirring until thickened. Mix well and correct the seasoning. Remove and serve.

◉◉ Silver Dollar Beef

Serves 2 as a main dish with rice and
vegetables
Time 20 minutes preparation
1 hour chilling
10 minutes cooking

銀元牛肉

This is a Cantonese dish based on American ground beef.

Ingredients	Seasonings	Sauce mixture
2 slices bacon	1 egg white	½ cup chicken stock
1 medium onion	1 teaspoon granulated	2 teaspoons tapioca
¾ pound lean ground	sugar	powder
beef	2 tablespoons light soy	2 tablespoons oyster
1 egg yolk	sauce	sauce
Cornstarch for coating	⅛ teaspoon salt	½ teaspoon granulated
3 tablespoons oil	1 tablespoon tapioca	sugar
2 tablespoons yellow	powder	1 teaspoon sesame oil
wine or pale dry	Dash of white pepper	Pinch of salt
sherry		

PREPARATION

1 Cut bacon into ⅛-inch shreds. Cut onion lengthwise in half and then cut each
half in ¼-inch slices. Separate the onion into strips and reserve the longer strips.
Chop the shorter strips into bits.

2 Set a heavy, small skillet over high heat and stir-fry the bacon until it renders its
fat. Add the onion bits and cook until onion is transparent. Remove and cool.

3 Mix beef with the seasonings in a bowl and then scoop up the meat by handfuls.
Beat it back into the bowl several times, then add the bacon and onion. Mix well
and repeat the beating several times until the mixture is firm. Chill at least 1
hour.

4 Divide the beef into 8 equal parts and shape each into a ball. Flatten each ball to
form a silver dollar shaped patty. Dip each silver dollar in the egg yolk, then coat
lightly with cornstarch. Set aside.

5 Mix ingredients for sauce in a small bowl and set aside.

COOKING

1 Set a heavy skillet over high heat. When hot, add the oil, spreading it evenly on
the surface with a spatula. Add the beef patties and pan-fry them until both sides
are brown.

2 Sizzle in the wine, cooking until evaporated. Remove patties to a serving platter. Add the onions to the skillet and cook until limp. Remove to surround the patties.

3 Restir the sauce mixture and add it to the skillet. Stir until it thickens, then pour it over the patties. Serve.

Spicy Beef Tongue

Serves 12 as part of a cold platter
Time 10 minutes preparation
20 minutes pressure-cooking
30 minutes resting

盐 水 牛 脷

Different versions of this dish are found in all Chinese regional cuisines. The American pressure cooker reduces the cooking time from hours to only 20 minutes.

Ingredients
1 beef tongue, about 4 pounds
2 tablespoons salt
¼ cup pale dry sherry
1 tablespoon granulated sugar

Spice mixture
1 whole star anise
2 teaspoons Sichuan or black peppercorns
1 2-inch piece of cinnamon
2 teaspoons aniseed
4 slices gingerroot
2 cloves garlic

1 tablespoon mustard seeds
¼ teaspoon cloves

PREPARATION AND COOKING

1 Trim excess fat from tongue, then blanch in boiling water for 5 minutes. Rinse in cold water.

2 Combine spices with salt, sherry, and sugar in a pressure cooker. Add the tongue and enough water to cover. Bring the pressure up to 15 pounds and cook for 20 minutes, then turn heat off. Let stand for another 30 minutes.

3 Remove tongue from pressure cooker and peel off skin. Place in a bowl and pour juice with spices to cover. Chill until needed.

4 To serve, slice crosswise vertically into thin pieces about ⅛ inch thick. Serve cold.

Note: The tongue should be prepared well ahead of time for the spicy flavor to permeate. Slice no earlier than 1 hour before serving to retain the best color.

◉ Sautéed Calves Liver in Wine

Serves 2 as a main dish with rice and vegetables
Time 10 minutes preparation
30 minutes soaking
30 minutes marinating
10 minutes cooking

酒爆牛肝

Calves liver is seldom used in Chinese cooking but works well in this recipe originally meant for pork liver. This is a dish from Fuzhou, Fujian.

Ingredients	Marinade	Sauce mixture
1-pound piece calves liver	1 egg white	2 tablespoons chicken stock
2 whole scallions, trimmed	1 tablespoon pale dry sherry	1 teaspoon tapioca powder
2 tablespoons cornstarch	Juice of 2 slices gingerroot	1 tablespoon dark soy sauce
4 cups oil	1 teaspoon granulated sugar	Dash of white pepper
1 clove garlic, shredded	2 tablespoons light soy sauce	½ teaspoon granulated sugar
2 tablespoons yellow wine or pale dry sherry		
2 teaspoons sesame oil		

PREPARATION

1 Soak the liver in plenty of cold water (keep refrigerated) for 30 minutes. Trim excess gristle of liver.

2 Pat liver dry with paper towels, then cut into slabs about 1 by 1¾ inches in size and ¼ inch thick.

3 Mix ingredients for marinade and add the liver. Use your fingers to mix the meat well with the marinade, then chill for at least 30 minutes. Turn liver pieces twice while marinating.

4 Cut the scallions into 1-inch lengths.

5 Mix the ingredients for the sauce mixture in a small bowl and set aside.

6 Just before cooking, drain the liver in a colander and then coat meat with cornstarch. Discard marinade.

COOKING

1 Set a wok over high heat. When very hot, add the oil. Wait for about 5 to 7 minutes, then test temperature by dropping a piece of scallion green into the oil. If it sizzles and moves about quickly, the oil is ready (about 350 degrees). Otherwise, wait a little longer and test again.

2 Put the liver into the hot oil, stirring constantly until the pieces lose their softness and the red color disappears. Then pour the liver and oil together into a strainer-lined bowl to drain, leaving about 1 tablespoon of oil in the wok.

3 Set wok again over high heat and when it is very hot and smoky, flavor the oil with garlic for 10 seconds. Return liver pieces to the wok and sizzle in the wine, stirring and turning until the wine evaporates.

4 Push the liver to the side of the wok and restir the sauce. Mix well and stream it into the center of the wok, stirring until thickened. Add the scallions, mixing together with the liver.

5 Add the sesame oil to the liver to glaze, then remove and serve immediately.

⊚⊚ Peppery Beef Tripe

Serves 6 to 8 as an appetizer
Time 15 minutes preparation
1 hour cooking
2 hours chilling

麻 辣 牛 肚

V ery inexpensive and yet special, this dish is marked by the Sichuan peppercorn which awakens the taste buds.

Ingredients	Seasonings	Braising sauce
1¼ pounds honeycomb beef tripe	1 tablespoon light soy sauce	4 cups chicken stock
2 teaspoons Sichuan peppercorns	1 tablespoon red rice vinegar	1 tablespoon yellow wine
4 stalks scallion (white part only)	1 teaspoon granulated sugar	1 tablespoon distilled vinegar
2 tablespoons oil	2 (or more) teaspoons hot chili oil	2 whole scallions, trimmed
2 cloves garlic, minced	1 teaspoon chicken bouillon powder	4 slices gingerroot
1 tablespoon yellow wine	¼ teaspoon salt	
1 tablespoon sesame oil		

PREPARATION

1 Blanch beef tripe in boiling water for 5 minutes, then drain and rinse.

2 In a 4-quart saucepan, bring braising sauce to a boil over high heat. Add beef tripe and bring sauce back to a boil. Cover and cook over medium-low heat for 1 hour (or longer, depending on the quality of the beef tripe) or until a chopstick can go through the beef tripe easily. Chill in refrigerator for 2 hours for easy slicing.

3 In a small skillet roast the peppercorns over medium heat until the fragrance escapes, about 1 minute, then remove to a small bowl. Use the handle of a cleaver to smash the peppercorns into granules, and put them through a fine-mesh sieve.

You should have about 1 teaspoon powdered peppercorns. Discard the husks left in the sieve.

4 Cut scallion whites into 1½-inch lengths, then shred them finely.

5 After chilling, cut the beef tripe into strips about 1¾ inches wide, then slice each strip diagonally into 3⁄16-inch lengths.

COOKING

1 Set a wok over high heat. When very hot, add oil. Flavor oil with minced garlic until light brown, about 30 seconds.

2 Add beef tripe, stirring constantly until every piece is well coated with oil. Sizzle in the wine along the edge of wok, adding seasonings.

3 Sprinkle in powdered peppercorn and stir to mix well. Add scallion shreds, stirring until limp. Test for salt. Glaze with sesame oil and serve hot.

◉◉◉ Deep-Fried Beef Brains

Yields 24 pieces—serves 6, 8, or 12
as an appetizer
Time 4 hours soaking
30 minutes preparation
30 minutes cooking

炸牛腦

The beef brains are first made into a pâté, then deep-fried. The crust is crisp to the bite but the inside is delicate and smooth.

Ingredients

1 pound beef brains
4 cups water
2 tablespoons distilled vinegar
2 eggs + 2 egg yolks
1 can (13½ ounces) clear chicken broth
¼ cup cornstarch
¼ teaspoon salt
¼ teaspoon + 2 tablespoons granulated sugar

1 teaspoon sesame oil
2 tablespoons vegetable oil
Cornstarch for coating
6 cups oil
2 tablespoons oyster sauce (optional)

Seasonings

1 teaspoon ginger juice
2 teaspoons brandy
1 teaspoon chicken bouillon powder
¼ teaspoon white pepper
¼ teaspoon salt

PREPARATION

1 Follow the recipe (page 279) for preparing pork brains to soak and remove the membranes of the beef brains. Add seasonings to the brains and steam in the same manner.

2 Set a fine-mesh strainer over a bowl, put in ⅓ of the cooked brains, and press them against the wall so as to mash the brains finely into the bowl. Finish the remaining 2 batches the same way. Discard the residues in the strainer if any.

3 Put eggs, chicken broth, and cornstarch in an electric blender. Beat on the lowest speed until well blended, adding ¼ teaspoon each of the salt and the sugar, the sesame oil, and 2 tablespoons of the vegetable oil. Pour egg mixture into the bowl to combine with the brain mash, using a wire whisk to mix well.

4 Set a 2-quart nonstick saucepan over medium heat. When hot, add the brain mixture, stirring constantly with a flat-edged wooden spoon for about 10 to 15 minutes or until it boils, then continue to stir and cook for 5 more minutes to assure doneness. Test for salt.

5 Pour mixture immediately into a well-greased loaf pan about 3½ by 8 inches in size. Shake the pan to level the mixture, then set at room temperature for 30 minutes. Wrap and chill at least 4 hours or overnight to firm into a pâté.

COOKING

1 Cut the brain pâté lengthwise in half, then cut crosswise into pieces about ⅔ by 1¾ inches in size. You will have altogether 24 pieces.

2 Put about ½ cup of cornstarch in a bowl and dredge each piece of brain evenly, adding more cornstarch if needed. Shake off the excess.

3 Set a wok over high heat. When very hot, add the oil. Wait for about 10 minutes, then test temperature by dropping a piece of scallion green into the oil. If the green turns brown quickly and a haze appears on the surface, the oil is ready, about 400 degrees. Dip a deep-frying strainer into the oil to coat it, then put in half of the brain pieces. Lower the strainer into the very hot oil and deep-fry until golden. Remove to drain on paper towels.

4 Finish deep-frying the remaining batch in the same manner. After draining the excess oil, transfer all the pieces to arrange on a serving platter. Serve while very hot with sugar and/or oyster sauce on the side.

❀❀❀ Wine-Blasted Tenderloin of Veal with Fresh Mushrooms

Serves 2 as a main dish with
stir-fried crunchy vegetables

Time 10 minutes preparation
30 minutes chilling
5 to 7 minutes cooking

鮮蘑菇炒嫩牛柳

Veal is relatively scarce in China but more plentiful, although expensive, in America. This light and flavorful dish is an example of how to adapt Chinese technique to essentially non-Chinese ingredients.

Ingredients

12 ounces tenderloin of veal (trimmed weight)
½ pound firm, large fresh mushrooms
2 tablespoons beef stock mixed with 1 teaspoon (rounded) tapioca powder
2 cups oil
2 large shallots, thinly sliced

2 tablespoons pale dry sherry
¼ teaspoon salt
1 teaspoon sesame oil

Seasoning mixture

1 egg white
1 tablespoon light soy sauce
2 teaspoons Maggi sauce
1 tablespoon pale dry sherry
⅛ teaspoon white pepper
½ teaspoon granulated sugar
1 teaspoon sesame oil
2 teaspoons tapioca powder
¼ teaspoon salt

PREPARATION

1 Trim all visible gristle from veal and remove membranes encased in the fillet. Straight-cut across the grain into ⅛-inch slices.

2 Mix ingredients for seasoning in a bowl until smooth, then add veal. Stir and mix with a wooden spoon, then chill for at least 30 minutes.

3 Remove stems from mushrooms. Wipe the caps with a dampened cloth to remove any dirt, then cut vertically into ¼-inch slices.

COOKING

1 Set a wok over high heat. When very hot, add the oil. Wait for about 3 minutes, then test the temperature of the oil by dropping a small piece of scallion green into the oil. If the green moves around immediately and sizzles, the oil is ready (about 350 degrees).

2 Add the mushroom slices, stirring quickly, for about 10 seconds. Using a deep-frying strainer, remove the mushrooms and rest the strainer on a plate to drain the oil.

3 Heat oil in wok for 1 minute more, then add the veal. Stir constantly to separate the slices and cook for about 30 seconds, then pour the meat and oil together into a strainer-lined bowl to drain, leaving about 1 tablespoon of oil in the wok.

4 Set wok back on high heat. When oil is very hot, add the shallots, stirring for 25 seconds. Return the veal to the wok and immediately sizzle in the wine along the edge. Add mushrooms, season with salt, and stir continuously until the wine is evaporated.

5 Push the ingredients in the wok to the side and restir the tapioca powder mixture. Stream the mixture into the center of the wok, stirring until it thickens. Glaze sauce with sesame oil and stir to mix all ingredients. Serve hot.

LAMB

⊚⊚⊚ Wooly Lamb

Serves 4 as a main dish with rice and a thick soup
Time approximately 30 minutes preparation, depending on shredding skill
30 minutes chilling
10 minutes cooking

炒綿羊絲

This dish is believed to add body warmth in the winter, although it is commonly made with pork rather than lamb. The recipe offers a contrast of texture between the stir-fried ingredients and the coat of a wooly lamb, made of crispy deep-fried rice sticks.

Ingredients

1 pound lamb, cut from loin
4 medium black mushrooms
2 leeks (white part only)
½ medium carrot
½ cup bamboo shoots
4 hot chilies, or to taste
2 cups + 1 tablespoon oil
1 ounce rice sticks
½ teaspoon salt

1 teaspoon granulated sugar
1 clove garlic, finely shredded
1 tablespoon pale dry sherry
1 teaspoon tapioca powder mixed with 1 tablespoon chicken stock
1 teaspoon sesame oil

Marinade

1 egg white
1 tablespoon tapioca powder
1 tablespoon light soy sauce
2 teaspoons dark soy sauce
1 teaspoon granulated sugar
¼ teaspoon salt
⅛ teaspoon white pepper
1 teaspoon ginger juice

PREPARATION

1 All ingredients used in the recipe are cut into fine shreds about ⅛ by ⅛ by 1½ inches.

2 Trim all visible fat from the meat and remove any gristle; there should be about 12 ounces of meat after trimming. Slice the meat as thinly as possible, then shred finely.

3 Mix the marinade in a bowl and add the lamb. Mix with your fingers until well blended, and then set in the refrigerator for at least 30 minutes.

4 Soak the mushrooms in warm water until soft. Trim the stems and squeeze to extract moisture. Shred finely.

5 Use the lower 4 inches of the leeks. Cut each lengthwise in half and separate the layers and rinse thoroughly to remove any sand. Shred finely.

6 Shred the carrot.

7 Blanch the bamboo shoots in boiling water for 1 minute, then rinse with cold water. Shred finely; drain and pat dry with a paper towel.

8 Remove seeds and pulp from chilies. Shred finely.

COOKING

1 Set the wok over high heat. When very hot, add 2 cups of oil. Wait for about 5 minutes, then test temperature by dropping a few inches of rice stick into the oil. If it puffs up immediately, the oil is hot enough (about 400 degrees).

2 Put in rice sticks, turning over quickly when puffed up. Deep-fry for 5 more seconds and then remove to drain on paper towels. The color of the rice sticks should be creamy white, resembling lamb's wool.

3 Remove wok from heat and strain sediment from oil with a fine strainer.

4 Add the lamb shreds to the wok, stirring to separate, then pour oil and lamb into a strainer-lined bowl to drain, leaving about 2 tablespoons of oil in the wok.

5 Set wok over high heat again. Add the leeks to the oil, stirring until limp. Add mushrooms, carrot, bamboo shoots, and chilies in succession, stirring after each is added. Season with salt and sugar, then remove to a bowl.

6 Rinse wok and wipe dry. Set over high heat. When very hot, add remaining 1 tablespoon of oil. Flavor oil with garlic for 10 seconds, then return lamb to wok. Stir and sizzle in the wine along the edge. Add the cooked vegetables, stirring again. Push all the ingredients to the side, restir tapioca mixture, and stream mixture into the center of the wok. Stir until thickened, then add sesame oil. Mix ingredients with sauce.

7 Line a serving platter with the rice sticks, pressing down to break the sticks into smaller pieces. Place the lamb shreds on top and serve while still hot.

WOOLY LAMB
PAGE 311

SICHUAN SPICY FRIED BEEF SHREDS
PAGE 289

◎◎Vinegary Lamb

Serves	2 as a main dish with rice and vegetables
Time	10 minutes preparation
	30 minutes chilling
	5 minutes cooking

醋 淄 羊 肉

Lamb is a tradition in Peking, and here it is given the vinegar-slipped treatment reserved usually for fish, to bring out the fresh flavor of lamb.

Ingredients	Seasoning mixture	Vinegar sauce
12 ounces lean lamb, cut from loin	1 egg white	2 tablespoons red rice vinegar
2 whole scallions, trimmed	1 tablespoon tapioca powder	1 tablespoon dark soy sauce
2 cups oil	½ teaspoon salt	1 tablespoon brown sugar
2 cloves garlic, minced		1 teaspoon tapioca powder
3 slices gingerroot, grated		2 teaspoons chicken stock
1 tablespoon pale dry sherry		Dash of white pepper
2 teaspoons sesame oil		

PREPARATION

1 Trim excess fat from meat and remove any gristle. Cut across the grain into thin slices about ⅛ by 2 by 1 inch in size.

2 Mix seasonings in a bowl, then add the lamb. Mix with your fingers until blended, and refrigerate for at least 30 minutes.

3 Mix ingredients for the sauce in a small bowl. Set aside.

4 Cut scallions into 1-inch lengths.

COOKING

1 Set wok over high heat. When very hot, add the oil. Wait for about 1 minute, then add the lamb, stirring until the slices separate. Pour oil and lamb together into a strainer-lined bowl to drain, leaving about 1 tablespoon of oil in the wok.

2 Reheat oil in the wok until very hot. Flavor oil with garlic and ginger for 15 seconds, then sizzle in the wine. Add the vinegar sauce immediately and stir until bubbly.

3 Return lamb to the wok, stirring to mix with the sauce. Add the scallions, glaze sauce with sesame oil, and mix. Serve hot.

Lamb Chops, Cantonese Style

Serves 2 as a main dish with vegetables and rice
Time 15 minutes preparation
30 minutes marinating
7 to 10 minutes cooking

煎 羊 排

Lamb chops are uncommon in Canton, but this is what the Cantonese would do if lamb chops were available. The gamey taste is neutralized by ginger juice perhaps more effectively than the mint jelly so common in America.

Ingredients

6 center-cut lamb chops, about 1 inch thick
3 cups oil
5 scallions (white part only)

Marinade

2 teaspoons ginger juice
1 tablespoon Fen liquor or brandy
1 teaspoon granulated sugar
1 tablespoon light soy sauce
2 teaspoons dark soy sauce
1 egg white
2 tablespoons cornstarch
¼ teaspoon white pepper
2 teaspoons sesame oil
¼ teaspoon salt

PREPARATION

1 Bone the chops and trim all visible fat and gristle. Cut the meat vertically across the grain into ⅓-inch slices. Tenderize each piece with the blunt edge of a cleaver, making criss-cross marks on both sides.

2 Mix the marinade in a bowl. Arrange 6 slices of lamb in 1 layer on a shallow baking dish, then add enough marinade to cover the surface. Layer more slices on top and repeat with marinade; continue until all slices are coated and end with marinade on top. Chill the meat for 30 minutes.

3 Cut scallion whites into 2-inch strips.

COOKING

1 Set a wok over high heat. When very hot, add the oil. Wait 5 minutes, then test the temperature by dropping a piece of green into the oil. If green sizzles noisily and soon turns brown, the oil is ready, about 375 degrees.

2 Deep-fry half the lamb until golden, then remove the meat to drain on paper towels. Deep-fry the remaining pieces in the same manner.

3 Serve with scallion strips.

⊚Tasmi

Serves 2 as a main dish with
stir-fried vegetables and rice
Time 10 minutes preparation
30 minutes chilling
5 minutes cooking

The name of this lamb dish (meaning "it is like honey") was given by Empress Dowager Ci-Xi for reasons obvious to the taster. The use of sesame oil in cooking belongs to the tradition of the Moslems.

Ingredients	Marinade	Sauce mixture
12 ounces lean lamb, cut from loin	1 egg white	1 tablespoon red rice vinegar
1 cup sesame oil	2 teaspoons tapioca powder	1 tablespoon dark soy sauce
1 tablespoon oil		1 teaspoon ginger juice
2 tablespoons sweet bean paste		1 tablespoon yellow wine
1 tablespoon granulated sugar		1 teaspoon tapioca powder

PREPARATION

1 Trim excess fat off meat and remove any gristle. Cut across the grain into thin slices about ⅛ inch thick or thinner and 1 by 2 inches in size.

2 Combine marinade in a bowl, mixing with a wire whisk until smooth. Add the meat. Mix with your fingers to blend well, and keep refrigerated for 30 minutes.

3 Mix sauce in a small bowl and set aside.

COOKING

1 Set a wok over high heat. When very hot, add the sesame oil and swish it around to coat the wok evenly. Wait for 1 minute, then add the lamb, stirring until the slices separate. Pour lamb and sesame oil together into a strainer-lined bowl to drain.

2 Heat the wok until very hot, then add the oil. Put in sweet bean paste and sugar; stir continuously until sugar dissolves. Return lamb slices to wok, mixing with the bean paste. Push the lamb slices to the side, leaving a space at the center of the wok. Restir the sauce mixture, stream it into the wok, and stir until bubbly. Serve.

Note: Reheat sesame oil over low heat to evaporate moisture, then store in the bottle and refrigerate for later use.

Soybean Products, Gluten, and Seaweeds

The soybean has been a basic food source for the Chinese since prehistoric times. It is one of the five staples in ancient historic records, and the use of brown bean paste is at least two thousand years old. The making of bean curd (tofu) was attributed to Prince Liu An of the Han Dynasty (about 100 BC).

Through the generations, soybean products have supplied needed protein to the otherwise undernourished Chinese. In fact, soybeans produce more protein per acre and per pound than any other commonly edible crop, including meat. But protein is not all that soybeans offer. The bean sprouts, for example, are very high in vitamin C, greatly appreciated during barren winter months. The Chinese use soybean products, one way or another, all year round. The versatile soybean is an integral part of the Chinese diet.

In China, the soybean became known as the "poor man's cow," and its use spread throughout the Orient, from northern Japan to southern Vietnam. Paradoxically, the soybean has been grown in the United States only since 1854, yet we are now the largest producer in the world.

Fresh beans, called "hairy beans" because of their fuzzy pod, are a specialty of eastern China, where they are often stir-fried with a preserved turnip green called red-in-snow. When soybeans are soaked and allowed to germinate, the robust sprouts with crunchy, meatlike heads are used in stir-fries, also for making a vegetarian soup stock. (The usual bean sprouts in most American markets, however, are from mung beans.)

Dried soybeans are yellow in color, great for making soup with beef or pork. Well-soaked dried soybeans can be cooked in a spicy sauce until tender, then roasted to dryness. This is the favorite snack of Chinese children, especially when lightly glazed with sugar.

Cooked soybeans are fermented and processed into soy sauce. The Cantonese like the lighter variety, called "fresh," "superior," "light," or "thin" soy sauce. It is light brown and nearly transparent in color. The more common Chinese soy sauce is a more viscous, dark brown, opaque liquid, usually sold with no extra qualifying English adjective (though the Chinese label may declare it to be "head" or "first," "dark," or "thick" sauce). The first extraction yields the darker sauce, and later extractions give the lighter ones. The Japanese soy sauce, incidentally, is somewhere in between.

Cooked soybeans are also mixed with salt and flour and fermented for weeks to become a soft paste called brown bean paste; it is sold in cans, either with ground or whole beans, and is an important seasoning.

Soaked soybeans are ground to a purée and squeezed through cloth; the liquid after boiling becomes bean milk. Hot bean milk, either sweetened or seasoned with dried shrimps and scallions, is common in North China breakfasts. Coagulated bean milk becomes bean curd, and its consistency depends on the proportion of ingredients used. Homemade bean curd is especially good because you can control the texture.

An array of soybean products is obtained in primitive Chinese factories by boiling a large quantity of bean milk in a big wok over an even, low heat. Layers of skin appearing on the surface are skimmed off carefully and hung to dry. The first layer, transparent and yellow in color, is called bean sheets or *fupi* (bean curd skin) and is sold in large, 18-inch rounds used as wrappers or for vegetarian dishes. The second layer is gathered into sticks which are called *fuzhu* (bean curd sticks). Often the layer is not gathered, but folded, and is called three-sided floating skin.

After several layers of skin have been peeled off, the consistency and color of the bean milk in the wok changes. The bean milk is cooked until the liquid is reduced to a thick layer on the bottom of the wok, then it is removed, dried, and cut in pieces. They are called sweet bean sheets (*tianzhu*).

The bean lees, a by-product of bean milk manufacturing, are as versatile as the soybean itself. It is human food, animal feed, and fertilizer, thus many poultry farms or pig farms are located right next to the bean sheet factory. Poultry and pigs fed this way are known for their fine texture and better flavor. If not used immediately, the bean lees are pressed into bricks and dried as fertilizer to be shipped to distant farms.

In the United States, there is a new Chinese soybean product called *soy-tin*, actually solidified soybean protein. It may be more nutritious than the other soybean products, but it has a slight metallic taste and the texture is spongy. Even the Chinese have to acquire a taste for it.

Bean cheese is fermented hard bean curd that has been marinated with strong liquor and salt. It comes in different flavors, and it can be used either as seasoning or as a tangy side dish for plain congee.

◉◉ Soybean Sprout Fluff

Serves	4 to 6 with other dishes in a Chinese family meal	
Time	20 minutes preparation 20 minutes seasoning 10 minutes cooking	大豆芽菜鬆

This is a country dish from Phoenix City, near Canton. Traditionally served with white rice, this dish can be served wrapped in fresh lettuce leaves instead, for an elegant setting.

Ingredients

¾ pound soybean
  sprouts
½ pound lean ground
  beef
2 whole scallions,
  trimmed
2 teaspoons tapioca
  powder
2 tablespoons chicken
  stock
3 cups + 3 tablespoons
  oil
1 ounce rice sticks
2 cloves garlic, minced
1 tablespoon pale dry
  sherry

Seasonings

1 tablespoon tapioca
  powder
Juice of 2 slices
  gingerroot
2 teaspoons pale dry
  sherry
2 teaspoons light soy
  sauce
1 tablespoon oyster
  sauce
1 teaspoon granulated
  sugar
1 teaspoon sesame oil
2 tablespoons oil
¼ teaspoon salt

PREPARATION

1 Rinse the sprouts. Take a handful of sprouts and put them together so roots are all on same side. Cut off about 1 inch of the ends and repeat this until all sprouts are trimmed. Chop finely into bits the size of rice.

2 Mix meat with seasonings in a bowl. Set at room temperature for 20 minutes.

3 Chop scallions finely.

4 Combine tapioca powder with chicken stock in a small bowl.

COOKING

1 Set a wok over high heat. When very hot, add the 3 cups of oil and wait for about 7 to 8 minutes. Test the temperature by dropping in a few inches of rice sticks into the oil. If the rice sticks puff up immediately, the oil is hot enough (about 400 degrees). Otherwise wait a little longer and test again.

2 Add half the rice sticks to the oil. They should puff up and cover the surface. Turn quickly to the other side and deep-fry for 3 to 4 seconds, making sure not to brown the sticks. Remove to drain on paper towels while you deep-fry the remaining portion.

3 Pour oil out and set wok on high heat again. Add the sprouts, stirring for 3 minutes or longer, until the moisture is evaporated. Remove. Rinse wok and wipe dry.

4 Set wok over high heat. When very hot, add remaining 3 tablespoons of oil. Flavor oil with garlic for 10 seconds, then add meat, stirring and turning until the bits are separated.

5 Sizzle in the wine along the edge of the wok, stirring a few times, then add the sprouts and scallions, mixing and turning well. Restir the tapioca powder mixture and add to the center of the wok, stirring until bubbly.

6 Mix all ingredients together and arrange on top of fried rice sticks on a serving platter.

Note: Soybean Sprout Fluff can be served together with lettuce leaves as wrappers (see Lettuce Wraps, p. 283).

◉Soybean Snacks

Yields 4 cups
Time 6 hours soaking
2 hours cooking
1 hour baking

蠔油荳

The Chinese have had more than three thousand years to find new ways to use the nutritious soybean. This snack is great with the children in Canton, and could be a hit at your next cocktail party. The use of an oven at low temperature replaces the tedious job of traditional sun-drying, plus makes the product more uniform.

Ingredients

1 pound dried
soybeans
6 cups water
¼ cup light soy sauce
1 tablespoon dark soy
sauce

¼ cup pale dry sherry
8 slices gingerroot
¼ cup granulated
sugar
2 tablespoons oyster
sauce

PREPARATION

1 Wash and pick over soybeans and discard the bad ones.

2 Soak in plenty of cold water for about 6 hours or until the beans are double their original size. Drain thoroughly.

COOKING

1 In a 4-quart nonstick saucepan, add soybeans, water, light and dark soy sauces, sherry, and ginger. Bring water to a boil over high heat, then cover pan and simmer for 1 hour, 30 minutes.

2 Raise heat to high and add sugar and oyster sauce to soybeans. Cook with the pan uncovered until all the moisture is absorbed, about 20 minutes. Stir several times during cooking.

3 Preheat oven to 200 degrees.

4 Line a baking sheet with aluminum foil and spread on the soybeans evenly. Bake for 1 hour, then turn off heat and let the soybeans cool in the oven.

5 Transfer soybeans to an airtight container. They can be kept fresh for up to a month. Refrigerate if you can.

◉◉◉Vegetarian Roast Duck

Serves 6 to 8 as part of a Chinese
multi-dish meal, or as a cold
platter
Time 15 minutes preparation
45 minutes soaking
20 minutes cooking

Looking somewhat like sliced pieces of roast duck, this dish shows how Chinese vegetarians satisfy both their protein requirements and their palates for fine food. The true vegetarian version, however, uses neither the chicken stock nor oyster sauce.

Ingredients

1 ounce dried straw
    mushrooms
1 pound sweet bean
    sheets
¼ cup + 4 tablespoons
    oil
2 teaspoons pale dry
    sherry
2 teaspoons sesame oil
6 bean sheets

Seasonings

1 cup chicken stock or
    water
2 tablespoons oyster
    sauce or dark soy
    sauce
1 tablespoon light soy
    sauce
Salt

PREPARATION

1 Soak straw mushrooms in cold water until soft. Trim dirt from ends and beat with chopsticks to loosen sand. Soak again in 1 cup of warm water for 20 minutes, then drain, reserving soaking liquid. Strain soaking liquid to remove any sediment. Cut mushrooms in half.

2 Rinse sweet bean sheets and soak in cold water for 30 minutes or until soft. Drain.

3 Set a heavy Dutch oven over high heat. When very hot, add the ¼ cup of oil, then sizzle in the wine and add the mushrooms. Stir constantly for 1 minute.

4 Add the seasonings to the pot along with the mushroom soaking liquid. Bring liquid to a boil and add the sweet bean sheets.

5 Bring to a boil, then turn heat to low. Cover pot and cook until the moisture is almost absorbed, about 15 minutes.

6 Stir in the sesame oil and let the mixture cool.

7 Lightly dampen a bath towel with hot water. Line a tray with half the towel and arrange all the bean sheets on it. Cover with the remaining half of the towel and let set for 30 minutes. Alternate the sheets so that the dry ones in the center will be turned out and moistened. Set for 10 minutes more.

ASSEMBLING

1 Divide the sweet bean sheet mixture into 4 equal portions.

2 Put half a bean sheet on the center of another as reinforcement. Add 1 portion of sweet bean mixture and wrap it up as you would a spring roll (page 78). Seal with some liquid from the bean sheet mixture.

3 Repeat for remaining rolls; you should have 4 rolls.

COOKING

1 Using a nonstick skillet, pan-fry the rolls over medium heat using the remaining 4 tablespoons of oil. Brown on all sides and remove.

2 Arrange rolls side by side, in 1 layer of a large piece of aluminum foil. Fold all sides up to enclose the rolls loosely. Place the package on a tray and lay a heavy board on top. Put some weights on the board and press the rolls until they are cool and flat. If not to be used immediately, chill in the refrigerator for up to 3 days.

3 When ready to serve, you'll note that the pressed rolls now resemble the breast of roast duck. Cut in slices about ⅝ inch thick and serve cold.

BEAN CURD (TOFU)

Bean curd made its formal appearance in books dating from the Sung Dynasty a thousand years ago, when it was already the food of the masses. Poets praised its jade-slab appearance and its yielding texture. The only things wrong, it seems, were its low cost and easy accessibility. Thus it was not worthy of being served at a banquet.

This lowly recognition for the bean curd remained the case for centuries; occasional attempts to imitate it using expensive ingredients (such as pork brains) to humor the *nouveau riche* could not shake off its humble peasant origin. My grandfather finally did it in Canton fifty years ago, by simmering true bean curd in a concentrated Supreme Stock at a banquet.

More commonly known in this country by its Japanese name of tofu, bean curd has become very popular in recent years. Quite a few large U.S. supermarkets now regularly supply tofu in sealed plastic boxes, often in three texture grades:

soft—soft and smooth, used mostly for soups and steamed dishes

semi-soft—the Japanese favorite, not too often used by the Chinese

hard—more substantial, used mostly for cutting into slices and cubes; or pressed and then shredded

Other commercial products include the deep-fried bean-curd puff, great for stuffing and braising with vegetables, meat, or fish. Another newcomer to the market is the deep-fried hard bean curd, which comes in cakes about 5 by 3 inches and ¾ inch thick, best for vegetarian stews.

The fortunate reader who has access to the commercial bean curds should buy them by all means for the recipes given in this book. However bean curd is not difficult to make, and a simple method starting from soybeans is described here for those who live in areas where it is not readily available.

One advantage of making your own bean curd is the chance to vary the texture by controlling the proportion of the ingredients. At one extreme is the extra-soft and delicate *Flower of Bean Curd*, which is smooth as silk and light as a dream. While Flower of Bean Curd is sometimes available in the Oriental markets, its flavor depends on its freshness and can be best assured when home-made. At the other extreme is the *heavy bean curd* with a chewy consistency, made with more solid ingredients and less water. *Old bean curd* is the product of prolonged boiling. The *bean curd biscuit* is made by first soaking the pressed bean curd in a spicy sauce, then baking. It is shaped like a thick soda cracker, and is nibbled by children in China in much the same way as crackers are nibbled by American children.

Dried soybeans are available at all Oriental markets or health food stores. Some supermarkets carry soybeans on their gourmet food shelves, in boxes or bags.

Caution: Soybeans kept too long after harvest do not coagulate well.

All bean curd is processed from bean milk, and the consistency of the latter dictates to a large extent the varieties of bean curd obtained. In the home, the bean milk is obtained by grinding the soaked soybeans in a blender; the thin, soft purée is then put in a muslin sack and squeezed. The solid leftovers are edible, though not esteemed by the Chinese.

Bean curd is coagulated from boiled bean milk. For home-made bean curd, the coagulant used is mainly calcium sulfate, sold as plaster of paris at any American drugstore. It is gypsum with the water content removed by roasting. (In commercial bean curds, other coagulants are also used, such as brine, calcium chloride, epsom salts, or vinegar.)

Once you know the basics you can easily prepare your own bean curd at any level of consistency. Home-made bean curd can be kept as long as from seven to ten days in the refrigerator, but change the water every day to preserve freshness. It can also be frozen; then it acquires a honeycomb texture and becomes highly absorbent.

◉ Light Bean Milk

Yields about 2 quarts
Time 6 hours soaking
20 minutes preparation
15 minutes cooking

豆 漿

The common American breakfast uses crunchy cereals and milk. In Northern China the counterparts are fried oil-strips and light bean milk (sweet or salted).

Ingredients	Equipment
½ pound dried soybeans	Electric blender
3 quarts + ½ cup water	Muslin sack, 15 inches long and 9 inches wide
Sugar (optional)	4- to 6-quart saucepan

PREPARATION

1 Rinse the soybeans. Soak in water to cover for about 6 hours, or until expanded to double their original size. You should have about 3 cups of beans.

2 Drain beans and, if not to be used immediately, keep refrigerated to prevent fermentation.

3 Combine 1 cup of soaked beans with 4 cups of water in the blender. Whirl at high speed until the beans turn to a thin purée.

4 Have the saucepan ready, with the sack lining the bottom. Through the opening of the sack pour in the bean purée. Squeeze to extract as much liquid as possible into the saucepan. Discard the lees.

5 Finish processing the remaining soybeans, discarding lees each time.

6 Set the bean mixture in the saucepan over high heat. Do not cover, but cook for 10 to 12 minutes or until the liquid starts to boil over. Bring it down by pouring ½ cup cold water into the mixture.

7 Return liquid to a boil and then remove saucepan from the heat. (Continued heating from this point will cause the bean milk to boil over again.)

8 Store in a container in the refrigerator. It will keep for days. For Sweet Bean Milk, add sugar to taste before or after refrigeration, and use as you would milk.

VARIATION: Seasoned Bean Milk

Ingredients

¼ cup dried shrimp
½ cup hot water
2 ounces Sichuan
   preserved vegetables
2 whole scallions,
   trimmed
1 tablespoon oil
1 cup water
6 cups light bean milk

1 teaspoon chicken
   bouillon powder
Salt
2 teaspoons sesame oil

1 Soak shrimp in hot water until soft. Chop fine into bits; reserve soaking liquid.

2 Rinse vegetables under cold water to remove red pepper and spices. Chop finely.

3 Chop scallions finely.

4 Set a 4-quart saucepan over high heat. When very hot, add the oil. Stir-fry the shrimp and vegetables for 1 minute. Add the water and the reserved soaking liquid and bring to a boil.

5 Add the bean milk and reduce heat to low. Cook slowly until it boils, stirring constantly.

6 Add the chicken bouillon powder and a very small amount of salt. Correct the seasonings and add the scallions and sesame oil. Stir to mix.

◉◉ Flower of Bean Curd

Yields about 2½ quarts
Time 6 hours soaking
20 minutes preparation
20 minutes cooking
20 minutes coagulating

豆腐花

A favorite of Chinese children and adults alike, to be taken hot or chilled.

Ingredients	Equipment	Chinese brown sugar syrup
3 cups dried soybeans	Electric blender	4 ounces Chinese brown sugar
5 quarts + 1 cup water	12-inch-high pan	¼ cup water
1 tablespoon plaster of paris	8-quart saucepan	
2 tablespoons cornstarch mixed with 1 cup water	Muslin sack, 9 by 15 inches	

PREPARATION

1 Put soybeans in a large bowl and add water to cover well. Set at room temperature for 6 hours, or until the beans expand to double their original size. There will be about 8 to 9 cups of beans. If beans are not to be used immediately, refrigerate to prevent fermentation.

2 Combine 2 cups of beans and 4 cups of water in the blender. Whirl at high speed for 1 minute or until reduced to a purée.

3 Have the saucepan ready, with the sack lining in the bottom. Through the opening of the sack, pour in the bean purée. Squeeze out the liquid and then transfer the lees to a large pan. Rinse sack.

4 Repeat the above, blending beans with water and the puréeing, until all the beans are used. Reserve the lees and rinse the sack each time.

5 Pour 1 quart of water onto the lees and mix well. Strain the liquid (using the sack) and add it to the bean milk in the saucepan. Discard lees.

6 Combine plaster of paris with cornstarch and water in the tall pan, stirring to mix well.

7 Set the bean milk over high heat but do not cover the pot. Cook for 15 minutes or until milk is about to boil over; add 1 cup of cold water immediately and wait until liquid again returns to a boil.

8 Remove saucepan from the heat and restir cornstarch mixture. Pour the bean milk rapidly into the tall pan. Let rest and do not stir. The bean mixture will coagulate in about 15 to 20 minutes.

9 To serve, spoon out the top foamy layer and discard. Serve remainder with Chinese brown-sugar syrup, with portions in individual bowls.

Note: The syrup can be prepared easily by dissolving Chinese brown sugar with water over high heat. If not available, use American brown sugar instead.

◉◉◉ Home-Made Bean Curd

Yields   1 piece of bean curd about 10
              by 10 by 1 inch in size
Time   6 hours soaking
              20 minutes preparation
              20 minutes cooking
              1 hour pressing

Solid bean curd is obtained by pressing a thicker form of Flower of Bean Curd in a wooden mold. Using the diagram below, the interested do-it-yourselfer can build such a mold easily and make 1½ pounds of bean curd from 1 pound of dried soybeans.

The mold comes in 3 pieces: a frame, a supporting bottom, and a lid. The frame is set on the top of the supporting board to form a loose-bottomed container. A piece of over-sized cheesecloth is folded on top to wrap the Flower of Bean Curd securely. The lid is put on and weighted first with a heavy cutting board (roughly the size of the bottom, but smaller), then a large pot of water (at least an 8-quart pot) or a pile of books is set on top. Under the load, excess water will drain at the base.

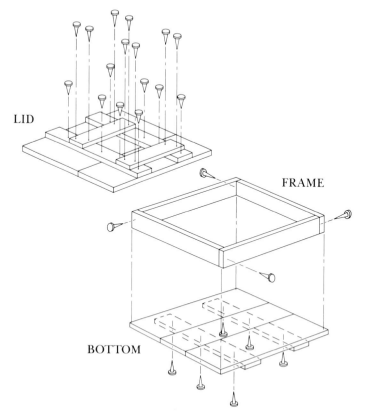

LID

FRAME

BOTTOM

In 1 hour, the Flower of Bean Curd is pressed into a thicker consistency, similar to the commercial semi-soft bean curd. For a soft bean curd, press with lighter weight; for a harder one, press longer with a heavier weight. Techniques are illustrated on pages 101–103.

PREPARATION

1 Prepare the curd for Flower of Bean Curd, using the ingredients and method described on page 325. For each batch, use 2 cups of soaked beans to 4 cups of water without rinsing the lees for a slightly thicker purée.

2 Omit the cornstarch from the ingredients and increase the amount of plaster of paris to 4 teaspoons. Blend in as directed.

3 After the bean milk has coagulated, remove the top foamy layer. Line the bottom and side of frame with a piece of cheesecloth (20 inches square). Scoop the bean curd into the mold.

4 Fold cheesecloth on top to secure curd. Then put on lid, top with cutting board, and weight as desired for 1 hour or longer.

5 Remove the weights, then the cutting board. Take the lid off and unwrap the cheesecloth to reveal the bean curd. Cut into 4 or more pieces and put in a container, covering them with water. Keep refrigerated and change the soaking water every day or use immediately.

◉Steamed Bean Curd with Fish

Serves	4 with other dishes in a Chinese family meal	
Time	10 minutes preparation 15 minutes cooking	老 少 平 安

In Canton this dish with soft texture is called Peace to Young and Old because it appeals to children too young to have teeth, old folks who have lost all their teeth, and adults in between. One generally serves it with other dishes that have a chewy texture for contrast.

Ingredients

2 tablespoons dried shrimp
½ cup hot water
1 package (12 ounces) soft bean curd
½ pound cod or sole fillet
½ teaspoon salt
4 teaspoons light soy sauce
2 teaspoons sesame oil

1 whole scallion, trimmed and chopped
1 sprig Chinese parsley, chopped

Seasonings

1 egg white
1 tablespoon tapioca powder
⅛ teaspoon white pepper
2 teaspoons pale dry sherry
¼ teaspoon salt

PREPARATION

1 Soak the shrimp in hot water until soft. Chop finely; reserve soaking liquid.

2 Drain the bean curd.

3 Rinse fish and pat dry. Cut coarsely into ½-inch pieces. Combine with the salt and the reserved soaking liquid in a blender, and whirl at high speed until reduced to a paste.

4 Add seasonings to the fish purée, then add bean curd and dried shrimp. Whirl in blender until smooth.

5 Remove purée from blender and pour into a well-greased 8-inch heatproof baking dish. Smooth the surface with a wet spoon.

COOKING

1 Line a 4-quart saucepan (its diameter should be 2 inches larger than that of the deep baking dish) with a kitchen towel. Set in a 2-inch rack. Add water to come up to half the height of the rack and bring to a boil over high heat.

2 Place dish on the rack and cover pan. Turn heat to medium-low and steam for 20 minutes, or until a chopstick inserted comes out clean. Remove dish from pan.

3 Pour soy sauce, spoonful by spoonful, over the surface of the bean curd to make a marble pattern. Whirl on the sesame oil and decorate with scallion and parsley. Serve hot.

◉◉◉Tai Shi Bean Curd

Serves 10 to 12 in a banquet
Time 30 minutes preparation
15 minutes steaming
15 minutes deep-frying

太 史 豆 腐

Only two dishes featuring the lowly bean curd are deemed worthy of inclusion in a Cantonese banquet. Both were invented in the kitchen of my grandfather, Supreme Scholar Kong Hungyan of the Qing Dynasty. This is one of them.

Ingredients
12 medium shrimp
⅜ teaspoon salt
3 ounces fillet of sole
  or pike
4 egg whites
1 package (12 ounces)
  soft bean curd
4 cups oil
Cornstarch for coating

Seasonings
½ teaspoon salt
1 teaspoon sesame oil
2 tablespoons tapioca
  powder
2 teaspoons pale dry
  sherry
¼ teaspoon granulated
  sugar
Dash of white pepper

PREPARATION

1 Shell, devein, and clean the shrimp (see page 151). Cut coarsely into ½-inch dice, then mince with a cleaver into a fine paste, adding about ¼ teaspoon of salt as you mince. Transfer paste to a mixing bowl.

2 Rinse and dry fish. Cut coarsely and mince to a fine paste, adding about ⅛ teaspoon of salt while mincing. Combine with shrimp paste in the mixing bowl.

3 Beat the egg whites until smooth, then add the seasonings. Mix with the shrimp–fish paste and stir with a wooden spoon in 1 direction until the ingredients hold together and are well blended.

4 Add bean curd, stirring until the mixture is smooth.

(Note: Another way to prepare the paste is to add the shrimp, fish, egg whites, ⅜ teaspoon of salt and seasonings to the container of a blender. Whirl at high speed until reduced to a smooth paste; then add the bean curd and continue to blend until all ingredients are well mixed and smooth.)

5 Remove mixture to an 8-inch square nonstick baking pan. Bring water in the base of a steamer to a vigorous boil and place baking pan in steamer. Steam over low heat for 15 minutes or until a chopstick inserted comes out clean.

6 When bean curd mixture is done, chill until cool and firm, about 2 hours.

COOKING

1 Blot the bean curd dry with paper towels. Cut into slabs about ⅜ by 1 by 2 inches.

2 Set a wok over high heat. When very hot, add the oil. While waiting for the oil to heat, coat the pieces of bean curd evenly with cornstarch, shaking off the excess.

3 Test temperature of oil by dropping in a piece of scallion green. If it sizzles, then turns brown, the oil is ready (about 375 degrees).

4 Add bean curd, piece by piece. Turn heat to medium-high and deep-fry until all the pieces rise to the surface and are lightly brown. Remove and drain. Serve immediately.

Stir-Fried Bean Curd with Fresh Mushrooms in Oyster Sauce

Serves 4 to 6 in a multi-dish Chinese family meal
Time 10 minutes preparation
5 minutes cooking

蠔油蘑菇豆腐

Button mushrooms are new to Chinese cookery but their use is spreading fast. The original version of this Cantonese favorite used fresh straw mushrooms.

Ingredients

1 package (12 ounces) soft bean curd
½ pound medium button mushrooms
2 whole scallions, trimmed
3 tablespoons oil
1 clove garlic, bruised
1 tablespoon pale dry sherry

Sauce mixture

1 tablespoon dark soy sauce
2 tablespoons oyster sauce
½ teaspoon granulated sugar
2 teaspoons tapioca powder
¼ cup chicken stock
1 teaspoon sesame oil

PREPARATION

1 On a cutting board, cut bean curd vertically into slices about ¼ inch thick, then cut slices into 1 by ½-inch pieces. Tilt the board slightly to drain off excess water.

2 Peel skin from mushrooms and trim the stems. Cut into ¼-inch-thick slices. (Or wipe the mushrooms clean with a damp cloth; do not rinse with water.)

3 Cut off a few inches from the greens of the scallions and chop the remaining portions finely.

4 Mix ingredients for sauce mixture in a small bowl. Stir to blend well.

COOKING

1 Set a wok over high heat. When it is very hot, add the oil. Flavor oil with garlic for 20 seconds, then remove and discard the garlic.

2 Add the mushroom slices, stirring constantly until each piece is well coated with oil. Sizzle in the wine along the edge of the wok and stir.

3 Add the sauce mixture and stir to thicken. Add the bean curd, stirring carefully. Cook for 4 to 5 minutes or until the bean curd is heated through.

4 Remove ingredients to a deep serving platter. Garnish with scallions and serve immediately.

◉◉ Stir-Fried Bean Curd with Tomato and Beef

Serves 2 as a main dish with rice
Time 10 minutes preparation
5 minutes cooking

蕃茄牛肉炒豆腐

The New World tomato has been firmly established as a Cantonese vegetable for close to a century. This dish is best served over white rice.

Ingredients

1 8-ounce piece flank
steak
¼ cup + 2 tablespoons
oil
2 pieces hard bean
curd, about 10
ounces total
2 large tomatoes
2 whole scallions,
trimmed
2 cloves garlic, sliced
2 teaspoons pale dry
sherry

¾ teaspoon salt
2 teaspoons granulated
sugar
2 teaspoons tapioca
powder mixed with 1
tablespoon water
1 teaspoon sesame oil

Seasonings

1 tablespoon dark soy
sauce
1 tablespoon oyster
sauce
1 teaspoon granulated
sugar
2 teaspoons tapioca
powder
1 teaspoon sesame oil
Dash of white pepper

PREPARATION

1 Slice meat across the grain into pieces about ⅛ by 1 by 1½ inches in size.

2 Combine meat with seasonings in a bowl, mixing with your fingers. Add 2 tablespoons of oil to separate the slices and mix again.

3 Cut bean curd into ¼-inch slabs about 1 by 1½ inches in size. Drain off excess water in a colander.

4 Put tomatoes in a large mixing bowl and pour boiling water over. Let stand for 5 minutes, then peel. Cut tomatoes crosswise in half. Squeeze out the seeds and cut pulp into wedges.

5 Roll-cut the scallions into 1-inch lengths.

COOKING

1 Set a wok over high heat. When very hot, add the remaining ¼ cup of oil. Flavor oil with garlic for 20 seconds, then add beef, spreading evenly along the bottom of wok. Pan-fry for 1 minute, then turn and pan-fry for 30 seconds more.

2 Sizzle in the wine along the edge of the wok, then add the scallions, stirring quickly to separate beef slices.

3 Remove beef, leaving as much oil in wok as possible. Add tomato wedges, stir for 1 minute, then add the bean curd. Turn and cook bean curd for 5 minutes, then season with salt and sugar.

4 Add tapioca powder mixture to the center of the wok, stirring until the sauce thickens. Glaze sauce with sesame oil.

5 Return meat to the wok, mixing all ingredients. Correct seasoning and remove and serve.

Braised Bean Curd, Family Style

Serves 4 as part of a multi-dish
Chinese family meal
Time 10 minutes preparation
10 minutes resting
15 minutes cooking

家常豆腐

Bean curd is not invariably soft and yielding, but firmer versions can complement or replace pieces of meat in the kitchen, in braised dishes like this one, or in sautéed dishes.

Ingredients	Seasonings	Braising sauce
4 ounces lean ground pork	1 tablespoon dark soy sauce	1 cup chicken stock
2 pieces hard bean curd, about 10 ounces total	1 teaspoon tapioca powder	1 tablespoon oyster sauce
¾ teaspoon salt	1 teaspoon pale dry sherry	1 teaspoon dark soy sauce
½ cup shelled green peas	¼ teaspoon granulated sugar	
3 cups oil	½ teaspoon sesame oil	
1 clove garlic, minced		
1 tablespoon pale dry sherry		
1½ teaspoons tapioca powder mixed with 1 tablespoon chicken stock		
1 teaspoon sesame oil		

PREPARATION

1 Mix ground pork with the seasonings. Set aside.

2 Cut bean curd into slabs about ¼ by 1 by 1½ inches. Sprinkle salt evenly on the surface and set for 10 minutes in the refrigerator.

3 Blanch peas in boiling water for 1 minute. Drain and run cold water over to stop the cooking.

4 Mix ingredients for sauce in a bowl and set aside.

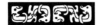

COOKING

1 Set a wok over high heat. When very hot, add the oil. While waiting for the oil to heat, pat the bean curd gently with paper towels to absorb excess moisture.

2 Test the oil temperature by dropping in a piece of scallion green. If bubbles appear around the green, which soon turns brown, the oil is ready (about 375 degrees).

3 Put in the bean curd pieces and deep-fry until light golden, about 5 to 7 minutes.

4 Remove bean curd and pour oil out, leaving about 1 tablespoon of oil in the wok.

5 Reset wok over high heat. Flavor oil with garlic for 20 seconds, then add the meat, stirring constantly until the bits separate. Sizzle in the wine and then add the braising sauce.

6 Return bean curd to the wok and cover. Cook for 4 to 5 minutes or until the sauce has almost been absorbed.

7 Add the peas, mixing together with the other ingredients, and cook for 1 minute more. Add the tapioca mixture and stir until bubbly. Glaze sauce with sesame oil and mix and serve.

⊛ Bean Curd Meatloaf

Serves   4 as a main dish with vegetable and rice
Time   15 minutes preparation 80 minutes cooking

焗豆腐肉餅

In this adaption of the Western meatloaf, half of the traditional beef and all the bread crumbs have been replaced by nutritious bean curd. The texture is unchanged, yet the taste is now Chinese.

Ingredients	Seasonings	
1 package (20 ounces) hard bean curd	2 tablespoons light soy sauce	⅛ teaspoon white pepper
1 large onion	1 tablespoon dark soy sauce	2 teaspoons sesame oil
4 tablespoons oil	1 tablespoon tapioca powder	1½ teaspoons chicken bouillon powder
1 pound lean ground beef	1 tablespoon pale dry sherry	2 teaspoons granulated sugar
2 whole eggs		

PREPARATION

1 Wrap bean curd 1 piece at a time with a kitchen towel. Squeeze to extract moisture and to break up the bean curd into fine bits.

2 Chop the onion finely. Stir-fry over high heat with the oil until limp. Remove onion and oil together and set aside.

3 Combine ground beef and seasonings in a large bowl, stirring with a wooden spoon in 1 direction until all ingredients hold together. Add eggs, bean curd, and onion and stir again, about 2 minutes.

4 Put beef and bean curd mixture in a greased 9 by 3 by 3-inch loaf pan.

COOKING

1 Preheat oven to 375 degrees

2 Bake bean curd meat loaf for 1 hour, 20 minutes or until a chopstick inserted comes out clean.

3 Serve with either of the following sauces: tomato sauce (see Fillet of Fish in Tomato Sauce, page 141); or sweet and sour sauce (see Sweet and Sour Pork Balls, page 277); or oyster sauce (see Crab Foo Yung, page 167).

◉◉◉Buddha's Delight

Serves 6 as a main dish with rice
Time 30 minutes preparation
35 minutes cooking

羅 漢 齋

This is adapted from *Louhan Zhai*, or the vegetarian dish for the five hundred disciples (louhans) sworn to protect the Buddhist way. This dish, featuring many ingredients each providing its own texture, is enjoyed by all Chinese. The truly vegetarian recipe would use neither chicken stock nor garlic.

Ingredients

½ ounce dried snow
 mushrooms
8 black mushrooms
¼ cup cloud ears
32 tiger lily buds
3 cups warm water
½ cup hair vegetable,
 about ¼ ounce
3 cups hot water
¼ cup + 4 tablespoons
 oil
6 sweet bean sheets
3 soybean sticks
1 piece hard bean
 curd, about 5 ounces
3 pieces deep-fried
 bean curd puff
1 can (16 ounces) straw
 mushrooms
1 can (8 ounces) sliced
 bamboo shoots

18 fresh snow peas
12 medium button
 mushrooms
½ carrot
8 deep-fried Gluten
 Puffs (see page 338)
2 ounces cellophane
 noodles
2 cloves garlic,
 flattened
2 cups chicken stock or
 water
1 slice gingerroot
½ teaspoon salt
2 teaspoons sesame oil

Seasonings

¼ cup light soy sauce
1 tablespoon
 granulated sugar
1 cup chicken stock or
 water
½ teaspoon salt

PREPARATION

1 Soak snow mushrooms in cold water until soft. Trim tough ends and blanch in some boiling water for 30 seconds. Rinse with cold water and drain.

2 Soak black mushrooms, cloud ears, and tiger lily buds individually in 1 cup each of warm water for about 15 minutes, or until soft. Trim stems and tough ends. Squeeze to extract moisture from black mushrooms. Rinse and drain cloud ears and lily buds thoroughly. Reserve mushroom liquid.

3 Soak hair vegetable in hot water for 30 minutes. Rinse with 3 to 4 changes of hot water, then put hair vegetable in a bowl, adding 1 tablespoon of the oil and 1 cup of hot water to cover. Beat vegetable repeatedly with a fork or a pair of chopsticks to loosen sand. Squeeze to extract moisture.

4 Soak the sweet bean sheets and bean sticks in separate bowls of cold water. Drain, then leave sheets whole and break sticks into 2-inch lengths.

5 Cut hard bean curd into slabs about 1 by 1 by ⅜ inch.

6 Soak the deep-fried bean curd puff in hot water and squeeze to eliminate excess grease. Cut into ⅜-inch slices.

7 Separately blanch the straw mushrooms and bamboo shoots in boiling water for 1 minute. Run each under cold water to rinse, then drain.

8 String the snow peas and rinse.

9 Wipe the button mushrooms clean with a dampened cloth; trim off tough ends.

10 Slice the carrot into ⅛-inch pieces.

11 Cut each gluten puff in half. Soak in a pot of boiling water, then squeeze to remove the grease when the water has cooled.

12 Soak the cellophane noodles in cold water until soft. Cut into 4-inch lengths.

COOKING

1 Set a 4-quart Dutch oven over high heat. When hot, add ¼ cup of oil. Flavor oil with 1 garlic, then remove garlic when brown. Add the black mushrooms, cloud ears, tiger lilies, and canned straw mushrooms, stirring for 5 minutes.

2 Add the mushroom soaking liquid and water. Bring to a boil, then turn heat to low. Add the gluten puffs and bean sticks. Cook for 20 minutes.

3 Add the seasonings, sweet bean sheets, hair vegetable, and cellophane noodles. Cook slowly until the liquid is almost absorbed.

(Note: the above steps can be prepared ahead of time or could be refrigerated overnight at this point. Before serving, set dutch oven over medium heat. Bring ingredients to a boil.)

4 Set a wok over high heat. When hot, add 1 tablespoon of oil. Flavor oil with ginger until brown, then add the peas, stirring until every piece is coated with oil. Remove and set aside; discard the ginger.

5 Add remaining 2 tablespoons of oil to wok. When hot, flavor oil with remaining garlic until brown, then discard. Stir-fry the button mushrooms, bamboo shoots, and carrot; also add snow mushrooms. Season with salt.

6 Transfer all cooked ingredients to wok and combine with vegetables, stirring and turning to mix well. Add the snow peas, stirring again.

7 Test for saltiness and add more light soy sauce if necessary. Whirl in the sesame oil. Mix and serve hot.

◉◉Bean Curd Salad

Serves 4 to 6 as a cold platter with other hot dishes
Time 15 minutes preparation
1 hour pressing

涼拌豆腐絲

Ingredients
¼ cup dried shrimp
½ cup hot water
2 tablespoons oil
Salt
2 pieces hard bean curd, about 10 ounces total
½ medium carrot
1 whole scallion, trimmed
2 sprigs Chinese parsley

Dressing
1 tablespoon sesame oil
1 tablespoon oil
1 teaspoon chicken bouillon powder
2 teaspoons red rice vinegar
2 teaspoons granulated sugar
1 teaspoon light soy sauce
1 clove garlic, minced
Few drops of hot pepper oil (optional)

PREPARATION

1 Rinse the dried shrimp, then soak in hot water for 1 hour or until soft. Mince finely; discard soaking water.

2 Set a small heavy skillet over high heat. When hot, add the oil. When oil is hot, add the minced shrimp, stirring constantly until golden. Remove and reserve.

3 Sprinkle about ½ teaspoon of salt evenly on the surface of the bean curd. Top with a heavy cutting board, then place books on top to press out moisture. When bean curd is pressed to half its original thickness (or about ⅜ inch), remove weights and cutting board. This takes about 1 hour. Shred bean curd finely into strips about ³⁄₁₆ by ³⁄₁₆ by 1½ inches.

4 Shred carrot finely, then add about ¼ teaspoon of salt and mix well. Set for 20 minutes, then squeeze to extract any moisture. Reserve.

5 Shred scallion finely into 1½-inch lengths.

6 Rinse the parsley and break into 1½-inch lengths. Combine ingredients for dressing in a jar and shake well.

7 About 30 minutes before serving, combine bean curd, carrot, scallion, parsley, and shrimp in a bowl. Add dressing and toss to mix well. Correct seasonings and serve cold.

GLUTEN

Gluten has been used by the Chinese for at least a thousand years. It is one of the three most important ingredients in Chinese vegetarian cuisine (the other two being bean curd and *fuzhu*). Its high protein content and low cost make it a bargain for tasty and nutritious meals. Unlike soybean products, gluten is usually appreciated on its first encounter. By itself, it has a delicate flavor which blends easily with seasonings of all kinds because of its spongelike absorbency. Gluten also has meatlike texture and chewiness. It is therefore the chief ingredient in vegetarian roast pork, vegetarian spareribs, vegetarian abalone, and many more.

Gluten as an ingredient is one of the better-kept secrets of Chinese cookery. Despite the textural similarity with meat, it is relatively unknown outside East Asia. Cooks in America cannot buy gluten from the corner grocery store, and often have to make their own. It is much harder to find than bean curd, partly because it is less popular; however, frozen cooked gluten from China is beginning to appear in some Chinese markets in large cities in the United States.

It is extremely simple to make gluten from a sack of flour. Our preference ranks the gluten flour first for its high yield, then the unbleached all-purpose flour for its natural flavor, and finally the bleached all-purpose flour.

Wheat flour contains ten to twenty-five percent gluten, depending on the variety. To make gluten, the nongluten ingredients are washed out of the flour as the gluten gathers into a mass. This requires mixing the flour with lightly salted water and kneading the mass until it becomes elastic. The by-product, which is mostly wheat starch, is the base for Cantonese dim sum wrappers.

The raw gluten obtained from washing the flour is called *original gluten.* (Often a further processing is applied.) Deep-fried, it becomes *gluten puff;* boiled, it becomes *cooked gluten.* So that it is seasoned uniformly, you should cut the gluten pieces into 1-inch cubes. Very often precooked gluten is sold in 1-inch balls, resembling Ping-Pong balls.

◉◉Home-Made Gluten

Yields 3 cups raw gluten
Time overnight resting
20 minutes washing

自 製 麵 筋

High-gluten flour is best for this, and you should be able to purchase it at a health food store or in a bakery. If you can't locate any, use unbleached all-purpose flour as a second choice. As a last resort, use standard bleached all-purpose flour. Techniques are shown on pages 100–101.

Ingredients
2 tablespoons salt
8 cups water

5 pounds high-gluten
  or unbleached
  all-purpose flour

PREPARATION

1 Mix salt with water and gradually pour in the flour. Mix thoroughly to form a round of dough; if time permits, knead the dough a little.

2 Cover dough with plastic wrap and keep refrigerated overnight.

3 Place the dough in a bowl or saucepan and set it in your kitchen sink. Hold the dough under gently running cold water and rub and squeeze as the water runs over. The starch will be washed out, making the water milky while the gluten becomes elastic and sticks together.

4 Keep washing and squeezing until the water in the bowl runs clear. Place the gluten mass in a colander to drain off excess water, then set in the refrigerator to firm. This is the raw, or original gluten.

Raw gluten can be processed further into several forms:

GLUTEN PUFFS

Break raw gluten into small balls about 1 inch in diameter. Deep-fry in moderately hot oil until each piece puffs up into a hollow ball. For details, see Braised Gluten Puffs in Shrimp Roe Sauce (pages 340–341). Gluten puffs are used quite often in braising. They freeze very well and can be kept for months. They can also be found in Oriental groceries.

COOKED GLUTEN

Break raw gluten into balls about 1 inch in diameter or keep the piece whole. Cook in plenty of boiling water for about 30 minutes over medium heat, or until the softness disappears. Store in refrigerator until needed or keep frozen.

STEAMED GLUTEN

Steam raw gluten for 1 hour. It will become spongy and absorbent like bread.

⊛Braised Gluten with Pork in Brown Bean Sauce

Serves 4 as a main dish with
vegetable and rice
Time 7 minutes preparation
1 hour cooking

麵筋炆豬肉

East China is renowned for its variety of dishes made with gluten. This is a fine example; the gluten has a meatlike texture and absorbs the seasonings readily. In this dish, the gluten is more than a meat extender or protein source—it adds to the variety of textures.

Ingredients

3 cups cooked gluten
(page 338)
1 pound lean pork, cut
from butt
3 tablespoons oil
2 cloves garlic, minced
3 tablespoons brown
bean paste
1 tablespoon
granulated sugar
1 tablespoon pale dry
sherry
1 cup chicken stock
1 cup water
2 teaspoons tapioca
powder mixed with 1
tablespoon chicken
stock
2 teaspoons sesame oil

PREPARATION

1 Cut gluten into 1-inch cubes.

2 Cut pork into cubes the same size as the gluten.

COOKING

1 Set a heavy Dutch oven over high heat. When hot, add the oil. Flavor oil with garlic for 20 seconds, then add bean paste and sugar, stirring until paste turns thin.

2 Add the pork, stirring for 5 minutes or until the pink color disappears. Sizzle in the wine, then add the gluten, stirring for 5 minutes more.

3 Pour in the chicken stock and water and bring to a boil. Turn heat to low and cover pan. Cook slowly until the pork is tender, about 40 minutes. Replenish with some water if needed.

4 Correct seasoning, then stream tapioca mixture into the pot. When sauce bubbles and thickens, glaze with sesame oil. Mix well and serve.

⊛⊛⊛Braised Gluten Puffs in Shrimp Roe Sauce

Serves 6 in a Chinese family meal
Time 30 minutes rinsing
overnight + 2 hours resting
20 minutes deep-frying
30 minutes cooking

蝦子生筋

This dish, common all over China, is indescribably tasty with the soft, chewy, yellow gluten puffs enveloped in brown shrimp roe sauce. Gluten Puffs with Frogs' Leg is a Cantonese banquet variant.

Ingredients

2 pounds unbleached all-purpose flour
6 cups + 2 tablespoons oil
1 tablespoon shrimp roe
2 teaspoons + 1 tablespoon yellow wine
1 teaspoon granulated sugar

2 slices gingerroot
2 cloves garlic, crushed
1 teaspoon tapioca powder mixed with 1 tablespoon water
2 teaspoons sesame oil
1 sprig Chinese parsley, leaves only

Braising sauce

1½ cups chicken stock
2 tablespoons oyster sauce
½ teaspoon granulated sugar
¼ teaspoon salt
Dash of white pepper

PREPARATION

1 Follow the master recipe (page 337) for preparing the raw gluten from the flour, then set the raw gluten in the refrigerator for 2 hours to firm.

2 Blot the piece of raw gluten dry with paper towels, then break into small balls about 1 inch in diameter. You will have about 40 balls altogether.

3 Set a wok over high heat. When very hot, add the 6 cups oil. Wait for about 3 to 4 minutes, then test the temperature by dropping a piece of scallion green into the oil. If bubbles appear around the green slowly, the oil is about 250 degrees. Turn heat to medium.

4 Divide gluten balls into 4 batches and deep-fry no more than 10 pieces each time. Drop gluten balls 1 at a time into the oil and separate them. When the balls start to puff and sizzle gradually, turn each piece over and press it against the wall of the wok so it will puff into a hollow ball. Stir the puffs constantly until the puffs do not inflate any further and the skin turns light yellow. Remove gluten puffs to drain in a colander set over a large bowl. Finish deep-frying the remaining 3 batches in the same fashion.

5 Cut each puff in half. Blanch them in boiling water for 2 minutes. Pour into a colander and run cold water over to rinse. Drain thoroughly. If not used immediately, chill in refrigerator; otherwise squeeze to extract as much moisture as possible.

6 Combine shrimp roe, 2 teaspoons of the yellow wine, sugar, and ginger in a small heatproof bowl. Steam over medium heat for 15 minutes. Discard ginger.

COOKING

1 Set a heavy 3-quart saucepan over high heat. When very hot, add the remaining oil. Flavor oil with garlic until brown and discard garlic. Sizzle in the remaining wine and immediately add the braising sauce. When sauce boils, add the shrimp roe, stirring a few times around, then add the gluten puffs. Bring the sauce back to boil. Turn heat to medium. Cover; cook 20 to 25 minutes or until sauce is almost absorbed.

2 Push the puffs to the side of the saucepan, leaving a space in the center. Restir the tapioca mixture and stream it gradually into the pan, stirring to prevent lumps.

3 Glaze sauce with sesame oil and mix it with the gluten puffs. Remove to a serving platter. Decorate with parsley leaves and serve.

Note: Gluten puff is available in some oriental markets.

SEAWEEDS

Seaweeds grown along the China coast provide nourishment for millions, as well as much needed organic iodine. The love for seaweeds is shared by the Koreans and the Japanese, and many seaweed products sold in U.S. markets are packaged in Japan.

Flaky purple *zicai* ("purple vegetable"; *nori* in Japanese), sold in thin sheets, burst into ten thousand flying veils in boiling stock to make a tasty soup. Another favorite soup ingredient is kelp, much more substantial and chewier. It is also tied in small knots in stews, the better to absorb the juices.

Dried agar-agar comes in slender strips like translucent spaghetti, or in blocks each roughly 1 inch thick and 8 inches long. Most Americans are familiar with it only as the base for bacteria culture, and may even shudder at the thought of eating it. But why not? It is tasty, nourishing, and one of the most sanitary foods obtainable (contains no bacteria; the latter have to be introduced artificially from the outside). Agar-agar makes a transparent jelly with an unusual texture; unlike animal-based gelatin which is elastic to the bite, agar jelly breaks cleanly and readily.

A freshwater weed bears mentioning here. Hair vegetable *(facai)*, which looks like a bundle of black human hair, is an alga found in streams in North China. It has an unusual texture, absorbs seasoning well, and is an important ingredient in Chinese vegetarian cuisine. Because it rhymes with "make money" in Chinese, *facai* is consumed in large quantities during the Chinese New Year holidays.

⊛⊛⊛ Seaweed Rolls

Serves 8 as an appetizer, or as part
of the hot platters in a
banquet
Time 40 minutes preparation
10 minutes cooking

This is a delicious hors d'oeuvre, also an elegant main dish.

Ingredients	Seasonings
1 pound shrimp in the shell	2 egg whites
Salt	1 tablespoon tapioca powder
6 sheets *nori*	1 teaspoon pale dry sherry
2 egg yolks, lightly beaten	1 teaspoon sesame oil
4 cups oil	Dash of white pepper
	¼ teaspoon granulated sugar

PREPARATION

1 Shell and devein the shrimp. Put in a colander and rub generously with salt a few times. Rinse off mucus with cold running water until the shrimp turns translucent, then drain and pat thoroughly dry with paper towels.

2 Mash the shrimp meat a small handful at a time with the flat side of a cleaver. Mince until fine, adding about ¾ teaspoon of salt while mincing.

3 Combine the shrimp with the seasonings in a large mixing bowl. Stir with chopsticks or a wooden spoon in 1 direction until the mixture is elastic. Scoop up the shrimp mixture with your hand and beat it back to the bowl several times to firm it. Chill for at least 2 hours or until ready to use.

4 Cut each *nori* sheet into 4 squares, each 3 inches in size.

ASSEMBLING

1 Spread about 2 tablespoons of shrimp paste along the lower edge of the *nori* sheet.

2 Roll firmly away from you. Seal the upper edge with egg yolk.

COOKING

1 Set a wok over high heat. When hot, add the oil. Wait for about 5 minutes, then test the temperature by dropping in a small piece of scallion green. If bubbles appear around the green and it sizzles and moves in the oil, the oil is hot enough (about 325 degrees). Otherwise wait a little longer and test again.

2 Drop all the rolls into the oil in succession, then turn the heat to medium. Continue to deep-fry until the rolls float to the top. Remove and drain; serve hot.

⊛Red-Cooked Chicken with Kelp

Serves 4 as a main dish with rice and vegetable
Time 20 minutes preparation
2 hours marinating
1 hour, 15 minutes cooking

海 帶 炆 雞

This dish is from East China, an area which uses a great variety of seaweeds. The kelp absorbs the juices of the chicken for a particularly flavorful treat.

Ingredients	Marinade	Braising sauce
1 small frying chicken, about 3 pounds	2 tablespoons dark soy sauce	2 cups chicken stock
2 ounces dried kelp	1 teaspoon ginger juice	1 tablespoon red rice vinegar
4 tablespoons oil	2 tablespoons pale dry sherry	1 tablespoon granulated sugar
5 whole scallions, rinsed and cut into 4-inch lengths		1 tablespoon dark soy sauce
2 tablespoons pale dry sherry		½ teaspoon salt
1 teaspoon sesame oil		

PREPARATION

1 Rub chicken with a Nylon scrubber to remove any yellow film on the skin. Rinse outside and cavity thoroughly, then split in half along the breast and back. Pat dry with paper towels and place in a bowl.

2 Mix ingredients for marinade and add to bowl with chicken. Turn chicken to coat evenly, then set at room temperature for 2 hours (or refrigerate overnight). Turn chicken pieces occasionally.

3 Soak kelp in boiling water to cover, then let sit until cool. Clean thoroughly, then cut into 2 by 1½-inch pieces. Drain.

4 Drain chicken and reserve marinade. Add marinade to braising sauce ingredients.

COOKING

1 Set a wok over high heat. When very hot, add 2 tablespoons of oil. Stir-fry the scallions until they are wilted, then remove.

2 Add remaining 2 tablespoons of oil to the wok. Place in the chicken, skin side down first. Turn heat to medium and brown the chicken on both sides.

3 Sizzle in the wine along the edge of the wok and then add the braising sauce, including the marinade. Also add the scallions, then place the kelp on top. Bring to a boil, then turn heat to low. Cover and cook for 1 hour, or until the chicken and kelp are soft. Correct seasoning and discard the scallions.

4 Remove kelp to line a serving platter. Bone the chicken and cut into 2 by 1-inch pieces. Arrange the chicken pieces on top of the kelp. If not to be served immediately, cover with plastic wrap and set at room temperature.

5 Just before serving, reheat the braising sauce. Glaze with sesame oil and pour on top of chicken. Serve hot or slightly warm.

◉Tossed Seaweed Salad

Serves 4 as an accompaniment to other dishes in a Chinese meal
Time 30 minutes preparation
10 minutes cooking

涼拌洋菜

Chinese salads often feature a blending of unlike textures. In this recipe, crunchy bean sprouts join up with chewy agar-agar strips in a salad of spinach which has been lightly blanched. A sprinkling of roasted sesame seeds makes every bite a discovery.

Ingredients	**Dressing**
1 pound fresh spinach	1 clove garlic
1 pound bean sprouts	1 scallion (white part only), chopped
1 ounce agar-agar strips	1 tablespoon red rice vinegar
½ teaspoon chicken bouillon powder	2 tablespoons light soy sauce
2 tablespoons granulated sugar	2 teaspoons granulated sugar
2 tablespoons toasted sesame seeds	1 tablespoon sesame oil
	4 tablespoons peanut oil

PREPARATION

1 Pick over the spinach and discard any withered leaves. Remove roots and stems. Use the leaves only. Rinse and drain thoroughly.

2 Remove roots from bean sprouts. Soak in cold water and keep refrigerated until ready to use.

3 Rinse agar-agar quickly with warm water. Squeeze to extract as much moisture as possible. Cut into 2-inch lengths. Put agar-agar into a bowl and sprinkle with chicken bouillon powder. Toss well.

4 Combine ingredients for dressing in a jar. Shake well and chill.

5 Half-fill a 4-quart saucepan with water. Set over high heat and bring to a boil. Add sugar, then spinach, stirring until leaves are wilted and water has returned to a boil.

BUDDHA'S DELIGHT
PAGE 334

BRAISED CAULIFLOWER IN HAM SAUCE
PAGE 361

EIGHT-TREASURE WINTER MELON SOUP
PAGE 114

STUFFED CRAB LEGS
PAGE 171

6 Pour spinach into a colander and rinse with cold water to stop the cooking process. Put a round pan under the colander to catch the drippings and keep refrigerated.

7 Drain sprouts in a colander and place colander in a large mixing bowl. Pour boiling water over sprouts, stirring with chopsticks several times. Remove colander from pot and drain and chill sprouts.

8 Squeeze as much moisture from the spinach as possible. Combine with bean sprouts, sesame seeds, and agar-agar in a salad bowl. Shake dressing and add to vegetables. Toss and correct seasoning. Serve.

Vegetables

Virtually the only thing the Chinese do not seem to do to vegetables is to eat them raw, yet traditionally even scallions and Chinese parsley leaves are eaten uncooked, as are cucumbers and white radishes (Chinese turnips), after pickling or marinating. As a result of Western influences, leafy vegetables, tomatoes, and cucumbers are now served uncooked in Chinese restaurants in Hong Kong, usually as garnishes. Lettuce is never cooked by Americans, yet in Chinese cookery lettuce is stir-fried or boiled, making it tender yet crisp.

There really is no one treatment for each class of vegetable; it depends on the purpose the cook has in mind. For example, vegetables are usually never overcooked because they become a mash, yet Mash-Paste Chinese Cabbage is a specialty of East China. We give a general classification of vegetables here, with some basic guidelines on how they are usually prepared.

STARCHY VEGETABLES AND ROOTS

This group includes such vegetables as taro, chestnuts, potatoes, and sweet potatoes. Normally, prolonged heating brings out the starchiness. Seasonings do not permeate the vegetables, yet these foods provide their own characteristic flavor; external flavorings are sometimes added with a gravy or sauce. Often the vegetables are cooked separately, then combined with meat in a second stage of cooking. Yams are not used in China and you should not substitute them for sweet potatoes, since the former has a pulpy consistency after cooking.

ABSORBENT ROOT VEGETABLES AND SQUASHES

This group includes such vegetables as turnips, radishes, carrots, melons, gourds, and squashes. They offer a texture base and they absorb flavors from the seasonings in which they are boiled, braised, or stir-fried. Braised Chinese Pumpkin with Spareribs in Black Bean Sauce is a great favorite around Canton. (The American pumpkin is very much looser in texture than the Chinese pumpkin and is not as suitable as the firmer-fleshed butternut squash.)

Unique Chinese vegetables in this class include the winter melon, the fuzzy melon, and the luffa (silk melon). Roll-cut young luffa when used in soups is zestfully green and very refreshing; zucchini can often be substituted. A whole steamed winter melon is a container for a fabulous soup—the Winter Melon Pond. The diner eats the container along with the soup, reminding one of how an ice cream cone is enjoyed.

FIBROUS VEGETABLES

These include green cabbage, Chinese cabbage (bok choy), celery cabbage, napa cabbage, mustard greens, onions, green beans, bamboo shoots, cauliflower, broccoli, and especially Chinese broccoli. To break down the fibers when stir-frying, add a little water in the later stages and cover; usually the degree of doneness can be judged by the color. Strong fibers often remain tough despite cooking; they should be removed first.

TENDER PARTS OF FIBROUS VEGETABLES

Vegetables such as snow peas, young asparagus spears, and young shoots of fibrous vegetables are kept crisp by very quick stir-frying. Sprinkle a little water during the last stage, but do not cover. Before cooking, remove any strings at the edge of the larger pea pods and cut off the tough bottoms of asparagus spears.

TENDER VEGETABLES

Bean sprouts, spinach, watercress, and lettuce are usually cooked only briefly, such as in stir-fries, with no covering and no water added. Tender green vegetables are often used to line a red-cooked dish so as to absorb the sauce.

DRIED VEGETABLES

These include black mushrooms, straw mushrooms, tiger lily buds, lotus roots, lotus seeds, red dates, and other dried foods. They need to be soaked before cooking to absorb moisture; the soaking juice for the mushrooms is flavorful and can be used in soups and sauces. In Chinese cooking, some dried vegetables are valued higher than their fresh counterparts.

CANNED AND FROZEN VEGETABLES

The Chinese do not use canned vegetables, preferring instead the fresh article. Nevertheless, some Chinese vegetables are available in the United States only in

cans. The most popular ones are bamboo shoots (several kinds), water chestnuts, miniature corn, and straw mushrooms. To remove the metallic taste imparted by the container, blanch the contents in boiling water and then rinse with cold water before using in a recipe. (We have found that American frozen green peas and broad beans are excellent for stir-fries, and both frozen and canned corn are good for soups.)

The following recipes are all meant as accompaniments to a selection of main dishes. You will also find that many of the recipes for main dishes feature vegetables.

⊚ Stir-Fried Tender Vegetables

Serves 2
Time 10 minutes preparation
3 minutes cooking

炒菜 (一)

This is a general recipe that can be used to prepare a wide variety of dishes.

Ingredients

3 cups vegetables
(lettuce, spinach,
watercress, zucchini
or cucumber, bean
sprouts, or fresh
mushrooms)

3 tablespoons oil
1 clove garlic, crushed
¾ teaspoon salt

PREPARATION

For *lettuce:* Separate leaves, rinse, break into 2-inch lengths, and drain. For *spinach:* Trim roots; cut the stems and leaves into 2-inch lengths, rinse, and drain. For *watercress:* Cut off the bunch just above the point where stem joins the leaves, and discard stems; rinse and drain. For *zucchini or cucumber:* Cut in half lengthwise; slice each half diagonally into slices ⅛ inch thick. For *bean sprouts:* Fill the sink with cold water and put in sprouts; green husks of the beans will sink to the bottom and the loose roots and sprouts will float to top and can be scooped up easily. Stir gently to loosen ends, then take a handful of sprouts at a time and put in a colander to drain. For *mushrooms:* Do not rinse. Trim tough ends and wipe mushrooms with dampened cloth or peel skin with a paring knife; cut caps vertically into ¼-inch slices.

COOKING

1 Set a wok over high heat. When very hot, add oil. Flavor oil with garlic until brown, then discard.

2 Sprinkle salt onto oil. Add vegetables, stirring and turning until each piece is well coated with oil and becomes soft, about 2 minutes. Remove and serve.

⊛Stir-Fried Fibrous Vegetables

Serves 2
Time 5 minutes preparation
5 minutes cooking

炒菜 (二)

This is a general recipe for vegetables such as cabbage, mustard greens, onions, bamboo shoots, cauliflower, or broccoli.

Ingredients

3 cups vegetables (bok
 choy, napa cabbage,
 mustard greens)
3 tablespoons oil
3 slices gingerroot
¾ teaspoon salt
2 tablespoons water or
 chicken stock

PREPARATION

Separate stalks or pieces of vegetable. Cut each piece into 2-inch lengths. Rinse and drain thoroughly.

COOKING

1 Set a wok over high heat. When very hot, add oil. Flavor oil with ginger until light brown, then discard.

2 Add vegetables, stirring and turning until each piece is well coated with oil.

3 Season vegetables with salt. Whirl in water or stock along edge of wok and cover immediately. Cook for 2 minutes, then turn off heat.

4 Keep wok covered for 1 more minute, then serve immediately.

◉◉Stir-Fried Mixed Chinese Vegetables

Serves 4 to 6
Time 20 minutes preparation
5 minutes cooking

炒雜錦菜

The taste of this colorful collection of crunchy vegetables is accented by the unique flavor of black mushrooms.

Ingredients

8 medium black
mushrooms
2 stalks young celery
½ cup bamboo shoots
6 ounces snow peas
4 water chestnuts
½ medium carrot
4 tablespoons oil
2 slices gingerroot

1 teaspoon granulated
sugar
½ teaspoon salt
½ teaspoon chicken
bouillon powder
1 teaspoon tapioca
powder mixed with 1
tablespoon water
(optional)

PREPARATION

1 Soak mushrooms in 1 cup warm water until soft. Squeeze to extract moisture, then trim and discard tough stems. Cut each cap into quarters. Reserve ¼ cup of the soaking liquid.

2 String fibers of celery. Rinse, then cut diagonally into ¼-inch slices.

3 Slice bamboo shoots into pieces 1 by 1½ by ⅛ inch. Bring some water in a saucepan to a boil and blanch shoots 1 minute, then remove to a colander. Run cold water over them to stop the cooking process and drain well.

4 Break off the tips of the snow peas and remove the strings. Rinse and drain.

5 Slice water chestnuts horizontally into ⅛-inch pieces.

6 Scrape carrot. Cut crosswise into ⅛-inch slices.

COOKING

1 Set a wok over high heat until the bottom turns a dull red. Add 3 tablespoons oil. When oil is hot and smoky, add ginger briefly to flavor oil, then discard when brown. Add mushrooms, stirring and turning, for 30 seconds. Add carrot and reserved mushroom liquid. Cook until moisture is evaporated.

2 Stir in, in succession, celery, bamboo shoots, and water chestnuts, making sure each piece is coated with oil. Add sugar and stir.

3 Push vegetables to the side of wok, add remaining oil, then put in snow peas. Season with salt and chicken bouillon powder. If a sauce is desired, stir in the tapioca mixture. Mix all ingredients together. Serve.

Stir-Fried Broccoli with Ginger and Brandy

Serves 2 to 4
Time 5 minutes preparation
3 minutes cooking

薑汁酒炒芥蘭

This is one of the dishes that made Cantonese cuisine famous in this country. The broccoli remains appetizingly green, and the texture is unusually crunchy.

Ingredients

1 bunch regular
 broccoli (about 1¼
 pounds, yielding 4
 cups)
2 teaspoons grated
 gingerroot
2 tablespoons brandy
1 tablespoon
 granulated sugar
3 tablespoons oil
¾ teaspoon salt
3 tablespoons water

PREPARATION

1 Separate broccoli stems from flowerets. Peel skin from stems. Cut flowerets into even sections, then cut stems diagonally into slices ¼ inch thick. Rinse and drain thoroughly.

2 Place ginger in a small bowl and add brandy. Mix together and put mixture through a fine sieve. Press grated ginger against the wall of the sieve to extract as much juice as possible.

3 Add sugar to mixture. Mix well. (Sugar helps keep the broccoli bright green.)

COOKING

1 Set a wok over high heat. When very hot, add the oil. When the oil is hot, sprinkle in salt. Immediately add broccoli, stirring and turning until each piece is well coated with oil, about 1 minute.

2 Sizzle in brandy mixture along the edge of the wok, stirring until evaporated. Sprinkle water onto broccoli, then cover wok. Turn off heat and wait 1 minute. Remove broccoli and serve.

◉ Stir-Fried Empty-Hearted Vegetable with Shrimp Paste

Serves 2 to 3
Time 10 minutes preparation
5 minutes cooking

蝦醬炒通心菜

This is a very appetizing dish in southern China, where the empty-hearted vegetables grow widely in the water fields. The shrimp paste compliments the vegetable just splendidly.

Ingredients

1 pound
  empty-hearted
  vegetable
3 tablespoons oil
2 cloves garlic, minced
1 tablespoon shrimp
  paste (page 43) or 3
  pieces bean cheese, 1
  inch square
2 teaspoons granulated
  sugar
1 red chili pepper
  (optional), shredded
  finely

PREPARATION AND COOKING

1 Rinse empty-hearted vegetable. Break into 3-inch lengths and discard the fibrous part near the end of the stalk. Drain thoroughly.

2 Set a wok over high heat. When very hot, add the oil. Flavor oil with garlic until light brown, then add shrimp paste (or bean cheese), sugar, and chili pepper, if used, stirring constantly until flavor escapes. Add the vegetable, stirring and turning until each piece is well coated with oil and is limp. Continue to stir and cook for 2 more minutes. Serve.

Note: The hollow stems of the empty-hearted vegetable capture a lot of water. You should drain it thoroughly before cooking or else the temperature of the wok will be brought down immediately. The best way is to spin off the moisture in a salad spinner.

◉Stir-Fried Zucchini with Garlic

Serves 2 as a vegetable dish
Time 5 minutes preparation
15 minutes salting
5 minutes cooking

蒜炒意大利絲瓜

Salting the shredded zucchini mellows the bitterness of the skin, and the added garlic flavor makes the dish unusual.

Ingredients
1 pound zucchini
1½ teaspoons salt
3 tablespoons oil
2 cloves garlic,
   shredded
1 teaspoon granulated
   sugar

PREPARATION AND COOKING

1 With a vegetable shredder, shred the zucchini into a colander and sprinkle on salt. Stir to mix the salt with the zucchini and set at room temperature for 15 minutes, then squeeze gently to extract excess moisture.

2 Set a wok over high heat. When very hot, add the oil. Put in garlic shreds, stirring for 20 seconds, then add the zucchini shreds. Continue to stir for 2 minutes, adding sugar. Remove and serve.

◉Stir-Fried Luffa Squash with Cloud Ears and Onion

Serves 4 as a vegetable dish
Time 10 minutes preparation
15 minutes soaking
7 minutes cooking

洋蔥雲耳炒絲瓜

Luffa squash is a southern vegetable for the hot summer. The country folks love to steam it plain, but it goes splendidly with cloud ears and onions in a stir-fry.

Ingredients

¼ cup cloud ears
1 pound luffa squash
1 medium onion
3 tablespoons oil
2 slices gingerroot

¼ teaspoon salt
2 cups hot water
1 teaspoon chicken
    bouillon powder

PREPARATION

1 Soak cloud ears in hot water for 15 minutes or until expanded. Trim tough ends and drain.

2 Scrape the tough ridges on the skin of the luffa squash, using a vegetable peeler. Roll-cut the squash into 1½-inch wedges.

3 Cut onion crosswise in half, then quarter each half. Separate layers.

COOKING

1 Set a wok over high heat. When the wok is very hot, add the oil. Flavor the oil with ginger until brown, then remove and discard ginger.

2 Add salt to the oil, then the onion and cloud ears, stirring constantly for 2 minutes. Whirl in the water along the edge of the wok, adding the squash wedges. Continue to stir until the squash is soft, about 2 minutes. Season with chicken bouillon powder. Stir to mix well and serve.

Note: Luffa squash is available only in the summer in Oriental markets. Cucumber is a good substitute for this recipe.

⊛Stir-Fried Cabbage with Tomato

Serves 4 as a side dish
Time 5 minutes preparation
5 minutes cooking

蕃 茄 炒 椰 菜

A very common family dish in South China.

Ingredients

1 small head of
    cabbage, about 1
    pound
4 medium, ripe
    tomatoes, about ¾
    pound
3 tablespoons oil

1 clove garlic, crushed
1 teaspoon salt
1 teaspoon granulated
    sugar
⅛ teaspoon white
    pepper

PREPARATION

1 Remove the outer layer of leaves from cabbage. Cut into strips about ½ inch wide and 2 inches in length.

2 Rinse tomatoes, then remove stems. Cut each tomato into 6 equal segments lengthwise.

COOKING

1 Set a wok over high heat. When very hot, add oil.

2 Flavor oil with garlic until brown. Add cabbage to wok, stirring and turning until each piece is well coated with oil and limp, about 3 minutes.

3 Add tomatoes, salt, sugar, and pepper. Continue to stir and turn for 2 minutes.

4 Cover wok. Turn heat off. Set for 1 minute. Serve.

◉Stir-Fried Tomato in Egg Sauce

Serves 4 as a vegetable dish
Time 10 minutes preparation
5 minutes cooking

蛋燴蕃茄

An appetite-promoting dish welcomed by people from all over China.

Ingredients

1 pound firm, ripe, medium tomatoes
2 whole eggs
3 tablespoons oil
½ teaspoon salt
1 clove garlic, minced
1 whole scallion, chopped finely
2 teaspoons pale dry sherry

⅛ teaspoon white pepper
2 teaspoons granulated sugar
1 teaspoon chicken bouillon powder
2 teaspoons tapioca powder mixed with 1 tablespoon water
1 teaspoon sesame oil

PREPARATION

1 Rinse tomatoes and put them in a large bowl. Pour enough boiling water to cover and set for 1 minute. Remove stems and peel skin of the tomatoes.

2 Cut each tomato crosswise in half. Squeeze each half gently to extract seeds and juice, then cut each half into 3 wedges.

3 Beat eggs with 1 tablespoon of the oil and a pinch of the salt.

COOKING

1 Set a wok over high heat, when very hot, add the remaining oil. Flavor oil with garlic and scallion for 10 seconds, then sizzle in the wine and immediately add the tomato wedges, stirring constantly until the natural juices escape, about 1 minute. Season with the salt, pepper, sugar, and chicken bouillon powder and stir to mix well.

2 Push tomato to the side of the wok and add the tapioca mixture to the center, stirring until bubbly.

3 Mix sauce with the tomato, whirl in the egg mixture around the wok, and continue to stir until the egg sets. Add sesame oil to glaze and serve.

◉Quick-Fried Broad Beans with Ham

Serves 4 as a part of a multi-dish meal
Time 25 minutes preparation
5 minutes cooking

火 腿 炒 蠶豆

Broad beans (fava beans) are known in southern China chiefly as the basis for inexpensive snacks, deep-fried or boiled. With their thick, tough skin peeled off, however, they are tender and sweet, and when accompanied by thin pieces of ham, they are fit for a North China banquet.

Ingredients

2 packages (8 ounces) frozen broad beans or 2 cups fresh broad beans
1 ounce Smithfield ham
1 cup oil for quick-frying
1 clove garlic, crushed

2 teaspoons pale dry sherry
½ cup chicken stock
¼ teaspoon salt
1 teaspoon granulated sugar
Dash of white pepper
1 teaspoon sesame oil

Sauce thickener

2 teaspoons tapioca powder
2 tablespoons chicken stock

PREPARATION

1 Thaw frozen broad beans completely. Remove skins and drain.

2 Cut ham into slices about ⅛ inch thick, then cut into ½-inch cubes.

3 Mix sauce thickener.

COOKING

1 Put a sieve over a bowl.

2 Set a wok over high heat. When very hot, add the oil. Use a spatula to swirl the oil around the wok twice. Add the broad beans, stirring constantly for 1 minute or until the beans turn bright green.

3 Remove beans and oil together into the sieve to drain, leaving about 1 teaspoon oil in wok.

4 Put in garlic and fry 10 seconds, then discard. Sizzle in sherry. Immediately add the chicken stock and ham. Bring to a boil. Cook 30 seconds. Season with salt, sugar, and pepper.

5 Give the sauce thickener a quick stir, then stream into the sauce, stirring until sauce is clear and thickened.

6 Return broad beans to wok. Mix together with sauce.

7 Glaze sauce with sesame oil and serve.

◉◉ Country-Style Potato Pancake

Serves	4 to 6 in a multi-dish meal
Time	30 minutes preparation
	30 minutes cooking

家鄉薯仔餅

Winter brings the northern wind, best suited for curing sausages. This potato pancake featuring sausages remains seasonal in Chinese tradition, even after these ingredients have become available year round. Pan-frying makes it crispy on both sides, to contrast with the soft interior of the chewy Chinese sausage.

Ingredients

3 medium black
   mushrooms
1 pound Idaho
   potatoes
1 sprig Chinese parsley
1 whole scallion, trimmed
2 Chinese sausages,
   about 2 ounces

½ teaspoon salt
⅛ teaspoon white
   pepper
1 teaspoon sesame oil
4 tablespoons oil

PREPARATION

1 Soak mushrooms in warm water until soft. Trim the stems, then squeeze water out of caps. Cut each cap into ⅛-inch bits.

2 Peel potatoes. Rinse, then grate potatoes coarsely into a mixing bowl. Spoon off about 1 tablespoon of the excessive juice.

3 Rinse parsley and scallion. Chop finely. Also chop sausages into fine bits.

4 Add salt, pepper, sesame oil, mushrooms, and sausages, to the bowl; mix well. Fold in scallion and parsley.

COOKING

1 Set a wok over high heat. When very hot, add 1 tablespoon of the oil. Swish the oil around the inside surface of the wok, using a spatula. Then turn heat to medium high.

2 Add one-fourth of the potato mixture to the center of wok. Press with the spatula to flatten the potato mixture to shape it into a pancake about 6 inches in diameter and ¼ inch thick. Pan-fry until the bottom side is brown, about 3 minutes, then turn to brown the other side for another 3 minutes. Remove to a platter.

3 Use 1 tablespoon of the oil to pan-fry each pancake in the same manner, to yield 4 pancakes in all. Allow to rest at room temperature for 5 minutes, then serve pancakes warm.

◉◉◉Fava Bean Pâté

Serves 6 in a family meal
Time 3 days to 1 week soaking
1 hour preparation
20 minutes cooking

豆 瓣酥

A year-round country cold dish from East China, with an interesting coarse texture.

Ingredients

1 pound dried fava
  beans
⅓ cup red-in-snow
  (packed)
¼ cup Sichuan
  preserved vegetable
3 cups water

6 tablespoons oil
2 teaspoons granulated
  sugar
1 cup chicken stock
Salt, if necessary
1 tablespoon sesame oil

PREPARATION

1 Rinse and check over beans; discard bad ones. Put them in a large bowl, adding cold water to cover. Soak at room temperature and change water twice a day. It takes about 3 to 4 days in the summer or 5 to 7 days in winter for the fava beans to sprout.

2 Select 4 cups of the sprouted fava beans for use in this recipe. Remove skins from the beans.

3 Reserve the remaining fava beans for other use (very good for soup, see page 118).

4 Soak red-in-snow in cold water for 20 minutes. Rinse well. Chop finely to the size of bacon bits.

5 Rinse off chili coating from the Sichuan preserved vegetable. Slice thinly first, then chop finely.

COOKING

1 Put skinless fava beans in a heavy 2-quart saucepan. Add water. Cook over low heat for 30 to 40 minutes or until fava beans are soft and the liquid is almost absorbed.

2 Use a potato masher to mash the fava beans coarsely while they are still hot; the mashed beans should resemble rolled oats.

3 Set a wok over high heat. When very hot, add 3 tablespoons of the oil. Stir-fry the red-in-snow and Sichuan preserved vegetable for 1 minute. Add mashed beans, sugar, and ½ cup stock, stirring and pressing with the spatula for 5 minutes over medium-low heat.

4 Add 3 more tablespoons of oil to the beans. Mix in remaining stock. Stir and press until the mashed beans turn finer and are pastelike, about 5 minutes.

5 Test for salt. (Note that no salt has been added so far owing to the salty taste of the preserved vegetables.) Add sesame oil. Mix well.

6 Remove mashed beans to a small loaf pan about 4 by 3 by 2¼ inches in size. Press bean mash firmly in with a serving spoon. Chill for at least 2 hours.

7 Turn fava bean pâté out onto a platter. Serve with a spoon.

⊚Braised Eggplant with Bean Paste

Serves 2
Time 5 minutes preparation
15 minutes cooking

麵豉炆茄子

A country dish for the average Chinese family, served with plain rice.

Ingredients

1 large eggplant, or 1 pound equivalent long eggplant
2 tablespoons brown bean paste
2 teaspoons granulated sugar
1 whole scallion, trimmed
3 tablespoons oil

1 clove garlic, minced
¾ cup + 2 tablespoons chicken stock
2 teaspoons tapioca powder
2 teaspoons sesame oil

PREPARATION

1 Cut eggplant lengthwise into 8 equal segments. Cut each segment diagonally into slices about 1 inch thick. (If long eggplant is used, roll-cut into uniform wedges.)

2 Mix bean paste and sugar in a small bowl.

3 Chop scallion finely.

COOKING

1 Set a heavy casserole or Dutch oven over high heat. When very hot, add oil. Flavor oil with garlic for 10 seconds, then add bean paste–and–sugar mixture, stirring until paste becomes thin and sugar melts—about 10 seconds.

2 Add eggplant, stirring until each piece is well coated with oil. Add ¾ cup chicken stock and bring to a boil. Reduce heat to medium and cover pan. Cook 10 minutes, checking occasionally. Replenish with more chicken stock if mixture becomes dry.

3 When eggplant is soft, mix together tapioca powder with remaining chicken stock. Push eggplant to the side of the pan and stream in mixture, stirring until bubbly. Add sesame oil to glaze, then mix in scallion. Remove and serve hot.

VARIATION
For a peppery taste, replace brown bean paste with 1 tablespoon Sichuan hot bean paste plus 1 tablespoon sweet bean paste.

❀❀Braised Cauliflower in Ham Sauce

Serves 4
Time 10 minutes preparation
30 minutes cooking

腿汁會菜花

Also called Red Plum Flowers over the Snowy Mountain.

Ingredients
1 small head cauliflower, about 1 pound
2 ounces Smithfield ham
2 cups Basic Soup Stock (page 118)
¼ teaspoon salt

Sauce
3 tablespoons oil
1 clove garlic, crushed
1½ tablespoons cornstarch
Dash of white pepper
¼ teaspoon salt
½ teaspoon granulated sugar
1 teaspoon sesame oil

PREPARATION

1 Trim green leaves and tough parts of stem from cauliflower. Rinse. Keep it in 1 piece.

2 Chop finely about 2 tablespoons of the ham and reserve. Thinly slice the remaining portion.

COOKING

1 Place soup stock and ham in a saucepan large enough to hold the cauliflower snugly. Set over high heat and bring to a boil. Add cauliflower and bring back to boil. Turn heat to medium, add salt, cover pan, and cook 20 minutes, or until a chopstick can go through the center part of cauliflower easily. Drain cooking liquid through a fine sieve and reserve. Keep cauliflower covered. Remove ham.

2 Prepare sauce. Set a small saucepan over medium heat. When hot, add 2 tablespoons oil. Flavor oil with garlic for 15 seconds, then discard garlic. Add cornstarch, stirring for about 30 seconds. Stream in hot chicken broth (from cooking cauliflower), gradually mixing it with cornstarch. Stir constantly until sauce thickens.

3 Mix chopped ham into sauce and season with pepper, salt, and sugar. Glaze the sauce with remaining tablespoon of oil and sesame oil.

4 Place cauliflower in a deep serving dish and pour sauce over. Serve whole, to be broken up with a spoon at the table.

⊛Braised Butternut Squash with Black Beans

Serves 6
Time   10 minutes preparation
            30 minutes soaking
            15 minutes cooking

豆豉炆南瓜

The Chinese pumpkin is an inexpensive and starchy vegetable used commonly in the southern China countryside, but it is different from the Western pumpkin. We found the butternut squash is a very close substitute.

Ingredients

1 mature butternut
  squash, about 2
  pounds
3 tablespoons
  fermented black
  beans
1 tablespoon warm
  water

3 tablespoons oil
2 cloves garlic, crushed
1 tablespoon pale dry
  sherry
¾ cup water
½ teaspoon salt
1 teaspoon chicken
  bouillon powder

PREPARATION

1 Wash the outer skin of squash well. Cut off stem and nearby tough parts. Cut squash in half. Remove seeds and pulp, then cut into 1-inch chunks.

2 Rinse black beans. Soak in warm water for 30 minutes.

COOKING

1 Set a wok over high heat. When very hot, add oil. Add garlic and fry 10 seconds. Add black beans, stirring once around, then add squash chunks. Stir constantly until every piece of squash is well coated with oil, about 1 minute.

2 Sizzle in the wine along the edge of wok and add the water. Season the squash with salt and bouillon powder.

3 Cover wok. Maintain high heat and cook squash for 5 minutes. Stir in a spading manner to turn the chunks around for even cooking. Cook 5 more minutes or until liquid is almost absorbed. Serve.

◉◉Braised Radish Balls with Dried Shrimp

Serves 4 to 6
Time 30 minutes preparation
       30 minutes soaking
       25 minutes cooking

蝦米蘿蔔球

Long white radishes in their original form are a lowly vegetable for the average Chinese. But when shaped into balls, they become a treasure. The milder taste, fine texture, and round shape of the American red radish is best suited for this recipe, except that the peeling of the skin takes a little time.

Ingredients

36 large red radishes
¼ cup dried shrimp
¾ cup warm water
2 tablespoons oil
1 clove garlic, crushed
1 cup thin chicken
    stock

½ teaspoon granulated
    sugar
½ teaspoon salt
1 teaspoon sesame oil

PREPARATION

1 Buy several bunches of fresh red radishes. Select the large and uniform ones; reserve the smaller ones for other use. Rinse, then use a vegetable peeler to remove the skins.

2 Soak the dried shrimp in warm water until soft, about 30 minutes. Drain and reserve soaking liquid.

COOKING

1 Set a heavy 2-quart saucepan over high heat. When hot, add 1 tablespoon of the oil. Flavor the oil with garlic until light brown. Add shrimp, stirring until flavor

escapes, for about 1 minute. Add chicken stock, shrimp-soaking juice, sugar, and salt. When the stock boils, add the radishes and bring back to a boil. Cover pan and simmer for 20 minutes or until a chopstick goes through the radish easily.

2 Turn heat to high to reduce sauce just to coat the radishes well. Mix in the remaining oil and sesame oil. Serve.

◉◉Black Mushrooms with Napa Cabbage

Serves 4 to 6
Time 30 minutes preparation
35 minutes cooking

北菇扒津白

When they are steamed with chicken fat, black mushrooms acquire a special luster and tenderness. And the natural juices of the napa cabbage flavor this dish as well. Even if made without the chicken fat, this dish is aromatic and elegant. It is deservingly one of the most popular banquet dishes, and since everything can be prepared in advance, it is also ideal for family entertaining.

Ingredients

2 ounces black mushrooms
2 teaspoons pale dry sherry
2 teaspoons granulated sugar
1¼ teaspoons salt
4 slices gingerroot
1 2-ounce piece chicken fat

1 head napa cabbage (about 2 to 3 pounds)
4 tablespoons oil
½ cup chicken stock
½ clove garlic, crushed
½ teaspoon sesame oil
1 sprig Chinese parsley

Sauce mixture

2 teaspoons tapioca powder
2 tablespoons oyster sauce
1 teaspoon pale dry sherry

PREPARATION

1 Rinse mushrooms. Put them in a bowl and add enough warm water (about 1½ cups) to cover. Soak until soft. Remove and then trim stems.

2 In a heatproof bowl, combine mushrooms, soaking liquid, sherry, sugar, ¼ teaspoon salt, and half the ginger. Mix well. Place chicken fat on top. Steam over medium heat for 20 minutes or until the fat has rendered. Discard the fat residue. Keep mushrooms in steamer.

3 Cut off about 2 inches of the leafy parts of cabbage and reserve for another use. Separate leaves but keep the heart intact. Cut each leaf lengthwise into strips about 1 inch in width. Cut cabbage heart in half, then cut each half into 6 to 8 slivers. Rinse and drain.

4 Drain juice from the steamed mushrooms, and combine with sauce ingredients in a bowl. Mix together.

COOKING

1 Set a wok over high heat. When very hot, add 3 tablespoons oil. Flavor oil with remaining ginger and discard ginger when brown. Add cabbage, stirring and turning until every piece is well coated with oil. Season with 1 teaspoon salt. Pour in chicken stock. Cover wok and cook for 10 minutes or until cabbage is soft. Remove to arrange on a serving platter. (If not used immediately, keep warm in oven.)

2 Set a heavy 2-quart saucepan over high heat. When hot, add remaining oil. Flavor with garlic and remove garlic when brown. Add mushrooms, stirring constantly. Restir sauce mixture and add to pan, stirring to prevent lumps. (If sauce is too thick, thin out with some cabbage juice.) Glaze sauce with sesame oil.

3 To serve, arrange mushrooms on top of cabbage, face side up. Pour sauce over and garnish with parsley leaves in the center. Serve hot.

⊚⊚Braised Winter Bamboo Shoots with Black Mushrooms

Serves 6
Time 30 minutes preparation
15 minutes cooking

紅燒雙冬

Bamboo shoots normally do not take on seasoning easily. Here they are deep-fried to a golden brown, then the grease is blanched off, the better to absorb the color and flavor of the soy sauce. Steamed black mushrooms are then added for the special texture and taste.

Ingredients

1 can (16 ounces) winter bamboo shoots
2 cups + 1 tablespoon oil
2 ounces medium black mushrooms
1 clove garlic, crushed

1 teaspoon granulated sugar
1 tablespoon dark soy sauce
1 tablespoon pale dry sherry
1 teaspoon sesame oil

Sauce

1 tablespoon oyster sauce
2 tablespoons chicken stock
1½ teaspoons tapioca powder

PREPARATION

1 Roll-cut the bamboo shoots into wedges about 1½ inches long. Blanch in boiling water for 2 minutes. Rinse with cold water, drain thoroughly, then pat dry.

2 Deep-fry bamboo shoot wedges in 2 cups of very hot oil over high heat until surfaces become wrinkled, about 5 to 7 minutes. Remove shoots and blanch in boiling water to degrease. Drain and reserve.

3 Follow basic recipe on page 364 to soak and steam the black mushrooms, using the same ingredients.

COOKING

1 Set a wok over high heat. When hot, add the remaining oil. Flavor oil with garlic until brown, then discard garlic.

2 Add bamboo shoot wedges, stirring constantly for 1 minute. Add sugar, then soy sauce, stirring for 30 seconds.

3 Sizzle in wine and immediately add black mushrooms and juice to wok. Bring to a boil, turn heat to medium, cover, and cook for 5 minutes.

4 Mix sauce ingredients and stream into wok. Glaze sauce with sesame oil and mix all ingredients well. Remove from heat and serve hot.

Note: This dish can be served over a bed of stir-fried leafy green vegetables.

◉◉ Dry-Braised Green Beans

		乾燒四季豆
Serves	4 to 6	
Time	15 minutes preparation	
	10 minutes cooking	

This is a tangy family vegetable dish popular in Sichuan.

Ingredients

Ingredients		Seasonings
1 pound green beans	1 teaspoon grated	1 tablespoon red rice
¼ cup dried shrimp	gingerroot	vinegar
½ cup hot water	1 tablespoon pale dry	1 tablespoon brown
¼ cup Sichuan	sherry	sugar
preserved vegetable	2 teaspoons sesame oil	½ teaspoon salt
3 cups oil		

PREPARATION

1 Select young and tender green beans. Remove any stringy fibers. Rinse and drain. Pat dry with a towel.

2 Soak shrimp in hot water until soft. Drain and reserve soaking liquid. Chop finely.

3 Rinse Sichuan preserved vegetable and chop finely.

4 Combine seasonings and set aside.

COOKING

1 Set a wok over high heat. When hot, add oil. Wait for about 5 to 7 minutes or until a green dropped into the oil sizzles noisily and soon turns brown; the oil is very hot, about 375 degrees. Then add all the beans, stirring until the surface of beans is wrinkled. Pour oil and beans together through a strainer into a bowl, leaving about 2 tablespoons of oil in the wok.

2 Set wok again over high heat and when hot, flavor oil with ginger for 10 seconds. Add the shrimp and preserved vegetable, stirring constantly for 1 minute or until golden but not brown.

3 Sizzle in the wine and immediately add the beans, shrimp soaking liquid, and seasonings, stirring until the moisture is evaporated.

4 Glaze the beans with sesame oil and remove from wok. Serve hot, warm, or cold.

◉◉◉ Hundred-Flower Stuffed Bitter Melon

Serves 4
Time 40 minutes preparation
2 hours chilling
20 minutes cooking

百 花 釀 涼 瓜

The pink shrimp paste is encircled by a green band of bitter melon, to make this an eye-pleasing dish with the bitterness of the melon still retained. The glossy veil on top is the clear sauce.

Ingredients	Seasonings	Sauce mixture
2 ounces pork fat	1 egg white	(for steamed version)
½ pound shrimp in the shell	½ teaspoon salt (scant)	¾ cup chicken broth
3 bitter melons, about 12 ounces	¼ teaspoon granulated sugar	1 teaspoon chicken bouillon powder
2 tablespoons granulated sugar	½ teaspoon sesame oil	2 teaspoons tapioca powder
2 teaspoons salt	1 teaspoon pale dry sherry	1 teaspoon granulated sugar
Cornstarch for coating	1 tablespoon tapioca powder	
3 tablespoons oil	Dash of white pepper	
1 cup chicken broth mixed with 1 teaspoon chicken bouillon powder		
1 clove garlic, crushed (for steamed version)		
1 tablespoon water mixed with 1 teaspoon tapioca powder		
1 teaspoon sesame oil		

PREPARATION

1 Follow the master recipe (page 161) to prepare the shrimp paste, using the seasonings of this recipe.

2 Cook pork fat in some boiling water for 10 minutes. Rinse with cold water, then mince finely.

3 Mix shrimp paste with pork fat. Cover and chill for at least 2 hours.

4 Trim the top and ends of the bitter melons. Cut each into 1-inch lengths. You will need 16 pieces. Remove the seeds and pulp from each piece so as to yield a hollow tube for stuffing.

5 Half-fill a 2-quart saucepan with water and bring it to a boil over high heat. Add sugar and salt, and then the bitter melons. Cook for 3 to 4 minutes or until the melon pieces are slightly tender and the color is bright green. Remove to a colander and run cold water over to stop the cooking process. Drain.

6 Take a piece of melon and use a paper towel to blot the inside surface dry, then coat evenly with cornstarch. Shake off the excess starch. Fill the hollow space with shrimp paste and smooth the top and bottom surfaces with a wet spoon. Arrange it on a platter.

7 Stuff the remaining melon pieces in the same fashion.

COOKING

1 Set a 9-inch nonstick skillet over medium heat until hot. Add the oil, spreading over the surface evenly. Arrange the stuffed melon pieces in 1 layer in the skillet, cut side down. Pan-fry the melon pieces until shrimp paste is set on one side, then turn to the other side and pan-fry the same way. Shake the pan to move the melon pieces around occasionally for even frying. Do not brown the shrimp paste and the melon, lest the pink and green color cannot be maintained.

2 Pour in the chicken stock mixture and turn the heat to medium-high. Cook 5 minutes, then turn melon pieces and cook 5 more minutes or until sauce is reduced to ½ cup and melon is tender. Push melon pieces to the side and leave a space in the center.

3 Restir the tapioca mixture and stream it into the skillet, stirring until the sauce thickens. Roll melon pieces in the sauce, then remove to arrange in a serving platter with cut side up.

4 Glaze sauce with sesame oil and pour over melon pieces and serve hot.

Note: Stuffed bitter melon pieces can be steamed. Arrange them vertically in a greased platter and steam over high heat for 10 minutes. To prepare sauce for the steamed version, use 2 tablespoons of the oil and heat in the wok until very hot. Flavor oil with garlic, and remove garlic when brown. Stream in sauce mixture, stirring until thickened. Glaze sauce with sesame oil. Remove the platter of melon from steamer and pour sauce over. Serve hot.

◎◎ Stuffed Winter Melon with Ham

Serves 6 as part of a Chinese meal
Time 15 minutes preparation
        30 minutes cooking

大 腿 冬 瓜 夾

A̲n elegant sandwich with two small translucent winter melon slices taking the place of bread, holding a piece of ham. Though served hot, it looks cool and is at its soothingly pleasant best on a warm summer evening.

Ingredients

2½ pounds winter
  melon
3 ounces Smithfield
  ham, from the
  center-cut portion,
  about 1 inch thick
1 cup chicken stock
2 tablespoons oil
2 slices gingerroot
2 teaspoons yellow
  wine

¼ teaspoon granulated
  sugar
Dash of white pepper
Salt
2 teaspoons water
  chestnut powder
  mixed with 1
  tablespoon water
½ teaspoon sesame oil

PREPARATION

1 Peel the skin off the winter melon. Remove seeds and the pulp. Cut the melon into ½-inch-thick slices about 1½ by 1¼ in size. Use a small knife to cut a slit from the middle of each slice ¾ths of the way down, forming a double-layered slice with the skin side not cut through. Make 24 slices.

2 Cut the ham across the grain into slices about ⅛ inch thick and 1½ inches wide. You also need 24 slices.

3 Take 1 piece of winter melon and stuff a piece of ham into the slit. Repeat with the remaining 23 slices.

4 Arrange melon pieces skin side down in a heatproof bowl, which should be large enough to hold the melon pieces snugly.

COOKING

1 Pour the chicken stock into the bowl to cover the melon. Steam over high heat for 30 minutes or until the melon becomes almost transparent and soft. Drain juices into a bowl and set melon back on the steamer.

2 Set a small saucepan over high heat. When hot, add 1 tablespoon of the oil. Flavor the oil with ginger for 10 seconds, then discard the ginger. Sizzle in the wine and at the same time pour in the melon juices. Bring juice to a boil, adding sugar, pepper, and a pinch of salt. Turn heat to low.

3 Restir the water chestnut mixture and stream it into the sauce, stirring to prevent lumps.

4 When the sauce thickens, test for seasoning, and glaze with sesame oil and the remaining tablespoon of oil.

5 Turn melon slices out by inverting the bowl into a deep serving platter. Scoop sauce evenly over and serve.

◉◉◉◉ Mashed Mound of Celery Cabbage with Jade Pillars

Serves 10 in a Chinese banquet
Time 1 hour soaking
50 to 60 minutes preparation
2 hours, 20 minutes steaming

爛 糊 干 貝

Country areas near Shanghai love Cabbage Mash, which is celery cabbage cooked slowly to a paste. With jade pillars as an added ingredient, this mash becomes a banquet dish—a mound of near-jelly, easily pried apart with chopsticks or fork. Every layer, made from a different part of the cabbage, is different in texture and has a subtly different taste.

Ingredients

2 ounces jade pillars
½ cup hot water
2 slices gingerroot
1 teaspoon granulated sugar
2 teaspoons pale dry sherry
1 large head celery cabbage, about 4 pounds

1 can (13¾ ounces) clear chicken broth
3 ounces chicken fat
1 teaspoon salt
1½ tablespoons tapioca powder
1 tablespoon oil
1 teaspoon sesame oil

PREPARATION

1 Soak pillars in a small heatproof bowl with hot water for 1 hour. Add ginger, sugar, and sherry. Steam over medium low heat for 1 hour. Flake all pillars but the largest one and reserve.

2 Remove celery cabbage leaves one by one but keep the heart intact. Rinse. Arrange leaves in a pile according to their original order.

COOKING

1 Have ready a heatproof bowl (a Pyrex bowl is suitable) about 8 inches in diameter and 3 inches deep.

2 Take a bunch of the first few layers of cabbage leaves and cut off the leafy end parts, leaving about 4½ inches of the stem portions. Cut each in half lengthwise.

3 Pour chicken broth into a deep skillet and bring it to a boil over high heat. Add the cabbage stems, cooking 5 minutes; the stems should become wilted and pliant. Take stems out with a pair of tongs and put into a colander, then set it over the skillet. Press with a slotted spoon to force the liquid back to the skillet.

4 Arrange cabbage stems lengthwise in an overlapping manner along the inside surface of the bowl, forming a spiral pattern. Place the whole pillar in the center and surround it with the flaked ones. Add jade pillar juice.

5 Cut chicken fat in ¼-inch slices. Put them sparingly over the cabbage stems. Steam over high heat for 30 minutes.

6 Meanwhile, cut the remaining cabbage, keeping the stem parts 4½ inches in length. Reserve the leafy parts. Wilt the stems in the same manner.

7 Discard residue of chicken fat and sprinkle ½ teaspoon of the salt on the steamed cabbage in the bowl. Arrange the just-wilted cabbage stems on top, this time more overlapping in the center. Steam 20 minutes over medium heat.

8 Cut the cabbage heart into 6 prisms lengthwise, then wilt them together with the reserved cabbage leaves in the same manner. Save all the excess juices for later use.

9 Sprinkle the remaining ½ teaspoon of salt on the cabbage in the bowl. Add all the wilted cabbage to fill up the center space in the bowl. Steam 30 minutes more over medium-low heat (for softer texture, steam 1 hour).

(Note: this dish can be prepared ahead of time up to this stage. Steam over high heat for reheating.)

10 Remove the bowl of cabbage from the steamer. Place a platter (about ¼ inch smaller than the bowl) over the cabbage. Press the platter gently, tipping the bowl to drain as much juice as possible into a small saucepan. Put the bowl of cabbage back into the steamer to keep warm.

11 Set the saucepan with cabbage juice over high heat and bring to a boil. Turn heat to low. Mix the tapioca powder with the leftover chicken broth from wilting the cabbage and stream it into the juice gradually, stirring until smooth and thickened.

12 Test for seasoning, then add oil and sesame oil to glaze sauce.

13 To serve, remove the platter that is placed over the cabbage. Cover the bowl with a round serving dish, about 12 inches in diameter, preferably with a slanted rim. Hold the platter and the bowl together firmly and flip them over quickly, then remove the bowl, revealing the cabbage. Spoon off excess juices to mix with the sauce, and pour sauce over the cabbage. Serve hot.

◉◉◉ Stuffed Fuzzy Melon with Pork

Serves 4
Time 30 minutes preparation
30 minutes soaking
40 minutes cooking

豬肉釀節瓜

Fuzzy melon takes on seasonings so well yet retains its firm texture that it, rather than the stuffing, is the best part of this dish. The stuffing, however, adds chewiness and subtlety. Select a uniform sized, green-skinned melon about 1¾ inches in diameter for cooking.

Ingredients		Seasonings
¼ cup dried shrimp	½ teaspoon salt	1 tablespoon light soy
1 cup hot water	1 cup chicken stock	sauce
6 medium black		2 teaspoons pale dry
mushrooms		sherry
½ pound lean ground		¼ teaspoon salt
pork		1 teaspoon granulated
1¾ pounds fuzzy		sugar
melon		1 tablespoon tapioca
Cornstarch for coating		powder
3 tablespoons oil		1 teaspoon sesame oil

PREPARATION

1 Soak shrimp and mushrooms in 2 separate bowls each with ½ cup of hot water for 30 minutes. Mince them finely and reserve the soaking liquids.

2 In a mixing bowl, combine pork and the seasonings, mixing with a wooden spoon in 1 direction until the pork holds together, then add the shrimp and mushrooms and mix some more. Scoop up the pork mixture by hand and beat it back to the bowl repeatedly until firm. Chill for at least 1 hour.

3 Using the blunt edge of a table knife, scrape away the fuzz and top green layer of the skin of the melon. Do not scrape too deeply into the meat, lest the green color completely disappear.

4 Cut melon into 1¼-inch lengths. With a vegetable corer, remove the center part of each section, leaving a hollow space in the center. The rim should be at least ⅜ inch wide. You will have about 12 pieces.

5 Blot dry the inside surface of each piece of melon with paper towels and dust with cornstarch. Pack the hollow space with pork stuffing and smooth the top with a wet spoon. Stuff the remaining melon pieces and arrange them on a platter. If not used immediately, wrap and chill in the refrigerator.

COOKING

1 Set a heavy 10-inch skillet over high heat. When very hot, add the oil. Spread the oil around with a spatula to grease the bottom of the skillet evenly. Arrange the

melon pieces in the skillet vertically in 1 layer. Pan-fry one side over medium heat until the pork stuffing is brown, about 2 minutes, then turn to brown the other side for another 2 minutes.

2 Lay each piece of melon down on the side and roll it in the hot oil so the skin will turn bright green.

3 Combine salt, chicken stock, and shrimp and mushroom liquids and add to the skillet. Bring the liquid to a boil. Cover and cook over low heat for 30 minutes or until a chopstick can go through the melon easily.

4 Remove melon pieces to a deep dish and arrange them vertically. Reduce sauce to about ½ cup and pour over melons. Serve immediately.

⊛⊛Jellyfish and White Radish Salad

Serves 12 as a part of a cold platter
Time 15 minutes preparation
overnight soaking
1 hour chilling

凉拌海蜇

This is a refreshing salad, East China style.

Ingredients	**Dressing**
½ pound pre-cut jellyfish shreds	1 tablespoon red rice vinegar
1 pound Chinese white radish	1 tablespoon sesame oil
Salt	¼ cup peanut oil
½ medium carrot	2 tablespoons fish sauce
2 whole scallions, trimmed	1 tablespoon granulated sugar
4 sprigs Chinese parsley	½ teaspoon chicken bouillon powder
	Dash of white pepper or cayenne

PREPARATION

1 Rinse jellyfish with cold water, squeezing and rubbing to remove salt. Soak in cold water to cover overnight, then rinse thoroughly. Drain in a colander for 1 hour, or until most of the moisture is gone.

2 Arrange jellyfish shreds in 1 layer on a kitchen towel. Pat dry and wrap with the towel to absorb moisture. Chill in refrigerator while you prepare rest of ingredients.

3 Peel skin from radishes and vertical slope-cut into ⅛-inch slices. Then cut vertically into ⅛-inch shreds. Rub with 1 tablespoon of salt and let stand at room temperature for 2 to 3 hours or until limp.

374

MAJOR CHINESE CUISINE

4 Rinse radishes with cold water to remove salt, then take a handful of shreds and squeeze to extract moisture. Repeat until all radish shreds have been squeezed.

5 Shred the carrot the same size as the radishes, then salt, rinse, and squeeze as with the radishes.

6 Cut off about 4 inches from the green end of the scallions and shred the remaining portions finely.

7 Rinse the parsley and break it into 2-inch lengths.

8 About 1 hour before serving, mix dressing and combine with all other ingredients. Toss well and chill.

Note: It is best to soak the jellyfish a night ahead. Keep it as dry as possible for the salad, so the dressing will not be diluted.

Marinated Mushrooms

Serves 12 as a part of a cold platter
Time 20 minutes preparation
overnight chilling

Choose fresh mushrooms that are closed on the underside and without blemishes on the cap. If the gills are exposed, the mushroom is overripe and does not have the firm texture needed in this dish.

Ingredients
36 medium fresh
button mushrooms
Juice of 1 lemon

Marinade
1 clove garlic, crushed
Juice of 1 lemon
2 scallions (white part
only), chopped
2 sprigs Chinese
parsley, chopped
1 tablespoon dry
mustard
1 teaspoon salt
1 teaspoon chicken
bouillon powder

2 tablespoons
granulated sugar
¼ teaspoon freshly
ground pepper
½ cup peanut oil

PREPARATION

1 Trim stems from mushrooms. Peel skin with a sharp paring knife or rub mushrooms with a damp cloth to remove any dirt.

2 Half-fill a 4-quart saucepan with water. Set over high heat and bring water to a boil. Add lemon juice and mushrooms and bring back to a boil.

3 Immediately pour mushrooms into a colander to drain.

4 While draining the mushrooms, mix ingredients for the marinade in a large bowl.

5 Using paper towels, blot moisture of mushrooms and then add them to the marinade. Toss well and cover and chill overnight. Turn mushrooms in the marinade at least twice.

Note: These are best made a day in advance to allow the marinade to permeate the mushrooms. But don't make them longer than 2 days in advance, lest the mushrooms become soggy.

⊚⊚Marinated Asparagus

Serves 12 as a part of a cold platter
Time 20 minutes preparation
2 hours chilling

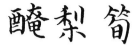

The Chinese version of asparagus vinaigrette. Asparagus is native to China but was known mainly as a drug until recently.

Ingredients
2½ pounds asparagus
2 tablespoons
granulated sugar

Marinade
Juice of 1 lemon
1 clove garlic, crushed
1 teaspoon light soy
sauce
1 teaspoon chicken
bouillon powder
1 tablespoon
granulated sugar

¼ teaspoon white
pepper
1 teaspoon salt
1 tablespoon sesame oil
4 tablespoons peanut
oil

PREPARATION

1 Break asparagus off at the point at which they will snap easily. Hold a spear by the tip and peel with a vegetable scraper, starting about 2 inches from the bottom. Peel as deep as ¹⁄₁₆ inch to remove the tough outer skin. Then turn and hold the asparagus by the bottom, making shallower cuts as you approach the tip. Shave off any scales. Wash and drain.

2 Half-fill a 4-quart saucepan with water. Set over high heat, bring to a boil, and add the sugar. Place asparagus in the boiling water and cook vigorously with the saucepan uncovered for 5 to 7 minutes. The asparagus is done when a bamboo skewer pierces the bottom easily.

3 Remove asparagus immediately to a colander and rinse with cold water to stop the cooking process. Drain and spread the spears in 1 layer on double paper towels to dry.

4 Arrange the asparagus alternately in an oval serving dish.

5 Mix the marinade and pour on top. Wrap with plastic wrap and chill for at least 2 hours or no longer than 6 hours. Serve.

Note: This dish is best prepared not too far in advance. Cook the asparagus during the morning and serve it in the evening.

◉◉ Marinated Cucumber

Serves 4 or as decoration for a cold
meat platter
Time 25 minutes preparation
40 minutes resting
overnight chilling

川辣黄瓜

Perhaps the most popular vegetable salad in northern China.

Ingredients
1 long cucumber,
about 1 pound
1 tablespoon salt
1 tablespoon oil
1 tablespoon sesame oil

Marinade
1 tablespoon Sichuan
peppercorns
2 dried red chili
peppers, broken into
½-inch pieces
3 tablespoons distilled
white vinegar
2 teaspoons water
3 tablespoons
granulated sugar

PREPARATION

1 Remove both ends of the cucumber. Place it between 2 chopsticks to guide your cutting and slice it thinly until the knife reaches the chopsticks. Cut 1 piece off after slicing 4 very thin slices, making a 4-layered cucumber piece. Continue to slice the remaining cucumber.

2 Dredge the cucumber slices with salt. Let stand at room temperature for at least 30 minutes or until soft. Drain and arrange cucumber pieces flat on a board and press with a heavy weight to expel moisture, about 10 minutes.

3 Meanwhile, prepare the marinade. Set a small skillet over medium-high heat. When hot, add the peppercorns and chili pepper, stirring until the spicy flavor escapes. Add the vinegar and water and turn the heat to low; cook for 1 minute.

4 Add the sugar, stirring until it dissolves, then strain the marinade and discard the solids.

5 Arrange the cucumber slices in layers in a glass container. Pour the marinade over, cover, and chill in the refrigerator for several hours or overnight.

6 To serve, drain the marinade and toss the cucumber slices gently with oil and sesame oil. Serve separately as 1 cold platter or use cucumber slices to surround another dish.

HUNDRED-FLOWER STUFFED BITTER MELON
PAGE 367

SICHUAN NOODLES
PAGE 387

⊛⊛ Pickled Napa Cabbage

Serves 12
Time 15 minutes preparation
6 hours pickling
overnight chilling

辣 白 菜

A favorite of North China. Excellent as an appetizer or as part of a cold platter.

Ingredients

1 head napa cabbage, about 3 to 4 pounds
2 tablespoons salt
3 cloves garlic
4 slices gingerroot
4 dried red chili peppers
⅓ cup peanut oil
3 tablespoons vinegar
4 tablespoons granulated sugar
2 tablespoons pale dry sherry

PREPARATION

1 Cut off about 2 inches of the leafy parts from the top of the cabbage. Reserve for another use.

2 Separate the leaves, keeping the heart intact. Cut each leaf into long strips about 1 inch wide. Cut the cabbage heart in half lengthwise, then cut each half into 8 to 10 lengths. Rinse and drain.

3 Arrange cabbage strips in a baking sheet in 1 layer. Add salt and toss well. Let stand at room temperature for 5 to 6 hours or until limp. Squeeze cabbage to extract as much moisture as possible. Set aside.

4 Shred the garlic and ginger finely.

5 Break the chili peppers in half.

COOKING

1 Set a wok over high heat. When the wok is hot, add the oil. Flavor oil with garlic, ginger, and chili peppers for 1 minute.

2 Add the vinegar and sugar and bring to a boil, then sizzle in the wine. Turn heat off and add the cabbage. Toss well to mix.

3 Remove cabbage to a container (preferably nonmetallic) and cover. Chill overnight and then serve cold.

Note: Allow at least 24 hours to marinate.

⊛Steamed Eggplant in Mustard and Sesame Sauce

Serves 4 as a cold vegetable dish
Time 10 minutes preparation
15 minutes steaming
30 minutes pressing
1 hour chilling

拌 麻 辣 茄 子

A delightful and refreshing cold summer dish for the southern Chinese family, nutlike yet mustard-hot at the same time.

Ingredients

1½ pounds long
　Japanese eggplants
1 whole scallion,
　trimmed
1 sprig Chinese parsley
½ teaspoon salt

Mustard and sesame sauce

2 teaspoons powdered
　mustard
2 teaspoons cold water
1 tablespoon sesame
　paste
1 tablespoon light soy
　sauce

1 tablespoon red rice
　vinegar
1 tablespoon
　granulated sugar
½ teaspoon chicken
　bouillon powder
1 tablespoon sesame oil

PREPARATION

1 Mix powdered mustard and cold water in a small bowl and stir with a teaspoon until smooth and hot, about 3 minutes. Set aside.

2 Combine the remaining ingredients for sauce in a mixing bowl. Use a wire whisk to blend them together, then add the prepared mustard and mix well.

3 Remove the caps and ends of the eggplants, then rinse. Cut them into 2 equal lengths if longer than 8 inches, otherwise use them whole.

4 Shred scallion finely into 2-inch lengths. Cut parsley the same length.

COOKING

1 Set a regular steaming rack in a saucepan large enough to hold the rack snugly. Add water to come up within 1 inch below the rack. Bring water to a boil over high heat and arrange eggplants in the rack. Steam for 15 minutes or until the eggplants are soft.

2 Remove the steaming rack with the eggplants from the saucepan. Use a soup spoon and a fork to transfer 1 piece of eggplant at a time to a platter. Hold the eggplant with the spoon at one end and use a fork to pry lengthwise to break the eggplant into several strips at once, each about ¼ inch wide. Push the strips from the platter into a colander.

3 Sprinkle the salt sparingly over the eggplant strips. Set the colander in the sink, and put a bowl of water on the eggplants so that excessive juice will drain off.

4 After 30 minutes, remove the eggplants to a deep dish. Pour the mustard and sesame sauce over. Wrap and chill for at least 1 hour.

5 When serving, add scallion shreds and parsley to eggplant. Toss at the table.

Small Eats

In Chinese, the term "small eats" covers a whole spectrum of foods not ordinarily served as main dishes at a meal.

Small eats can be found in big restaurants. Soup noodles and fried rice appear at the end of a banquet in case the diners still have an appetite. Some restaurants are known for their delicate pastries and sweet soups served as desserts. In Northern restaurants, upside-down *guo-tieh* (pan-stickers) and soup-filled buns are often appetizers to a meal. But in Canton, feather-light dim sums ("touch-the-heart") are a teahouse specialty for breakfasts and informal lunches.

Also in Canton, small specialty shops sell wontons and noodle soups. Some shops specialize in breakfast food: plain congee with deep-fried pastries or congee with meat and fish; also puddings made of turnip, taro, or water chestnuts. Northern breakfast food includes bean milk, roasted buns, and oil-fried strips. Western-style cafés, called "ice chambers," serve coffee, tea, and soda with toast and pancakes; they also carry traditional sweet soups, sometimes mixed with crushed ice.

Snack shops sell beef and pork jerky, meat fluff, also chewy vegetarian food made of soybean or gluten to suggest the flavor and texture of roast goose, abalone, duck gizzards, and pig's knuckles. Also sold are seasoned soybeans, deep-fried broad beans, vinegared ginger, and a wide array of preserved fruits, particularly plums and olives. Their salty-sweet licorice taste appeals to Chinese children just as chocolate or potato chips are favorites with American kids.

Peddlers in the street sell roasted or spicy cooked peanuts, roasted chestnuts, and roasted sweet potatoes. In the South, flower of bean curd is sold warm with syrup, while the brisk air in the cities of the North is filled with the aroma of deep-fried "smelly bean curd." Peking peddlers sell among other unusual specialties, boiled lamb intestines filled with lamb's blood.

Favorite Chinese candies include those made with peanuts and sesame seeds. The halvah, made of sesame powder and considered a Middle Eastern candy, is widely sold in North China, perhaps brought in from the Middle East centuries ago. As late as the 1940s the candy man chiselled out 1-inch chunks of hard candy from a round block four feet in diameter. The ringing sound of the hammer on the chisel was part of the streetcorner music, now largely forgotten.

RICE

The Cantonese enjoy long-grain rice, but elsewhere in China short-grain rice is more common. The Chinese usually wash their rice by stirring in water and rinsing twice. The amount of water is not measured for cooking, but rather tested by dipping the middle finger to touch the surface of the rice. The proper water level should just reach the first joint.

The size of your finger does not matter much, but that of the pot does. For 1 cup of raw rice, use a 1-quart saucepan; 2 cups of rice, a 2-quart saucepan; 3 to 4 cups of rice, a 3-quart saucepan; 4 to 6 cups or more, use a 4-quart saucepan or larger. A heavy cast-aluminum pot is preferable.

You can also measure the water as follows: for each cup of rice, add an equal quantity of water plus an extra half cup for the pot. No salt or fat should be added for Chinese-style rice; plain rice is wonderfully sweet and chewy.

To cook the rice, set the pot over high heat, uncovered, and bring to a boil. Continue boiling until small bubbling craters appear on the surface (the time varies from 10 to 15 minutes depending on the amount of rice cooked). This signifies the right time to cover the pot (also the time to introduce any dish to be steamed atop the rice). Turn the heat to simmer and keep the pot covered for 15 minutes. Loosen the rice with a fork or chopsticks before serving.

Electric rice cookers, very popular in Taiwan, Hong Kong, and Japan, dispense with guesswork and give consistent and excellent results. One would justify its cost if rice is cooked more often than once a week.

Yangzhou Fried Rice

揚州炒飯

Serves 6 as a main dish with vegetables

Time 30 minutes preparation
15 minutes cooking

This colorful fried rice had its start in Yangzhou, a city famous for Eastern cuisine, but the dish is also found all over China.

Ingredients

6 cups cooked rice, cooled
6 black mushrooms
1 whole chicken breast, about 10 ounces
3 ounces Cantonese Roast Pork (page 252) or 2 Chinese sausages
3 ounces cooked shrimp
1 egg yolk

3 whole eggs
Salt
4 whole scallions, trimmed
7 tablespoons oil
1 clove garlic, crushed
½ cup chicken stock
1 tablespoon oyster sauce (optional)

Seasoning

2 tablespoons water
½ teaspoon salt
1 egg white
1 tablespoon pale dry sherry
½ teaspoon granulated sugar
Dash of white pepper
1 tablespoon tapioca powder
1 tablespoon oil
1 teaspoon sesame oil

PREPARATION

1 Break the clumps of cooked rice to separate the grains.

2 Soak mushrooms in hot water until soft. Trim stems and squeeze caps to extract moisture. Dice.

3 Skin and bone the chicken. Trim fat and remove all visible gristle and membranes. Dice.

4 Put chicken in a mixing bowl and add water from seasonings. Add salt, egg white, sherry, sugar, pepper, and tapioca powder, then stir in the oil and sesame oil. Mix well and chill until ready to use.

5 Dice the pork or sausages. Dice the shrimp.

6 Add the egg yolk to the eggs and beat lightly with a pinch of salt until smooth but not foamy.

7 Chop scallions into ¼-inch lengths.

COOKING

1 Set a wok over high heat. When very hot, add 2 tablespoons oil. Flavor oil with garlic until lightly brown, then remove and discard garlic. Add chicken, stirring constantly until well separated and no longer pink. Remove to a large bowl.

2 Add 1 more tablespoon of oil to the wok, still over high heat. When oil is hot, add the sausage or pork and the mushrooms. Stir 1 minute or until the sausage turns transparent, then add the shrimp and stir a few times around the wok. Remove to combine with chicken in the bowl.

3 Rinse wok and wipe dry. Set over high heat and, when wok is hot, add the remaining 4 tablespoons of oil. Scramble the eggs in the oil until set, then turn heat to medium.

4 Break the eggs in the wok into small pieces about the size of the chicken, then add the rice and sprinkle salt over it. Turn rice repeatedly to ensure even heating (it takes about 5 to 7 minutes).

5 When the rice is heated through, whirl in half the chicken stock along the edge of the wok and stir. When moisture is absorbed, add remaining stock in the same manner and stir again.

6 Return all cooked ingredients to the wok, stirring constantly to mix with rice. Add the scallions and correct the seasonings. Add the oyster sauce also, if desired. Mix and serve.

◎◉Beef Fried Rice

Serves 3 as a main dish with
stir-fried vegetables, or 4 as a
luncheon with lettuce-leaf
wrappers

Time 20 minutes preparation
30 minutes chilling
10 minutes cooking

生 炒 牛 肉 飯

Ingredients

½ flank steak (about
  12 ounces)
4 cups cooked rice,
  cooled
1 medium onion
4 whole scallions,
  trimmed
2 whole eggs
1 egg yolk
Salt
⅓ cup + 2 tablespoons
  oil

1 teaspoon chicken
  bouillon powder
2 tablespoons chicken
  stock
2 teaspoons light soy
  sauce (optional)

Seasonings

1 egg white
1 tablespoon oyster
  sauce
¼ teaspoon salt
2 teaspoons tapioca
  powder
2 teaspoons pale dry
  sherry
½ teaspoon granulated
  sugar
1 teaspoon sesame oil
Dash of white pepper

PREPARATION

1 Trim meat of excess fat. Cut lengthwise into 1-inch strips, then slice diagonally across the grain into very thin pieces no thicker than ⅛ inch.

2 Mix ingredients for seasonings in a bowl and add meat. Chill for at least 30 minutes.

3 Break clumps of rice with your fingers to separate the grains. Reserve.

4 Dice the onion.

5 Cut scallions into ¼-inch lengths.

6 Beat the eggs with the yolk and add ⅛ teaspoon of the salt; mix until smooth.

COOKING

1 Set a wok over high heat. When very hot, add ⅓ cup of the oil. Put in the meat, stirring constantly until the slices separate, for 1 minute. Remove the meat with a strainer, leaving as much oil in the wok as possible.

2 Add onion to the wok, stirring until limp. Tilt the wok so that excessive oil will run to the center. Scoop the onion out with a slotted spatula, then add remaining oil to wok.

3 Scramble the eggs in the wok until set. Add the rice, ½ teaspoon salt, and the chicken bouillon powder, stirring and spading to ensure even heating, about 5 minutes.

4 Sprinkle the chicken stock along the edge of the wok, stirring until the moisture is absorbed. Return the meat and onion to wok, and add scallions. Mix well and check seasoning, adding soy sauce if desired. Mix and serve.

◉◉ Eight-Treasured Glutinous Rice with Sausage

Serves 5 to 6 as a main dish with leafy vegetables
Time 30 minutes preparation
2 hours soaking
40 minutes cooking

腊味糯米飯

This is a one-pot dish to add warmth during a cold winter night. It is popular in all parts of China with different versions; you also can make up your own combinations of ingredients. Incidentally, the finished product makes an outstanding stuffing for roast turkey.

Ingredients
3 cups glutinous rice
2 jade pillars (optional)
¼ cup dried shrimp
2 cups warm water
8 medium black mushrooms
6 Chinese pork sausages
½ cup diced lean pork, preferably cut from loin
½ cup cooked chicken, Cantonese Roast Pork (page 252), or ham
3 whole scallions, trimmed
2 sprigs Chinese parsley
2 tablespoons oil

Seasonings
1 teaspoon light soy sauce
1 teaspoon tapioca powder
Dashes of sugar, pepper, and salt
½ teaspoon sesame oil
1 teaspoon pale dry sherry

Rice seasonings
2 tablespoons light soy sauce
2 teaspoons oyster sauce
1 teaspoon sesame oil

PREPARATION

1 Soak rice in plenty of hot water for 2 hours. Rinse and drain thoroughly.

2 Soak pillars and shrimp, each separately, in ½ cup warm water until soft. Flake pillars into fine shreds; dice shrimp finely. Reserve both soaking liquids.

3 Soak the mushrooms in remaining warm water until soft. Trim stems, then squeeze caps to extract excess moisture. Cut mushrooms into ¼ inch cubes. Reserve soaking liquid.

4 Dice the sausages; dice the pork. Mix the meat with the seasonings and set aside.

5 Dice the chicken (or roast pork or ham) and set aside.

6 Chop the scallions finely. Cut the parsley into ¼-inch lengths.

COOKING

1 To steam the rice, combine it with the pillars in a heatproof bowl and add all the soaking liquids. Mix well. Steam over medium-high heat for 30 minutes, or until the rice is transparent.

2 Set a heavy skillet over high heat. When hot, add the sausages, stirring until the fatty parts turn transparent. Add the dried shrimp and mushrooms, stirring 2 minutes. Remove.

3 Add oil to the skillet and stir-fry the pork until the pink color disappears. Add the chicken and stir 1 minute.

4 Combine the steamed rice and all the cooked ingredients in the bowl, then add the seasonings for the rice. Toss and mix. Steam over high heat for 10 minutes. Add the scallions and parsley and mix again. Serve hot.

Note: If the steamed rice is wrapped with an egg sheet (see page 164), it becomes a Sweet Rice Roll, which could be served in ½-inch slices as a snack.

If the rice mixture is wrapped individually with *shao mai* wrappers (see page 408), they become Sweet Rice Shao Mais.

If the rice is packed tightly into small muffin tins to form cakes, they can be coated with a batter (see page 177) and deep-fried. These are Crispy Sweet Rice Cakes.

◉Rice Crust (Guoba)

Yields 12 pieces of crust about 1 by 2 inches in size
Time 1 minute preparation
25 minutes cooking
1 hour, 10 minutes heating

锅 巴

Rice improperly cooked often leaves a crunchy crust which nevertheless finds favor with Chinese children, who may eat it as is or soak it with soup or tea. It is only reasonable that chefs would deliberately cook their rice "improperly" for the crust.

Sizzling rice is rice crust made even crunchier by deep-frying. But while the crust keeps indefinitely, sizzling rice must be used scorchingly hot to guarantee the "sizzle."

Ingredients

2 cups raw or cooked
long-grain rice
2½ cups water

METHOD 1

1 Rinse the raw rice, and drain. Put it in a 10-inch frying pan and add the water. Cook over high heat, uncovered, until it comes to a boil. This takes about 10 minutes. When little craters start to form on the surface of the rice, turn heat to low, cover pan, and cook for 15 minutes.

2 Turn heat to simmer. Warm the rice slowly until a thick crust forms on the bottom, about 40 minutes.

3 Scrape out the soft rice, leaving the crust at the bottom. Turn the heat back to low and warm the crust until the edges separate from the pan.

4 Carefully turn the crust with a spatula. Cook for another 30 minutes, or until the crust is dry and crispy.

5 Break the crust into pieces about 1 by 2 inches. Keep in an airtight jar for later use.

METHOD 2

1 Put the cooked rice into an 8-inch nonstick frying pan. Moisten a spatula with water and pat the rice flat on the bottom of the pan to form a patty. The rice will be approximately 2 grains thick.

2 Set the frying pan over low heat. Cook the rice for 40 minutes or until the edges of the rice patty separate from the pan and a crust is formed.

3 Turn the rice crust over carefully and cook the other side for 30 minutes or until dry and crusty.

4 Break crust into small pieces about 1 by 2 inches. Keep in an airtight container.

NOODLES AND FEN

Noodles *(mein)* were invented in China two thousand years ago, in the later Han Dynasty, and found equal favor with Emperors and common folk.

The preparation of noodles in North China calls for skill and showmanship. Peking chefs start with a three-pound piece of dough and produce, after a sequence of pulling and folding by hand, thin noodles of uniform thickness. The record is twelve pulls (eleven folds) to yield 2,048 "dragon beard" threads, small twirls of which are fried a crisp golden yellow and served atop a pancake.

Shanxi chefs whittle a hand-held piece of dough rapidly into long prisms of noodles, straight into a wok of boiling water. But it is wasteful to commit a hand to holding the dough, hence the dramatic variation of putting the dough on (surprise!) the head. With two daggers whirling less than an inch from the temples and a waterfall of noodles flying into the pan, this dazzling act is not for the faint-hearted.

Zha Jiang Mein (fried soybean paste noodles) is famed in Peking; in West China highly seasoned small bowls of *Dan Dan Mein* is a well-known snack; in Canton *Wonton Mein* is justly famous; these local specialties are now found all over China.

Chinese-American *Chow Mein* (stir-fried noodles) use deep-fried noodles, but the true Chinese versions are pan-fried. East China chow mein is called "yellow on both sides" because the noodles are fried on both sides for crispiness.

Rice sticks (*fen*) are noodles made of rice. They come in a variety of forms. Shaho fen from a suburb of Canton is a ½-inch-wide rice stick, smooth and elastic. Uncut shaho fen can be rolled into one-inch diameter rolls called pig intestines, often filled with minced dry shrimp, pork, or beef. In scenic Guilin the food to match its mountains is a rice stick soup with paper-thin slivers of horsemeat. A far more popular ingredient in the same vein is *fensi* (cellophane noodles), a transparent mung-bean noodle which blends with everything and is found in soups, boiled dishes, and stir-fries. *Fenpi* (fen skin), a round thin skin also made of mung bean, is about 9 inches in diameter and is used in cooking in East China as an ingredient rather than as a staple.

⊛⊛ Home-Made Noodles

Yields 1¼ pounds noodles
Time 5 minutes preparation
30 minutes resting
35 minutes rolling and cutting

自 製 蛋 麵

Several types of fresh noodles are now available in many supermarkets in big cities of the United States. However, home-made noodles are inexpensive and actually fun to prepare, particularly with the convenience of the modern pasta machine.

Ingredients

2 cups + 2 tablespoons all-purpose flour
2 tablespoons gluten flour
3 large eggs

2 tablespoons water
½ cup cornstarch for dusting

Utensils

double-layered cheesecloth about 8 inches square
broom handle about 2 feet long and 1¼ inches in diameter

PREPARATION

1   Mix the flour with the gluten flour in a large mixing bowl, forming a well in the center. Into the well add the eggs and water, stirring in 1 direction with a wooden spoon to blend with the flour until it becomes a grainy piece of dough. Cover dough with a damp towel and allow to rest for 30 minutes.

2   Sprinkle about 1 tablespoon of flour evenly on a kneading board. Turn the dough out and knead for 10 minutes or until smooth. Sprinkle with more flour when needed. The dough now is stiff and elastic.

3   Put the cornstarch in the center of the cheesecloth. Bring the edges up and tie loosely into a bag for dusting.

4   Flatten the dough with your palm. Dust the dough with cornstarch by wiping the cheesecloth bag on both sides. Hold a rolling pin with both hands and press (but do not roll) the dough firmly, then repeatedly from one end to another. Turn the dough over and press the same way. Wipe the dough with the cornstarch bag between each turn and roll to smooth the dough occasionally with the rolling pin until it is about ³⁄₁₆ inch thick.

5 Dust the dough on both sides with cornstarch again. Roll it up with the broom handle, then pull the broom handle out, so that the dough is now a multi-layered tube.

6 Press and dust the multi-layered dough as described in step 4. Then unroll the dough into a thin piece and dust with cornstarch on both sides. Repeat the sequence: rolling on the broom handle, pressing and dusting 2 more times until the dough become a thin sheet about $1/16$ inch. Fold the sheet back and forth into a long pile about $2\frac{1}{2}$ inches wide, in approximately 12 layers.

7 Cut the piled dough sheet into $1/8$-inch strips. Loosen each strip into a 2-foot-long noodle. It can be used at once.

8 To save for later use, gather about 10 to 12 strips of noodles to form a 3-inch skein; you will have 4 skeins in all. Wrap the skeins of noodles in plastic. Keep refrigerated for up to 2 days or keep frozen indefinitely.

Note: After kneading the dough until smooth, the remaining procedures can be done in a pasta machine. Follow instructions given for the individual machine.

◉◉◉Dan Dan Mein (Sichuan Noodles)

Serves 4 as a snack
Time 20 minutes preparation
20 minutes soaking
15 minutes cooking

担 担 麺

One of the most celebrated eating places in old Chongqing (Chungking) in the 1940s was a bamboo hut in Lantern Lane which peddled nothing but Dan Dan Mein. These days the name could mean any informal noodle dish, but the genuine version uses dried shrimp, chopped peanuts, Sichuan preserved vegetables, red chili pepper oil, and sesame seeds. It is served moist, like a Zha Jiang Mein (see page 388), but with a bowl of soup on the side. The taste is typically Sichuan: chewy, sharp, and hearty.

Ingredients

¼ cup dried shrimp
¾ cup hot water
¼ cup Sichuan preserved vegetables
½ cup unsalted roasted peanuts
4 whole scallions, trimmed
1 tablespoon sesame seeds
6 tablespoons oil

4 cups chicken stock
1 pound Home-made Noodles (page 386)

Dan dan sauce

2 tablespoons dark soy sauce
2 tablespoons light soy sauce
1 tablespoon red rice vinegar
2 tablespoons sesame paste
1 tablespoon chili oil
2 tablespoons sesame oil
2 tablespoons granulated sugar

PREPARATION

1 Soak shrimp in hot water for 20 minutes. Chop finely and reserve the soaking liquid.

2 Rinse chili and spices off the preserved vegetables, then chop finely.

3 Put peanuts onto a board and use a rolling pin to roll over the peanuts repeatedly until they resemble coarse meal. Set aside.

4 Chop the scallions finely.

5 Roast the sesame seeds in a small saucepan over medium heat until golden, about 1½ minutes. Set aside.

COOKING

1 Mix the dan dan sauce in a bowl with a wire whisk until smooth.

2 Set a heavy 1-quart saucepan over high heat. When very hot, add 2 tablespoons of the oil. Put in shrimp, stirring for 2 minutes or until the shrimp flavor escapes, then add the preserved vegetables and stir for 1 more minute. Remove saucepan from heat.

3 Combine the dan dan sauce, the shrimp, and the preserved vegetables in the saucepan, adding 2 tablespoons oil. Set aside.

4 Half-fill a 4-quart pot with water. Set it over high heat and bring to a boil. While waiting, heat up the chicken stock along with the shrimp juice in a separate saucepan, warming it over very low heat.

5 Loosen the noodle skeins and drop noodles into the boiling water. Cook until the water returns to a boil. Add 1 cup of cold water to the pot, bring the water back to a boil again, then remove saucepan to the sink.

6 Use a strainer to remove the noodles to a colander, and run cold water over to stop the cooking process. Shake the colander to drain excess water.

7 Return noodles to the hot water in the pot and stir just once, then pour the noodles into the colander to drain. Toss in the remaining oil.

8 Serve the dan dan sauce in 4 separate bowls, and put in ¼ of the hot noodles. Sprinkle chopped scallion and sesame seeds on top. Serve with the chicken soup, also in 4 separate bowls. The eater should toss the noodles and the sauce well.

◉◉ Zha Jiang Mein (Noodles in Meat Sauce)

Serves 4
Time 1 minute preparation
15 minutes cooking

炸 醬 麵

As popular in Peking as spaghetti in meat sauce is in the United States, the sauce here has a tangy brown bean paste base.

Ingredients

4 whole scallions,
   trimmed
½ cup oil
1 pound lean ground
   pork
2 tablespoons yellow
   wine
½ cup brown bean
   paste
1 cup chicken stock
2 tablespoons
   granulated sugar
1 teaspoon salt
1 tablespoon sesame oil
1 pound plain noodles

PREPARATION AND COOKING

1 Chop scallions finely and set aside.

2 Set a wok over high heat. When very hot, add ¼ cup of the oil. Put in the pork and stir constantly until the moisture is evaporated, about 4 minutes. Then sizzle in the wine and stir 1 more minute.

3 Add the scallions and the brown bean paste, stirring constantly until the flavor of the bean paste escapes.

4 Add the chicken stock, sugar, and salt. When it boils, turn heat to low. Simmer sauce for 10 minutes or until the sauce is reduced just enough to cover the pork and is thickened. Stir occasionally while simmering.

5 Stir in the remaining ¼ cup of the oil. Simmer 1 more minute, then glaze sauce with sesame oil.

6 Bring at least 2 quarts of water to a boil in a large pot over high heat. Add the noodles and bring the water back to boil. Immediately add 1 cup of cold water to the pot and bring the water to boil again.

7 Remove the pot from the heat, using a strainer to transfer the noodles to a colander, and run cold water over to stop the cooking process. Drain excess moisture.

8 Return noodles to the pot, stir once, then pour into the colander. Shake the colander to drain as much water as possible and put noodles in a large bowl.

9 Each person puts his own share of noodles in an individual bowl and pours meat sauce on top.

◉◉ Stir-Fried Noodles with Pork Shreds

Serves 4 as a luncheon
Time 25 minutes preparation
15 minutes resting
15 minutes cooking

肉絲炒麵

Pan-fried noodles, crisp on both sides and topped with a stir-fried dish, is a common snack. Oil is needed for the crisping, but a nonstick pan conserves oil, facilitates flipping, and simplifies clean-up afterwards.

Ingredients	Seasonings	Sauce mixture
2 pieces extra thick center-cut pork chops, trimmed (about 8 ounces)	2 teaspoons tapioca powder	1 cup chicken stock
6 medium black mushrooms	1 tablespoon light soy sauce	1 tablespoon tapioca powder
½ cup hot water	1 teaspoon pale dry sherry	1 tablespoon oyster sauce
½ pound mung bean sprouts	½ teaspoon granulated sugar	Salt
4 whole scallions, trimmed	Dash of white pepper	
1 pound fresh Chinese noodles	1 teaspoon sesame oil	
2 teaspoons chicken bouillon powder	⅛ teaspoon salt	
8 tablespoons oil	2 tablespoons oil	
¼ teaspoon salt		
1 clove garlic, sliced		
1 tablespoon pale dry sherry		
1 teaspoon sesame oil		

PREPARATION

1 Remove bone and excess fat from pork chops. Cut into slices about ⅛ inch thick, then cut slices into shreds the size of a match stick.

2 Mix seasonings except the oil in a bowl and add pork shreds. Mix well and stir in the oil. Chill for 30 minutes.

3 Soak black mushrooms in hot water until soft. Squeeze to extract moisture and trim stems. Cut caps into ⅛-inch strips. Reserve soaking liquid.

4 Fill the sink with cold water and put in sprouts; green husks of the beans will sink to the bottom and the loose ends and sprouts will float to the top. Stir gently, then take a handful of sprouts at a time and put in colander to drain. You will have about 2 cups of sprouts.

5 Cut scallions into 2-inch lengths.

6 Half-fill a 4-quart saucepan with water. Set it over high heat and bring to a boil. Loosen the noodles and add them to the boiling water, stirring until water is about to boil again. Bring boiling water down by pouring in a cup or so of cold water. Bring water back to a boil, then remove quickly to drain noodles in a colander. Rinse with cold water to stop the cooking process and drain well.

7 Sprinkle chicken bouillon powder evenly on the noodles and toss well.

8 Combine ingredients for sauce with the mushroom liquid in a small bowl and set aside.

COOKING

1 Set a nonstick skillet over medium-high heat. Add 2 tablespoons of oil, whirling around to spread it evenly. Add half the noodles in 1 layer and pan-fry until the bottom is light brown.

2 Turn to brown the other side, slipping in 1 more tablespoon of oil. Remove noodles to one end of an oval serving platter.

3 Pan-fry the remaining noodles in the same manner and place noodle sheet on other side of serving platter.

4 Raise heat to high. Add 1 tablespoon of oil to the skillet. Put in bean sprouts, stirring about 1 minute. Season with salt. Stir to mix with the sprouts. Remove immediately to drain excess juices in a colander.

5 Rinse the skillet and wipe it dry. Set it over high heat. When very hot add the remaining oil. Flavor the oil with garlic for 5 seconds, then add the pork, stirring constantly until shreds separate. Add the mushrooms and scallions, stirring 20 seconds more. Sizzle in the wine, immediately add half of the sauce mixture to the skillet, then give the remainder a quick stir and stream it into the skillet, stirring until sauce boils and thickens. Return bean sprouts to skillet. Mix sauce with all the ingredients in skillet, adding sesame oil to glaze, then pour over fried noodles.

6 Cut noodles in quarters at the table with a kitchen scissors. Serve on individual plates.

⚙⚙⚙ Cold Tossed Noodles with Roast Chicken

Serves 4 as a luncheon dish
Time 20 minutes preparation
+ 1 hour to cook chicken

燒雞涼拌麵

This is a great recipe to utilize leftover roast chicken; for summer luncheons.

Ingredients

1 pound fresh egg noodles
1 cup cold water
¼ cup oil
1 tablespoon sesame oil
1 small frying chicken, about 2½ to 3 pounds
1 slim cucumber or 1 pound selected bean sprouts
2 whole scallions, trimmed
2 sprigs Chinese parsley

Seasonings

2 tablespoons chicken stock
2 teaspoons chicken bouillon powder
2 teaspoons dry mustard
2 tablespoons light soy sauce
1 teaspoon granulated sugar
1 tablespoon sesame paste
1 tablespoon red rice vinegar
Chili oil (optional)

PREPARATION

1 Half-fill a 4-quart Dutch oven with water and set over high heat. Bring to a boil, then loosen noodles and add to the pot. Have the cold water ready; when water is again beginning to boil, add the cold water immediately to bring down the temperature. When water again comes to a boil, pour all contents of the pan into a colander to drain. Run cold water over the noodles to stop the cooking and to rinse off excess starch. Drain thoroughly.

2 Put the noodles in a large bowl. Add ¼ cup of oil and the sesame oil and chill until ready to use.

3 Cook and bone the chicken as for Chinese Roast Chicken (page 193) or use leftover roast chicken. Shred meat finely into strips about 2 inches long and ¼ inch wide.

4 Shred the cucumber finely into julienne strips. Wipe and chill. If bean sprouts are used, pour boiling water over to wilt them. Put them in a colander and run cold water over to keep them crunchy. Drain and chill.

5 Mix ingredients for seasoning in a jar and shake well.

6 Shred the scallions into 1½-inch strips.

7 Break the parsley into 1½-inch lengths.

8 In a large salad bowl, combine noodles, chicken, cucumber (and/or sprouts), scallions, and parsley. Toss with seasonings and serve cold.

◉◉Stir-Fried Rice Sticks, Singapore Style

Serves 4 as a luncheon dish
Time 30 minutes preparation
10 minutes cooking

星 洲 炒 米 粉

Over 80 percent of the inhabitants of the Republic of Singapore are Fujian Chinese in ancestry. Fujian tradition and Malay ingredients yielded this dish, popular in Hong Kong cafes.

Ingredients

½ pound rice sticks
1 can (13¾ ounces) chicken broth + equal part water
4 medium black mushrooms
2 cups selected bean sprouts
2 whole eggs
Salt
Oil for greasing skillet
4 ounces Cantonese Roast Pork (page 252)
3 ounces cooked shrimp

1 large shallot
1 medium onion
¼ cup + 3 tablespoons oil
2 tablespoons curry powder
1 tablespoon light soy sauce or fish sauce

PREPARATION

1 Hold rice sticks in piles under cold running water and rinse quickly. Place rice sticks in a colander to drain.

2 Bring diluted chicken broth to a boil in a 3-quart saucepan, then remove saucepan from heat. Place in the rice sticks and soak until saturated. Drain thoroughly.

3 Soak mushrooms in warm water until soft. Trim stems and squeeze caps to extract moisture. Shred finely.

4 Remove heads and tails (optional) from the sprouts. Soak in cold water and keep refrigerated. Drain well shortly before using.

5 Lightly beat eggs with a pinch of salt. Grease a nonstick skillet thinly with oil and set over medium heat. When skillet is hot, add the egg mixture. Tilt skillet around so as to spread egg mixture evenly in a thin layer. Cook eggs until set. Remove and shred finely, about ⅛ by 1½ inches.

6 Shred the pork finely, the same size as the egg shreds.

7 Cut shrimp the same size as egg shreds.

8 Cut shallot crosswise into slices 1/16 inch thick.

9 Cut onion vertically in half, then shred crosswise into ⅛-inch strips.

COOKING

1 Set a wok over high heat. When hot, add ¼ cup of oil. Twirl oil around to coat the wok evenly, then add the rice sticks, spreading in 1 thick layer. Pan-fry for 5 minutes, then turn to fry the other side until heated through. Remove.

2 Add 2 tablespoons more oil to the wok and fry the shallot slices until golden. Remove.

3 Add onion strips to wok, along with mushrooms, stirring several times around the wok. Add the sprouts, stirring 30 seconds. Remove.

4 Add 1 tablespoon more oil to the center, then put in the curry powder, stirring once. Add the rice sticks, pork, egg, shrimp, onion, mushrooms, and sprouts, tossing and stirring to mix well.

5 Season with light soy sauce and salt. Decorate with fried shallots and serve.

◉Shahe Fen (Rice Sheet)

沙河粉

Yields 6 sheets, about 2¼ pounds
Time 5 minutes preparation
30 minutes steaming

Even though fresh shahe fen is available in Chinese grocery stores in the United States, it does not freeze as well as the noodles and therefore has to be consumed soon after purchase. Reconstituted dried shahe fen has a grainy texture that is a far cry from the fresh product. Fortunately, making your own is just as easy as making American pancakes. If the rice sheet is rolled up into a "pig-intestine" shape, served with a tangy sauce, it becomes a great breakfast item in South China.

Ingredients
1 cup rice flour
¼ cup wheat starch
¼ cup tapioca powder
2 cups water
1½ tablespoons oil
1 teaspoon salt
Oil for greasing pan

Utensils
1 round cake rack (8 inches)
2 baking pans (8 by 8 by 2 inches)

PREPARATION
Mix all ingredients except the greasing oil with a wire whisk in a mixing bowl until well blended.

COOKING

1 Set the cake rack into the wok and pour in water to come up just below the rack. Bring water to a boil over high heat.

2 Have a kettle of boiling water ready for replenishing.

3 Generously grease the baking pan. Restir the flour mixture, and add ⅓ cup to cover the bottom of the pan. Set the pan on the cake rack. Cover wok and steam over high heat for 3 minutes or until the rice sheet looks bubbly.

4 Remove the baking pan to cool in a sink filled with ½ inch of cold water for 1 minute. Loosen the 2 top corners of the rice sheet and peel gently half way down, then fold it over the lower half of the rice sheet. Transfer it to a platter.

5 While 1 baking pan is being cooled, use another baking pan for the next sheet and repeat steps 3 and 4. Finish all the sheets in the same manner. You will have very little waiting time in between preparing sheets. Pile the rice sheets up. Wrap in plastic and chill for at least 1 hour, or up to 2 days in the refrigerator.

VARIATION: Rolled Rice Sheet

The rice sheet can be rolled into a loose cylinder about 1¼ inches in diameter, then cut with scissors into 1-inch lengths. This is the Cantonese "pig-intestine fen." Serve it with the following sauce and sprinkle roasted sesame seeds on top.

Sauce

1 tablespoon prepared
  mustard
1 tablespoon hoisin
  sauce
1 teaspoon granulated
  sugar
1 tablespoon dark soy
  sauce
1 tablespoon sesame
  paste
2 tablespoons oil

Stir-Fried Rice Noodles (Shaho Fen) with Beef and Pepper in Black Bean Sauce

Serves 2 as a main meal
Time 10 minutes preparation
1 hour chilling
10 minutes cooking

豉椒牛河粉

Considering the ingredients, this dish is actually a meal in itself, although it is a Cantonese snack. Traditional pan-frying of the rice noodles requires much oil so that the noodles will not stick to the wok. Reheating the rice noodles in the oven or in the microwave oven proves far better than pan-frying without sacrificing the fine texture.

Ingredients
8 ounces flank steak
1 medium bell pepper
½ sweet red pepper
(or 2 red chili peppers)
1 small onion
3 tablespoons fermented black beans
2 cloves garlic, crushed
1 batch Shaho Fen (page 394)
2 cups oil
2 teaspoons pale dry sherry

Seasonings
2 teaspoons tapioca powder
1 tablespoons dark soy sauce
½ teaspoon granulated sugar
1 teaspoon sesame oil
Dash of white pepper

Sauce mixture
1 cup chicken stock
1 tablespoon tapioca powder
¼ teaspoon salt

PREPARATION

1 Slice steak across the grain into slices about ⅛ inch thick. Mix with seasonings in a bowl and keep refrigerated for 1 hour.

2 Remove seeds and pulp from bell pepper and red pepper. Cut them into 1 by ½-inch pieces.

3 Cut the onion crosswise in half, then cut each half lengthwise in half. Separate the layers.

4 Rinse black beans and put them in a small bowl. Add the garlic and smash with the end of the handle of a Chinese cleaver until black beans and garlic become a thick paste. Set aside.

5 Mix sauce in a bowl.

COOKING

1 Preheat oven to 300 degrees.

2 Line a baking pan with aluminum foil. Cut the shaho fen (rice sheets) into noodle strips about ½ inch wide. Loosen noodle strips and arrange them in 1 layer in the baking pan. Cover with another piece of aluminum foil. Bake in the oven for 10 minutes. If a microwave oven is used, arrange rice noodles evenly in a serving platter. Cover with plastic wrap; cook 2 minutes or until heated through.

3 Five minutes after the noodles are set in the oven, have a strainer placed over a bowl ready for oil-dipping the beef.

4 Set a wok over high heat and, when very hot, add the oil. Wait for about 2 minutes, then give the meat in the bowl a quick stir and put it in the oil, stirring constantly until slices separate, about 30 seconds. Remove the meat with a deep-frying strainer and rest it on a platter to drain oil.

5 Reheat the oil in the wok until a piece of scallion green dropped in sizzles and moves about quickly (about 350 degrees). Add the peppers and onion to the oil, stirring just a few times, then pour the vegetables with the oil into the strainer-lined bowl to drain, leaving about 1 tablespoon of oil in the wok.

6 Set the wok back on high heat. When the oil is very hot, add the black bean paste, stirring constantly for 30 seconds or until flavor escapes. Return meat to wok and sizzle in the wine.

7 Restir the sauce mixture and stream it into the wok, stirring to prevent lumps. Add the pepper and onion to mix with beef. Turn heat off.

8 Transfer the rice noodles to a serving dish. Pour the meat and vegetables over. Serve hot.

SPRING ROLLS, WONTONS, AND DUMPLINGS

Spring Rolls

Yields about 2 dozen
Time 30 minutes preparation
30 minutes chilling
20 minutes assembling
15 minutes cooking

Also known as egg rolls in the United States, as one version uses a sheet of pan-fried eggs for the skin. The best wrapper, however, is in the Shanghai style, made with flour and water but no eggs at all. Now available in frozen form, these wrappers can be kept indefinitely in the freezer and are thin and strong. Besides, they do not turn brownish-black as readily as the other kinds.

There are no rigid rules for ingredients in the stuffing—any kind of cooked or raw meat (even leftovers) and any crunchy vegetables will make a wonderful combination. Techniques for shaping are shown on pages 78–80.

Ingredients

1 whole chicken breast, about 12 ounces
6 medium black mushrooms
⅔ cup warm water
1 cup bamboo shoots
2 whole scallions, trimmed
½ medium carrot
1 stalk celery
3 sprigs Chinese parsley
½ cup chopped cooked shrimp
½ cup shredded Cantonese Roast Pork (page 252) or ham
2 whole eggs + 1 yolk

Salt
6 cups + 4 tablespoons oil, approximately
1 clove garlic, shredded
½ teaspoon granulated sugar
24 spring roll wrappers
1 teaspoon tapioca powder mixed with ½ egg white

Seasonings

1 tablespoon oil
½ egg white
2 teaspoons tapioca powder
1 teaspoon pale dry sherry
½ teaspoon granulated sugar
2 teaspoons light soy sauce
¼ teaspoon salt
Dash of white pepper

Sauce mixture

1 tablespoon tapioca powder
1 tablespoon light soy sauce
1 teaspoon sesame oil

PREPARATION

1 All ingredients used are to be cut into fine shreds about ⅛ by ⅛ by 1½ inches.

2 Remove skin from chicken and bone the meat. Trim fat, gristle, and membranes, then shred finely. Mix seasonings in a small bowl, adding chicken shreds. Mix well and chill for at least 30 minutes.

3 Soak mushrooms in warm water until soft. Trim the stems, then squeeze the caps to remove excess moisture. Shred finely; reserve soaking liquid.

4 Shred the bamboo shoots finely. Blanch in boiling water for 1 minute, then rinse with cold water. Drain.

5 Cut scallions, carrot, and celery into 1½-inch lengths, then shred.

6 Rinse parsley and break into 2-inch lengths.

7 Shred the shrimp meat.

8 Shred the pork.

9 Beat the eggs and yolk lightly with a pinch of salt. Set a nonstick pan over medium heat and spread about 2 teaspoons of oil over the surface. Add the egg mixture, twirling to form a thin layer. Remove when set and cool. Shred finely.

10 Combine sauce mixture with the reserved mushroom soaking liquid.

COOKING

1 Set a wok over high heat. When very hot, add 2 tablespoons of oil. Flavor oil with garlic shreds for 10 seconds, then add the chicken, stirring constantly until the shreds of chicken separate. Remove and reserve.

2 Add 2 additional tablespoons of oil to the wok. Add the mushrooms, stirring a few times, then add the bamboo shoots, carrot, and celery in succession. Season with salt and sugar and keep stirring for about 1 minute.

3 Add the pork, shrimp, and chicken to the wok and stir to mix well. Push the ingredients to the side, leaving a space in the center.

4 Restir the sauce mixture and add to the wok in a gradual stream, stirring until thickened. Remove wok from the heat and add the egg shreds and scallions. Toss to mix and keep refrigerated until ready to use. Mix in the parsley leaves.

ASSEMBLING

1 If frozen wrappers are used, thaw completely. Cover with a towel and separate carefully 1 at a time.

2 Place wrapper with smooth side down. Put about 2 tablespoons of the filling on the lower center (right below the diagonal). Lift the corner near you and turn to cover the filling.

3 Bring the side corners to overlap each other. Tuck securely.

4 Roll toward the tip to form a 4 by 1½-inch envelope. Keep it as firm as possible, and, at the same time, press to eliminate excess air inside the envelope.

5 Seal by moistening the far edges with tapioca and egg mixture. Arrange the rolls flat on a tray with the sealed side down. Cover with a kitchen towel if to be used immediately, or cover with plastic wrap and refrigerate (no more than 4 hours) until ready to use.

FINAL COOKING

1 Heat remaining oil in a wok to 350 degrees. Deep-fry the egg rolls in 2 batches until light golden.

2 Turn rolls occasionally for even browning.

3 Drain spring rolls on paper towels and serve hot.

VARIATION: Miniature Spring Roll

Conveniently finger-sized for easy serving, these are favorites in cocktail parties in Hong Kong. Use the same ingredients as the regular spring rolls and prepare the filling the same way.

1 Cut the wrapper diagonally into 2 triangles. Trim off the 2 corners, using the cut-out portions to form a small rectangle for reinforcement at the center of the envelope-shaped skin (see page 79).

2 Put about 1 tablespoon of filling on the reinforced area. Bring the bottom edge up to fold over the filling, matching the top of the reinforcement.

3 Fold about 1 inch from the left side and right side, overlapping one another. Roll toward the tip of the triangle and seal with a dab of beaten egg.

4 Set a wok over high heat and bring oil to 350 degrees. When ready, deep-fry the rolls in 3 batches.

5 Drain on paper towels and keep warm in the oven if not to be served immediately.

◉◉◉ Wontons in Soup

Serves 4 as a luncheon dish
Time 1 hour preparation and
assembling
3 hours chilling
15 minutes cooking

The traditional Cantonese wonton is a light snack, rather than a soup in a full meal. There should be more shrimp meat than pork in the stuffing, and the use of the great earth fish (dried flounder) lends a subtle flavor. Wonton skins available in the United States will do, though they are a bit too thick by the Cantonese standard, but you can always make your own (same as the shao mai skin, only cut into squares rather than in rounds, page 408). The techniques for shaping are shown on pages 84–85.

Ingredients
12 ounces shrimp in
the shell
Salt
1 great earth fish,
about 2 to 3 ounces
1 tablespoon oil
3 ounces lean ground
pork
½ package wonton
wrappers (about 40)
1 egg white, beaten
lightly

3 cups Basic Soup
Stock (page 108)
3 cups cold water
2 teaspoons sesame oil
2 tablespoons light soy
sauce
1 whole scallion,
trimmed and
chopped

Seasonings
1 egg yolk
2 teaspoons tapioca
powder
2 teaspoons sesame oil
1 teaspoon light soy
sauce
½ teaspoon salt
⅛ teaspoon white
pepper

PREPARATION

1 Shell and devein the shrimp. Put them in a colander and rub generously with salt. Rinse with cold water to remove mucus, then drain and pat dry with paper towels. Chill in the refrigerator for at least 1 hour.

2 Roast 1 side of the great earth fish over low heat directly on the stove until pleasant fishy flavor is detected, then turn and roast the other side the same way for a total of 2 minutes. Bone fish while hot by tearing the meat from the skin and the bone. Reserve the bones, head, skin, and all. Break the fish meat into ½-inch pieces.

3 Set a small heavy saucepan over medium heat. When the pan is hot, add the tablespoon of oil. Add fish pieces, stirring constantly for 1 minute, and remove from the oil. Cool fish for 5 minutes, then chop it finely into bacon-bit pieces. You will have about 2 tablespoons.

4 Split each shrimp along the back and dice.

5 In a mixing bowl, combine the pork and the seasonings. Stir in 1 direction with a wooden spoon until the pork holds together in a paste. Add the shrimp and the fish bits and stir some more. Scoop up the meat mixture by hand and beat it back to the bowl several times until the mixture is elastic. Chill for at least 2 hours.

6 Combine the reserved fish bones and scraps with 2 cups of water in a small saucepan and cook over medium heat until water is reduced to 1 cup, about 20 minutes. Strain soup through a strainer to combine with the soup stock in another saucepan and set aside.

ASSEMBLING

1 Place 1 full teaspoon of filling into the center of the second quarter of a wrapper. Fold the first quarter (with the corner) over to cover filling.

2 Fold the first and second quarters over the third, leaving the top corner as a flap.

3 Bend the 2 angles at the base inward, pressing with 2 thumbs to expel the air inside.

4 Moisten 1 angle with egg white to paste to the other angle.

COOKING

1 Heat the stock over high heat until it comes to a boil. Turn the heat to a simmer.

2 On another burner, place a 4-quart (or larger) saucepan, half-filled with water, and set it over high heat. Bring the water to a boil and, when boiling vigorously, add the wontons. Bring back to a boil, then bring it down by adding a cup of cold water. Continue to cook until the wontons rise to the surface. Remove wontons •with a deep-frying strainer to a large bowl of cold water, then drain immediately.

3 Bring chicken stock back to a vigorous boil and add the sesame oil and soy sauce, then the wontons.

4 Pour wontons and soup into a serving bowl, sprinkle chopped scallion on top, and serve in individual bowls.

◉◉◉Vegetable and Pork Wontons

Yields 4 dozen
Time 30 minutes soaking
15 minutes preparation
1 hour chilling
15 minutes assembling
15 minutes cooking

菜肉雲吞

While Cantonese wontons are light and good for a summer day, the more substantial Shanghai wontons here are suited for cool evenings. Real Shanghai wonton skins are even thicker and larger in size, but not as readily available as the Cantonese skins. Pork and green vegetables make a typical filling.

Ingredients

¼ cup dried shrimp
½ cup hot water
1 tablespoon oil
1½ pounds fresh
  spinach
2 tablespoons
  granulated sugar
½ pound lean ground
  pork
4 slices gingerroot,
  grated
4 whole scallions,
  trimmed and
  chopped
48 wonton skins
6 cups chicken stock

Seasonings

1 whole egg
1 tablespoon tapioca
  powder
1 tablespoon light soy
  sauce
¾ teaspoon salt
1 teaspoon pale dry
  sherry
1 teaspoon granulated
  sugar
2 tablespoons sesame
  oil

PREPARATION AND COOKING

1 Soak shrimp in hot water for 30 minutes or until soft. Drain and mince finely and reserve the soaking liquid.

2 Stir-fry the shrimp with the oil over high heat. Stir constantly until shrimp flavor escapes, then add the soaking liquid and cook to evaporate moisture. Remove and set aside.

3 Break leaves off the spinach and rinse well. You will have about 4 cups of spinach leaves. Blanch leaves in 2 quarts of boiling water with the sugar until leaves are bright green and wilted. Pour spinach into a colander and run cold water over to stop the cooking process. Squeeze to extract as much moisture as possible. Pile spinach leaves into a block and chop finely.

4 Mix ground pork with seasonings in a large bowl. Stir with a wooden spoon in 1 direction to firm up meat, then add ginger, chopped scallions, dried shrimp, and spinach. Continue to stir until ingredients hold together for 5 more minutes. Chill in refrigerator for 1 hour.

5 Use 1 tablespoon of filling for each wonton. Assemble and cook the same way as Wontons in Soup (page 400).

◉◉ Wonton Ears with Lychee Sauce

Yields about 60 ears
Time 10 minutes preparation
   20 minutes assembling
   20 minutes cooking

荔枝雲吞

Fried wontons shaped to scoop up the lychee sauce make this Cantonese appetizer fun and tasty. The techniques for shaping are shown on pages 85–86.

Ingredients	Seasonings	Lychee sauce mixture
½ pound lean ground pork	1 tablespoon light soy sauce	2 tablespoons red wine vinegar
2 scallions (white part only)	¼ teaspoon salt	1 tablespoon brown sugar
1 can (20 ounces) lychees	1 whole egg	2 tablespoons tomato catsup
1 package wonton wrappers	2 teaspoons tapioca powder	2 teaspoons chicken bouillon powder
4 cups + 3 tablespoons oil, approximately	2 teaspoons sesame oil	½ cup water
1 clove garlic, crushed	1 teaspoon pale dry sherry	2 tablespoons tapioca powder
2 teaspoons sesame oil	1 teaspoon granulated sugar	
	Dash of white pepper	

PREPARATION

1 Mix seasonings and pork together in a bowl. Stir in 1 direction with a wooden spoon until the meat holds together. Scrape by hand and beat meat back to the bowl several times until firm.

2 Chop scallion whites finely and add to the pork.

3 Drain lychees and reserve juice. Quarter each lychee.

4 Mix ingredients for sauce in a bowl; add lychee juice and stir.

5 Use a 2½-inch cookie cutter to cut the square wrappers into rounds.

COOKING

1 Set a wok over high heat. When very hot, add 4 cups oil. Wait for about 4 minutes, then test the temperature by dropping a piece of scallion green into the oil. If small bubbles appear around the green immediately with sizzling, the oil is ready, about 300 degrees.

2 Drop in wonton ears 1 at a time for a total of 15 ears, stirring constantly. Deep-fry until golden, then remove in succession to drain on paper towels.

3 Deep-fry the remaining 3 batches in the same manner. Keep them warm in the oven.

4 Pour oil out and wipe wok clean. Set the wok back on high heat. When hot, add 1 tablespoon oil. Flavor oil with crushed garlic until brown. Restir sauce mixture and stream into the wok, stirring constantly to prevent lumps. Turn heat to medium. Add the lychees and bring sauce to a boil. Correct seasoning. Glaze sauce with the remaining oil and sesame oil.

5 Pour lychee sauce into a sauce bowl and serve as a dip for the wonton ears.

◉◉◉Cantonese Soup Dumplings

Serves 6 as a luncheon dish
Time 40 minutes preparation
30 minutes soaking
15 minutes cooking

羊城水餃

Similar to wontons and sold in wonton restaurants in Canton, soup dumplings are more substantial by the use of black mushrooms and bamboo shoots, also by adding your choice of flavoring ingredients. The techniques for shaping are shown on pages 83–84.

Ingredients

½ pound shrimp in the shell
Salt
½ pound lean pork, cut from the loin
2 ounces pork fat
8 medium black mushrooms
1 cup bamboo shoots
3 scallions, green and white parts separated
2 tablespoons tapioca powder
1 package round dumpling skins (about 60) or wonton wrappers cut to a circle with a cookie cutter
4 cups Basic Soup Stock (page 108)
Soy sauce
Sesame oil

Optional shrimp flavor

2 tablespoons dried shrimp powder
1 tablespoon oil

Optional fish flavor

2 to 3 ounces great earth fish
1 tablespoon oil

Optional jade pillar flavor

1 ounce jade pillars
1 slice gingerroot
1 teaspoon pale dry sherry

Seasonings

2 tablespoons light soy sauce
¼ teaspoon salt
1 whole egg
2 teaspoons sesame oil
1 teaspoon granulated sugar
¼ teaspoon white pepper
1 tablespoon oil (2 tablespoons oil if jade pillar flavor is used)

PREPARATION

1 Shell and devein the shrimp (see page 151). Rub generously with salt and rinse with cold running water, removing film until the shrimp meat turns translucent gray. Drain and pat dry. Cut into ¼-inch cubes. Chill until ready to use.

2 Cut pork into ³⁄₁₆-inch cubes. Reserve.

3 Blanch pork fat in boiling water until it is no longer soft and white. Soak in cold water for 30 minutes to keep it crispy. Cut into the same size as the pork.

4 Soak the mushrooms in warm water until soft. Squeeze to extract moisture; cut into ⅛-inch strips and then into ¼-inch lengths.

5 Slice the bamboo shoots into ⅛-inch pieces. Blanch in boiling water for 1 minute, then rinse thoroughly with cold water. Drain and pat dry with paper towels. Shred into strips the same size as the mushrooms. Put in a clean kitchen towel and squeeze out as much moisture as possible.

6 Use about 4 inches of the white part of the scallions and shred into strips first, then cut into the same size as the mushrooms. Chop the green parts fine.

7 In preparing optional flavor, choose one from among the 3 versions given. If dried shrimp flavor is preferred, set a small heavy saucepan over high heat. When hot, add the oil. When the oil is very hot, stir in the dried shrimp powder and remove the saucepan immediately from the heat. Set aside. For fish flavor, follow instructions given in Wontons in Soup (page 400) to prepare the great earth fish. For the jade pillar flavor, soak pillars with ½ cup of hot water, then add ginger and sherry. Steam over high heat for 20 minutes. Flake pillars and cut into ¼-inch lengths. Reserve soaking liquid and add to the soup stock.

8 Add the soy sauce and salt for seasonings to the pork in a large bowl, mixing with your fingers until the meat holds together. Combine with the next 5 seasonings ingredients and mix again.

9 Add the pork fat, diced shrimp, mushrooms, bamboo shoots, scallion whites, and one of the flavoring ingredients if used. Sprinkle tapioca powder on top, then mix in 1 direction until all ingredients hold together. Chill until firm, about 2 hours.

ASSEMBLING

1 Place about 1½ tablespoons of the filling on the center of the upper half of the dumpling skin.

2 Fold the lower half over and press lightly to help the skin adhere to the filling and expel air. A half-moon shape is now formed.

3 Gather the edges toward the center as you would draw a string purse. A dumpling is now formed. Repeat for remaining dumplings.

COOKING

1 Add the soup stock to another saucepan and set it over medium heat. Bring to a boil. Season with salt. Turn heat to simmer.

2 Half-fill a 6-quart saucepan with water, setting it over high heat. When water comes to a boil, add all the dumplings at once. When water returns to a boil and dumplings float to the top, add a cup of cold water to the pot. Bring water back to a boil and pour dumplings immediately into a colander.

3 Serve soup in individual bowls. Put several dumplings in each bowl and pour hot soup over to cover. Add 1 teaspoon each of soy sauce, sesame oil, and scallion greens.

Note: Dried shrimp powder, great earth fish, and jade pillars are available in Chinese markets.

⊚⊚⊚ Cantonese Steamed Dumplings (*Shao Mai*)

Yields	40 dumplings
Time	1 hour preparation
	2½ hours chilling
	30 minutes assembling
	15 minutes cooking

燒 賣

This is a typical Cantonese dim sum dish, meaning "cook and sell." It is too delicate for the regular wonton wrapper but the special *shao mai* wrappers are now available in most large Chinese markets. Make your own if there are none available in your area, or dust enough cornstarch between several pieces of wonton skin and roll them hard to make them thinner, then trim to the desired shape and size. The techniques for shaping are shown on pages 91–92.

The secret in making good *shao mai* is the firm packing of the stuffing, which can be done conveniently in the cavity formed between the thumb and index finger. The appetizing-looking dot of orange used to be the coral from crabs, but is now colored shrimp meat.

Ingredients	Seasonings
40 *shao mai* wrappers	1 teaspoon salt
8 ounces lean pork, cut from loin	1 tablespoon light soy sauce
8 ounces shrimp in the shell	1 egg white
3 ounces pork fatback (optional)	2 teaspoons sesame oil
8 medium black mushrooms	1/8 teaspoon white pepper
3 scallions (white part only)	2 teaspoons pale dry sherry
1 or 2 drops orange food coloring	1 teaspoon granulated sugar
	1 tablespoon tapioca powder

PREPARATION

1 Use a 2¼-inch cookie cutter to trim each wrapper smaller.

2 Remove excess fat and gristle from meat. Cut into 3/16-inch cubes.

3 Shell, devein, and clean shrimp with salt (see page 151). Rinse thoroughly under cold water, then pat dry with paper towels. Chill at least 30 minutes or until used.

4 Blanch pork fat in boiling water for 10 minutes. Rinse and soak in cold water. Chop finely.

5 Soak mushrooms in warm water until soft. Trim stems. Cut caps into cubes the same size as the pork. Squeeze to extract moisture.

6 Cut scallions into bits. Dice all but 4 shrimp.

7 In a large bowl, add the pork, salt, and light soy sauce, mixing with a wooden spoon until the pork holds together. Then add the next 6 seasonings. Mix.

8 Add the shrimp, pork fat, and mushrooms to the pork mixture, mixing well. Scoop up with your hand and beat mixture back to the bowl repeatedly until it is firm and elastic, about 5 to 7 minutes. Add in the scallions. Chill until firm, about 2 hours.

9 For decorative purposes, mash the reserved shrimp with the flat side of a cleaver. Chop finely, then remove to a small bowl and add 1 or 2 drops of orange food coloring. Mix well, wrap and chill.

ASSEMBLING

1 Place a wrapper upon your slightly cupped palm. Using one hand, scoop up with a butter knife about 1 tablespoon of the filling and place it on the center of the wrapper.

2 Insert the knife downward into the bulk of the filling; both the filling and the wrapper will stick to the blade of the knife.

3 Withdraw your palm and form a ring with your thumb and index finger. Gently push the wrapper and filling together toward the knife. The filling now assumes roughly the shape of a circular cylinder encased in the wrapper.

4 Withdraw the knife. Use the flat side of the blade to pat the filling, packing and increasing the contact between the filling and wrapper and also to smooth the top of the *shao mai*.

5 Place a small dot of orange shrimp paste (about the size of a soybean) on the smooth top of the *shao mai* for decoration.

6 Arrange the *shao mais* close together on a well-greased plate.

COOKING

Set the plate with the *shao mais* in the steamer. Pour enough boiling water into the base of the steamer to come up within 1 inch of the rack. Cover steamer tightly and steam over high heat for 12 minutes. Wrap the cover of the steamer with a kitchen towel to prevent the dripping of condensed steam on the *shao mais*.

SHAO MAI WRAPPER

Ingredients
1 cup unbleached flour
1 tablespoon gluten
   flour
2 whole eggs, lightly
   beaten
cornstarch for sprinkling
   (optional)

1 Sift the 2 kinds of flour together into a mixing bowl. Add eggs gradually, stirring with a wooden spoon to form a dough. Knead until smooth.

2 Cover dough with a dampened kitchen towel and let sit for 20 minutes. Divide dough into several portions and roll each portion into small dough rods about ½ inch wide. Cut the rods into discs about ¼ inch thick. With a rolling pin, roll each disc into rounds. Sprinkle discs with cornstarch when necessary and sprinkle cornstarch on board.

3 Accumulate about 12 rounds, sprinkling cornstarch between each, to form a pile. Roll the whole pile to make the individual rounds thinner. With a cookie cutter, cut each round into 2¼-inch circles.

4 Continue to make the wrappers in batches. Wrap and chill until ready to use (or freeze).

SHAO MAI (CANTONESE STEAMED DUMPLINGS)
PAGE 406

CURRIED CRESCENTS
PAGE 417

⊛⊛⊛Pan-Stickers (*Guo-tieh*)

Yields 48
Time 30 minutes preparation
20 minutes resting
1 hour chilling
30 minutes assembling
15 minutes cooking

鍋貼

A North China appetizer, these pan-fried dumplings are habitually made with a thick, doughy skin and a meat–vegetable filling. They are packed tightly in 1 layer, pan-fried on the bottom side, but served upside down to show the charred bottom. The techniques for shaping are shown on pages 89–90.

Ingredients	Seasonings	Dough
½ pound napa cabbage	½ teaspoon salt	3 cups all-purpose flour
½ teaspoon salt	2 tablespoons light soy sauce	¼ teaspoon salt
2 whole scallions, trimmed	⅛ teaspoon white pepper	¾ cup boiling water
1 pound lean ground pork	2 teaspoons grated gingerroot	¼ cup cold water
6 tablespoons oil	1 tablespoon pale dry sherry	**Ginger and vinegar sauce**
1 cup water	1 tablespoon sesame oil	2 tablespoons finely shredded gingerroot
2 teaspoons distilled white vinegar	2 tablespoons tapioca powder	¼ cup red rice vinegar
		1 tablespoon sesame oil

PREPARATION (FILLING)

1 Rinse cabbage and chop into small bits the same size as a soybean. Stir in the salt and mix. Let sit for 10 minutes, then squeeze to extract moisture.

2 Chop scallions finely.

3 In a large mixing bowl, combine pork with salt and soy sauce for seasonings. Stir for 30 seconds, then add next 5 seasonings, plus the cabbage and the scallions. Stir in 1 direction until all ingredients hold together, about 5 minutes. Chill until firm, about 1 hour.

PREPARATION (DOUGH)

1 Sift the flour and salt together in a large mixing bowl. Make a well in the center and add boiling water. Mix flour with a wooden spoon.

2 Cover bowl with a towel for 5 minutes, then add the cold water, mixing again with the flour mixture. Cover and let sit for 15 minutes.

3 Turn dough out on a floured board. Knead until smooth, sprinkling additional flour on the board if necessary.

ASSEMBLING

1 Divide dough into 4 equal parts. Roll each part by hand into a rod, then cut each rod into 12 small pieces.

2 Roll each small piece into a round wrapper about 3 inches in diameter. Sprinkle flour lightly on the kneading board if necessary.

3 Place about 1 tablespoon of filling in the center of a wrapper and shape the filling into a strip.

4 Fold the wrapper in half and pinch the edges together at the center of the arc, leaving the 2 ends open.

5 With your fingers, make about 3 to 4 pleats in 1 side of the opening at each end. Pinch all along the edges to seal.

6 Remove the finished pan-stickers to a floured tray. Keep covered with a dry cloth as you finish making the rest.

COOKING

1 Set a heavy 10-inch skillet over high heat until drops of water sprinkled into it sizzle and dry up. Add 3 tablespoons of oil and spread it around to grease the bottom evenly.

2 Add half the pan-stickers, arranging them closely together, with pleated sides up. Pan-fry over medium heat for 2 minutes, or until the bottoms are lightly browned.

3 Add ½ cup of water and 1 teaspoon of the vinegar. Cover the skillet and cook for 8 minutes, or until the liquid is evaporated.

4 Remove cover and continue to pan-fry until the pan-stickers can be moved around easily. Remove skillet from heat, and cover it with a 12-inch serving platter.

5 Flip skillet to turn the pan-stickers out, showing the browned sides up.

6 Pan-fry the remaining pan-stickers in the same manner and serve all hot with ginger and vinegar sauce on the side.

VARIATION: Boiled Dumplings (*Jiaozi*)

Here 1 cup of cold water is used to mix with the dough instead of using ¾ cup of boiling water and ¼ cup of cold water, as in preparing the dough for *Guo-tieh*, thus the dough is more pliable. Also, the same filling can be used.

The assembling of the *jiaozi* is made simple by pinching the edges together instead of pleating. Just put a tablespoon of the filling in the center of the wrapper and fold the wrapper in half. Pinch to seal the edges to form a *jiaozi* in a half-moon shape.

To cook, bring a pot of water in a 6-quart saucepan to a vigorous boil over high heat. Add the *jiaozis* in 1 batch, stirring with a wooden spoon a few times around until the water boils back, then add 1 cup of cold water to the pan to bring down the temperature of the cooking liquid. Cook for about 5 minutes or until *jiaozis* float on top of the water. Skim with a deep-frying strainer to 2 separate platters, keeping the *jiaozis* in 1 layer to prevent sticking together. Serve hot with ginger and vinegar sauce.

◉◉ Mandarin Pancakes

Yields 40 pancakes
Time   30 minutes preparation
            20 minutes resting
            40 minutes cooking

單餅

These pancakes can be prepared ahead of time and refrigerated for 2 to 3 days or kept frozen for months. Steam them until hot and serve. The technique for shaping is shown on pages 94–96.

Ingredients

3½ cups all-purpose
  flour
1 cup boiling water
⅓ cup cold water

½ cup sesame oil
Oil for greasing

PREPARATION

1 Sift the flour into a large mixing bowl. Make a well in the center and add the boiling water, a little at a time, incorporating the flour by stirring it into the water with a wooden spoon or chopsticks.

2 Cover bowl and let sit for 5 minutes, then add the cold water, mixing well.

3 Turn the flour mixture out and work with your fingers to blend until a dough is formed. Cover with a dampened towel and set aside for 15 minutes.

4 Remove dough to a board and knead for 10 to 12 minutes or until smooth.

5 Divide dough into 4 equal portions. Roll each part into a rod, then divide each dough rod into 10 equal pieces.

6 Grease an area of the kneading board about 10 inches square with oil to prevent sticking. Flatten each piece of dough into a 2-inch round and brush evenly with sesame oil on the surface. Place another round on top, forming a 2-layered round. Roll into a thin pancake about 6 inches in diameter and ⅛ inch thick. Grease the board with more oil if needed.

7 Roll 2 pancakes, then proceed with the cooking. Continue to roll and cook, 2 pancakes at a time, until all the dough is used up.

COOKING

1 Set a griddle (or heavy skillet) over medium heat. Pan-fry each pancake for 1 minute or until the surface bubbles and brown spots appear on the bottom side. Turn to brown on other side for about another 30 seconds.

2 Remove pancake and pull the 2 layers apart while hot. Stack pancakes on a platter and cover with a lightly dampened cloth.

3 Finish pan-frying the remaining pancakes.

Note: Cooking time can be cut in half if 2 griddles are used simultaneously.

◉◉◉◉ Cantonese Flat Bread

Yields 4 dozen pieces
Time 20 minutes preparation
40 minutes resting and rolling
25 minutes steaming

What is baked in the West is often steamed in Chinese cookery. The flat bread (Cantonese call it "thousand-layer bread") was originally meant to complement the crispy skin of roast duck and roast suckling pig. However this dough can be used to make stuffed steamed buns as well. Techniques for shaping are shown on pages 93–94.

Ingredients

2 cups all-purpose flour	½ cup granulated sugar
2½ teaspoons baking powder	1 tablespoon lard or vegetable shortening
¾ teaspoon distilled white vinegar	½ cup lukewarm water
2 egg whites	Flour for sprinkling
	Peanut oil for greasing

PREPARATION

1 Sift the flour and baking powder together onto a kneading board, making a well in the center. Into the well place the vinegar, egg whites, sugar, and lard. Use your fingers to mix the ingredients in 1 direction, gradually also pouring in the warm water. Incorporate the flour from the side while mixing, and continue to mix until all the flour has been lumped into a piece of dough.

2 Knead the dough, rolling it toward and pressing it away from you for 10 minutes or until smooth. Cover with a damp towel and let rise for 15 minutes.

3 Roll the dough out into a very thin long strip (thinner than ⅛ inch and about 4 inches wide). Sprinkle flour lightly and evenly over and under the dough strip while rolling. Roll the strip from one end onto a rolling pin for easy handling.

4 Grease a piece of wax paper for lining the steamer. Lay 1 end of the dough strip to line the center surface (see page 93). Brush oil on dough, then fold dough back and forth until the whole strip is used up, making sure to brush oil between the layers.

5 Pierce holes through the layers of dough with a trussing needle so the bread will rise evenly when steaming. Set the pile in the steamer. Steam 25 minutes.

COOKING

1 Fill the base of the steamer with water. Bring to a boil over high heat. Wrap the cover with a kitchen towel. Cover steamer and set it on the base.

2 Remove bread and separate the layers. Cut each into pieces about 3½ by 1½ inches. Wrap tightly in plastic wrap.

Note: The flat bread can be prepared ahead of time and kept frozen. Thaw and reheat before serving by steaming.

◎◎◎◎ Char Siu Buns

Yields 24
Time 40 minutes preparation
overnight chilling
3½ hours dough rising
30 minutes assembling
30 minutes resting
30 minutes cooking

义燒包

Moist and flavorful, these roast pork buns are a specialty of Cantonese tea houses, and always a great favorite with children. The techniques for shaping are shown on pages 86–88.

Ingredients
1 pound Cantonese
Roast Pork (page
252)

Seasonings
2 tablespoons oyster
sauce
¼ cup granulated
sugar
3 tablespoons peanut
oil
2 teaspoons sesame oil

Bun dough
1 tablespoon
granulated sugar
¼ cup warm water
(105 degrees)
1 package active dry
yeast
4¼ cups all-purpose
flour
2 tablespoons lard or
Crisco
½ cup extra-fine sugar
1 cup milk, heated to
lukewarm
1 tablespoon oil
3 teaspoons baking
powder and ¼
teaspoon baking
soda mixed with 1½
tablespoons water

Master sauce
¼ cup peanut oil
1 ounce shallots,
minced
3 tablespoons
all-purpose flour
¾ cup chicken stock
2 tablespoons dark soy
sauce

PREPARATION (FILLING)

1 Set a heavy saucepan over high heat. When very hot, add the peanut oil for the sauce. Flavor oil with shallots until light brown, then turn heat to medium and add the flour. Stir and cook 1 minute.

2 Stream in the stock gradually, stirring until the sauce has thickened and is smooth. Season with soy sauce and set aside.

3 Cut pork into ½-inch pieces about ⅟₁₆ inch thick. Put meat in a large mixing bowl and add the seasonings and master sauce, mixing with a wooden spoon or by hand until all are blended. Keep refrigerated for at least 5 hours or overnight until very firm for easy stuffing.

PREPARATION (DOUGH)

1 In a small bowl, dissolve the sugar in the warm water. Sprinkle the yeast on top and let stand for 2 to 3 minutes, then stir to mix well. Let sit until doubled in size, about 15 minutes.

2 Sift 4 cups of the flour onto a kneading board and make a well in the center. Add in lard and sugar, and the yeast mixture, then add the milk gradually. Blend with the flour, using a swirling action, and gradually incorporate the flour with the liquids.

3 Squeeze dough into a ball. Scrape the board clean, then sprinkle some flour on top to prevent sticking. Knead the dough by rolling it toward and away from you for 10 minutes; sprinkle with the remaining flour during kneading.

4 In a mixing bowl, add the oil. Put in the dough, rolling it around to grease the top. Cover with plastic wrap and place in a draft-free spot (or warm oven) for 3 hours, or until the dough has doubled in size.

5 Punch dough down and flatten dough into a piece about ¾ inch thick. Spread the baking powder–baking soda mixture evenly on the dough (acts as a stabilizer). Roll dough up and knead about 15 minutes, or until smooth and satiny. The dough should be firmer than a regular white bread dough.

6 Cover dough and let rise again for 30 minutes, or until doubled in size. It is now ready for buns.

BREAKING DOUGH
(Note: Dough-breaking instead of cutting is a traditional Cantonese practice in dim sum restaurants. The breaking leaves no sharp cutting edges, which would require longer time for the dough to round out.)

1 Divide dough into 4 equal parts. Roll 1 part by hand to form a rod approximately 9 inches long and 1¼ inches in diameter.

2 Lightly mark the rod with a small knife to divide the dough into 6 equal portions of 1½ inches each.

3 Hold the dough in one hand, with 1 section sticking out from the opening formed by the thumb and index finger, and tear away briskly with the thumb and index finger of the other hand to break off a small dough piece.

4 Continue to break the dough in the same manner to give 6 uniform small cylindrical pieces for each dough rod, yielding altogether 24 pieces.

ROLLING THE DOUGH
1 Flatten each small dough rod with your palm.

2 With a rolling pin, roll each rod out into a round disc, making a quarter turn after each rolling.

3 Roll to leave the center thicker, while the edges are thinner for easy pleating.

ASSEMBLING
1 Place about 1½ tablespoons of filling at the center of each dough round, with the flat side up.

2 Gather the edges by first pleating counterclockwise, then twisting to seal securely.

3 Place the bun with pinched side up on a piece of wax paper about 2 inches square.

4 Finish all the buns, keeping them covered and letting them rest for at least 30 minutes, or until the dough is light.

COOKING

1 Arrange buns in the steamer, keeping them 1 inch apart. Half-fill the lower part of the steamer with water and set it over high heat.

2 Bring water to a vigorous boil and set steamer on. Steam over high heat for 15 minutes. Be sure to have boiling water ready for replenishing; and do not uncover the steamer any time during the steaming. (If a bamboo steamer is used, the water in the wok on which the steamer stands should come up within 1 inch of the first layer of the steamer. If a flat-lid steamer is used, wrap the lid with a kitchen towel to prevent condensed steam from dripping on the buns.) You may have to steam the buns in several batches depending on the size of the steamer. Allow 15 minutes steaming for each batch.

VARIATION: Chicken Buns

A chicken filling can be used instead of the pork. Lighter in taste and more subtle in flavor, these chicken buns are as popular as the pork versions in Canton.

Ingredients	Sauce base	Seasonings
1 whole chicken breast, about 1 pound	⅓ cup peanut oil	1 egg white
2 pairs chicken legs and thighs	4 tablespoons all-purpose flour	1 teaspoon salt
1 ounce black mushrooms	¾ cup chicken stock	2 teaspoons brandy
4 Chinese sausages	½ teaspoon salt	2 tablespoons light soy sauce
4 scallions (white part only)		⅛ teaspoon white pepper
		2 teaspoons granulated sugar
		2 tablespoons tapioca powder
		1 tablespoon sesame oil

1 Prepare the sauce base as you would the master sauce for the pork buns, using salt to replace the dark soy sauce.

2 Follow the instructions for boning the chicken breast and legs (pages 64 and 72). Dice meat and mix with seasonings. Chill.

3 Soak mushrooms in warm water until soft. Squeeze to extract moisture, then trim stems. Dice the caps.

4 Steam the sausages for 20 minutes. Dice.

5 Chop scallions finely.

6 Combine the sauce base, chicken mixture, mushrooms, sausages, and scallions in a large mixing bowl. Stir with chopsticks or a wooden spoon in 1 direction until ingredients hold together. Chill for at least 5 hours or until very firm for easy stuffing.

7 Continue with instructions as for preparing the pork buns.

FLAKY PASTRIES

Though similar to French puff pastry, the classic Chinese flaky pastry is different and takes less time to prepare. The French version incorporates layers of butter between layers of dough, and needs hours of chilling to harden the butter after each folding, whereas the Chinese layer with lard, which requires no chilling.

The classic method described below is suited for hand processing. This yields a batch of small rolls about 1½ inches long and ¾ inch wide.

It is actually the rolling process rather than the folding which gives the "thousand-layered" effect. Starting with a triple-folded piece of dough, you finish with about 200 layers of pastry. The number of layers increases to about 600 if the flattened roll is triple-folded again for a finer pastry.

There is no reason, however, to stick to the classical method completely. It is possible to make the rolls twice as long, for example, without loosing the desired flakiness. The lard can be replaced with vegetable shortening, though the result will tend to be less flaky. Lastly, the pastry can be baked in the oven, rather than fried in the classical Chinese dim sum tradition.

⊛⊛⊛⊛ Classic Chinese Flaky Pastry

Yields 36 rolls
Time 1 hour preparation
20 minutes resting

酥 皮 製 法

Water dough
2 cups all-purpose flour
4 tablespoons lard
⅓ teaspoon salt
8 tablespoons water

Shortening dough
1 cup all-purpose flour
6 tablespoons lard

PREPARATION

1 Sift flour for water dough on a board. Make a well in the center and put in the lard and salt. Add the water gradually, mixing with your fingers in a circular motion until the lard blends with the water. Incorporate the flour from the sides a little at a time until all the flour is incorporated. A soft water dough is now formed.

2 Knead water dough until smooth. Cover with a dampened cloth and rest for 20 minutes.

3 Sift flour for shortening dough onto the board. Cut the lard into the flour and blend gently with your fingers (do not knead) to form a crumblike dough. Shape into a ball. See pages 96–98 for illustrated techniques.

4 Divide water dough into 4 equal parts. Roll each part by hand into a solid rod, 9 inches by ¾ inch. Cut each rod into 9 equal pieces, for 36 pieces altogether.

5 Flatten the shortening dough into a 9-inch square. Cut square into 36 equal squares, each 1½ by 1½ inches.

6 Take a piece of the water dough and press it flat with the palm of your hand to form a disc. Roll a piece of the shortening dough between your palms to make a small ball.

7 Place the ball atop the disc.

8 Bring the edges up, pleating and clipping to seal the ball into a nugget.

9 Roll the nugget into a roll 3 inches long and ½ inch wide between your hands.

10 Lay roll flat on a kneading board and flatten it with a rolling pin to make a very thin dough strip about 12 inches by 1½ inches.

11 Roll up strip with your fingers, starting at the narrow end. This multi-layered dough roll can now be shaped into flaky crescents, buns, and rounds.

Note: The roll can be cut crosswise into circular discs, which become tight spirals upon heating. These spirals are used often for sweet pastries.

The dough rolls can be wrapped individually with plastic wrap and kept frozen for months. Thaw in the refrigerator until soft, then shape.

⚙⚙⚙Curried Crescents

Yields	36 crescents
Time	15 minutes preparation
	4 hours chilling
	40 minutes assembling
	30 minutes cooking

咖喱角

Flaky crescents are generally meat-filled. The most popular version is the curried beef crescent, sold widely in Chinese pastry shops. Sometimes the same pastry can be shaped into buns or filled with pork, chicken, or shrimp. Techniques for making are shown on pages 90–91.

Ingredients	Seasonings	Sauce mixture
1 pound lean ground beef	2 tablespoons dark soy sauce	⅓ cup chicken stock
6 cups + 4 tablespoons oil	1 tablespoon pale dry sherry	1 tablespoon tapioca powder
1 medium onion	1 tablespoon tapioca powder	
36 rolls Classic Chinese Flaky Pastry (page 416)	2 tablespoons curry powder	
1 egg yolk, lightly beaten	2 teaspoons granulated sugar	
	1 egg white	
	½ teaspoon salt	

PREPARATION

1 In a mixing bowl, combine seasonings with the meat, stirring well with a wooden spoon.

2 Add 2 tablespoons of oil to meat mixture and mix well.

3 Chop onion finely and mix ingredients for sauce. Set both aside.

4 Set a skillet over high heat. When very hot, add 2 tablespoons of oil. Put in the onion and cook until limp, about 5 minutes.

5 Add the meat mixture, stirring constantly to break up any lumps. When the color of the meat changes, restir the sauce mixture and add it to the skillet. When the sauce thickens, remove the meat to a platter. Chill for at least 2 hours or until firm.

ASSEMBLING

1 Flatten a spiral dough roll and bring both ends up. Press to taper both ends and make them overlap at the center.

2 Roll the dough out into a round disc about 3 inches wide with a thinner edge for easy sealing and ridging.

3 Place the pastry disc on your palm. Brush half of the edge with beaten egg yolk. Put about 1 tablespoon of the filling in the center.

4 Fold the pastry disc together and press the edge firmly to make a half moon. Make ridges along the edge. Continue making remainder of pastries.

COOKING

1 Set a wok over medium heat. When hot, add the remaining 6 cups of oil. Wait for about 5 to 7 minutes, then test the temperature by dropping in a small piece of scallion green. If bubbles appear around the green, which also sizzles, the oil is ready (about 275 degrees).

2 Slip 12 crescents into the oil. Spade with a spatula to prevent crescents from sticking to the bottom of the wok. Deep-fry slowly until light golden, about 7 minutes. Remove crescents to drain on paper towels.

3 Continue to deep-fry the remaining crescents in 2 batches. Serve warm as snacks.

VARIATION: Flaky Pork Buns

Ingredients
12 ounces lean ground pork
6 medium black mushrooms
1 cup bamboo shoots
2 whole scallions
1 whole egg
¼ cup sesame seeds
2 tablespoons oil
¼ teaspoon salt
½ teaspoon granulated sugar
36 rolls Classic Chinese Flaky Pastry (page 416)

Seasonings
1 tablespoon light soy sauce
2 teaspoons oyster sauce
¼ teaspoon salt
1 teaspoon sesame oil
1 tablespoon pale dry sherry
½ teaspoon granulated sugar
1 tablespoon tapioca powder
Dash of white pepper

Sauce mixture
¼ cup chicken stock
2 teaspoons tapioca powder

1 In a mixing bowl, combine seasonings with pork. Stir with a wooden spoon to mix well.

2 Soak mushrooms in warm water until soft. Trim and discard stems, and chop caps finely into bits the same size as the ground pork.

3 Blanch bamboo shoots in boiling water for 1 minute. Run cold water over to stop the cooking, then drain thoroughly. Chop finely, then put on a kitchen towel, wrap, and squeeze to extract moisture.

4 Cut off about 3 inches of the green ends from the scallions, then shred remainder.

5 Mix ingredients for sauce and set aside. Beat egg until smooth. Place sesame seeds on a small platter for coating buns later.

6 Set a heavy saucepan over high heat. When hot, add the bamboo shoots, stirring constantly until most of the moisture is evaporated. Add the oil, salt, and sugar, then the mushrooms. Stir ingredients around the saucepan several times.

7 Add the pork, stirring to separate the lumps. When the pink color of the meat disappears, restir the sauce mixture and add it to the center of the pan. Stir until the sauce thickens, then add scallions and mix well. Remove saucepan from the heat and stir in the beaten egg. Chill until firm, about 2 hours.

8 Form the pastry disc as for Curried Crescents, and fill with meat mixture. Instead of folding the disc in half, gather the edge up. Twist at the top to seal securely. Turn the sealed side down.

9 Flatten the top surface of the bun and lightly brush with water. Sprinkle on the sesame seeds, pressing gently to help them adhere.

10 Preheat the oven to 275 degrees.

11 Arrange the buns on a greased baking sheet at least 1 inch apart. Bake for 30 minutes, or until light golden. Serve warm or cold.

Sweets

Sweet desserts are not a tradition in Chinese family cooking. A number of sweet preparations, however, are served in the Chinese household as snacks taken outside regular meals. Banquets usually end with sweet dishes, but many of these are actually soups which the Chinese call sweet teas.

Ingredients for sweet teas could be walnuts, almonds, peanuts, or black sesames all ground with rice into a puree and cooked with sugar water into a thick soup. Sometimes mung beans, red beans, lotus seeds, gingko nuts, dates, and jujubes are cooked in sugar water too. More unusual sweet teas also served at the banquets include the use of a kind of brown freshwater algae called Fairy Ge's rice; bird's nests; or hasma, the ovaries of the Manchurian tree frog. The more modern version of the sweet tea is snow mushrooms served with chilled fresh fruits.

Next in line in frequency are sweet pastes which serve as stuffing in cakes, buns, pastries, and moon cakes. These are made of red beans, chestnuts, sesame, Chinese jujube dates, even winter melon meat. Lotus seed paste is often accompanied by the yolks of salted ducks eggs.

Some pastes are served as is. In Chaozhou (in Guangdong province) the common banquet desserts are the taro paste, which is reddish purple in color, the bright green pea paste, and the golden pumpkin paste. All are infinitely delicious—also enormously rich with lard.

Then there are sweet cakes and sweet pastries. The Cantonese favorite is Malayan Cake, which is a steamed cake sweetened with brown sugar. Smiling Face is a cookie shaped like a cracked baseball with a sesame covering. Coconut Milk Cake is actually jelled coconut milk with yellow split peas.

In Hong Kong, an expensive sweet dessert these days in a banquet is Slow-cooked Pear Stuffed with Bird's Nest. The most common North China desserts are (sweet) Eight-Treasure Rice, which is a sweet glutinous rice pudding, and Sweet Almond Bean Curd, which is a pudding made of agar-agar and the juice extracted from almonds.

⦿Steamed Sponge Cake

Yields one 9 by 3 by 2-inch cake
Time   20 minutes preparation
           40 minutes cooking

清 蒸 蛋 糕

Although like the French genoise in texture, the Cantonese sponge cake is steamed, not baked, and is quite moist.

Ingredients

6 whole eggs, at room
    temperature
1 cup extra-fine sugar
1 cup cake flour
1 teaspoon almond
    extract

PREPARATION

1 If possible, remove embryonic cord from the eggs. Add eggs to a large mixing bowl and beat with an electric mixer at high speed for 2 minutes, then at low speed for 3 minutes.

2 Stream in the sugar gradually and continue to beat at low speed for 3 minutes, or until color of egg mixture turns a pale yellow and a ribbon is formed when the beater is lifted.

3 Add the flour, a little at a time, until it is all incorporated. Stir in the almond extract.

4 Pour batter into a 9-inch loaf pan lined with wax paper.

COOKING

1 Bring water in the bottom of a double-layered steamer to a vigorous boil over high heat. Place in the loaf pan and cover steamer tightly. If the steamer has a flat lid, wrap the lid with a kitchen towel to absorb condensation.

2 Steam cake for 40 minutes, or until a toothpick inserted comes out clean. Remove to cool on a cake rack.

3 Slice and serve warm or cold.

⊚ Steamed Brown Sponge Cake

Yields   one 10-inch cake
Time   20 minutes preparation
          1 hour steaming

黃糖蛋糕

This is a firmer version of the Steamed Sponge Cake. In Canton it is called "Malayan Cake," conceivably invented by the Chinese in Malaya during the last century.

Ingredients

3½ cups all-purpose
   flour
3 teaspoons baking
   powder
½ teaspoon baking
   soda
½ teaspoon salt
½ cup granulated
   sugar

1 cup brown sugar
¼ pound lard or
   margarine
⅓ cup peanut oil
5 large eggs
2 tablespoons honey

PREPARATION

1 Combine flour, baking powder, baking soda, and salt in a bowl. Sift twice.

2 Beat the sugar, brown sugar, margarine, and peanut oil with an electric mixer set on medium speed until smooth, about 2 minutes.

3 Add eggs to the batter, 1 at a time, and continue to beat for 2 minutes more.

4 Turn speed to low and add the honey. Stream the flour mixture into the batter gradually. Scrape the bowl and beat 1 minute more, until well blended.

5 Pour the batter into a greased and floured 10-inch round baking pan.

COOKING

1 Line a stockpot with a small kitchen towel and set the steaming rack (see note) onto it. Bring water to a boil in a kettle and then fill stockpot with the boiling water to 1 inch below the top of the steaming rack. Bring water in stockpot to a boil again.

2 Place another small kitchen towel on the steaming rack in the pot to prevent the cake pan from slipping. Then place the cake pan on the rack and cover pot.

3 Steam cake over high heat for 1 hour. Do not remove the cover at any time unless the water is used up (that is unlikely if the pot is large enough). Replenish with boiling water only.

4 The cake is done if a bamboo skewer inserted into the center comes out clean. Cake can be served warm or cold.

Note: An 8- to 10-quart stockpot with a diameter of at least 12 inches or a large

lobster pot are suitable for the steaming. You could use 2 empty cans with both ends removed to serve as a rack, but the height of the cans should be about half the depth of the pot so that there will be enough water underneath the cake pan for steaming. If the pot has a flat lid, wrap the lid with a kitchen towel to absorb condensation.

◉◉◉◉ Thousand Layer Cake

Serves   8 as dessert
Time   50 minutes preparation
              2 hours chilling
              40 minutes steaming

蛋 黃 千 層 糕

"Thousand" is the exaggerated way to say "more than five." This Cantonese delight has only nine layers, but each bite wakes up a thousand taste buds by offering an unforgettable interplay of saltiness against sweetness and crunchiness against moist softness. The "exotic" ingredients are actually quite inexpensive in an Oriental market, and this is not really difficult to prepare as long as you know how to prepare the Cantonese Flat Bread.

Ingredients

3 ounces pork fatback
1 tablespoon brandy
½ cup + 1 tablespoon
    extra-fine sugar
6 salted duck eggs
3 ounces candied
    winter melon
⅔ cup olive nuts

1 cup oil
2 tablespoons lard
2 tablespoons cake
    flour
1 batch Cantonese Flat
    Bread dough (page
    412)

PREPARATION

1   Cook pork fat in some boiling water for 10 minutes. Soak in ice water until cool, then cut into small bits the same size as a mung bean. Mix with brandy and 1 tablespoon of the sugar. Set aside.

2   Separate salted duck eggs. Steam egg yolks for 20 minutes. Reserve the egg whites for other use. Cut egg yolks into ¼-inch dice.

3   Cut candied winter melon the same size as egg yolks.

4   Fry olive nuts in moderately hot oil (350 degrees) for 1 minute or until light brown. Remove and dice into the same size as egg yolks.

5   Set a 1-quart nonstick saucepan over medium heat and add the lard. When it is hot, add the cake flour, stir, and cook 1 minute, then add the remaining sugar.

6   Remove the saucepan from the heat. Add egg yolks, candied winter melon, and pork fat to mix with the flour and sugar. Fold in olive nuts. Chill in the refrigerator for at least 2 hours.

7 Follow the recipe for Cantonese Flat Bread to prepare the dough. After resting, roll dough out in the same manner into a long thin strip. Cut out 5 pieces each 4¼ by 9 inches in size.

8 Grease a 4 by 9-inch straight-sided loaf pan with oil. Divide the filling into 4 equal parts.

9 Line 1 piece of flat bread dough on the bottom and spread on ¼ of the filling evenly. Top with another piece of dough and spread on another ¼ of the filling. Layer the remaining dough and filling in the same fashion, ending with a piece of dough on top. You will have altogether 9 layers.

10 Pierce the dough layers with a bamboo skewer all the way down, from top to bottom. This creates holes for the air to escape and provides for evenness in shape during steaming. Holes should be punched no more than 1 inch apart.

COOKING

1 Wrap the cover of the steamer with cloth to absorb condensation during steaming.

2 Bring water in the base of the steamer to a vigorous boil. Set the loaf pan in the top layer. Cover and steam the layer cake for 40 minutes.

3 Remove loaf pan from the steamer. Cool the cake in the pan for 30 minutes, then invert to turn out the layer cake onto a serving platter. Cut into ½-inch-thick slices and serve.

◉◉◉Sugar Puffs

Yields	2 dozen puffs
Time	15 minutes preparation
	15 minutes cooking

糖 沙 翁

Apparently adapted by the Cantonese from the French *pâte à choux*, this sugar puff is deep-fried rather than baked.

Ingredients

¾ cup water
2 tablespoons lard or
  margarine
⅛ teaspoon salt
1 cup sifted
  all-purpose flour

3 whole eggs, at room
  temperature
7 cups oil
Extra-fine sugar

PREPARATION

1 Combine water, lard, and salt in a heavy 2-quart saucepan and set it over high heat. Bring to a boil, then remove from the heat.

2 Add the flour all at once, stirring vigorously in 1 direction until the mixture leaves the sides of the pan and forms a ball. Add the eggs, 1 at a time, and stir with a wooden spoon until the mixture is smooth and glossy.

3 Place 1 cup of oil in a deep dish. Scoop up a handful of the dough and squeeze it through your fist until it reaches the size of a small walnut. Scrape it off with an oiled spoon and drop it into the oil in the dish. Continue to make dough balls in the same manner until all the mixture is used up.

COOKING

1 Set a wok over high heat. When hot, add the remaining oil. Wait for about 7 minutes, then test the temperature by dropping in a piece of scallion green. If the green sizzles noisily and soon turns brown, the oil is ready (about 375 degrees).

2 With a spatula, push all the dough balls and the oil together into the wok. Turn heat to medium. Stir constantly until the balls puff up and roll around slowly in the oil.

3 When the puffs turn golden, remove and drain on paper towels. Roll puffs in sugar and serve.

⊚⊚Smiling Faces

Yields 40
Time 10 minutes preparation
20 minutes resting
15 to 20 minutes cooking

笑 口 棗

These small balls, made from a quick dough, burst into smiling faces when heated in hot oil. They are a favorite Cantonese snack.

Ingredients

1½ cups granulated
  sugar
¾ cup boiling water
4 cups all-purpose
  flour
3 teaspoons baking
  powder
½ teaspoon baking
  soda
3 tablespoons lard,
  softened

2 whole eggs
½ cup sesame seeds
6 cups oil

PREPARATION

1 Dissolve the sugar in boiling water. Let cool.

2 Sift the flour, baking powder, and baking soda onto a kneading board. Make a well in the center and put in the lard and eggs. Pour the sugar mixture in a gradual stream to mix with the flour. Blend well into a dough.

3 Lightly knead the dough for 30 seconds; do not over-knead. Cover dough with a kitchen towel and set at room temperature for 20 minutes.

4 Divide the dough into 4 equal parts. Roll each part by hand to form a long tube about 1 inch in diameter. Break the tube into 10 equal parts; there should be 40 total.

5 Take each piece of dough and rub it between your palms to shape it into a ball.

6 Spread the sesame seeds on a dish and roll the dough balls, 1 by 1, in the seeds. Press and roll until their entire surfaces are covered. Press seeds in as firmly as possible.

COOKING

1 Heat the oil in a wok over medium heat. After 6 to 7 minutes, test the temperature by dropping in a small piece of scallion green. If bubbles appear around the green immediately with sizzling, the oil is ready (about 300 degrees).

2 Add 10 balls in succession; do not stir. Dough balls will soon roll and turn in the oil, and split into smiling faces. Deep-fry until golden.

3 Deep-fry the remaining batches; remove and drain on paper towels.

Note: Smiling Faces can be served with bean milk, plain congee, or tea for breakfast or as a snack.

◉Ginger-Curdled Milk

Yields   4 servings
Time   10 minutes preparation
             10 minutes cooking
             3 minutes resting

Daliang, alias Phoenix City, is one of the few places in Guangdong Province known for milk dishes. The milk of Daliang is from the water buffalo, rich with butterfat and vitamins. It is delivered to the small eateries direct from the farm without sterilization, fortification, or dilution. The tradition is to serve the milk hot after boiling; it is normally sweetened. Well-known milk dishes include Ginger-Curdled Milk and Doubled-Layered Milk, given here, and Steamed Almond Custard (page 429) and a banquet dish, Stir-Fried Milk (page 248). Also famous is salted cream sheets, looking like thin, small pancakes to be mixed with hot congee.

The sharp ginger juice here acts as a coagulant and at the same time is mellowed by the creamy light custard. Getting the milk to curdle at the right time was once a chef's secret. This recipe was shared verbally by a group of Daliang chefs when I was invited to hold a conference with them early in 1980.

With the help of a candy thermometer, temperature control is made easy but the consistency of the milk is hard to define. It is close to the American "half and half," or in between a whipping cream and an extra-rich milk. Also, the ginger-root should be mature enough or else the milk will not curdle. Select a knob with crinkled skin and which looks dry and fibrous.

Ingredients

1 knob gingerroot, about the size of a walnut	2 eggs
	½ cup half and half
	1 cup extra-rich milk
¼ teaspoon distilled vinegar	⅓ cup superfine sugar

PREPARATION

1 Scrape the skin of the gingerroot and grate root into a small bowl, then strain the juice through a very fine mesh strainer, pressing the ginger pulp against the wall to extract as much juice as possible. You should have about 2 teaspoons. Mix ginger juice with vinegar and set aside.

2 Have 4 small Chinese rice bowls or custard cups ready.

3 Break eggs and remove the embryonic cords and put them in a mixing bowl. Beat with a wire whisk gently until smooth, then add half and half and milk, a little at a time, to mix with the eggs. The mixture should be smooth but not foamy.

COOKING

Put the egg mixture in a heavy 2-quart saucepan, preferably with a pouring lip. Set the pan over medium heat and stir constantly with a flat-edged wooden spoon very gently. The mixture will thicken in 4 to 5 minutes. Insert a candy thermometer and continue to stir until the temperature reaches 170 degrees. Remove the pan immediately from heat. Sprinkle in the sugar, then whirl in the ginger juice mixture, stirring quickly a few times around until the sugar dissolves. Pour milk into individual bowls. Set for 2 to 3 minutes; the milk will curdle. Serve hot.

◉◉Double-Layered Milk

Serves	4 as snack or dessert	雙 皮 奶
Time	1 hour resting	
	15 minutes preparation	
	30 minutes cooking	

A sweet hot snack from Phoenix City, the milk is made into a hot custard, with a two-step process that provides layers of cream in the bottom and on top. This version eliminates the bottom layer for simplicity.

Ingredients

4 egg whites	¼ teaspoon distilled vinegar
½ cup superfine sugar	
¼ cup half and half	4 tablespoons heavy cream
1½ cups extra-rich milk	

PREPARATION

1 Beat whites gently in a mixing bowl with a wire whisk until smooth but not frothy.

2 In another mixing bowl, combine sugar with half and half and milk, stirring constantly until sugar dissolves. Stream in egg whites gradually, whisking until well blended. Stir in vinegar.

3 Pour milk mixture into 4 individual Chinese rice bowls (about 3¾ inches in diameter) or custard cups.

COOKING

1 Take the cream out of the refrigerator and rest at room temperature while the steaming is in progress.

2 Half-fill the base of a steamer with water and bring it to a boil over high heat, then turn heat to medium-low. Put the bowls of milk in the top layer of the steamer and wrap the lid securely with a kitchen towel. Cover and steam for 25 minutes or until a toothpick inserted comes out clean.

3 Shake the cream in the container and spoon 1 tablespoon (or more if needed) to cover the entire surface of the custard in each bowl. Cover steamer and steam for another 5 minutes.

4 Remove bowls from steamer. Rest for 3 to 5 minutes. A wrinkled layer of cream will form on the surface.

5 Serve hot. The excess cream under the layer will run into the bowl to enrich the custard upon the first spooning.

⊛⊛ Steamed Almond Custard

Serves 4
Time 10 minutes preparation
1 hour soaking
25 minutes steaming

杏 汁 燉 奶

The gentle steaming retains the velvety texture of this custard, which is lightly accented by home-prepared almond juice. A delightful snack for the Cantonese family.

Ingredients

2 tablespoons blanched
  Chinese almonds
¼ cup boiling water
3 whole eggs + 1 egg
  yolk

½ cup superfine sugar
1¾ cups extra-rich milk
  (or regular milk)
¼ teaspoon distilled
  vinegar

PREPARATION

1 Soak Chinese almonds in boiling water for 1 hour, then purée them in an electric blender with the soaking water.

2 Over a bowl, set a strainer which is well lined with double cheesecloth. Pour the almond purée into the strainer to drain juice into the bowl. Gather the edges of the cheesecloth to form a bag. Twist to extract as much almond juice as possible. You will need 1 tablespoon; the remainder (also about 1 tablespoon) can be frozen for later use.

3 Break whole eggs and remove embryonic cords.

4 In a large mixing bowl, add the eggs, egg yolk, and sugar. Beat gently with a wire whisk until sugar dissolves and the egg mixture is smooth but not foamy. Gradually stream in the milk, stirring to mix with the egg until well blended. Mix in almond juice and vinegar. Pour egg mixture through a fine-mesh sieve into 4 individual small Chinese rice bowls/custard cups.

COOKING

1 Bring water in the base of a steamer to a vigorous boil over high heat, then turn heat to medium-low.

2 Put the bowls of egg mixture in the top layer of the steamer and wrap the lid securely with a kitchen towel. Cover and steam for 20 minutes. Remove the lid and cover again immediately to release steam every 5 minutes for a total of 3 times so that no condensation will drop on the surface of the custard. Test for doneness by inserting a toothpick into the custard. If it comes out clean, it is done; otherwise, steam for another 5 minutes. Serve hot.

◉Sweet Snow Mushrooms with Oriental Fruit

Serves 8
Time 30 minutes preparation
2 hours soaking
20 minutes cooking

銀耳鮮果羹

Snow mushrooms are mixed with fruit for an interesting texture. The fruits are excellent conversation-starters; all except the four cherries are Chinese in origin. Hawaiian pineapples were transplanted from Taiwan, and the earlier name for New Zealand kiwifruit is Chinese gooseberries.

Ingredients

1 ounce Fujianese snow mushrooms	1 small can (10 ounces) Mandarin oranges
1 cup granulated sugar	1 small can (12 ounces) pineapple chunks
4 cups water	1 kiwifruit, peeled
1 can (16 ounces) lychees	4 preserved cherries (optional)

PREPARATION

1 Soak snow mushrooms in cold water for 2 hours, or until expanded. Trim and discard the tough ends.

2 Cook mushrooms in boiling water for 10 minutes, then cover and remove from heat. Let stand until the water becomes cool. Rinse mushrooms and drain thoroughly.

3 In a 3-quart saucepan, combine sugar, water, and mushrooms. Bring to a boil over medium-high heat. When sugar dissolves, remove to a fruit bowl. Keep refrigerated.

4 Drain juice from lychees and reserve. Cut each lychee in half. Drain Mandarin oranges and pineapple chunks and discard canning liquid. Slice kiwifruit thinly crosswise. Cut each cherry in half. Mix fruit.

5 Add lychee juice and mixed fruit to snow mushrooms. Mix and serve cold.

⊚⊚⊚ Sweet Almond Curd

Serves 6 to 8 as dessert
Time 2 hours soaking.
30 minutes preparation
30 minutes cooking
3½ hours chilling

杏 仁 豆 腐

Once very popular in Peking, the almond bean curd is now replaced by the almond flavored gelatin for convenience. This is the original version in which the essence is from home-ground Chinese almonds, and the coagulant is the agar-agar.

Ingredients

3 ounces Chinese
  almonds
2 cups boiling water
½ ounce agar-agar

4 cups water
1 cup granulated sugar
1 cup milk

PREPARATION

1 Rinse and pick over almonds; discard bad ones. Soak in boiling water for 2 hours.

2 Soak agar-agar in plenty of cold water for at least 1 hour. Squeeze dry before using.

3 Put almonds and their soaking liquid into an electric blender. Whirl with high speed for 5 minutes or until almonds turn into a fine purée, then pour mixture through a fine-mesh sieve to drain into a large bowl.

4 Put the residue of almond back into the blender, and add 2 cups of water. Whirl 5 more minutes. Drain liquid also into the large bowl. Discard residue.

5 In a 3-quart saucepan, add 2 cups of water, the sugar, and the agar-agar. Bring to a boil over high heat, then turn heat to low. Cook until agar-agar is dissolved, about 20 minutes.

6 Rinse the strainer and line it with double cheesecloth, then set it over another bowl. Pour the almond liquid into the strainer to strain the second time, gathering the cheesecloth to form a bag. Twist to extract liquid into the bowl. Discard the second-pass residue.

COOKING

1 Add almond liquid and the cup of milk to the agar-agar mixture, stirring all the while until liquid returns to a boil.

2 Pour almond mixture again through a very fine mesh sieve (this time to strain the agar-agar) into a baking pan, 9 by 9 inches in size. Set at room temperature to cool 30 minutes, then chill in the refrigerator for at least 3 hours. Almond mixture now curdles like a bean curd.

3 When served, prepare Oriental Fruit (page 430). Cut almond curd into ½-inch cubes to combine with the fruit.

SWEET PASTES FOR STUFFING

In China sweet desserts are served at the end of banquets, but very seldom at the end of a family meal. They are actually part of the small eats tradition. Many of these dishes involve a sweet stuffing which differs from one region to the next owing to climatic difference. Jujube dates and chestnuts are widely found in the north, and pastes made of them are common there. East China is known for lotus seeds, hence lotus seed paste. In the south, sweet red bean paste (not sweet soybean paste) and sesame seed paste are common. These pastes used to be made to order. Canned versions are now available, but we found them too soft to be perfect.

◉◉◉Red Bean Paste

Yields 6 cups
Time overnight soaking
30 minutes preparation
4½ hours cooking

紅豆沙

Ingredients
1 pound dried red
  beans
2 cups granulated
  sugar
2 cups peanut oil
2 tablespoons wheat
  starch or cake flour

PREPARATION

1 Pick over beans and discard foreign matter and bad beans. Rinse, put into a large bowl, add cold water to 2 inches above the beans, and soak overnight. The beans will expand to double their size after absorbing most of the water. Drain well.

2 Put beans in a 4-quart nonstick pan. Add about 2 quarts of water and set over high heat. Bring to a boil, then turn heat to low. Simmer for 2 hours or until very soft.

3 Place a metal mesh strainer over the large bowl. Scoop about ¾ cup of the cooked beans into the strainer. Use a wooden spoon to press the beans against the wall of strainer repeatedly until most of the paste has dropped into the bowl. Remove the residue to a separate pan.

4 Continue to press the remaining beans in the same manner, each time using ¾ cup of the beans. You will have about 4 cups of very fine bean paste. Reserve.

5 The residues still contain much usable paste. To extract it, add 4 cups of water and the residues to a pan. Cook over high heat for 5 minutes to yield a thick mixture.

6 Press the bean mixture through the strainer into another bowl in 3 or 4 batches, resulting in a much thinner paste in the bowl. The residues this time can be discarded.

COOKING

1 Put the thin bean paste into a nonstick pan. Cook over high heat for 5 minutes, then add the sugar. Continue to cook for 5 more minutes.

2 Add the thicker (first round) bean paste to pan. Bring back to boil, turn heat to low, and add ½ cup of the oil, stirring constantly with a wooden spoon until oil is absorbed.

3 Simmer the bean paste for 30 minutes. Stir in 1 direction at least twice, then add another ½ cup of the oil. Stir until oil is absorbed. Do this simmer-pour-stir sequence a total of 3 times. By this time, the 2 cups of oil will have been mixed into the paste.

4 Sift the wheat starch into the bean paste. Raise heat to high. Stir until bean paste clears the sides of the pan and becomes smooth and thick, about 5 to 7 minutes.

5 Transfer the bean paste to a container and chill. It can be kept in refrigerator for 2 to 3 weeks or can be kept frozen indefinitely.

◉◉◉Lotus Seed Paste

Yields 2 cups packed
Time 4 hours soaking
20 minutes preparation
3 hours, 20 minutes
  simmering
4 hours chilling

Ingredients

1 pound dried lotus
  seeds
4 cups water
1¼ cups granulated
  sugar

½ cup oil
1 tablespoon wheat
  starch

PREPARATION

1 Rinse lotus seeds and put in a bowl, adding enough boiling water to cover. Soak at room temperature for 4 hours, then open each seed and remove the green bud in the center, if any.

2 Combine lotus seeds and water in a 3-quart saucepan. Bring the water to a boil, then turn heat to low. Cover the pan and cook for 2 hours or until lotus seeds are very soft and half the water has evaporated.

3 Use a potato masher to mash the lotus seeds in the pan (the mash will be very thin because of the cooking liquid). Pour the thin mash through a fine-mesh strainer into a nonstick 2-quart saucepan, pressing the mash with a wooden spoon against the wall of the strainer until the starch of the lotus seeds almost goes into the saucepan. Discard the residues in the strainer.

COOKING

1 Set the nonstick saucepan over high heat. Bring the lotus mash to a boil. Turn heat to low and simmer for 1 hour, stirring every half hour to prevent sticking.

2 When most of the moisture has evaporated, add the sugar, stirring until dissolved. Add ¼ cup of the oil to the mash, stirring until the oil is absorbed, then add the remaining oil. Continue to stir until the oil is absorbed, then sprinkle in the starch. Keep on stirring until the lotus seed mash turns thicker, now to a paste. (Total stirring time is about 20 minutes.)

3 Remove the saucepan from heat. Cool lotus seed paste at room temperature, then store in a container and keep refrigerated for at least 4 hours before using. If not used immediately, the lotus seed paste can be frozen indefinitely.

◉◉◉ Jujube Date Paste

Yields 1 cup
Time 30 minutes preparation
1 hour, 20 minutes cooking
2 hours chilling

棗泥

Ingredients

½ pound Chinese
  jujube dates
3 cups water
¼ cup brown sugar

3 tablespoons oil
1 tablespoon wheat
  starch or cake flour

PREPARATION AND COOKING

1 Rinse dates and put them in a nonstick 2-quart saucepan. Add water and cook over medium heat for 40 minutes or until soft and water is almost absorbed.

2 Remove skin and pits from dates and put the dates back into the saucepan. Cook over low heat for 20 minutes or until moisture has almost evaporated. Add the brown sugar, stirring to mix with the dates. Add the oil, stirring constantly until blended with the dates, about 15 minutes.

3 Sprinkle the starch over the dates, stirring until dates turn thicker, into a paste. Cool at room temperature. Chill to firm for at least 2 hours or put in a container and freeze indefinitely.

⊛⊛⊛Cassia-Flavored Chestnut Paste

Yields 2 cups
Time 30 minutes preparation
30 minutes roasting
2½ hours simmering

桂花栗蓉

Ingredients

1¼ pound chestnuts in the shell
6½ cups water
1 tablespoon preserved cassia blossoms
1¼ cups granulated sugar
½ cup lard
½ cup peanut oil
2 tablespoons wheat starch

PREPARATION

1 Preheat oven to 450 degrees.

2 Rest chestnuts on their flat side. Use a knife to cut a shallow cross on top of each; be sure to cut through the shells.

3 Arrange chestnuts in 1 layer on a roasting pan, sprinkle with a few teaspoons of water, and roast for 30 minutes. The shells should burst.

4 Remove the shells with the skin attached to extract the chestnut meat.

5 Cook chestnuts with 4 cups water over medium heat for about 40 minutes or until very soft.

6 Put chestnuts and cooking juices into the blender. Whirl at high speed for 2 minutes or until the chestnuts are reduced to a thin purée; add 2 cups of water, a little at a time, to ease blending.

COOKING

1 Boil preserved cassia blossoms with remaining ½ cup water for 1 minute. Drain juice into a bowl and reserve. Discard cassia blossoms.

2 Combine chestnut purée and sugar in a 2-quart nonstick saucepan and set it over high heat. When it boils, turn heat to very low. Cook chestnut purée for 30 minutes. Add the lard, stirring constantly until lard is absorbed. Cook 30 minutes and add ¼ cup of the oil, stirring to blend with the purée. Cook 30 minutes, then add the remaining oil. Stir and cook for 30 minutes more, then mix in cassia juice.

3 Continue to cook the chestnut purée for 20 minutes or until moisture is almost evaporated. Sprinkle in the starch and mix well. The chestnut purée should become pastelike. Remove to a container. Cover and cool, then chill in refrigerator until firm. Use immediately or put in the freezer.

◉◉◉ Sesame and Cashew Paste

Yields 2 cups
Time 10 minutes roasting
25 minutes resting
15 minutes preparation
2 hours chilling

蘇 蓉

Ingredients

1½ cups sesame seeds
¾ cup cashew chips
2 tablespoons lard
   (margarine, butter,
   or shortening)
1 tablespoon
   all-purpose flour
1½ cups extra-fine
   sugar

PREPARATION

1 Put sesame seeds in a heavy saucepan. Set the pan over low heat and stir sesame seeds all the while until light golden in color, about 5 minutes. Rest to cool 20 minutes.

2 Roast cashew chips in the same manner for 5 minutes; let set for 20 minutes.

3 Put sesame seeds in a blender. Whirl at high speed for about 7 to 10 minutes. Stop the machine every now and then to mix the sesame seeds well. Add cashew chips and beat for 3 to 4 minutes more until a thick paste is formed. Remove sesame-cashew paste from the blender; scrape to clean the sides.

4 Set a small saucepan over low heat. Add lard, stirring until it melts. Sprinkle in flour, stirring for 2 minutes or until the mixture turns bubbly.

5 Remove saucepan from heat. Add sugar, then the sesame-cashew paste. Mix well with a wooden spoon. Put in a container and chill to firm, at least 2 hours.

◉◉Date-Filled Crêpe

Yields 4 servings
Time 20 minutes preparation
10 minutes resting
10 minutes cooking

枣 泥 锅 饼

This is one of the best-known sweet preparations in Peking. It is date paste wrapped in pancakes, looking somewhat like a jumbo-sized spring roll. Restaurants now invariably deep-fry their pancakes for mass production. The original pan-fried version, while almost completely forgotten, is better as shown below.

Ingredients

¾ cup all-purpose
flour
1 whole egg
1 cup water
3 tablespoons oil
8 tablespoons Jujube
Date Paste (page
434)

1 egg yolk mixed with
1 teaspoon water for
sealing

PREPARATION

1 Sift the flour into a mixing bowl. Make a well in the center, into which put the egg. Incorporate the egg gradually with the flour with a wooden spoon.

2 Stream in water a little at a time, stirring all the while until batter is smooth. Add 2 tablespoons of the oil and mix well. Set batter for 10 minutes.

3 To make thin pancakes, set a 10-inch nonstick skillet over medium heat for 1 minute. Pour in ⅓ cup of the batter in the center and twirl it around the skillet so that batter will spread out to form a thin cake about 8 inches in diameter.

4 When the edge of the thin cake leaves the skillet, in about 30 seconds, slip it ¼ of the way to the far end of the skillet; flip and turn it over as you would an omelette. Cook the other side for 15 seconds and remove to a platter. The thin cake should be very light in color with no brown spots. Cover with a kitchen towel. (Wrap with plastic if you are using it later.)

5 Continue to fry the thin cakes in the same manner, each time using ⅓ cup of the batter. You will have 4 thin cakes. They can be prepared 3 to 4 hours ahead of time if wrapped properly to keep moist.

ASSEMBLING

1 Spread 1 thin cake flat on a platter. Put 2 tablespoons of date paste to cover the center area, about 1¾ by 6 inches.

2 Fold both the left and right sides over and brush the folded surface with egg-yolk mixture.

3 Fold the near side over to cover the filling in the center, adhering to the 2 sides.

4 Brush egg-yolk mixture on the just-folded area. Turn the far side of the thin cake down to form an oblong package, about 2 by 6½ inches in size.

5 Assemble the remaining 3 packages.

COOKING

1 Dip a pastry brush in the remaining oil. Grease evenly the inside surface of the nonstick skillet with 1 teaspoon oil, adding ½ teaspoon more oil if needed. Set over medium-low heat.

2 Arrange thin cake packages in 1 layer in the skillet. Pan-fry packages 1 minute or until small brown spots appear on the underside. Turn packages to the other side and pan-fry in the same manner. Remove to a serving platter. Cut each with scissors into 1-inch widths. Serve hot.

◉◉◉ Deep-Fried Lamb's Tail

Yields 12
Time 30 minutes preparation
10 minutes deep-frying

炸羊尾巴

This North China sweet favorite, fluffy and off white, resembles a lamb's tail but with no lamb in it whatsoever; the stuffing used is said to have been chopped lamb's tail meat, but is now generally sweet red bean paste.

Ingredients

4 ounces sweet Red
Bean Paste (page 432)
1 tablespoon
cornstarch +
cornstarch for
coating (about 2
tablespoons)
6 extra-large egg
whites

1 tablespoon
all-purpose flour
4 cups oil for
deep-frying
2 tablespoons
confectioner's sugar

PREPARATION

1 Roll Red Bean Paste into 12 balls, each about 1 inch in diameter. Coat evenly with cornstarch.

2 Beat egg whites with electric mixer until stiff peaks are formed, about 5 minutes. Sprinkle in cornstarch and flour. Beat 1 more minute.

3 Use a ladle to scoop up about 3 tablespoons of the egg white mixture. Push a red bean ball into the center. Smooth out the surface to make a snowball about 2 inches in diameter.

4 Altogether make 12 snowballs. Arrange them on 2 separate platters.

COOKING

1 Set a wok over high heat. When the wok is hot, add oil and turn heat to low. Wait 2 to 3 minutes or until a deep-frying thermometer registers 250 degrees.

2 Dip a spatula into the oil to grease it well, and use it to push 6 snowballs from the platter, 1 at a time, into the oil. Deep-fry evenly until snowballs turn firm and off-white in color, resembling a lamb's tail—about 3 minutes. Remove to drain oil.

3 Maintain low heat throughout. Deep-fry the remaining 6 snowballs in the same manner. Sprinkle with confectioner's sugar and serve immediately.

◉◉◉◉Flaky Lotus Pastry

Yields   18 pastries
Time   10 minutes preparation
       30 minutes assembling
       1 hour chilling
       30 minutes cooking

This is an elegant sweet pastry shaped like a lotus flower, served at Cantonese banquets. The sweet filling is made of lotus seeds but you can also substitute sweet Red Bean Paste (page 432).

Ingredients

18 rolls Classic Chinese
 Flaky Pastry (page
 416)
6 ounces Lotus Seed
 Paste (page 433)

Beaten egg yolk for
 sealing
6 cups oil

PREPARATION

1 Keep pastry rolls chilled and ready.

2 Take about 1 tablespoon of the lotus seed paste and roll it between your palms to shape it into a ball. Take more lotus seed paste and make 17 more balls.

ASSEMBLING

1 Flatten the roll of pastry dough with a rolling pin and bring both ends up. Press with your fingers to taper both ends and make them overlap at the center.

2 Roll the pastry out into a disc about 3 inches in diameter, making the edge much thinner for easy sealing. Brush the edge of the disc with egg yolk.

3 Place a ball of lotus seed paste in the center. Bring the edges up by gathering and pleating. Twist to seal securely.

4 Turn the sealed side down and place balls on a platter. Continue to make remaining pastries. Wrap and chill until ready to deep-fry, at least 1 hour (so lotus petals will open beautifully).

COOKING

1 Make a series of 3 criss-cross incisions on the top of each pastry, using a sharp knife. Cut them as deep as to the filling, about 2 inches long, so that there are 6 equal segments.

2 Set a wok over medium heat. When hot, add the oil. Wait for about 5 to 7 minutes, then test the temperature by dropping in a small piece of scallion green. If bubbles appear around the green, which also sizzles, the oil is ready (about 275 degrees).

3 Slip six of the pastries into the oil, so the lotus petals have enough space to open up. Each will open into a multi-layered pastry resembling a flower. Remove and drain on paper towels. Deep-fry the remaining pastries in small batches of 6 each.

4 Serve warm as a dim sum for banquets.

Note: Sweet lotus seed paste is sometimes available in large bakeries in Chinatown during the Mid-Autumn Festival time. It is the major ingredient for the mooncake.

Flaky Spiral Filled with Date-Nut Paste

Yields	18 spirals
Time	10 minutes preparation
	2 hours chilling
	30 minutes assembling
	25 minutes cooking

棗仁酥盒

The intriguing spiral pattern adds to the charm of these tasty after-dinner snacks, and can be the start of a guessing game: how was it made? Techniques are shown on pages 98–99.

Ingredients

1 ounce pine nuts
1 cup Jujube Date
　Paste (see page 434)
18 rolls Classic
　Chinese Flaky Pastry
　(page 416)

1 whole egg, lightly
　beaten
6 cups oil

PREPARATION

1 Roast the pine nuts over low heat in a small skillet for 2 minutes, stirring constantly until nuts are light brown. Remove to cool, then chop into small bits.

2 Mix pine nuts with the date paste. Divide the date-nut paste into 18 equal parts. Shape each part into a ball, then flatten it into a round piece about 1½ inches in diameter. Arrange on a platter in 1 layer and wrap and chill for at least 2 hours.

ASSEMBLING

1 Cut the pastry roll in half crosswise, then flatten each half into a disc.

2 Roll out each disc, about 2 inches in diameter (note that the pastry for a disc is much thinner than for a crescent). Place 1 disc on your palm and brush the edge with beaten egg in a band about ¼ inch wide. Put a piece of date–nut filling in the center and cover with the other pastry disc.

3 Press the edge firmly to make it thinner and to seal. Make ridges along the edge.

4 Continue to make remaining pastries.

COOKING

1 Set a wok over medium heat. When hot, add oil. Wait for about 5 to 7 minutes, then test the temperature by dropping a small piece of scallion green into the oil. If bubbles appear around the green, which also sizzles, the oil is ready (about 275 degrees).

2 Slip half of the pastries, fluted sides up, into the oil. Spade with a spatula to prevent discs from sticking to the bottom of the wok. Deep-fry slowly until light golden, about 10 minutes. Remove to drain on paper towels.

3 Finish deep-frying the remaining discs. Serve warm as a dessert in a banquet or as a snack.

◉◉Glutinous Dumplings Filled with Sesame and Cashew Paste

Yields 1 dozen
Time 30 minutes preparation
10 minutes resting
7 minutes steaming

椰 絲 蘇 糰

Interestingly chewy, these are more for snacks than for dessert. A favorite sweet dim sum from Canton.

Ingredients

¼ cup rice flour
1 cup glutinous rice flour
¼ cup boiling water
¼ cup cold water
4 ounces Sesame and Cashew Paste (page 436) (about ½ cup packed)
¼ cup water

¼ cup granulated sugar
¾ cup shredded coconut

PREPARATION

1 Mix rice flour and glutinous rice flour in a mixing bowl. Make a well in the center and add boiling water. Stir with a wooden spoon to mix with the rice flour, then add cold water, stirring to mix into a lump. Turn flour mixture onto a board and knead it until smooth and satiny, about 5 minutes. Cover with a dampened towel. Rest 10 minutes.

2 Divide Sesame and Cashew Paste into 12 equal parts. Roll each part between your palms to make a ball the size of a concord grape.

3 Roll rice dough into a rod, 12 inches long, about 1¼ inches in diameter. Divide the rod into 12 equal parts.

4 Dust one palm lightly with glutinous rice flour and place in 1 piece of rice dough with the cut side up. Dust the other palm also lightly with glutinous rice powder and press on the dough to flatten it into a 2½-inch round.

5 Place a ball of sesame and cashew paste in the center of the dough round. Bring the edges up by gathering and pleating; twist to seal securely. Roll between your palms to make it into a round dumpling.

6 Finish for the remainder of the rice dough.

COOKING

1 Lightly grease a perforated steaming plate with oil. Arrange the dumplings seal side down about ¾ inch apart. Steam over high heat for 7 minutes.

2 Boil water with sugar. When the sugar dissolves, pour this sugar water into a small bowl.

3 Dip a dumpling in sugar water, then roll it in coconut shreds to coat evenly. Do all 12 dumplings, then serve immediately or cool to room temperature and then serve.

◉◉◉Glutinous Rice Pudding Stuffed with Chestnut Paste

Serves 8 as dessert in a banquet
Time   4 hours soaking
            10 minutes preparation
            1 hour, 30 minutes cooking

Two northern Chinese rice dishes have the same name, "Eight-Treasure Rice." The one introduced elsewhere is a main dish or a stuffing for braised duck. This one is a snack or banquet dessert. It is fragrant with cassia flowers, sweet with chestnut paste, and chewy with glutinous rice and nuts; it gives ample chance for the host or hostess to demonstrate artistry in creating floral patterns from colorful pieces of food. This recipe shows a foolproof technique to ensure that the pattern is not destroyed by the cooking process.

Ingredients

1 cup glutinous rice
8 blanched almonds
16 lotus seeds
1 Peking date
  (California dates
  make a fair
  substitute)
3 red maraschino
  cherries
4 green maraschino
  cherries
½ cup hot water

2 tablespoons lard or
  peanut oil
1 cup granulated sugar
6 jujube dates
½ cup Cassia-flavored
  Chestnut Paste (page
  435)
½ cup water
2 teaspoons tapioca
  powder mixed with 1
  tablespoon water

PREPARATION

1 Rinse glutinous rice and put in a bowl, adding cold water to cover. Soak rice for at least 4 hours. Drain.

2 Soak almonds and lotus seeds in boiling water for 1 hour. Split each nut in half. Cook over low heat for 30 minutes or until soft, then drain.

3 Pit the date. Cut the 2 kinds of cherries crosswise into slices about ⅛ inch thick.

4 Put glutinous rice in a heatproof bowl, about 7 inches in diameter, and steam over high heat for 20 minutes or until rice is soft and no longer opaque. Sprinkle with 2 tablespoons of hot water every 5 minutes, up to ½ cup water. Remove the bowl of rice from steamer and mix in half the lard and half the sugar. Press with a wet spoon to pack the rice.

5 Invert the bowl to turn out the rice into a dome shape on a platter. Rinse and dry the bowl, then grease it with the remaining lard. Set the bowl aside.

6 Arrange the date in the top center of the rice dome, then arrange the almonds, cherries, lotus seeds, and jujube dates in separate circles to surround the date center, forming a circular pattern.

7 Put the bowl over the rice dome on the platter. Hold them together and turn upside down, then remove the platter. The rice is now back into the bowl.

8 Scoop out with a spoon ½ cup of the glutinous rice from the center of the bowl to leave a hollow space. Pat the chestnut paste into a half-moon piece and put it into the hollow, then cover the chestnut paste with the glutinous rice. Smooth the surface of the rice with a wet spoon.

COOKING

1 Cover the bowl with aluminum foil and set it into a steamer. Steam over medium heat for 1 hour.

2 Shortly before serving, combine remaining sugar and water in a small saucepan and cook over medium heat until the sugar dissolves. Stir the tapioca mixture and stream it into the sugar water, stirring to prevent lumps. Turn heat to very low.

3 To serve, turn the bowl of rice onto a deep dish, pouring sweet sauce over, and spoon it into individual bowls at the table.

◉◉◉ Sweet Almond Tea

Serves 6 to 8
Time 20 minutes preparation
4 hours soaking
10 minutes cooking

杏仁茶

Sweet teas are made from powdered walnuts, almonds, peanuts, sesame seeds, lotus seeds, or even diced sweet potatoes. They are served after dinner, but also in the afternoon.

Ingredients

¼ cup long-grain rice
3 ounces Chinese
    almonds
6 bitter almonds
    (optional)
6 cups water
1 cup granulated sugar

PREPARATION

1 Rinse rice, then soak in water to cover for 4 hours. Drain.

2 Soak almonds and bitter almonds in boiling water for 10 minutes. Remove skins.

3 In the container of a blender, put 2 cups of water, the rice, and the almonds. Whirl at high speed for about 4 to 5 minutes or until the rice and almonds are reduced to a fine purée.

4 Add 1 additional cup of water to blender and whirl 1 more minute.

5 Line a colander with cheesecloth and set it into a 4-quart nonstick saucepan. Pour the almond purée into the colander and follow with remaining 3 cups of water. When liquid has almost completely drained into the saucepan, bring the edges of the cheesecloth together and squeeze to extract as much moisture as possible.

(Note: The almond milk can be used immediately or stored in the refrigerator for up to 2 days.)

COOKING

1 Set the saucepan over medium heat, stirring all the while. When mixture turns bubbly, add the sugar, stirring until dissolved and thickened.

2 Serve almond tea hot.

VARIATION: Sweet Walnut Tea

Substitute 1 cup of walnut meats for the almonds. Blanch them in boiling water for 2 minutes, then rinse with hot water and drain. Remove the skins and let dry at room temperature.

Heat a wok over high heat until very hot. Add 1 cup of oil. Wait until a piece of scallion green dropped into the oil sizzles and moves about quickly (about 350 degrees), then add the walnuts, stirring constantly for 40 seconds or until the walnuts turn light brown. Remove walnuts immediately with a deep-frying strainer. Cool at room temperature for 15 minutes.

Combine the soaked rice and fried walnuts in the blender and proceed as for almond tea.

VARIATION: Sweet Peanut Tea

Substitute 1 cup of raw peanut meat for the almond. Put peanuts in a small heavy saucepan and roast over medium low heat for 10 minutes or until the skin of the peanuts comes off easily. Remove skins of the peanuts and proceed as for almond tea.

VARIATION: Sweet Sesame Tea

Substitute 3 ounces (½ cup packed) of black sesame seeds for the almonds. Rinse and pick over the sesame seeds; remove and discard foreign particles if any. Drain in a fine-mesh strainer first, then spread them on double paper towels to dry. Roast in a small heavy saucepan over medium-low heat for 10 to 12 minutes or until sesame seeds start to pop. Stir seeds constantly while roasting. Proceed as for almond tea.

Part 3

Food in the Chinese Context

Planning a Chinese Meal

Menu planning is more critical, and much more fun, in Chinese cooking than in most Western-style meals. In Western meals the cook plans a small number of dishes, to be served more or less one at a time. The Chinese, however, cherish the tradition of serving several different main dishes together or in rapid succession, as in banquets, to be shared family style.

The Chinese cook must consider not only the effects of this simultaneous offering of dishes on the guests, but also the required scheduling in the kitchen. The latter is especially important when he or she is the only cook. There is also the additional demand that the cook should not ignore the guests, but should appear often if only to receive compliments. Lastly, there is the demand for balanced nutrition, which for a multi-dish meal is relatively easy to meet. The difficulty is more in the art of making the selections than in scheduling their preparation.

HARMONY THROUGH CONTRAST

The average menu for a lower-middle class Chinese family of three to six persons consists of four dishes of modest size, one soup, plus white rice. The Chinese living in the United States often reach a balance in their meals of fewer but more substantial dishes. Except for informal one-pot meals such as curried chicken and Chinese beef stew, a good Chinese meal should have at least two main dishes for variety and contrast. This contrast of tastes and textures is to be savored by the diners again and again in the same meal. The purpose is to achieve harmony through contrast, rather than merely being different.

Do not serve all soft-textured dishes; allow at least one dish to exercise the jaw. The Chinese usually solve the texture–variety problem with the same dish by adding chewy and crunchy ingredients (pork shreds, bamboo shoots, black mushrooms) to soft foods.

Use a different main ingredient for each dish, with the exception of pork and pork products (ham, sausages, and pork organs), which play a special role in Chinese cuisine; the main ingredient of a soup could also match that of one of the dishes.

Avoid repeating the same seasoning (for example, two sweet and sour dishes) in the same meal. Do not overpower delicate dishes by highly spicy ones, particu-

larly hot-pepper dishes; if one must have both, serve the delicate ones first. Try to have a stir-fry as part of the meal; it is easy to do, and can accommodate virtually any meat and vegetable ingredients.

Americans may serve water during the meal, but we strongly prefer soup. The Cantonese family-style soup tends to be bland, but delicate and thirst quenching (see our recipes for minute soups). A thick, hearty soup such as Pungent and Hot Soup is great for a winter evening, but its preparation will take more time.

COORDINATING THE COOKING PROCEDURES

The proper blending of dishes can greatly affect the efficiency of preparation. Some dishes (stir-frying, pan-frying, and deep-frying) require periods of critical timing which demand the undivided attention of the cook; clearly no two such dishes should be prepared at exactly the same time.

Fortunately, the demands for variety naturally rule out many possible clashes. Also, many cooking steps can be done ahead of time, allowing much better meshing of the schedules.

On the other hand, if several dishes have similar preparation steps (cutting, for instance), do them together or in rapid succession. For example, one dish may be stir-fried, another may be steamed on top of the rice, and a soup may be simmered over a separate stove. A braised dish may take hours, but once started, it requires no particular attention. The oven is an added asset for keeping food warm before their last-minute preparations. Ingredients for several dishes can be set up together to save time. But remember that all dried ingredients have to be soaked at least an hour before using.

Most Chinese homemakers seem to coordinate the time requirement instinctively. This skill actually is acquired with practice.

SERVING THE FOOD

Chopsticks, having been in use for over 3,000 years, have deeply affected the eating habits of the Chinese. Accordingly, solid food is presented to be picked up by chopsticks. Narrow strips are designed to be scooped or pulled up in a bundle with the chopsticks. Slender green vegetables are usually cut into lengths of no more than two inches, probably because of the diameter of the rice bowl. To eat rice, the bowl is raised to lip level, and the rice is pushed into the mouth by chopsticks. When the Chinese roast an entire fowl, fry a whole fish, and steam large, thick slices of pork, the fowl is often cut up in the kitchen before serving and large but tender pieces of other foods are broken up with chopsticks and occasionally with spoons at the table.

While some Chinese consider the knife and fork to be leftovers of barbarism, Americans complain that in Chinese food bones are left in. The practice is to pick up the morsel with bones and nibble on it; this goes not only for chicken but also for one-inch-long spareribs. For fish, it is proper to extract the finer bones before, during, and after nibbling. It is the same with lobster chunks and pan-fried jumbo shrimp with shells.

The Chinese spoon holds twice as much as the Western version, and it has a flat bottom so that it can rest on the table without spilling its contents. Most Chinese consider the Western spoon grossly inefficient, but—on the other hand—the very delicate Chinese soups, such as shark's fin soup and bird's nest soup, are served in undersized bowls, with smaller spoons.

The Chinese dinner is seldom served in an atmosphere of intimacy or extravagance. The emphasis is on the food, and the ambience is largely furnished by the eaters themselves. The dining room is adequately lit to enable the guests to select the morsels from the shared dishes.

BEVERAGES

Soup is present throughout a Chinese family meal, and for quenching thirst, the diner need look no further. (Tea used to be served before and after, but seldom during meals.) In traditional banquets, where dishes are presented one at a time, there may be more than one soup.

Grain-based wines heighten the enjoyment of food, and counteract the cloying effect of rich foods. The sweet rice wine and yellow wine are prewarmed in a hot water bath before serving. Fiery grain liquors like *moutai* (more than 100 proof) require no warming; they supply their own warmth, so to speak.

During the summer, traditionally the Chinese would dissipate body heat by drinking steaming-hot liquids to induce sweating. Western civilization brought in an alternate philosophy, using cold drinks as body-coolers. The old order having been breached, the Chinese dinner table is now flooded with beverages of all kinds: beer, tea, yellow wine, *moutai*, cognac, Scotch, soft drinks, and occasionally even grape wine. But unlike Americans, the Chinese almost never drink ice water with their meals. For information on serving wine with Chinese meals, see pages 469–473.

SUGGESTED MENUS

In Chinese meals, there are three major requirements, namely quality, variety, and quantity. Within limitations of budget and availability, the cook tries to produce the best food. But with two or more people at the same table, the food is shared family style and variety becomes an important concern. The lone eater misses a lot, and he (or she) knows it.

Usually one tries for contrast and avoids the repeated use of the same major ingredient or the same cooking technique. But more of this later.

Quantity is less a concern with the Chinese, who can fill empty spaces in the stomach with rice and save extra food as leftovers for the next day. There should be about three servings for each adult. We recommend for variety:

> *1 dish, 1 soup and rice for 2 people*
> *2 dishes, 1 soup and rice for 3 people*
> *3 dishes, 1 soup and rice for 4 people*
> *4 dishes, 1 soup and rice for 5 to 6 people*
> *5 or 6 dishes, 1 soup and rice for 7 to 8 people*

In dinner for four, the call for variety usually leads to four servings per adult. For eight to twelve persons, especially in the case of a home banquet at which dishes are served one at a time, the Chinese homemaker may find it difficult to sit with the guests. The menu should be planned to allow the cook some respite.

To relieve the pressure, serve cold platters that have been prepared ahead of time at the beginning of the meal. The cook can join the party while the soup and some other dishes are being warmed. Also, there should always be a planned intermission between servings, so the host or hostess can have a chance to chat, pour the wine, and receive compliments. Don't be overly ambitious to entertain a large group, however, unless you are experienced and confident. A buffet dinner often is a better answer than a formal banquet.

DINNER FOR 4

Hand-Shredded Chicken in Oyster and Ginger Sauce
Fillet of Fish in Tomato Sauce
Stir-Fried Minced Beef with Green Peas
Minute Spinach Soup with Pork Slices

Early Afternoon

Marinate chicken for 2 hours, then steam. When the chicken is done, brush the skin with sesame oil and let cool. Mix oyster sauce. Crush the garlic. Shred scallions. Cut Chinese parsley. Soak black mushrooms. Rinse spinach.

1 Hour, 15 Minutes Ahead

Season beef and chill. Slice fish fillets. Season and chill. Debone the chicken by tearing the meat into bite-sized pieces. Cut the skin into pieces about the same size. Arrange chicken pieces on a serving platter and place the skin on top. Wrap and set at room temperature. Simmer the chicken bones in the cooking liquid to yield about 3 cups of stock for the soup.

45 Minutes Ahead

Remove scallion whites from the fish fillets and chop them fine. Also chop the scallion greens. Mix tomato sauce. For the beef dish, cut and blanch carrots, dice black mushrooms and the onion, and blanch green peas. Mix sauce. Have minced garlic ready for the fish and the beef.

30 Minutes Ahead

Cook the rice. While cooking the rice, add egg white to the fish, mixing well, then coat each piece with cornstarch. Slice pork and season.

15 Minutes Ahead

Drain the stock into a saucepan and heat it over low temperature. Deep-fry fish fillets. Cook the tomato sauce. Keep both warm in the oven. Cook oyster sauce for chicken in a saucepan. Cover.

7 Minutes Ahead

Resteam chicken. Bring the soup stock to a vigorous boil. Add spinach to soup and bring it back to a boil, then add pork slices and season. Keep soup uncovered. Stir-fry the beef with green peas. Pour oyster sauce over the chicken. Pour tomato sauce over fish fillets. Serve the 3 dishes and the soup together with rice. Brew tea during dinner and serve it with fresh fruit after dinner.

DINNER FOR 4

Red-Cooked Duck with Napa Cabbage
Stir-Fried Beef Shreds with Pepper
Scrambled Egg with Crabmeat
Mock Bird's Nest Soup
Rice, Tea, Fruit

Early Afternoon

Marinate the duck for 1 hour. Rinse and cut cabbage. Drain well. Mix the braising sauce, then cook the duck. While cooking the duck, purée the winter melon. Drain melon juice off to cook with ham slices for 30 minutes. Chop ham fine. Mix soup thickener. Separate eggs for the soup. Beat egg whites with 1 tablespoon water. Set the egg yolks aside.

1 Hour Ahead

Sliver the fillet of beef. Season and chill. Shred peppers, garlic, carrots, and scallions. Cook the cabbage and keep warm in the oven. Beat the eggs with the reserved egg yolks, oil, and salt. Have shredded scallions and parsley lengths ready for the scrambled egg. Cook the winter melon purée in the stock with the ham juice until soft. Set aside.

30 Minutes Ahead

Cook the rice. While the rice is cooking, degrease the duck sauce, reheat the duck, and arrange it in a serving platter; then thicken the sauce. Keep the duck and the sauce separately warming in the oven. Season the crabmeat. Reheat the winter soup.

15 Minutes Ahead

Arrange the cabbage to surround the duck. Pour the sauce over and put the platter back in the oven. Thicken the soup. Keep warm over low heat. Stir-fry the beef.

5 Minutes Ahead

Scramble the egg, whirl egg whites into the soup. Serve the 3 dishes together with the soup and the rice. During dinner, brew tea and serve it with fresh fruit after dinner.

DINNER FOR 4

Deep-Fried Chicken Breast in Lemon Sauce
Pearly Balls
Stir-Fried Mixed Chinese Vegetables
Pungent and Hot Soup
Rice, Tea and Fruit

Early Afternoon

For pearly balls, soak the glutinous rice, chop bamboo shoots and scallions. Mix the pork with seasonings, adding bamboo shoots and scallions. Chill for at least 2 hours.

2 Hours Ahead

Shape pork balls and roll them in glutinous rice. Arrange the balls on a steaming platter. Cover and chill until they are used. Soak black mushrooms and cloud ears for soup. Also soak black mushrooms for the mixed vegetable dish. Debone chicken breasts, then score and season. Simmer the bones with the mushroom liquid to yield about 2 cups of thin stock.

1 Hour Ahead

Prepare the lemon sauce mixture for chicken. Cut mixed vegetables for stir-frying. For the soup, shred and blanch bamboo shoots. Trim cloud ears. Shred and season pork. Mix soup thickener and the pungent and hot mixture. Beat the eggs. Have the shredded scallions and the Chinese parsley ready.

35 Minutes Ahead

Start rice cooker. Steam pearly balls. While steaming the pearly balls, strain the soup and mix with 3 cups basic soup stock in a saucepan. Bring the soup stock to a boil, adding black mushrooms, cloud ears, and bamboo shoots. Shred the bean curd.

20 Minutes Ahead

Deep-fry the chicken breasts for the first time. While resting the chicken in the strainer, remove sediments from the oil, then deep-fry the chicken the second time. Pour oil out and prepare the lemon sauce.

10 Minutes Ahead

Chop chicken breasts into pieces. Arrange them in a serving platter; keep warm in the oven. Stir-fry the mixed vegetables. Add pork to the soup, stirring until shreds are separated. Thicken the soup, then whirl in the eggs. Stir in pungent and hot mixture, and sprinkle with scallion and parsley. Pour lemon sauce over the chicken. Remove pearly balls from steamer. Serve the 3 dishes together with the soup and the rice. Brew tea during dinner and serve with fruit after dinner.

DINNER FOR 4

Soy Sauce Chicken
Steamed Bean Curd with Fish
Stir-Fried Beef Slices with Snow Peas
Pork and Winter Melon Soup with Salted Duck Eggs
Rice, Tea and Fruit

3 Hours Ahead

Prepare the spicy mixture, then cook the chicken in the spicy soy sauce. When done, brush the chicken skin with sesame oil. Cover it loosely with aluminum foil. Let cool at room temperature. Soak the dried shrimp.

1 Hour Ahead

Chop the dried shrimp fine. Purée fish in the blender and mix with the bean curd, adding dried shrimp and seasoning. Arrange the bean curd mixture in a deep dish, cover, and chill until needed. Slice and season the beef, then chill. String and rinse snow peas.

30 Minutes Ahead

Cut the winter melon. Slice and season the pork. Cook the winter melon with the salted egg yolks in the soup stock. Keep the pot of soup over low heat. Have the water in the base of the steamer ready for steaming.

15 Minutes Ahead

Place the dish of bean curd in the steamer. While the bean curd is steaming, chop the soy sauce chicken. Warm some sauce and pour it over the chicken. Stir-fry the beef with snow peas. Whirl the salted egg whites into the soup. Serve the 3 dishes at the same time with soup and rice. Brew the tea and serve with fruit.

DINNER FOR 4

Five-Spiced Beef Shank
Steamed Minced Pork with Dried Shrimp and Black Mushrooms
Almond Chicken
Minute Watercress Soup with Fish Slices
Rice, Tea, Fruit

Evening Before

Marinate the beef shank. Debone the chicken breast and dice. Season and chill chicken dice. Simmer chicken bones to yield about 2 cups of thin stock.

Early Afternoon

Cook the beef until tender, about 2 hours. Keep the beef in the refrigerator. Soak black mushrooms, dice vegetables, blanch the almonds. When the mushrooms are soft, dice. Have the scallions and garlic ready for stir-frying the almond chicken. Soak dried shrimp and black mushrooms for steamed pork.

40 Minutes Ahead

Mix minced pork and arrange the pork mixture in a heatproof dish. For the soup, slice the fish. Have the watercress, Chinese parsley, and preserved cucumber shreds ready. Start the rice cooker.

25 Minutes Ahead

While the rice is boiling, set a steaming rack in the rice cooker. When craters appear on the surface of the rice, place the dish of minced pork on the rack. Cover the rice cooker. Slice only 1 beef shank, arranging the slices in a serving platter. Brush beef slices with sesame oil first, then pour some braising sauce over. Freeze the remaining beef shank in the spicy sauce for other use.

10 Minutes Ahead

Strain the thin stock into another saucepan, adding 1 more cup of chicken stock. Bring the soup to a boil then heat it over low heat, putting in the preserved cucumber shreds. Deep-fry the almonds first, then finish with stir-frying the chicken dish. Turn the temperature to high to heat up the soup, adding watercress, then the fish slices and parsley. Remove the minced pork from steamer and serve together with the cold beef shank, almond chicken, soup, and rice. While serving dinner, brew the tea and serve it after dinner with fruit.

DINNER FOR 4

Strange-Flavored Chicken

Clear-Fried Shrimp in Yellow Wine

Silver Dollar Beef with Stir-Fried Zucchini

Red-in-Snow and Fava Bean Soup

Rice, Tea, Fruit

(Note: In this dinner, it is assumed that the fava beans have been sprouted in advance and kept in the refrigerator.)

Early Morning

White-cook the chicken. Shell, devein, and clean the shrimp. Drain shrimp well, then wrap and chill. When the chicken is done, rest it on a rack to cool, brushing with sesame oil to prevent the skin from drying.

3 Hours Ahead

Chop the chicken up into bite-sized pieces and arrange in the serving platter. Wrap the chicken and set at room temperature. Simmer the chicken bones in the cooking liquid to yield about 4 cups of thin stock. Prepare the strange-flavored sauce. Have scallions and the garlic ready for stir-frying. Soak dried shrimp. Remove the skin from fava beans. Cut the Sichuan preserved vegetable and the red-in-snow.

2 Hours Ahead

Season the shrimp. Refrigerate until needed. For the silver dollar beef, chop the whole onion (no need to reserve); cut bacon into strips. Brown the onion with bacon. Season the beef, adding bacon and onion. Cover and chill. Mix sauce in a small bowl. Shred the zucchini, stirring in salt and rest in a colander at room temperature, then squeeze off excess moisture. Shred the garlic.

30 Minutes Ahead

Start the rice cooker. Stir-fry the dried shrimp in a saucepan until flavor escapes. Strain the stock through a fine-mesh sieve into the saucepan and bring the stock to a boil, adding the fava beans and the shrimp juice. Cook the soup for 5 minutes, then add the preserved vegetables. Simmer 10 more minutes. Keep soup warm over very low heat, uncovered. While cooking the soup, shape the

beef patties into "silver dollars," coat with cornstarch, and pan-fry them until both sides are brown, then remove. Cook the sauce and pour over beef. Keep warm in the oven.

10 Minutes Ahead

Stir-fry the shrimp. Stir-fry the zucchini and arrange the zucchini to surround the beef patties. Pour the strange-flavored sauce over chicken and serve the 3 dishes together with the soup and the rice. Brew tea and serve it with fruit after dinner.

DINNER FOR 4

White-Chopped Chicken with Broccoli
Sautéed Calves Liver in Wine
Deep-Fried Oysters
Egg Flower and Minced Beef Soup
Rice, Tea, Fruit

Early Afternoon

White-cook the chicken, cooling it by running cold water over the skin and into the cavity. Brush the chicken skin with sesame oil. Cover and let set at room temperature.

2 Hours Ahead

Chop chicken and arrange pieces in a serving platter. Simmer the chicken bones in the cooking liquid to yield about 4 cups of thin stock. Shred scallions and grate the gingerroot and put them in a small bowl, sprinkling salt on top. Rinse and cut broccoli. Have ginger juice and brandy ready for stir-frying. Clean oysters, blanch, drain, and pat them dry. Season. Chill until needed. Mix batter; also chill. Soak calves liver in water.

45 Minutes Ahead

Drain the liver and slice it into slabs, adding the marinade. Mix sauce and have scallions and garlic ready for sautéing.

35 Minutes Ahead

Start the rice cooker. Strain the stock into a saucepan and set it over low heat. Season minced beef, beat the eggs, chop scallions, and mix soup thickener.

25 Minutes Ahead

Coat oysters with cornstarch. Shred lettuce to line a serving platter. Ready oil for deep-frying. When the oil is hot, scoop some hot oil to pour over the shredded scallion and grated gingerroot. Dip oysters in the batter and deep-fry. Drain oysters in a colander. Remove sediments from the oil. Cook the soup and keep it uncovered.

3 Minutes Ahead

Drain marinade from the liver and add cornstarch to coat. Immediately put the liver pieces into the hot oil for oil-dipping, then finish with the sautéing procedure. Serve the soup first. While serving soup, stir-fry the broccoli, arranging it to surround the chicken pieces. Pour scallion and ginger sauce over chicken. Put

the deep-fried oysters on the shredded lettuce and put a small dish of five-spice salt on the side. Serve the 3 dishes together. Brew tea during dinner and serve it after dinner with fruit.

DINNER FOR 4

Steamed Chicken Soup with Black Mushrooms
Leek-Stuffed Short Ribs of Beef
Stir-Fried Luffa Squash (or Cucumber) with Cloud Ears and Onion
Ginger-Curdled Milk
Rice, Tea

Early Morning
Soak black mushrooms in hot water. At the same time, clean and blanch chicken. Trim mushroom stems. Put chicken, ham, mushroom liquid and boiling water into the casserole. Steam the soup for 2 hours. While steaming the chicken, prepare the stuffed beef ribs. Soak the cloud ears.

30 Minutes Ahead
Add black mushrooms to the soup and continue to steam. Start the rice cooker. Trim tough ends of cloud ears. Cut luffa squash and onion. Have gingerroot slices ready for stir-frying the vegetables. Grate gingerroot and squeeze off juice for the curdled milk.

10 Minutes Ahead
Reheat the stuffed ribs. Stir-fry the luffa squash. Serve these 2 dishes with the soup and the rice. Brew tea during dinner. After dinner, mix ginger juice with vinegar in a bowl. Boil the milk, adding ginger juice and vinegar mixture. Then pour into 4 separate bowls and stir well. Serve tea with the curdled milk.

DINNER FOR 6

Crab Foo Yung
Sichuan Spicy Fried Beef Shreds
Steamed Chicken with Chinese Sausages and Black Mushrooms
Stir-Fried Pork Slices with Snow Peas
Seaweed Soup
Rice, Tea, Steamed Brown Sponge Cake

Early Afternoon
Shred beef, then marinate; refrigerate. Soak black mushrooms and dates. Slice the sausages. Soak some black mushrooms separately for the crab foo yung. Prepare the brown sponge cake. Soak dried shrimps for the soup.

2 Hours Ahead
For the foo yung, shred bamboo shoots and blanch, drain, then pat dry. Shred black mushrooms and scallions. Cut the parsley. Chop and season chicken. Cut black mushrooms and dates, adding to chicken and mix well. Wrap and chill.

Have scallions and gingerroot ready. For the beef, shred the celery, carrot, and fresh hot chili pepper; flatten the garlic. For the soup, shred and season pork, chop dried shrimp, cut the *nori*, beat eggs, and mix soup thickener.

1 Hour Ahead

Fry the beef and set at room temperature. Slice and season the pork. String the snow peas, rinse, and drain. Season the crabmeat.

30 Minutes Ahead

Start the rice cooker. Beat the eggs and add seasonings. Mix the sauce and set aside. Stir-fry the bamboo shoots and black mushrooms, then add to the egg mixture with the crabmeat, scallion shreds, and parsley. Pan-fry the crab foo yung, then cook the sauce. Keep the foo yung and the sauce warm separately in a 175-degree oven. Have water in the base of the steamer ready. Cook the soup up to adding the nori squares.

15 Minutes Ahead

Spread the chicken pieces in one layer in a heatproof dish, putting the sausages on top. Place the dish in the steamer when the water boils.

12 Minutes Ahead

Reheat the Sichuan beef in the wok. Keep it warm in the oven. Rinse the wok, then stir-fry the pork with snow peas. Pour the sauce over the crab foo yung. Remove the chicken from the steamer when done. Reheat soup and whirl in eggs. Serve all 4 dishes at the same time with soup and rice. Brew tea during dinner. Slice the brown sponge cake and serve with tea.

DINNER FOR 8

Salt-Water Chicken
Oil-Blasted Shrimp
Red-Cooked Duck in Yellow Wine with Napa Cabbage
Deep-Fried Spicy Livers
Beef in Oyster Sauce
Scrambled Egg with Crabmeat
Spinach Velvet Soup
Rice, Tea, Sweet Sesame Tea

Evening Before

White-cook the chicken. Prepare salt water to marinate the chicken. Set at room temperature until chicken is cool, then refrigerate. Trim and devein the shrimp and marinate them in wine. Soak the rice and black sesame seeds separately and refrigerate.

Early Morning

Purée the rice with the sesame seeds. Slice and tenderize beef. Blast shrimp in oil and refrigerate. Chop the ham.

3 Hours Ahead

Cook the duck. Neutralize, then season the beef. Refrigerate. Mix oyster sauce. Have the garlic, scallions, and gingerroot ready for stir-frying the beef. Rinse

spinach leaves. Blanch and chop them fine. Refrigerate. Wrap and chill. Chop up the salt-water chicken and arrange pieces in the serving platter. Wrap and set at room temperature. Marinate chicken livers.

1 Hour Ahead

Cook the napa cabbage in chicken broth, leaving it in the skillet. Season the crabmeat. Beat the eggs and mix in crabmeat, shredded scallions, and parsley. Refrigerate the mixture. Drain marinade from livers, add a beaten egg, and mix well. Chop the duck and arrange on serving platter. Wrap and leave at room temperature.

30 Minutes Ahead

Start the rice cooker. Coat chicken livers with cornstarch and deep-fry them in 2 batches. After draining the excessive oil on paper towels, keep the livers warm in 175-degree oven. Ready the soup stock and bring it to a boil.

10 Minutes Ahead

Add chopped spinach to the soup. Thicken soup,then whirl in egg whites. Serve the soup first. While serving soup, stir-fry the beef in oyster sauce, then scramble the egg mixture. Reheat napa cabbage, arranging it to surround the duck. Serve the 6 dishes with rice. After dinner, brew the tea and cook the sweet sesame tea. Serve them together.

DINNER FOR 10 TO 12

Egg Pâté
Drunken Chicken
White-Cooked Pork in Garlic Sauce
Marinated Asparagus
Tossed Seaweed Salad

Deep-Fried Beef Brain
Miniature Crab Casserole (2 × the recipe on page 173)

Eight-Treasure Winter Melon Soup

Onion-Stuffed Duck with Napa Cabbage
Wine-Blasted Tenderloin of Veal with Fresh Mushrooms
Steamed Whole Fish

Rice, Tea, Smiling Faces (½ the recipe on page 173)

Two Evenings Before

White-cook the chicken and marinate it in wine. Keep the chicken refrigerated until it is used. Soak beef brains first in water, then in vinegar water, and refrigerate overnight.

Evening Before

Prepare the egg pâté. Cook the pork and leave it in the saucepan with the soaking liquid. Refrigerate when cool. Clean beef brains. Steam brains with seasonings, then mash fine. Cook the brain custard. Cover and refrigerate.

PLANNING A CHINESE MEAL

Next Morning

Marinate the duck. Peel onions. Mix braising sauce. Soak black mushrooms separately for the soup and the miniature crab casseroles. Mix the dough for smiling faces, then deep-fry them. After the smiling faces have cooled off completely, store them in an airtight jar. Cook the duck. Marinate the asparagus.

Afternoon

Rinse and cut the cabbage. Dice ingredients for the winter melon soup. Blanch bamboo shoots, pork dice, chicken dice, and green peas. Cook the shrimp; shell and devein them, then dice shrimp. Slice and season the tenderloin of veal, then refrigerate. For the seaweed salad, soak the agar-agar; select the bean sprouts; rinse and cut spinach. Blanch the sprouts and spinach separately. Refrigerate. Mix the salad dressing. Roast sesame seeds. Cook the pork fatback for the crab casserole and chill to firm. Prepare garlic sauce.

2 Hours Ahead

Mince black mushrooms, scallions, ham, and pork fat. Prepare the crabmeat mixture and refrigerate. Slice fresh mushrooms. Ready the fish on a heatproof platter for steaming, wrap it, and refrigerate. Shred scallions, gingerroots, and parsley. Cook the napa cabbage, keeping it covered in the skillet.

1 Hour Ahead

Grease 12 small ramekins. Divide the crab mixture into 12 equal portions and put 1 portion into each ramekin. Coat the top of the crabmeat mixture with bread crumbs, then brush with oil. Set the ramekins aside. Slice the pork, chop up the drunken chicken, slice the egg pâté, and arrange them on separate serving platters. Wrap and set these 3 cold platters at room temperature. Preheat oven to 375 degrees.

20 Minutes Ahead

Bake the crab casseroles. Cook the winter melon soup up to the adding of the crabmeat and green peas. Cut the brain custards into pieces and coat with cornstarch. Toss the seaweed salad. Arrange the marinated asparagus to surround the pork. Start the rice cooker.

Cooking While Serving

1 Serve the 4 cold platters at the same time. Check the crab casseroles; if done, turn oven temperature to the lowest. (Serving time: 20 minutes)

2 Heat the oil for deep-frying. Remove crab casseroles from the oven and serve. (Cooking time: 5 minutes)

3 Deep-fry the brain custards and serve. (Cooking time: 10 minutes)

Intermission (10 minutes for cooking the soup)

4 Bring the soup back to a boil, adding crabmeat and green peas. Serve. While serving, ready the water in the base of the steamer for steaming the fish. (Serving time: 10 minutes)

5 Reheat the duck and the cabbage separately, then combine them in a serving platter and serve with rice. (Cooking time: 5 minutes; serving time: 10 minutes)

6 Set the smiling faces in the oven to warm. Bring water in the steamer to a vigorous boil over high heat. Put in the fish, cover, and steam. Meanwhile, stir-fry the veal tenderloin and serve. (Cooking time: 10 minutes; serving time: 5 minutes)

7 Heat oil for pouring over fish. When the fish is done, add the seasonings; spread the scallions, gingerroot, and parsley on top. Pour the hot oil over the fish and serve. (Cooking time: 5 minutes)

Intermission (Total serving time: about 1 hour, 30 minutes)

8 Brew tea. Serve tea with smiling faces.

CLASSIC CHINESE BANQUET FOR 12

Stuffed Mushrooms with Crabmeat
Emerald Shrimp
Ham in Candy Sauce
Braised Abalone with Black Mushrooms

Chicken Velvet and Jade Pillar Chowder

Oil-Poured Fish Chunks
Lemon Chicken
Northern Lamb Chops with Asparagus

Rice, Tea, Sweet Almond Bean Curd with Oriental Fruit

Ingredients from an Oriental Market
Smithfield ham: center cut and ham hock; canned abalone; black mushrooms; lotus seeds; preserved cassia blossoms; jade pillars; water chestnut powder; Chinese almonds; canned lychees and mandarin oranges.

Ingredients Which Could be Purchased Ahead of Time and Kept Frozen
Lace fat; Gulf shrimp; chicken breast; stewing hen; leg of pork; loin of lamb.

2 Days Before the Banquet

Stock Prepare the supreme stock. Cool, then refrigerate overnight.

Flat Bread Prepare the flat bread. Cut into pieces 3½ by 1½ inches in size. Wrap and refrigerate.

Almond Bean Curd Soak Chinese almonds and prepare almond liquid. Refrigerate.

Ham in Candy Sauce Soak and rest the ham in baking soda water. Clean and trim, then soak in cold water at room temperature overnight.

Evening Before

Stuffed Mushrooms Clean lace fat. Drain. Cover and refrigerate.

Emerald Shrimp Shell, devein and clean. Drain and pat dry. Wrap and chill.

Ham in Candy Sauce Soak lotus seeds. Split seeds in halves and remove the greens in the center. Simmer ½ hour. Drain. Cover and refrigerate. Do the initial cooking of the ham, then refrigerate.

Lamb Chop Slice the loin of lamb and marinate. Cover and refrigerate.

Soup Prepare chicken velvet. Cover jade pillars with water in a bowl and soak in refrigerator overnight.

Almond Bean Curd   Soak agar-agar in cold water for 1 hour, then cook with almond liquid and sugar to form almond bean curd. Rest. Cover and refrigerate. Keep all the canned fruit in the refrigerator.

Morning Before

Fresh Ingredients   Shop for crabmeat, fillet of fish, fresh chicken, fresh mushrooms, asparagus, spinach, and kiwifruit. Refrigerate all ingredients if not used immediately.

Stuffed Mushrooms   Remove stems from fresh mushrooms. Chop the stems finely. Prepare crabmeat stuffing. Wipe mushroom caps to clean. Cover them separately and refrigerate.

Emerald Shrimp   Prepare spinach paste, then use it to tint the shrimp. Mix seasonings and add to shrimp. Cover and refrigerate until used.

Lemon Chicken   Clean and pat the chicken dry. Marinate. Turn chicken in the marinade occasionally. Mix braising sauce. Have lemons, shallots, garlic and gingerroot ready.

Early Afternoon

Abalone and Black Mushrooms   Soak and ready the black mushrooms for steaming.

Ham in Candy Sauce   Slice the ham. Arrange pieces in a bowl. Steam with crushed rock candy until dissolved, about 15 minutes, then drain the sweet ham juice. Arrange part of the lotus seeds on top of the ham slices. Add sherry and the remaining rock candy. Steam 45 minutes. Remove and cover the bowl. Set at room temperature.

Lemon Chicken   While steaming ham the second time, cook the lemon chicken. When done, rest chicken on a rack and brush with sesame oil to prevent the drying of the skin. Do not cover at this moment. Slice the remaining half lemon. Wrap lemon slices and refrigerate.

Stuffed Mushrooms   Spread lace fat on racks to dry. Then stuff the mushrooms and wrap them with lace fat. Refrigerate.

Lamb Chop   Clean and cut asparagus. Drain, then chill.

2 Hours Ahead

Oil-Poured Fish Chunks   Wipe fish fillets clean and cut into chunks. Chill until ready to use. Mix sauce, cut scallions, and have garlic and ginger ready.

Soup   Simmer jade pillars in soup stock for 20 minutes. Prepare water chestnut powder mixture. Beat eggs.

Ham in Candy Sauce   Cook the remaining lotus seed with ham juice and flavor the sweetened ham juice with preserved cassia blossoms. Keep the lotus seeds and the ham juice separate. Prepare the sauce thickener.

Abalone and Black Mushrooms   Steam black mushrooms. Slice abalone, wrap and chill. Prepare sauce thickener.

30 Minutes Ahead

Stuffed Mushrooms   Dip stuffed mushrooms in egg whites first, then coat with wheat starch.

Ham in Candy Sauce   Reheat the bowl of ham in the steamer over low heat. Preheat oven to 175 degrees.

10 Minutes Ahead

Ham in Candy Sauce   Remove the bowl of ham from steamer. Drain juice,then keep warm in the oven. Arrange flat bread in a serving platter, covering with a paper towel. Steam over low heat until ready to serve.

Stuffed Mushrooms   Deep-fry stuffed mushrooms the first time.

5 Minutes Ahead

Rice   Start the rice cooker.

Stuffed Mushrooms   Finish the second-time deep-frying. Drain oil on paper towels. Pour used oil into a bowl. Wipe the wok clean.

Lemon Chicken   Wrap the platter of chicken loosely with aluminum foil. Keep warm in oven, lowering the temperature to 150 degrees.

Cooking While Serving

1 Serve the stuffed mushrooms. (Serving time: 5 minutes) Reheat lotus seeds and cassia-flavored sauce. Heat soup over low heat with chopped ham.

2 Stir-fry the emerald shrimp and serve. (Cooking time: 5 minutes; serving time: 5 minutes)

3 Turn the ham out from the bowl to a serving platter. Arrange lotus seeds around the ham dome. Thicken the sauce and pour it over. Serve with flat bread. (Cooking and serving time: about 10 minutes)

4 Final touch with the abalone and black mushrooms. Serve. (Cooking and serving time: about 10 minutes)

Intermission (10 minutes for cooking the soup)

5 Bring soup back to a boil. Thicken the soup. Beat in chicken velvet. Whirl in the eggs. Pour into a serving tureen. Decorate with the remaining chopped ham and serve. (Serving time: 10 minutes)

6 While serving soup, mix fish chunks with salt and give them an oil-dip. Serve immediately. (Cooking time: 5 minutes; serving time: 5 minutes)

7 Reheat and thicken lemon sauce. Remove chicken from oven and pour sauce over. Decorate with lemon slices. Serve with rice. (Cooking time: 5 minutes; serving time: 10 minutes)

8 Deep-fry lamb chops. While draining chops on paper towels, stir-fry asparagus. Arrange lamb chops in the center of the serving platter and surround them with asparagus. Serve. (Cooking time: 15 minutes; serving time: 5 minutes)

Intermission (10 minutes)

9 Brew tea.

10 Cut almond bean curd into cubes to combine with the mixed fruit in a salad bowl. Cut kiwifruit and preserved cherries. Toss all ingredients together and serve. (Total serving time: about 1 hour, 45 minutes)

Tea, Wine, and Liquor

TEA

The Chinese certainly take tea for granted. Most of them were puzzled by the coffee crisis of the late 1970s. Why would a shortage of coffee be so important if tea is plentiful? On the other hand, the historic significance of the Boston Tea Party is readily grasped by the Chinese, who drink tea every morning, afternoon, and evening—before and after and sometimes during meals.

Tea has been used as a drink for untold centuries. The amazing fact is not its use, but its predominance to the virtual exclusion of the other ninety-nine "grasses" sampled by Shen Nong, the legendary founder of agriculture. Tea was mentioned in texts dated to the Spring-Autumn Era (722 BC–418 BC) under an alternate name; and the official history of the Three Kingdoms Period (220–265 AD) contained the first explicit mention of tea. It relates the story of the last Wu Emperor, who reigned in the present Nanking, and his habit of forcing quantities of wine on all guests in his banquets—except for one highly respected teetotaling official, who would always be served a pot of tea (undoubtedly disguised as yellow wine). He had anticipated the practice of many barmaids all over the world.

The planting of tea started in the Yangtze Valley and later spread through China. In seafaring Fujian, one of the greatest tea producers, tea is called by its ancient pronunciation, *deh*. Elsewhere in China it is called *cha*. Consequently, Western Europe—which receives its tea shipments by sea—uses the name *tea*, or something similar, while Russia—trading with China through the overland Silk Road—calls it *chai*. Armenia—equally inaccessible from China by either route—uses both terms.

During Tang days (618–907) tea was important enough to merit a monograph (*The Classics of Tea* by Lu Yu), also a special tax. Trade along the Silk Road began to involve great quantities of tea. The Sung Dynasty (960–1297) nationalized the tea trade, and used tea to barter with nomads for horses. And both tea and salt had been used to back the Sung paper money.

The Mongols resisted all Chinese culinary enticements save one: they became great consumers of tea, which they boil first, then mix with milk, salt, and noodles. For centuries after the Mongols departed, special tea plantations were maintained in northern China for the Mongolian trade, producing tea pressed into bricks which were used as Mongol money until the 1920s.

Brick tea is also favored by the Tibetans, who mix very strong boiled tea with yak butter and salt. In Burma and Thailand, tea leaves are often treated as a vegetable. Some Russians—as well as some local groups in China—also chew their tea.

Tea was brought into Western Europe in the seventeenth century. Housewives of wealthy Dutch merchants held the first tea parties at about 1635, when tea was retailing at $100 per pound. Tea was popularized in England by Catherine of Braganza, a Portuguese princess who became queen to Charles II in 1662. The unshakable habit of afternoon tea was started by Anna, the Duchess of Bedford, early in the nineteenth century. Shortly thereafter the British East India Company found the tea trade so lucrative that it planted tea in India and Ceylon to vie with the Chinese original. However the tea dumped into Boston Harbor in 1773 was indubitably Chinese in origin.

Since the first shipment of tea after harvest always fetched higher prices, sailing speed became very important and the tea trade greatly influenced shipbuilding. In 1848, and loaded with tea, the American clipper ship *Rainbow* sailed from Canton to New York via Cape Horn in a record 88 days. The British later copied the clipper design. Other American contributions to tea in history include iced tea, tea bags, and instant tea.

Over the centuries, Western tea merchants have adopted Chinese tea terms and given them new meaning. Examples are *pekoe* ("white hair") meaning small leaves, *hyson* ("bright spring") meaning green tea from young leaves, *congou* ("effort," the same words as *kung fu*) meaning hand roasted, *Bohea* (the name of a mountain in Fujian province) meaning black tea.

In the beginning, tea was boiled, not steeped. Boiling was the only method recommended by Lu Yu, the Tang author of *The Classics of Tea*. Later, people began to experiment with new methods of tea-making. A Sung emperor advocated beating a mixture of scalding water and powdered tea into a froth; this technique, appealing to the nose as well as the eyes, is practiced even now by the Japanese in the ritual-laden tea ceremony *(chanoyu)*. The current method of steeping appears to have been invented in the early days of the Ming Dynasty.

Tea is roughly divided into three types: green, black (red),* and oolong ("black dragon"). Green tea is just dried tender leaves; the most famous green tea is probably Dragon Well from near Hangzhou. It is pale yellow and refreshingly astringent. The topmost grade of Dragon Well tea uses only the top three little leaves of every branch.

Black tea—or more properly, red tea—is from toasted fermented leaves, and it is red, robust, and hearty. The popular Keemun from East China is said to be the model for English Breakfast tea; it is bright red with a pleasing aroma considered by many as the height of red tea perfection.

Pu Erh tea from Yunnan province is rich in tannin yet mellow in taste. Lychee red tea has the fragrance of lychees. Lapsang Souchong has a smokey flavor like that of bacon.

Oolong (Black Dragon), made from partially fermented leaves, is produced in Fujian, Taiwan, and Guangdong. It is said to combine the good features of both green and red teas, and is deservedly popular in China and abroad. By 1982, the

---

*The Chinese do not understand how anyone can look at a cup of red liquid and call it black tea. The word *black* probably refers to the dark color of the dried, fermented tea leaves.

TEA, WINE, AND LIQUOR

---

price of Chilled Peak Oolong in Taiwan had skyrocketed to US $600 per pound, but good oolong can already be had at less than 1 percent of the cost. Ti Kuan Yin (Iron Buddhisattva, Iron Goddess of Mercy) belongs also to the oolong family; its leaves have been rolled tightly before drying, and are hard as iron *(ti)*. Orange Pekoe from Ceylon is classified as black tea despite its light color.

As mentioned before, *pekoe* means white hair. Very young tea leaves do have white hair on them, and make an unusually light "green" tea, called "white tea" by professionals. Silver Needle Pekoe (Yinzhen Baihau) leaves are thick with silvery hair like the ears of albino guinea pigs.

Dried tiny white chrysanthemums from Hangzhou produce the only "tea" to be sugared by the Chinese; it is fragrant and light, delightful to the eye. Chrysanthemum-Dragon Well is a mixture of the two, usually blended to order. A ready-mixed flower-tea combination is jasmine tea with an oolong or green tea base, an aromatic favorite of Americans and Chinese alike. Another kind, called rose red tea, is black tea mixed with rose petals; it is not as common as the jasmine tea.

Why is tea so popular in China? Tea has a mild diuretic and laxative effect; it is said to dissipate body heat, clear the voice, brighten vision, and promote digestion. It contains B-complex vitamins and is certainly a handy mild stimulant. At the very least, the practice of tea drinking ensures that the Chinese quench their thirst with boiled water, thus reducing their chance of catching dysentery or cholera. But the Chinese almost never think about their health while sipping tea.

Tea blends well with all cultures, philosophies, and most religious beliefs. People can inhale its aroma, contemplate its color, savor its taste, and meanwhile warm their hands. (The reading of tea leaves, however, seems not to be a Chinese invention.) Tea is enjoyed by both the very rich and the very poor, since the price of tea can vary greatly from the most nondescript warehouse sweepings to the exotic-breed Iron Buddhisattva collected from sheer cliffs by trained monkeys.

The water for making tea does make a difference: it should not be too hard, leaving deposits of scum, nor artificially softened. Until the turn of the century many Chinese households collected rain from their roofs for tea, a delightful custom. Many mountain temples in China are known not as religious shrines, but for their scenery and the quality of their spring water for tea. Fifty years ago, one tea house in Canton achieved renown by hiring coolies to carry spring water down from the White Cloud Mountain, ten miles away.

There is no set formula for tea-making: one teaspoonful of leaves per measured cup is considered adequate. A usual tea cup, incidentally, holds only half a measured cup. When in doubt, use more tea leaves, since concentrated tea can be diluted but there is no remedy for weak tea. Some people make very strong black tea in the morning, to be diluted and sipped throughout the day. The Chinese do not keep their tea overnight; it turns sour unless refrigerated.

Use a clean kettle and fresh water from the tap, and pour when the water just begins to boil. Over-boiling removes the dissolved oxygen, making the tea taste flat. (A common suggestion is not to boil the same water twice.) The tea pot and cups should be porcelain, earthenware, or glass; metal or plastic may affect the taste. And the cups should not deny the sipper visual enjoyment by masking the color of the tea.

The vessels should first be rinsed with boiling water. Pour scalding water over the tea leaves in the vessels, rather than add tea leaves to hot water. Steep for five

minutes before serving; do not judge the timing by the color of the tea, unless the drinker is very familiar with the particular kind of leaves. A refill using the same leaves is advocated by tea fanciers: the first steeping brings out the aroma, the second brings out the taste. Most Chinese drink tea plain, though some drinkers of black tea have adopted Western habits and use milk and sugar or lemon, the latter particularly with iced tea.

The people who live near Swatow (Shantou) in eastern Guangdong, near the Fujian border, have their special brand of cookery (Chaozhou cuisine). They are also perhaps the most punctilious tea drinkers. Their art of tea drinking is called Kung Fu Tea, for like the martial arts, it takes constant practice to maintain proficiency. Mountain spring water is heated to a boil in a small brass pot, then poured into a pre-scalded, fist-sized red clay teapot half-filled with the choicest tea leaves. The highly concentrated tea gives a special twinkle to the tongue. It is sipped a drop at a time from tiny cups, and only the thumb and forefinger are used to hold the cup. The purists assert that the other three fingers, as well as the elbow, should flare out in an exaggerated posture to show respect for the tea being sipped; any deviation from this posture reveals to the host that the nectar is

WELL-KNOWN
CHINESE TEAS

Type	Origin	Remarks
GREEN TEAS		
Dragon Well (Long Jing)	Zhejiang	connoisseur's favorite
Longevity Eyebrow (Shou Mei)	Guangdong	large leaves
Pi Lo Chun	Jiangsu	delicate leaves
Look On	Anhui	often with twigs
OOLONGS		
Oolong (Black Dragon)	Fujian, Taiwan	universal appeal
Ti Kuan Yin (Iron Buddhisattva)	Fujian, Taiwan	connoisseur's favorite
Shui Xian (Water Nymph)	Fujian, Taiwan, Guangdong	
BLACK (RED) TEAS		
Keemun	Anhui	England's favorite tea
Lapsang Souchong	Fujian	smokey taste
Pu Erh	Yunnan	aids digestion
OTHERS		
Chrysanthemum	Zhejiang	to be taken with sugar
Jasmine	(all over)	oolong or green tea with jasmine petals
Lychee Red	Guangdong, Fujian	red tea with lychee syrup
Rose Red	Guangdong	red tea with rose petals
Brick Tea	Central, North and West China	tightly compressed bricks
Silver Needle Pekoe (Yinzhen Baihau)	Fujian	leaves coated with silvery hair

being squandered on an ignoramus. A different pot is used for each kind of tea, and the pots are never washed. Old pots become treasured heirlooms. Thick with deposit, they can yield tea with hot water alone.

In daily life, tea is consumed by the Chinese with little ritual, except in a business appointment. The host often signals the end of the meeting by raising his cup to suggest one more sip of tea, just like the "one for the road" in American drinking.

It may surprise some that until recently tea was *not* featured during formal banquets—only before and after. On the other hand, tea is very often an important part of ritual. A marriage is officially consummated when the new parents-in-law formally accept the cup of tea offered by the bride. A bride-to-be is said to have "spilled her tea" if her intended dies before her wedding.

Tea is also used for cooking. Tea Leaf Eggs are eggs hard-cooked in a spiced tea broth. Tea leaves are the smoking agent in Camphor and Tea Leaf Duck and My Lord's Smoked Chicken. In the dish Dragon-Well Shrimplets, tea leaves are stir-fried with shrimp; the best leaves for this purpose are fresh Dragon Well tea leaves just harvested from the field in Hangzhou.

Leaves from other plants are often made into "substitute" teas. Examples are leaves of mango, lychee, longan (dragon-eye), and young mulberry, but these are far less popular than real tea. Other plant parts are boiled into herb teas, of which chrysanthemum tea is perhaps the most popular. Herb tea ingredients may include mint, licorice, honeysuckle, tangerine peels, lotus seeds, barley, gingko, lychees, hibiscus flowers, and ginseng. Some herb teas are not really pleasant to drink, but are household remedies—patent medicines, if you like—for common ills. Their recipes are often secret, passed from one generation to the next.

CHINESE WINE AND LIQUOR

Wine has been in use in China for four thousand years or more. The Chinese use the word *wine* loosely to cover all alcoholic drinks made with any ingredient. The wine with which the deposed Shang king (1122 BC) was accused of over-indulging was probably a millet-based beer. Present-day undistilled wine is made from regular rice, glutinous rice, kaoliang, wheat, barley, and even soybeans, with 8 to 20 percent alcohol. Distillation produces what should perhaps be called whiskey, up to 130 proof (65 percent alcohol by volume).

Li Bai, often considered to be the greatest Tang poet, was the most renowned admirer of wine in China. It was said that he would not write without it, and some of his best works were written in praise of wine itself, including a glorious ode about drinking in the company of the moon and his own shadow. Legends say he drowned in a lake while trying to rescue the (reflection of the) moon from drowning.

Though it contains little about food, Chinese literature is full of references to wine. Food, however, almost invariably accompanies wine; the Chinese abhor drinking on an empty stomach. Drinking alone is also frowned upon. With food and company, the chance of becoming drunk is sharply reduced. The solitary alcoholic is not a native Chinese phenomenon.

At banquets, a noisy guessing game (trying to guess the total number of fingers from the two hands of the participants) livens the atmosphere. The loser is penalized by drinking; therefore the skillful player should learn how to lose as well as win. Probably volumes can be written to associate this with the Chinese national character. There is a saying, "advance through retreating."

Fermented glutinous rice yields a wine mash important in Chinese cookery. The liquid from the mash is simply called "glutinous rice wine." It is sweet and light, and low in alcohol (about 8 percent). More potent (about 18 percent) is yellow wine, the best of it from Shaoxing, near Hangzhou. Its taste is acquired, and those expecting the taste of a grape wine will be disappointed at first for it is dry, yet low in tannin, pale like a white wine, but served warm rather than chilled. Many books suggest it be treated like a hot, dry sherry.

Chinese connoisseurs take their yellow wine seriously, as do Western counterparts their grape wines. Until recently, most Chinese bought their wine by the ounce from the local grocer, and the fastidious ones would ask for special offerings at a wine shop. The quality of wine depended on the reputation of the wine merchant, surely, but apparently on the reputation of the customer as well. Regardless of price, ethical merchants simply would not waste good wine on those who had no appreciation of it.

One way to guarantee quality is to age one's own wine. This is practiced in wine-growing Shaoxing. When a daughter is born, the father seals and buries a quantity of the best new wine in ten-gallon earthen urns, to be opened only at her wedding. This is called *Nüer Hong* (Daughter's Red); the red refers not to the color of the wine, but the prevailing color of the wedding celebration.

Grape wine was known in the Han era (206 BC–22 AD), and was popular during Tang (618–907). But viniculture and the art of grape wine-making in Ancient China were limited to the Turkic people along the Silk Road. Even roadside taverns were tended by "foreign damsels." Each time the Silk Road was blocked by invading nomads, the flow of grape wine stopped.

Within the past century, grape wine was re-introduced into China, this time from Europe. French wines appeared in major cities open to foreign trade, and the brief presence of the Germans in Qingdao, on the Shandong Peninsula, has indirectly fostered a wine industry. Even today, the total production of grape wine is small, and is limited largely to northern China and Taiwan; but the potential is there.

Very strong distilled liquors are produced in China. The technique of distillation apparently was invented in Sichuan about 800 AD, but again introduced from the Middle East during the Mongol Yuan Dynasty (1271–1368). *Moutai* from the mountainous southwest is colorless, fragrant, and pungent (110 proof). Fen liquor, equally transparent and even more powerful (130 proof), is the standard ingredient for Five-Spiced Beef Shank. Bamboo Leaf Green, an herb liquor based on Fen liquor and bamboo leaves, is pale green and smooth, but could not be the same as its namesake fifteen centuries ago, before distillation was invented in China.

A variety of fruit liqueurs are made: black plum, orange blossom, lychee, dragon-eye, apricot, Chinese gooseberry (kiwifruit, called "monkey's peach" in China). Many specialty liqueurs are drunk for their medicinal value—for example, ginseng liqueur, deer-tail liqueur, tiger-bone liqueur, silkworm pupae liqueur, and the orange-brown Ng Gar Pay. In Canton the gall bladder of a poisonous snake is drained into a cup of colorless liquor, creating a liquid emerald, bitter as quinine. Drinking it may or may not improve one's courage, but is by itself proof of bravery.

Wine is important in Chinese cooking. It softens the fibers of vegetables, breaks the tissue of meats, quickens the cooking process, and improves the aroma, appearance, and taste of food. For stir-frying, a technique of "sizzling in the wine" is commonly used. The wine is whirled onto the rim of the wok, runs into the hot center part from all directions, making a loud sizzle while vaporizing the alcohol, and leaves only the aroma behind. Yellow wine or a pale dry sherry do the sizzling job well, although stronger "wines" up to whiskey strength are also used. Even the wine mash is important in Chinese cooking. It is used as a dessert, as a seasoning in preparing meat, fowl, fish and shrimp, and as a preservative for goose eggs. Red mash from Fujian is red in color, and adds a special zing to food.

Wine is used for marinating. Five-spiced Beef Shank is marinated in Fen liquor, and Drunken Chicken in yellow wine.

Since true Chinese wine and liquor may be hard to get, substitutions may be needed. Yellow wine often can be replaced by a pale dry Spanish sherry. The strong Fen liquor can be approximated by brandy, vodka, whiskey, or rum.

BEVERAGES WITH CHINESE FOOD

In old China the only liquids served during a meal were soup and grain-based wines. Westernization has brought many new beverages to the dinner table, incidentally creating a problem of beverage selection.

Soup is present throughout a Chinese family meal, and for quenching thirst the diner need look no further. Because of this, tea is usually not served during meals—only before and after. In traditional banquets, where the dishes are presented one at a time, there may be several soups.

Grain-based wines heighten the enjoyment of food, and counteract the cloying effect of rich foods. The sweet-rice wine and yellow wine are prewarmed in a hot-water bath and served in thumb-sized porcelain cups. Fiery grain liquors like *moutai* require no warming; they provide their own warmth, so to speak.

In the summer, traditionally Chinese would dissipate body heat by drinking steaming-hot liquids to induce sweating. The Western world has brought the alternative philosophy of using cold drinks as thirst quenchers and body coolers. Excellent Western-style beers and sodas are now made in China, and they have found their way into modern Chinese banquets, together with tea, yellow wine, *moutai*, cognac, whiskey, and occasionally grape wine. Modern Chinese diners agree only in one respect: they do not drink cold water with their meals as Americans do.

In affluent Hong Kong, quality French cognac is served undiluted in water tumblers. To us, however, gulping cognac half a tumbler at a time is not to taste cognac—nor the food afterwards.

Some food experts assert that the only drinks fit to accompany Chinese food are beer and tea. Grape wine, in limited supply and even more limited promotion, is nearly unknown in China. Nevertheless, we are convinced that grape wine goes splendidly with Chinese food. In the Western world, where good grape wines are in abundant supply, a suitable choice can add immensely to dining enjoyment.

Western tradition generally favors serving white wines with fish and poultry, red wines with meat. But there are no hard and fast rules, and a red, for example, may be a fine choice with Camphor Tea Leaf Duck. Chinese food spans a tremendous spectrum of ingredients, techniques, textures, and tastes. In the same dish you may find several different ingredients and even several cooking techniques, and also dishes of contrasting flavor may be served together. The choice of beverages can indeed be a problem.

Take, for instance, a dish featuring beef as the only meat ingredient. This would appear to favor a red wine, but when the beef is cut into slivers, mixed with twice the amount of green vegetables, and then stir-fried, a switch to white wine might be appropriate. Suppose, further, the dish is flavored with curry. The added piquancy would have a drastic effect on the choice of wine.

Such a dish may only be one of four on the dinner table. The ideal choice for the curried beef with vegetables could conceivably be a poor one in terms of another dish. But there are simple rules based on common sense and, more important, wide latitude in applying them.

Sweeping generalizations are possible. Cantonese and Fujianese cuisines are light in general; they usually are best with fruity white wines. On the other hand, East China cuisine tends to be substantial, and Sichuan-Hunan food is heavily seasoned and often done with much oil; medium red wines such as burgundies and chiantis are good choices. North China cuisine is somewhat in between, and is best enjoyed with a rosé or light red wine such as beaujolais or zinfandel.

Other commonly available beverages can be served similarly. Green tea is refreshing and stringent like a dry white wine. Tannic black tea is like a light red wine, and Oolong occupies an intermediate position. Pu Erh is tannic and mellow, comparable to an aged claret. Lapsang Souchong is smoky like bacon, and is ranked with heavier wines like a burgundy.

A Pilsner beer is lighter than a lager, and goes better with lighter food, but either beer spans the range of food.

A very dry sherry—in small sips—is appreciated like a dry white wine. The nutty amontillado goes well with heavier foods.

Very sweet fortified wines, such as port and oloroso (cream) sherries, should be reserved for the dessert. Chinese sweet rice wines, however, are gentle and unobtrusive, like a fruity white wine, and yellow wine covers the domain of the lighter sherries.

Potent grain liquors, valued for their grease-cutting effect, are ranked with bordeaux for that reason. By the same token, whiskies, if consumed with the same respect as the Chinese do their *moutai* in small quantities, cleanse the palate between foods and amid friendly conversation.

Some food-beverage combinations are particularly suited for each other. We have become very fond of combining fruity white German rieslings, especially moselles and rheingaus of *kabinett* class, with the fresh simplicity of Cantonese food. The Red-Cooked Pork Shoulder with Rock Candy from Shanghai, with crystalline fatty skin which melts in the mouth, is well matched by a good French red burgundy. A spicy gewürztraminer (the Californian type has an aroma like lychees) can hold its own against a mild curry; so can lapsang souchong tea, which blends nicely also with the smoked Camphor and Tea Leaf Duck or My Lord's Smoked Chicken. A pepper-hot dish from Central China dominates all, and the palate should be soothed between mouthfuls with bland, starchy food such as

white rice or flower buns. Beer or a tannic beverage, such as a California cabernet sauvignon, or Pu Erh tea, from Yunnan, would then be reasonable.

While some experts frown on serving wine with salad or vinegary food, we often accompany lightly pickled vegetable salads and sweet and sour dishes with fruity white wines or gewürztraminers.

The best way to serve several wines in one meal is to present them with matching dishes in sequence, with lighter food-wine combinations first. But this is practical only in banquets. With several dishes on the table, as is usual in Chinese meals, problems arise. Should one serve several different wines together, each earmarked for a particular dish?

Though a diner can mix the dishes on his plate, wines of different character certainly do not blend well in the same glass or in rapid rotation even in different glasses. A reasonable strategy is to aim for the average. This is not as difficult as it sounds, especially if all dishes are from the same regional cuisine. Or, the host may choose the wine to emphasize some of the dishes or even one major ingredient in a dish. In any case, once a decision has been made, do stick by it unflinchingly. The presence of many possible choices actually gives the host latitude in selection.

Food as a Chinese Tradition

Every day (and dare one say in every way?) a billion mouths are helping to make Chinese food better and better. While it is often said that a common written language holds the Chinese civilization together, chopsticks perhaps play a stronger role as cultural cement than the Chinese writing brush.

Over the years, the use of food has permeated Chinese culture. It has led to a plausible (but unproven) theory of medicine, with taboos not all of which have rational explanation and practices for which the origins are veiled in half-forgotten history.

FOOD—MEDICINE IN FOLKLORE

When a Chinese person takes ill, a traditional doctor may prescribe a dozen or more dried herbs, which are boiled together for hours into a bowl of dark brown soup to be swallowed hot, perhaps twice a day. This soup-medicine is invariably very bitter. It would be vastly more desirable to regulate the body in some way against incipient attacks of illness via the more pleasurable means of proper food intake.

The Chinese diet for health follows a Taoist perception of cosmic equilibrium. Unlike the experienced herb doctor who commands a vast repertoire of ingredients, the average person uses a limited list of milder ingredients but has more time to make the proper adjustments. There is the additional requirement that most of food-medicine be palatable.

In the simplest form, the Taoist world is composed of two intertwining forces: *yin*, the feminine component, and *yang*, the masculine. These are parlayed into cold and hot humors in the human body, which in the normal state should be in balance. Deviation in either direction upsets the equilibrium and leads ultimately to disease, unless countered in time by food with the opposite tendency.

All matter—whether animal, vegetable or mineral—is said to possess an inherent humor temperature, broadly classified into seven grades: very cold, cold, cool, neutral, warm, hot, and very hot. Even though ice is considered cold and water neutral, the classification is usually based on the item's effect on the human body after cooking, and is independent of actual temperature.

Hot-humored food increases body energy, blood circulation, and pulse rate and/ or raises the body temperature. The opposite effect results from cold-humored food, which in addition can cleanse the body without being necessarily laxative. Those prone to nosebleeds are to avoid hot-humored food, even on a cold winter day. Those with cold feet should consider taking more hot-humored food.

Beef is warm, lamb is hot; but pork, chicken and most other fowl, and fish are neutral or very nearly so. Most green vegetables, especially green melons and squashes, are cool or cold. But yellow vegetables (pumpkin, for instance) tend to be neutral or warm. Garlic and chives are considered warm; peppers (red, green, black, or white) are hot, as are most spices. Fruits are cool, especially if eaten raw. Shrimp is hot, but the freshwater hairy crab, a famous Chinese delicacy in the fall, is considered cold. Most beans are neutral or warm, but mung beans are cold, as are fermented black beans and bean curd. Minerals tend to be cold.

The same food may have been ascribed different humor temperatures by different scholars, and many new foods have never been rated at all. The home-remedier does not memorize a whole list of humor temperatures; most foods are nearly neutral anyway. He or she just uses a handful of ingredients for corrective measures. For example, take mung bean and fruits for more coldness, but lamb and red pepper to add warmth.

The Cantonese are probably the firmest believers in this temperature school of self-cure. Canton is hot and humid during the summer, and "cool-teas," featuring herbs with a cooling humor, are sold in the streets. These cool teas, either sweet or bitter, are served hot from huge charcoal-fired brass samovars. Tea-houses feature chrysanthemum tea; it is cool and is said to improve vision. Cafes offer *lookdou sa* (Cantonese; green-bean silt), a porridge made with cold-humored mung beans for the lazy summer afternoon. A similar porridge of red beans would be improper; red beans are believed warm, suitable only for a cold day. Modern technology has allowed red-bean silt to be served with crushed ice; the combination is thought to be more or less neutral.

In the winter, the tendency is to take hot-humored foods to improve circulation and to keep warm. It is also the time to take tonic food, as the harsh cold depletes body resources. Tonic herbs are slow-cooked for hours with lamb, black-legged chicken, or pork livers; the resultant soup is drunk for its medicinal effect. Not all tonics are warm: for instance, though all ginseng are tonic, the American version is cool, unlike its warm Asiatic cousins. Most exotic food ingredients are believed to be tonic; these include shark's fin, bird's nest, bear's paw, and hasma—the gland from the Manchurian tree frog.

Yet another folk belief is the strengthening of a part of the human body by eating an animal's counterpart. The tail of a pig, however, is not believed to enable a human to grow a counterpart—only to strengthen the backbone. This analogous thinking can be overdone, when carried to analogs in *shapes*. Ginseng root was probably first used because it has the appearance of a human body. Walnuts, looking like miniature brains, are fed to students by anxious parents the week before final examinations.

TABOOS

It would appear that the Chinese will eat anything. Certainly, the repertoire of Chinese food ingredients probably exceeds that of any other cuisine. On the other hand, certain foods are avoided for ethical or religious reasons, or just owing to hearsay evidence.

Ethical Restraints During the Warring States period (475–221 BC), when King Hui of Wei saw a cow being led away for ritual sacrifice, he was overcome by pity and ordered its release. But when asked whether the ritual should be abolished, he said, "How can it be abolished? Use a goat instead." He was laughed at by his countrymen as a miser.

Many Chinese will refrain from eating beef on the ethical grounds that the cow has already toiled enough during life, and it would be shameful to consume it after death. These moralists will not touch beef even when they know it comes from nonworking cattle; the latter, it is argued, have been redeemed by the toil of their kin. This sentiment against eating beef is similar to the Western aversion to eating horsemeat.

Dog fat in cooking was recommended in *Li Ji*, believed to have been written in the Spring-Autumn Era (before 476 BC). In recent centuries, however, few people are motivated to consume man's best friend, despite the common belief that dogmeat is a great tonic for the winter.

Religious Avoidances In ancient times, auspicious ceremonies were preceded by a period of vegetarianism and bathing, to cleanse the body inside and out. This practice has been continued by adherents of Taoism.

Vegetarianism is practiced by all Buddhist monks and a number of Buddhists in China. The original reason is ethical: a love for all animal life. Manichaean sects once thrived in parts of China; their followers were said to "eat vegetables and serve the devil." This religion no longer exists.

The Chinese Moslems, like their brethren elsewhere, avoid pork as unclean.

The Taoists were experimental alchemists fifteen centuries ago. Scholarly life in the Jin Dynasty (265–420) was affected by the practice of eating mineral powder as a means toward longevity; some of these were actually poisonous arsenic compounds.

Hearsay Taboos Strangely, some edible foods are often believed as poisonous in combination. The most common taboo is the eating of crabs and persimmons together. Controlled experiments have shown the groundlessness of such belief. A Northern taboo is sugar with thousand-year-old eggs; the Cantonese have been mixing the two for generations. Some people also believe that pork and beef should not be cooked together. The official cookbook of the Mongol court, written seven hundred years ago, is full of these taboos.

Of course, there are poisonous substances which should not be eaten, however harmless their appearance. In Canton in the 1930s, people regularly poisoned themselves with the puffer fish, called *fugu* in Japan where it is a great delicacy. Its liver and ovaries are highly poisonous, and it takes an expert to clean the fish properly. Poisonous mushrooms certainly grow in China, but those purchased in stores are all edible.

HOSPITALITY AS A CHINESE TRADITION

When two friends meet in China, the traditional greeting is, "Have you eaten rice yet?" This is often taken as symptomatic of the food-conscious Chinese, but that is only half the story. In the old days, the hungry friend probably would be brought home for a meal. It is nevertheless strange, when the same greeting is being used at all hours of the day, even at midnight.

The Chinese are hospitable people. When a friend arrives unexpectedly during a meal, the host will offer to "add an extra pair of chopsticks" to share the food. Also added might be a pair of Chinese sausages, perhaps a few "egg-purses" (fried eggs in half-moon form) or Assorted Egg Pâté with salted duck eggs, thousand-year-old eggs, and regular eggs.

Home-cooked meals often are not really considered adequate for hospitality, and the middle class usually call feasts in large restaurants. But as late as a quarter century ago, opulent gourmets with private kitchens would set the standard for restaurants.

The prosperous Chinese Mandarins and merchants used to feast often. Any notable event, good or bad, is a cause for a feast. Thus a wedding is celebrated, a birthday, an anniversary of an ancestor, the passage of an examination, or even a death in the family. It can become overdone, as people may strive for face and spend beyond their means. In Hong Kong even today some people will remark that they cannot afford to marry because of the expenses needed for the feasting. It is a Chinese custom that the family of the bridegroom should pay for the wedding feast.

In Taiwan there is a traditional village festival called "Bye-Bye," during which all strangers are invited to a sumptuous feast. To decline is to insult the genial but proud hosts.

FESTIVE FOOD

Folk festivals furnish the proper setting for special food preparations. Three of the most important festivals are listed below. It is noted that the lunar calendar is used with 30-day months.

The Dragon Boat Festival

Alternate Names: High Noon Festival (Duanwu Jie), Fifth Moon Festival

Date: Lunar calendar—Fifth day of the Fifth Moon
     Western calendar—Early June

Special Food: Zong (steamed rice pudding wrapped in bamboo leaves)

The memory of a loyal minister who died two thousand years ago has been transformed into a day of sports competition.

During the Warring Kingdom era, Qu Yuan (about 300 BC) served as a minister of King Huai of Chu, the largest kingdom along the Yangtze Valley. He tried to counter the treachery of corrupt officials, but was in turn accused of high crimes and exiled from the court. Inconsolate, he wandered the countryside and composed some of the greatest long poems in Chinese literature. The most famous is the ode "Li Sao" (The Parting Sorrow) in which the king was referred to either as

a beauteous maiden or a fragrant herb—both, however, insensitive to his declared devotion. He became the father of the Chinese metaphoric poetry.

Finally Qu Yuan drowned himself in a small river, but the grateful people never stopped looking for him. They combed the rivers and tributaries on boats, dropping food along the way in case he were alive and hungry. This was no mean task to the superstitious Chu folk, for lurking behind the lush Yangtze vegetation were man-eating animals and perhaps even evil spirits; surely they would devour the unlucky intruders or at least the food intended for the wandering poet! This search became an annual regatta of long rowboats in the shape of dragons, where oarsmen row to the beating of drums and gongs, all designed to scare away evil spirits. The food for the poet evolved into zong, a glutinous rice and mung bean pudding wrapped with bamboo leaves into a unique tetrahedron shape and filled either with sweet bean paste or with pork, black mushrooms, chestnuts, and salted duck eggs. Large zongs call for wrapping of lotus leaves more than a foot in diameter. The zongs are tasty and filling, and last for weeks without refrigeration.

The Moonlight Festival

Alternate Names: Mid-Autumn Festival (Zhongqiu Jie), Eighth Moon Festival

Date: Lunar calendar—Fifteenth day of the Eighth Moon
          Western calendar—Mid-September

Special Food: Mooncakes

The full moon always falls on the fifteenth of the lunar month. The China night becomes clear in the cool, still air of early fall, and on the fifteenth day of the Eighth Moon, the moon is at its roundest—well, at least at its brightest. Children on that night gaze at the changeless moon, trying to spot Wu Gang, the Chinese Sisyphus, wielding his axe on the self-healing magic osmanthus tree; or catch a glimpse of Chang'E, the beautiful girl who stole the elixir of life from her despotic husband and flew with the wind into the Lunar Palace of Spacious Chill. If these fairytale personages could not be seen that clear night, there would be little hope for another lunar year. And the ardor of the kids will not be deterred by Neil Armstrong and his eleven fellow astronauts.

Moon-gazing is not limited to children, of course. Grown-ups think of loved ones far away yet sharing the same moonlight. The roundness of the moon reminds families to hold reunions ("union in the round" in Chinese). Most travelers will try to return before this day, if humanly possible. The old folks at home will be waiting, so will the squatly cylindrical mooncakes. Each mooncake is more than three inches in diameter and more than an inch thick; the baked brown skin is filled with a quarter pound of nuts, glazed melon slices, and sweet lotus seed paste. Some mooncakes even have moons inside—up to four brightly yellow spheres which are actually yolks from salted duck eggs. It is the nearest thing to an American fruitcake in Chinese cookery.

Was the mooncake really invented to transmit messages for simultaneous uprisings against the Mongols 700 years ago? While it may be difficult to prove this to be true, it is equally difficult to prove otherwise. Under the magic spell of the full moon, it is far easier to believe a good story.

The Chinese New Year (Yuandan)

Date: Lunar calendar—First day of the First Moon
          Western calendar—Early February

Special Foods: Deep-Fried Jiandui (heaps), Youjiao (crescents), Yuxia (taro

shrimp), and Qiaoguo (artful fruits—decorative knicknacks)
Steamed, then Pan-Fried Niangao (New Year Pudding), Luobo-
gao (Turnip Pudding), and Yutougao (Taro Pudding)
Boiled Dumplings
Fruit—Tangerines

The Chinese New Year is a month-long festival for the children, but it can be a period of trial for grown-ups. All business debts are to be settled before the New Year, and undesirable employees are given notice on New Year's Eve to leave the next day.

Even accounts with Heaven are settled during the Twelfth Moon. On the evening of the twenty-third day, the Kitchen Lord, a minor deity stationed in every kitchen, flies heavenward to make an annual report to the Jade Emperor. A ceremony (The Thanking of the Kitchen) features sticky, sweet paste to glue the Kitchen Lord's mouth shut. Even his picture in the kitchen is smeared with sticky molasses. In this way, surely, bad reports against the household will not be uttered, nor will good ones perhaps. Nevertheless, the Chinese are content to survive another year no better than the last one; they are more fearful of disasters as punishments for reported misdeeds.

The Kitchen Lord returns on New Year's Eve, which calls for another family celebration. In the stores, the owners will have a feast also. If the owner of the store takes the first piece of chicken himself, every employee heaves a sigh of relief; for a leg offered to an employee, called "unimpassioned chicken," signifies dismissal.

During the Twelfth Moon, perhaps for the first time during the year, children are actually welcome in the kitchen to try out their proficiency with chopsticks, fishing out funny-looking sizzling things from boiling oil under Mother's watchful encouragement.

These oddities include Fried Heaps, which are bloated dumplings of glutinous rice flour half-filled with sweet bean paste; Oil (fried) Crescents, which are crescent-shaped versions of the same thing, giving young girls a chance to learn to flute the edges; a salty variety with dried shrimp, pickled turnips and pork, under the name of Salt Water Crescents; Taro Shrimps are slivers of taro irregularly stuck together; Artful Fruits are small colorful knicknacks made of seasoned dough.

After the deep-frying is done, Mother steams huge puddings made of turnips and rice flour, seasoned with scattered dried shrimp, minced Chinese sausage, dried marinated pork, and dried black mushrooms, all diced. She might use taro instead of turnips, producing a purple pudding. These puddings can be kept for weeks without refrigeration in the cold winter. Though edible after steaming, they are usually cut into slices a quarter-inch thick and pan-fried to lend a golden, crisp crust, contrasting with the soft, yielding texture and the chewy dried shrimps inside. Another pudding is the ubiquitous New Year's Pudding, which is brown and sweet in Canton, but white and salty-sweet in the North.

On New Year's Day only good omens are permitted. Good luck slogans are posted all over the house, including "Ever Full" on the rice jar. One shuns both unlucky sounding words (like *deadly*) and the local undertaker, who usually avoids being seen by staying home. Outside, the colorful Chinese Lion dazzles the crowd by its dancing antics to the throbbing rhythm of a huge drum. It feeds itself from time to time by gobbling a head of lettuce tied to offerings of good luck money, hung high on store fronts, just above a long string of live, blasting firecrackers.

Citrus fruits are in season: a must is tangerine, whose Chinese name sounds the same as "good fortune." Fish to the Chinese sounds the same as "surplus." Both tangerines and fish are put in the rice jar. As the word *fu* in tofu sounds the same as "riches," a tofu fish dish signifies "Riches and Honors in Surplus." Other dishes are given propitious names, such as Chicken (sounds in Mandarin like "good fortune") with Chestnuts ("profit"). The puddings are easily explained, as gao (pudding) sounds like "high (honors)". Incidentally, the Chinese use the same word *gao* to mean leavened cakes or unleavened pudding.

For the first ten days of the New Year, relatives and friends visit one another, exchanging good wishes, presents, and food. The children receive from married grown-ups good luck money in tiny red envelopes.

Dumplings of glutinous rice flour resembling the full moon, called Yuanxiao, originally were intended for the Yuanxiao—First Moon Evening or Lantern Festival—which falls on the fifteenth day of the New Year. Now their use is spread all during the New Year Season.

More than any other festival, the Chinese New Year reveals the Chinese psyche: a longing for good fortune, which may never come; an acceptance of unexplained disaster without warning; and a preoccupation with food—perhaps the only item under control by the household. Food is thus made into lucky omens, even a weapon of bribery to the Kitchen Lord.

Chinese Food and Health

One of the questions people often ask is, "Is Chinese food really good for you?" We have often been led to believe that nutritious foods are uninteresting. Following this logic, one may ask, "If Chinese food is delicious (as it certainly is), then is it nonnutritious?" The answer is, of course, no.

We only need to look at Chinese history. The Chinese people have been health-conscious for thousands of years, practicing constantly and gradually refining their methods and food selections. When we examine their dietary patterns, selection of ingredients, and cooking techniques, we see that their culinary development coincides with that of the development of nutritional science. By trial and error, prudence, and concern for health, the Chinese eventually adapted the most efficient and nutritious methods of cooking.

BASIC NUTRITION CONCEPT

The food one eats must provide energy for one to stay alive and carry on daily activities. A growing person needs the nutrients in food to promote growth and build body tissues. We also need specific amounts of nutrients to enable the body to regulate thousands of internal processes that occur daily.

Carbohydrates, proteins, and fats are called the "energy nutrients" because they are the means by which the body receives the fuel it needs. A gram of carbohydrate or protein each supplies the body 4 kcals., while a gram of fat, a much more concentrated source of energy, supplies 9 kcals. Weight will be maintained only when total energy consumed (as food) is equal to total energy used by the body. Therefore, it stands to reason that weight gain will result when intake consumption is more than expenditure. Contrary to some popular beliefs, "calories do count" in weight control. As people mature, they may tend to gain weight because their activity level decreases while their food consumption remains constant. The best way to maintain weight after the 20s is to remember that food consumption and activity levels must proceed together in the same direction.

As noted above, carbohydrate foods contain approximately the same number of kcals. per gram as protein foods. However, many people consider carbohydrate

foods to be "fattening." In reality they contain fewer kcals.than foods high in fat content. Foods containing large amounts of complex carbohydrates (starch foods such as grains, vegetables, and legumes) often contain high percentages of fiber and water compared to foods high in fat (such as cream cheese), which are much more concentrated.

In addition to carbohydrates, proteins, fats, fiber, and water, one's food must also provide a variety of vitamins and minerals. There is no one perfect food that supplies all the nutrients essential to life. The secret of a good diet is to eat a wide variety of foods which contain a wide variety of nutrients. This variety principle should be applied on a daily basis and also at each meal throughout the day. This is the best way to assure that the body is achieving the broad range of nutrients it requires. This is the essence of Chinese cooking.

PROTEIN AND THE CONCEPT OF COMPLEMENTATION

In many parts of the world, protein is the nutrient in the shortest supply, and protein deficiency is a fact of life. By looking at the protein component of certain foods, one can better understand the reason why various cultures combine foods in unique specialized patterns.

Protein is composed of twenty-two amino acids (or building blocks) which are combined in various ways in the body. Hair protein is different from muscle protein because of the number and construction of those building blocks that make up each protein. Of the twenty-two amino acids, one's body can manufacture all but eight from other substances. Because these eight amino acids must be provided directly from food, they are called the "essential amino acids." Animal protein (meat, fish, poultry, eggs, dairy products, etc.) usually contains all of the eight essential amino acids one needs in the proper amounts, while many plant proteins are deficient in one or more of these essential amino acids. Fortunately, not all plant proteins are deficient in the same amino acids. When one eats two or more kinds of plant proteins, the essential amino acid requirement can be met easily through complementation. By combining different vegetables such as beans and wheat or soybean and rice, which contain those building blocks in different proportions, one can get a sufficient quantity of all the essential amino acids for building body protein.

MAIN FOODS IN THE CHINESE DIET

Rice and Other Grains

Grains and starch have always played a major role in the Chinese diet. In the *fan-cai* (rice and main dishes) principle of cooking, the fan or grain has been the fundamental portion of the meal; the grain most widely used throughout the centuries has been rice. Rice is principally a starch (complex carbohydrate) and has traditionally provided most of the calories in the Chinese diet. However it also contains some plant protein, B vitamins, calcium and iron, and virtually no fat. Rice protein is a higher quality than wheat protein (the combination of amino acids in rice is better than wheat—for example, it has more of the essential amino

acid lysine). Rice is a very high-yield food, producing more calories per acre than any other grain. It is an efficient crop that has enabled China to sustain its dense population for centuries.

Although rice is certainly the most popular grain, people from northern China also include large amounts of wheat and millet in their diet. These are starches with similar vitamin and mineral contents as rice. Wheat tends to have more protein than rice but, in any case, the main protein requirements are generally satisfied by other means, notably by soybean products.

Soybean and Soybean Products

Rice may indeed be a high-yield food, but the soybean produces more protein per acre and per pound than any other commonly edible food—plant or animal. It is an integral part of the diet in both northern and southern China and represents the most important protein source in the entire country. Soy products are high in protein, iron, thiamin, riboflavin, vitamin A, calcium, and fiber. In fact, the soybean is richer in protein than equivalent amounts of red meat and richer in digestible calcium than equivalent amounts of milk. In addition to the quantity of protein, soybean has very good amino acid ratios (except being slightly low in amino acid, methionine) and is considered a high-quality protein source, especially when eaten with rice. Most of the soybeans consumed in China are fermented, ground into flour, processed, sprouted, or milled. The following are some of the forms in which soybeans are commonly used:

1 *Plain fresh soybeans,* boiled for breakfast, and so on.

2 *Soybean sprouts,* in soups (perhaps with a few spareribs or meat bones), salads, or mixed with meat slices and many stir-fried dishes. Bean sprouts are extremely low in calories (35 kcal./100 g), high in protein and fiber, have sufficient iron, and are a good source of vitamin C. They are available even in the winter when other vegetables are not in season.

3 *Soybean curd* (tofu), used plain in many dishes or with soy sauce, with meat, in soups, with mushrooms, with thousand-year-old eggs, as hot spiced bean curd, and in literally hundreds of other creative dishes. It is high in protein, calcium, iron, and fiber; and low in fat. Bean curd also has a very good calcium to phosphorus ratio, which is important for the proper function of bones and teeth. In China, bean curd is made by using a calcium salt (not to be confused with table salt) to coagulate the protein first; this is an important factor in increasing the calcium content. However, recent studies have found that although most brands of bean curd in the United States also are made with calcium salt, there is at least one that is very soft and slippery, which uses a noncalcium substance (glucono-lactone), as the coagulant. This soft version has only about one-third of the calcium as the regular and one should therefore read the label before buying bean curd (or use calcium salt to coagulate when making homemade bean curd), especially when one depends on this food as the major calcium source.

4 *Flower of bean curd,* an amorphous form of wet bean curd served in hot soup with sesame oil and spices. This product is high in calcium, and is easy to digest and absorb.

5 *Bean curd bisquit or pressed bean curd,* made by adding pressure to the bean curd to reduce the water content, it is sliced into stir-fried vegetable and meat dishes and used in cold-cut combination dishes; it can be nibbled as a snack.

6 *Bean curd sheets,* another pressed product, can be folded into different shapes and is often molded to simulate chicken and duck to embellish vegetarian dishes.

7 *Soybean milk,* a very popular drink in China among all ages. It is given to babies upon weaning and is higher in protein and lower in saturated fat than cow's milk. In addition, it contains no cholesterol and is less allergenic. Soy milk does not contain the milk sugar—lactose—which can cause diarrhea. (This is a common problem in a large part of the world; it appears only people of northern Europe are found to be free of this problem.)

Fish and Other Seafoods

Freshwater and saltwater fish are used in countless Chinese dishes in many forms—fresh, cured, dried, and salted. Literally hundreds of species of fish and seafood can be found in Chinese cuisine, running the gamut from small freshwater fish and fish maw to shark's fin, shrimp, oysters, abalone, and squid. In general, fish contains a good amount of high-quality protein, vitamins, and minerals and is lower in saturated fat and (except for shellfish) lower in cholesterol than meat. Fish, especially the small fish that are eaten with bones, are also a very rich source of calcium and phosphorus.

Poultry

In China, chicken is considered a "higher class" food than beef and pork. The cooking process utilizes most parts of the chicken, and techniques used are usually stir-frying, steaming, or white-cooking rather than deep-frying. Generally, the skin is removed when stir-frying chicken breasts, thereby decreasing the amount of total consumable fat. From a nutritional standpoint, poultry is similar to fish in that it contains high-quality protein, vitamins, and minerals and is lower in saturated fat and cholesterol than meat.

Other forms of poultry used are duck and, to a lesser extent, goose. Both duck and goose contain higher overall levels of fat than chicken.

Vegetables, Legumes, Fruits

Vegetables, other legumes (in addition to soybeans), and fruits are also used extensively in the Chinese diet. They are extremely nutritious foods; besides containing substantial amounts of protein, they are quite high in vitamins, minerals, and fiber. Since beans, vegetables, and rice are often consumed in one meal, the principle of protein complementing (discussed earlier) comes into play, thereby enhancing the overall value of the foods. Because of the emphasis placed on using fresh vegetables and because of the cooking techniques used, the Chinese are quite successful at protecting these foods against undue nutrient losses. Mung bean sprouts, like soybean sprouts, are a good source of vitamin C. Many dark green vegetables are used in a variety of daily dishes. They contribute significantly to the daily need for vitamin A, vitamin C, calcium, and fiber.

Meat, Oils, Lard, Nuts, and Seeds

These are the principle sources of fat in the Chinese diet. Although meat is the major protein source for Westerners, Chinese cooks use meat mainly for flavor, texture, and color to augment the *cai.* The protein needs are met easily by soybean products, eggs, poultry, fish, and a variety of vegetables. Pork is used more commonly than beef and lamb. Traditionally, lard rather than butter was the fat commonly used by the rich, however in recent years peanut, soy, and corn oils have been used by most Chinese cooks.

Additionally, many different types of seeds and nuts are used to provide the fat and some protein for the *cai,* mainly to enhance texture and flavor and to render variety.

Gluten

Gluten is one of the major proteins found in wheat. Other ingredients in wheat flour can be removed easily and cheaply so that only the wheat gluten remains. In this case, the product is all protein and has a meatlike texture. It is then added to stews, vegetables, and rice dishes to enhance the protein value of the meal. It is commonly used in combination with soy products as a high-protein food in many everyday dishes as well as in vegetarian cuisines. It gives the meat texture and provides more satisfaction than starchy foods.

Seaweed

Another food used extensively in Chinese cuisine is seaweed, which can be found in several forms:

1 *Agar-agar* is a complex carbohydrate that contributes to the diet primarily by adding bulk. Nutritionally, it contains no particular magical properties but, because it is such a high bulk food, it tends to decrease a person's overall caloric intake.

2 *Kelp* is also quite high in fiber content. Additionally, it contains some protein and vitamins and a substantial amount of minerals. It is especially rich in iodine, needed to prevent goiter. In the Western world iodized salt is a major iodine source, whereas in China people depend on seafood to meet their daily iodine requirement.

3 *Nori* is another form of seaweed that is often used in soups, also as a wrapping for shrimp and rice. It too is rich in minerals, especially iodine.

CHARACTERISTICS OF CHINESE MEALS

Nutritional Effects

Among the nutritional benefits from Chinese meals are low levels of saturated fats and cholesterol in the diet. Cholesterol, the substance that accumulates in the arteries and is often associated with atherosclerosis, can be found to some degree in all animal fats. Plant foods, on the other hand, are cholesterol-free. People like the Chinese, who consume low amounts of cholesterol and saturated fat, would seem to run less risk of developing coronary heart disease.

Fish and poultry contain mostly polyunsaturated fats rather than the saturated fat found in most meats, especially beef and lamb. The blood cholesterol level is lowered when one increases the proportion of polyunsaturated fats over saturated-fat consumption.

Butter is not used on rice nor indeed in any other dish. In fact, except in the far North, dairy products in general are not commonly utilized in most parts of China. This further reduces the intake of saturated fat and cholesterol (except pork fat, sometimes used in cooking).

Since dairy products are good sources of calcium, are the Chinese in danger of developing a calcium deficiency? Calcium absorption and utilization by the body are very complicated mechanisms, and studies have shown a decrease in calcium absorption in the presence of a high fat diet. Thus, a lower overall fat intake may help the Chinese absorb required amounts of calcium more easily than is true

with Westerners. Other studies have shown that when the protein intake is lowered, there is less calcium lost in the urine and therefore better calcium utilization. Many Americans consume two to three times the protein required. By eating Chinese food and reducing meat intake, they could avoid the excess protein consumption and might improve calcium utilization.

Chinese meals normally contain large amounts of rice, fruits, vegetables, and beans which are generally high in fiber or bulk. They require more chewing, are less concentrated in calories, and are high in volume, thereby filling the stomach faster. It normally takes a person longer to finish a meal of grains and vegetables than one of meat and other types of animal products. This factor is important in weight control. Researchers looking at the eating habits of obese individuals have found that they tend to eat very quickly and allow no time for the brain to signal satisfaction and to turn off the hunger stimulus. A Chinese diet would tend to lessen overeating (there would be less room for dessert), thus aiding in weight control.

Fiber-rich food definitely reduces intestinal "retention time." The reduction in retention time lessens the chance for carcinogens to be produced and retained in the colon, thereby lessening the chance for colon cancer to develop. Similarly, the reduction in retention time lessens the chance of developing diverticular disease problems and constipation.

It should be noted, however, that in recent years, as the level of affluence and Westernization has risen, there has been increased consumption of red meat, eggs, and organ meats among the Chinese people. Results have been an increased intake of saturated fats and cholesterol and increased incidences of obesity and the obesity-related diseases: diabetes, hypertension, and coronary heart disease.

Unlike many Westerners, Chinese seldom eat sweet desserts. In most families, fresh fruit—which supplies vitamins, minerals, and fiber—is a daily part of the diet. Use of table sugar among Chinese is quite low. Sugar itself has no nutritional value except to supply energy in the form of calories, and it has been found that foods high in sugar increase the chances of developing atherosclerosis. Foods high in sugar have also been associated with the development of dental caries, and can also cause a sudden increase in insulin secretion which can quickly lower the blood sugar level and cause adverse physiological symptoms. High sugar intake for a long period of time has been shown to be associated with hypoglycemic symptoms and adult-onset diabetes. It is hoped the Chinese will not be "Westernized" and adopt the sweet tooth while the rest of the Western world is finally realizing the problems of excess sugar consumption.

CHINESE COOKING TECHNIQUES AND THEIR INFLUENCE ON NUTRITION

Stir-frying
Many Chinese households use only a wok for cooking. The wok has been uniquely designed for stir-frying, and most dishes (with the exception of rice which is boiled or steamed) are usually stir-fried. The purpose of stir-frying is to shorten the cooking time (thus retaining more nutrients). This results in food

that is not overcooked and with vegetables that also maintain their fiber content. Furthermore, coating small pieces of food with a thin layer of oil is a way to prevent further nutrient loss.

Another advantage is that as a rule, oil instead of butter is used. Soybean and corn oils are used most frequently because they are cheaper and most readily available, and vegetable oils usually are high in polyunsaturated fatty acids which play an active role in lowering blood cholesterol levels. Peanut oil, which is also used, is a little higher in saturated fat content. Linoleic acid, a polyunsaturated oil and the essential fatty acid required by the body, is found in high amounts in most vegetable oils. Lard has been used as cooking fat by some Chinese people; however, in recent years owing to nutrition awareness and the lower cost of good quality oils, most Chinese are using vegetable oils.

Stir-frying food has still another virtue. The ingredients used are usually a mixture of a variety of vegetables, beans, and slices of meat or fish. When these foods are cooked in the same pot and eaten together, the complementary protein value of the meal is really optimized. For example, a few slices of meat or fish would go a long way in supplementing the specific amino acid deficiency of certain vegetables, thereby enhancing the utilization of the vegetable protein.

White-cooking
White-cooking is a technique that is sometimes used to prepare poultry and fish. The water is brought to a boil, the heat is then turned off, and the food cooks via residual heat. This process will involve some loss of water-soluble nutrients leeching into the water. However, because the food is not cooked in a continuous boiling process like simmering, it will be protected against the loss of nutrients—such as vitamin C—that are destroyed by oxidation.

Steaming
The Chinese use the technique of steaming in making bread and a variety of dumplings (for example, dim sum). Wheat protein is low in the essential amino acid lysine. In the baking process, the crust of the bread forms a lysine-carbohydrate complex which is hard for the body to digest. Thus, much of the lysine in baked products becomes unavailable. This decreases the protein score of wheat. However, when bread is steamed it is easier to digest and absorb, and the protein score is somewhat higher.

Contrary to Western belief, Chinese seldom steam vegetables. Vegetables are almost always stir-fried or are sliced thin and eaten raw in salads. Steaming can be the method used for cooking poultry, spareribs, pork, beef, and desserts made of sweet rice with dried fruits, however the food most suitable for steaming is fish. The fish is steamed for just a few minutes, thereby preserving the freshness and tenderness of the flesh.

Nutritionally, steaming is somewhat better than many other methods of cooking. It is less greasy than frying, and the food is much easier to absorb. Compared to boiling, the nutrients in steamed food are fairly well retained because there is no direct contact with the boiling water, which can dissolve and wash away many vitamins and minerals.

Oil-dipping
This method is mainly used to preserve the tenderness of food. The food—which is usually meat (either shredded, sliced, or in chunks), fish or shellfish—is dipped into heated oil and immediately removed. This process preserves juiciness while allowing the outside oil to drip off. The direct contact of the food with

the heated oil cooks the food quickly and protects against nutrient losses. The trick to oil-dipping is to drain off the oil as much as possible. If it is not done properly, a considerable amount of oil will be retained and add to the calorie content of the food.

Use of Iron Utensils

Most Chinese cooking can be done with the use of a wok which is often large and made of iron. Studies have shown that the iron content of food can be increased when it is cooked with iron utensils. Iron is the nutrient that is hardest to get in a sufficient amount in a typical western diet. Any addition in the iron content to a daily diet would be beneficial to most people, especially women.

SOME NUTRITIONAL CONCERNS IN CHINESE CUISINE

Although the Chinese diet is a very nutritious one, there are some concerns, mostly owing to Westernization or modernization,that must be kept in mind. The first is the matter of what appears to be a large intake of sodium (salt). As an example, soy sauce has an extremely high sodium content. Traditionally, Chinese people eat large amounts of *fan* (plain rice with no soy sauce or salt added) and small amounts of *cai* (courses of meat and/or vegetables seasoned with soy sauce, placed in the center of the table for sharing). However, in recent times, the proportion of *cai* to *fan* consumed in the diet has greatly increased, causing an increase in sodium consumption. Other sodium-rich foods commonly eaten by the Chinese are seaweed, oyster sauce, many types of bean paste, preserved vegetables, salted fish, and fermented soybean curd.

When one opens up a Chinese cookbook, one often sees MSG, or monosodium glutamate, as an ingredient in many dishes. Monosodium glutamate is not a foreign substance, but is an amino acid and a natural ingredient found in mushrooms and a variety of common vegetables. But when used in large amounts in its pure chemical form (as the white powder that one uses), it often causes certain allergic-like responses in some individuals (the so-called Chinese restaurant syndrome) and it increases the sodium intake.

Traditionally, MSG has not been used extensively in Chinese home cooking. Rather, it is used in restaurants to cover the poor quality of their ingredients or to "enhance" the flavor of the food. Actually most Chinese housewives are very fussy about the freshness of the ingredients they use, and would only choose fresh vegetables, fish, and poultry for their meals, thereby eliminating the need to add MSG.

Why worry about a high sodium intake? Most of us consume much more sodium than we need. Increased sodium consumption is related to increased water retention and an elevated blood pressure which can lead to a variety of diseases. All foods high in sodium should be eaten sparingly and with consideration for the total sodium content of the diet.

Another nutritional concern of Chinese food is the use of lard as a cooking medium. Traditionally, it was the more affluent people in China who preferred lard as the fat used in stir-frying, deep-frying, and even in making desserts. The practice was not very widespread, probably because the majority of the people were not well-to-do. Today virtually everyone is familiar with the potential dis-

advantages of eating large amounts of saturated fat and cholesterol and its relationship to atherosclerosis, and fortunately lard is seldom used. An interesting point is that lard is not as saturated a fat as butter, beef fat, or lamb fat and it contains more of the polyunsaturated linoleic acid than beef and lamb.

A third area of nutritional concern has to do with the main staple in the diet—rice. Many Chinese seem to favor the unenriched over the enriched grain, and the iron and some of the B vitamin contents are lower in the unenriched product. The enrichment of grains in the United States involves adding back to the grain some of the B vitamins and some of the iron that was lost in the milling process.

Another concern is that most Chinese people prefer rice that is highly polished. Polishing virtually eliminates the majority of the B vitamins and reduces the nutrient content of the grain significantly.

The fourth possible concern of Chinese cooking is the use of baking soda. Although it helps in denaturing and tenderizing meat, when it is added in cooking vegetables it does destroy many vitamins. However, this is a practice that most modern Chinese cooks have decided to abandon. Instead of using baking soda to maintain the green color of the vegetables, uncovering the wok in stir-frying will have the same effect.

CONCLUSION

Does one meet daily nutrient requirements by eating Chinese food? The foregoing information suggests the benefits to be gained from Chinese cooking. This variety of ingredients, cooking techniques, colors, textures, and taste are for all to enjoy, as we seek good health and a better way of life. Equally important is the enjoyment gained in preparing, serving, and providing for our families new ways of eating. If you try some of the recipes in this book and follow the general advice included here, you and your guests will benefit—from the food's nutritional value and also from an understanding of how millions of people from a vast continent have not only survived but also found pleasure from food.

Index